THE CHINA CONSULS
BRITISH CONSULAR OFFICERS,
1843–1943

The CHINA CONSULS

BRITISH CONSULAR OFFICERS,
1843–1943

P.D. COATES

HONG KONG
OXFORD UNIVERSITY PRESS
OXFORD   NEW YORK

Oxford University Press

Oxford   New York   Toronto
Petaling Jaya   Singapore   Hong Kong   Tokyo
Delhi   Bombay   Calcutta   Madras   Karachi
Nairobi   Dar es Salaam   Cape Town
Melbourne   Auckland

and associated companies in
Berlin   Ibadan

First published 1988
Published in the United States
by Oxford University Press, Inc.,
New York
Second impression 1991

British Library Cataloguing in Publication Data
Coates, P.D. (Patrick Devereux), 1916–
China consuls: British consular officers,
1843–1943.
1. China. British consular service,
1843–1943
I. Title
327.2
ISBN 0-19-584078-X

Library of Congress Cataloging-in-Publication Data
Coates, P.D. 1916–
The China consuls: British consular officers, 1843–1943/
P.D. Coates.
p.   cm.
Bibliography: p.
Includes index.
ISBN 0-19-584078-X
1. Great Britain—Commerce—China—History.
2. China—Commerce—Great Britain—History. 3. Great
Britain—Diplomatic and consular service—China—History.
I. Title.
HF3508.C5C6 1988   88-515
CIP

Printed in Hong Kong
Published by Oxford University Press, Warwick House, Hong Kong

To the consular colleagues and Chinese friends of my youth

PREFACE

DURING the hundred years in which Britain enjoyed extraterritorial rights in China the China consular service, that stepchild of the Foreign Office, played a significant part, but the work of generations of its officers, good, bad, and indifferent, has been swept aside by the march of events. Nothing remains but thousands of dusty volumes in the archives. So forgotten is the service that in referring to it modern academic works abound in errors.

In 1937 I entered the amalgamated British consular service which had recently been created and was posted to Peking. I served in China for some years before transferring to busy but more humdrum duties in departments at home. In a vastly changed postwar world I increasingly felt that the vanished China service deserved some memorial. Retirement gave the leisure to explore the archives and to piece together the story of the service. It is an unusual and curious story which has not been told before.

This book is not designed as a contribution to academic understanding of extraterritoriality, of treaty port life, or of British merchants or missionaries, though as all these were central to consular life much is necessarily said of them. It is not even designed to contribute to the history of British administrative machinery, though data about recruitment to the service and about Foreign Office management are probably novel. It is simply an account of a small group of British officials whose working lives were spent in alien surroundings far from home, and of the way they behaved in most abnormal conditions. It is a book about men.

No apology is offered for giving more space to some minor posts than to some major ones. Small happenings at small posts often revealed character more clearly than the larger events on which history likes to dwell.

The opinions of consular officers are for the most part

reproduced without comment. Their strictures on a China which, once ahead of Europe, had fallen behind were often severe. It may therefore be salutary to recall how relatively recently in Britain witches had been burned, political offenders had been hung, drawn, and quartered, men and women had been publicly flogged and hanged, administration had been corrupt, and sanitation had barely existed.

For the benefit of the general reader Chinese personal names, so bafflingly unpronounceable to the uninitiated, have been kept to a minimum. Wade-Giles romanization (see pp. 83–4) is used for personal names except in the case of well-known names normally written otherwise, such as Chiang Kai-shek, and of the occasional early name the correct form of which is not known. The former Chinese Post Office spelling is used for familiar place-names and the Wade-Giles system for less familiar ones.

The reference notes are provided only for academics. Other readers should disregard them.

P.D. COATES

CONTENTS

CONTENTS

PLATES

ACKNOWLEDGEMENTS

I am extremely grateful to the Nuffield Foundation for so broadmindedly giving a retired non-academic the grant, covering fares to London and incidentals, which made possible the necessary long research at the Public Record Office; to the School of Oriental and African Studies, who kindly agreed to administer the grant and made me an honorary visiting fellow while it lasted, and to Professor W.G. Beasley for his kindly welcome at the School; and to the staff of the Public Record Office, especially Mr E. Odell, for making research there convenient and agreeable. Crown copyright material in the Public Record Office is reproduced by courtesy of the Controller, HM Stationery Office.

I am much indebted to help from former China consular officers, or from their widows or descendants, in particular from the late Sir Alwyne Ogden, who preserved into his nineties a notably accurate memory and who spared no trouble in answering queries; and to the schools, colleges, local record offices, and other institutions or individuals who so patiently and helpfully supplied, or tried to supply, information about the early lives of long dead officers. They are too numerous to be listed, but to all of them I express my warm thanks.

Without the encouragement given at the outset by the late Sir Robert Scott and by other distinguished public servants, some like him now dead, I would perhaps not have ventured to start work, and I gratefully record the keen and helpful interest shown while work was in progress by the late Sir Edward Youde.

Above all I am grateful to my wife, on whom the making of this book often imposed unfair burdens and who nevertheless always urged me to continue.

PROLOGUE

BRITISH consulates in China were a product of the first war between Britain and China. The immediate cause of the war was a dispute about opium, the basic cause a conflict of cultures. Surrounded on their land frontiers throughout their history by less advanced races, the Chinese regarded those beyond the pale of Chinese civilization as barbarians, sometimes formidable in a barbarous way but by definition morally and intellectually inferior. Through a mist of ignorance and cultural arrogance they saw in Western civilization, fatefully advancing towards them in a shrinking world, no more than further barbarism, and met it with their traditional airs of lordly superiority. The British, arrogant too, fretted under pretensions which to them were ridiculous in theory and odious in application. In their eyes China was a backward oriental state, untouched by Christianity or by the new gods of science and technology.

By far the largest part of Western trade with China was British. The East India Company had traded profitably in China since the early eighteenth century, but on humiliating and frustrating terms. The company's trade, and the sea-borne trade of all other Western countries, was officially confined to the single port of Canton in the extreme south. Foreign traders were allowed to reside in Canton for only part of each year. While at Canton they were cooped up outside the city walls in a tiny though not uncomfortable ghetto, which they were allowed to leave three times a month for an escorted walk in a pleasure-garden. Foreign women were prohibited from sullying Canton with their presence and during the Canton trading season had to be left behind at a minute Portuguese coastal settlement which the Chinese tolerated at nearby Macao. Trading otherwise than through a dozen or so approved Canton merchants was prohibited. All communications

to the Chinese authorities had to be made in the form of petitions and channelled through these merchants. There was no way of finding out which of the multifarious exactions levied on the trade were legal, which extra-legal, and which illegal.

In the hope of establishing official relations with the Chinese government, the British had sent two pompous missions by sea to north China. Lord Macartney, leading the first, did succeed in 1793 in obtaining audience of a powerful emperor who had already reigned for more than half a century and who, perhaps so sated with power that he felt able to indulge his whims, waived the prostrations (kowtows) exacted by China from all such petty tribute-bearers; but audience and a patronizing message for the barbarian chieftain George III was all Macartney did obtain. In 1816 Lord Amherst, on declining to kowtow, was hustled ignominiously away from the succeeding ruler's court without having seen him.

In 1834 the East India Company's monopoly over British trade at Canton was brought to an end by Act of Parliament, and the powers of the company's select committee at Canton to control British subjects trading in China lapsed. To replace the select committee of merchants as an instrument of control, royal commissions were issued to three official superintendents of the trade of British subjects in China. The attempts of the chief superintendent, Lord Napier, to establish with the Chinese viceroy at Canton the direct relations considered appropriate for the holder of a royal commission were fruitless. The viceroy insisted that the new barbarian headman should continue to deal through the approved Canton merchants. Napier died at Macao, baffled and unsuccessful, within three months of his arrival. In the absence of instructions from home to pursue a forward policy his successors in the office of chief superintendent lay low, remaining in Macao without visiting Canton until 1837.

Meanwhile, outside the official Canton trade, a profitable illicit trade, again largely in British hands, had been growing up along the China coast. This was the trade in opium, the main producer of which was India.

The growth in China of the new vice of opium-smoking, as inexplicable as the growth of twentieth-century drug addiction in the West, had caused sporadic concern to Chinese emperors in the eighteenth century. At the end of the century an imperial edict

wisely banned opium imports. The wisdom was confined to paper. There was little genuine attempt to enforce the edict, which remained a dead letter. With the connivance or encouragement of a multitude of Chinese officials the nominally prohibited trade continued, and indeed continually grew. So long as the unwritten rules of a well-understood official farce were observed and the right palms were crossed with silver, the foreign sellers had little to fear from official action and had only to be beware of armed robbers.

At length, however, the yearly increasing outflow of silver in payment for the inward flood of opium came to be seen in the highest Chinese quarters as an economic menace. Having lengthily considered and finally rejected arguments that the trade should be legalized and taxed, the court determined on decisive action to stop it. In 1839 an imperial commissioner, Lin Tse-hsü, arrived in Canton with orders to put an end to the importation and smoking of opium. Soon the British at Canton and the chief superintendent, Captain Elliott, found themselves under a form of house arrest. Lin restored their freedom to leave Canton only after Elliott had, under duress, agreed to obtain and surrender to Lin for destruction the many million dollars' worth of British-owned opium in Chinese waters.

In carrying out his instructions Lin had up to this point been firm and successful but, by Chinese standards, moderate. The British in Canton were not thrown into prison, still less tortured. The mildest weapons in the customary Chinese official armoury were used; pressure was applied, increased until the barbarians yielded, and then removed. To a society in which collective responsibility was a fundamental concept there was nothing unreasonable in detaining the whole community until the point had been gained. Had Lin acted similarly towards a group of Chinese merchants his proceedings would have been accepted by Chinese public opinion.

The British judged Lin's proceedings otherwise. To them collective responsibility and justice to the individual were incompatible, and to bring even an individual to account facts must be established through regulated procedure in a court of law. Although the British government would have welcomed a move to legalize and tax opium imports they did not deny China's right to prohibit the trade and were not prepared to support officially British traders in illicit goods who were caught by legitimate Chinese preventive methods. However, they regarded Lin's actions

not as legitimate but as outrageous. Instead of apprehending
smugglers he had arbitrarily seized and held to ransom a whole
community, some of whose members had not the slightest connection with the opium trade. The British government's patience with
China was exhausted. They took standard action to ensure the
future personal security of British subjects trading in China and to
normalize, as Europe then understood normality in its contacts
with less advanced states, relations between Britain and China. In
other words, the British government resorted to arms.

Before the leisurely hostilities were over Lin had been disgraced
and Elliott had been recalled under a cloud and succeeded by Sir
Henry Pottinger. Inevitably, the Chinese were defeated by superior
weapons. When the British navy forced its way up the Yangtze river
in central China the Chinese capitulated. The war ended with the
signing at Nanking in 1842 of a treaty the very form of which was
designed to assert Britain's equality of status with China. So slow
were communications with Britain that ratifications were not
exchanged until June 1843. Later in the same year the original
treaty was supplemented by a second one. The British government
sought no exclusive advantages in China, and the United States and
French governments peacefully obtained from China treaties on
similar lines.

The British victors failed to secure Chinese agreement to the
the removal of the ban on opium, but China had to pay a war
indemnity and to cede the island of Hong Kong, which was
intended to provide a secure base for British merchants, vessels, and
goods. The Chinese would not accept the presence in Peking of a
barbarian representative, so the chief superintendent remained in
Hong Kong and dealt with an imperial commissioner stationed at
Canton. The five ports of Canton, Foochow, Amoy, Ningpo, and
Shanghai were opened to British merchants and the import and
export duties payable there were defined. Britain was to enjoy all
privileges granted by China to other powers. British subjects were
placed, as in the Ottoman empire, in an extraterritorial position,
subject to English law and to British courts and excluded from the
jurisdiction of Chinese officials and courts. And China agreed to
accept a British consulate at each of the five ports opened to trade.

Part I
The First Five Ports

THE OPENING PHASE

THE exchange of ratifications of the Treaty of Nanking meant that the five consulates could be opened. That in turn meant appointing staff to man them. At each consulate the generous initial complement, later severely cut back at some ports, was a consul, a vice-consul, an interpreter, and a senior and junior assistant. All were full-time salaried officials, prohibited from trading on their own account. Although all appointments to the posts were in the gift of the Foreign Secretary, Lord Aberdeen, he used his patronage surprisingly little to oblige political or personal friends.

In practice, Aberdeen's freedom of personal choice was greatly restricted. It had been decided to delegate to the chief superintendent control over the five consulates and to prohibit direct consular correspondence with the Foreign Office.[1] It was therefore only reasonable to take account of the chief superintendent's views on staffing. Further, the chief superintendent being on the spot in distant Hong Kong, which Foreign Office despatches took months to reach, he was able to act more promptly, and was better placed to find serviceable men with that rare qualification, previous experience of China. He was therefore authorized to make provisional appointments, the Foreign Secretary's confirmation of which was more than a formality but was not usually withheld. More than half the new posts were in effect filled by the chief superintendent and not by Aberdeen. Equally, Aberdeen's department, the Foreign Office, had claims to appointments. Men already in Foreign Office employment applied for posts in China which they considered to be better or more secure than their existing posts. Applications for junior posts for the sons of living or dead Foreign Office officials had to be considered too. The Foreign Office had a good reputation for looking after sons.[2]

At the end of 1843 there was a flurry of appointments by the

Foreign Secretary. They included only one consul. Macgregor, a 60-year-old veteran whose long and useful consular service had been mainly in Germany and Denmark,[3] was selected for Canton, the senior consulate. This apparently respectable choice was not a success. Before Macgregor reached Canton the Foreign Office learned with displeasure that his son was going into business in China, no doubt the reason why a consul who had not served further afield than the Canaries had put his name forward for Canton. They warned Macgregor that if British merchants there remarked invidiously on the situation he would be transferred to a lesser China consulate, and that if his son had any connection whatever with the prohibited opium trade Macgregor's continued presence in China would be incompatible with what was due from the British government to the Chinese government.[4] Nor did Macgregor give satisfaction once he had taken up his post, at which his considerable experience of shipping and trade negotiations in Europe was wasted. He was 'a very nervous man',[5] not at his best in dealing with unruly British and unruly Cantonese, he incurred official censures, and the chief superintendent's final verdict was that he lacked the energy needed at Canton.[6] Within four years he retired and was forgotten in China. His tenure of the highly paid Canton post at least earned him a greatly increased pension, which he survived to draw for nearly thirty years.

Of the four vice-consuls selected in London, only Layton had no previous Foreign Office experience. Formerly a highly paid tea-inspector for the East India Company at Canton, he persuaded Aberdeen by long unsolicited letters that he was an expert on China. Jackson, who had started in the Foreign Office Slave Trade Department in 1825, had been ousted by a quirk of the government machine from an apparently secure slave trade post abroad and, back in the Slave Trade Department, had only temporary work. Sirr and Robertson were barristers, working for the Foreign Office on an Anglo-Portuguese claims commission. The commission's work was coming to an end and both men sought more permanent positions in China. Robertson's career was to prove outstanding but had so far been the reverse of promising. A letter from a Queen's Counsel supporting Robertson's application for an assistant's post stated that Robertson had gone out to India in the mercantile naval service but had left it when the death of his maternal grandfather, a clergyman who had had the Duke of Cumberland's ear, spelled the

loss of the influence through which a fair share of promotion in India could be looked for; then he had tried the Bar, where his practical knowledge, sound judgement, and gentlemanly manners had not enabled him to compete with men more used to artificial thinking, sophistry, and ready elocution; and now he was employed in the commission only in matters of minute detail. The Foreign Office first intended to tell Robertson that all vacancies for assistants had been filled, but a minute to that effect was crossed out and replaced by one noting his appointment to the higher grade of vice-consul.

Six assistants, a term which the Foreign Office decided was preferable to 'clerks', were selected in London. Pottinger was told that they were to be treated like gentlemen and that, considering the distance separating many of them from friends and guardians, they were strongly recommended to his protection and consideration. Four were Foreign Office sons. The sub-librarian Hertslet, pointing out that he had a large family and had not had a pay increase for four years, begged a China appointment for his eldest son. Sir Woodbine Parish, a successful negotiator abroad, asked with an air of some confidence that his third son, who had acted as his secretary at Naples, should receive an appointment with reasonable prospects of promotion. Backhouse, the younger son of the former permanent secretary, had first been a midshipman and was now out of work after three unpaid years in a merchant's office in Liverpool. On the strength of this commercial experience his father asked for him to be given the vacant vice-consul's post at Rio. The death of F.E. Harvey's father, formerly a Guards officer and then consul at Bayonnne, had obliged Harvey to take a £25-a-year position in a Rotherham business which was closing. Harvey was on the Foreign Secretary's list of candidates for future vacancies among the permanent Foreign Office clerks, and in his extremity now appealed to be given a £50 temporary clerkship. The Foreign Office response to the Backhouse and Harvey applications was to appoint both as assistants in China. The last two assistants appointed had no Foreign Office connections. Hague had been nine years in business and had risen to the position of managing clerk. His application for a China post came in through the member of Parliament for York, who stated that Hague's father was chairman of the Yorkshire visiting magistrates and a gentleman of high respectability. Only to fill the final vacancy did Aberdeen turn to his private acquaintance.

He appointed a 16-year-old younger son of the Scottish painter Giles, from whom Aberdeen commissioned a number of works.[7]

In Hong Kong Pottinger's problems of selection were different. He not only held under the Foreign Office the temporary office of plenipotentiary concurrently with the permanent office of chief superintendent, but was also governor of Hong Kong under the Colonial Office. He had therefore to fill posts in the new colony as well as in the consulates, and the local field of choice was narrow. The tiny nucleus of permanent officials serving him as chief superintendent had been too hard hit by death and disease to be a possible source of consuls or vice-consuls. The senior superintendency official, Johnston, who had come out as private secretary to his cousin Lord Napier and had risen rapidly, had been in Pottinger's mind as his second choice for the Canton consulship[8] but instead went home, still only just over 30, on a sick leave which lasted two and a half years. J.R. Morrison, who while still a minor had been appointed Chinese secretary in succession to his father, a Nonconformist minister and eminent Chinese scholar, died suddenly in August before even reaching 30. (While Morrison was still alive the Foreign Office rewarded his valuable services by sending out his 15-year-old half-brother M.C. Morrison at the public expense to employment in the superintendency, and after he had died they showed their appreciation further by a peculiar undertaking that M.C. Morrison, who at the time knew no Chinese, should when qualified as an interpreter be appointed assistant Chinese secretary.)[9] E. Elmslie, the secretary to the superintendency, likewise under 30, had gone home, sick in body and permanently affected in mind, leaving his son by a Chinese mistress unsupported.[10] His younger brother, A.W. Elmslie, was only 23.

Pottinger therefore had to look in other quarters. He vainly tried to recruit, perhaps as Shanghai consul or perhaps as Shanghai interpreter, another scholarly Nonconformist missionary, Medhurst.[11] His offer of consulships to some others likewise came to nothing, and his unsuccessful approaches to men with scanty qualifications were later considered to have lowered consular prestige, for some of those who had turned up their noses at consular posts did not allow their refusal of offers to be forgotten.[12] Pottinger wished a Pomeranian tailor's son, Gutzlaff, to get the Foochow consulship but the Foreign Office rejected the proposal. Gutzlaff, first a brazier's apprentice and then a missionary, had been a magistrate

under the British during their wartime occupation of Chusan, a large island off Ningpo. The extortions of the Chinese with whom he had staffed his magistrate's office had disgusted even one of his close personal friends,[13] and his previous missionary activities had also been criticized. In his zeal to survey the potential mission field he had taken passage as interpreter on opium ships sailing north-wards up the coast from Hong Kong, so that the Chinese were simultaneously supplied with opium and with Christian literature; these proceedings were viewed askance by some other missionaries. An informed review of a Gutzlaff book on China had accused him of unblushing plagiarism and found nothing more flattering to say than that some parts of the book were less bad than others.[14] It seems as well that Gutzlaff, in spite of marrying three British wives in succession, had remained an alien. While acknowledging his services the Foreign Office ruled that as an alien he could not exercise magisterial functions over extraterritorialized British subjects, so instead of receiving a consulship he succeeded J.R. Morrison as Chinese secretary.[15] His performance in the post attracted more criticism. Palmerston, as Foreign Secretary, advised him to condense his material and adopt a simpler style of composition, for the simpler and more concise the language of a report the more useful Palmerston considered it likely to be.[16] A consular colleague wrote more acidly after Gutzlaff's death that few had exceeded his capacity for rapidly inditing sentences con-taining a number of propositions not one of which should be true.[17]

Pottinger eventually recruited as consuls Balfour, an army staff officer; Thom and G.T. Lay, two of the interpreters serving him as plenipotentiary; and Gribble,[18] a former captain of an Indiaman who had turned to commerce. What manner of men these amateur consuls were, and how they performed their new duties, will be seen later. He also recruited Sullivan, once a master in the navy, as vice-consul at Amoy, and St. Croix, another former captain of an Indiaman, as consular agent at Whampoa, an outpost of the Canton consulate. Both men were looking for openings. An attempt by the Hon. James Murray to open up trade in wildest Borneo with two small vessels, one commanded by Sullivan, left Murray dead in a brush with Malays[19] and Sullivan without an employer. St. Croix, who had lost by speculation a fortune gained in many voyages,[20] had come out in his own ship[a] seeking a fresh start for himself and

for seven accompanying boys, the sailor sons of his relatives and friends; after arrival most of the boys imitated St. Croix by starting a new life ashore.[a] Both men's long experience of shipping and seamen was a useful qualification in their new positions.

In selecting interpreters and assistant interpreters Pottinger could do little other than appoint any available young man tackling the language seriously. Medhurst's son, born in Java and speaking Dutch and Malay, had at the age of 16 been brought to Macao by his father. Parkes, early orphaned, had at the age of 13 come out to Macao, where his sisters and he had been given a home by a cousin married to Gutzlaff. In Macao both boys had been put to work at Chinese, had learned enough to be useful during the war, and consequently were natural choices for interpreterships after it; Medhurst was paid more than the other interpreters not because he knew more Chinese but because his father had refused payment for wartime services to the plenipotentiary.[21] T.T. Meadows had fallen in love with the language as instantly and irrationally as others fall in love with a woman at first sight. After attending a single lecture at Munich University by a professor who strangely combined the teaching of Armenian and of Chinese, Meadows abandoned all studies other than Chinese,[22] took himself out to China intent on a government post and, after a brief spell as an assistant, was found competent to be an interpreter. Wade, an army lieutenant of good Irish family who during the war had likewise started a lifetime's love-affair with the language and who had been interpreter to the Hong Kong garrison, was obliged to go home because of illness and to let slip his intended appointment as Amoy interpreter,[23] but he was to return and force his way into the service. Medhurst, Parkes, and Wade all earned entries in the *Dictionary of National Biography*, and Meadows is still remembered as a sinologue. Gingell, an assistant army surgeon who had learned enough during the war to be made an assistant interpreter, was a competent man whose career was cut short by death. The only unfortunate interpretorial appointment was that of Sinclair, whose lack of judgement and faults of character plagued the service for forty-three years. Impecunious though connected with well-to-do landed gentry, orphaned at the age of 5, brought up in Brussels by a widowed aunt previously married to an artillery officer, Sinclair came out to Hong Kong with a five-year spell of work in Koblenz behind him, a good knowledge of French and German, and an introduction to the

admiral from his well-bred connections. These qualifications procured him temporary work in the Canton consulate, and he soon learned enough Chinese to become an assistant interpreter.[24]

Eight consular and superintendency assistants were selected in Hong Kong. Bird had joined Pottinger's wartime staff from Bombay, where he had probably been in business.[25] Warden's father had captained an East India Company ship during the war.[26] Hale, the surgeon son of a clergyman who became British Embassy chaplain in Paris, came out from England at Pottinger's invitation to be appointed medical officer to the Shanghai consulate. Medical officer posts were soon abolished, but Hale was reappointed as an assistant, receiving an addition to the normal assistant's salary in return for giving medical assistance to the consulate staff.[27] The same readjustment was made in favour of the Amoy medical officer, Winchester, a naval assistant surgeon who had for a year been colonial surgeon in Hong Kong.[28] Why Connor and Meredith were in Hong Kong and available for selection by Pottinger is not clear. Connor, whom Sir John Davis, Pottinger's successor as chief superintendent and governor of Hong Kong, found very well educated and indefatigable, had arrived there in 1842.[29] Meredith, of whom Davis also thought highly, was one of at least eight children in a middle-class Lambeth family and had just reached Hong Kong, barely 17 years old.[30] Davis appointed the other two assistants, Oakley and J.T. Walker, after Pottinger's departure. Both had, like Sinclair, come from Europe to remote Hong Kong looking for work and armed only with introductions. Oakley's introduction was from the Home Secretary, in whose constituency his father, a clergyman of socially undistinguished origins, held a living.[31] Walker, an attorney's son, had an introduction from his father's neighbour, Sir George Staunton, whose long experience in China made the recommendation weighty.[32]

Such were the methods employed in London and Hong Kong to select the consular staff who at the five ports were to represent their country in alien and unfriendly China. The staff selected in England in December were hustled away with little time to prepare for a long voyage and years of exile. Early in January 1844 most of them sailed from Portsmouth in a vessel of 535 tons. She carried Jackson, his wife, and two children; Sirr, with wife and maid; Robertson, whose baby fell ill at the last moment and whose wife had to be left behind with the baby to follow on a year or so later; and the six

unmarried assistants. The absence of Robertson's baby cannot have been unwelcome to the others during a journey which took all but five months by the old route round the Cape of Good Hope.[33] Layton travelled separately, in a style reflecting the past spaciousness of his East India Company days. He took out with him the wife he had married in Macao before the war, their Macao-born daughter, a governess, the wife's sister, a Chinese female servant whose son acted as servant boy, and an English female servant.[34] Macgregor too travelled separately. He took the new Suez route, which involved travelling in four different ships and crossing Egypt overland.[35] By the middle of the year all had reached Hong Kong, with much of the exhausting, humid hot season before them. Money did not go so far as had been imagined at home, and on being refused extra allowances Sirr promptly resigned to practice law in Hong Kong. After he and his wife had been fined for beating their landlord the resignation itself was seen by the chief superintendent as a good riddance, but as Sirr had received free passages for himself and his wife, a quarter's salary, and an outfit allowance the chief superintendent invited the Foreign Office to consider proceedings for breach of contract. The Foreign Office confined themselves to ruling that Sirr was on no account ever again to be employed by them. So watertight were departmental compartments in Whitehall that not long afterwards Sirr became deputy Queen's advocate in Ceylon, which was a Colonial Office responsibility, but when he later brazenly sought reappointment to the China consular service the Foreign Office did not overlook their earlier ruling.[36] The other recruits from England proceeded to consulates, all of which except Foochow had been opened many months before the recruits had reached Hong Kong.

G.T. Lay opened the first consulate, at Canton, in July 1843, though his appointment by Pottinger was subject to Foreign Office confirmation, which was not forthcoming. A Nonconformist of unknown but probably humble origins, Lay first emerges in his twenties as a private tutor in Cambridge.[37] He knew some Latin, Greek, and probably Hebrew.[38] He was said to have received a medical education, which may possibly mean that he had been apprenticed to a medical practitioner,[39] and at one period was joint editor of a musical encyclopaedia.[40] As the naturalist on Captain Beechey's 1825–8 expedition to the Pacific he had already shown a tendency towards misfortune by nearly drowning on an unin-

habited coral island and spending almost a year ill in Hawaii.[41] Back in England he resumed tutoring, combining it with literary engagements and with superintending a Hampstead Sunday school. Then, inexplicably described as professing a knowledge of Eastern languages, he was recommended to the British & Foreign Bible Society, who were looking for an eastern Asia agent.[42] He held this post, based in Macao, from 1836 to 1839, studied Chinese, and on his return published a book on China. On the strength of the book and of his ability to speak Chinese he secured appointment in 1841 as an interpreter on Pottinger's mission, Lay even then hoping that the appointment would lead to permanent consular employment.[43] The war brought him a wound and the opportunity to dabble in Chinese dialects, although his translations of written Chinese remained unreliable.[44] The conclusion of hostilities brought a mild Foreign Office reproof. The home press had printed a letter to the Tract Society in which he wrote that although the warrior's prowess had helped to secure the settlement the hand of God had been at work and that God required from the victor not the abuse of power but tracts, bibles, and missionaries. The Foreign Office warned Lay and Gutzlaff, who had also got into the home press, that they should be more discreet in private correspondence and that missionary pursuits would be incompatible with Foreign Office employment.[45] Lay would have done better to stick to missionary pursuits, for he was not cut out for consular duties.

Lay had no trouble in opening the Canton consulate. Canton was easily reached by river from Hong Kong, there was an established foreign community, and he could move straight into a comfortable building designed for foreign occupation. The building soon burnt down, forcing the consulate to function for a time in boats,[46] but Lay's ten months in Canton were generally uneventful. The Chinese authorities expressed their regret when he left at the end of May 1844 to make room for Macgregor. Pottinger, on the verge of going home, praised Lay's conciliatory manners and perfect acquaintance with the Chinese character and appointed him officiating consul at Foochow. He recommended Foreign Office confirmation, a recommendation which Davis strongly endorsed.[47] Lay's habitual bad luck was, however, operating. A Foreign Office despatch sent off early in May, and now somewhere at sea, was bringing the news that Alcock, for the last three years British commissioner in the Anglo-Portuguese commission, had been appointed Foochow

consul. Alcock's career as a surgeon had been ended by muscular trouble in the hands, but not before he had made his mark by his organization of British military hospitals in Spain and Portugal amid scenes of exceptional medical horror.[48] His experience in the Peninsula had led to his appointment as commissioner, and when he now put in for a China consulship the Foreign Office rewarded his successful settlement of over 2,000 contested claims[49] by giving him the post. The choice of a man of 34 without any relevant experience except this limited previous service under the Foreign Office proved inspired, but Alcock was wholly unknown in China. When the despatch reached Hong Kong Davis replied irritably that Alcock's unexpected appointment had considerably embarrassed him, that Lay, who had very strong claims, would now have to go to Amoy, thereby displacing Gribble from the service altogether, and that he sincerely hoped Lay would be confirmed at Amoy.[50] The Foreign Office did then at last confirm Lay as consul, but meanwhile he had been having a dreadful time at Foochow.

Lay with two assistants reached Foochow in July 1844 to find that opening the consulate there was a very different matter from opening at Canton. Foochow lay some 30 miles up-river, and navigation in the river was difficult and dangerous for foreign shipping. Presumably for that reason the warship bringing the first British consul to Foochow dumped him, his assistants, and their luggage at the river mouth and left the party to get to the city by native boat.[51] In imperial China pomp and circumstance attended the public appearance of any official of standing, and the un-dignified arrival of a personally unimpressive man cannot have encouraged the authorities to take Lay seriously. They provided HM Consul with what Lay chose to call the best house at their disposal, though he admitted it was small, very humble in appearance, and partly constructed of boards. When Davis toured the new consulates he found that the house was built on piles over a mud bank and was flooded every high tide, and considered it so disgraceful that Lay could not be allowed to remain unless something better was procured. Lay himself now described it as a wretched building, disreputable in appearance and situated in a very low-class suburb. Stiffened by Davis, Lay temporarily broke off relations when the authorities, arguing that foreigners were not allowed inside the city, still refused him a building in it. He did then obtain what he described as a consulate in a very eligible position

inside the city. He was easily satisfied. The site was picturesque, but on succeeding Lay, Alcock reported that the consul and senior assistant had been occupying a single moderate-sized first-floor room with two closets attached, the whole so constructed as to keep out neither sun nor rain.[52] The improvement, such as it was, came too late for Meredith, the junior assistant. He went home with chronic dysentery, returned to China for eighteen months, and then went home again to die of the dysentery at the age of 21.[53]

In the absence of trade or a foreign community Lay had little work and little society. A European had hardly ever been seen at Foochow and an immense mob treated his every appearance as a circus side-show. Under the mental and physical strain Lay's reporting became increasingly unbalanced. From his shameful riverfront shack he wrote of the respect to be gained among the people by the sight of a resident British officer exercising judicial control over his countrymen and corresponding honourably with the province's highest authorities. From the new consulate he reported that the Chinese characters at his front door displayed the British nation's independence and the royal dignity of his Gracious Sovereign, and that as the people who came in thousands to see him would not leave without being gratified he was obliged daily to take a seat on some elevated part of the grounds to be gazed at. In reality, Lay finished by finding mob exigence intolerably inconvenient and was reduced to ejecting intruders with his own hands, on one occasion being thrown down in the attempt. On reaching Foochow Alcock considered the crowd of noisy curiosity-seekers anything but good-humoured and when Lay spoke to them without effect Alcock went to the magistrate, who came in person to disperse them and sent a guard to prevent recurrence. Davis condemned as extremely dangerous and mistaken Lay's stated policy of trying to win over the populace as a means of influencing unfriendly officials. It was not a policy pursued by other consuls.[54]

Lay himself was so pleased with his performance that to Davis' irritation he suggested his own retention at Foochow, which as the provincial capital he considered the place to settle all difficult questions, and the posting to Amoy of a mere vice-consul to handle ordinary business in correspondence with Lay. Lay was already in bad odour with Davis, who had just rebuked the Foochow consulate for corresponding privately with a Hong Kong newspaper hostile to Davis and had given a warning that anyone

detected in secret correspondence with newspapers, contrary to one of the strictest rules of the public service, would be instantly dismissed. It was therefore magnanimous of Davis to procure an increase in the pay attached to the Amoy post to which Lay was made to go. Lay did not benefit much. He was there long enough to quarrel with the police chief, who frankly admitted that his small salary obliged him to take bribes and who, duly bribed, was slow to abate the nuisance caused to Lay by a fleet of nightsoil boats operating during the hottest part of the day. After that Lay died, aged 45, of what was variously diagnosed as bilious fever or climatic fever. By a final stroke of misfortune he had on reaching Amoy fetched from Hong Kong the wife whom he had not seen for four years, with the result that he left her not only destitute with five children but also far gone in pregnancy.[55]

Gribble opened Amoy in November 1843, accompanied by Sullivan as vice-consul, Winchester as medical officer, and two temporary British clerks. Like Layton he reflected East India Company style and his arrival was more impressive than Lay's subsequent arrival at Foochow. Himself a tall, fine-looking man,[56] he landed from a warship with his pregnant wife and their four little girls, a European woman servant, a Chinese manservant, and a West India servant.[57] On inspecting Amoy, more than once to be described as notoriously the filthiest town in China, Winchester found no locality fit for immediate European residence in narrow streets full of decaying vegetable matter, without sewerage or drainage, and with a most abominable and universal stench. While the office was established in Amoy, Gribble and his staff therefore set up house on Kulangsu, a small island in the harbour which had been occupied during the war by the British and which, pending Chinese payment of the war indemnity, had not been finally evacuated.[58] Kulangsu eventually became the preferred residence for foreigners at Amoy and a charming, quiet, healthy place in which to live. As yet it was quite otherwise. In the opinion of a consul some years later, when the staff were living in Amoy, no European could reside on Kulangsu without risking his life, and Gribble and his staff might have been bent on demonstrating this. Within three months everyone had been ill except Winchester, who before long was also constantly suffering from intermittent fever. Sullivan had been at death's door for weeks, both clerks had been down with fever, malignant Kulangsu fever had killed a Chinese

servant, and iritis had prevented Gribble from reading or writing for five weeks.[59] The illnesses continued, and to make Kulangsu life still more uncomfortable a small dispute between Mrs Gribble and Mrs Sullivan, a dozen years her junior, led to coldness between the two husbands.[60]

In the midst of all the illness there was a good deal of foreign shipping, ten vessels calling in the first month, and accordingly early need for Gribble to use his magisterial powers. A drunken ship's carpenter, for example, assaulted the mate, bit the captain's finger, and desisted from demolishing the hatch with an axe only when covered by the captain's pistol. On the intercession of the captain, who said the carpenter had a good name and a large family, the corporal punishment first in Gribble's mind was replaced by a temporary reduction in wages. He did, however, order two men from a British ship two dozen lashes after a shipboard disturbance with which British marines had had to deal.

Gribble was heavily handicapped by not having been allocated one of the new consular interpreters. Two Cantonese he had brought with him could communicate in bastard English but could not understand either the Amoy dialect, in which all ordinary affairs were conducted, or Mandarin, the form of Chinese obligatory in official business. A well-disposed American missionary who spoke the dialect but not Mandarin tried to help, and Gribble engaged two local men, one of whom had learned some English in Singapore but could speak no Mandarin and the other of whom could speak Mandarin but had no English. Gribble's means of communicating with the Chinese authorities were thus absurdly unsatisfactory and were in the hands of Chinese staff who he feared might be suborned. He was further handicapped by the constant staff illnesses and by the lack of anyone on his staff used to official accounts and to the procedures of government offices. His performance as an office man in these circumstances left a good deal to be desired.[61] Pottinger was reduced to fury and to a series of inexcusably rude despatches to Gribble. He was extremely surprised that Gribble could for one moment have imagined that the Amoy accounts could possibly be sent to England in their present slovenly state, and was obliged distinctly to intimate that failing improvement it would be his unpleasant but imperative duty to make other arrangements for the discharge of Her Majesty's service at Amoy; the plan enclosed with Gribble's letter was totally unintelligible to

Pottinger and to everyone else who had seen it; Gribble's proposal was entirely premature and uncalled for; and, in a despatch made public in Hong Kong by Pottinger's order, Gribble's action was unaccountable and non-receipt of an earlier despatch could not excuse Gribble's neglect. Pottinger petulantly reported to the Foreign Office that Gribble was unsatisfactory, that he entirely overlooked most clear and explicit instructions and went out of his way to give unnecessary trouble. Less than four months later Pottinger, in handing over to Davis, told him and the Foreign Office that he had altered his opinion and now thought Gribble suitable to be a consul.[62] By that time, however, the Foreign Office had made up their minds about Gribble, and Alcock had been appointed; and although Davis called attention to Gribble's zealous services and recommended that he should succeed to the next vacancy, the Foreign Office refused to give Gribble the expectation of reappointment.[63] Pottinger's treatment of Gribble confirms Pottinger's reputation as a poor administrator.[64] Fortunately Gribble was resilient. He reappeared as superintendent of a large steam fleet for the Peninsular and Oriental line,[65] and could afford to educate his son at Harrow and Cambridge.[66]

Ningpo was opened by Thom in January 1844. He was the son of a Glasgow merchant[67] and his own business career, started at the age of 14, had taken him successively to Venezuela, Mexico, France, and China.[68] In China, which he reached in 1834, he had acquired a Chinese mistress and, with the encouragement of his employers, a creditable acquaintance with the written and spoken language. He had just published at his own expense a Chinese-English vocabulary, of which he distributed thousands of copies free,[69] and later produced a colloquial reader, based on a Chinese work, on which new entrants to the service for some years cut their teeth.[70] Patriotism and a wish to enjoy the freer intercourse with Chinese which he hoped an official position would afford induced him to accept at considerable financial loss the hazards of a temporary wartime government post as an interpreter.[71] In it he encountered imaginary as well as real hazards. He possessed a Chinese picture depicting his own death with an arrow through his heart; his head, pickled in oil, was allegedly on display at Foochow; and a Chinese officer was decorated for killing so prominent a barbarian, an incident to which neither the officer nor Thom referred when they later met at a conference.[72] Thom's stated

object in life was health, not wealth, enough money for his few wants and a little over to help a friend now and then, and some leisure for reading. Acting on this urbane philosophy he refused Canton, where he found the Cantonese too hostile, and asked not to be considered for Foochow or for the Chinese secretaryship in Hong Kong, partly because he could not understand the Foochow dialect and because Hong Kong was so unhealthy but partly because his appointment to either post would mortify his dear friend Gutzlaff. He said he would have been happy to serve as interpreter at Ningpo had there been some elderly, quiet, good-tempered man as consul. No such person being in sight he accepted the Ningpo consulship in the modest belief that although he lacked many of the necessary qualifications others might be still less qualified.[73]

A warship brought Thom to Ningpo with his medical officer, two temporary British clerks, and Sinclair as assistant interpreter.[74] M.C. Morrison, now 16, who was not on Thom's staff, came with the party to see whether a change of air would cure dysentery which had already lasted eight months and to study Chinese under Thom.[75] Baggage and furniture were stored by an obliging Cantonese merchant and the four juniors, one with dysentery, were stowed away in a miserable little house inside the city. Thom and the medical officer were fortunate in being lodged on board a warship, but after days of trudging the streets in a vain search for premises to rent Thom contemplated retreat from Ningpo. Then he came upon an unoccupied woodyard with a small house attached. The Chinese authorities said that if Thom wanted the premises he would be installed whatever the owner's wishes, and Thom was inducted with a large posse of police. Two months later he moved into the house of a once wealthy Chinese. It was situated among ricefields outside the city, and was approached only by narrow footpaths between the crops. Davis found its position highly objectionable, although he implied that locating the consulate in the extremely dirty and crowded city might have been worse.[76]

One of Thom's first steps was to issue some sensible regulations for British subjects. They were not to go further than 3 miles from the city without permission from the consul, who would provide a guide, or to shoot anywhere without his permission; they were not to enter houses, offer wanton disrespect to temples or tombs, or shock the people's prejudices; and finally they were not to enter cities or large villages without the permission of both the consul

and the Chinese authorities.[77]

A year after the port's opening there were still only three British residents, two of them spinster missionaries and the other a merchant who soon gave up and moved to Shanghai.[78] Thom found his post sad and lonesome at times,[79] but in spite of an almost entire absence of foreign trade enough British shipping called to give him trouble. Although he confessed to ignorance of seamen's ways, during his first quarter in office he had to deal with five cases of drunken seamen who had been riotous, insubordinate, or abusive, and to fine a captain for flogging a drunken steward. After the withdrawal of the warship which had been at Ningpo during Thom's first months the lack of physical means of enforcing his authority on seamen worried him. He arranged for six men who refused duty on their ships to be escorted to the consulate by Chinese police, ordered their confinement on bread and water in the Chinese gaol, and took an early opportunity of shipping them over to the British authorities still occupying Chusan. He remarked that it would have been very awkward if the men had not obeyed his orders, for the staff were not remarkable for their physical strength and some of them might have been soundly thrashed; like all persons whose nominal authority was not backed by physical force, he measured his man to calculate the chances of victory or defeat before venturing to engage with him; a quiet person would probably be sentenced to a fine and imprisonment, and a trouble-some fellow likely to cause a disturbance might escape punishment, 'which might be excused on the plea of expediency but it can hardly be called distributing justice with an even hand'.[80]

Thom's distribution of justice escaped rebuke, but his protection of a young Chinese named Lu Ming (alias Le Lu-ming), who had been his right-hand man in occupied Chusan during the war, brought a ponderous Foreign Office reprimand. The British authorities in Chusan handed Lu over to the Chinese on an un-verified charge that he was the leader of a robber gang, as well as handing over on similarly unverified charges some men who had served under Gutzlaff as policemen on the island. One morning Lu was dragged through the streets of Ningpo in chains, the Chinese staff of the consulate prepared to flee, and Lu's mother, wife, sister, and family came screaming to the consulate to implore help. Thom saw in the charges against Lu the threat of a systematic campaign of revenge against Chinese who had assisted the British, and he

considered that the British reputation would be tarnished and that his own position in Ningpo would become intolerable unless the assurances of immunity for such men which had been sought and obtained during the peace negotiations were honoured. He therefore made immediate representations. He was promised that Lu would be kindly treated but within two hours learned that he was being beaten. At a personal interview with the magistrate he obtained sight of Lu, in chains, having gone without food for three days, and unable to stand without being supported, but could not obtain his release. That evening Lu's family came screaming back to Thom, alleging a plan to flog Lu into a confession and ship him away that night. In a midnight interview with the magistrate Thom announced that he would not again lose sight of Lu and that if Lu were not released he would spend the night with Lu in prison. He found that after his previous interview the chains had been removed and that Lu had been fed and moved from the gaol to the police office. There Thom spent the night on a borrowed stretcher in the same room as Lu. The next morning he sent for his bedding, writing-desk, and clean clothes, and temporarily established his consulate in the police office, suspending his flag over the inner door and calling two sailors from a British ship to attend him. Terribly annoyed by the crowds which came to see the fun and by their comments, which on the whole favoured Thom, the magistrate capitulated after twenty-four hours and agreed to release Lu into Thom's custody if Thom would remove flag and sailors. After protracted further negotiations the Chinese acquitted Lu of the charges against him, and those of Gutzlaff's policemen who had survived imprisonment and beatings were released. Thom in return agreed to make no use of evidence that Lin, the official who had instigated the arrest of Lu, had conspired against Lu's life, Lin resigned, and friendly relations with the authorities were resumed.

Davis was scandalized. He told the Foreign Office that he entirely condemned the methods employed by Thom, whose right course would have been to lodge a protest, or at most to have struck his flag and retired to Chusan; his first impulse to suspend Thom had been checked only by reluctance to be harsh on any occasion and by the fact that Thom's formal commission had just been received. Thom stood his ground. He stoutly asserted to Davis that he had been guilty only of saving an innocent man, and one whose immunity had been guaranteed by treaty, from being unjustly

murdered under the form of law. Whatever Davis' immediate reactions to Thom's methods he ended by supporting Thom's objective and the results achieved, and, asking the Foreign Office how far he could go in seeking Chinese assurances against such persecution, expressed his satisfaction at Lu's acquittal and Lin's resignation. His satisfaction at the resignation was marred by a subsequent report that Lin had had three audiences of the emperor and had been promoted.[81]

Months after Lu's rescue the Foreign Office replied to Davis that the account of Thom's extraordinary proceedings had been read with the utmost surprise. They could not understand how Thom could have so far forgotten himself as to degrade the office which he held and the flag of his country by establishing himself in a Chinese police office and hoisting the flag over a doorway of that building; he was to be told in the strongest terms that Aberdeen entirely disapproved his conduct and that he was to be more circumspect in future; Thom's previous behaviour had not led Aberdeen to anticipate the possibility of his being an actor in such a scene and, trusting that the severe censure now conveyed would have a salutary effect, Aberdeen willingly refrained from visiting more severely the serious misconduct of which he had been guilty.[82]

Thom's spirited eccentricity had succeeded, whereas prompt and vigorous action on conventional lines taken by Sullivan at Amoy in a similar case failed resoundingly in 1851. The Chinese arrested at day-break a Singapore Chinese named T'an (or Tan) King-chin, a quiet, inoffensive, and timid young employee of a British firm whose chief interest was his little library of well-chosen English books; in retrospect the Chinese authorities were believed to have confused him with his brother, a man of very different character whom they may have had sound reason to suspect of sedition. In the morning Sullivan's vice-consul and interpreter called on the appropriate official and demanded release, which was refused on the ground that T'an was a Chinese and not a British subject. Sullivan with his whole staff came shortly after noon to renew the demand, and after four hours' discussion secured agreement that T'an would be returned. The party got back to the consulate at five o'clock. T'an was returned between six and seven o'clock in a sedan-chair, dead. The British medical report, which makes gruesome reading, was that he had been dead for an hour and had died from very extensive beating.[83] The affair was long remem-

bered as a perfidious atrocity.[84] More than twenty years later Chinese ministers in Peking were visibly discomposed by an emphatic warning that a repetition might have the most serious consequences for China.[85] But for Thom, Lu's fate and its effect on relations would probably have been similar.

This was not the only time Thom got into official trouble. Out of the goodness of his heart he involved himself more deeply than Davis considered advisable in the fate of three shipwrecked Japanese sailors, and he took the blame when in his absence on duty his vice-consul Layton and his interpreter Sinclair, both inveterately quarrelsome, had a ridiculous dispute about flying the consular flag, which went up and down, down and up, as the two men gave conflicting orders to the Chinese staff. Davis, a cold man, had warmed to Thom, as many people did,[86] and paid handsome tribute to his memory twenty years later.[87] Now he informed the Foreign Office that he considered Thom one of the best-intentioned people in the world, although the eccentricity of proceedings caused by a lack of official training gave on occasions such as these considerable trouble and anxiety. This time the Foreign Office reaction too was more kindly; Thom's conduct in their employment had been so meritorious that Aberdeen was spared the necessity of taking particular notice of the incidents.[88]

After two and a half years at Ningpo Thom applied for home leave, describing his constitution as shattered by over twelve unbroken years in China and forwarding a medical certificate which referred to fever, diarrhoea, dropsy, debilitation, and emaciation.[89] As others were to do, he had put off his leave application too long. He died at his post almost at once, aged 39, leaving a few hundred pounds for the support of a son and daughter by his Chinese mistress. His elder brother, a Nonconformist minister in Liverpool, undertook to bring the children up with his own children. A Foreign Office official recommended that a small lump sum should be paid to the minister out of Secret Service funds (if 'SS' in his minute stands for 'Secret Service') in recognition of Thom's very meritorious services, but it seems possible that the recommendation was not accepted.[90]

Balfour opened Shanghai in November 1843. The 34-year-old son of a Scottish artillery captain, he had joined the Madras Artillery at 14. As a staff officer in the war he had made his mark by competent handling of the Chinese war indemnity payments,[91] had

picked up some of the language, and had impressed Pottinger by his reasonable attitude towards the Chinese.[92] Within a week of reaching Shanghai he had arranged to rent a house and had agreed the port limits and the places for loading and unloading cargoes. He was also quickly resisting the standard Chinese attempts to channel foreign trade into a Chinese monopoly group, to levy duties above the treaty rates, and to prevent foreigners from leasing houses. The next year he procured the release of an arrested Chinese in British service by threatening to leave the port forthwith. This was one of the courses which a few months before Davis had thought open to Thom in the Lu case, but Davis now much doubted whether Balfour should have gone so far without prior approval.[93] Nevertheless on visiting Shanghai soon afterwards he was well satisfied with Balfour's judicious and conciliatory conduct. He found the consulate in a large and commodious house inside the city, a British residential settlement on an open airy site outside the city, and fifteen British subjects, whose families included six females, already living there.[94] The attitude of the Chinese authorities being 'Having obtained ground you had better manage it yourselves'[95] Balfour obtained their agreement that roads and bridges in the settlement should be the responsibility of the residents, acting through a committee elected from their number.[96] He thereby without premeditation laid the constitutional foundation for foreign administration of the settlement at Shanghai.

Balfour's combination of resolution and conciliation may account for his success with the Chinese. At least equal firmness was needed to control the British community, members of which went so far as to challenge the consulate staff to duels. Balfour did not reply to a merchant who called him out in a letter reminding him that besides being a consul he was a soldier, but he recorded his determination to control the merchant and secured a withdrawal and apology. A clerk in a British firm was apprehended for writing to Hale, the senior assistant, in terms construed as a challenge. He was released only on substantial bail and was fined $100. Davis had advised imprisonment but Balfour considered imprisonment inexpedient; in his view it would have excited the local British to have a man of the clerk's social standing in a Chinese gaol and British prestige would have suffered.[97]

Within a year Balfour, though successful, had had enough of the constant anxiety due to difficulties with the Chinese and to what he

called the peculiar vexations caused by his own countrymen. After twenty years constantly on duty and away from his native land he felt the need for relaxation and tendered his resignation. It was accepted with reluctance and his departure was delayed for many months while arrangements were made to replace him. By that time his health was giving trouble. He had had repeated attacks of inflammation of the spleen and a doctor now certified that consequent upon intense application to official duties he was labouring under a complicated and obstinate derangement of the digestive system, particularly impeding the action of the liver. He left China for ever, noting that had he speculated in land at Shanghai, something to which he was opposed in principle and had forbidden to his staff, he could have left with a large fortune.[98] When Macgregor retired, Balfour was offered Canton but refused.[99] He stuck to the army, became a full general and a KCB, and after retirement sat in the Commons for fifteen years.

Within scarcely more than three years, two of Pottinger's four consuls had died, one had resigned in disgust, and one had been got rid of. The amateur phase was ending.

2
THE CHINESE

IN the seventeenth century China had been conquered by the Manchus, robust nomads from the north-east. The now decadent Manchu dynasty was still on the throne, decadent Manchu garrisons were still dotted about China, and intermarriage was still prohibited, but the Manchus had become barely distinguishable from the Chinese, who were assimilating these conquerors as they had assimilated earlier ones. The Manchus had always governed on Chinese lines, taking over *en bloc* Chinese institutions. Officialdom remained, as it had been before the conquest, the top of the Chinese social ladder, and to become an official remained the goal of clever and ambitious youth. China had concluded, long before the Victorians did so, that success in competitive literary examinations qualified men to undertake whatever tasks the state might lay upon them. As in Britain the greatest merit of the examination system was that it opened a way, however difficult that way might be when obstructed by poverty, for men of the humblest origins to reach high office. The Manchus modified the system to give some preferential treatment for Manchus and Mongols but otherwise retained it intact, though in their decline they increasingly watered it down by raising funds through the sale of honorary or actual offices. The path to examination success was excessively thorny, requiring many years of dedicated study on prescribed lines of classical Chinese, a dead language written and understood only by the educated élite. The wastage was enormous. A series of progressively stiffer examinations, in all of which nearly all the competitors failed, ended for the lucky few in qualification for office. It then still remained actually to obtain a post and to rise through the official hierarchy, and the office-holder at all times risked being cashiered if something went wrong, or was thought to have gone wrong, in his area of responsibility or if he displeased a superior.

An incoming provincial official took over from his predecessor the seal and yamen belonging to his post. The yamen was a walled series of courtyards containing his offices and living quarters for himself, any family he brought with him, and his staff and servants. To Chinese eyes a yamen was a place of much dignity, even though to consular eyes it might appear 'an assemblage of miserable sheds, straggling gateways and half-ruined barn-like buildings'.[1] It was the local nerve-centre, from and into which reports and orders, in rigidly prescribed form, were continually passing. The strict 'rule of avoidance' prohibiting anyone from holding office in his native province went far to ensure that the newly appointed official, arriving after perhaps weeks of uncomfortable travel, was ignorant of local conditions and unduly dependent on underlings inherited from his predecessors. In the coastal belt in which the five consulates were located this rule had an additional disadvantage. Over most of China a form of Chinese, called in this period Mandarin because of its use in the oral transaction of all public business, is spoken with local variations perhaps not much greater than the difference between the broadest Scots and the broadest Devonshire. However, the coastal belt speaks a variety of dialects which differ more widely from Mandarin and from each other than Dutch does from German. In the coastal belt the official could normally communicate freely only with the tiny educated minority who had learned Mandarin. He required an interpreter to communicate with the rest of the population. If exceptionally he could speak the local dialect he might well think it unbecoming to use it officially, so that in his court evidence given in dialect which he had already understood might still be rendered into Mandarin for his benefit by an interpreter.[2]

The primary tasks of the official in his yamen were to keep everything quiet, to avoid criticism, to satisfy his superiors, and to remit fixed sums in taxes. Provided he fulfilled these tasks and provoked no serious complaints among the local gentry or serious uprisings among the local people he had in practice very wide administrative and judicial latitude. His official salary was derisory, and he could not pay his staff or maintain himself without taking money on the side. An honest official took only what public opinion considered reasonable, an avaricious one took a great deal more. Competence varied. There were able officials, who might or might not also be honest, with formidably keen minds, and there

were others who were inept bookworms. None of them knew anything of the world outside China.

Consular contacts with Chinese other than teachers, consulate employees, personal servants, and possibly mistresses were in the main confined to these products of a centuries-old and ossified selection system, though exceptionally gifted linguists like T.T. Meadows could establish wider contacts which were recognized to be valuable.[3] Officials with specialized functions, such as provincial treasurers and provincial judges, had little contact with consuls, who normally dealt with a hierarchy of all-purpose territorial officials ranging from viceroys and governors at the head of provinces through intendants and prefects in the middle to district magistrates at the bottom. Consuls were left in no doubt as to what was expected of them. They must, wrote Aberdeen, avoid giving just cause of offence to officials or people, and they were always to behave courteously towards officials.[4] Immediately on taking over Davis instructed them that among their chief duties was the attainment of the goodwill and esteem of officials and people.[5] Layton was reprimanded for being in constant altercation with the Amoy officials.[6] Bowring, Macgregor's successor at Canton, was told by Palmerston on appointment to remember that in dealings with Chinese officials temper and discretion were, above all things, requisite and that he was to try to cultivate a good understanding, discountenancing and repressing to the utmost of his abilities any proceedings of British subjects calculated to give just cause of complaint to officials or people.[7] Wade's manner to officials, praised as being firm and impressive yet courteous and gentleman-like, was evidently considered model.[8]

Well-intentioned instructions were easier to issue from headquarters than to carry out in the field across a cultural gulf. China had been defeated in the field, but foreigners remained by definition inferior beings, to whose officials the superiority of the Chinese government and of its officials should be demonstrated at every safe opportunity. The tone was set by Peking, where it took some thirty more years of argument before foreign representatives were received in audience by the emperor. Provincial officials who exposed themselves to a charge of making concessions considered unnecessary by the court jeopardized their careers. As a result they would, as one consul put it, turn a deaf ear to the most energetic protests against treaty violations if by affording relief they would

have to incur responsibility with their own people.⁹ A standard defensive tactic was to downgrade the level at which consular representations were handled; at Foochow viceroys passed them down to intendants who in turn tried to fob successive consuls off with mere deputies. ('Deputies' were men qualified for office who, pending appointment to substantive posts, were deputed by local officials to perform miscellaneous functions.)¹⁰

The instinctive attitudes of early Victorian consuls, and their reactions to Chinese official superciliousness, were for the most part what might have been expected, and references to China as a half-civilized country and similar expressions are recurrent in their despatches.¹¹ In a book written only three and a half years after his arrival in China, T.T. Meadows did show sympathetic insight. The Chinese, he wrote, were often unreasonable towards foreigners because they believed foreigners a coarse, rough lot; steady urbanity, not reactions confirming their belief, could make insolent Chinese look very foolish; lies and false promises were in a Chinese not incompatible with high principles, which were met as often in China as in Europe; in social intercourse an undisturbed manner, expressive of placid delight in Chinese company, was to be recommended; a man without all his wits about him could not hope to prevail against them in argument on any subject which they understood; they had a great fund of funny stories, which they told well; and on the whole they were not disagreeable to associate with, in spite of occasional qualms caused by their dirty habits. The dirty habits he had in mind were probably hawking and spitting; many years later Meadows did his best to be polite, but feared he might have to run out to be sick in the courtyard, when an official paying a cheerful and civil call brought his own spittoon, a dirty-looking pewter vase which his servant placed on the table between the two dignitaries and which he lifted from time to time to spit into. Meadows, whose own behaviour as the years went by became more and more eccentric and was far from steadily urbane, showed himself even in his youth a man of his time by assuming that the circulation of good European works on natural law, political economy, metaphysics, and science would eventually demonstrate Europe's mental superiority as its superior physical power had already been demonstrated, and that China would then bow before the civilized West's moral power. Still, he was in advance of most of his colleagues in his recognition of Chinese qualities.¹² At the

other end of the consular spectrum was Parkes, whose notoriously overbearing manner towards Chinese officials did not prevent him from becoming successively minister to Japan and to China. To the 25-year-old Parkes the shrill whistling and belching of steam by a high-pressure British steamer at Canton seemed a tangible contradiction of his fusty, malodorous teacher's belief that Confucius was the ruling genius of the world.[13]

Urbanity was noticeably lacking in a series of consular reactions at Foochow. The chief superintendent disapproved when Sinclair broke off relations because an official had not returned Sinclair's call, and the Foreign Office considered that Hale, breaking off relations later, had been injudicious and hasty. The Foreign Office endorsed the chief superintendent's disapproval of an unduly strong letter from J.T. Walker to the viceroy, and stated that Her Majesty's government could never approve of violent and intemperate language, which in any case tended to defeat its own ends. Hale was told that he had shown lack of courtesy and dignity by tearing in half, and sending to the viceroy, a letter from the prefect in which the term 'barbarian' was frequently used.[14] On the other hand, both chief superintendent and Foreign Office with apparent inconsistency approved Medhurst's reaction to a proclamation referring to the British as barbarians and to the Queen's officers as barbarian headmen. Medhurst informed the prefect that he would not put up with this insulting designation; 'we are not barbarians but in civilisation and everything else that constitutes the greatness of a nation undoubtedly your superiors. This is patent to the whole world, and we might call you barbarians, yet we do not do so, because we are a courteous nation'. The Foreign Office even suggested that such counter-statements to offensive proclamations might be made public.[15] Medhurst considered that the viceroy was served by a villainous crew of subordinates remarkable for administrative imbecility, corruption, and contempt for foreigners,[16] and his tone continued correspondingly abrasive. At one interview with a sub-prefect he taxed the sub-prefect and his superior, the prefect, with deceit and falsehood, with cringing servility in a previous application for British naval assistance against pirates, and with impudent evasion of treaty rights in a current case. He added for good measure that the case showed what a double-faced dishonest set Chinese officials were and why rebellion was successfully wresting the empire from their injustice and vicious mismanage-

ment. The unhappy sub-prefect said 'Quite true, quite true' and, begging to be excused, took his leave.[17] It is hardly surprising that Medhurst described himself as treated by Foochow officials with that sort of doubtful courtesy which was never accorded without suggestion, and then only in scant measure.[18]

Formal introductory calls when a new consul or new Chinese official took over a post were a fruitful source of real or imagined slights. A sedan-chair was indispensable for consular calls, and except at Foochow, where blue covers were used for years, the covers had to be green, the colour used in the chairs of those Chinese officials with whom consuls claimed equality of rank. Uniform too was indispensable, although it looked outlandish to Chinese eyes and in no way impressed them.[19] Receiving a call at his first post, Alcock wore a cocked hat, a blue coat with silver lace and gold buttons, blue trousers with a broad silver stripe, and a number of Spanish and Portuguese decorations,[20] probably creating much the same impression as a Zulu chieftain in ceremonial finery would have done. Sweating in his heavy uniform, the consul paying or returning a call clambered into his chair and was borne off by the consulate chair coolies, his dignity possibly supported by a retinue on foot drawn from the consulate's Chinese staff. After a lengthy journey through the noise and smells of crowded alleyways he reached the yamen. There, if all went well, the twin main gates were opened for him, petards were ceremonially exploded, he dismounted in the courtyard, and he advanced, his host coming forward to meet him at the point in the yamen prescribed by Chinese protocol for a meeting between officials of their respective ranks. He was seated at the appropriate position in the reception hall and sweetmeats and tea were put on the table. After a suitable time the official lifted his teacup for the first time and sipped it, as a sign that the call had lasted long enough. The consul rose, he was escorted out by his host for the right distance, neither more nor less, the two men took leave of each other with bows and stereotyped phrases of courtesy, and the consul was borne back to the consulate. Medhurst's initial call on the viceroy at Foochow in 1855 went admirably. An appointment was immediately made for his call, and on his arrival at the main gate with the vice-consul they were most politely received by no less than three deputies; then the prefect received them in the main audience hall; and finally the viceroy met them under the eaves of his inner court, whence he led them in

person to his inner room, seating them above him and conversing affably and courteously for twenty minutes. The round of calls on leading Foochow officials which Medhurst paid on his return from home leave in 1858 was less successful. After a little pressing they all agreed to receive him and most were civil enough, but the governor was so cool and ungracious that Medhurst remonstrated with him.[21]

If things did not go well the consul, trying to look impassively dignified, might be kept waiting in his chair outside the yamen gates for five or ten minutes while the riff-raff stuck their noses into the chair and commented on its strange occupant; or only a side gate might be opened; or his reception inside the yamen might be inappropriate.[22] Worse, a Chinese official might indicate that he was too busy for calls,[23] in which case a formal protest might be made. A Chinese call on the consul was similarly formal. No detailed description of a Chinese call in the early days seems to have survived, but the call would probably not have been very different from one described later in the century. The official, wearing his official robes and official hat, arrived at seven o'clock in the morning and was invited to a seat; the consul, who had been waiting in uniform, sat down in his cocked hat, failure to wear which throughout the call would have been gravely discourteous; and then the consul offered a sweet foreign liqueur and foreign biscuits, feeling a fool to be wearing a hat in his own drawing-room and to be drinking a liqueur before breakfast.[24] Chinese officials, like the consuls, were prompt to take offence, justifiably or otherwise, at the manner of their reception. One complained that no petards had been fired in honour of his arrival and rejected the explanation that this was not a foreign custom.[25]

Business with Chinese officials was conducted by interviews and by written communications, both time-consuming. The journey by chair to and from an interview might well be wearisomely lengthy. All correspondence had to be translated. A consul competent in the written language did not need a translation to comprehend inward communications, but translations had to be made for the consulate archives; the Ningpo archives were found difficult to use[26] because translations had not been made and filed. Not infrequently slights implying inequality of status between China and Britain were seen in the form or wording of Chinese official documents, which then again led to protests.[27] A consul or interpreter, however skilled,

always needed assistance to turn into acceptable official Chinese the communications drafted in English in the consulate. Originally the interpreter seems to have written out a translation which the consulate's Chinese writer then amended stylistically.[28] Later the writer, who understood no English, was told in the spoken language what was to be said and submitted for approval a draft in the very different written language of Chinese bureaucracy. After the translation had finally been approved a fair copy was made in the writer's best handwriting and dispatched. Although at first not all consulate writers were sufficiently well educated for their functions, as surviving specimens of poor style and handwriting show, the class soon became indispensable and respected members of every consulate's staff.[29] One experienced writer later became famous in the service for an uncanny ability to deduce from oral explanations in halting Chinese exactly what needed to be written and was regarded as almost a thought-reader.[30]

Relations with Chinese officials were generally limited to calls of ceremony, calls about current business, and written communications. An 'inhospitable exclusiveness' was regarded as a Chinese characteristic. Chinese officials would have risked their social reputations and their careers by being on noticeably friendly personal terms with a foreigner. An educated Chinese employed in the Ningpo consulate showed the state of public feeling, and earned instant dismissal, by saying that to be seen at the local examination hall with a foreigner would be degrading and refusing to take a consular officer there.[31] The obstacles in the way of a relaxed social relationship would in any case have been great even if the Chinese had been willing to contemplate it. Upbringing, education, tastes, and domestic habits were too dissimilar for common ground to be readily found. A major barrier was the different position of women in the two societies. Upper-class Chinese women lived virtually in purdah, and the freer life of foreign women must constantly have shocked Chinese susceptibilities. (As recently as the 1930s an elderly Chinese in a Peking park saw two Chinese students of opposite sexes walking decorously hand in hand. 'Look at them, just like two dogs', he said bitterly.)[a] Yet even without social contacts individual Chinese officials soon ceased to be seen as stereotypes. Many, perhaps most, were found unfriendly, ignorant, and obstructive. Some seemed merely ridiculous, like the aged Shanghai magistrate whose predecessor's death had been attributed

to the malign geomantic influence of an American mission steeple. His fear of similar building and similar effects on his life expectancy led him to arrest Chinese who had sold land near his yamen to British missionaries, thereby causing a dispute settled by Alcock's tactful assurance that no steeple would be built on the site.[32] Others were respected, witness a succession of judgements expressed by Winchester, himself a well-educated and able man. At Ningpo the intendant had in his opinion always been courteous and fair to foreigners. At Canton, effusively embraced by a departing high official, Winchester made allowance for the finesse and diplomacy usual in China but parted with regret from a Manchu gentleman who had so interestingly combined elegant and courteous manners, a readiness to gain the personal goodwill of foreign officers, intelligence and quickness, curiosity about foreign arts and sciences, and harmless vanity and ostentation. The Canton viceroy, with whom Winchester had been in frequent official contact, seemed to him a man of conduct and ability, quick to apprehend questions and to settle complicated issues, and a potentially most dangerous opponent.[33]

A consul who failed to obtain satisfaction by badgering the local authorities at interviews and bombarding them with despatches and letters had reached the end of normal procedures. In theory the dispute could then be referred to the chief superintendent and raised by him with his opposite number, the imperial commissioner at Canton, but Alcock roundly asserted that this was quite ineffective,[34] and frustrated consuls were apt to risk disapproval and take matters into their own hands. It was often effective to direct British subjects to stop paying customs duties locally until redress was obtained. Alcock did so once at Shanghai without being reproved, but his view that it was a course which should be adopted wherever necessary was not accepted.[35] At least five other officers in charge of posts were at different times reproved for adopting it.[36] Those who had got what they wanted by this means probably thought their success worth a reproof. The Foreign Office were finally driven to include in consuls' letters of appointment a specific prohibition against a practice regarded as irregular and objectionable.[37]

It was also often effective to call in the navy, or threaten to call in the navy, but this form of consular pressure was even less likely to be favourably viewed by superior authority. A.W. Elmslie, tem-

porarily in charge at Canton, seems to have escaped rebuke for getting a naval party forcibly to release a Parsee arrested for debt, but it was a different story when he threatened naval action unless an armed robbery were punished and the stolen property returned. He was told that his threat was futile, as the navy could not operate so far up the river, and that, as he should have known, unexecuted threats weakened one's position.[38] J.T. Walker asked for naval support at Foochow, where he wished to make a decided stand against tyrannous Chinese encroachments, but the navy complained and his action was not well viewed.[39] The Chinese authorities having failed to remove some squatters' huts from land purchased by British subjects at Foochow the navy at Hale's request landed thirty-five unarmed men and demolished them; Hale was told that except in extreme circumstances no hostile acts should be engaged in without reference to the chief superintendent, who as a general rule would not sanction any act of violence until he had applied for redress to the highest Chinese authority.[40] T.T. Meadows, having expressed readiness to seize with an armed force a well-known Ningpo pirate should the pirate's acts in the city lead to the murder of a respectable British subject, was peremptorily prohibited from such unlawful proceedings.[41]

Almost immediately afterwards, the crew of a wrecked British vessel, on reaching an inhabited island near Ningpo, were robbed and stripped. To prevent further mistreatment of British subjects, and being convinced that application for redress to the Chinese authorities would have been utterly useless, Meadows proceeded in HMS *Cormorant* to the spot. The offending village was surrounded with a strong guard and the houses in which most stolen property was found were pulled down, with dire warnings for the future should there be a recurrence. The chief superintendent, Bowring, told Meadows that the preferable course would have been for the captain of *Cormorant*, accompanied by a consular interpreter, to have called the people together, lectured them, and promised rewards for kind treatment of shipwrecked men. The captain got into hotter water; the admiral found the action an indefensible breach of the treaties and ordered *Cormorant* to be relieved at Ningpo. Meadows, always argumentative, was not disposed to kiss the rod and sought to justify himself. Immediately on his return to Ningpo he had told the intendant that he had been violating the treaties; the intendant had smiled and on hearing Meadows'

narrative had declared that he entirely approved and that moderation and leniency had been shown. It would not have been possible,
Meadows argued, to ask the intendant to act, for the building of
houses on the island was prohibited and officials permitting it were
supposed to be cashiered or degraded; the legal punishment on the
villagers, a hundred blows of the heavy bamboo and transporta-
tion, would have been unduly severe; as things were the villagers
only had to rebuild their houses with materials that had not been
destroyed. Bowring was wearied by such controversies with his
subordinate and the Foreign Office found Meadows' action highly
irregular and culpable, and calculated to lead to very serious international difficulties with China.[42]

M.C. Morrison did apply to the Amoy authorities for redress
when villagers in search of plunder attacked a grounded British
vessel, killing three of the crew and severely wounding the master
and five others. He was told that the local magistrate would have
difficulty in collecting a sufficient punitive force but that the
Chinese would co-operate with a British naval vessel, and the
intendant agreed the text of a proclamation drafted by Morrison
which demanded the surrender of the ringleaders and the payment
of compensation. The Chinese force assembled to meet Morrison
and the navy near the spot was derisory, but the officer in charge
and a few men were taken on board the British vessel and carried
the proclamation to the first of the two villages concerned. On the
village opening fire it was burned. At the second village the
headmen were told that the compensation would be $10,000, or
$6,000 if the ringleaders were surrendered. They offered only $100,
and after due warning the village of 1,500 to 2,000 stone houses
was fired, with some loss of life. Six Chinese war junks then arrived
and the commandant expressed his thanks for the action taken. The
Chinese in the Amoy area were said to be pleased at the chastise-
ment inflicted on villages which had hitherto paid no revenue and
had defied the government. Presumably because Morrison had
acted in consultation and in nominal co-operation with the Chinese
authorities, the Foreign Office approved his action.[43]

There was some sense, as there often was, behind Meadows'
wrong-headedness. The normal Chinese official was constitutionally averse to avoidable action and avoidable responsibility,
and usually had such insufficient means of enforcement that direct
confrontation with rioters, bandits, pirates, and other groups of

sturdy malefactors was hazardous if not impossible. His ragged staff of yamen runners and police, notable for 'dirt, cunning, ferocity and cruelty',[44] was geared only to wreak his vengeance against scattered individuals who might later fall into his hands. A consular application for redress after some attack on a British subject was therefore apt to be fobbed off with an interim reply saying that an immediate investigation had been urgently ordered and with a later substantive reply containing some such statement as that the culprits had fled and could not be apprehended. Still more frustrating was a bland denial that anything untoward had occurred. A British cutter was boarded in the Canton river by a large number of cut-throats and the vessel was burned, some of the crew being killed or drowned and nearly all the others severely wounded. The Chinese reply to representations was that on enquiry a foreign vessel was found to have accidentally caught fire and that no robbery or fighting had been seen or heard of at the time.[45] Even where malefactors were apprehended they were not necessarily punished. Two bands of pirates captured at sea by the British navy were successively handed over to the Foochow authorities. The first band were said to have repented of their evil course, were pardoned, and were drafted into various regiments. The official taking delivery of the second band 'met them as friends and equals, bowing in a most ceremonious style and drinking tea and *samshoe* with them, and taking them away more as companions than as prisoners' (*samshoe*, or *samshui*, is a potent Chinese spirit).[46]

On the other hand, if punishment was inflicted its severity tended to shock. All but 3 of a group of 28 suspected pirates handed over by the navy to the Amoy authorities were beheaded within three days, and in Foochow a group of 170 pirates was beheaded in half an hour, one man despatching 62 with a single sword.[47] Palmerston issued orders for decapitation to be sought only where such examples might really be required for the protection of British subjects and by the gravity of the offence, as the Chinese seemed to inflict capital punishment to an extent not in harmony with the British nation's feelings.[48]

Chinese courts and judicial methods were likewise not to the British taste. The accused and witnesses were examined on their knees, the presiding official was prosecution, jury, and judge all in one, and the use of torture was routine. Palmerston initially gave instructions that the consul or his representative should be present

at any punishment inflicted on Chinese for assaults or outrages on British subjects. Alcock objected that examination under torture, brutal punishments, the substitution of bogus criminals for the real culprits, and the possible condemnation of the innocent were all factors which might make consular attendance incompatible with British standards or, if the innocent were condemned, might be disadvantageous to British interests. Palmerston backed down and in effect left it to consuls to decide when consular representation was desirable.[49] One such occasion arose in Shanghai in 1858. Reporting the piracy of a British vessel there D.B. Robertson said he had seen death in many forms but nothing so fearful as the pool of blood which covered the deck, and that it would be his duty to press for capital punishment. He was present in the intendant's yamen when three apprehended men were sentenced and led out to their execution, which on Robertson's orders was witnessed by the consulate gaoler. The rapid capture and immediate execution indicated to Robertson a friendly disposition on the part of the Chinese authorities, and to encourage this he gave the intendant $200 for distribution among the police.[50]

Official powerlessness in the face of local disturbance was described from Ningpo by J.A.T. Meadows, who had followed his younger brother T.T. Meadows out to China and like him had secured appointment to the service by intensive application to the language. Villagers incensed by a new tax-collectors' device which increased their tax burden threatened to burn out the Ningpo magistrate and his collectors. Asked to protect a British missionary who lived next door to one of the collectors, the acting intendant said on the one hand that the villagers would not dare and on the other hand that calling out the soldiers, who would not act against the people, would be useless. The villagers did dare and there was commotion in the city the next day, throughout which Meadows pushed himself into every place where there was any stir, meeting with not the least insolence or insult but constantly being asked by the villagers whether they did not have right on their side. He found the rioters burning everything in the yamen of the magistrate, who had fled with all his people, and in the houses of two tax-collectors. The acting intendant was pulled out of his chair and very roughly handled, his yamen was gutted, and he and his family lost everything except the clothes on their backs. During the destruction of the two yamens the city's normal life continued within 50 yards,

shoe-makers, barbers, carpenters, and the like plying their trades as usual, while in the general's yamen a couple of dozen officers and men squatted peacefully around without a weapon in sight. Meanwhile, the newly appointed prefect had agreed to go with the mob to a temple for discussion, and there Meadows saw him surrounded by a crowd of countrymen, some of whom clapped him on the back and bawled into his ear while he every now and then smiled and replied. The prefect gave a written undertaking to revert to the former tax-collection system and two days later offered a large reward for the apprehension of two tax-collectors, with whom he was however understood to have had a conversation the previous evening.[51] Such rude democracy not infrequently tempered autocracy and arbitrary rule in China.

Consular officers were not at risk of physical violence being directed against them by Chinese officials. Official reluctance to use physical force was demonstrated during a journey which Gingell made overland without having any treaty right to do so. He was transferred from Foochow to Amoy and in the absence of any foreign vessel perforce took passage in a salt junk. Two days out the junk anchored indefinitely on account of unfavourable winds and pirates, so Gingell went on by land, hoping to be helped towards Amoy by a prefect three days' journey away. The prefect did provide an escort of two policemen but the next day, no doubt thinking on reflection that he might get himself into trouble, sent a deputy in pursuit who woke Gingell up in the evening first to say that the prefect invited him to return to the prefectural city for an entertainment and then to say that Gingell must return to it. Gingell refused and headed for Amoy next morning, but suddenly realized that his chair-bearers had left the Amoy road and were carrying him back to the prefect. Gingell staged a sitdown strike and the following day received from the prefect presents of a chair, wine, food, and so on, and a further invitation to return. Gingell declined everything except the chair, in which he went forward, and had no further difficulties, but the Chinese authorities maintained their objections to his overland route and complained formally.[52] In later periods it would have been exceptional for a consular officer in such a predicament not to have been helped out with good grace.

The risk of physical violence came not from officials but from the unlettered masses. The masses were often, perhaps usually, 'harmless and inoffensive'.[a] In the countryside near Hong Kong the

very young children and the dogs ran off howling at the approach
of one student interpreter, and the older people examined him most
minutely from head to foot, but there was not the slightest incivility
and he was invited to take food or join in a pipe.[a] On other
occasions reactions were different. China saw nothing like the
professional ferocity of Japanese attacks on foreigners during the
opening of Japan, but Chinese attacks, which were most frequent in
Canton and Foochow, were unpleasant enough. In Canton, Vice-
consul Jackson, going with a Chinese official to the site of an attack
on British subjects, had to retreat for a mile under a continuous and
well-directed volley of stones; he was assaulted and robbed on
one walk and on another walk with Macgregor both men were
menaced with constant cries of 'Slay the thievish devils'. Returning
from a 5-mile walk along the crest of a hill M.C. Morrison, a
missionary, and another companion were overtaken by several
hundred villagers, many of whom had swords, spears, and shields;
at first they were stoned, then Morrison and the missionary were
knocked down, the missionary was wounded on the head with a
sword, and the whole party were robbed of their clothes, beaten,
and threatened with death. The delightful walking country round
Canton was evidently considered hazardous, for the chief superintendent considered that Morrison had been imprudent and the
Foreign Office that his conduct had been most foolish and culpable.
The usual practice of the Meadows brothers at Canton was to go
out together armed and to pick their way along crests so that they
could always see any attack being mounted and could get back to
their boats before being overtaken.[53] Yet Bowring, despite warnings, took many walks, often alone, within a 20- to 30-mile radius
of Canton while he was consul there, and far from being assaulted
was always courteously treated as he stood to watch such features
of local life as outdoor plays and executions.[54] The discrepancy is
difficult to explain, unless it was that the country people paid their
customary respect to grey hairs even on Bowring's foreign head.
Cantonese pirates were no respecters of consular officers' persons,
although their attacks were recognized not to be specifically anti-
foreign in intention. T.T. Meadows, returning one evening by river
from Whampoa to Canton, was assailed by a piratical craft containing about thirty men. He had armed himself with a rifle, two
pistols, and a sword, but the rifle jammed and the pirates obtained
possession of his boat after he had shot one pirate dead and

wounded another with the pistols. He jumped into the river, hid, and reached the consulate, wounded and exhausted, three hours later. Oakley and three companions were attacked lower down the river one evening. The pirates boarded without warning and commenced a discharge of stinkpots (sulphur-based incendiaries emitting noxious fumes) and spears, one of which buried itself in the stock of Oakley's gun. The foreigners were well armed and after a constant fire had been kept up for some twenty minutes the pirates disengaged. They carried off most of their dead and wounded but left one body behind, and one of the British party's servants was missing.[55] Foochow was no better than Canton. Parkes was stoned by soldiers, Jackson was repeatedly hooted and pelted, M.C. Morrison and Meredith were pelted with stones while walking in the city's streets, Markham was assaulted and pelted by villagers. Parish had difficulty in escaping when stoned by some 150 people, receiving some heavy blows. He had often been stoned before but had not reported the earlier attacks to the consul, who he doubtless feared would prohibit his walks, and a couple of months later was again pelted and hooted while walking on the shore.[56]

Some attacks may have been provoked by arrogant behaviour. The attitude of British officials towards Chinese was not always what it should have been. An incident at Ningpo leaves a disagreeable impression of Davis' attitude as chief superintendent, an attitude all the more surprising as he had spent a large part of his working life in responsible positions in China and was literate in Chinese. The rudder of HMS *Ringdove*, under repair on shore, was being guarded against theft by a marine. The marine's orders were to load and to hail, and then to fire, if anyone approached the rudder, but the officer who had given him these orders was afterwards not sure whether he had told the marine to load with blank or ball. While on guard the marine shot and seriously wounded a Chinese. Sullivan, the consul, arranged for the marine to be held in naval custody pending instructions from Davis as to whether he should be tried in Hong Kong or in the consular court. In a sensible report he doubted the power of any naval officer to station an armed guard on shore without the privity of consul and local authorities, and doubted any officer's authority to issue the ill-judged and thoughtless orders to which the occurrence was mainly attributable. Davis' reply quite concurred in the opinion of Hong Kong's acting attorney-general that the marine, who deserved

commendation for his strict obedience to orders, must immediately be released and discharged from all charges for this imaginary offence; the officer's orders were justified, given the thievish propensity of the Chinese; if the Chinese had entered the enclosure to steal he had very properly been shot, and if he had entered by mistake the shooting was a mere accident; the Chinese propensity to lie was so notorious that their evidence could not be used with too much caution.[57] In an Amoy case the reaction of Bonham, who succeeded Davis as chief superintendent and governor of Hong Kong and whose previous post in the Straits Settlements should have taught him something about Chinese, was equally disagreeable and did not commend itself to the Foreign Office. A Straits Chinese employee of Muir and Syme, an Amoy firm with whom Layton had been having one of his usual quarrels, approached Layton improperly dressed and smoking a cigar. Instead of throwing the cigar away when ordered to do so he whiffed the smoke into Layton's face. Layton jumped up, boxed the man's ears, and kicked him two or three times. Layton could scarcely imagine that anyone so insulted could have refrained from acting in the same way, though he admitted that his action, committed in momentary irritation, had been hasty; and as for the firm's allegation that the consulate staff often smoked in the consulate office, it was an utter falsehood that the staff so far forgot themselves. Bonham assured the Foreign Office that any person in a similar situation in life who had behaved like that in a merchant's office in Singapore would have had the same treatment as Layton had given, either from the owner of the premises or from a servant. Palmerston told the firm that while Layton's act of violence was regretted, their employee's conduct had not been becoming, and that it would be to the advantage of all parties to let the matter drop, but he instructed Bonham to point out most strongly what a false position Layton had put himself into by allowing himself to be betrayed into violence; this was at all times mistaken and undignified, and in an official was calculated to diminish usefulness.[58]

Physical violence towards social inferiors or servants is not behaviour usually associated with the Victorian gentleman. Alcock was not expressing a merely personal view when in fining a British subject for beating a servant he declared in his Shanghai consular court that disobedience in a servant in no way justified violence, more especially in the circumstances in which the foreign com-

munity in China was placed.[59] Nevertheless, some entries in private consular diaries show regrettable lapses. Satow of the Japan consular service, destined to become successively minister to Japan and to China, in his aloof maturity a fearsomely correct figure, was briefly posted to China in his arrogant youth and booted his disobedient boy downstairs with two good kicks.[60] A coolie was beaten for smashing a lamp;[a] a boy was thrashed when his master was overcharged by boatmen;[a] and two new recruits threatened to kick a servant for an inflated bill as late as 1903, by which date, it is true, a third recruit who witnessed the scene feared that neither of his colleagues would ever be conspicuous for treating the natives with tact.[a] Inexcusable though such conduct must now seem, and justified though Alcock's contemporary condemnation was, kicking or otherwise maltreating servants was at least no very shocking thing in imperial China. An affecting scene in China's most famous novel describes the remorse of the sensitive hero after kicking his favourite maid in the dark when he had meant to kick a skivvy.

Some attacks on consular officers resulted from failure to keep cool under provocation. One attack on Parish at Foochow might not have occurred if he had not first pushed, and then kicked, a villager abusing and threatening to beat a Chinese accompanying Parish.[61] Returning to their boat after a trip into the country three student interpreters, Adkins, Webster, and Payne, were faced with demands for about five times the correct payment from their village porters, who to enforce their demands laid hold of the boat's ropes. Webster and Payne, both of whose subsequent careers in the service were short and disgraceful, wanted to land and start a fight. Adkins kept his head, went ashore alone, and by 'a little management' gradually got the porters to let go of one rope after another. The boat dropped quietly down river amid the porters' parting imprecations, but Adkins was sure that if the party had struck one blow or fired one shot it would immediately have been stoned.[a]

In most cases of attack, however, consular officers were probably the scapegoats for the behaviour, at times inconsiderate, at times unwise, at times bad, and at times atrocious, of other foreigners.

3

THE BRITISH COMMUNITIES

AT the ports consul and naval officer, both holding the Queen's commission, stood in a relationship to each other which was close but not invariably happy. At Shanghai Alcock was once told that unless he hauled the Union Jack down from his official boat a naval party would be sent to haul it down,[1] and he had a notable brush with a peppery commander-in-chief. Nettled by Alcock's criticism of his orders, the admiral declared that so long as he held his command no man living should use such language without being held accountable. He complained to the Admiralty. Alcock responded that gratuitous charges levelled by one so much higher in rank and so much more advanced in years required an answer in terms no less direct and unhesitating, and he analysed over seventeen pages 'the succession of erroneous premises on which all His Excellency's arguments are founded, and the mistaken inferences and conclusions to which they lead him'. Admiral and consul were induced to bury the hatchet in a courteously worded exchange of apologies, in which however each man managed to restate his original position.[2] Such clashes were fortunately unusual. Normally consular relations with the navy were excellent, and if consuls often called for naval help the navy were not infrequently glad of consular help. When a fisherman was accidentally killed during gunnery practice off Amoy they turned to the consul, who settled with the dead man's parents for $25 down and $5 a month for five months,[3] and when off on a pirate hunt they were apt to beg the loan of a Chinese-speaking junior as interpreter. The junior might find himself at some risk in volunteering to go along with a boat party attacking pirate junks or with a landing party attacking several hundred pirates on shore, but it was a change from office work.[4]

The remainder of the British communities consisted of constantly

changing faces from merchant ships and of resident missionaries and merchants. Consuls had the twin functions of trying to ensure that the Chinese authorities accorded the communities protection and that legitimate British aspirations were as far as possible furthered, and of trying to enforce British good behaviour and British observance of the treaty provisions. Neither function was made easier by the presence of lawless non-British foreigners, perhaps without consuls in China and probably inadequately controlled by their consuls if they had any. Chinese officials had difficulty in distinguishing between different foreign nationalities and ordinary Chinese could not distinguish between them, so that the unpunished misdeeds of a foreigner of whatever nationality tended to be laid at the door of foreigners collectively. As Alcock put it, the Chinese suffered most, but every European nation also suffered, both in character and in their interests in China, from the activities of worthless foreigners not under effective consular control who converted their treaty privileges of access and trade into means of fraud and violence.[5] When a Chinese at Ningpo was violently pushed overboard by a Portuguese and drowned, Sullivan's consulate was besieged by the dead man's friends and relatives, as in his experience usually happened in cases of assault by foreigners on Chinese at Ningpo. He had difficulty in persuading the complainants that he had no jurisdiction over the Portuguese but managed to send them all to the intendant. The relatives were bought off by the other side for $20, and the intendant duly pronounced that it had been an accident. In this instance the only immediate sequel was Sullivan's lament that life was held cheaply enough in China for it to be purchased for a few dollars, but in every such incident there was a potential risk, immediate or delayed, to all foreigners.[6]

Looking after British merchant seamen was an important consular duty, on which consuls reported to the Board of Trade and not to the Foreign Office. D.B. Robertson considered seamen as a class to be shameless scroungers who drank away their money and then got undeserved relief from the consulate.[7] All too often they were also exceedingly violent and troublesome. In 1847 Alcock described the vessels in Shanghai as manned by the lowest class of London and Liverpool seafaring men or by Lascars and Manilamen whose knives were always ready for service. In 1852 he reported that it was no uncommon thing for a whole suburb of Shanghai to

be put in terror of their lives by the drunken violence of some of Sydney's and San Francisco's most dissolute men, armed with bowie knives and revolvers. In 1853 he was trying to arrange the apprehension of a hundred or so seamen, mostly British or American but including some Germans, Swedes, and French, who were plundering in the suburbs and the surrounding country. In 1855 Robertson reported that it was sometimes dangerous for Europeans, and generally dangerous for Chinese, to walk down Shanghai's streets at night owing to drunken and insubordinate seamen, and in 1857 that he and the United States consul had difficulty in keeping order with some 2,000 seamen, chiefly British and Americans of the worst class, in port. In the latter year a respectable Chinese peasant was murdered by a number of European seamen, and Robertson feared that evidence to convict would be wanting, although a more cruel and outrageous murder could hardly have been committed; he had given some temporary assistance to the destitute and pregnant widow and would try to collect a small sum for her. Following the unprovoked murder of an innocent Chinese by rampaging liberty men from British naval vessels, Robertson asked in 1858 that the landing of these men should be more strictly regulated; men from merchant ships, he said (with some appearance of inconsistency), were generally orderly and with them an assault was rare, but the naval men seemed to consider themselves free from all restraint on shore and to consider the persons and property of Chinese to be entirely at their disposal. The following year T.T. Meadows likewise accused seamen from men-of-war of causing more trouble in the Shanghai settlement than any other class.[8] Looking back later in life, C. Alabaster remembered the British man-of-war's crew of his youth as slaves who on their very rare trips on shore got drunk at once and pitched into every foreigner they met.[a]

The deplorable Shanghai picture was repeated at all the other ports. A glimpse of seamen ashore in China came from Ningpo in 1859. One Sunday night a Yorkshireman serving on a Danish ship fatally knifed an American seaman in a Swiss grog-shop where a mixture of Chinese spirits and gin was sold at $1 a bottle. The grog-shop consisted of three rooms. In the bedroom on the right German crews were having supper at the time; in the centre room there was drinking and dancing; and the third room, where the murder took place, was a bar 8 feet square. At Amoy Layton was

pleased that he had so few serious cases when in a year there might be over a thousand seamen, British, Arabs, Lascars, Manilamen, Malays, Hindus, and Muslims, in the port, but he had had to deal with two masters who were notorious drunkards; one frequently lay in his own vomit on the deck and the other, after lying in bed unwashed for ten days, had to be cleaned up by the mates before appearing in the consular court. He had found a British merchant who spoke Bengali useful, as an interpreter in that language was often needed. Sullivan, who at times had up to 700 seamen in port at Amoy, and who took on a constable speaking Malay, Bengali, and Portuguese, gave a master two months for taking an armed boat's crew on shore at midnight, breaking open a house, and assaulting the inmates. M.C. Morrison at the same port had to pay a British master to interpret in Malay after a quarrel between Malay and Javanese seamen had left several dangerously wounded. At Foochow a seaman's death was ascribed to arsenic administered in a Shanghai brothel. A mate searching with an armed boat's crew among the harbour's floating brothels for an abducted prostitute caused so much alarm that another prostitute was drowned; the Chinese officials half hinted that compensation would be the best settlement, and Medhurst was glad to find that the mate's payment of $50 to the relatives arranged the matter. At Canton trouble was incessant. In one of the earliest incidents men from a British naval vessel murdered an American baker in cold blood after a drinking quarrel, throwing him into the river with his arms and legs tied together and rowing off. Bowring soon concluded at Canton that British vessels trading with China were often commanded by unfit persons, brutal, poorly educated, and indifferent seamen, with re-sults only too apparent in the consular court's records.[9]

At first consuls were ill-equipped to deal with a tide of violent or refractory seamen, for they lacked physical means of enforcement, as Thom had found, and had nowhere to confine prisoners. Chinese officials might oblige by making room for British prisoners in Chinese prisons, but Chinese prisons were unspeakable. When Layton took six sailors to the Chinese prison in Amoy in 1845 he found a state of misery and filth almost too shocking for him to behold and far too horrid for him to narrate. He suspected that his sailors were supplied in prison with prostitutes, Chinese spirits, and provisions, and if the sailors had money on them the suspicion was probably well-founded; treatment in a Chinese prison varied

according to the ability to pay. By 1846 Layton was punishing most petty crimes by imprisonment in his own consular gaol; the prisoners were usually kept in irons for the first twenty-four or forty-eight hours and were then put on parole and made to spend eight hours a day clearing the compound and doing other similar work. As there was neither gaoler nor constable, Layton visited the prison room himself once or twice a day and the consulate's Chinese servants fixed and removed irons. Sullivan in 1850 considered this gaol grossly unsatisfactory. It consisted of a single room about 11 feet square, ventilated only by a 6-inch grating on the door and without means of removing nightsoil. The whole space was so small and its tainted smell so overpowering that Sullivan hesitated to keep any human being in it for more than one night during the hot season, and for that reason had let off with a fine one delinquent who deserved imprisonment. The following year Sullivan was forced with the utmost reluctance to send to the Chinese prison three men for whom he had no accommodation. Sullivan's first plea for permission to spend $70 on providing proper accommodation was turned down flat by Bonham, who replied that it would be improper to spend public money on improving private property and that in any case the Parliamentary grant was insufficient to meet even really needful and pressing contingencies. Sullivan returned to the charge and Bonham then undertook to consider plans and specifications but typically combined his undertaking with a complaint, which Sullivan demonstrated was ungrounded, that Sullivan seemed much more disposed than his predecessors to propose the spending of public money. Within ten years, it is regrettable to find, a successor at Amoy had nothing good to say of Sullivan's gaol; prisoners so frequently broke out that a sentence of imprisonment was a mere form, and the cells were so unhealthy that many of the prisoners who did not break out had to be sent to hospital or released for reasons of health.[10] At his previous post in Ningpo Sullivan had already built a consular gaol. On seeing the Chinese prison to which he had sent an Indian for theft he was determined to use it again only in the direst necessity and applied to Davis for authority, which was promptly given, to build cells for six. The result was a room 14 feet by 16 feet divided into two and opening on to an enclosed court 16 feet square. Soon after its construction a British master guilty of acts of violence was sentenced to a month's

imprisonment in it. He was allowed to exercise in the consulate gardens before 8 a.m., to see his friends daily between 12 and 3, and to have whatever provisions he wished, other than wines and spirits, sent in. Lenient though sentence and conditions of imprisonment were, Sullivan had to be supported by Bonham against complaints by the prisoner after his release and against complaints by a local resident that he had not been allowed to visit the prisoner at the time of day that he wished to visit him. Ten years passed, and this gaol too, in which a successor at Ningpo was holding two Britons and three Malays, came in for criticism; it was considered very insecure and very small. By that time, however, such small gaols were mainly being used for those awaiting trial or for short-term prisoners and longer sentences were being served in Hong Kong.[11]

In Shanghai recourse was again first had to the Chinese prison, but the competent Balfour arranged with the magistrate for suitable rooms to be set aside where British prisoners were visited daily by the consulate staff. Shortly before handing over he asked that a consulate gaol should be built. In referring the request to London Davis noted that there was no gaol at Canton and that in the Levant consuls were understood to have places of confinement in the lower part of their own residences, but something seems to have been sanctioned, for in 1850 two seamen in a temporary gaol fell ill and their hospital expenses had to be paid. By 1851 there was a permanent gaol, and by 1853 there were prisoners in it during most of the year and it was often full to capacity with a dozen or so inmates. Suits of coarse woollen prison clothing, together with underclothing, were found necessary for prisoners with insufficient garments for inclement weather, and could be used too to clothe distressed British subjects. Two or three of the prisoners were usually ill, and medical attention had to be arranged. By 1855 the doctor considered the gaol overcrowded and unhealthy; on one occasion thirty-two men had been confined in it for some days, it was very damp, and nobody could be confined there for a few weeks without getting ague, diarrhoea, or dysentery; most of the prisoners had recently had to be discharged on account of fever and dysentery; more accommodation was imperative, and also an assistant gaoler, for one man could hardly keep twenty prisoners in order even if he had not been an invalid for the previous six weeks.[12] Most of the prisoners were seamen guilty of insubordina-

tion or breach of contract. Alcock found it very difficult to check the tendency of seamen who disliked their ship to render their discharge compulsory by getting themselves a sentence from the consular court; neither solitary confinement nor corporal punishment was possible, and imprisonment under not very rigorous conditions was not an effective deterrent. Robertson likewise concluded that sailors had no objection to a month's idleness in prison and that a treadmill would do more than anything else to keep order in Shanghai.[13]

The implications of demanding an extraterritorial position for British subjects in China do not seem to have been thought through in advance, for there is no evidence that any of these pressing practical questions received the slightest consideration before consuls were confronted with them and obliged to improvise. Similarly no prior thought seems to have been given to the need, which soon made itself felt, for a consular constable to serve legal notices, summonses, and warrants. Robertson as vice-consul in Shanghai had much difficulty in making prisoners when he was summoned to deal with the not infrequent cases of insubordination and mutiny on board British ships; the Chinese whom the consulate employed as police were good in their way but not suitable for handling Europeans, the well-disposed part of the ship's company were little inclined to secure their shipmates, and the mates were too often utterly useless or in tacit league with the men. European constables were before long taken on at the ports most frequented by seamen, but Ningpo lacked one in 1855. With forty or so badly behaved deserters in port who for an infinitesimal sum could get drunk on Chinese spirits, and with an alarming increase in crime, unidentified foreigners having three times in a week stabbed, cut, and maimed Chinese by night, Winchester would rather have had his Ningpo staff deficient in any other department.[14] A constable's duties were difficult and responsible, but for many decades the posts were so miserably paid that recruits were frequently poor types addicted to drink. Four days after having been prevented from using violence on the prison cook the Shanghai constable, one of many constables who over the years came to grief, addressed the consul about the matter most violently and disrespectfully under the influence of liquor, tearing the badge of office from his cap and throwing it on the consul's table. He had to be discharged immediately. Fortunate was the consulate which had a constable

like Pereira, a Corsican who in the 1860s was serving at Amoy. He spoke French and tolerably good English, Italian, Spanish, Portuguese, and Amoy dialect and, being himself an ex-seaman, knew how to handle sailors. One day from his veranda the consul saw three seamen, an Englishman, a Jamaican negro, and a Manilaman, turn on Pereira, who was taking them to gaol. The negro and the Manilaman had their knives out. Pereira gave the Manilaman a blow with his fist and doubled the negro up with a kick while he closed with the Englishman and threw and handcuffed him. Before the other two could recover he wrenched their knives away, tossed them into the harbour, and said very quietly 'No more of that nonsense! It will only get you into trouble if you stick me'. He led the men off without having received a scratch himself and never mentioned the matter to the consul, who he did not know had been a witness.[15]

A determined consul could sooner or later lay by the heels his local British desperadoes, whatever the deficiencies in the consular gaol and whether or not he had an effective constable. Inflicting adequate punishment for serious crimes was another matter. Consular power varied somewhat from time to time, but broadly speaking the maximum penalty which a consul sitting with local British assessors could inflict on a criminal was twelve months' imprisonment plus deportation. Until the Supreme Court for China and Japan was established at Shanghai in 1865 the Hong Kong Supreme Court dealt with murders and other major crimes committed in China.[16] These arrangements frequently resulted in a failure of justice, particularly where serious violence had been done to a Chinese. The Hong Kong Supreme Court proceeded according to the letter of English law and the chief justices' opinions were not always helpful. Winchester, the son of a Scottish advocate and no stranger to the law, complained that the Hong Kong bar had the reputation of being none too scrupulous and that Hong Kong jurors, taken from the motley local foreign population, included Portuguese and Parsees who understood English imperfectly and grog-shop keepers.[17] It was extremely difficult to procure the attendance in Hong Kong of Chinese witnesses to a crime committed by a British subject in China. Bitter experience had taught the Chinese to avoid wherever possible any proceedings in Chinese courts, and they were at least as reluctant to become involved with British courts. In 1849 employees of a Ningpo British merchant injured

some Chinese in a fight, but the injured men, far from accepting
Sullivan's invitation to come forward, secreted themselves for fear
of being compulsorily sent to Hong Kong as witnesses. Sullivan had
regretfully to dismiss the case, and noted that the only wish of the
Chinese officials had been to keep out of the matter, as in their
corrupt form of government any collision with foreigners always
became a source of trouble and of thankless responsibility.[18] At
Amoy M.C. Morrison went to a village where a Malay had inexplicably run amok and had killed one child and very severely
wounded another child and a man, but he met with complete
refusal to sign any statement, the fear here being that the $300
compensation paid by the Malay's brig might thereby be jeopardized.[19] Winchester merely reflected common service experience in
saying that the acquittals in Hong Kong of a seaman who had
murdered another seaman, and of a master who had killed a
Chinese at Swatow, cast doubt upon the effectiveness of criminal
justice as administered in Hong Kong over British subjects in
China.[20] It became accepted that a serious offender was better dealt
with in a consular court on a minor charge, on which he could be
convicted, than sent to Hong Kong to escape all punishment. In
1855 Bowring had had to leave in consular hands for minor
punishments two men who had been engaged in piracy and murder in the Canton area and a man in Shanghai who had been
kidnapping Chinese and handing them over to other Chinese to be
murdered. The kidnapper escaped from the consular gaol, though
handcuffed and in irons, after confederates had broken through the
planks of the cell floor. On recapture he was given twelve months
for kidnapping and twelve months for forcing the gaol, the best that
a determined consul could do.[21] Morrison could do no better with
his Malay than give him twelve months for wounding and stabbing.
Even such light sentences might encounter obstacles; an assessor in
an earlier Amoy case[22] considered twelve months with hard labour
too severe a sentence on a drunken seaman who had fired a pistol
down a hatch and wounded several Chinese. In 1858 a Manilaman
from a British ship knifed and killed a British seaman in a trifling
dispute over a prostitute, and Bowring accepted Morrison's suggestion that as Spanish procedure was simpler and less likely to
enable a criminal to escape, the murderer should be handed over to
the Spanish authorities. In making the suggestion Morrison said
that owing to the peculiarities of the British legal system as applied

to China three murderers in the Amoy district had escaped capital punishment within the last two years, and two of them had escaped almost without any punishment whatever.[23] The breakdown in the system was so notorious that Sinclair was officially rebuked for not having acted himself after the knifing in the Swiss grog-shop at Ningpo. He was told that speedy conviction in a consular court was a better way of checking crimes arising from drunken quarrels than trial in Hong Kong, where 'it is well known that the prisoner has a much better chance of escaping than he has before the consular court'.[24]

As some consuls' letters of appointment stated, the extensive consular judicial powers were not normally put into the hands of professionally unqualified persons. The letters went on to enjoin the combination of firm administration of justice with temperate and considerate indulgence, but the risk of blunders and of ignorance was not removed by such pious platitudes. Some guilty men escaped on account of procedural errors by consuls. In his knifing case Sinclair had not taken the depositions in front of the prisoner, had given him no opportunity of cross-examining, and had issued no warrant in despatching him from Ningpo for trial, lapses which ruled out the possibility of a trial in Hong Kong. Hart, in charge at Ningpo after two years in the service, sentenced a man to six months' hard labour for assault and robbery when implication in the robbery had not been proved and without realizing that consular powers had recently been found not to extend to hard labour; the chief superintendent felt obliged to discharge the offender. Robertson, who had sent six convicted prisoners off from Shanghai to serve their sentences in Hong Kong but had sent no committal orders with them, so that on arrival in Hong Kong they were perforce set at large, regretted that he could not account for his omission and could only throw himself on the chief superintendent's favour to pardon what he confessed to be a great oversight. Blunders in consular cases were not confined to consuls. A naval officer who obliged by taking a convicted prisoner from Ningpo to Hong Kong had so much trouble in getting the gaol to take delivery of the prisoner that he was more than half-inclined to set him at liberty. When the prisoner had been safely lodged in the gaol his presence there was officially denied by the Hong Kong authorities, whose later excuse for this error was that the gaoler's health had been very bad at the time.[25]

If some guilty men escaped their deserts others received heavier punishments than consuls had legal power to inflict. It took some years for it to be realized that consuls had no power to order floggings. The mild Lay as consul at Canton had two men flogged, to which St. Croix attributed the good order among Whampoa crews. Flogging apparently then ceased at Canton because the navy, taking the view that the infliction of corporal punishment on merchant seamen by the navy was illegal and derogatory to the service, refused further co-operation. At Amoy, Gribble, Lay, and Layton all sentenced seamen, some European, to be flogged, but Sullivan used this punishment, which was most repugnant to him, only on Asiatics, as the only one likely to have much effect on the Asiatic mind. Thom had similarly thought that Lascars would be delighted with imprisonment, which meant no work and free food, and that flogging, which he too disliked, might be necessary. From 1852 consular flogging of British subjects ceased, although on the establishment of the Supreme Court the newly arrived chief judge checked piracy among them by sentences of fifty lashes, a penalty which had no statutory backing but which he justified by construing widely his commission to prevent and punish crimes and to maintain order.[26] In the navy flogging remained normal along the China coast. One martinet captain ordered a flogging almost daily, and men were still flogged for being last aloft or last down.[a] The Chinese were used to brutal punishments and would not have been shocked, and civilian Victorian nerves were strong too. On board HMS *Actaeon* Adkins saw nothing inappropriate in writing home to his mother that a marine sentenced to four dozen for drunkenness on duty had kicked up enough row to be heard on the lower deck, whereas another man flogged for desertion had not even winced.[a]

Missionaries were the second element in the consul's flock. He was not directly concerned with Roman Catholic missionaries, as all Roman Catholic activities in China, irrespective of the national status of individual priests, came under French protection, although indirectly he might be concerned because Catholic and Protestant missionaries were, like their respective converts, often on very bad terms. Among the Protestants there were personally awkward customers, such as the man who, having had his claims against the Chinese ruled out, addressed to Alcock several letters of 'a reproachful not to say vituperative character'.[27] Others gave trouble

by deliberate disregard of treaty restrictions on their activities. When Medhurst, the very missionary to whom Pottinger had offered an official post, illegally ventured in disguise into the interior from Shanghai Davis' instructions to Balfour were forceful. If the Chinese complained, Balfour was to disavow and condemn in the strongest terms this breach of the treaty; if they apprehended Medhurst the maximum permitted consular penalties were to be inflicted on him; and Balfour was to exact rigid observance of treaty restrictions from all British missionaries, the more adventurous of whom were in Davis' opinion carried by fanaticism and an appetite for notoriety far beyond the bounds of ordinary reason and common sense.[28] On the whole, however, missionaries were as yet the least troublesome part of the British communities to consuls. In contrast to later periods their numbers were small, a good proportion were educated men, some being notable Chinese scholars, and their activities were confined to the treaty ports and to their immediate vicinity.

Nevertheless, from the outset the Foreign Office, who as time went on were pushed into supporting missionary activities and pretensions the dangers of which they foresaw, viewed missionaries unenthusiastically. In 1848 they apprehended that much inconvenience might arise if consular officers took a prominent part in any missionary proceedings in China, and Alcock was told that although he might seal the land deeds for the site of a proposed Shanghai church he should not be a party to negotiations with the Chinese proprietors or with Chinese officials. Alcock's own view was that with three missionary establishments already inside the walled city, a large missionary settlement in the foreigners' area, and a Roman Catholic cathedral on the other side of the city, the spiritual wants of the Chinese population seemed to have been anticipated for a long period ahead, far in excess, indeed, of all probable demand; he doubted the expediency or prudence of adding yet another place of Christian worship in the heart of a pagan population, and apprehended mischief if missionary zeal outran discretion.[29] In 1851 the premises of a British medical missionary who had settled in Foochow the previous year were damaged in a disturbance after a missionary colleague had distributed tracts to the crowd at a festival. J.T. Walker was in charge at Foochow. He obtained compensation from the Chinese authorities but told the two missionaries that greater precautions would

have been desirable. Bonham instructed him to follow up his rebuke with a warning from Bonham that if indiscretion caused further trouble Bonham would not feel bound to intervene. In 1855 the same missionary was rebuffed when he wished to establish a hospital and asked for consular help. Hale declined, holding that the judicious course was to avoid any interference in missionary undertakings. Bowring supported Hale; consular aid would be improper if the hospital were immediately associated with purposes of conversion and with interference with Chinese religious opinions or practices. The Foreign Office agreed that there should be no unnecessary excitements about missionary proceedings in China.[30] In 1858 Lord Malmesbury, the Foreign Secretary, yielded to the importunities, backed by members of Parliament, of W.C. Milne, a missionary of more than ordinary attainments in Chinese, and appointed him an interpreter. He did so against the advice of Hammond, his formidable permanent secretary, who distrusted Milne's missionary background. In informing Milne of his appointment Hammond wrote that Milne was to abstain altogether from missionary pursuits, which must materially influence the Chinese people's social habits and which might in some instances tend to engender angry feelings; HM servants in China would be in a position most effectively to protect the missionaries' interests and promote the spread of Christianity if they abstained from any active participation in such proceedings. Very soon after Milne's arrival in China Bruce, who had taken over from Bowring, reported that Milne's missionary background, combined with poor health, was much in the way of his promotion to higher rank. Hammond did not fail to point out to Malmesbury's successor that his disregarded advice about the appointment had been justified.[31] Milne's early death solved the problem.

In 1860 Medhurst supported with great vigour missionary efforts to obtain a foothold in Foochow city against the wishes of the authorities, but was warned off by Bruce. In Bruce's view missionaries did only harm to their cause by standing on their undoubted treaty rights and trying to force their way in, a line of conduct which could not conciliate Chinese opinion to their teaching; the more silently and unobtrusively the missionaries' operations were effected the more their cause would be advanced; their first rule of conduct should be to avoid conflict with the authorities.[32] The tide of evangelical fervour later swept aside the

wisdom and caution shown by Alcock, Hammond, and Bruce, but for the moment wisdom and caution held the field. When the Chinese sent to Canton in custody the Revd William Burns, 'a most zealous but by no means prudent person', whom they had apprehended on an illegal journey through the interior, even the fire-eating Parkes, personally a devout Victorian in the style of family morning prayers,[33] saw no cause to object. He accepted delivery of Burns in a civilized exchange of letters with the Chinese, and was instructed to warn Burns not to repeat the offence.[34]

If brutalized British seamen were the most difficult class of British subjects to keep in order, merchants, the third element in treaty port life, ran them close. After long years of experience Alcock considered treaty port society about as bad as it could be, with little public opinion and a very low moral tone.[35] He was speaking of a society in which merchants set the style. Culture, and even education, were in short supply. Adkins found the people at Ningpo, his first port, a decent enough set, civil and hospitable, but not at all polished; he did not much care about what very little society there was, and most of the ladies addressed him as 'Mr Hadkins'.[a] Bruce, pleading to the Foreign Office that consular recruits should be of liberal education and gentle birth, described the merchant princes as being generally as deficient in education as they were flush of cash and as generally yielding (Bruce may have been optimistic here) to the influence of a gentleman.[36] Lack of intellectual interests showed itself in the almost universal refusal to learn Chinese. Bowring, himself an exceptional linguist, was the first of many consuls to lament that the tone of society was against learning Chinese and that none of the merchants was interested in learning it.[37] The treaty port merchants were young. Youth and excess do not necessarily go together, and there must have been others like the young Scottish tea merchant whose published correspondence shows him living quietly in Canton and making money;[38] nevertheless violence and intemperance were marked features of port life. Leaving aside a substantial Parsee or Indian group at Canton, not 30 of some 350 other British residents at the ports in 1851 were over 40 years old. There were less than 50 adult women.[39] The majority of the bachelors who were not missionaries kept mistresses.[40] Some mistresses may have come from Macao, where the Portuguese, according to Thom,[41] preferred prostituting their sisters to working, and an occasional Englishwoman could be

picked up. Mary Jones, a maidservant in her forties, distressed
Layton by taking up residence in Amoy with Syme, a 28-year-old
British merchant. Layton enquired whether this disgrace upon the
English name and the outrage upon public morals caused by open
fornication and criminal cohabitation could be dealt with by
deporting her, but Bonham replied that in such cases in England
only the ecclesiastical courts had jurisdiction, which was seldom or
never used, and that there was no ecclesiastical jurisdiction in
China.[42] Mary Ann Leisk from Batavia, presumably also British,
was living in 1847 with the only British merchant at Ningpo; unlike
Layton Sullivan was not worried, and in any case within two years
Mary Ann had moved to Shanghai and had died.[43] The majority of
the mistresses were Chinese. Communication with them must
normally have been in pidgin English, a barbarous hybrid in which
the grammar and syntax were Chinese and the vocabulary an
English eked out with Malay, Portuguese, Indian, and Chinese
words, and which was more apt for commercial transactions than
for tender emotions. The mistresses were certainly low-class, for no
respectable Chinese family would have consented to a daughter
becoming the wife, let alone the concubine, of a foreign devil.[44] For
many years to come, the entries in consulate marriage registers
show that where relationships were regularized the Chinese brides
were illiterate, whereas Japanese girls marrying British subjects
could often sign their names. Some Chinese girls, whatever their
origins, may have been full of virtues; as a young assistant, Hart
had three children by one and later in life remembered with warmth
her amiability and good sense.[45] Generally speaking, however,
relationships cannot have been of a type calculated to raise the tone
of society, witness an affair in Foochow. A gang of Cantonese
servants had for two years been annoying foreigners who kept
Chinese mistresses by tempting the women to infidelity and rewarding constancy with beatings and extortion. Foreigners surprised the gang feasting on foreign premises with some women.
Their leader was severely flogged and was humiliated by having his
queue cut off. He was about to be spirited away from the port in a
foreign ship when Medhurst got wind of the incident and demanded that the man should be brought before him. Having
failed to get the parties to settle amicably, in other words having
failed to procure a cash settlement out of court, Medhurst fined the
assailants $100 each; a third was fined only $50, as he had had

much provocation in finding his mistress in dalliance on his own premises with the plaintiff. The first two assailants were further condemned to pay $25 each to the plaintiff.[46]

Merchants were hardly to be blamed for smuggling. It seemed to Sullivan at Amoy in 1851 that in reality they reached a composition with Chinese officials who were universally venal, who were very alert to stop genuine smuggling where no composition fee had been agreed, and who would not receive favourably active consular interference; the consul, he thought, was not called upon to be a Chinese customs officer and should restrict himself to tariff violations brought officially to his notice. These were practical views and a fair representation of consular attitudes, but things got progressively worse. By 1854 Alcock considered that at Shanghai customs inefficiency and corruption, combined with foreigners' readiness to use force, had made waste paper out of the treaty tariff, and that the only alternatives for the honest merchant were to withdraw from trade or to smuggle too. Smuggling was not confined to the treaty ports. An assistant travelling in a naval vessel to Formosa in 1857 counted eleven vessels, most of them British, at the unopened port of Tamsui, and it can confidently be assumed that they were all smuggling with the connivance of local officials.[47]

The consul might wring his hands or shrug his shoulders, according to temperament, at the venality and inefficiency which prompted the smuggling of legal goods, but he could do even less about the smuggling of prohibited opium, still a vast and profitable trade and still mainly in British hands. The British government's attitude was that no support would be given to British subjects detected by the Chinese in smuggling opium, but that it was for the Chinese to detect the smugglers and to bring them before the consular courts. Local Chinese officials had no wish to stop a trade so profitable to themselves, and it was carried on almost openly, the opium traders paying an unofficial tariff which went into the officials' pockets. Opium was delivered in bulk by foreign ships to permanently based opium receiving-ships, from which it was delivered to Chinese opium dealers. The receiving-ships were positioned either just outside the limits of the treaty ports or at places, such as the neighbourhood of Swatow, which were not officially opened to foreign trade. Officially, consuls had no knowledge of the prohibited trade, although their mail might be brought by opium ships and although at the less frequented ports

they might on occasion be obliged to travel to or from their posts by
opium ships, whose masters made an expensive favour of carrying
passengers.[48] It was an unhappy situation, which consuls like their
government considered could be put right only be legalizing the
trade and subjecting it to a legal tariff. It was rare to find any
consular condemnation on moral grounds of trade in opium. Soon
after his first arrival in Hong Kong, C. Alabaster did write in his
diary that it was a gigantic evil, those engaged in which dis-
honoured themselves and disobeyed their God, but most consular
officers were concerned not with the inherent morality or immorality of the trade but with the abuses stemming from its theoretical
invisibility. Because the trade had to be officially ignored it is
inadequately documented in consular reports, but consuls believed
it to be at the bottom of many acts of foreign and Chinese violence.
Gangsterism flourished, as it did during the Prohibition era in the
United States, on a trade which handled a valuable substance in
great popular demand and which was outside the law. The hope of
an opium haul was blamed for a naval surgeon on a professional
visit to the Foochow consulate being held up in his boat by fifteen
Chinese; after his pistol had twice misfired, which the consul
thought perhaps fortunate in view of the disparity of numbers, his
hands were severely cut while he held a blunt spear off from his
chest.[49] A Chinese gang who boarded a British ship down river
from Canton and accounted for most of the crew were believed to
be officially sanctioned opium smugglers resentful of being under-
cut by foreign smugglers.[50] At Shanghai Alcock complained of the
difficulty of controlling the violence to which the trade gave rise
because the trade's illegality precluded recourse to legal remedies;
his principle was to refuse as far as possible to recognize officially
opium transactions but to act vigorously against overt intimidation
or violence, holding all offenders legally responsible for such acts
but without referring to the transactions underlying the offences.[51]

Whereas consular condemnation of the opium trade was notably
lacking, consular officers unanimously condemned in the strongest
terms what was euphemistically called coolie emigration and what
was in reality a traffic in human beings. Illiterate Chinese men were
driven by over-population and the resulting poverty voluntarily to
seek a livelihood overseas, or Chinese crimps enticed, tricked, or
kidnapped them on to some foreign vessel loading a human cargo.
Once on board they were transported overseas under atrocious

conditions in voyages marked by deaths, suicides, and successful or unsuccessful risings. Those bound for California or Australia were over the worst if they survived the voyage, but those conveyed to destinations such as Chile, Peru, or Cuba were liable to find that they had bound themselves to serve for a period of years as indentured labourers for a monthly pittance and that they were in effect barbarously mishandled slaves. British merchants, British ships, and British masters of foreign ships were involved in the traffic. Even viler, if possible, were the Siamese vessels trafficking in small boys and girls, often orphaned beggars; Robertson reported in 1856 that no Siamese vessel left Shanghai without a cargo of forty to a hundred boys aged from 6 to 10, some bought but most kidnapped, and that the masters were usually British.[52] The coolie trade was on a very large scale. Bowring reported in 1852 that 16,000 men had left the Canton area for California in a very short period, and in 1855 the treaty port of Amoy and the unopened Swatow area were respectively reported to have shipped 2,500 and 5,300 indentured labourers on seven United States, one Chilean, three Peruvian, and four British ships, all bound for Cuba, Chile, or Peru.[53] Alcock called from Canton for the international action imperatively necessary to put down a traffic worse than the slave trade.[54] Robertson at Shanghai called it an abominable traffic and referred to atrocities committed by British and Americans.[55] At Amoy Winchester, who made his mark with the Foreign Office as a man who had paid special attention to the trade, felt unable within the limits of official decorum to express his shame and disgust and at Canton thought that the Chinese had done justice in 'their own horrible wild way' by drowning two crimps and crucifying two others.[56] With Foreign Office encouragement[57] consuls acted vigorously. Learning in 1856 that a British merchant had collected about 160 men in a Shanghai godown (warehouse) for shipment to Swatow and thence to Cuba, Robertson confirmed from the intendant that the traffic was illegal, told the merchant that he would use every means in his power to prevent it, and considered it his duty, should the men be surreptitiously shipped, to teach the merchant to respect China's laws.[58] (In 1859 the French consul-general at Shanghai was still facilitating the trade in the face of Chinese protests and British subjects were injured in the ensuing riot.)[59] Winchester strongly warned a Ningpo British merchant against shipping coolies to Peru.[60] At Amoy Gingell, who by

personal inspection of the execution ground had verified that one crimp had been beheaded and another crucified, aimed at getting a local British merchant convicted in Hong Kong under the Slave Trade Act instead of inflicting minor punishment in the consular court. Unfortunately he got his legal procedure wrong, and the man escaped with a warning that a repetition of the offence would subject him to trial under the Act. Gingell was more successful in rescuing kidnapped coolies bound for a British steamer chartered to transport them to Cuba, and had no sympathy with the great loss of the charterer, Syme, in a trade so repulsive to Christian feeling.[61] M.C. Morrison broke off relations with the Spanish consul at Amoy after a Spanish coolie ship bound for Cuba had caused dangerous local feeling. The Foreign Office approved his efforts to prevent abuses but warned him not to go too far where non-British shipping was concerned.[62]

Events at Amoy in 1852, three years before the passing of the Chinese Passenger Ships Act gave some protection to emigrants on British ships, showed how easily feebleness in combating the traffic could put a treaty port community at risk. Syme and Connolly, who was a partner in Tait and Co., the principal local shipper, were the British merchants involved. The Chinese authorities arrested one of Syme's coolie-brokers, a euphemism for crimps, a class whom Morrison while at Amoy later described as capable of any atrocity. Syme took it on himself to rescue the man from the yamen; in the resulting riots two British subjects were violently assaulted; the navy had to be called in for protection; and a naval landing party shot and killed several rioters and four innocent bystanders. Bowring was not satisfied with the reports received from Backhouse, the vice-consul in charge, and sent F.E. Harvey from the superintendency to investigate. Harvey reported that the barracoon (receiving depot) for the people Syme had 'amiably called applicants for emigration' was a disgrace to the British name and character; that Backhouse's failure to act immediately after Syme's illegal rescue was probably responsible for the rioting; and that Backhouse had left the superintendency completely in the dark about the reckless way in which coolies had been obtained and shipped at Amoy. Stimulated by the investigation Backhouse belatedly convinced himself that there was enough evidence for proceedings against Syme and Connolly. Syme was fined $200, and although Connolly got off because the witness against him had 'in a

most unaccountable manner' been allowed to escape from the consulate gaol, Tait's coolie operations were for some time transferred to the Swatow area, outside consular control. The Foreign Office, whose judgement was that Syme and others concerned had disgraced their country and endangered its interests, commended Harvey.[63] They seem to have let Backhouse escape with this oblique censure, possibly remembering that he was physically and perhaps mentally ill. Soon after reaching Amoy as vice-consul in 1847 Backhouse very nearly died from an illness which followed a fall and which seriously affected his mind and paralysed his right side. He returned from a year's sick-leave in 1849, but lameness required three more months' sick-leave in 1850. For a large part of 1851 and 1852 he was being treated for partial paralysis of the right leg and foot, and for debility. By the second half of 1853 he was quite confined to bed and had to be given a year's sick-leave. He was back in Amoy early in 1855, but the next year was so shattered bodily and mentally that he once more went on twelve months' sick-leave.[64] This time, still only 37, he at last went into retirement, in which he survived for less than five years. The Foreign Office were always far too reluctant to retire compulsorily consular officers whose duties had got beyond them.

In Alcock and Robertson the Shanghai merchants had to reckon with men very different from Backhouse. Alcock asserted his authority vigorously and ostentatiously. A clerk in one of the big firms refused Vice-consul Robertson's request to stop exercising his horses on the public road. Alcock regarded this deliberate flouting of authority in public, in front of Chinese and Europeans, as a grave misdemeanour; his power to watch over British interests depended in part on respect for the authority vested in him, for if British subjects could flout consular authority with impunity it would soon be treated with contempt by the Chinese. He fined the clerk and bound him over to keep the peace. He sentenced to seven days' imprisonment without the option of a fine a merchant who had carried off a boat in the Chinese magistrate's custody and who had previously annoyed the Chinese authorities by high-handed proceedings. The chief officer of a ship belonging to a major British firm was similarly given seven days for throwing on the ground a warrant brought by the constable for the arrest of a crew member. The firm complained, but Alcock maintained that when his authority was treated contemptuously he was bound to vindicate it

without hesitation. The real danger, he considered, was not abuse of consular power; the danger lay rather in weakness in exercising it resulting from a reluctance to incur animosity in small communities which viewed with the most watchful hostility the exercise of any legal control and in which the absence of any just cause of complaint was no impediment to a specious grievance. Promoted to consul, Robertson still found the Shanghai attitude trying. A British merchant failed in 1856 for nearly £120,000 and, after promising not to leave Robertson's jurisdiction, fled to Hong Kong. He was followed there by his Chinese creditors, who as merchants were readier than Chinese officials to use foreign inventions and hired a steamship for the pursuit. On the merchant's return Robertson remanded him in custody for a few hours before releasing him on bail, and received a protest from two British subjects who, instead of being satisfied that they had not had to pledge themselves, complained that theirs was not the security which had been accepted. There seemed to Robertson to be 'a spirit of opposition abroad which can be satisfied only by making grievances out of nothing...there is an opportunity for cavil, and it must not be lost'. Months afterwards Robertson was still being abused by both plaintiffs and defendants, and was determined not to have a single dollar wrung from him until he was assured that such a course would be legally correct. His troubles were increased because the Hong Kong attorney-general, who in a private capacity was acting for the Chinese creditors, refused in his official capacity to give Robertson legal advice and confined himself to acid comments.[65]

The hostile attitude of merchants was not confined to Shanghai. Bowring, writing while chief superintendent without having forgotten his experiences as Canton consul, said that throughout China nothing was more difficult than to discharge public duties and to obtain the approval, or at least escape the hostility, of part of the commercial community, who were as peremptory in insisting on extreme and doubtful rights against the Chinese as they were loose and careless in observing responsibilities obligatory upon themselves. The smaller the port and the community the more powers exercised by an official with whom the community was daily on familiar social terms might be resented.[66]

Consuls were expected to demand from merchants proper behaviour towards the Chinese. Davis deplored the merchants' contemptuous and aggressive conduct and the violent demeanour

towards Chinese so unfortunately characteristic of the British, and spoke of the need to protect the Chinese from the provoking insolence of British residents. He found an ally in Cochrane, the commander-in-chief, who was convinced that the merchants would find circumspect conduct their best protection, and urbanity and goodwill more persuasive advocates than any amount of naval force.[67] Palmerston's views were clear and were expressed more than once. Macgregor under instructions from Davis fined a young merchant, Compton, whose violent reactions to the raucous cries of Chinese hawkers had provoked a serious riot at Canton, but slipped up procedurally, and the Hong Kong Supreme Court allowed Compton's appeal. Palmerston had Compton informed in a letter which was made public that the fine had been thoroughly approved and that his escape owing to a procedural defect was regretted.[68] Palmerston told Davis confidently to rely on support in suppressing most promptly and vigorously any tendency among the British community to provoke wanton collisions with the Chinese. He also expressed displeasure at Macgregor's lenient treatment of two merchants who in a drunken frolic assaulted a Chinese; he could not admit Macgregor's doctrine that the offence of getting drunk was a palliation of any offence which the drunken person might happen to commit; the government looked for enough energy and determination in the consul to keep British subjects in order and enough firmness to keep the Chinese authorities to their duty and to hold the mob in check; there was no doubt that by proper firmness and activity the consul should be able to make a sufficient stand against either party. On Bonham's appointment as chief superintendent Palmerston directed him to use his powers to maintain order among British subjects, whose reckless behaviour had more than once jeopardized peace between Britain and China, and about whose conduct the British government were not without apprehensions.[69] In reporting minor anti-foreign incidents at Amoy M.C. Morrison accused local foreigners of riding fast through streets and villages, and referred to his own efforts to persuade them that it was expedient to respect the feelings and sometimes even the prejudices of a half-civilized population. Bruce replied that respect for Chinese customs by the handful of foreigners in their midst was essential to security and good feeling; conduct such as reckless riding through crowded places must eventually end in some disastrous collision; reckless riding was punishable under English

law and the legal penalty should be rigidly enforced.[70] Medhurst at Foochow was told by Bruce to repress stringently violence by British subjects, punishment as well as compensation being desirable, and was encouraged in his efforts to check the regrettable lack of respect for Chinese persons and property through habits such as trespass on fields and dangerous riding.[71] Lord John Russell, the Foreign Secretary, entirely endorsed Bruce's attitude, and gave instructions that every outrage on Chinese property or persons should be punished criminally, mere payment of compensation being wholly inadequate.[72]

The condemnation by Bruce and Russell of compensation as a means of settling criminal cases had no lasting effect. Chinese tradition looked favourably on out-of-court settlements, and in purely Chinese cases manslaughter or even murder might be hushed up by a payment to relatives who preferred cash to doubtful retribution in the courts. Assimilating the Chinese attitude, consuls continued to pride themselves on skilfully promoting out-of-court settlements where Chinese had been injured, or alleged they had been injured, by British subjects.[73] Chinese officials rarely saw objection to a practice which saved them trouble. It also saved consuls trouble.

No objection was ever seen to civil cases being settled out of court. Alcock claimed credit for having brought many parties to amicable understandings at Shanghai,[74] and every good consul tried to do the same. Nevertheless, there was substantial civil litigation in consular courts. In a single year at Canton there were twenty-four cases in which altogether some $24,000 were claimed; Indian fondness for litigation may have contributed, for they were defendants in nearly all the cases, the plaintiffs being other British subjects, Chinese, and other nationals, but even at Ningpo, where there was little trade, some $60,000 were claimed in fourteen civil cases.[75] Consuls did not always like the decisions which English law compelled them to give; Medhurst at Foochow was indignant at being obliged to leave a British subject in possession of property of which Chinese owners had in his opinion been cruelly defrauded, and had to be advised by Bruce to avoid appearing a partisan rather than a judge.[76] On the whole, however, consuls may have been justified in claiming that their courts were cheap, prompt, and much more satisfactory than the always expensive, often dilatory, and sometimes vexatious proceedings in the lawyer-dominated

Hong Kong courts.[77] Bowring, who as consul at Canton had more than once excluded an attorney from pleading in his court, deplored the subtleties and refinements of professional men, and as chief superintendent thought it would be a calamity if professional lawyers were admitted to practise in consular courts and that it would be unfair to Chinese plaintiffs, who had no means of consulting Hong Kong lawyers.[78]

The Foreign Office sympathized with consular distaste for lawyers, but when three Hong Kong barristers formally applied to be heard in consular courts the Law Officers advised that they should be heard and it was not felt possible to stand out against their advice.[79] Although himself a barrister, Robertson was still maintaining from Canton in 1861 that the appearance of barristers in consular court cases involving Chinese would be a calamity, but he was told that it could not be prohibited.[80] Lawyers largely based on Shanghai eventually played an important and not always beneficial part in treaty port life. Some, notably American and Italian lawyers, were said, in a 1929 Foreign Office minute, to be 'among the shadiest characters who have ever come to Shanghai'.[81]

4

THE INFANT SERVICE

FROM its inception the China consular service was treated as a self-contained body of specialists, vacancies in the higher ranks being filled by promotions from within the service. Pottinger was told that the assistants sent out from home were to be given the utmost encouragement to qualify themselves for higher duties, and that while no Foreign Secretary could bind himself or his successors to give eventual promotion to any person it could hardly be doubted, considering the peculiar nature of the duties which would devolve on public servants in China, that the claims of anyone who had qualified himself for promotion would be duly taken into consideration when a suitable opportunity offered.[1] This laboured wording amounted to a cautious undertaking that Foreign Secretaries would not appoint outsiders over the heads of serving officers. In large parts of the world, patronage appointments of outsiders to senior consular posts continued throughout the nineteenth century and caused resentment and demoralization in the general consular service.[2] In the China service the only two outsiders ever commissioned were Bowring, a radical member of Parliament, and C.B. Hillier, chief magistrate of Hong Kong, a post under the Colonial Office. After Balfour had refused the offer of Canton in succession to Macgregor, Palmerston appointed Bowring, rejecting Davis' recommendation of Alcock.[3] Bowring's finances were sufficiently embarrassed to make a well-paid government post attractive, but the appointment was not mere jobbery. He was an economist and businessman with considerable knowledge of international trade and had been showing a particular interest in China.[4] Alcock was not pleased to find his path to promotion barred by the unexpected appointment and Robertson complained that a consulship, something which was still eluding him, had gone to someone who had shared none of the difficulties

and disagreeables of a newly opened country.[5] Their reactions no doubt typified service reactions, but Bowring's paper qualifications were good and his performance at the post was satisfactory. When chief superintendent and governor of Hong Kong, Bowring recommended Hillier for Bangkok, where the consulate was then being staffed from the China service. The previous year the Foreign Office had replied to Bowring's recommendation of a senior superintendency post for Hillier that unlike men in the China service Hillier had no claims for appointment under the Foreign Office. Why Bowring's second recommendation was not rejected on the same grounds is not clear.[6] The appointment did the service little harm and Hillier no good, for he died at his new post within a few months.

The decision to fill vacancies only from within the service was a progressive one, but it did not by itself make promotion procedures satisfactory. At least the Foreign Office had no truck with attempts to bring external influence to bear. When Staunton as a member of Parliament solicited promotion for his protégé J.T. Walker, Hammond forbiddingly minuted that if Walker were deserving his claims to promotion would doubtless be advocated by the chief superintendent in due course and with reference to the just claims of others;[7] and parents, uncles, and aunts who urged their relatives' claims did so in vain.[8] Internal problems however remained. The easiest to dispose of was the status of interpreters. There was a sharp distinction initially between the functions of interpreters and those of assistants. Interpreters had little to do with general consular business, some working in their own houses without entering the general office, and assistants had even less contact with interpretorial work.[9] There was doubt as to whether interpreters were eligible for promotion to the commissioned ranks of vice-consul and consul. The Foreign Office were not ill-disposed towards interpretorial claims, but Bonham had the strange notion that vice-consular vacancies should be reserved for assistants and that interpreters should be eligible only for consulships.[10] A turning-point came with his appointment of Oakley as acting vice-consul at Canton in preference to Parkes. Parkes was patently able, whereas Oakley had not distinguished himself, had not applied himself to the language, and must surely already have been showing signs of the alcoholism which caused his hurried retirement less than four years afterwards. The Foreign Office overruled Bon-

ham.[11] Complete integration of the interpreters followed, and by the mid-1850s new entrants assumed that successive promotion to junior assistant, senior assistant, interpreter, vice-consul, and consul awaited them.[a]

Other internal problems were less easily solved. Each consulate was constitutionally a little world on its own linked only to the superintendency, so much so that it was for long doubtful whether one consul could properly write officially to another or whether the correspondence should be routed through the chief superintendent.[12] Appointments were not made to a grade generally but to a particular post of that grade at a specific consulate. A few months after being appointed senior assistant at Amoy, Parish had to go home on sick-leave, on returning from which he was reluctant on health grounds to go back to Amoy. As no senior assistant's post was vacant elsewhere he had to accept demotion to junior assistant at Ningpo. It took him nearly eight years, and service at five ports, to be reappointed a senior assistant. (At this point Parish left China on appointment as vice-consul at Buenos Aires. After a number of years at the consulate he retired and made money in Argentine railway development. His father had been a successful Foreign Office representative in Argentina, and the father's merits no doubt procured the son's appointment.)[13] So strong was the emphasis on the separate identity of each consulate that on a vacancy occurring the officer of the same consulate next in succession was treated as having a preferable claim to the succession unless sufficient grounds for deviating from this official rule were seen.[14] Grounds for deviation were not infrequently seen in filling senior vacancies, but for juniors the application of the rule produced some odd results. In a service in which nearly everyone was young vacancies usually occurred only when disease brought premature retirement or death. As for years there were no premature retirements at the Shanghai consulate and the only person to die was its most junior member the remaining Shanghai staff went short of promotions. Even at posts where deaths were frequent they might occur at the wrong level to benefit a particular junior. Winchester at Amoy had no benefit from the successive deaths of three consuls, obtaining promotion from junior to senior assistant only when the senior assistant also died.[15] Slow communications caused inequities. Eligible officers usually took the initiative themselves by applying for vacant posts, and a vacancy might be filled before an appli-

cation was received from a port with slow communications.[16] The earlier an application could be got in the better, so much so that on a consul's death his vice-consul might get off two despatches, the first decorously reporting the death and the second applying for the succession.[17] The most favourable position was to be on home leave when someone on sick-leave at home retired or died. Direct application to the Foreign Office might then secure appointment to a vacancy long before its occurrence became known to other eligible officers in China.[18] It is fair to say, however, that the Foreign Office, in the person of the indefatigable and omniscient Hammond, were well informed about the merits of even junior officers in China. Alcock as minister in Peking once wrote to Hammond that although Hammond's manner to subordinates might not always be very pleasant he never wittingly did them an injustice, a left-handed compliment which Hammond preserved among his personal papers.[19] With such a man to advise, Foreign Office decisions were more likely to rectify injustice by superintendents than to cause it. While Pottinger, Davis, Bonham, and Bowring were in Hong Kong the Foreign Office kept a close watch on their recommendations and sometimes made promotions without consulting them.[20] Bowring in particular had a bad reputation in the Foreign Office for favouritism, and one Foreign Secretary declined to consult Bowring about filling a vacancy, preferring to rely on Hammond's advice.[21] As soon as Bruce had replaced Bowring the Foreign Office attitude changed. Bruce was a reliable man, well-known to the Foreign Office, and he was told that the Foreign Office must largely rely on his recommendations about junior staff.[22] From then on the Foreign Office progressively opted out of responsibility for postings and promotions in China, confining themselves more and more to automatic confirmation of whatever recommendations the minister at Peking made. By 1868 Hammond was minuting that in all such matters they should be guided by the minister, who knew the qualifications of his flock and the circumstances which entitled everyone to consideration in his turn.[23]

Initial arrangements for recruiting and training, for pay, leave, and pensions, for accommodation and medical care were all to a greater or lesser extent unsatisfactory. Although exceptionally Wade and J.A.T. Meadows were appointed for their knowledge of the language,[24] for some years after 1843 nearly all recruits were

appointed in recognition of services rendered in China by their relatives. To honour an undertaking given by Aberdeen after J.R. Morrison's death another of his half-brothers, G.S. Morrison, was appointed,[25] as were two of Lay's sons, H.N. and W.H. Lay.[26] Pedder, the Hong Kong harbour-master, Fittock, a master in the navy with much service in China, and Colonel Caine, the colonial secretary at Hong Kong, each obtained a son's appointment.[27] D.B. Robertson when vice-consul at Shanghai secured an appointment in the consulate for one of his brothers, though his attempt when consul there to introduce another brother failed.[28] Chief superintendents had their own axes to grind. Bonham provisionally appointed Woodgate, a young relative of his wife, to a superintendency vacancy and sought confirmation on the ground that it was most conducive to the public interest to appoint a gentleman of birth and education who would have promotion before him as an incentive. Palmerston replied that he was happy to do what was agreeable to Bonham, but the following year rejected Bonham's application to promote Woodgate over the heads of officers with longer service.[29] Bowring sought appointment for Lane, a relative whom he had brought out as his private secretary. Although Hammond minuted that Bowring needed to be closely watched about appointments, Bowring obtained the appointment not only of Lane but also of Gower, his subsequent private secretary and a member of a banking family with which Bowring had presumably had dealings.[30] There was no test of these entrants' education, ability, or physical fitness, nor were entrants who proved below standard weeded out. Watkins, appointed by Davis, was for many years unique in having been sacked, also by Davis, merely for inadequacy, namely, bad handwriting.[31]

In 1852 Lord Malmesbury became Foreign Secretary. He was old-fashioned about patronage and simply gave the Foreign Office the names of 'two lads' whom he had personally decided to appoint.[32] One, Markham, became a useful officer apart from a total disinclination to learn Chinese.[33] The other, Thompson, a poorly educated and sickly orphan aged only 15, resigned within two years with the backing of a medical certificate stating that one so young and delicate should not have been sent to Hong Kong and would risk his life by staying there.[34] Markham owed his appointment to 'Mr George Harris's interest with Lord Malmesbury', George Harris very probably being Malmesbury's uncle.[35]

Who approached Malmesbury on Thompson's behalf is nowhere stated.

Early in 1854 Hammond recommended that the entrants then needed should be taken from the Chinese language class at King's College, London, the only institution in Britain then teaching the language. A draft submitted to Lord Clarendon, the Foreign Secretary, invited nominations from King's College and from University College, which had a fine collection of Chinese books but whose chair of Chinese was vacant. Clarendon was chancellor of the Queen's University of Ireland. He amended the draft so as to invite nominations likewise from the Queen's Colleges at Belfast, Cork, and Galway, an illogical addition which nonetheless produced recruits of good quality.[36] The five institutions selected their men with conscientious care. University College even deputed a committee member to converse with Gregory, their nominee, in order to form some judgement of his bodily qualifications, after which they informed the Foreign Office that Gregory was apparently in sound health and of vigorous constitution.[37] Each of the five nominees was duly appointed.

Later in 1854 more entrants were needed. A letter to the Treasury, which was published and which was doubtless a response to pressure for improved methods of recruiting public servants, stated that Clarendon in selecting recruits would be influenced by their having already acquired a certain proficiency in Chinese and that he therefore intended to apply to King's College.[38] The service was substantially expanded in the next four years to meet needs in China and to prepare for the opening of Japan, posts in which country, it was envisaged,[39] would initially be filled from the China service. All the twenty-two juniors appointed in the period came from the King's College class except Hance, who was permitted to transfer from a Colonial Office post in Hong Kong,[40] and Bowring's protégé Gower. In recommending students for appointment by the Foreign Secretary the principal of King's College claimed that he took into account not only their performance in the Chinese class but also intelligence, aptitude for business, steadiness of character, gentlemanlike manners, and above all moral and religious principles. Sometimes he mentioned that they were in good health.[41]

The decision to recruit from the class was enlightened and deserved to be successful. Unfortunately the teaching given to the

class was useless. The man in charge, a bigoted missionary named Summers, whose refusal to take his hat off to a Roman Catholic procession in Macao had once led to a serious international incident, knew very little Mandarin and spoke principally Cantonese and Shanghai dialect. His luckless class studied eight chapters of the New Testament in what purported to be literary Chinese and twelve chapters of St. John's Gospel in Shanghai colloquial dialect, while Summers purported to teach them Mandarin, Cantonese, and Shanghai dialect simultaneously. Bowring reported that they reached Hong Kong unable to pronounce anything correctly and that they had derived little benefit from the teaching of a man ignorant of official Chinese matters.[42]

Malmesbury returned to the Foreign Office in 1858. The recently established Civil Service Commission were pressing government departments to adopt competitive entry, preferably the open competition already in force for the Indian Civil Service or at least 'limited competition', that is, competition between a limited number of nominated candidates.[43] Malmesbury paid no attention and was attacked by *The Times* for appointing to a vice-consular post in the now separate Japan service an unknown outsider, whose discreditable conduct was later to end in enforced resignation.[44] In the China service Malmesbury did make five appointments from the King's College class but then brushed aside Hammond's recommendation of continued recruitment from the class and made four purely personal appointments.[45] This time his bounty fell on the sons of 'an excellent portrait painter', of a deceased surgeon, of the sheriff substitute of Sutherland and Argyllshire, and of the Revd J. Mayers, consular chaplain at Marseilles. 'I will ever make it my endeavour', wrote the chaplain in a letter of obsequious gratitude, 'to invoke at the throne of grace God's choicest blessings on Your Lordship'.[46] The painter's son was a conscientious dullard, the bottle ended prematurely the careers of the surgeon's son and the sheriff substitute's son, but Mayers turned out to be outstanding. The first three travelled out to China with Bruce, who was on his way to take over from Bowring. He cannot have been impressed, for soon after his arrival he recommended to Malmesbury that entrants should be examined before appointment.[47] It is unlikely that in making the recommendation he was unaware of the methods Malmesbury had employed.

In 1860 a Commons select committee agreed with the Civil

Service Commission that open competition was the best method of procuring competent public servants, but did not advise its immediate adoption. The disappearance of simple nomination, the committee noted, disturbed private interests and prescriptive rights of patronage, 'and many persons exercising local influence find themselves no longer able to obtain for relatives and dependants that ready admission into public offices which was formerly within their reach'. As a temporary compromise the committee recommended limited competition, not less than three nominated candidates competing for each vacancy. They did not point out that limited competition increased rather than decreased ministerial opportunities of doing favours, as three or four persons could be obliged by nominations for a single vacancy.[48]

When in the following year more recruits were needed for China and Japan Lord John Russell had replaced Malmesbury. He acted on the select committee's recommendation. The Foreign Office told the Civil Service Commission, who were to undertake the examination, that general intelligence, in testing which great importance should be attached to précis writing, was a primary qualification; that examination in orthography, handwriting, arithmetic, Euclid, modern geography, and translation from Latin and French would test whether candidates had had a liberal education; and that steady character, habits of application, and good health were important.[49] The Commission acted accordingly. As there were few applications for nominations on the Foreign Secretary's personal list he made up the necessary number by inviting names from the English, Scottish, and Irish universities and from Wellington College. All other requests for nomination were turned down; a William Jones protested in vain from the Conway telegraph office that competition should be open and that many young men in the oppressed working class capable of passing the examination were excluded for want of the influence necessary to procure a nomination.[50] Twenty-seven candidates sat for ten places. A curious feature of the results was that three successful candidates respectively got 4, 1, and 0 marks out of 100 in a supplementary arithmetic paper.[51] Those who passed with the highest marks were allowed to choose whether to go to China or to Japan.[52] The new method of entry remained largely unaltered until open competition was substituted in 1872. Recruits for the tiny Siam service, a separate organization from 1858 onwards, were obtained through the same

examinations. The Siam service did not stand high in esteem, and throughout its history consisted mainly of competitors who had not passed high enough to have the option of China or Japan. Russell's opinion in 1862 was that the least promising candidates would do for Siam, and he marked his approval of the Oxford First which Vidal took shortly after winning a Siam place in the 1863 examination by giving Vidal a China place instead.[53]

The original age limits of 16–20 were criticized by Wade, the Chinese secretary, as too low. The entrants' lives, he said, were to be spent in a remote and semi-barbarous country and they should therefore bring with them to China as large an experience of their own country's usages as possible. He favoured attracting public-school boys for two reasons. First, the analytical approach to language emphasized in public-school Latin and Greek facilitated the study of written Chinese. Second, a public-school education discredited bullying and the belief that might made right; young men on getting to China soon acquired the notion that violence and intimidation were the only course, whereas 'justice apart, there is nothing so impolitic as bullying a Chinese'. In forwarding Wade's views to the Foreign Office Bruce said that the desiderata were good sense, conciliatory manners, a liberal education, and an aptitude for languages. Which of these various opinions carried most weight at the Foreign Office does not appear, but Russell decided that time for 'a public-school and something beyond' would be given by age limits of 18–24, which accordingly applied from 1862 onwards.[54] This change had one advantage which no one mentioned. It stopped any more boys leaving England at about 16, as C. Alabaster had done, and suffering acute homesickness in Hong Kong. He had not even had the break with home life represented by a boarding-school education, and his first Christmas out East made him so miserable that he felt like running away.[a]

The Foreign Secretary kept a list of persons to be nominated when the next examination was to be held, which happened not at predetermined intervals but whenever one or more vacancies had been caused by death or retirement. A place on the list could be obtained either by direct approach to the Foreign Secretary or by application to him through a member of Parliament or other influential person. The varying grounds on which a place was sought rarely if ever had any relevance to prospective consular duties. A merchant who had offered a broker's office place for an

18-year-old had not kept his word; a consul's widow had bought army commissions for five sons but could not afford one for the sixth; a half-pay naval commander, nephew of the late chaplain of the House of Commons, said he was supporting a wife and eleven children on £200 a year.[55] Among the successful candidates B. Brenan was nominated because his father, a retired lieutenant-colonel who had commanded a regiment of the Imperial Osmanli Cavalry, had a large family to provide for, and B.C.G. Scott and G. Brown were nominated because their fathers were respectively a very active and influential Liberal supporter in Suffolk and one of the few Liberal supporters in Rugby; the plea on which a peer, whose support had been enlisted through family connections, obtained Crawford's nomination has not been preserved, but the true situation was that having rejected the army and failed in New Zealand Crawford was left with only two visible alternatives, the Post Office or the Far Eastern consular services.[56] The resulting list was predominantly English and south country, and was essentially middle-class,[57] although H.B. Bristow who obtained a place on it and competed successfully was the son of a King's Lynn inn-keeper. (Bristow was being educated at a minor school in Harrow, and Hammond had strong links with Harrow. Bristow's father had been a near neighbour in King's Lynn of the Lay family. Either factor may explain his nomination.)[58] Nominations were given first to those on the list. If the requisite three competitors for each vacancy were still lacking, the number was made up by inviting names from selected universities and occasionally from Wellington or Marlborough.[59] Among the universities the Queen's University, having previously produced good recruits, was specially favoured.[60]

In the first limited competitions candidates whose names had been put forward by universities, particularly Scottish and Irish universities, did better than those on the Foreign Secretary's list. Seven of the fourteen China recruits from the first three competitions were Scottish or Irish, and six of these had been at Scottish or Irish universities. Alcock protested from Peking that Chinese spoken with a broad Scotch or Irish accent must be very unintelligible and suggested that the Civil Service Commission might be instructed to insist on the absence of a provincial accent in entrants. All the five China recruits from competitions in the following two years were Scottish or Irish, all except one having been to Scottish

or Irish universities, and Alcock, asking for a nomination for the son of an English friend, deplored the scarcity of English entrants. Whether by accident or design, so large a proportion of the nominations for subsequent limited competitions came from the Foreign Secretary's list that less room was left for plebeian candidates from the Scottish and Irish universities and most entrants from these examinations were English. Restricted though competition was under the limited system it markedly affected the service's composition both by increasing the Scottish and Irish element and by decreasing in-breeding. Before the introduction of competition the service had in fifteen years seen seven pairs of brothers and a half-brother. Only two pairs of brothers got in through competition as long as the service lasted.[61]

In accepting limited competition Russell had reserved the right to appoint without competition persons well suited for the public service.[62] Three appointments of young men already in China were subsequently made without competition, but subject to qualifying examination papers sent out by the Civil Service Commission being passed. The appointments on this basis in 1861 of W.T. Lay, yet another of G.T. Lay's sons, and in 1865 of Lowder, one of Alcock's stepsons for whom it had not been possible to make room in the Japan service, were a final flicker of the old Foreign Office attitude towards recruitment.[63] The old attitude was particularly marked in Lowder's case. After he had failed the qualifying examination Hammond suggested that although now over age Lowder should be allowed to sit again. Clarendon rejected this as a dangerous precedent, but a post not subject to the new examination system was found for him in the Supreme Court office at Shanghai, and when addiction to drink obliged him to return home after only nine months in the post his enforced resignation was discreetly managed.[64] Egan, who had sold his lieutenant's commission and was learning Chinese in Hong Kong, was appointed in 1865 on the strength of a character reference from D.B. Robertson and of Wade's suggestion that it would save money to recruit a man already in China whose passage out would not have to be paid. Delirium tremens three years later, at the age of 27, proved Robertson and Wade wrong. The Foreign Office were minded to make an example of Egan by dismissing him but his pleading induced them to relent and to allow him to resign.[65] W.T. Lay resigned little more than a year after his appointment and without sitting the qualifying

examination.[66] All three appointments were thus complete failures, and the Foreign Office never again experimented with bypassing the competitive entrance system.

It was one thing to recruit, another thing to turn recruits into efficient officials. There was little purposeful training in general duties. Juniors in China, like their counterparts in Whitehall, spent much of their time on mindless routine, principally in making beautifully written fair copies of drafts. Fair copies had to be made, and by a convenient rationalization the Foreign Office and other departments had persuaded themselves that this drudgery acquainted young men with all aspects of office work and thereby equipped them in due course for promotion.[67] The sole functions allocated to the Shanghai junior assistant in 1853 were copying and the preparation of the consulate's quarterly accounts with the Foreign Office and Board of Trade.[68] At posts with smaller staff the juniors' work was slightly less monotonous; at Ningpo in 1858 accounts and copying were varied by 'bullying sailors, writing letters on business for the consul and taking minutes of trials'. Another deadening chore for assistants was acting as Post Office packet agent, which meant stamping and despatching to Hong Kong the community's outward mail and distributing its inward mail from Hong Kong. By 1859 the Shanghai postal work had grown so much that it kept an assistant fully occupied on four days a month; the noisy crowd of foreigners and coolies besieging the office at mail-time was found unpleasant and undignified, and in such matters the Shanghai community was 'not remarkable for amenity or consideration'. Assistants acting as packet agents did have the consolation of an additional allowance from the Post Office.[69]

Language training, on the other hand, received much thought. To function effectively the consular officer needed to be able to express himself orally in Mandarin and to be able to read documents written in officialdom's formal style. An 1844 circular from Davis promised that language competence would be the best claim to promotion; Palmerston, who in his jaunty way told Hague in 1847 that the best way to obtain the promotion sought by Hague was to deserve it, added that knowledge of Chinese would always be an important qualification; and the Foreign Office repeatedly ruled that assistants must learn Chinese.[70] Promises and rulings to this effect remained dead letters for years. F.E. Harvey, who during

his voyage out taught himself the elements of Chinese writing, and Parish were the only two original assistants who consistently worked at Chinese. Both were above average in ability, but though their diligence was eventually recognized by monetary awards both were for years left behind by assistants who, put off by the difficulties and the absence of incentives, had learned little or nothing.[71] In favourable circumstances Chinese is difficult for Europeans. It takes as long to reach a tolerable standard as it does to reach a first-class standard in two, three, or more European languages. In speech the varying voice inflections ('tones') on which meaning depends are not easy to distinguish and reproduce, and memorizing thousands of symbols ('characters') in the originally pictographic script is wearisome and time-consuming. In the early days circumstances were extremely unfavourable. Teaching Chinese to foreigners was no longer prohibited but there were no adequate teachers, textbooks, or dictionaries; the Foreign Office made no contribution towards the considerable cost of teachers and books, and initially gave no time off for study;[72] and the geographical location of the first consulates was a major obstacle to learning fluent Mandarin, which was not native to any of the five ports. At Amoy Winchester in fourteen months learned nearly 1,500 characters, a substantial start, but the tones seemed almost impossible to a man with a poor ear, he could practise with nobody but his teacher, he found nothing he said was understood, and he decided to give up. Ten years later Cooper found learning Mandarin there almost like learning a dead language; he could speak it with practically no one but his teacher, who was himself not a native Mandarin speaker.[73] Had Winchester and Cooper tackled Amoy dialect instead of Mandarin nothing they said would have been understood on their transfer to another port. (Very few early officers spoke a dialect in addition to Mandarin. Wade and H.N. Lay spoke Cantonese and Swinhoe and Pedder Amoy dialect, but it was more typical that after years in Canton neither of the Meadows brothers, both notable Mandarin speakers, had learned Cantonese.[74] An officer who spoke anything besides Mandarin always remained a great rarity. From start to finish the dialect-speaking southern ports were normally staffed by officers unable to communicate with ordinary local people.)

In 1846 Balfour urged the need for incentives, of which he considered promotion the most effective.[75] Alcock, in spite of

speaking several European languages, found the tones very difficult and considered learning Chinese more arduous and repulsive than any of his other work, but characteristically he worked hard at it and from Shanghai twice urged the need for incentives.[76] In 1847 the Foreign Office mooted an annual prize, but Davis made difficulties about adjudicating between assistants at widely separated ports.[77] The Foreign Office then announced that lack of language competence would be a bar to promotion and with a show of vigour purported to implement their ruling when Foochow, at the time downgraded to a vice-consulate, fell vacant. Both J.T. Walker and Hale had claims to the post, and Bonham was told to promote the one more proficient in Chinese. Hale, who had learned practically nothing, was the loser, but Walker, who got the post, knew very little more. To make their point effectively, the Foreign Office should have passed both men over. Worse was to come. On Walker's death Hale, as ignorant as before, was on leave in England, and from there the Foreign Office appointed him to succeed Walker. The appointment was not calculated to convince juniors that they must learn the language, and moved Bowring, who considered a knowledge of Chinese particularly important at Foochow, to protest.[78]

As chief superintendent Bonham did nothing to encourage the acquisition of the language, and as governor of Hong Kong reputedly preferred men who had not learned it, believing that study of Chinese warped the intellect and undermined the judgement.[79] Bowring attached great importance to Chinese, but his influence was in practice not wholly beneficial. His suggestion that juniors should prepare for the opening of Japan, Korea, Indo-China, and Siam by learning one or more of these languages as well as Chinese was deservedly still-born, but his hardly more realistic notion that they should learn Mandarin and a dialect simultaneously impeded the studies of those who acted on it. Above all, he kept entrants making fair copies of his draft despatches instead of leaving them free to study.[80] It was Wade who put the teaching of Chinese to student interpreters, as entrants were styled, on a sounder basis.

Wade, throughout his career nearly always at the centre of diplomatic activity in China, eventually served for many years as minister in Peking. He is remembered both as a diplomatist and as the inventor of a system, which with modifications by H.A. Giles

became standard among English-speakers for more than a century, for representing ('romanizing') Mandarin sounds in alphabetic script. His career was a long conflict between the rival charms of sinology and diplomacy. More or less free of the malaria which in 1843 had nearly cost him his life and had cost him his appointment as interpreter at Amoy he returned to Hong Kong in 1846, prepared to sell out of the army if he could get a Foreign Office post in which he could study Chinese and meanwhile filling in as interpreter in the courts. Davis spoke so highly of Wade, as Pottinger had done, that the Foreign Office found an interpretorial post for him in the superintendency, where he remained for years, indifferent to promotion and spending much of his income on Chinese books. When renewed malaria, 'chiefly affecting his brain', forced him home again on sick-leave he took a Chinese teacher with him.[81] He returned as vice-consul at Shanghai. This was the only consulate post he ever filled; he found consulate work uncongenial and would have preferred retirement to a consulship.[82] He was not vice-consul for long. With his superiors' encouragement he took a lucrative and undemanding post as a Customs inspector at Shanghai (see p. 137). He hoped thereby to save enough quickly to retire and then to study in China undistracted by official duties and to publish language textbooks for interpreters and missionaries. Instead, he soon threw the post up and asked for a Foreign Office subvention which would supplement his own modest means sufficiently to enable him to carry out his plan. Hammond after some hesitation advised against a subvention; although Wade was clever and very zealous, and would be excellent as Chinese secretary, he was unsteady; he might again grow restless and start after something else.[83] The refusal deterred Wade from devoting himself entirely to study. He applied for the vacant Chinese secretaryship, which he said was the only official post he had ever coveted, and after the Foreign Office had overcome renewed doubts about his steadiness he was substantively appointed to the post in 1856.[84] In 1861 he again came home on sick-leave, and the Foreign Office, with whom he was now in high favour, obtained Treasury agreement to financial arrangements permitting him to pursue long-term language studies in England on a salary of £1,000 a year. He was persuaded by Bruce that it would be an inopportune time for his services to be lost to Bruce and to the Legation. While remaining Chinese secretary he became concurrently secretary of the Lega-

tion, with diplomatic status in both capacities.[85] Despite this dual harness he found time to continue work on his valuable textbooks of colloquial and documentary Chinese[86] and in 1865, after a period as chargé d'affaires in Peking, he was again ready to relinquish his official prospects, believing that as an official he was replaceable whereas no one else competent was prepared to sacrifice his career to undertake philological work of lasting utility. This time the Foreign Office, loath to lose Wade's services at Peking, declined to approach the Treasury.[87] In 1869, when his forthcoming appointment as minister was widely expected,[a] he was still in many moods considering retirement preferable and once more reverted to the 1861 proposal, only to be told that in the current climate at the Treasury it was utterly hopeless to expect agreement.[88] At length his shoulders grew accustomed to the diplomatic yoke from which he had failed to escape, and when replaced as minister on reaching the age of 65 he was disappointed not to be accredited to some minor European court. He became professor of Chinese at Cambridge instead, but he was mentally exhausted. Leisure for scholarship had in the end come too late, he published nothing more, and he had no pupils.[89]

In 1856, however, the newly appointed Chinese secretary, 36 years old, was a live wire, quick-tempered, and much given to oaths. In a student interpreter's diary he is to be seen bolting into students' rooms, blowing up teachers, looking the rummest monster imaginable half-shaved in shirt and 'putgamas', tackling three curries at a breakfast party, and forming ever-changing plans for a new dictionary, new vocabularies, and new linguistic methods.[a] He failed to persuade the Foreign Office that a properly organized initial Chinese course should be instituted in England to weed out those would-be student interpreters who lacked language aptitude, but he did persuade them that on arrival in China the prime duty of entrants was to study Chinese, not to make fair copies of drafts. (This battle had however constantly to be renewed; latterly it was typing and cyphering which competed with language study.)[90] The Chinese secretary was made responsible for the student interpreters during their initial period of language study, a period which became fixed at two years, and in 1859 was given an extra £250 a year in recognition of the additional responsibility. Wade, known in the service as quixotic over money,[a] spent all the allowance on Chinese teachers for the students. On its cession Hong Kong had

been sparsely populated by fishermen, and Bowring, who oblivious
of Chinese reluctance to mix with foreigners had given instructions
that at the ports students should cultivate the acquaintance of
educated Chinese, accepted that in Hong Kong itself there were no
Chinese with whom a gentleman could associate. The teachers
whom Wade had been able to get together in Hong Kong had
therefore been imported and were a scratch lot.[91] According to the
same diarist old Ying, who was Wade's own teacher, was a jolly old
fellow and tremendously polite, and old Hao was rather a good
teacher; but old Hsiao was an obstinate, conceited old fool so
ignorant that he could hardly write and although old Miao's
pronunciation was magnificent he was very dirty and kept dropping
off to sleep during lessons.[a] The opening of the Legation in Peking
removed such difficulties, and Wade soon reported that the new
students there would in eighteen months learn as much as their
south China predecessors had done in eight years.[92]

Responsibility for the student interpreters was no sinecure. Their
high spirits were apt to lapse into hooliganism. In Hong Kong the
eminently sensible Adkins had started his first visit to Macao by
announcing to four Portuguese soldiers that he was a free-born
Englishman and would knock them all down for one dollar.[a]
In Peking Satow, who has already been seen kicking his boy
downstairs, was one of a wild set. He and H.J. Allen spent a Sunday morning shooting at the roof ornaments of a famous institute
of Chinese learning; eight students caused three accidents in a day
by cantering round street corners; and the Chinese complained of
student behaviour in a temple. On instructions from the disgusted
Bruce, Wade told them that anyone offending the Chinese again
would be severely disciplined, and particularly warned them
against entering the Temple of Heaven unless the gate was willingly
opened in return for a gratuity. The students, including Satow,
commented by climbing over the Temple of Heaven wall again that
same afternoon.[93] One wonders whether Satow, controlling the
service from Peking with humourless strictness forty years later,
ever recalled his own youth.

Few people think themselves paid enough for their work, and
there were constant complaints, which lasted as long as the service
itself, about pay. Bruce in 1859 considered current salaries, taken in
conjunction with the prestige of a consulship, enough to attract
well-educated men, but in the changed conditions of 1863 he

considered that a married man could hardly live respectably.[94] Some at least of the complaints ring true. Statements of income and expenditure submitted by student interpreters in dire financial straits show that on £200 a year rigid economy did not necessarily prevent indebtedness.[95] One student interpreter wrote home a few months after arrival in 1857 that no one could live on that pay.[a] Another student, posted to Shanghai, found that he was paid less than the consulate's Chinese linguist.[96] Promotions, which came reasonably fast in the early service, brought successive and considerable salary increases, but Treasury insistence on economies kept reducing the salaries at the top. Gingell, for example, on joining the service could have expected his eventual consulship to be worth £1,500 a year, but by 1860, when he had become consul at Amoy, he was getting only £900. Foochow had gone down to £900 too, and Ningpo was worth only £800. The progressively lessening value of long-sought prizes just as they came within reach caused understandable dissatisfaction.

The apparent value of consular salaries was reduced by the expenses of expatriate life in China. Official entertaining had to be met out of salary, and on Sullivan's death his widow put his failure to provide for her down to the expensive hospitality with which he had felt bound to uphold a consul's rank and position.[97] Imported household requirements were dear. Life insurance cost more, and doctors charged more, than at home.[98] The bigger firms met their clerks' medical bills, but in 1864 the Treasury still maintained that a contract at each China consulate with a local doctor for free attendance on the staff would create a precedent for other countries and that undue expense would result.[99] Then there was United Kingdom income tax, which government servants were the only British subjects in China to pay, the losses when the value of silver rose against sterling, and the irritating loss incurred through the method of paying salaries. The Chinese had never developed a silver coinage and payments too large to be made in their copper coins were made by weighing and assaying lumps of silver. At the treaty ports they quickly took to foreign silver dollars as a convenient medium of exchange, but for no better reason than local usages a particular type of silver dollar might stand at a premium at one port and at a discount at another. The colonial treasurer at Hong Kong took no account of this on receipt of the quarterly salary bills drawn in sterling on Hong Kong, the only way in which

consular officers were paid. He paid out in whatever coinage he had available. This might be a locally unacceptable type of silver dollar, or rupees, or English coins, and a loss of 5 per cent, 12 per cent, or even 20 per cent might be incurred in changing them into acceptable coins. Macgregor's Hong Kong agent once had un-willingly to accept on his behalf 309 crowns, 407 half-crowns, 643 shillings, 50 sixpenny pieces, and 1 halfpenny, and in order to minimize his losses Elmslie, who in 1854 was still getting all or part of his Canton salary in coins such as rupees, sovereigns, shillings, sixpences, and halfpence, shipped them to Singapore, Calcutta, or London to reduce the loss in converting them into the Spanish dollars favoured at Canton.[100]

All these drains upon salaries paled in comparison with the cost of home leaves and transfers.

Local leave of up to three months was obtainable from the chief superintendent,[101] but there was nowhere much to go. The Canton staff could slip down to Macao for a change, an officer at one port might visit another port, a run at sea, possibly provided free by the navy, was favoured by some. Others chose to remain uninter-ruptedly at their posts, working a six-day week, until home leave was possible.[102] Primitive arrangements for home leave reflected the vanishing age when a large part, or even the whole, of a working lifetime might be spent in unbroken service overseas. Except for the ten months immediately preceding his appointment to China Pottinger had been uninterruptedly abroad for over thirty-eight years and Colonel Caine spent forty-five years in the East without going home.[103] Although home leave was readily granted on production of a medical certificate, home leave for healthy men was almost an act of Foreign Office grace. In 1860 the impression in China was that without a medical certificate it would be granted only after nine or ten years' service, and the Foreign Office were still declining to define any given period of service as entitling a healthy man to leave. True, casualness about making home leave possible was matched by an agreeable Foreign Office casualness about the length of leave allowed to those who had managed to get home. A genuine or bogus plea of ill-health almost automatically obtained one or more six-month extensions of the twelve months for which permission to absent oneself from China had been granted in the first place.[104] During the 1850s T.T. Meadows stayed on leave for three years, and even in the 1880s Baber did the same.[105] Whether

long or short most home leaves were no doubt spent in quiet domesticity, but there are references to travel on the Continent, to presentation at court,[106] and to hospitality extended by the families of colleagues still in China. Adkins, for example, asked his father to put up and mount Parkes, who was far senior to Adkins, and warned him against inviting another senior, that 'worthless ass' Sinclair, or Adkins' alcoholic contemporary Payne.[a]

Before 1861 the Foreign Office paid not a farthing towards the cost of home leave, whether a man was sick or healthy. For a man with dependants the cost was huge; Jackson paid £700 to get himself, his wife, and two children home from Foochow.[107] How men repeatedly forced by illness to go home, or to send wives and children home, could raise the money is a mystery. Faced with such expense the robust put off leave far too long. Alcock after eight years saw little possibility of ever being able to afford home leave and went home only after twelve years, Sinclair and Robertson were out for thirteen and fourteen years respectively, and J.A.T. Meadows, who arrived in China in 1845 and had not been home when he resigned in 1861, seems to have died in China in 1875 without ever having seen his native Northumberland again.[108] At last in 1861 a substantial concession was made in response to collective service representations supported by Bruce. The Treasury agreed to payment of half an officer's travelling expenses, and a third of his family's expenses, if home leave was taken for personal convenience after five years in China or on a medical certificate at any time.[109] The overdue concession was termed an 'indulgence', a revealing term which survived well into the twentieth century as the official description of financial assistance towards the cost of hard-earned home leave. Indulgence did not go so far as to remove another iniquitous obstacle to home leave. Seniors still went on half-pay for the whole of any leave lasting more than three months, a cut escaped by juniors only because they could manifestly not have existed on half their small salaries.[110] And finally, as there were no facilities for storing belongings, departure on home leave meant selling everything up at a loss among the local foreign community and equipping oneself again at heavy cost on return.[111]

Travelling expenses on transfer between ports were met from public funds except where an officer was transferred on promotion,[112] but indirectly transfers were most expensive. The cumulative cost of furnishing afresh after a series of transfers from one

unfurnished house to another could be crippling. How people elected or afforded to furnish varied between individuals. A student interpreter who lost practically everything in a typhoon valued the property at only $80. Wade was surrounded chiefly by books; by 1857 he could speak of having a not inconsiderable Chinese library and later said that during his first twenty years in China he had as a bachelor existed with little more than bed, table, and two chairs. Hance, senior assistant at Canton and a married man, put in an itemized claim for compensation after the Chinese burned the factories in 1856. Hance's botanical work in China earned him a European reputation and an entry in the *Dictionary of National Biography*, and Mrs Hance was musical. Some of their possessions reflected these interests. Solid books in English, French, Latin, and Greek had included among other works on natural history the 1481 Parma edition of Pliny, all capitals illuminated by hand and valued at 10 guineas, and there had been a Broadwood grand piano, a mahogany cottage piano, and vocal and instrumental music. The rest of the claim does not suggest luxury. The drawing-room had been furnished with four chairs, two with cushions, two footstools, four lamps, two flower-stands, two rugs, and matting. Bedroom furniture had consisted of four-poster and wardrobe, both from Calcutta, two children's beds, and a bidet with mahogany stand. The main bedroom and the dressing-room had both contained a Shanghai porcelain bath, a wash-stand, and a commode. The spare room, where Mrs Hance kept her saddle and embroidery frame, had offered visitors only a camp-bed and the spare commode. Miscellaneous items included a black lacquered child's carriage with its case and a sedan-chair. Even such modest equipment re-presented a large outlay from an assistant's modest salary, and consuls inevitably spent more. Layton, according to his widow, had before his death spent a large part of his private means on the endless extra expenses of fitting up houses in China. Alcock, a reliable witness, was more specific. He had received £750 by way of outfit allowance and had fitted up five consulates at a total cost of about £2,500. He blamed himself for having misguidedly ex-hausted his private resources in this way; he was living in Shanghai without personal extravagance, keeping neither horse nor boat and avoiding the expense of local leave, but retrenchment which would affect his official standing had become inevitable.[113]

Travelling between posts on transfer was uncomfortable and

occasionally hazardous. Passage had to be taken in whatever vessel might be available. To reach Ningpo Sullivan chartered a small brig to carry himself, family, and 80 tons of luggage, which implies that on this occasion furniture was not left behind. Gingell reached Foochow by lorcha (a small sailing vessel with a foreign-style hull and Chinese-style rigging), Connor by opium ship. Medhurst lost all his belongings, for which he was refused compensation, in a ship wrecked in the Yangtze. D.B. Robertson was lucky to escape with his life while transferring from Shanghai to Canton in a steamship which struck a reef in a heavy sea and gale. The sea rushed into the saloon within a few minutes, thirty-one of the crew were lost, and the passengers and remaining crew with great difficulty reached a barren island. After two days of suffering and exposure they were rescued, but Robertson lost everything he owned in the world.[114]

Full pension, from 1859 onwards two-thirds of the final salary, was reasonable for the minority who survived to earn it but until 1875, when two years' service in unhealthy Chinese posts became reckonable as three for pension purposes,[115] the pension of a man whose health had prematurely broken in China was calculated on exactly the same basis as that of a Whitehall clerk. Vice-consul Elmslie after seventeen years' service got £250 a year on retiring at 35 and Vice-consul Hague, who retired at 38 with twelve years' service, got £193 a year on which to support a wife and at least four surviving children. The medical records show that premature retirement was forced on both men by their health breaking in China.[116] Their pensions should have been calculated on a basis which recognized this.

Similarly the health hazards of China should have been recognized by some financial provision for widows and dependants. In the days of the East India Company the widow of their Chinese secretary, the Revd Robert Morrison, had been granted £100 a year for life, with an additional £25 for each child until the age of 18 was reached,[117] but after the Foreign Office, with the Treasury behind them, took over, the families of dead men were left to fend for themselves. An officer's pay ceased abruptly on the day of his death, and that was that. The Treasury adamantly refused to budge on this issue. In 1880 a member of the service made proposals for a widows and orphans fund, to be financed by deductions from salaries and to be run without any official guarantee and without any official assistance in the fund's administration. The only

request for official assistance was that deductions from salaries should be made compulsory on future entrants. The Treasury response was a refusal to consider any proposal committing the government 'to any interference whatever with provision for the families of any class of persons in the Civil Service of the State', and the scheme failed to get off the ground.[118] Even in the twentieth century widows got at best a small lump sum, and in the service and among the always open-handed treaty port communities the whip-rounds, one of which had produced £500 for G.T. Lay's widow in 1846, continued.[119] No married consul or vice-consul who died in the first twenty years after the opening of the consulates had provided adequately for his widow. Mrs Hillier was left with less than £1,000 to support herself and four young sons. Mrs Lay with her six children had only £200. Mrs Layton and Mrs Sullivan had only one child each, but Mrs Layton was in great need and Mrs Sullivan was reported to be as badly off as Mrs Lay and Mrs Layton (Sullivan's will suggests that the widow exaggerated her predicament). Mrs Connor, married as a minor less than a year before her husband's death, was left absolutely destitute and pregnant; his estate did not even cover the £100 6s. 8d. which the Foreign Office had advanced to him for his recent passage back to China. There was one helpful precedent. Lady Napier had been left without money on her husband's death as chief superintendent and a passage home had been provided from public funds. The precedent enabled the Foreign Office to provide passages home for the widows of less exalted officials.[120] Once the widows had got home, however, Foreign Office help was at an end, except that in the 1840s Secret Service moneys (if 'SS' does indeed stand for 'Secret Service') were here and there drawn on for a small lump-sum payment, such as £300 to Mrs Lay,[121] and that before competitive entry was introduced a son on reaching a suitable age might be found a Foreign Office berth. Mrs Hillier and Mrs Connor improved their circumstances by remarrying at home, but Mrs Lay and Mrs Layton were not so fortunate. Mrs Lay was said in 1849 to be destitute of support and on her death in 1882 left less than £150, and Mrs Layton, vainly appealing in 1870 for a pension to keep her from absolute want, wrote of twenty years of long weary struggle in broken health. Mrs Sullivan withdrew only to Macao and remarried into the service, but on the death at his post of her second husband, Gingell, she again urgently needed money to support eight children.[122]

After Alcock had made a spirited protest against being asked to pay for his own accommodation at Foochow it gradually became accepted in principle that free accommodation would be provided, but it was a long time before free accommodation was available everywhere for juniors.[123] The accommodation provided varied from the indifferent to the intolerable. At Shanghai purpose-built consular premises provided no married quarters for vice-consul or interpreter, and the interpreter, and probably the vice-consul too, shared with his servants a privy which was in immediate contact with his cookhouse.[124] At posts without purpose-built premises the Shanghai defects would have been considered minor. On the opening of the Peking Legation all the student interpreters complained of languor and dyspepsia in the single attic rooms which served each of them as sitting-room and bedroom, and the medical officer considered that given their teachers' habits and the Peking climate their health was being seriously undermined; he found a marked improvement in health after he had had the ceilings removed and roof windows put in for light and ventilation, though the rooms still remained too small.[125] In 1858 water was pouring into the Amoy consulate through innumerable holes in the roof. In 1861 its doors and windows were off their hinges, the roof still leaked, there were holes in the floor, the beams were rotting or being destroyed by white ants, plaster was falling off by the square foot, and the building was so near total collapse that another building, this time on Kulangsu, had to be hurriedly bought.[126] At Ningpo, where it took a couple of decades to provide a decent consulate, conditions were vividly documented. On succeeding Thom and moving into the consul's house with his wife and young daughter, Sullivan complained that the pond on its east side had overflowed twice in their first month, completely 'innundating' (*sic*: Sullivan was an indifferent speller) the house; those rooms which were floored were so rotten and wet that heated pans of charcoal placed on them for days had failed to dry them; the roof leaked in every direction; and the local doctor had certified that in its present condition the house was uninhabitable. The water from the nearby public well being almost unfit for use in summer Sullivan requested sanction to spend $120 in sinking a well, as 'bad water is so highly prejudicial to the health of Europeans in this climate', but Bonham replied that sanction was altogether out of the question. T.T. Meadows found that there was still no drinkable water and

suffered severely from what he diagnosed as a species of incipient cholera caused by drinking water from almost stagnant pools. As the river-water was brackish and there were no springs he sought permission to buy eighteen to twenty large jars in which to collect rain-water, but sanction was again refused. (Even in 1898 drinking-water was still 'gathered' from the consulate roof or in a drought fetched in from the country.) Sinclair's description of the house was even more lurid than Sullivan's had been; it was shut off from cool air by high walls round it; it was flanked on two sides by ricefields which were under water for most of the year and which stank of rotting vegetation and liquid manure; there was a green pond of stagnant water immediately under the drawing-room windows and an even worse one behind the house; and in the hot season there was the smell from the nearby graves, some of which were crumbling and exhibited ruined coffins and their decaying contents.[127] Houses of this sort were not constructed to withstand the vagaries of the south China climate. At the Foochow consulate Hale lost his china, glass, floor coverings, and other property in a typhoon which blew down two walls. The reaction to his claim for compensation was that there would be no end to such claims in China if he were compensated.[128]

Office accommodation and furnishings were no better. The first waterside office at Amoy had been a single ground-floor room in a godown used mainly for storing raw cotton and dried fish, and the constant movement of both commodities by scores of noisy coolies had made it difficult to get into the office and almost intolerable to work in it. After nearly twenty years during which a variety of inconvenient and sometimes discreditable office accommodation had been used the waterside office was still abominably housed. The building was constructed directly against a nearly perpendicular cliff which prevented ventilation and from which masses of damp rock, one dimly lighted ledge of which was used for baths, protruded into the building. The adjacent hillside was a favourite place for the poorer classes to bury their dead at the rate of 600 to 700 a year, and contained scores of large nightsoil pits. An assistant required to live in the building for the convenience of shipping, which tended to call at Amoy in the early morning, pleaded for a move before his gradually failing health was irretrievably weakened, a plea strongly endorsed by his doctor. The furnishings of the Shanghai consul's office, where Alcock penned so many historic

despatches, consisted in 1859 of an iron safe, an iron money-chest, a writing-table in very bad condition, three nearly worn out rattan chairs, and a clock; and they moved T.T. Meadows, for once incontrovertibly sensible, to comment that public interests must in some degree suffer if consular offices were not equipped to the standard considered decent in the most modest mercantile establishment. Thirteen years after the establishment of the Ningpo consulate there were still so few chairs that when mandarins called on the consul the juniors temporarily lost their seats and had to stop work; and the juniors, who lived three-quarters of a mile away and who must from time to time have suffered from dysentery, still had no closet accommodation. T.T. Meadows had a small room cleared out for them 'and the necessary chair, etc.' provided, but this was ruled to be private expenditure which could not be met from public funds. Medhurst was only partially successful in urging that the Foochow consulate should have its own boat for visits to shipping instead of borrowing a merchant's boat, which at least once had taken the opportunity of running goods past the customs post under this unwitting consular protection; an official boat was sanctioned but Medhurst was told that he must pay the boatmen himself.[129] Public funds did run to the provision of flag-poles and sedan-chairs, which were evidently considered more essential than closet accommodation or boats, but only at the price of extensive and sometimes venomous correspondence about the cost of purchase and maintenance.[130]

By 1859 the Foreign Office had accepted the need for decent purpose-built housing, but Bruce was enjoined to be very cautious and economical, and to see that the size and number of rooms was limited to what was necessary for health and reasonable comfort.[131] This was a sensible warning. Although Alcock recognized that it was in a consul's financial interest to be modestly lodged he considered that for reasons of prestige consulates must stand comparison with the merchants' handsome mansions, and the ideas of at least some consuls were grandiose, Robertson planning a billiard-room for the Canton consul and Medhurst recommending for Foochow drawing-room, breakfast-room, and dining-room, pantry, library, five bedrooms, and five dressing-rooms. Bruce was specially cautioned against building separate houses for juniors, who required two or three rooms at most and would otherwise be encouraged to indulge in expensive habits they could ill afford.

W.H. Fittock's application to have his Shanghai accommodation made suitable for a married man was turned down on the ground that the Foreign Office could not undertake to provide an assistant with more than an unmarried man needed.[132] This was a much less sensible Foreign Office attitude. At 30, so senior an assistant that he was promoted to vice-consul a year later, Fittock was surely entitled to his wife and two young children. The Foreign Office, however, apparently shared Alcock's earlier belief that Shanghai juniors might generally be expected to be single, a view hardly more realistic than Davis' still earlier wish that in a country so full of disgusts and privations for European females the whole service should be unmarried.[133]

The health of the service was deplorable, due primarily, in so far as surviving medical certificates are capable of being construed in modern medical terms, to malaria and intestinal diseases, and certainly made worse by the infrequency of home leaves away from the damp heat, inimical to northern Europeans, of south China. Of the thirteen young assistants appointed in 1843 eight were dead by the age of 45 and three others had retired in broken health before reaching that age.[134] Far too much food and alcohol cannot have helped. Throughout the nineteenth century consumption seems to have been gargantuan. Around the turn of the century tiffin (lunch) and dinner at Shanghai were described as being practically the same, each comprising soup, fish, entrée, joint, sweets, curry, cheese, salad, and dessert. Some forty years earlier a Shanghai doctor castigating local indulgence at the table nevertheless recommended a moderate amount of wine, and by moderate meant up to half a dozen glasses of port or sherry daily.[135]

The causes of common diseases were still unknown and treatment was primitive. As medical attendant to the Amoy consulate Winchester indented for 8 lbs. of castor oil and 2 lbs. of Seidlitz powder, and Alcock, that once rising surgeon, recommended in 1867 that the newly appointed Legation doctor should bring with him enough leeches to start a leech pond. There were occasional flashes of medical inspiration. The same Shanghai doctor who recommended too much daily port or sherry concluded that every local case of dysentery or cholera occurring during the hot season could be traced to eating fruit or vegetables; although he could offer no explanation for so curious a linkage he confidently ascribed his own good health to not eating them.[136] On the whole,

however, the most useful service rendered to consular officers by their doctors may have been the issue of medical certificates on the strength of which leave was obtained. The certificates were often alarmingly outspoken. Hertslet cannot have been cheered by reading that staying in China would certainly be fatal, nor Connor by reading that the preternatural induration of his spleen indicated a state of lesion premonitory of malignant disease which in Hong Kong's climate would probably be fatal.[137] Pedder's career showed how little doctors could help. At 15 he injured his leg in a fall in Hong Kong, where he was living with his father and studying Chinese, had to be sent home, and spent over three years in bed with pieces of bone constantly coming away. Returning to Hong Kong reputedly quite well and strong again he entered the service at 21. Eighteen months later he started to vomit after the smallest quantity of food and had heart palpitations and pains in the chest. He continued to vomit for three years with little intermission; one diagnosis was chronic gastritis and duodenitis, a second was chronic stomach disease, an enlarged liver, and lungs not entirely free from disease. Four years later he was still vomiting after meals and was suffering from heart palpitations, pains in the liver area, inability to lie on the right side, nervous headache, and constipation followed by diarrhoea; the diagnosis now was sluggish secretion of the bile and indurated state of the liver. How many more years the vomiting continued is not recorded, but Pedder remained 'a confirmed invalid' with constant and varied illnesses.[138] Astonishingly, it was only failing eyesight which forced retirement at 52,[139] and he lasted for over twenty years in retirement. Even more astonishingly, he was an excellent consul, his informative despatches were enlivened by humour, and he worked indefatigably.

Amply as the archives document those aspects of the infant service which were of official interest, they and other sources throw only haphazard gleams of light upon leisure activities and domestic life.

In the treaty port communities, made up of various nationalities but with the British predominating and with English serving as the lingua franca, life varied between the narrow and the extremely narrow. The rigid treaty restrictions on travel outside the immediate vicinity of the ports were not enforced by the Chinese, but consuls rarely had a change of scene; Alcock was eighteen months in Shanghai before ever leaving the city, and then he thought it advisable to notify the intendant before travelling 22 miles into the

country.[140] There are recurrent references to the tedium of the life.[141] Parkes' boredom with the incessant shop-talk of the merchants was doubtless shared by others.[142] Some exceptional officers had interests which filled their leisure, with results that impressed even an occasional Chinese contemporary.[143] Wade and T.T. Meadows threw themselves into sinology, Hance into botany. Swinhoe's interest was zoology. As an entrant Swinhoe struggled with a standard Chinese natural history instead of keeping to his syllabus of set books, and as a junior at Amoy he kept a civet cat, a pangolin, a great owl, and young falcons.[144] The average man made do with whatever distractions his port had to offer. The distractions invariably centred round the club, that ubiquitous creation of the Victorian expatriate, and sport. In Shanghai a club was functioning by 1848 or earlier, and by the mid-1860s Foochow's foreign population of about a hundred, which was supporting a billiards club, a fives court, a bowling-alley, a racecourse, and a reading-room, was sneered at for failing to provide the general club which was by then customary. Each port had its favourite sport, such as boating at Amoy, but shooting was universal.[145] The earliest photographs from all parts of China include groups of bewhiskered foreigners with guns in their hands and dogs at their feet.[a] Shanghai was famous for an abundance of pheasant, partridge, woodcock, quail, and wildfowl,[146] but in less favoured Hong Kong four student interpreters out for a day's shooting were content to slaughter a dove, a shrike, a ricebird, two sparrows, and a heron.[a]

In such small communities people might see too much of each other, recreations might become monotonous, and even the solace of domestic life might be wanting, for it was not easy to come by a wife in a society which was so largely male. Suitors had to move fast. In the 1850s a visitor to Shanghai from Ningpo, where there were then no unmarried women, married within twenty-four hours a previously unknown girl.[a] Another Ningpo resident got his sister in England to select and ship out a suitable bride, rejected her on arrival because she squinted (she retreated to Hong Kong, where a Dutchman was less fussy), and instead married a girl who had meanwhile arrived in Ningpo and to whom Hart had become engaged against strong competition and with her father's consent.[a] No wonder that of some seventy unmarried men who entered the service before 1860 nearly thirty were still unmarried when they

died or left the service. China provided the others with only a dozen or so wives, who included four or more missionaries' daughters, a consular widow, a consular sister, and the two Chinese married respectively by J.A.T. Meadows and Webster.[147] Most of those who married found their wives during home leaves, the best opportunity for wife-hunting. C. Alabaster's diaries show him on his hunt, untypical in that it was unsuccessful. On his first leave, when he was 25, he first vainly proposed to his boyhood friend Ada and then flirted with other possibles, who included Miss Sinclair, the charming Nelly, the charming Caroline, the fair Gertrude, and Seraphina, 'by no means averse to me'. On his second leave, seven years later, Ada first accepted and then jilted him, and he returned in much distress to China,[a] where after four more years he did succeed in marrying the daughter of an American ex-missionary.[148]

Little can be learned about family life. For some time there seems to have been a taboo on despatches acknowledging in plain English the very existence of wives and children, and curious circumlocutions, such as 'the illness of a principal member of my family' or 'the death of a member of my family', were used to report a wife's illness or a child's death.[149] Through the obscurity shadowy wives can be discerned in prematurely failing health or dying painfully young; Medhurst lost his first wife when she was 17, the year after their marriage, and again lost his second wife the year after their marriage;[150] Hertslet lost two 24-year-old wives before dying himself at 28.[151] Throughout the nineteenth century medical certificates avoided indelicate precision about ladies' illnesses. The certificate stating that the first Mrs Hertslet had suffered 'several very serious attacks of complicated disease' was unusually specific, the standard formula being a bald statement that the wife's state of health made her return home necessary, and it comes as a shock to find one certificate actually referring to uterine disease.[152] As for the children, one cannot discern even dimly how many survived infancy, at what age they were sent home, and what happened to them when they got there. There are only sad little glimpses. Medhurst applied for home leave to arrange the education of a son already in England, where there was neither friend nor relative capable of acting, and Winchester had his two sons, aged 4 and 3, brought back to him in China because their guardian in England had died. Many unrecorded pangs can be represented only by Winchester's complaint that his quarter-century of eastern service

had had 'more than its share of those painful domestic separations which are its curse'.[153]

Early bachelor officers seem not infrequently to have kept mistresses; C. Alabaster in 1874 wrote that such connections had once been common enough, though now almost unknown.[154] The mistresses surface in the archives only where the relationships caused scandal. A Chinese woman with whom Carroll lived for years did cause scandal by using her position to maintain an illegal gambling-house.[155] When in 1853 Sinclair as Foochow interpreter wished to import his Chinese mistress into a temple in which an Anglican missionary was living his superior at Foochow found the affair exceedingly discreditable and disgusting, and the Bishop of Hong Kong forwarded a complaint to the Foreign Secretary. Sinclair, who was not an Anglican, disputed the bishop's authority over his morals. Bonham with evident relief left this nice point for consideration in Whitehall, where, he said, Sinclair could give any necessary information during his forthcoming home leave. Sinclair cancelled his home leave, the matter was dropped, and in rapid succession Sinclair was given two promotions. His unabashed claim that such intercourse with the Chinese people deepened knowledge of their language, customs, and mentality, and therefore made for better interpreters, attracted no comment.[156] Bruce might have viewed Sinclair's behaviour more seriously. He told the Foreign Office in 1862 that the relationship between the sexes in China was not such as to render habitual immorality politically innocuous and that although he did not pry into the student interpreters' lives he preferred them to vent the exuberant vigour of youth in other ways and therefore encouraged them to keep horses and ride about the country.[157] The Foreign Office, on the other hand, seem to have been quite relaxed on such matters. There is no evidence that the Chinese marriages of J.A.T. Meadows and Webster, or the illegitimate families which Thom and Hart had by Chinese mistresses, prejudiced their careers, even though Mrs Meadows, a grasping illiterate, was eminently unsuitable as a consular wife. (In widowhood her life was notorious, there were strong rumours of infanticide, and her three daughters by Meadows were removed to Europe to safeguard their moral welfare.)[158] The Foreign Office attitude towards Chinese wives later became very different.

THE FIVE PORTS

THE five treaty ports, each with its little foreign community perched on the edge of China's vastness and isolated among her teeming multitudes, might all have been expected to make much the same demands on consuls. The contrary was the case. Each port developed its own character and made different demands. The local political and economic situation and local personalities varied from port to port, and so did the impact of the great Taiping rebellion and of other smaller rebellions which plagued the later Manchu rulers of China.

Canton steadily lost commercial ground to Hong Kong and Shanghai, and its titular rank as the senior consulate was for other reasons undeserved. It was within much easier reach than the other ports of instructions from the chief superintendent. In 1848 it took on average six to eight weeks for the Shanghai consul to get an answer from Hong Kong, and Hong Kong's communications with Amoy and Foochow, although both were so much closer than Shanghai and Ningpo, were unreliable. At Amoy Gribble was often out of communication for three or four weeks, and in 1852 one Hong Kong despatch to Amoy took two and a half months aboard a vessel which made an unusually long passage from Hong Kong. In contrast a letter between Hong Kong and Canton took from eight to fifteen hours.[1] The Canton consul therefore lacked the scope for initiative and the freedom of action enjoyed by more distant colleagues, who in an emergency had to act on their own responsibility. As the Foreign Office put it, he had readier access to the chief superintendent in case of difficulty. As Alcock put it, the Canton consul was a mere registering clerk for the chief superintendent's decisions.[2] In Macgregor's day Canton produced numerous incidents involving British residents, who in some cases had started the trouble or made it worse by ill-judged reactions; in the worst

incident Davis supposed that the fate of six young men murdered
by villagers would have been very different if they had not had
recourse to their pistols and shot several villagers.[3] The situation
became so strained that Davis made a dash at Canton with a small
force and briefly occupied the factories, a pointless episode which
did not improve the situation. In all these affairs Macgregor played
a subordinate role.

So powerless a position was not suited to his successor at
Canton, Bowring, who accepted the consulship in the evident belief
that he could through private correspondence with the Foreign
Secretary help from Canton to shape China policy. A shower of
private letters to Palmerston followed his arrival in 1849, and
showed almost immediate resentment of his position. After only
three months he rhetorically asked Palmerston what knowledge of
Chinese affairs the British government could have if there were a
consul at Canton who was not in personal touch with Palmerston
and whose access to the Foreign Office was therefore confined to
whatever parts of his official communications might be sent home
by the chief superintendent.[4] Bonham, then chief superintendent
and not the man to fail to detect intrigue by a subordinate,
responded with cautious denigration and mistrust. Bowring's first
trade report, which was in fact readable and interesting, was
described by Bonham as very voluminous and going beyond
commerce to other subjects already covered by Bonham's own
despatches; but as Bowring had taken great trouble the whole
report was being forwarded, although the last few pages afforded
all the required information about Canton trade. After Bowring
had been at Canton twelve months Bonham, before going to
Shanghai for six weeks, cautioned Bowring to have as little correspondence as possible with the imperial commissioner, as in
any important matter proceedings must be governed by instructions
from home which were to be found only in Bonham's office.[5] Even
outsiders could detect that Bonham found his subordinate tiresome
and that relations between the two were very cold.[6] Bonham can
therefore hardly have been best pleased by Palmerston's decision
that Bowring should act at Hong Kong when Bonham went on
home leave in 1852. For the duration of the leave Bowring became
a superintendent of trade, the only post-war occasion on which the
power to appoint one or more superintendents in addition to a chief
superintendent was exercised.[7]

Bowring leaped at the opening which he saw for making good his frustrations as consul. He had arrived at Canton at a most unfavourable juncture. Treaty or no treaty the Cantonese had obdurately refused to allow foreigners, whose presence even in the factories' ghetto was disagreeable enough, to enter the walled city itself. The special Cantonese antipathy towards foreigners was well known, but its causes are a matter for speculation. Perhaps the Cantonese had had more reason to resent foreigners' actions in peace or war. Perhaps they merely had a stronger tradition of irrational prejudice; certainly almost a century later the foreigner entering any village near Canton was pursued by hordes of children yelling 'Foreign devil',[a] a tedious habit by then out of fashion in most of China. Changes among top Chinese officials in Canton had recently strained local relations more than ever, and all British attempts to meet senior Chinese officials were systematically brushed aside. Bowring had formed the fateful notion that mild pressure would induce the Canton authorities to allow foreigners into the city and to concede normal working relations between officials. He started off in Hong Kong with a bounce, immediately telling the Foreign Office that the right of entry into the city could be made effective without serious difficulty and that no more appropriate time could be found for urging it peremptorily upon the Chinese. How Palmerston would have responded cannot be said, but Palmerston had left the Foreign Office. Bowring was told not to raise the question and a succession of further rebuffs when he proposed to initiate other lines of action culminated in instructions that while in Hong Kong he was to keep everything as quiet as possible. A letter sent as his term at Hong Kong was running out to a transient Foreign Secretary, who passed it to his successor Russell with a gibe at Bowring's 'prolific pen', complained that his hopes of doing any good in China had vanished; he had vainly hoped that during his short incumbency he could have settled the questions pending between Britain and China, and believed he could have done so peacefully to the benefit of Britain and mankind, but he had been prevented by peremptory orders; now he hoped that on Bonham's return some other field might be found for him, or that at least he might have twelve months' home leave, although he would not wish to quit China if the power of usefulness were in his hands. Russell's only apparent reaction was to authorize Bonham to grant the leave, which Bowring took three weeks after Bonham's return.[8]

Thirteen months later, in April 1854, he was back in Hong Kong as substantive successor to Bonham, whose ill-health had forced retirement. He may well have owed the appointment to the accident of long intimacy with Clarendon, the new Foreign Secretary.[9] His appointment was made against the wishes of Foreign Office officials, whose judgement was shown by events to be sound.[10]

Consular life at Canton had long been frustrating and now became extremely uncomfortable. In 1854 rebels came so close that skirmishing within a mile or two of the city walls occurred almost daily, the wealthier Chinese left, and movement on the river became risky even in an armed ship's boat. Order was gradually restored by a river victory over the rebels, a victory which was watched by Vice-consul A.W. Elmslie, and by the ruthless extirpation of suspects by Yeh Ming-ch'en, the imperial commissioner. Alcock, transferred to Canton in 1855, reported that year that there had been 70,000 public executions in the city and in early 1856 that excursions in the country were no longer dangerous. Alcock then went on home leave and Parkes became acting consul in June 1856.[11] Parkes was a dangerous official. He was an energetic, efficient, and brave man whose only interests were work and responsibility, but he was quick-tempered, humourless, narrow-minded, and the reverse of farsighted. Within four months he and Bowring had between them taken steps which led to a second Anglo-Chinese war.

The lorcha Arrow, owned by a Chinese at Hong Kong and registered at Hong Kong, with an entirely Chinese crew of twelve men but with a British master, was lying off Canton in October. She was only technically British. Everything about her was Chinese except her flag and her master. Nothing seems to be recorded about the master's character and his true position on board. He may have been a respectable and competent seaman genuinely in command of the vessel, but Chinese who wanted the advantages of British protection for their vessels were not slow to hire dummy British masters of low character.[12]

The Chinese authorities suspected the Arrow of piracy. Fifteen months later Alcock was telling the Foreign Office that lorchas were smugglers and pirates all and that they grossly abused foreign flags and their immunities.[13] C. Alabaster, who was in Hong Kong at the time, said in a private document written later in life that probably the Arrow was, as most Chinese boats were when they got

the chance, a pirate.ᵃ After his retirement Wade, who had also been in Hong Kong at the time, stated in evidence to a royal commission that very possibly the *Arrow* had been a pirate and very possibly was then smuggling.[14] Evidently contemporary service opinion was far from convinced of her innocence, but it was never to be firmly established whether Chinese suspicions were justified.

The Chinese authorities treated the *Arrow* as a Chinese vessel, came aboard, and arrested all the Chinese crew. Parkes was bound to have regard to her formal status as a British vessel and therefore to treat arrests on board her as a breach of extraterritorial rights, but with cool handling a more or less satisfactory settlement could have been quietly reached. Parkes instead took a high line. He demanded from the imperial commissioner public atonement for the public insult to the British flag and the return in the consul's presence of the arrested men to the *Arrow*, from where any of the men charged with crime could then be conveyed to the consulate and the case against them examined by the consul in conjunction with Chinese officials. He thereby put both Yeh and himself into a position from which neither could retreat without loss of face. Bowring made things worse by instructing Parkes to demand a written apology. Yeh did finally have all the men returned, but not in the formal and face-losing manner demanded. Parkes refused to accept such a delivery. Innocent or guilty the men vanish from the story at this point, some or all of them returning to the horrors of a Chinese prison, for Parkes apparently cared little about saving them from such a fate; he seems to have treated them as pawns in a power struggle. The situation progressively deteriorated into a state of war. As Yeh made no further move Bowring called in the navy to bombard Canton and for good measure made admission of the right of entry into the city a condition for ceasing naval operations. Yeh remained obdurate. In December the Chinese burned the factories and Lane was killed by a falling wall which narrowly missed Winchester and the admiral.[15] The consulate was closed and the staff withdrawn to Hong Kong. Without knowledge of what may have passed between Bowring and Parkes in private letters and meetings their respective shares of responsibility cannot be determined, but Parkes was complacently satisfied at the outcome. 'The finger of One who rules the destinies of races is clearly traceable in the whole affair', he wrote to a missionary brother-in-law. 'It is the cause of the West against the East, of Paganism against Christen-

dom, and what may we not look to see as the result? The opening of China indeed, I trust'.[16] It is much to Wade's credit that he tried, unsuccessfully, to stop Bowring from making it ever more difficult for Yeh to give way without loss of face. Although notoriously peppery Wade was not given to intemperate language on paper, and the unusual terms of a letter which he addressed to Bowring and which he asked should be placed in the archives show how indignant he was. He had stated that morning, he wrote, that he was wholly against publication of the letter to Yeh demanding entry to the city for all foreigners as opposed to the admiral's demand for entry of officials to discuss official business; he might on occasion have spoken too frankly to Bowring in imparting his views; it had certainly not in general been to any advantage of the questions discussed; and unless specially called on he asked to be exempt from the obligation of troubling Bowring with his sentiments on any subject.[17]

It is strange that the *Arrow* affair ruined Bowring but made for Parkes' advancement. The government found it politically inexpedient to remove Bowring but they drew all his teeth. In March 1857 Lord Elgin was appointed ambassador to handle relations with China. On Elgin's appointment Bowring was told that his functions were in abeyance in respect of the Canton trouble, military and naval operations, negotiations for peace, and the revision of the treaties. A rapid succession of further humiliating despatches followed. Elgin's younger brother Frederick Bruce, British agent and consul-general in Egypt, who was accompanying Elgin as the embassy's secretary, was given full power to act if Elgin became incapacitated; Bowring was ordered not to leave Hong Kong and not to correspond with the Chinese; Elgin was given full powers in relation to Japan, and Bowring's functions in relation to Japan were to remain in abeyance; Bowring's political functions in relation to Siam were to cease on the arrival in Bangkok of a consul newly appointed by the Foreign Office; Elgin was to have the services of China consular officers as necessary.[18] Bowring was thus stripped of every important function under the Foreign Office, yet as he was still chief superintendent he remained in charge of the consulates' ordinary business and remained responsible for managing the service except in so far as Elgin drew men off for his own purposes and did not overrule Bowring's decisions. This anomalous and unsatisfactory situation, which left the service under a discredited

chief and yet directed to attend to any instructions from Elgin, lasted until the spring of 1859, when Bruce reached Hong Kong as minister to China and concurrently chief superintendent.[19] Parkes on the other hand was instructed on Elgin's appointment to hold himself in readiness to give his services. Elgin considered that the *Arrow* affair had been most discreditable and was initially of the opinion that Parkes, like Bowring, had shown utter want of judgement, but Parkes rehabilitated himself in Elgin's eyes. Before long Elgin thought him clever, though exceedingly overbearing in his manner to the Chinese, and his final judgement was that Parkes was one of the most remarkable men he had ever met, with extraordinary energy, courage, and ability.[20]

By the end of 1857 a force sufficient to take Canton had been mustered by the British and the French, who had found the trial and execution of a French missionary a reason for joining in the hostilities. Yeh was captured and sent to Calcutta and a puppet local government was 'assisted' in maintaining order in the city by three allied commissioners. Parkes was one of the three. Force of character and knowledge of the language concentrated the commissioners' powers in his hands, and everything concerning relations with the Chinese was referred to him. Elgin procured for him as a commissioner large additions to his consular salary. This generous treatment at the expense of the Chinese authorities, from whom reimbursement was apparently claimed, made the man who was at least partly responsible for an unnecessary war the best-paid consular officer in China.[21]

After two years' home leave Alcock returned in the middle of 1858 to Canton, where following the allied occupation of the city the consulate had been reopened in cramped accommodation in a chop-boat[22] (a vessel of 50–100 tons with one deck).[23] Canton was in such a state of unrest that all trade had gone and with it virtually the whole foreign commercial community. Left wholly without official information about steps taken by civil or military authorities and therefore unable to keep either Bowring or Elgin informed, Alcock rightly saw no fitting place or intelligible meaning for the consular flag and within a month had with Bowring's approval moved the consulate back to Hong Kong. The Foreign Office approved the withdrawal from Canton, but before their approval became known Elgin had, perhaps for no better reason than his distrust of Bowring as 'a most dangerous person', ignored

Alcock's arguments and overruled Bowring's decision; although Elgin gathered that, for reasons which Bowring had deemed sufficient, Alcock had been authorized to haul down his flag, he trusted that Bowring would see the necessity for reopening the consulate at Canton without delay. Three months after moving to Hong Kong Alcock had to move back again.[24] He spent some more unhappy months at Canton, his period at which was a dreary and frustrating blank in an otherwise uniformly successful life. He had covered himself with glory as consul at Shanghai, during his recent leave his copious and cogent views on China policy had been welcomed by the Foreign Office,[25] and he was about to become successively Britain's first minister to Japan and her minister to China. In contrast he never met the Chinese authorities at Canton, and however friendly his personal relations might be with the allied commanders he was officially ignored by them. He left for his post in Japan with a strong parting protest against the false position in which the consul at Canton was placed. Winchester, who took over from him temporarily, and D.B. Robertson, in substantive charge from 1860, were equally irked. Although Robertson was responsible to the new minister, Bruce, and not, as Alcock had been, to the discredited Bowring, he still found that he was not consulted by the British commanders and that in the eyes of the Chinese authorities he held a very secondary position. The consulate did not regain its proper standing until the allied commission was dissolved late in 1861 and the city was handed back to the Chinese.[26]

Remote from any influence on political events an officer, at first a consular agent and later a vice-consul, was in charge of the Canton consulate's branch establishment at Whampoa, 12 miles down river. There he led an isolated and eminently disagreeable water-borne existence between the two Anglo-Chinese wars in a post described by Bonham as onerous and most unenviable.[27] There was plenty of room for ships to berth at Canton but, unless towed, large sailing-vessels could not make their way there through the narrow gaps in the defensive stone barriers which the Chinese had thrown across the river during the first war. They came no further than Whampoa, where they lay at anchor over 3 miles of reaches. To board them the officer spent much time in his boat, often against the current and sometimes in so heavy a swell that boarding became dangerous or even impracticable. Along the river a collection of temporary shacks, known as Bamboo Town, catered for the crews

when on shore. The anchorage and Bamboo Town, whose dilapidated and decaying tenements were described as inspiring unmitigated disgust, were considered a blessing to Canton, in as much as they spared it the loose population inseparable from merchant shipping. There were few permanent residents and their company cannot have been exhilarating. Apart from the vice-consul and his constable, the British community in 1851 consisted of three shipwrights, two surgeons, one master mariner, one ship's chandler, and one clerk.[28]

The first consular agent, St. Croix, resigned in 1847 and was replaced by Bird, lured by higher pay from the superintendency to a post which he found particularly disagreeable and which he would not have accepted had he been fully aware of its nature.[29] His blunders, complaints, misfortunes, and quarrels filled many despatches.

In matters of law Bird was accident-prone. He exceeded the powers of a consular agent by fining a master under the Mercantile Shipping Act for not providing the crew with lime and lemon juice, and was promoted to vice-consul so that he might have the necessary powers under the Act. As vice-consul he then was deemed to have trespassed upon the consul's jurisdiction by giving a seaman six months. Bonham ruled that Bird's judgements were subject to the consul's supervision, but he had not ended the confusion about Bird's powers. By mid-1852 Bird had dealt with 33 civil cases as well as 46 criminal cases, 585 police cases, 6 inquests, and 5 naval courts, and he presumably continued on the same lines until in 1856 it was belatedly realized that he probably had no civil jurisdiction.[30] In his private capacity he was sued in the Hong Kong courts for $20 by his predecessor St. Croix and had judgement given against him in absentia because the lawyer whom he had instructed by letter to defend the case happened to be away and the letter remained unopened; and he had to be officially discouraged from instituting libel proceedings against a Hong Kong newspaper which accused him of homicide after the death of an imprisoned seaman.[31] He was himself victimized by a libel action against him in Hong Kong. An American named Hunt, who combined keeping a floating store with being United States consular agent at Whampoa, had been tempting sailors from British naval and merchant ships to desert and to take better-paid jobs in American ships. Bowring as consul and Elmslie as acting consul at Canton

had refused to act, so Bird suggested to two British ship's masters that they should boycott Hunt's business. Hunt claimed $10,000 damages and withdrew the proceedings after Bird on legal advice had apologized and had agreed to pay £310 costs. The Hong Kong attorney-general, who had not been able to advise Bird at the time because he had been acting chief justice, advised Bonham on Bonham's return from home leave that judgement would have been in Bird's favour if the case had gone forward. Bonham expressed surprise to the Foreign Office that Bowring had in Bonham's absence not taken some decisive step through the United States consulate to stop such disgraceful proceedings and deplored the legal trickery and stratagems by which Bird had been forced to pay so large a sum for acting faithfully and honestly in advising the two masters on a question of public importance. The Foreign Office replied that it was wholly impossible to give Bird relief, however much his heavy pecuniary loss was to be regretted. The prosecution had not arisen from any act which it was his public duty to perform; helping Bird would tend to establish the principle that a consular officer could look to the support of the public against the consequences of any legal proceedings to which he might, without reference to his public duties, have made himself liable.[32] While this unhelpful ruling was *en route* to China Bird pursued his campaign against deserters by sending the constable to arrest one Achong, a Chinese who had been harbouring a British deserter. Achong was out, but his wife, or a prostitute with whom he was living, came back with the constable to demand $20 for the deserter's keep. Bird detained her, hoping thereby to secure Achong's appearance, and while attempting to escape by swimming she drowned. Achong threatened to kill Bird and the constable unless $100 were paid in compensation, and came alongside Bird's boat in the small hours with half a dozen men, pulling off when the alarm was given but leaving a stinkpot with lighted fuse in a porthole. The consul, Parkes, commented acidly that he differed from Bird as to both the propriety and the expediency of detaining the woman.[33]

Quarrels were many. An angry correspondence between Bird and T.T. Meadows, the Canton interpreter, was on Bonham's instructions removed from the archives as unsuitable for preservation there.[34] Elmslie in two spells as acting consul showed unmistakeable personal animus. In 1849 Bird, on the unsupported evidence of a Chinese pedlar, sentenced two apprentices to a month's solitary

confinement for robbing the pedlar of a cap and a pair of trousers, one witness remaining unexamined because he did not profess any religion and doubted a future state of rewards and punishments. The boys' captain was morally convinced of the innocence of two well-behaved boys from respectable families, and Elmslie, who thought the evidence insufficient, instructed Bird to release the boys forthwith. When Bird complained to Bonham Elmslie charged Bird with having in many cases seriously involved himself with British subjects and foreign governments, and claimed that Bird had invariably been extricated from these difficulties by Elmslie's personal influence with the aggrieved parties. Worse was to follow. After a squabble over an official triviality Elmslie accused Bird of habitual insubordination. Bowring, on resuming charge of the Canton consulate, was directed by Bonham to hold an inquiry at which Meadows, J.T. Walker, and Oakley gave evidence on their honour in the presence of accuser and accused. Bonham, who heartily disliked Elmslie, reported that Elmslie had manufactured the charge and brought it forward in Bowring's temporary absence in order to injure Bird, but his only specific recommendation was that the two men should no longer serve together. Palmerston expressed strong disapproval of Elmslie having used temporary and accidental possession of authority to vent long-harboured malice and to make groundless charges, and warned Elmslie that he would be dismissed if there were any recurrence. Bird too was censured. The want of judgement in his conduct, and of temper and propriety in his language, led Palmerston greatly to doubt Bird's fitness for his present position; his post, placing in his hands management and control of a great number of sailors, particularly required temper and judgement, 'for it is essential that the person who has to control uneducated men should be able to command his temper...if he loses his temper and gets into the wrong, he will necessarily cease to be respected and obeyed'. There was some inconvenience, Palmerston wrote, in leaving the two men in official relations with each other, but neither deserved removal by promotion, and he had no present means of moving either to an exactly similar post; he trusted that the present severe admonition would be a sufficient corrective of their future conduct without the punishment of removal to a place of inferior rank or emolument.[35]

Some of Bird's irritability may have been due to the deficiencies in his floating accommodation. In 1848 Bonham requested sanction

to buy a prison hulk for Whampoa because the existing vessel was so unsatisfactory. To accommodate prisoners, whose number had on one occasion reached fourteen, there were only four very small and wholly unventilated compartments in the hold, so low that the prisoners had either to sit or to recline and so insecure that they had to be kept in irons. The portion of the vessel set apart for Bird consisted only of two small rooms and was altogether insufficient. Not only was it insufficient, but the annoyance to him from drunk and disorderly seamen confined in close proximity was often so great that he could not do his work. By 1850 he was heartily sick of living so close to his gaol; a seaman in it had just had delirium tremens, and until death ended the man's ravings Bird could neither work nor sleep. He suggested that the best replacement would be a flower-boat, that is, one of the ornamental barges in which the Cantonese were accustomed to dine, gamble, and whore. He conceded that 'there is a certain association of ideas connected with flower-boats incompatible with the respectability of a magistrate's residence', but Bonham authorized the hiring of one, stipulating however that Bird must personally pay for any necessary internal fittings.[36] The following year the Foreign Office decreed that as soon as possible a proper residence, office, and gaol should be provided. To circumvent Chinese objections to land being acquired for these official purposes a British shipwright at Whampoa was induced to acquire land in his own name for subsequent transfer to government use, but just as the transfer was on the point of completion the shipwright disappeared, feared murdered, after leaving Whampoa for Canton with a valuable cargo of cochineal. It took six more years to acquire a site.[37] Meanwhile Bird remained afloat. In 1853 he was in a chop-boat so old and rotten that she sprang a leak one night when he was in bed, and he had great difficulty in beaching her and effecting an escape. Six months or so later he went on sick-leave to Australia, where he had already unsuccessfully applied for a job on account of the great dislike for him which he said prevailed at Whampoa; the medical certificate mentioned nervous irritation and mental depression.[38] First Oakley acted briefly in his absence and then Winchester.[39] Bird had hardly left when an old navy store-ship, the *Alligator*, a three-deck vessel of some 500 tons, was made available for the vice-consulate. She was received unenthusiastically. The unmarried Oakley asked permission to defer moving into a ship which 'was so filthy and

incommodious as to be totally unfit without considerable altera-
tion for a comfortable residence'. Winchester, a married man with
children, complained that the *Alligator* was too large for his
boatmen to keep wholesomely clean and that plagues of mosquitoes and cockroaches made life almost intolerable. Even the Treasury consented to the large sum of £250 being spent on fitting her
up for the vice-consulate. Bird cut his leave short and moved into
her just in time for her to be struck by more than twenty shots in a
battle between Chinese government junks and a large piratical fleet.
In little more than a year after that the vice-consulate was closed
following the *Arrow* hostilities, the *Alligator* reverted temporarily
to the navy, and Bird was given another twelve months' leave, this
time on account of deranged digestive organs and a disturbed
nervous system.[40] His day was nearly over. He again came back
from leave early, spent a few months in Hong Kong and at the
reopened Whampoa vice-consulate, became aggrieved at lack of
promotion and insubordinate, was pensioned off on a medical
certificate recommending a change from China's climate, reappeared within twelve months as a ship's chandler at Shanghai, and
died there soon afterwards at the age of 45.[41] He had not been the
'wee judge Jeffries' that a Hong Kong newspaper dubbed him.
Bowring was nearer the mark in calling him an honest but irascible
man whose lack of suavity of deportment, discretion, and self-
control had inflicted much disagreeable correspondence on his
superiors. In one respect he had been unexpectedly competent; he
had insured his life adequately and left nearly £2,000 as provision
for his widowed mother and unmarried sister, both of whom his
will advised to return to Britain.[42]

   During Bird's first leave Winchester did not find Whampoa a bed
of roses. He had difficulty in managing a numerous and increasing
body of seamen at a time when China was so disorganized that
local government had ceased to exist at Whampoa. A lawless
foreigner named Suicar, who was thought to be a papal subject and
whose vocation was crimp and harbourer of deserters, obtained his
deserters by open patrols of the shipping. He kept a chop-boat and
six boarding-houses, usually occupied by thirty Europeans and by
Lascars in addition; he boasted that he could call in five hundred
Chinese as well; his armed attack on another boarding-house
caused an American's death; and four of his men armed with knives
boarded a British vessel and aided the gunner to desert. The

Whampoa constable, who was also gaoler, boarding officer of shipping, and dogsbody in the office, and whom Winchester praised as the most hard-working public servant imaginable, must also have been a brave man, for he proceeded to Suicar's and took the gunner into custody.[43]

After Bird's retirement the next man to languish at Whampoa, again in the *Alligator*, was Hale. The navy had restored her to civilian use as consular 'locomotive accommodation' in time for Alcock to use her when Elgin required the consulate to leave Hong Kong for Canton, but they had first stripped the copper off her bottom. Alcock lost no time in renting premises on land when she started sinking under him and had to be kept afloat by four pumps working day and night. After recaulking she reverted to the vice-consulate.[44] Hale had been ensconced in relative comfort as vice-consul at Foochow. He had married in England during a leave, had lost his wife in Shanghai two years later, and had left his infant daughter at home.[45] What were described as very serious charges were now made against him at Foochow. Hale's official account was that he had treated the unmarried sister-in-law of a British resident, Caldecott Smith, with unwarrantable and indecent freedom, kissing her and attempting to put his hand under her clothes, but that he had never contemplated any such criminal act as seduction. His unofficial version was known in the Foreign Office to be that he had produced a contraceptive without disapproval having been expressed. Caldecott Smith was legally advised that as his sister-in-law had left for England immediately afterwards and was not available to give evidence criminal or civil proceedings against Hale could not be instituted in Hong Kong, and at home the Law Officers advised that there was not enough evidence to convict Hale of criminal assault. The view of a junior in China was that as poor Hale had got into a scrape and lost caste among the Foochow community he could naturally not be left there, and the Foreign Office expressed the same view in officialese. Caldecott Smith was told that the Foreign Secretary did not feel called upon to interfere further between Caldecott Smith's family and Hale, but that as the matter seemed to have occasioned much comment at Foochow it had been thought right to move Hale to Whampoa.[46] The earlier intention had been that on Bird's retirement he should be replaced by some naval officer combining firmness with gentlemanly bearing, and the Foreign Office had been prepared, if no such

person was available in China, to look at home for a person with maritime experience used to policing shipping. The need to move Hale into the only vice-consular vacancy put a stop to that. Although after little more than a year at Whampoa Hale's health broke and he retired, to die at the age of 45, no suggestion of recruiting a specialist from outside the service to replace him was made.[47]

At Amoy the resident British community was slow to grow. In 1851 there were only thirty-one persons and in 1857 still only thirty-six.[48] Three successive consuls, Lay, Layton, and Sullivan, died at their posts, the eldest aged 47, without leaving any permanent mark on the port. In 1852 Parkes, then the interpreter, induced Sullivan to send him inland to the intendant to deal with current difficulties about British subjects obtaining land. His forcefulness extracted from the intendant agreement to the definition of a waterfront area to be set aside for British residences and godowns. The Foreign Office ruled that when the land was divided up among British subjects its demise to other foreign nationals should be prohibited, the lack of such a precaution having in the Foreign Office view caused inconveniences at Shanghai. All the land, except for a site reserved for a consulate, was let to British subjects through the consulate within three years. This was the first of the treaty port areas, so dear to China hands and so obnoxious to later generations of Chinese, afterwards known as British concessions, though this term had not yet been borrowed from the French and the implications were not yet seen. It was also the first of the six such areas which Parkes was to extract from the Chinese within a decade. It was of minimal significance. It was so small that it consisted of only ten lots. Its origins were so obscure that in the twentieth century, when China was struggling to regain full control over her own territory, the area's legal status as a concession, about which the Legation had had serious doubts as early as 1877, was considered by the British to be incapable of documentary proof.[49]

Backhouse, left in charge of Amoy by Sullivan's death, became the first consular officer whose port fell to rebels. In a local insurrection Amoy was captured suddenly and almost painlessly, but the recapture some months later was protracted and bloody. The arrival of a fleet of government junks to drive the rebels out heralded an immediate artillery duel with a vast expenditure of ammunition and little damage. Two or three shots came through

the consulate roof and several fell in the compound, which contained a house each for consul and vice-consul and a third house for the rest of the staff. Another shot took off the arm of a carpenter aboard HMS *Rapid* and Backhouse pointed out to the Chinese admiral the need for more careful aim, 'the shots being at present merely cast into the air to fall where they may, independent of any particular aim'. Growing illness confined Backhouse to his bed and he was relieved by D.B. Robertson. Within three weeks Robertson had vacated the consulate, the ground surrounding which had been taken by government troops and which had been considerably damaged in cross-fire. He took up residence in HMS *Hermes*, the wear and tear he had gone through from the perpetual attacks round the consulate both by day and by night making him feel that a little rest would be most welcome, but the intrepid constable elected to stay at the consulate, looking after the buildings and Robertson's personal effects. Some days afterwards the insurgent fleet and the insurgent leaders sailed away after dawn and panic broke out in the town. Hundreds put off on boats, rafts, boards, and even doors, and many tried to swim to Kulangsu, the greater part of whom drowned round *Hermes*. Landing in the town Robertson found the streets empty except for flying parties of insurgents being mercilessly speared. British seamen and marines guarded the entrances to the tiny concession and warned government troops to keep out, an early example of innumerable actions taken to keep Chinese unrest out of foreign areas in the treaty ports. By mid-morning the town had been completely taken. Robertson reported that a most cold-blooded and barbarous slaughter followed. On the waterfront government troops beheaded by the score everyone on whom they had managed to lay hands. On board the admiral's junk, to which he had gone to rescue some captured employees of British firms, Robertson led the admiral from his cabin, showed him the fearful spectacle, and begged him to show mercy. The admiral promised, saying that a few must suffer, and Robertson returned to *Hermes*. The bloody work still went on. When the troops wearied of the slowness of decapitation they destroyed dozens with bill-hooks, spears, and clubs. Finally they fell to work on board junks within 50 yards of *Hermes*. Some victims were slashed with a knife and knocked overboard, others tied by one arm and leg and hove into the water. The harbour was covered with struggling human beings, many of them boys about

12 years old. Deeply conscious of the responsibility that he would incur by intervening Robertson unwillingly watched for four hours scenes of the greatest barbarity and horror. At last, when whole boatloads were being mutilated and drowned alongside *Hermes*, Robertson felt interference a duty. Such proceedings, which he had told the admiral were most repugnant to Europeans, were, he considered, an outrage upon British humanity, for the people might have been taken elsewhere to be killed. He therefore sent a message to the admiral that he would not permit the carnage to proceed further. The admiral ordered it to be stopped and boats sent from *Hermes* rescued from drowning more than 300 people, numbers of whom were fearfully wounded. Several of the rescued were recognized as coolies employed by foreign firms, and certainly many of them were not insurgents. The following day Robertson sent a further message that he would not answer for the results if such scenes were repeated, as he had already had great difficulty in restraining his countrymen from overt actions which might have compromised friendly relations. He understood that the slaughter was then continued in a place remote from European shipping or residences and heard a fortnight later that numerous executions were still occurring daily. Bonham approved all Robertson's proceedings.[50]

After this gory interlude Amoy's business grew fast. The 50 British ships which called in 1854 became over 100 in 1855 and over 200 in 1856, in which year their crews numbered nearly 4,500.[51] With so many British ships along the coast a proportion came to grief, and villagers plundering wrecked vessels and stripping or murdering survivors gave recurrent trouble.[52] Replying in 1869 to a circular Foreign Office enquiry about local life-saving arrangements Pedder wrote with gusto that in the Amoy consular district there were none; on the contrary the property of all those whose lives were in danger was regarded as fair prey and if they resisted they were killed; a Chinese going to a wreck first provided himself with an offensive weapon to use against any wrecked person who resisted being stripped.[53] More unusual shipping cases occurred too; after the master of a dismasted British vessel had had for the ship's safety to throw overboard chests belonging to Chinese deck passengers the supercargo was kidnapped to enforce claims for compensation.[54] It was however the coolie trade which gave the consulate most concern. A particularly horrifying case on the

Ingelwood, a British vessel, was brought to the consulate's attention by some of her own crew. She was found on inspection to
have on board over forty female children, the eldest aged 8, who
had been kidnapped or purchased at Ningpo. The doctor who went
on board reported that the illness of the captain and some of the
crew had evidently been caused by the stench from the children and
that when their cabin door had been opened he immediately smelt
such an oppressive stench that he suffered from a serious headache
during the whole day and had several times felt sick.[55]

Foochow was the port least affected by armed commotions and
for years was wrapped in slumbers broken only by an occasional
incident. Although it was the natural port for a tea trade which for
a time was to bring to Foochow the famous tea-clippers and a
community of foreign merchants living in lavish style, the Chinese
during the port's first years channelled the tea trade elsewhere and
Foochow saw no foreign trade other than that in opium. Alcock
managed to produce a report of nearly a hundred double pages on
Foochow's trade prospects, but even so prolific a writer could
produce no half-yearly return of foreign trade, for there had been
absolutely none. He tackled his duties with his customary vigour at
a post which on leaving he described as agreeable but more or less
a sinecure.[56] Taking the view that influence and respect could
hardly be attained in a half-civilized country without something of
an appearance being made he disregarded instructions about the
size of the consulate's establishment and to procure respect took on
fourteen Chinese as messengers, coolies, watchmen, and the like.
He acted to stop the pelting, hooting, and rude hustling of British
subjects. He was not surprised that strange-looking Europeans,
unable to speak Chinese, should be objects of the greatest curiosity
in an arrogant and ignorant population of many hundred thousand,
but considered that the sooner the Chinese put a true value on
European nations the more certainly commercial, social, and political intercourse would improve; with such considerations in mind he
first induced the viceroy to issue a general proclamation and then
secured adequate public punishment of soldiers who had stoned
Parkes. Arriving at Foochow with his wife and her maid, he
then brought his mother-in-law and sister-in-law there. When Mrs
Alcock and the maid arrived whole streets were blocked with the
inquisitive crowd and Mrs Alcock was sufficiently alarmed for
Parkes, who handed her out of her chair at her new home, to regret

having no smelling-salts on him, but behaviour improved; when Alcock later saw the maid off to Hong Kong boys shouting after her were chastised by their fathers.[57] After a year in Foochow Alcock rashly reported that hostile feeling among the people had entirely disappeared, almost at once had to report serious riots against local British opium traders, and again almost at once reported an utter absence of hostile words, jests, or looks during his walks. Puzzled, as many others were to be over the years, by the suddenness with which an alarming and unexpected squall had blown up and blown itself out, Alcock tentatively and probably correctly surmised that the local people were normally indifferent to the presence of foreigners and became hostile only when their interests or prejudices were roughly disregarded.[58] He claimed to have left Foochow on the best of terms with the Chinese authorities,[59] a claim which for many years to come few of his successors could reasonably have made.

Jackson, a sensible and competent successor without Alcock's commanding personality, found Foochow even more of a sinecure than Alcock had done. During the whole of his first year not a single foreign merchant ship called, and the consulate business was so trifling that he hardly had to indent for stationery.[60] His main anxiety was the absence of a doctor, who became available only when a naval vessel with a surgeon on board paid a hasty and unheralded visit. Lay with his 'medical education' and Alcock as a surgeon had been regarded by Davis as providing the consulate with a resident doctor, but Jackson was not qualified to play the dual role. He believed that he had been within twenty-four hours of death from epidemic fever when HMS *Scout* providentially arrived and provided skilled attention. The next naval visit was five months later, and in that period Jackson had been convalescing, J.T. Walker's life had been in extreme danger, M.C. Morrison had been in constant ill-health, and Mrs Jackson had been suffering from a troublesome disorder needing skilled treatment. Jackson ascribed the frequent staff indispositions more to the morbid sensibility induced by wearisome monotony and by a life without any kind of society than to insalubrity of climate, and he deplored the cruel position of a little group left for long periods without medical aid or any personal intercourse whatever with their countrymen. Davis asked the admiral that Foochow should be visited as often as possible and even hoped that a sloop might be permanently

stationed there. The Foreign Office concluded that if visits were from now on to be more regular there seemed no immediate necessity to appoint a medical officer. A few months after this complacent conclusion had been reached *Scout* sank in the river during a visit. She was raised, but the incident and the absence of trade made the admiral decide that future calls should be only occasional and should be off the entrance to the river. After this there was at least once a gap of over seven months between the visits of a ship and surgeon. Another well-meant contribution by Davis to improving the medical situation was to give Jackson liberty whenever necessary to leave his post to seek medical advice at Amoy or elsewhere. Jackson thanked him sincerely for this fresh proof of thoughtful consideration and hoped that his restored health would make it unnecessary to take advantage of the offer, 'though, were it otherwise, the impossibility of obtaining a conveyance would effectually frustrate your kind intentions'. Bonham eventually provided a solution by transferring Gingell to Foochow to combine the functions of interpreter and surgeon. After three and a half years in Foochow, and six in China, without ever leaving his post, Jackson's state of health was known to be very precarious. He applied for home leave, saying with moderation that he had suffered from the climate and the monotony and that he and his wife needed a change; he was however utterly unable to determine how the family could get to Hong Kong; unless a naval vessel called the only alternatives seemed to be to hire a junk and risk pirates or to ask a passage in an armed Chinese craft, the latter course being one which as consul he would be very reluctant to adopt.[61] After Jackson's departure thought was given to the possibility of obtaining another treaty port in exchange for Foochow, a proposal which the Chinese refused to consider, or of simply closing the consulate, but it was reduced to a vice-consulate instead. The reduction in the post's status enabled Jackson as the commissioned consul at Foochow to obtain at an early age the advantageous retirement terms available to public servants on the abolition of their offices, apparently to compensate them for the loss of something to which they had a permanent right. He got £600 a year, half his salary, considerably more than he would have received had he retired on health grounds at that age. He lived to draw the compensation allowance for thirty-four years, during nearly all of which Foochow was again a full consulate.[62]

Jackson left behind at Foochow a community which in the fifth year of the port's opening still consisted of some American missionaries, a Spanish Catholic priest, and the British masters of the two opium receiving-ships lying some distance from Foochow. Compton, the Canton merchant, for whom Jackson professed a sincere regard, in spite of the past condemnation by Palmerston, Davis, and Macgregor, explored Foochow's trade potential and did do some business, although according to Gingell he found the local merchants smooth-tongued, prodigious liars, 'which however being the national character cannot be wondered at'.[63] At last in 1853 three ships with cargoes of tea left Foochow, heralding her transient glory in the tea trade. The hitherto neglected port was visited in 1854 by 55 vessels and in the following year by 132.[64] In 1855 there was a full consul again, in 1856 three British tea-inspectors were resident, and with more foreigners present the troublesome curiosity of the Chinese population began to abate.[65] The community even had a resident Irish doctor, who responded to the termination of his services by calling another resident a craven-hearted, hypocritical, low-born knave, no gentleman, and a coarse vulgar animal; the resulting $25,000 libel action was settled by his publishing an apology. A parallel increase in American residents and the arrival of a full-time United States consul, Caleb Jones, were not an unmixed blessing. British interests were adversely affected by Jones' reactions when an American merchant, who had fired into the air to disperse a crowd discharging crackers in the street, was beaten to death.[66] Jones' official methods proved troublesome to the United States minister and to the British consulate, where one of his letters was found so peculiarly offensive that it was left unanswered.[67] The style of Jones' consular establishment can be deduced from his marshal's method of serving a warrant on an American, who happened to be in the company of a British naval surgeon. The warrant was served by the marshal clapping pistols to the heads of both men; the surgeon took this for an assault and defended himself; and in the British consular court Jones brought an unsuccessful action against the surgeon for assault.[68]

The consulate struggled to get Chinese officials to approve land transactions giving the suddenly growing British community suitable premises in which to trade and to live. It was a long battle. One magistrate having been dismissed for placing his official seal

on a contract to let premises in the city to British missionaries other officials were reluctant to expose their own careers to similar hazards. The foreign community eventually settled in Nantai, on the other side of the river from the city, in an area which was nothing but a huge graveyard devoid of houses. The foreigners' voluntary subscriptions for road building and similar works eventually made the area, which became the permanent focus of Foochow's foreign life, a pleasant place in which to live. Although the common people were by now on the whole civil, there were constant petty insults and, as Bruce pointed out to the consul, it was in practice safer and more comfortable for foreigners at the ports to congregate in places set apart for them than to exercise, if they could, their treaty right to live inside Chinese cities, a right which no merchant wished to exercise. It became inconvenient for the consulate to be isolated in the city away from the new centre of foreign business at Nantai and newly built consular premises at Nantai were occupied in 1859. To maintain the barren principle that foreigners were entitled to live in the city itself the expense of retaining additionally the old consulate in the city was with increasing reluctance incurred by the Foreign Office for some thirty years longer.[69]

Ningpo was too close to economically booming Shanghai, with which it could not compete, for much legitimate trade to develop. Sullivan had so little to do at Ningpo, and considered the prospect of trade there so distant, that after four years he successfully applied to be removed into active employment at Amoy, and the consulate, which like Foochow would have been closed entirely if the Chinese had been willing to open another port in exchange, was reduced to a vice-consulate.[70] Sullivan was in Ningpo long enough, however, to see the beginning of activities which during the 1850s made Ningpo notorious for a foreign-run convoying racket. The racket, which caused concern at other ports but whose stronghold was Ningpo, consisted of extracting payments from Chinese vessels in return for defence against other racketeers and against pirates.[71] William Davidson, a Scot whose methods did not seem to Sullivan ever to have been very scrupulous and whose dubious activities at Ningpo enabled him to leave well over £100,000 on his death at Torquay in 1887, was apparently one of the pioneers of the racket and he was a smuggler both of legitimate goods and of opium.[72] (Pottinger regretted that a 'Mr. Davidson, a very respectable and

well-informed merchant' from Batavia declined his offer of the Amoy consulship in 1843. A modern academic work has wrongly deduced that the shady Ningpo adventurer might have become a consul. The offer was almost certainly made to one G.F. Davidson, an experienced and mature merchant fitting Pottinger's description. William Davidson was too young in 1843 to have been considered.)[73] Lower down the treaty port social scale was Webster, an early specimen of Ningpo's British undesirables. His two years in China had been chequered. Disrated as a mate for dishonesty, he had escaped from the Shanghai consulate gaol, had been successively mate and captain on vessels owned by Davidson, had then been discharged, had got into debt at Hong Kong, had come to Ningpo from Shanghai posing as an American, and in Ningpo had been trying to collect a Portuguese crew to run his convoying racket among the Chinese fishing fleet. Sullivan gave him three months for assaulting a Chinese.[74]

Briefly in charge after Sullivan's transfer D.B. Robertson feared that as the Chinese could not distinguish between Europeans the activities of a score of Portuguese, Goans, and Manilamen in violently collecting spurious debts would lead to an explosion affecting other Europeans; he got the gang out of one respectable shop by sending a uniformed messenger to the shop with strict orders not to intervene but to watch the gang's proceedings. Under Robertson's successors law and order continued to deteriorate. During Hague's incumbency Portuguese lorchas forcibly took over the protection of vessels which Davidson's men had been convoying; a Chinese was brought in with a fearful wound from a Portuguese belaying-pin; a Maltese was brought in with fourteen spear wounds inflicted by local people when he landed for an assignation with a Chinese woman; a piratical fleet with over 1,000 men defeated a government naval force and threatened Ningpo; and on land rebels advanced too.[75] J.A.T. Meadows, interpreter at the consulate, acted as vice-consul when Hague went home sick. He had much to say about the rebels but more to say about Portuguese misdeeds. His particular aversion was Marques, who filled the new post of Portuguese consul at Ningpo. The governor of Macao denied Meadows' allegations, which Bowring had seen fit to pass to the governor, that Marques got a commission on all money collected by Portuguese convoyers, and in return accused Meadows, accurately enough, of being anti-Portuguese. Meadows showed

where his sympathies lay in reporting a clash between the Portuguese and locally based Cantonese pirates. A notorious Cantonese pirate had come over to the government three years before, had been given official rank, was employed by the intendant to control the local population, and practised every kind of extortion on his own account. Now he was joined by a pirate brother-in-law, fresh from defeating a Portuguese lorcha fleet, and a pirate cousin. The Portuguese were afraid to put to sea but knifed two of the Cantonese in Ningpo. As Marques took no action, professing not to know who the murderers were, to have no police, and to have no gaol, the Cantonese took matters into their own hands. Chinese merchants and foreign missionaries were considerably excited to see well over a hundred 'ex-pirates armed with guns, swords, spears and stinkpots running and shouting through the streets with red handkerchiefs on their heads and red sashes round their waists'. After a brisk exchange of fire, houses inhabited by Portuguese were rushed and two Portuguese killed. The Chinese authorities sent not a man to the scene of the disturbance. According to Meadows' version of events the Portuguese gunboat which in due course reached Ningpo made a most treacherous and cowardly attack on the Chinese lorchas and killed innocent people by firing into the city, and the United States gunboat which arrived later came to protect American and British residents from the ruffianly Portuguese proceedings.[76]

A Portuguese named Bemvindo attacked a Chinese servant of the consulate. Meadows' experience, like that of the Cantonese, was that Marques invariably failed to act in such cases and like the Cantonese Meadows took the law into his own hands. At the head of the consulate's entire Chinese staff he carried Bemvindo forcibly off from the lodging-house where he was living, had him tied to a post at the consulate, and had the head Chinese servant give him thirty-five lashes with a rope. A prompt complaint from the governor of Macao reached Bowring, and Meadows was greatly annoyed to be suspended before his own account had reached Hong Kong. In dudgeon he announced that he had decided to retire from his post for a time. Quoting Bowring's standing instructions that consuls should report any new forms of trading he reported in a Parthian despatch a new form of trade opened up at Macao, namely, a Portuguese slave trade in male and female children aged between 5 and 8, whom Portuguese bought for $3 to $4 and shipped

via Macao to Timor or Manila; three Portuguese were involved, including Marques, who got a commission, probably 8 per cent, on the lorchamen's profits; 'as these gentlemen — Portuguese gentlemen, of course — are all officials of the Macao government' doubtless the governor of Macao was well acquainted with the trade and would on request take pleasure in giving Bowring more detailed information than Meadows could collect in Ningpo.[77]

Despite Meadows' indignation at his suspension Bowring had been decidedly helpful to him. The acting attorney-general at Hong Kong had advised that if Bemvindo died from this most serious outrage Meadows would be guilty of murder and had recommended that Meadows should be brought before the Supreme Court, where any suit for pecuniary compensation by Bemvindo should be conducted free for him by the colony's legal staff, with witnesses receiving free passages to Hong Kong.[78] Instead, Bowring in consultation with the governor of Macao suspended Meadows for six months so that Meadows could make arrangements with Bemvindo, the governor for his part undertaking that meanwhile there would be no proceedings in the Hong Kong courts and that no report would be made to Lisbon.[79] T.T. Meadows gave Bowring no credit for helpfulness. While on home leave he wrote to Hammond deploring Bowring's woeful indiscretion, against which when serving under Bowring he had constantly battled and which had now been responsible for his brother being suspended unheard. He took the opportunity of correcting his previous statement to Hammond that his brother's excellent relations with the Ningpo missionaries were partly due to an exemplary private life; his brother, having decided to give up all hope of ever being able to return to England, had now followed treaty port practice and taken a Chinese girl. He was in fact still out of touch with his brother's private life, for J.A.T. Meadows had before the Bemvindo incident acknowledged the girl as his wife in the presence of his subordinate Hart, the only other British member of the vice-consulate's staff. How Hammond replied is not known. The only Foreign Office reaction preserved is a straight-faced docket saying that the letter *inter alia* pointed out Bowring's unfitness for office. To Bowring the Foreign Office wrote that although J.A.T. Meadows' conduct had been wholly unjustifiable, sufficient reparation had been afforded by his suspension and resignation, and that the governor of Macao should therefore be invited to let the matter rest.[80]

The story did not finish there. Winchester, hastily sent to replace J.A.T. Meadows, had long ago given up trying to learn Chinese, and as no interpreter could be spared to fill the gap at Ningpo Winchester and Bowring accepted an offer by Meadows, who had gone into business at the port, to lend his services as interpreter. They also accepted as authoritative his very favourable report on Hart's language studies and on at least one expedition against pirates the navy were glad to accept his proferred services as interpreter. After a year of this Meadows applied to be reinstated as acting interpreter. Bowring considered that reinstatement at Ningpo might give umbrage to the Portuguese but hoped that the Foreign Office would agree to so useful an officer being reinstated elsewhere. The first Foreign Office reaction was that this would not be right to the Portuguese government, but some months later they changed their minds; if Portuguese susceptibilities could be managed they were now disposed to reinstate him at Ningpo, since before the unfortunate incident he had as far as they knew always been diligent and behaved with propriety. Bowring was instructed to ask the governor of Macao whether Meadows had not made sufficient atonement. The governor obligingly intimated that he was thoroughly satisfied with the punishment inflicted and would with pleasure see Meadows restored to the public service. Meadows was taken back first as acting, and then as substantive, interpreter at Shanghai, a key interpreter's post.[81] To Foreign Office regret he resigned abruptly in 1861 on being ordered to Canton. He went into business at Tientsin, made money, was bankrupted by a speculation in Korea, made more money, and was described by Wade as a very honest man. At Tientsin he acted for years as United States vice-consul, and also became consul for Denmark and the Netherlands.[82]

Immediately after taking over, Winchester reported that over forty children in Portuguese hands were still awaiting shipment and that Marques, though without a financial interest in the trade, was fully aware of it and was permitting or ignoring it for as long as he could safely do so. He secured evidence confirming the long-held local belief that Bemvindo and associates let boats out to pirates and disposed of the plunder in Ningpo on the pirates' behalf and, presuming that there must be some limit to local Chinese long-suffering, he feared an eventual catastrophe. His summing-up of the situation was that although Marques had been sent to repress

Portuguese misconduct the misconduct continued as before with the additional advantage of official approval, and that 'Mr. Marques' idea of the nature and object of his functions is certainly very different from those which we attach to the office'. Temporarily in charge during an interregnum between Winchester and Sinclair, Hart had no greater Portuguese trouble than the beating of a British sailor by two Portuguese in Marques' office and in Marques' presence; fortunately the sailor, who like all foreigners in Ningpo went about armed, did not attempt to use his revolver. Sinclair on arrival thought he could manage Marques, who after a British subject had been killed by a Portuguese knife in a brothel actually took two Portuguese into custody. Sinclair changed his tune when both men broke out and got clean away and asked that the governor of Macao should consider action to deter further murderous Portuguese assaults.[83]

Bowring selected T.T. Meadows to take charge of Ningpo during Sinclair's home leave. He fondly believed that he had during discussion at Hong Kong convinced Meadows that his brother had been treated with much leniency, that there had been no injustice, and that there were no grounds for complaint against the Portuguese.[84] Bowring was rapidly disabused. At all T.T. Meadows' independent posts, of which Ningpo was the first, the misdirection of an acute brain made him a thorn in his superiors' flesh; he had not been more than two weeks in Ningpo before seeking guidance on no less than twelve doubtful points about the exercise of his judicial powers.[85] Now unjustified resentment against Bowring, his bad relations with whom became notorious along the coast,[86] made him more than usually awkward to handle. Very soon Bowring was deciding not to encumber a despatch to the Foreign Office with copies of Meadows' reports, so lengthy as to make a large volume, about local lawlessness. Meadows' subsequent correspondence on the same subject became so bulky and diffuse that a resumé of it had to be prepared in Hong Kong, where the staff complained of having to copy such elaborate and voluminous outpourings and where Bowring wished in vain that in dealing with specific issues Meadows would avoid the vast sea of generalities which flowed from his pen. Voluminous and diffuse, too, were the complaints against Bowring himself which were directed from Ningpo to the Foreign Office. A wealth of unnecessary detail and a lively style make Meadows' despatches

enjoyable reading today. Contemporaries were less pleased to be confronted with thirty-nine foolscap pages controverting, all too convincingly, Bowring's contention that prior sanction should have been sought before Meadows dismissed a Chinese and a constable on the Ningpo staff. Bowring seems to have silenced his subordinate only once. Meadows had asked permission to buy a special burial-ground for coloured seamen, alleging that burying them close to the graves of Thom and other respected persons was repugnant to Ningpo residents. Bowring replied that 'white men and black are entitled to equal justice when living and to equal regard when dead'; he did not believe that Thom's repose would in the slightest degree be disturbed or degraded by the adjacency of the mortal remains of those whose living frames had been clad by heaven in a darker colouring; and people who thought otherwise were free to spend their own money buying themselves a separate burial-ground.[87]

Retribution overtook the Ningpo Portuguese in mid-1857. Forty to fifty were killed in an attack on them by the Cantonese expirates, aided by ten to fifteen Europeans and Americans. Meadows considered the Cantonese almost respectable in comparison with the cowardly but ferocious Portuguese, and having ascertained that the Cantonese intended to avoid attacks on British subjects refused, as did the United States consul, either to intervene or to shelter fleeing Portuguese. Marques and his family got away in time from the Portuguese consulate, where in an oddly international shootout an American or Irishman hauling down the consular flag was shot dead by a pro-Portuguese Italian, who was then killed by two Cantonese. Bowring charged Meadows with having been actuated by personal dislike in refusing Marques shelter. The Foreign Office rejected the charge and considered that Meadows had shown a wise discretion in recommending that Marques should look for asylum to the Catholic bishop and not to the British consulate. It was not long, however, before they felt called upon to express regret at Meadows' disrespectful, antagonistic, and insubordinate tone to Bowring; Meadows' proper course, they wrote, would have been to represent to Bowring in temperate and respectful terms the grounds on which he thought he had been judged hardly and to ask that his representations in vindication of his impugned conduct should be submitted to the Foreign Secretary.[88]

This major affray, after which Marques was recalled, was the end

of Portuguese dominance in Ningpo's foreign ruffianism, but the British share in the ruffianism was by no means ended. The very next month a Frenchman sent a British ex-convict up-country with a gang of a dozen armed Cantonese and Ningpo men to commit armed robbery. After killing one man the ex-convict was taken prisoner by villagers and so tightly bound that five days later he was brought dying to the consulate, with hands, forearms, shoulders, back, and hips sloughing away. Although the treatment had been cruel Meadows could not detect any specific anti-foreignism; the man was dead; and had he lived he would very probably have been hanged in Hong Kong. Meadows therefore confined himself to drafting a proclamation, which the intendant issued, prohibiting further breaches of the treaties, and to going in person to the village and reading the villagers a lecture against taking the law into their own hands. Convinced that he had thus made it as safe as before for British subjects to go into the country he earnestly hoped that the Chinese authorities would not be pressed to punish the villagers. Bowring thoroughly approved of Meadows' actions and considered that nothing further need be done.[89]

The following year a defendant in the consular court admitted striking someone a severe blow on the head with a slingshot but added in palliation that he had mistaken the injured man for someone else; three naval ratings out on a robbing spree were drowned while fleeing from angry villagers; a group of British seamen were fighting among themselves and robbing the Chinese down river at Chinhai, where Meadows had no constable and where he expected only the most listless kind of passive co-operation from the Chinese authorities; one of the Chinhai group was first starved for seven days by Cantonese who boarded his lorcha and was then murdered by them; no evidence about the murder could be obtained from a British subject who had been on board one of the vessels involved but who had been too opium-sodden to be aware of the proceedings; and in spite of Meadows' warnings two former masters of British coasters settled at Chinhai to run a convoying racket. One of these two masters got blown up in a powder explosion. The survivor took on a new partner, and within two years of starting from nothing the pair ran five boats, owned three other armed boats, and employed fourteen foreigners, including British, German, American, Chilean, and Portuguese nationals. At this point they were charged with blackmail, the navy

seized them, and they were brought before the consular court and prohibited from further convoying. Another year, and one of the pair was murdered by a Spaniard and a Sardinian and the life of the other was being threatened by one Roberts. Roberts was deported to Hong Kong for making the threat, similarly threatening the constable, associating with pirates, and being unable to give security for good behaviour. He was then penniless but six months later he reappeared as the owner of a junk which he was presumed to have robbed from Chinese, was given six months for robbing a British lugger of two guns and their carriages, very nearly escaped from the consular gaol, and had to be sent in handcuffs to the Chinese prison for custody. The next pair of British adventurers to appear, one a former private soldier with a Chinese father-in-law and the other a former merchant seaman, established themselves profitably in the Chinhai convoying business and employed among others Portuguese, Greeks, Italians, and Turks.[90] It is a sufficient commentary on the China coast of the day that in 1859 Wade called Ningpo a quiet post.[91]

Shanghai's trade and the foreign community dependent on it were for a century to show an almost unlimited capacity for growth, and the Foreign Office by 1846 already saw Shanghai as promising to rank second in importance only to Canton. Davis considered Alcock the ablest consul in China, but mindful of the claims of seniority recommended Johnston, at last back from sick-leave, as Balfour's successor. The Foreign Office rejected the recommendation, conceiving Alcock best qualified.[92] Alcock's notable term of office at Shanghai confirmed the rightness of their judgement. Humiliated by failure to emerge from a very well-paid but subordinate position at Hong Kong, Johnston soon sought retirement on health grounds, but not until 1852 did the Treasury agree to pension arrangements which he was prepared to accept. Soon after retirement he made an absurd application to be appointed chief superintendent. He died in well-to-do obscurity many years later.[93]

Alcock's most sensational exploit as consul in Shanghai came in 1848. Three British missionaries distributing tracts outside the city were attacked with poles, iron bars, swords, and a heavy iron chain, and in Alcock's view owed their lives to their Christian forebearance and to their ability to remonstrate and parley in Chinese. Attaching no credence to the intendant's report that the

chief offenders could not be found, Alcock concluded that a denial of justice would be fatal to the British position in Shanghai and that regardless of danger to himself and his family, living in isolation in the centre of the Chinese city and away from the foreign settlement, he must take upon himself all the responsibility of coercive measures. He informed the intendant that until some of the ringleaders had been arrested and punished the British navy would stop any junk loaded with grain passing down the river. The ultimatum was preposterously daring. The movement of grain was a vital Chinese necessity, there were some 1,400 grain junks and 50 war junks in the area, and the physical means of enforcing the prohibition consisted of one small naval vessel, whose commander was acutely aware of the great responsibility he was assuming. Alcock, however, was convinced that although some hazard of a serious collision was unavoidable there were many probabilities against it and in favour of a satisfactory settlement. Alcock had an unrivalled ability to gauge risks accurately. The intendant ventured on nothing but delay and subterfuge. Stepping up his war of nerves, Alcock dispatched the vice-consul and interpreter up the Yangtze to the viceroy at Nanking. They were satisfactorily received and the provincial judge was sent post-haste to Shanghai. Some of the attackers were promptly arrested, identified, and punished, Alcock removed his embargo on junk movements and on British payment of customs duties, which he had also suspended, and the intendant and district magistrate were removed from office. The bold, incisive, and successful action was no more typical of Alcock than were his pains throughout to minimize his opponents' loss of face and to maintain outward courtesies. He assured the intendant that he bore him no personal ill-will; he explained his course of action to a deputation of junk-owners, whom he found very pleased to think that the intendant's removal might result; and on the conclusion of the affair the provincial judge was escorted to the consulate for refreshments, to the printing-press run by one of the assaulted missionaries, and to the hospital run by another of them, movements which Alcock said attracted much attention among the Chinese and which he believed were calculated to indicate perfect resumption of harmony. He also believed that the Chinese would not again lightly venture upon a denial of justice for outrages against British subjects, and that Chinese weakness, ordinarily astutely masked by contempt and arrogance, had been demon-

strated. The whole affair was over within a month.[94]

The reactions of Bonham in Hong Kong, where he had taken over from Davis only days before the first reports of Alcock's actions came in from Shanghai, were equally typical of the man. He was as averse to expressing decided opinions to his superiors as he was given to bullying junior subordinates. His initial report to Palmerston was that although every allowance should be made for a trying and embarrassing situation Alcock had exceeded his authority, and he told Alcock that the dispute should have been referred to Hong Kong for settlement with the imperial commissioner and that no aggressive act possibly endangering peaceable relations with the Chinese government would have been sanctioned. Soon he was awkwardly excusing himself to Palmerston for any appearance of timidity and was conveying the 'gratifying' news that all Alcock's demands had been met. Alcock's action, Bonham now said, would tend materially to ensure peaceable relations at Shanghai and at other ports; as Alcock had embarked on his action before Bonham had taken over from Davis and had most successfully concluded it Bonham 'had no particular remark to make'; but as less competent gentlemen might be emboldened by Alcock's success to imitate him, probably less successfully, Bonham desired to be instructed about the relative responsibilities of consuls and chief superintendent. Even Palmerston seems to have been a little at a loss. In all the circumstances, he wrote, the government approved Alcock's action and did full justice to his vigour and firmness, but the case must be considered as an exception to the rule and not as a precedent; and 'no doubt' on any future occasion of difference between himself and the Chinese authorities Alcock would conform strictly to his instructions.[95]

After such a start it is not surprising that relations between Bonham and Alcock lacked cordiality. Friction showed in a series of exchanges in 1850. First, information about a land transaction which Alcock had approved in Shanghai reached the Foreign Office in a form which led Palmerston to express 'entire disapproval', a set Foreign Office formula of strong rebuke. Few Palmerstonian rebukes can have met a more spirited rejoinder. If it had been borne in mind, Alcock wrote, that he had been given contradictory information about the government's intentions and kept in total ignorance of facts of which he might easily have been informed, Palmerston, instead of passing a totally unmerited aspersion on a

distant official unable to communicate with his own government, might have allowed that Alcock had acted to the best of his judgement. In transmitting this defence, some of the barbs in which were probably aimed more at Bonham than at the Foreign Office, Bonham commented that although there had been no element of jobbery Alcock had acted inadvisedly, precipitately, and without his usual good judgement. The Foreign Office however backed down completely, exculpating Alcock with the further set formula that his explanation was quite sufficient.[96] Next, Bonham, a man for inessentials, recommended in the interests of economy that Alcock's indent on the Stationery Office in London should be cut by half, as Shanghai should be able to manage on the same quantity for which Canton had indented. Alcock's remonstrance was filed in Hong Kong with angry marginalia; Alcock had no alternative to continuing to indent annually for adequate supplies ('exceedingly impertinent') and while he did not presume to question Bonham's authority ('you had better try') he doubted whether the superintendency were in a position to estimate Shanghai's stationery requirements ('doubt as you please — but it *shall* be done') which the consul was better placed to do ('he be damned'). The Foreign Office agreed that the indent had evidently been excessive, but in a curious sequel Canton was later found to have underindented and Bonham was obliged to seek sanction for Canton to purchase stationery on the commercial market.[97] Then Bonham, who had misread a Shanghai despatch about the probable cost of purchasing surveying instruments, was invited to explain how the mistake, totally inexplicable to Alcock but evidently the foundation for a tone of disapprobation in Bonham's reply, had originated.[98] Finally, Bonham reported that the imperial commissioner denied without qualification the authenticity of an imperial edict to the importance of which Alcock had drawn attention. He followed this by complaining that Alcock had reacted to Bonham's report in a very objectionable strain; if Alcock had not asked for the matter to be laid before the Foreign Office Bonham would himself have addressed to him a sufficient rebuke; and Bonham hoped that Palmerston's remarks might be so framed as to prevent recurrence of something so disagreeable and so prejudicial to the public service. The Foreign Office reply distributed blame with an equal hand. While Alcock had been needlessly tenacious Bonham had been unnecessarily sensitive; Palmerston was inclined to agree with

Alcock that the Chinese denial of authenticity had been evasive and
that had it been ever so positive it might still have been untrue; on
the other hand Alcock seemed to 'have a good deal of spare time on
his hands to be enabled to swell out into such long detail matter
which might better have been comprized [sic] in a much smaller
space'.[99]

Criticism of the length of Alcock's despatches was a recurrent
theme. In 1847 Davis did not burden Palmerston with Alcock's
'very voluminous despatch, forming with its enclosures of correspondence a Book'. In 1849 Bonham turned down Alcock's request
for an additional assistant and advised him to write less instead. In
1852 Bowring did not feel justified in troubling Palmerston with a
very elaborate and voluminous Alcock despatch. In 1853 the
Foreign Office were minuting that the only fault in Alcock, a man
of intellect who had served well and faithfully, was excessive zeal
leading to over-voluminous writing. So it went on. After Alcock
had become minister in Peking Hammond warned the Foreign
Secretary in 1868 that a despatch from Alcock about missionary
activities was most wearisome reading, and even fifteen years after
he had ceased to be minister a letter once again castigating Roman
Catholic proceedings in China took up over two columns of small
print in *The Times*. During Peking's summer heat Legation juniors,
for ever making fair copies with blotting-paper under their forearms to prevent sweat marks on the paper, groaned at their otherwise kindly chief's interminable and none too legible drafts.[100]
Today the chorus of criticism seems ungrateful. Alcock was no
devotee of concision, but he expressed forceful opinions in lucid,
distinctive, and masculine prose.

The Foreign Office rebuke to Alcock on this occasion had no
effect. Like most officials who write more than their superiors wish,
he continued to write at undiminished length. Bonham on the other
hand may have taken note of the Foreign Office failure to support
him. Friction between the two men ceased to be so apparent, and
shortly before retiring Bonham, in endorsing Alcock's plea for a
transfer to a healthier climate, volunteered that Alcock had always
shown himself zealous and able.[101] Nevertheless at no time can
Alcock have felt confident of whole-hearted support from Bonham.

In his despatches from Shanghai Alcock frequently went beyond
his local responsibilities to consider British policy towards China.
He combined bold strategic thinking with bold tactical recommen-

dations, while recognizing that the Chinese government submitted to intercourse with foreigners only as a necessary evil and 'would be only too happy if either Earthquake, or Deluge, would relieve them for ever, both of us and our Trade', and that more concessions might be extorted from the Chinese than it would be wise or profitable to accept. His strategic recommendations, made in 1850, were to diversify a trade based on exports of tea, which India was now trying to grow and tastes in which might alter, and on imports of opium, which China might start growing for herself, and to obtain trading access to the Yangtze and connected waterways; Chinese reluctance to concede this trade access might be overcome in three months in negotiations backed by a show of naval force. Tactically, he had concluded by 1852 that systematic Chinese obstructionism and refusal to redress grievances had reached a pitch calling for action, since in China temporizing or submitting merely led to further pressure. He recommended that either payment of customs duties by British subjects should be withheld, 'with a distinct intimation that if this does not suffice other and more determined measures should follow', or that the treaty provisions should be regarded as in abeyance and their enforcement on British subjects should cease. The strategic recommendations were prophetic, the tactical ones were rejected. As far as Shanghai was concerned the rejection was immaterial, for in September 1853 the tactical situation there changed entirely. The Chinese city suddenly fell to local rebels, who held it against government troops for nearly a year and a half. Although Alcock had been hard hit by his wife's death six months before and was now very ill for several weeks with severe dysentery, his response to the crisis was incisive enough to have lasting effects in Shanghai and in all the treaty ports.[102]

The area in Shanghai obtained by the French for French residents, the French concession, always remained a purely French responsibility. Balfour's area, which had subsequently been extended in agreement with the Chinese authorities, had similarly been envisaged as a purely British responsibility. By accident it had developed differently. Although two-thirds of the residents were British, it had become an international settlement in which residence was open to all foreigners and for which the treaty power consuls at Shanghai, at this time the British, French, and United States consuls, had a joint responsibility.[103] Under the handicaps, as he put it, of having to work with many incoherent elements in a

cosmopolitan community and of having to avoid too obtrusive an
appearance of being in charge, Alcock acted to save the settlement
from being sacked by troops whom he considered as lawless a
horde of semi-savage soldiery as he had ever met, even in the
mountain wilds of Spain. Dangers from which there was no escape,
he told the community, were best met boldly; he prohibited the
entry of armed Chinese into the settlement; and he even warned
both sides not to fire on foreigners taking their daily boating
exercise. Bonham, who reasonably took the view that foreign
oarsmen would have only themselves to blame if they were shot,
was alarmed by so much vigour, and it was fortunate for Alcock
that when a clash did occur Bowring had replaced Bonham. Armed
troops from a government encampment entered the settlement.
Hurrying to the spot Alcock found volunteers under Wade, who
combined normal vice-consular duties with commanding a community volunteer force, already there. The incursion was checked,
and the next day Alcock called on naval forces and the volunteers
to destroy the encampment. The operation succeeded at the cost of
four foreigners dead. Having so forcefully made his point Alcock as
usual became conciliatory. He pointed out a suitable site for a new
encampment further from the settlement. The government authorities agreed to put their men there if protected from rebel attack
during the move, Alcock warned the rebels that for thirteen days
no attack in that direction would be permitted, the move was
made, and the settlement remained inviolate until the rebellion collapsed early in 1855. Bowring and the Foreign Office successively
approved Alcock, who was considered to have shown prudence,
vigour, and great courage.[104]

The area intended for exclusive British occupation had by one
accident become a settlement for all foreigners, and by a second
accident the majority of the settlement's residents became Chinese.
Now and during ensuing troubles Chinese poured into the neu-
tralized settlement, as an oasis of peace, and foreign landholders
made fortunes by running up houses for the refugees. The incoming Chinese found in the settlement security and a comparatively
efficient and honest administration, but the anomaly of a foreign
minority controlling an area henceforward inhabited mainly by
native Chinese created incessant problems. This fundamental
change was an unplanned by-product of Alcock's defence of the
settlement and was unwelcome to him.[105] His other two lasting

innovations during the Shanghai confusion were not fortuitous. His relations with the intendant, a former merchant who had purchased rank instead of earning it by examination success, had not been smooth. Alcock had described the intendant as an ignorant, intriguing Canton trader, unacquainted with official ways and unable even to speak Mandarin, who in a few months had committed more blunders and slighted foreign representatives more often than all his predecessors put together.[106] Adversity made the intendant more malleable. He agreed to widen the powers of the foreign community's elected representatives to administer the settlement, thus making possible the development of an increasingly effective foreign municipal council.[107] He also agreed to the introduction of a foreign element into the customs. Deprived through the rebellion of control over the custom-house the intendant could not collect duties and could therefore not remit to his superiors the sums expected from him. Alcock, long intent on diminishing customs malpractices as impediments to honest trade, proposed the employment of foreigners as customs inspectors. The intendant accepted the proposal as a way out of his immediate embarrassment.[108] The resulting increase in the Shanghai customs revenue was so marked that the device temporarily employed at Shanghai was permanently adopted at all treaty ports, where the Maritime Customs, administered by foreigners of many nationalities in the service of the Chinese government, became an essential feature of business and social life. The first inspectors at Shanghai were an international triumvirate of whom Wade was one. Bowring wished Gingell to succeed Wade but the Chinese insisted on appointing the youthful H.N. Lay, who was favoured by Alcock.[109] They discovered him to be too ambitious a servant. After a brief meteoric career at the head of the Customs he was dismissed, to die many years later in obscurity and straitened circumstances.[110] Lay was succeeded by Hart, inspector-general from 1863 to 1911. Hart, autocratic towards his subordinates in his highly efficient Customs organization, was the supple and trusted adviser of his Chinese employers on many matters, and died wealthy and loaded with honours. He took with him to the Customs contemporary Foreign Office concepts of patronage and over the years offered Customs berths to numerous sons and relations of his former consular colleagues.

Immediately after his wife's death Alcock had applied for a transfer to Europe or to the Levant. The Foreign Office were

sympathetic towards so deserving an officer, but after long delay could offer only promotion to Canton, which he accepted unenthusiastically. On his departure from Shanghai immediately after the rebellion's collapse a subscription among the foreign community to provide him with a service of plate raised £700. The Foreign Office permitted him to accept the plate as a highly honourable testimonial and expressed entire satisfaction with his conduct at Shanghai, but to his disappointment would not recommend him for the Order of the Bath.[111]

D.B. Robertson was the right successor for a further tense period when Shanghai was threatened by the Taiping rebellion (see p. 142). Like Alcock he was a firm man whose views were respected in the Foreign Office, and he had a flair for establishing personal relations with Chinese officials. He had known Shanghai intimately from its first days as a treaty port; using his own instruments he had personally made the first survey of the settlement and accompanied by Parkes he had, at the cost of three hours of extreme peril during a sudden gale, supervised the erection of possibly the first shipping beacon in the river.[112] Below the now peaceful surface of a Shanghai being rebuilt at astonishing speed by a race not shackled by caste or religion he detected a deep stream of dissatisfaction; the Chinese saw their shortcomings in comparison with the West, but 'the wave of civilisation which would otherwise pass over the country' was broken by the government's opposition to every change. In order to protect life and property in the small areas where foreigners were allowed to reside he recommended that the three treaty powers should make it plain that interference with the settlement from any quarter would be prevented; in making the recommendation he evidently had the Taiping threat to Shanghai mainly, but not exclusively, in mind. He was authorized to make it known to all parties that Shanghai was not to become a battle area and that any attack on Shanghai would be deemed a hostile act by the British government.[113]

The collapse of Chinese authority in the city in Alcock's day had made the maintenance of law and order among the settlement's new Chinese residents a pressing problem. Alcock had met the situation by bringing them under temporary foreign jurisdiction and declaring that no Chinese could be arrested in the settlement without foreign consent, a daring move which alarmed both Bonham and Bowring but which was justified by the emergency.[114]

The settlement police force, created to protect respectable foreigners against lawless foreigners, had previously handed over to the Chinese authorities any Chinese offenders against foreigners. (The system had not always worked satisfactorily. A coolie from under whose bed a large sum of stolen money had been recovered came back to the consulate a week after being handed over to the magistrate and demanded the return of clothing he had left there. The only explanation obtained from the Chinese authorities was that they did not know the man was at liberty.)[115] Now the settlement police brought arrested Chinese before consuls, mainly the British consul, on charges which in 1855 included four murders and thirteen kidnappings. By 1857 there was a European force with a superintendent, two sergeants, and fourteen men, presumably supported by Chinese constables. There was no reason why on the restoration of Chinese administration in the city the previous Chinese jurisdiction over the settlement Chinese should not have been reinstated, but the imperial officials had no wish to be bothered with work which the foreigners were prepared to undertake. The new magistrate suggested to Robertson that Robertson and his colleagues should deal with minor settlement crimes and that those convicted should be put to work on the settlement's roads, in irons where appropriate. Robertson acted accordingly, passing only grave crimes on to the magistrate. The Foreign Office in due course ruled that even with Chinese sanction the employment of Chinese prisoners in irons was *ultra vires* and must cease forthwith, but did not express any general disapproval of Robertson's arrangement, which he himself seems to have adopted for practical reasons and without ulterior motives. Thus the Chinese through inertia, and without realizing the importance of the ground they had yielded, had taken a major step towards losing their jurisdiction in the settlement. As Carles, assistant Chinese secretary in 1883, put it, the Chinese in agreeing to European policing of the settlement certainly never contemplated that a warrant issued by the local viceroy could by that date be executed in the settlement only 'by a person in the pay of a Committee of foreign merchants [the elected members of the Shanghai municipal council] and that consent to its execution at all was by no means a matter of course'.[116]

Robertson took home leave in 1859. T.T. Meadows was sent to Shanghai as acting consul. From Foochow Medhurst, who as the senior of the two had already twice succeeded in getting interesting

temporary assignments taken away from Meadows and allocated to himself, protested so violently that Bruce made him rewrite the protest in more decorous terms.[117] Whether this tactlessness had put Bruce's back up, or whether for other reasons, Bruce misguidedly stuck to his original decision. Meadows was far too erratic and eccentric for a key post. His vagaries, and in particular his attitude towards the Taipings, whom he would unhesitatingly have admitted into Shanghai, alarmed Bruce, who complained that he had never had to deal with so impracticable and mischievous a subordinate and who begged Elgin to find some pretext for sending Meadows to the north and out of Shanghai.[118]

WAR AND REBELLION

CHINA'S defeat in the *Arrow* war was as inevitable as it had been in the first war. In mid-1858 an allied force landed near the mouth of the river leading up to Tientsin, which is within easy striking distance of Peking. After a trifling engagement the Chinese took fright. They negotiated with Elgin and other foreign representatives and were bullied into peace treaties in which an article particularly odious to the Chinese court provided for the presence of foreign envoys in Peking. Elgin went home, his task apparently completed, and a year later Bruce, now the newly appointed British minister, arrived with a naval squadron off the river-mouth, expecting to proceed to Peking and to exchange ratifications. A party at the court remained opposed to receiving barbarian envoys on an equal footing. Bruce's way up the river was barred, and an over-confident British attempt to capture the forts commanding the river and to force a passage up it was ignominiously repulsed with heavy casualties. Elgin was reappointed special ambassador, and after yet another year had elapsed a more substantial allied force successively captured the forts, Tientsin, and Peking. The 1858 treaties were ratified and additional concessions were made by the defeated Chinese. Besides accepting the envoys and agreeing to pay a war indemnity China undertook to open more ports, to permit foreigners to travel in the interior for trade or pleasure, to legalize the importation of opium, and to cede a small area adjacent to Hong Kong. Elgin again went home, leaving Bruce to function as minister.

Hostilities between Britain and China in Canton and the north left the consulates other than Canton anomalously undisturbed. As soon as the Canton hostilities became known the Foochow viceroy passed a message that amicable relationships with the consulate ought not to be in any way affected by such unfortunate hap-

penings. There were no repercussions at Amoy. At Ningpo the intendant expected only peaceful orders from Peking and T.T. Meadows asserted that in return for immunity from hostile operations the provincial authorities would discreetly allow the allied forces to provision themselves.[1] At Shanghai the intendant's first reaction was to quote a Chinese proverb, 'Let everyone sweep his own floor'; as preparations for attacking Canton were mounted he expressed the earnest hope that peace and quiet would be maintained at Shanghai; and after the fall of Canton he said that the Canton trouble was entirely Yeh's personal responsibility. Still more anomalously, the allied forces assembled at Shanghai in 1860 to attack the north were requested by the local authorities to protect Shanghai against advancing Taipings.[2]

During the long Taiping rebellion whole provinces were overrun and devastated, tens or scores of millions perished, and the existence of the Manchu dynasty was threatened. Influenced by brief youthful contact with an American Protestant missionary, the Taiping leader proclaimed himself the Younger Brother of Jesus, and foreigners debated whether the distorted Taiping Christianity made the rebels acceptable or made them detestable blasphemers. More pragmatically, Alcock had argued in 1853 that commercial concessions might be won in return for rescuing China from disintegration, that England might throw a sheathed sword into the balance with decisive effect and dictate her own terms, and that failure to intervene might result in anarchy and the ruin of English interests.[3] After years of hesitation the British government decided, for very much the reasons Alcock had advanced, to support the dynasty against the rebels. The Shanghai request for protection was met,[4] and although at the end of 1860 Bruce still considered himself without authority to protect Ningpo from the Taipings[5] the Foreign Office by the beginning of 1862 had convinced themselves that the Taipings were 'Revolters not only against the Emperor but against all Laws human and divine' and should be kept away from the treaty ports.[6] In 1862 allied troops and the Ever-Victorious Army, a disciplined force of 4,500 Chinese officered by a motley crew of foreign mercenaries in Chinese pay and initially commanded by an American, went over to the offensive against the Taipings in the Shanghai area. In 1863 Major Gordon, a British regular officer, was given permission to enter the imperial service and took over command of the force. Its success in the field

contributed to the fall of the Taiping headquarters at Nanking in 1864 and the subsequent crushing of the rebellion.

T.T. Meadows seems to have been alone among consular officers in believing that a Taiping victory would be to the West's advantage.[7] D.B. Robertson did not consider that it would bring China within the pale of civilization.[8] Medhurst despised the Taipings. Those he met in 1854 were nearly all uncouth and ill-conditioned fellows evidently gathered from the lowest classes of the people, their religious publications were written in a diffuse, ungainly style, and the Eastern King, one of the Taiping leaders, was obviously a man of most ordinary literary attainments whose blasphemous assumptions of Divine Power proved him deprived of all moral principles.[9] This shallow report was regrettably considered by the Foreign Office to do Medhurst great credit.[10] C. Alabaster in 1861 was equally contemptuous and equally shallow. He noted in his diary that the first Taiping chief he met was 'a dirty devil',[a] and he recorded officially his disgust at the universal coolie look, the want of intelligence in the higher ranks, and the difficulty with which the chief wrote even his own name.[11] At Ningpo, where during the Taiping troubles a succession of consular officers were for four years 'constantly engaged in duties rather befitting the staff of an irregular army than a service of sober civilians',[12] F.E. Harvey was more perceptive. During his incumbency the Taipings succeeded in taking the city, which they held for five months until with his encouragement British and French naval units picked a quarrel with them and drove them out. Reporting in 1862 after three months' experience of Taiping occupation Harvey said that unlike many foreigners he did not condemn the Taipings because their chiefs were not well-born or well-educated. The chiefs had treated him very courteously and with a rough, blunt honesty alien to the effete imperial mandarins, but there was a fume of blood and a look of carnage about them from which he recoiled in horror; their troops were undisciplined savages; and the movement was merely a destructive anarchy.[13] Pedder's reactions at Amoy were similar to those of Harvey. After the fall of Nanking a Taiping force, in a dying flicker of the rebellion, threatened Amoy. Pedder made immediate plans against possible attack; he would send his family away and would deter any thoughts of looting the consulate by arming his staff with rifles and revolvers, and arming the Malays in his gaol with cutlasses and pikes. Later he made his way, at the cost

of a 36-hour wetting and a resulting bout of fever, to the rebel base and received an assurance that Amoy, by then under British naval protection, would not be attacked. He was impressed by the chief's terse and vigorous speech and simple, unassuming manner, reminiscent of that of an English gentleman, and by the alertness of the troops, but he did not see how society, which somehow managed to exist under mandarin misrule, could exist at all under the rule of mere fighting men.[14] This was a common consular reaction. If the imperialists failed to govern, said Parkes, they at least knew how to govern, whereas the Taipings were incapable of governing.[15]

Hostilities against the Chinese government and the Taipings demanded Chinese speakers. Parkes and Wade were attached to Elgin's headquarters and many juniors were lent to the forces. An episode which nearly cost Parkes his life made him famous at home. During the allied advance on Peking in 1860 he acted as spokesman for Elgin in discussing with Chinese negotiators terms for a cessation of hostilities. He was seized during the negotiations, separated from all but one of his companions, half of whom were not seen alive again, chained, roughly handled, and thrown into a Peking prison. After some ten days his coolness and presence of mind secured transfer to relatively honourable confinement while the Chinese argued his fate among themselves. A peace party in Peking favoured returning him alive, whereas orders for instant execution were momentarily expected from the court, which had prudently retired to Inner Mongolia. Release allegedly came only a quarter of an hour before the order for his execution reached Peking. In the final hours of confinement, when he knew life or death to be in the balance, he stayed cool enough to debate with a Chinese official, who was taken aback by such detachment, whether the earth revolved round the sun and whether the moon rotated on its own axis.[16] He was eventually awarded at China's expense £8,000 for his sufferings[17] and was made a KCB.

What war meant to the juniors lent to the forces cannot be coherently pieced together from the civilian archives, which afford only occasional and disconnected glimpses. One glimpse, probably not untypical, is of Mongan in the south. Although the allied advance on Peking was assisted by a train of Cantonese coolies, who saw no harm in being paid to help their emperor's enemies or in looting their northern compatriots,[18] around Canton itself some

resistance followed allied occupation of the city. In 1858 a British gunboat was dispatched to a troublesome nearby town bearing a notification that peace had been concluded and that the menaces of the local authorities and gentry could not be tolerated. The gunboat landed a party consisting of Mongan, armed with a revolver, a Hong Kong newspaper editor armed with a dagger, two unarmed naval officers, and a bluejacket carrying a white flag. While pasting up copies of the notification outside the town the party were rushed by armed men from inside it. They retreated to the boats and rowed off under rather sharp and well-directed fire, which killed one man and wounded another.[19]

Fortunately Adkins' lengthy letters home, and scrappier personal papers left by C. Alabaster, do provide a coherent picture of two juniors in wartime. On both the impact of war was profound.

Early in 1857, fifteen months after his first arrival in Hong Kong, Adkins vomited profusely after a walk and hearty breakfast and discovered that nearly all the foreign community were similarly afflicted, all the colony's bread, a foodstuff not eaten by Chinese and therefore baked in Hong Kong solely for foreign consumption, having been liberally dosed with arsenic as a contribution to China's war effort. The druggists' shops were full of people with very long faces buying emetics and comparing symptoms, and round a doctor who was analysing the bread Adkins found residents drinking jorums of mustard and water and then vomiting. Like C. Alabaster, who had seen sixteen leading citizens swallowing emetics in a group, he thought the scenes comical in retrospect, but the community were so alarmed that for months afterwards revolvers were worn even in church. In 1858 Adkins, then at Ningpo, was ordered north at a moment's notice to assist in interpreting, but by the time he had got as far as Shanghai the negotiations at Tientsin had been concluded and he was ordered straight back. A year later, however, he was interpreter on board HMS *Opossum*, one of the gunboats attempting to remove the river barriers which blocked Bruce's way to Tientsin. She came under so hot a fire that in the first half hour her hull was riddled and half her crew were killed or wounded. Adkins busied himself with tourniquets and sherry for the wounded and counted himself fortunate on having 'stood for upwards of three hours under as heavy a fire as ever an amateur was exposed to' without being hit. The unsuccessful attack was abandoned. In a very small boat which nearly

sank and which was narrowly missed by a parting Chinese shot, and holding in his arms a marine half of whose leg had been carried away, he got off to a makeshift hospital ship and spent the night listening to the cries of wounded men whose limbs were being amputated by five surgeons. The rest of his summer was spent more peacefully in a warship surveying the coast northward from the scene of the repulse. One of his functions was to obtain local provisions; the navy paid a good price but being a farmer's son he regretted extremely orders which obliged him to bully villagers into surrendering their stocks of vegetables and their tillage oxen. Reverting to civilian work in Shanghai in September, he prepared for the expected 1860 campaign by asking his mother to select and send out a sword, straight, double-edged, well-balanced, and not too heavy. In February he was back in a survey ship and for months was bored by idleness and a diet of salt beef, salt pork, brackish water, and bad tea. The bustle of the campaign itself was a welcome change. He was worked off his feet obtaining supplies and managing the baggage train but to his regret missed any serious fighting. In war, he concluded, the British were cruel and the French barbarous.[a]

When the allies were about to withdraw from Peking in the autumn of 1860 Elgin introduced him to Prince Kung, the emperor's brother, and he was left behind in the capital, all alone, ostensibly to get the Legation's future quarters ready for spring occupation but in reality to get the Pekingese used to an English presence. The Prince had handled the peace negotiations and was for many years to remain in charge of China's foreign relations. Wade considered that the Prince at 28 was as young a gentleman as he had ever met, not unintelligent but with so much levity and insincerity as to baulk all interest in his conversation, and that his manners were not very well bred for a Chinese.[20] Now, however, the Prince undertook to look after Adkins and subsequently treated this visible reminder of China's defeat with condescending kindness. The condescension was mutual. At first Adkins wrote 'I am safer without his troubling his imperial noddle about my concerns, I imagine', and then 'for a Chinese I rather like him, though I am afraid that like most Chinese he is a bit of a rogue'.[a] For a fortnight or so Adkins still had the company in Peking of a Russian ambassador and his suite. Their attentive hospitality made him feel quite at home with them,[a] but according to a Russian source these

attentions were not disinterested; he was suspected of having been left behind to spy on Russian diplomatic moves, the friendly hospitality was intended to lull his suspicions, and on the day the Russians signed their treaty with China pains were taken to make him drunk at dinner.[21] On the Russian embassy's departure he had no foreign company left except the members of a long-established Russian ecclesiastical mission, who were friendly and kept him supplied with bread but with whom he could communicate only in Chinese, that barbarous lingo. He felt lonely in a huge city which after nightfall seemed the quietest place in the world, with never a sound reaching his room. Chinese grub was not to his taste, his cook could not make soup and alleged that 4 lbs. of mutton and 10 lbs. of beef had been eaten in four days, the fumes from his brazier gave him headaches, he was reduced to smoking a Chinese brass pipe, and an English grate, lamp, carpet, chair, and book would have been welcome. At least the personal hazards which he had feared were non-existent. He rode all over the city without molestation and the people were very well-behaved; 'I would not be the only Chinese in London under similar circumstances for any consideration'. He struck up conversations about the war with the Chinese military, and his written and spoken Chinese improved.[a]

The following May his reward came. As acting vice-consul he took charge of Chinkiang, a newly opened treaty port up the Yangtze. Once a flourishing trade centre Chinkiang had been devastated during the rebellion and was still closely invested by 10,000 Taipings. Its walls enclosed only ruins and a single straggling and very dirty street, there was no trade, there were no foreign merchants, and the countryside was a deserted wilderness in which a few old people scratched a living.[a] A luckless assistant, G. Phillips, had after only three years in China been landed there in February from a warship to open the consulate and had set up in a ruinous temple. In Adkins' first week the firing during a Taiping night attack was so heavy that he moved the consulate a mile down river to safer but uncomfortable quarters on an island.[22] There he remained for three years, all alone after Phillips had been transferred in the following spring to the relative comforts of Amoy. Visiting gunboats, anchored protectively fifty yards from his front door, provided chances of cricket and medical attention, but in their absence 'Robinson Crusoe was hardly more lonely' and he took to Chinese poetry to pass the time. He was always on duty at his one-

man post, and if he left the consulate he might be out when needed; if he did go out shooting he risked being shot himself; he nearly drowned when out sailing with a gunboat commander; his home mail failed to arrive; his servants were scoundrels. Villainous foreigners, who were sometimes the perpetrators and sometimes the victims of piracies and murders, infested the river. By confiscation of boats and sentences of imprisonment he tried to bring the British element to book, making himself 'very obnoxious ' but not caring what people said or thought so long as his conscience was clear. Nevertheless the bigger fish escaped his net and the Yankees, none of whose consuls he thought worth a rap, continued to do just as they pleased. He longed for home life in Worcestershire but did not dare to apply for leave until confirmed as a substantive vice-consul. Occasional journeys to Nanking in British warships were not agreeable breaks in the monotony of Chinkiang life. While Nanking was still in Taiping hands Adkins went there to demand compensation for the plundering of British junks. With some difficulty he persuaded the senior naval officer that a Taiping invitation to enter the city for discussion could safely be accepted and a Taiping prince, wearing cloth of gold and a head-dress covered with valuable pearls, received the British visitors very politely in a sumptuously decorated palace. Without spending undue time on ceremony the prince had the compensation weighed out in silver and indicated that the principal offender would be beheaded. Adkins had hardly finished asking for leniency when an executioner entered with dripping sword and knelt to report execution of the sentence. The prince ordered the head to be brought in and on the visitors demurring had it placed just outside the outer door, where they could barely avoid trampling on it as they left. A visit immediately after the fall of Nanking was worse. To call on the victorious imperial commander Adkins had to walk over 6 miles in a temperature of 105° in the shade through a deserted city filled with heaps of corpses and an overwhelming stench. On reaching the imperial commander he drank an infinity of cups of tea, got a mount, and rode back with a very empty stomach. The sights, the smells, and the mosquitoes allowed him no rest day or night until he left Nanking.[a]

In October 1865 the Foreign Office at last appointed him a substantive vice-consul.[23] The good news took over five months to reach him[a] and before it arrived he had been forced to put in a

medical certificate and to apply for home leave. He was suffering from rheumatism, leg ulcers, and frequent fevers, and reached home in such poor health that he remained on leave for two and a half years.[24] His eventful first tour of duty, which had lasted ten years, had scarred him in other ways too. Outwardly he remained a resolute, fair-minded, and hard-working official whose tact and temper conciliated Chinese officials and in Alcock's view marked him out as far the best man to succeed Wade as Chinese secretary.[25] Inwardly he had had enough. Before his leave he was already 'beginning to loathe China and all it contains'. When he got back to China he loathed 'the vilest of all vile countries' more every day.[a] It was a blessing in disguise that continued ill-health first dimmed his service prospects and then at 44 brought premature retirement and three pensioned decades of useful, kindly, and respected local activities in Worcestershire.[26]

C. Alabaster, aptly nicknamed 'the Buster',[27] was undersized,[28] fiery, and ambitious. From his first attachment to the navy in 1857 he remembered the admiral as the kindest old gentleman who ever lived but also remembered with bitterness a flag captain's unmeasured denunciation when, almost too weak to stand, he had leant against a gun for support.[a] Then he was attached to the captured commissioner Yeh, who with some Chinese attendants was shipped off to Calcutta as a prisoner of state. The enforced company of a brash 19-year-old stripling can hardly have been particularly congenial to Yeh, especially as Wade had recently described Alabaster as having so poor an ear that he could not in the least distinguish the differing tones in spoken Chinese.[29] On Alabaster's side, however, the incongruous relationship became almost affectionate. Instead of the ferocious monster depicted in the British press he found a very fat, very apathetic, kindly man given to poetry and devoted to religion. He heartily approved of Yeh's Draconian measures against rebellion round Canton; by lopping off countless thousands of heads Yeh had, he considered, saved the province from the fate of other provinces where rebellion had flourished and where in consequence millions had been killed and other millions had died of starvation. In Calcutta Yeh declined to leave his house, refusing even such quaint invitations as the offer of a seat on the bench should he wish to visit the Supreme Court. Alabaster complained that he himself was thus virtually a close prisoner, on duty from five in the morning until midnight with

never a day off. The days, weeks, and months must indeed have dragged. He read Yeh the newspapers or Wheaton's *International Law* and similar works 'which sometimes appear to amuse him but without inducing conviction'. He talked with him about Buddhism or politics (asked why the opium trade was not legalized, Yeh replied that the Chinese government neither permitted nor forbade it, they simply disregarded it — *yeh pu-shih chun, yeh pu-shih pu-chun, pu-kuan chiu shih la*).[30] He chatted too with Sergeant Lan, who was a cross between aide-de-camp and batman to Yeh, and he studied Confucius by himself. Still, he exaggerated the rigours of his life and mixed sufficiently in Calcutta society to be blackballed at the club.[a] Release came unexpectedly. Early in 1859 'poor Lan' died of cholera and then in April Yeh, 'poor old man', fell ill, rallied, relapsed, and died. It was decided to ship the body to China without a post-mortem which, as Alabaster rightly advised, would have outraged Chinese susceptibilities. The body was soldered into a metallic coffin, no Chinese one being available among the local Chinese community, and the undertaker poured arsenic into the mouth to preserve the features. In the next three days the body twice burst the coffin, which had twice to be soldered down again. On his mettle, the undertaker then put the coffin into a mahogany chest, with six inches of charcoal between the two, bound the whole with iron bars, covered it with gunny bags, and sent in a grossly inflated bill. Alabaster's plans for an adventurous overland return to China were vetoed by the viceroy of India and he accompanied Yeh's maltreated remains back to Hong Kong, glad to see the China coast again although he did not love the Cantonese and expected to regret India.[a] His fifteen months with Yeh left him with an abiding interest in Chinese philosophical concepts, about which he later went into print.[31]

Promoted to interpreter and posted to Canton for the second half of the year he accompanied several gunboat expeditions, on one of which the whole party would, he said, have been cut off if he had not kept his head while in very considerable personal danger.[32] The year 1860 saw him transferred successively to Amoy, where he briefly had a quieter spell, and then to the newly opened port of Swatow. At Swatow he was stoned twice in a single week, accompanied gunboats in attacks on pirate villages, once having with 15 men to fight his way through 500, was praised by the navy for his courage, and was described by the consul as a perfect little

demon.[33] Transferred to Shanghai in 1861 he found that attempting to parley with Taiping forces under a flag of truce was dangerous; the Taipings opened heavy fire on Alabaster and an unarmed naval captain as soon as they and their flag came within range and rapid retreat became necessary, whereas on a second attempt some days later the flag was discreetly hidden behind a rock, they were therefore not potted at, and an interview with the local Taiping leader was obtained safely.[a] As the British forces came into more direct conflict with the Taipings in the Shanghai area Alabaster's life became increasingly unconsular. Official military expeditions took him away from the office so much that the consul asked, unsuccessfully, for a replacement and had to do much of Alabaster's office work.[34] He took part in at least one less official expedition, going out with seven other mounted men and madly charging and scattering band after band of rebels.[a] He boasted that he had seen one admiral killed and another wounded, 'a fortune which happens to few',[35] and he treasured a British officer's letter saying that in 1862 and 1863 he had been more often under fire than perhaps any man alive.[a] After the Ever-Victorious Army's American commander had been killed in action there were difficulties between the force and its Chinese paymasters, Alabaster slid into the position of mediator between the two, and late in life claimed practically to have held the force together until Gordon took command six months later. The Chinese were so pleased with these services that they made him an offer of employment under the Chinese government. He was tempted to accept but instead applied for home leave. Besides general debility he was suffering from an anal fistula, inflammation of the bladder, and retention of urine, conditions the treatment of which had repeatedly been interrupted by military expeditions, and longer residence in Shanghai, he wrote, would be likely to lead to his leaving Her Majesty's service and the world together.[36] He returned from leave to altered conditions and had so much difficulty in adjusting to a new style of life that he nearly ruined his career prospects before the adjustment was made.

Alabaster was not alone in having to readjust. The service as a whole had to do so. The older consuls seemed to Bruce reactionaries who instead of cultivating friendly relations with Chinese officials stood on their dignity behind barriers of formality and sought to impose solutions instead of persuading. He deplored consular unwillingness to follow a recent Foreign Office directive

that consuls were to resort to force only where British lives were threatened or British property endangered, and in 1862 sought the Foreign Secretary's personal support in his efforts to stop persistent acts of violence by consuls and navy. Even more fundamental changes in the service's standing were implied by the peace settlement. The chief superintendents in Hong Kong had resided not in China but in a British colony, had never had direct dealings with the central government, and had latterly been without direct channels of communication with any Chinese authorities. Neither superintendents nor the Foreign Office could ignore views expressed by able consuls who did reside in China and who did have constant contact with provincial officials. Now the Tsungli Yamen, a new Chinese organization with some resemblance to a Ministry of Foreign Affairs, was functioning in Peking and Bruce, in his equally new Legation in Peking, soon claimed to be on an easy and familiar footing with the Yamen ministers.[37] The consuls had lost their advantage over the superintendents. Bruce now wanted them to alter their ways and attend to details, their proper province, and leave principles to diplomatists; led astray by Alcock's example, he wrote disapprovingly, China consuls were regrettably more apt to write speculative general despatches than to carry on with routine business.[38] Henceforward consuls were tamer officials who were expected to deal with local issues in accordance with general Legation guidance, to negotiate as many local settlements as they could, and to refer unresolved disputes to the Legation. Direct influence from the consulates on the shaping of British policy towards China had virtually ceased.

Part II

From the Second Peace Settlement to the Boxers

THE CHANGED FRAMEWORK OF
CONSULAR DUTIES

FROM the second peace settlement to the turn of the century the response of a stagnant Chinese government to external pressure was ineffectual and uncomprehending resentment. Obscurantism ruled, centred round an empress dowager who maintained her personal autocracy through successive minorities. Reluctant diplomatic representation abroad, and study abroad by students, brought small enlightenment, for the travellers on their return were distrusted. The superiority of foreign technology in war had become so clear that arms were bought and arsenals and shipyards built, but ignorance, incompetence, corruption, and nepotism made them ineffective, and there was little acceptance that China had anything to learn in other fields. Traditional methods crushed more internal rebellions, but no answer was found to mounting external pressure. Even the government machinery remained wholly inadequate for dealing with foreigners. The Tsungli Yamen was a half-hearted innovation and its communications to provincial authorities were liable to be ignored if inconvenient. In 1866 the Foochow viceroy told the acting consul that he was answerable only to the emperor and would not abide by any Yamen decision conflicting with his own opinion.[1] Weak from the start the Yamen became weaker still after the empress dowager in 1884 dismissed Prince Kung who, in spite of Wade's unfavourable first impressions, had as its head shown some capacity for decision. The principle laid down to consuls by Bruce that unresolved disputes were to be referred to the Legation, which would hold the imperial government responsible for the misconduct of local agents, would have been easier to implement had the Yamen been more effective.

External pressure was symbolized by the treaty power ministers at Peking. Sometimes the ministers made individual representations

on behalf of their own governments, sometimes in temporary
unison they made joint representations through the dean of the
diplomatic body, an office held by the minister who had been
longest in Peking. Whatever form the representations took their
content was usually unwelcome and their tone became more and
more minatory. After leaving Peking Bruce in 1864 lamented to the
Foreign Secretary, Russell, the tradition among British consular
officers of imposing settlements on the Chinese without seeking to
persuade them, a method which might carry particular matters
through but could not achieve friendly relations. Russell the
following year told Alcock that the government could not too
strongly inculcate the importance of consular officers cultivating
friendly relations, adding that the Chinese were not barbarians but
according to oriental notions highly civilized and that in recent
years they had been perfectly disposed to listen to reason. By 1899
the Legation were saying that remonstrances were practically
disregarded unless accompanied by threats and that only force was
respected.[2] The decline in the ethical standards applied to dealings
with China is painfully apparent.

The second peace settlement imposed on China by victorious
Britain and France, onerous though it was, had included only one
insignificant cession of territory, a tongue of land sticking out from
the mainland opposite the island of Hong Kong. Non-combatant
Russia used China's negotiations with Britain and France as a lever
to obtain for herself the cession of a vast but sparsely populated
area, the potential importance of which was not appreciated by the
Chinese, along the Siberian border. Subsequent Russian designs on
Chinese Turkistan, part of which Russia occupied for years, came
to nothing, but a shadowy suzerainty over the Liuchiu islands was
lost to Japan, over Indo-China to France, with whom there were
unsuccessful hostilities, and over Burma to Britain. Suzerainty over
Nepal was lost, sovereignty over Macao was ceded to Portugal.
Full-scale war with Japan in 1894 over the status of China's vassal
Korea brought an ignominious Chinese defeat which signalled to
the world that Japan had successfully modernized and that China
had not. Under the peace terms China recognized the so-called
independence of Korea, in reality the first stage towards outright
Japanese annexation; ceded to Japan Formosa and the neighbouring Pescadores islands; and even gave Japan the same extraterritorial rights in China as all major and some minor Western

powers were already enjoying. Japan also obtained the cession in Manchuria of the strategically vital Liaotung peninsula but was bullied by Russia, backed by France and Germany, into waiving the cession. China's collapse against Japan showed her to be an easy prey. Various powers claimed huge areas of China as their spheres of influence, in which trespassing by other predatory powers was strongly discouraged. In 1898 Germany found a pretext to extort a lease of Tsingtao in Shantung and of a surrounding area, as well as railway and other concessions in the province. Other powers were not to be outdone. Russia extorted a compensatory lease of Port Arthur in the very Liaotung peninsula Japan had been forced to disgorge. Britain extorted compensatory leases of territory adjoining Hong Kong and of Weihaiwei on the Shantung coast, France extorted a compensatory lease of Kwangchowwan on the coast of south-west China, the whole of which she aimed to dominate. There was an unsavoury international scramble to obtain concessions for railways and mines and to make China loans on terms advantageous to the lenders.[3] The total dismemberment of the Chinese state seemed possible or even probable and to be prevented primarily by international jealousies. A confidential handbook prepared under Foreign Office auspices was in 1919 still stating that any first-class power could undoubtedly establish a supremacy in China similar to British rule in India but that domination by any one power would hardly be acquiesced in peaceably by the rest.[4]

In all this the British minister was brought under the home government's progressively more effective control by the growth of the international telegraph system. By 1871 the network had reached the Mongolian border and Shanghai, London telegrams to Peking taking about fourteen days by the cheaper Russian route and about nine days by Shanghai, and by 1884 an internal link connected Shanghai with Peking. The minister's control over consuls in time of crisis was similarly revolutionized by the rapid extension of the internal network, which by 1885 had reached all but two of the treaty ports then open.[5]

Chinese disgust at national humiliation became a swelling tide after the Japanese war. Just after it two members of the official élite, talking to H.B. Bristow at Tientsin, criticized the throne's undue power and the ignorant incompetence of provincial authorities and expressed the hope that China would soon become a republic. The disconcerted Bristow, to whom after thirty years in China this was

a wholly new experience, hurriedly broke off the conversation.[6] In
1898 an abortive attempt at reform came from the centre. K'ang
Yu-wei, an untried reformer, obtained the ear of a young emperor
who had come of age, and procured a flood of imperial decrees
making fundamental changes. The arrest of the empress dowager
was planned. She struck first, imprisoned the emperor, and had
those reformers on whom hands could be laid summarily executed.
At Shanghai, where it had been planned to arrest the unsuspecting
K'ang as he landed from a British steamer, B. Brenan arranged for a
launch to intercept him at sea and transfer him to a second British
steamer already *en route* to Hong Kong. Consular help at Canton
saved most of his family too, Mansfield sending a secret warning to
the family to flee instantly and briefly sheltering one of K'ang's
young cousins in the consulate.[7] The crushing of reform left
xenophobia in the ascendant. In parts of north China the Boxer
secret society, pledged to exterminate foreigners and claiming
magical power to make initiates invulnerable, attacked missionaries
and converts. The court did not put them down and in 1900
allowed them into Peking. There converts were massacred, the
German minister was done to death in the streets, and with
wavering court encouragement Boxers and soldiery besieged the
legations, which were defended by a few hundred regular soldiers
of various nationalities hastily brought up from the coast as danger
became imminent and by all available foreign civilians. Viceroys
and governors in central and south China, conscious of the implications of the court's folly, protected foreigners. In some parts
of north China foreigners were also protected, in other parts they
were put to death by Boxers or officials. In Peking the siege of the
legations was protracted but incompetent. Against the odds the
defenders held out. An international relief force was landed at
Tientsin and fought its way through to occupy Peking. The court
fled to a distant province, leaving the population, who had already
suffered from the Boxers, to suffer from the misbehaviour of
foreign troops. The disastrous blind fury of 1900 did China's
reputation great harm and the victors' punitive terms left her
weaker than ever.

  Britain and to a lesser extent other powers had been obliging
China to open further treaty ports. British manufacturers and
merchants, overlooking the infinitesimal purchasing power of the
Chinese peasant, were under a persistent delusion that further into

the interior, always just out of immediate reach, lay vast markets where British manufactures could be profitably sold once restraints on access had been removed. Consular officers were not immune from the delusion. Medhurst's 1872 commercial report from Shanghai stated that a large increase in Chinese consumption of foreign goods required access to new markets, an access which could be got by opening new ports and by obtaining the right to navigate inland waters and to improve inland communications.[8] Pipe-dreams of boundless trade round the corner reached a peak of absurdity in the paper which a Dr M'Cosh, formerly of the Bengal Medical Staff, read to the British Association in 1873. Disregarding unimaginable engineering difficulties and unimaginable construction costs he looked forward to the extension of the Bengal railway system through Manipur, northern Burma, and Yunnan to the Yangtze, and he ecstatically foresaw the day 'when the prodigious commerce of the Indus, the Ganges and the Brahmaputra, the Ningtee, the Irrawaddy and the Yangtze shall be hoisted upon trucks, and rolled from east to west, from west to east, in one grand tide, ever ebbing, ever flowing, everlasting, and when London and Liverpool, Manchester and Bradford, Glasgow and Paisley, Dundee and Aberdeen, shall dip their pitchers into the sacred stream, and deal out its bounty to the people of the land'.[9] In fact foreign trade proved negligible at most of the additional treaty ports, whose prospects had been assessed with unfounded optimism. In 1896 there were in all ten British merchants at five of the ports then open and none at all at six others.[10] Nevertheless there was a British consulate at each port.

Although the Treasury greatly disliked the cost of the China service the Foreign Office laid down in 1869 that a consulate at every treaty port was essential to control and protect British subjects, among whom 'the class of persons connected with shipping is...least safely to be left without control'.[11] An 1870 decision to close the consulates in Formosa, where trade had not come up to expectations, was first suspended and finally cancelled following objections from the Board of Trade and from Wade, but in reaching the original decision the Foreign Office had considered that continued use of Formosan ports by British subjects after the closure would be a disaster and had intended to prohibit British trade there. The service, Wade told the Foreign Office in 1873, was the sole safeguard against collisions which might lead to wars, a

consul was needed at every port, and Shanghai might much more safely be left without one than Formosa.[12] In those early days the insistence on consulates at all ports was probably politically correct, but it had an adverse effect on the service. It condemned men to serve at one-man posts, supported only by Chinese staff and perhaps by a constable, in obscure backwaters where in other circumstances no one would have dreamed of maintaining a consulate, where there was not enough work, not enough society, and not enough recreation, and where accommodation was often scandalously unsuitable and unhealthy. It had been Alcock's opinion that it was always undesirable to have only one officer at a post, and particularly at posts where the tedium was intolerable, but where there was not enough work for one officer a larger staff could not be justified. Some of these consulates might have been expressly designed to breed ill-health, indolence, eccentricity, and alcoholism.[13]

Consuls took for granted treaty port society and rarely described it. Even their not infrequent statements about the size of communities are puzzling. Sometimes the statements relate to treaty ports and sometimes to consular districts, and apart from this basic discrepancy they are usually bafflingly vague about occupations, the number of missionaries representing different missions, and the non-British element. It is at least clear that as the century advanced the smugglers and ruffians of the earlier period faded away. Ports with reasonable-sized communities ran instead to sport, amateur theatricals, fancy-dress parties, calling-cards, clubs, cliques, and class distinctions. It was usual for a port of any size to have one club ('the club') for the élite of consuls, Customs commissioners, and merchants, and for their respective juniors, and another ('the Customs club') for tide-waiters, consular constables, and others below the salt. In 1870 the annual consular registration of British subjects, obligatory throughout China and costing $5, reduced to $1 for artisans, gave Medhurst social worries at Shanghai. Some kindly consuls were classing missionaries, and even bishops, as artisans and letting them off with $1, and there were no consular objections to socially ambitious tide-waiters insisting on paying $5, but Medhurst faced up to the duty of deciding who was a gentleman and who was an artisan. One applicant, he said, '[may be] essentially an artisan but driving a thriving business and...seen airing his wife and family every evening in a carriage on the [race]

course. The other may be a gentleman by birth and mixing in all the best society of the place but known none the less to be struggling for a livelihood and taking his daily constitutional as a pedestrian. The former jocosely claims to be charged the lower fee and the latter ventures to hint his inability to pay the higher'. Medhurst, who advocated the uniform fee eventually introduced, reluctantly charged the former $1 and the latter $5 'in accordance with their several positions in the social circle'. His quandary underlines not only Victorian class consciousness but also the fluidity of the Victorian class structure, for his own father had started as an artisan. Similarly T.T. Meadows, who at least in boyhood had had a Northumbrian accent, carefully distinguished in enumerating British subjects at Newchwang between two English ladies and two English women of lower station.[14] Treaty port foreigners, among whom the British still predominated, remained, unless they were missionaries, as cut off from Chinese society as modern Chinese communities in Britain are from surrounding British life. Foreign merchants were in China to make money, but the 1872 entry in C. Alabaster's diary that Shanghai foreigners were demoralized, given over to the devil, and devoid of energy or interest in aught beyond money probably reflected, like an earlier entry's dismissal of Hong Kong as a detestable island where murder, immorality, and mis-government reigned unchecked,[a] a passing mood rather than a settled opinion. He was nearer to the mark two years later in mentioning in an official despatch the 'customs of exuberant hos-pitality' which made it almost impossible for consular officers to avoid liquor.[15] Drink was always the curse of treaty port society and open-handedness its virtue.

In the treaty port context the terms 'concession' and 'settlement', originally used interchangeably, acquired precise and distinct meanings. A concession, a word which to Wade in 1864 was still an objectionable Gallicism,[16] was an area leased from the Chinese government by a foreign power, which paid a trifling ground rent and sublet plots to its own nationals and, perhaps, to the nationals of other powers. A settlement was an area which the Chinese government set aside for foreign residence and within which foreigners leased plots from Chinese landholders. At some ports there were concessions, at some there were settlements, and at others, such as Foochow, no area was formally defined for foreign residence and there was neither concession nor settlement. At the

time of the second peace settlement previous difficulties over obtaining leases for British residence and trade were much in the British mind and concessions, of which there was already one at Amoy, were the favoured solution. British concessions were accordingly forced out of the Chinese at Canton and at five of the additional treaty ports then opened, Chinkiang, Hankow, Kiukiang, Newchwang, and Tientsin. When on British insistence four more ports, Ichang, Pakhoi, Wenchow, and Wuhu, were opened in the 1870s Whitehall doubted whether plots in concessions at these ports could be sublet on terms which would give an adequate return for exchequer expenditure on essential infrastructure such as bunds (embanked quays).[17] For these purely financial reasons the establishment of more concessions was first deferred and then shelved. Whitehall thrift thus operated to spare later Chinese nationalism yet more of the thorns in the flesh which concessions represented. No more new British ones were established, though the thriving ones at Tientsin and Hankow were extended. In 1897 the attitude of the British government was described as very averse to their establishment.[18] No reasons for the aversion were stated, but regard for Chinese susceptibilities is unlikely to have been among them.

The British consistently tried to produce a trained body of Chinese-speaking officials not only to secure Chinese observance of treaty provisions but also to control British subjects. None of the other treaty powers did nearly so much. Some were readier to enjoy the privileges of extraterritoriality than to take on the corresponding obligations. In 1867 a Dane who murdered a British subject at Shanghai was expected to escape justice in the absence there of a Danish tribunal competent to try him, and nearly sixty years later Jordan in his retirement could still express the opinion that the judicial procedures in China of all the treaty powers except Britain and the United States left much to be desired.[19] It was common for one or another understaffed treaty power to seek the Legation's sanction for a British consul to accept concurrent appointment at his port as that power's consular representative. An 1866 Foreign Office instruction to the Legation that foreign consulships should not be held on a permanent basis was either withdrawn or became a dead letter. In 1885 Spence, the acting consul at Taiwan (see pp. 319–21), reported that successive British incumbents had concurrently been consuls for Denmark since 1864 and for Austria-Hungary since 1869, vice-consuls for Germany (originally for Prussia and the

Hanse towns), France, and Spain since 1865, 1868, and 1877 respectively, and United States consular agents since 1876; he judged from his experiences elsewhere that the absence of a German colleague was ample compensation for the considerable German work; duties in respect of the non-existent Austro-Hungarian interests were confined to submitting an occasional nil return; and duties for the other countries were light or negligible.[20] The other powers made no money payment either to the British government or to British consular officers for services rendered. Most of them were ready to pay in decorations, of which C. Alabaster claimed to have been offered ten or so,[21] but to comply with a strict rule first laid down by Queen Elizabeth I foreign decorations had to be refused. Initially foreign fees could be pocketed, but even this trifling recompense vanished after a ruling that they had to be remitted to the exchequer in the same way as British fees.[22] A concurrent position as a foreign power's representative had its drawbacks. There were merely linguistic ones. H.J. Allen, faced at Newchwang with the bankrupt estate of a deceased Dane, applied to Copenhagen for instructions about Danish law and received guidance in Danish which he could not get translated even in Shanghai, and at Taiwan Hurst could correspond with his Spanish missionary flock only in Latin and received incomprehensible communications in Spanish from the Spanish consul at Amoy.[23] It could be embarrassing to be simultaneously responsible for protecting the interests of foreign Roman Catholic missionaries and those of British Protestant missionaries, two groups still apt to be bitter enemies.[24] Worse, defending or promoting a second power's interests might injure British interests.[25] Nevertheless Legation enquiries in 1886, when a multiplicity of concurrent appointments was automatically going with some posts, revealed that most consuls considered the system expedient. Their fear was that unsuitable British or other treaty power merchants would otherwise be appointed, and it was also felt that a consul unhampered by consular colleagues had more influence with the Chinese.[26] In 1895 O'Conor, the minister of the day, put a stop to the system.[27]

At a port with more than one consulate the incumbents addressed to each other communications opening with the not always truthful formula 'Sir and dear Colleague', and they collectively constituted that port's 'consular body', headed by the senior consul. At times consular bodies addressed through senior

consuls representations to the local authorities or to the dean of
the diplomatic body at Peking, but they were only pale little local
imitations of the diplomatic body and were normally significant
only in their own eyes. At Shanghai the international settlement's
peculiar status made the consular body a convenient forum for
jealous sniping at British preponderance.[28]

By the end of the century the service was staffing posts in all
China's main regions except the north-west. Its officers were liable
to postings over an immense area whose climate ranged from the
sub-Siberian to the subtropical, whose terrain ranged from endless plains to endless hills and mountains, and whose apparently
homogenous culture concealed substantial regional variations. Members of a Chinese consular service administering Chinese extraterritoriality in an area extending from Lisbon to Moscow and
from Stockholm to Palermo would hardly have had to make greater
official and personal adjustments on being re-posted. Nevertheless
some common factors applied to nearly every consulate nearly all
of the time. The chief ones were the Legation at Peking, the
Supreme Court at Shanghai, trade and taxes, opium, missionaries,
and relationships with Chinese officials.

The most important common factor was the personality of the
successive ministers at Peking who were responsible for the local
administration of the service, to whose varying styles the service
had to adjust, and to whom it had to look for instructions and
support in official matters and for help and sympathy in personal
ones. Between Bruce's departure and the end of the century there
were six ministers. First came three ministers who had been
promoted from the China service into the diplomatic service,
Alcock (1865–70), Wade (1871–82), and Parkes (1883–5). All
three had intimate knowledge of the China service's work and of
many of the men in it, and Wade indeed could write as minister[29]
that there was only one officer of whom he had no personal
knowledge. Alcock was a firm, fair, and efficient chief, a doughty
defender of his officers against any Foreign Office criticism he
considered misplaced, and a determined remover of black sheep.
Wade was a man of honour and delicacy,[30] so unassuming in
personal matters that whereas the normal Legation group photograph displayed a centrally seated minister surrounded hierarchi-
cally by his staff Wade was photographed standing off-centre in the
back row.[a] His constitutional failing was irascibility. He was

sufficiently aware of it to write to a Tsungli Yamen minister in 1865 that he was 'unfortunately irritable' by temperament.[31] Much more serious for subordinates than the short temper of a kindly and decent man was the decline in his powers. By 1873 he was complaining that long service in China had told on his energy and temper and that he had less heart to roll stones uphill. He could not delegate and unremitting labour broke him down.[32] Alcock, quitting Peking with unimpaired energy, filled his retirement with a multitude of activities, ranging from authorship to charitable works and from official committees and the presidency of the Royal Geographical Society to a leading role in the establishment of the British North Borneo Company.[33] Wade left the Legation in a different state. He admitted to ever-increasing difficulty in discussing business, putting pen to paper, or even reading a book, and this had been coming on for a considerable time. In 1882 Spence, informing a Foreign Office official semi-officially from Ichang that Wade had not replied to his application for home leave, said that Wade nowadays replied to nothing, and it was common knowledge in the Foreign Office, where the position was considered most grave, that consuls could extract no Legation replies to their representations. Wade had always been an unsystematic deskworker, and in a raid on his office during one of his absences a member of the Legation staff had retrieved many missing documents which Wade had been swearing were not with him. Now he left behind a chaos of arrears in Peking. On his return to England the Foreign Office, hoping to expedite urgently needed reports based on papers in his hands, lent him the services of Spence, whose leave had eventually been granted and was now specially extended for the purpose, but though able and energetic Spence could extract neither reports nor papers. Wade had held up for three years the transmission from Peking of China service complaints, which the Foreign Office considered justified, about inadequate pay and delays in promotions and it took him seventeen more months to comment on the complaints from retirement. Missing 1877 Foreign Office papers about Chinese-language training for entrants were tracked down to him and his comments obtained in 1887.[34] The service can hardly have regretted his departure. If, as is not unlikely, the Chinese too were glad to see him go they erred, for he was the last nineteenth-century British minister to have at heart China's interests, as he perceived them, as well as British interests. Parkes

had a reputation for being a slave-driver. To judge from the regime he had instituted when consul at Shanghai his concept of staff management and leadership was crude, for his Shanghai subordinates had been required to submit each morning for his scrutiny an itemized and signed record of their previous day's work. As minister to Japan he had caused discontent in the Japan service by promotions which disregarded seniority. He did not last long enough in Peking to leave his mark on the China service. Like Wade he had overworked and his health was deteriorating. Less than two years after arrival he took to his bed and was dead in three days.[35]

Officially and socially the diplomatic service stood high during the nineteenth century and the Foreign Office had a built-in prejudice against promoting mere consular officers into it. Only exceptional consular ability, combined with exceptional consular opportunity for demonstrating that ability, stood a chance. When Parkes died the era in which some China consuls had figured prominently in diplomacy was past and the current seniors were not notably able. Two career diplomatists, Walsham (1886–92) and O'Conor (1892–5), in turn succeeded Parkes. They were followed by a curious intruder into diplomacy, MacDonald (1896–1900), a former army officer whose previous military and civil experience had been in Africa and who seems to have been the personal choice of Salisbury as Foreign Secretary.[36] All three came to China, took charge of the China service, and left China again without so much as clapping eyes on most of the consular officers whose careers and well-being lay in their hands.

Walsham was hopelessly idle. In 1891 the Foreign Office sent him a biting reprimand. They listed their numerous despatches and telegrams to which no reply whatever had been received, drew attention to the almost entire absence of reports from him, and warned that so serious a neglect of duties ought not, and indeed could not, be allowed to continue.[37] After such a reprimand they might have been expected to require his resignation, but instead they posted him to Bucharest on his return from China and procured a KCMG for him two years later. China consuls suffered from him even more than the Foreign Office. They experienced the same neglect, but for them it was punctuated by petulance.[38] O'Conor was a shrewd judge of men, knew a good deal about the personal circumstances of consular officers he had never met, had a happy touch in correspondence with them, and was vigorous and

efficient. MacDonald too was vigorous and efficient but was less likeable. The hectoring tone he adopted towards the Chinese spread over into some of his communications to subordinates, and he was a dreadful snob. In 1899 he wrote semi-officially to the Foreign Office about three recently arrrived entrants, Oliphant, who came of a good Scots family, J.L. Smith, a tea-planter's son, and H.E. Sly, the son of a valet and the nephew of a uniformed Foreign Office menial. Oliphant, said MacDonald, was a gentleman and would do all right, but Smith and Sly, 'pronounced by himself Sloy', were '*quite* impossible'; neither of the two could ride; Smith had tumbled seven times in a single hour off one of the ponies sent to meet the party at the railway station (then some four miles outside the walls of Peking) and Sly's virgin efforts at riding had since put him in hospital three times.[39] Although Smith had nervous breakdowns during his career and committed suicide he was courageous and conscientious, and Jordan when minister praised him for good sense,[40] while Sly's career was above average. Oliphant was killed during the siege of the legations, so what his career might have been cannot be guessed, but a brother in the Customs, who would also have been socially acceptable to MacDonald, was later thought rather a ne'er-do-well.[41] The conclusion of the letter shows Mac-Donald in a better light. Tours, an 1893 entrant who had been badly knocked about by soldiers in Peking the following year, had after enduring a five-year wait brought out the fiancée he had left at home. Now six weeks after marrying her he was down with smallpox and was being nursed by the bride; if she too contracted smallpox, MacDonald wrote, his wife, the only other woman in the Legation, would nurse her. During the siege MacDonald as a former regular had been invited to take overall charge of the defence and had acquitted himself creditably, but his comment after the siege was over jars. Of the little band of defenders over seventy were dead.[42] Among the Legation staff an assistant and two student interpreters had been killed and the survivors, weakened by the ordeal, were in MacDonald's phrase going down like ninepins with disease (three more student interpreters would succumb). The resolute Mrs Tours, whose siege diary had austerely recorded that an atmosphere of dead pony and decaying Boxer was not the right thing for children[a] and who had despaired of saving her baby, now had her husband lying between life and death with acute brain inflammation, and other members of the staff had been invalided.

An unknown number of converts had been slaughtered. A twice-wounded student interpreter wrote angrily home that Russian troops were shooting harmless countrymen on sight, that both the Russians and the French were inhuman brutes, and that the Japanese were as cruel as could be.[43] Yet in a private letter to the Foreign Office MacDonald could say that the siege had on the whole been very good fun.[44]

In the exercise of their judicial functions consular officers were from 1865 answerable not to the minister but to a chief judge in Shanghai, from whom they received instructions and guidance and to whom they reported, and the Hong Kong Supreme Court passed unregretted from their scene. In that year a supreme court under the chief judge was established at Shanghai by an order-in-council making provision for the exercise of British extraterritorial jurisdiction in China and Japan, in other words, for trying civil or criminal cases in which British subjects were the defendants or the accused and for dealing with such matters as lunacies among British subjects. Exclusive jurisdiction over all cases arising in the Shanghai consular district rested with the Supreme Court. In other consular districts consuls continued to be responsible for trying most local cases in their provincial courts, as consular courts were now styled, appeals lying to the Supreme Court. Admiralty, lunacy, and some other specialized jurisdictions rested exclusively with the Supreme Court, and Supreme Court judges, who had a concurrent original jurisdiction in provincial courts, sat in them for murder trials and other important cases.[45] Subsequent amendments of the order-in-council did not fundamentally alter the Supreme Court's functions in China. In the wider legal world the chief judge at Shanghai did not rank high. The Foreign Secretary was told in an 1891 minute that the post had not always been satisfactorily filled from the legal profession 'in consequence of the frequent dearth of highly qualified candidates', and one chief judge who wished to transfer to a home appointment was not considered eligible for anything more elevated than a county court.[46] In the eyes of the British in China, however, the chief judges occupied positions of prestige and honour. The potential awkwardness of being subordinate in one capacity to the minister and in another capacity to the chief judge rarely surfaced. On one occasion in 1871 when there was a serious difference of opinion between Legation and Supreme Court the Legation were anxious to avoid this becoming publicly known, and

Wade censured Parker for lack of decorum in letting it be known in 1873 that in another matter the chief judge held one view and the minister another.[47] There is very little to indicate how well or badly consular officers got on with the Supreme Court. J.T. Pratt complained in 1908 that he had been contemptuously criticized in public by the chief judge, and the minister, who sympathized, offered to hint to the chief judge that more moderate language and greater consideration were desirable. It is reasonable to infer from a much later Foreign Office minute of 1922 mentioning a long-standing feud between Legation and Supreme Court that the consular officers of that period were caught up in the feud.[48] Otherwise all is almost complete silence. The state of relations between consulates and Supreme Court was in any case much less important than the state of relations between consulates and Legation, for most provincial courts rarely sat. In the early 1880s the eccentric H.J. Allen fitted his Newchwang courtroom up as a miniature theatre for the community's amateur dramatics and at least six years went by before the courtroom's dignity had to be restored by a successor needing it for its proper purpose.[49]

The establishment of the Supreme Court was seen by some in the service as disadvantageous for Chinese seeking to sue British subjects. Most chief judges had no previous knowledge of China before their appointment and none of them knew the language. The procedural formalities which they brought with them were incomprehensible and irksome to Chinese plaintiffs, and expensive too. In 1868 Winchester at Shanghai noted a great stock of rough contempt for everything Chinese in a cumbrous and expensive establishment where the Chinese believed justice to be obtainable only at enormous expense. Davenport said in 1872 that Shanghai Chinese regarded the Supreme Court rule which obliged them, if more than trifling sums were claimed, to employ British lawyers charging $25 for an interview and $50 for a court appearance as no more reasonable than it would have been to require British plaintiffs in a Chinese court to kneel in the Chinese fashion. In 1879, again at Shanghai, W.C. Hillier recorded that after a junk had been run down by a British steamer with the loss of two lives the owner, who knew no English, had abandoned his claim because he could not afford a lawyer and could not comply with the requirement that all petitions and complaints should be in the prescribed form and that a competent interpreter should be

provided. In 1880 a British subject of poor reputation was successfully sued in the Tientsin provincial court and appealed. Faced with incomprehensible rules and great expense the Chinese plaintiff eventually abandoned his valid case. H.B. Bristow commented that if the appeal from his provincial court had lain to the minister, as it would have done before 1865, it would have been decided in ten days without expense to either party. Still critical of legal charges Bristow wrote from Chefoo in 1886 that while the Chinese plaintiff in a British court was at every step met by fees, damages, costs, and expenses a British plaintiff in a Chinese court would have his case determined without fee of any kind, but Bristow should have qualified the criticism by adding that the Supreme Court was not corrupt and was able to enforce its judgements, neither of which was by any means always the case with Chinese courts. The same type of criticism continued. In 1900 Little at Samshui said that, faced with procedural rules, court fees, and lawyers' fees, an indigent Chinese plaintiff in the right could hardly get justice against an obstinate British defendant in the wrong, whereas a British plaintiff merely put the matter in his consul's hands.[50]

There were doubts too about the justice obtainable in the Supreme Court in serious criminal cases. In 1883 Logan, a British tide-waiter, shot and killed one Chinese and wounded two others at Canton. Popular anger was exacerbated by another incident and a riotous mob destroyed sixteen houses in the British concession. The viceroy and the Tsungli Yamen protested bitterly that the seven-year sentence then passed on Logan was far too lenient. Although Parkes received the Yamen's complaint unsympathetically, at the Foreign Office Pauncefote, who had once been attorney-general at Hong Kong and was now the permanent under-secretary, considered after reading the evidence that the complaint was justified and that Logan should have got twenty years. The Law Officers likewise considered the sentence too light.[51] The attitude of British juries was also questionable. Garstin, acting consul-general at Shanghai in 1929, thought it most unlikely that a Shanghai British jury would find one of their countrymen guilty of the murder or manslaughter of a Chinese. In 1936 J.F. Brenan, then the consul-general, went almost as far. He said that in such cases juries were most reluctant to convict a white man on Chinese evidence.[52] The attitude of nineteenth-century juries is not likely to have differed.

For a considerable time consular promotion of British trade seems to have been largely confined to recommendations and hints in the annual trade reports sent by each consulate to the Foreign Office, who had the reports printed and put on sale. There were good trade reports and there were trade reports dismissed by a twentieth-century scholar as rubbish.[53] The verdict is perhaps unduly harsh, for there was often nothing to be said. Some trade reports, C.F.R. Allen wrote in his 1889 Kiukiang report, might be able to give useful intelligence for merchant or manufacturer, but at ports like Kiukiang there was nothing to put in that had not been written a dozen times before. It probably mattered little whether the reports were good or bad, for the printed versions were poorly publicized. A travelling representative of the chief British cotton-thread manufacturers, who were energetic and enterprising enough to be seeking new markets throughout China, told the Chungking consul in 1896 that until reaching China he had thought the consular reports were confidential and that very few people knew copies could be purchased. The Board of Trade waited until 1912 to make the discouraging pronouncement to the Foreign Office that the annual trade reports were in general chiefly valuable as a historical record and for reference. In such matters consuls got little Foreign Office encouragement or guidance. In the experience of Hosie, the author of some excellent commercial reports, the Foreign Office took little or no interest, and he found it exceedingly disheartening that after he had slaved to collect information his reports were looked on as a nuisance by the Foreign Office officials dealing with them, who would apparently have been much better pleased had the reports never been written. The truth of the matter was that Hosie's reports were rightly considered much too long, but the Foreign Office waited until he was on the verge of retirement before asking the Legation to hint at this.[54]

For the rest consular officers initially tended to act much like referees in a football match, trying impartially to ensure that Chinese authorities and British merchants observed the treaty rules for the commercial game and not themselves participating in the game. D.B. Robertson told the Canton viceroy in 1867 that he knew little of commercial matters, and his language was approved by Alcock. Free trade ideas were ingrained. Middleton's 1865 trade report from Chefoo, after recording that British shipping was not doing so well there as that of other European countries and that

British merchants were suffering severely from Chinese competition, concluded that as the situation was 'in accordance with the
principles of free trade it must eventually produce beneficial results
to all concerned'. Similarly in 1879 the Foreign Office circulated a
memorandum stating that while a tariff intended simply to bring in
revenue was a tolerable evil a tariff imposed to injure foreign trade
or to protect native industry necessarily did most harm to the
country which imposed it and was therefore both mischievous and
injudicious. Well into the 1870s British trade looked after itself
successfully in China. In 1872 Medhurst's Shanghai trade report
called foreign goods and British goods nearly synonymous terms,
and Wade reported that three-quarters of the trade, and half the
shipping carrying it, was British.[55]

As all over the world competition ate away at British commercial
and manufacturing predominance there began to be calls for
diplomatic missions and consulates to give more active support
and more information about marketing opportunities. An early
indication of changing attitudes came in C. Alabaster's 1880
Hankow trade report. He expressed a cautious hope that as the
officials of other powers untiringly pushed the interests of their
nationals the strict rule against British officials mixing themselves in
any way in commercial enterprises could be somewhat relaxed;
consuls who sat as judges in trade disputes should not be personally
interested in trade, 'but if a way could be found of encouraging
them to find new outlets for the industry of their countrymen it
would be advantageous'.[56] In 1886 O'Conor, who had received
confusing and possibly contradictory guidance from successive
Foreign Secretaries, took the attitude, which was approved, that
consuls should be ready to point out commercial openings 'and, if
necessary, to introduce British commercial agents willingly, yet
with just discrimination, to the local authorities'. This and other
correspondence about consular assistance to British commerce was
published by the government,[57] and when copies reached China
later in the year there were critical and pertinent reactions. A
leading Shanghai broker said that consular officers, who were not
commercially trained, should devote themselves to enforcing just
British rights. Spence took the view that British merchants did not
need consular nursing, and his views, expressed in a sensible and
amusing speech to a large gathering at Shanghai, were endorsed by
his audience. From Pakhoi C.F.R. Allen argued against any course

of action which might bring the suspicion of giving or receiving commissions or bribes on British consuls, who at present stood proudly above any such suspicion. In his 1886 Chefoo trade report H.B. Bristow, who like Spence eventually entered business in China, poured scorn on the idea that he should travel round his consular district making trade enquiries which local British merchants were far better qualified to make. At his one-man consulate, he said, he was always on call; during the year his personal intervention had halted a pitched battle between foreign sailors and several hundred Chinese during which fifteen men had been badly wounded; he had empanelled a jury and held an inquest so quickly on a British ship's officer who had committed suicide that the ship had been able to leave the same day; an immediate application by him to the Chinese authorities had nipped in the bud a plot to murder missionaries; none of these emergencies could have been dealt with had he been in the interior enquiring into the price of razors, into the markets for flannels or mining machinery, or into the locally acceptable marking of bales; he had a great variety of other duties and no help in the office; instruments professing to combine hammer, screwdriver, gimlet, pincers, file, scissors, and bootjack never fulfilled any of these purposes satisfactorily, and a consul trying to rival such an instrument would have the same defect.[58]

In 1896 an admirable review by B. Brenan of British trade in China accepted as a fact of life that the consul who in other countries directed his attention chiefly to commerce had in China too little time for commercial duties to do them justice. He recommended that a new post should be created to take over the responsibility, which he considered was being carried out piecemeal and inadequately by consulates, for trade promotion throughout China. It was decided to accept the recommendation and to recruit a commercial attaché from within the service, but the salary was fixed too low to induce Brenan himself to accept appointment. In suggesting to the Foreign Office the names of six other possible consular candidates MacDonald could from personal knowledge express an opinion of the suitability of only one of the six, a striking indication of the gulf separating the minister from his flock. Henceforward a few members of the service received specialist commercial appointments of a similar character, but varying from time to time in status, nomenclature, and pay, and were removed from

ordinary consular duties for as long as they held the appointments. Pressure of events or of work usually continued to relegate trade promotion, as opposed to the protection of existing trade, to a secondary place in the thinking of other consular officers, and indeed Cockburn was surely right in saying in the late 1890s that in China a British merchant's opinion of his consul was based almost entirely on the ability shown in handling Chinese officials and that knowledge of commercial details was of comparatively small importance. One rare exception to this limited consular vision came in a quarterly Canton report by Bourne in 1894. Foreseeing that cheap Asiatic labour might threaten dear European labour and that Manchester might not be able to retain a monopoly of cheap cotton, he suggested that the British would nevertheless profit from the probably immense growth of production in China if they concentrated on those things which the Chinese could not do, namely, large-scale importing and exporting, the provision of capital, banking, shipping, insurance, the supervision of labour, and joint-stock enterprise. Buried in a routine report Bourne's views seem to have attracted no attention.[59]

The framework of consular duties continued to be provided by the treaties. The second peace settlement radically altered the treaty position about inland taxation of foreign-owned goods, about opium, and about missionaries.

China was covered with a dense network of tax barriers collectively known to foreigners as the native customs (here spelled with a small 'c' to distinguish them from the foreign-officered Maritime Customs operating only at treaty ports). At the barriers all manner of goods in transit paid all manner of customs duties, the official and unofficial rates of which varied from barrier to barrier and from time to time. The minor customs officials at the barriers lived on the difference between the amount they remitted to their superiors and the amount they collected. The first peace settlement had vaguely provided that foreign-owned goods should not pay more than the allegedly moderate but unspecified native customs duties then current. It proved impossible for the foreigner to ascertain what rates had then been current and what rates were subsequently in force. B. Brenan described the mystifying jungle of customs charges levied at Wuhu in 1877 by two parallel customs branches. The first branch started by assessing basic duty, levied at varying rates on different articles, on all merchandise. To the basic

figure it then made two very substantial percentage additions, respectively for the cost of remitting to Peking the money collected and for a freight tax varying according to the total weight of the merchandise. Then came a series of lesser charges for the costs of bankers, clerks, accountants, bookkeepers, gaugers, servants, and 'inner waters remittance'. Every one of these charges was separately shown on the receipts issued by the customs. Finally a last fee of 12½ per cent was collected for which 'no receipt is given, for the reason, I am told, that it is quite illegal'. The second branch assessed the taxes on boats, on masts, and on the varying materials in which the merchandise was packaged, and then proceeded to make additions similar to the additions of the first branch. Brenan estimated that the total effect was to increase an apparent tax of 10 taels to an actual tax of about 25 taels.[60]

The new treaty provision was intended to cut a way through the jungle for the foreigner. In return for a supplementary 2½ per cent payment on top of the 5 per cent *ad valorem* import or export duties an inward transit pass giving free passage through tax barriers in the interior was available for foreign-owned imports moving between port of entry and point of destination and an outward transit pass was available for foreign-owned exports moving between point of purchase and port of export. The concession was valuable. One estimate was that goods under transit pass paid five times less than other goods, and in spite of transhipment costs it was worthwhile sending Swatow sugar to Hong Kong to be reimported as foreign sugar under transit pass.[61] The transit pass system, however, frequently failed to operate satisfactorily and not infrequently did not operate at all. The 2½ per cent supplementary payment was, like the 5 per cent basic payment, assessed by the Customs in accordance with a published tariff and the payments received were remitted in full and without peculation to the central government. The money collected by the native customs, on the other hand, was provincial revenue or the perquisite of provincial officials great and small, and further money could be made by winking at smuggling for a consideration. The provinces stood to lose by every transit pass issued.[62] For this reason ingenious devices were consistently employed in some provinces to frustrate the intention of the treaty provision, and other provinces simply ignored the provision. Consular officers probably used more paper in expostulating about transit pass difficulties, or in reporting

unresolved difficulties to the Legation, than on any other single subject. The correspondence makes tedious reading. Where, as on the Yangtze, the transit pass system operated reasonably freely[63] it was extensively abused by foreigners. They obtained passes in their own names for goods owned by Chinese merchants who paid them a fee for the service. The practice was so widespread that the expression *lie hong* ('bogus firm') was coined to denote a firm which existed solely by such abuses. C. Alabaster's opinion at Hankow in 1883 was that 99 out of 100 outward passes were fraudulent. His efforts to curb the irregularities were endorsed by the Legation but served only to put the profitable malpractices temporarily into American hands.[64]

Opium was no longer a prohibited import. The revenue from opium shipped to China was so essential to India's finances that the Indian government met part of the cost of running the China consulates. Consulates had to watch the state of the trade on behalf of the Indian government, who complained of inconvenience when not regularly informed how much opium was being imported, where it was coming from, what price it was fetching, and what competition Chinese opium was offering.[65] Opium was excluded from the transit pass system. At the treaty ports it was sold to Chinese dealers, who alone were permitted to move it into the interior and who sought by smuggling to avoid heavy internal taxation. The service had few serious qualms about the morality of the trade. The explanation for this apparent insensitivity casts a lurid light on contemporary British society. Officer after officer forcefully expressed the opinion that opium in China was far less evil than alcohol at home. J. Scott said at Hoihow in 1879 that opium did not produce half the misery and crime of alcohol. Spence on home leave in 1883 said that opium was injurious and opium in excess pernicious, but infinitely less injurious to the public than whisky in excess; 'the excessive opium-smoker is a perfectly harmless creature, whose kindly instincts, if he has any, are not even dulled by indulgence in his vice, whereas the drunkard is too often a terror to his wife and children, a pest to his neighbours and a disgrace to his country'. C.M. Ford wrote from Amoy in 1894 that although excessive smoking led to utter moral and physical degradation moderation in smoking was common, and that if the Chinese knew what alcohol did in Europe he had not the slightest doubt which of the two they would consider the worse. The three

officers quoted were all Scots, but members of the service coming from other parts of the British Isles expressed similar opinions.

Acceptance of opium contrasted with immediate condemnation of trade in morphia. In 1885 R.J. Forrest reported from Amoy that Chinese were importing from England large quantities of morphia, a drug originally introduced as an antidote to opium-smoking, and he feared panic should it become generally known that a foreign poison was being extensively sold. The Legation warned the Tsungli Yamen, so that they might take steps to prevent the circulation of so dangerous a substance, and promised British co-operation in necessary restrictions, but although the Yamen expressed gratitude the importation of morphia into Amoy and the habit of injecting it were still greatly increasing ten years later.[66]

Among consular officers themselves addiction to opium was very rare. Smoking it was not socially acceptable among the British in China, but it was not prohibited by English law and does not seem to have been automatically regarded as a major breach of written or unwritten Foreign Office codes. In 1874 Wade called on consuls to report to him juniors whose misconduct endangered the repute and efficiency of the service. He expatiated on the evils of drink and debt. Smoking was mentioned much more briefly, though he required consuls to inform him of anyone thrown into the disreputable company associated with the habit. On the other hand the Foreign Office did not delete before publication of C.T. Gardner's 1878 Chefoo trade report a passage in which he described, with the intention of correcting misinformation and misconception, how he had some years previously taken to opium during an apparently hopeless illness, what effects he had experienced, how long it had been before he became addicted, and what the withdrawal symptoms had been. In conversation in 1881 with Li Hung-chang (see pp. 285–6) H.B. Bristow said that although he had not tried smoking he was an English official and might smoke opium as much as he pleased so long as it did not interfere with the proper discharge of his duties.[67]

The new treaty provisions opened the whole of China to missionaries. Like traders and travellers they could now go anywhere in the interior when provided with consular passports countersigned by the Chinese authorities, a provision of dubious authenticity in a French convention gave them the right to lease or buy land in the interior, and they and their converts had a treaty

right to practise Christianity. It was some time before Protestantism took much advantage of the new openings, and the seventy or eighty missionaries of the 1850s had by 1871 become only a hundred or so, about half of them British but only fifteen Anglicans. Then came an explosion, and in the 1890s there were more than 2,800, over half of them British.[68] Consular reports contain no systematic account of Roman Catholic missionaries, and usually describe their behaviour only when it threatened to provoke, or did provoke, riots endangering other foreigners, or when relations with Protestants were particularly bad. There are only occasional specific glimpses, such as that of the Church Militant provided by E.L.B. Allen from Pakhoi in 1886; a French father, using two revolvers and a sword to beat off an attack on his house by some twelve men armed with guns and axes, had probably killed two attackers and had returned to the area with a shotgun, a repeating carbine, and two revolvers, 'so I trust he may be able to make his position good'. The unsystematic references, perhaps coloured by unconscious Protestant prejudice among consular officers, very few of whom were Roman Catholics, imply that Roman Catholic missionaries tended to regard their converts as a special group in the body politic and to support them in secular matters against Chinese officials and Chinese neighbours, and that French officials supported rather than discouraged such pretensions. Unless the French altered their policy towards Catholic missions, D.B. Robertson wrote from Canton in 1874, peace with China would rest on a very slender base.[69] British missionaries too were frequently tempted to support their converts, and consistent consular discouragement was frequently ill-received.[70] In 1899 a missionary told W.H. Wilkinson at Ningpo that if not supported his converts would go over to Rome or to some other more helpful mission, a statement which Wilkinson regarded as a striking commentary on missionary methods and on converts.[71]

Overbearing officials, crooked merchants, and lawless ruffians were comprehensible, if unwelcome, Western imports into a China whose own society also bred such men, whereas the motives which inspired missionary work were outside Chinese experience and were incomprehensible and suspect. As a doctrine Christianity, particularly when dogmatically and intolerantly presented, seemed an alarming challenge to conservatism and orthodoxy, and Christianity in practice seemed to the Chinese authorities a political

engine weakening their control and establishing foreign influence. At lower levels suspicion and fear found their voice in rumours, placards, and pamphlets. These typically accused missionaries and converts of sexual orgies and of kidnapping and killing children for food or as ingredients in magic potions. As the number of missionaries increased so did suspicion and fear, and anti-missionary unpleasantnesses, assaults, and riots, culminating in much trouble along the Yangtze in the 1890s and then in the Boxer outbreak. C. Alabaster's Swatow trade report for 1868 asserted that merchant, traveller, and official would always find their way smoother where an honest missionary had gone before, but in 1883 he was more sombre at Hankow, where his own relations with the missions were excellent. He accepted that there was considerable truth in the Chinese view of Christian churches as political organizations under foreign control, wished he could impress on missionaries and converts that in becoming a Christian a Chinese did not acquire a semi-foreign character, and warned that outbreaks could at any time result from the missions' *imperia in imperio*. An episcopal assertion to Ningpo missionaries in 1874 that in Ireland the minister of the Gospel was exposed to far more difficulty and danger than the missionary in China would hardly have been repeated twenty years later by the most polemical supporter of the Protestant ascendancy in Ireland.[72]

The Foreign Office as a body remained cool towards the missionaries. They laid down in 1864 that the claim to acquire land in the interior should not at present be asserted, in 1869 spoke of injudicious missionary proceedings, and in 1871 correctly forecast that unchecked Christian propaganda would either end in the expulsion or massacre of missionaries or end in more hostilities, ruinously expensive and disastrous both for the Chinese state and for trade. Hammond's personal attitude can be deduced from the freedom with which D.B. Robertson at Canton voiced heterodox views to him in personal correspondence. Missionaries, Robertson wrote in 1870, were greatly to blame for their utter disregard of Chinese temper or feelings. They committed a social offence by trampling on national prejudices, and the Chinese had a perfect right to resist; 'religion is, after all, only a political institution and has no other status or authority'; he had recently suggested to one reverend gentleman, who had complained of persecution, that if Buddhist or Taoist priests built temples in England and went round

the country to denounce Christianity as a farce they would be killed perhaps and their temples pulled down — 'that's just what you do in China and what the Chinese do to you in return. I don't see what you have to complain of'. In 1873 he wrote that bishops were only inconvenient articles of social furniture and gave themselves great airs, and in 1874 that Protestant missionaries lived too comfortably and maintained a benevolent neutrality between the flesh and the spirit. Currie, a later occupant of Hammond's seat, does not seem to have been any greater lover of missionary endeavour. He was superciliously disdainful in intimating to Walsham in 1887 the desire of one clergyman to travel in Chinese Turkistan: 'I believe he occasionally distributes bibles and tracts but in other respects he is a respectable and harmless traveller'.[73]

Equally the Legation long resisted the spread of permanent mission stations in the interior. In dealing with his local missionaries Everard as acting consul both at Kiukiang in 1886 and at Wuhu in 1890 was still trying to stand on Wade's ruling, long overtaken by events, that missionaries had no right to reside outside the immediate vicinity of treaty ports and that consuls should not sanction their doing so at places so isolated that control and protection were both impossible. In the first instance Everard's attitude was specifically approved by the Legation.[74] The official resistance was in vain. The largest missionary society, the China Inland Mission, had as its name implied been founded to carry the Gospel message into the heathen interior. Its dedicated members were not to be deterred by assaults and riots or by official disapproval. Other missions were not far behind. The one mission station established in remote Szechwan in 1881 had become nine stations by 1890, and five different Protestant missions were soon established in the province. Reporting from Chungking on the expected arrival there of over a dozen young China Inland Mission ladies E.D.H. Fraser submitted that some further instructions about residence in the interior were desirable; if missionaries had no right of residence they had in theory only themselves to blame if they got into trouble; on the other hand, it was in practice hard to pass over in silence the public thrashing of a lady, and if a life were lost redress surely had to be sought; the current system of leaving missionaries to find out for themselves whether they could establish themselves in a new place made hard-worked magistrates, naturally reluctant to be saddled with the protection of alien propagandists, look suspicious-

ly at visitors and at least wink at hostile demonstrations; a compromise might be to secure the right to reside at existing stations and a few other suitable locations and to forbid settlement elsewhere. At about the same time as Fraser was making his suggestions and before they were received O'Conor was instructing Hurst, who at Foochow had still been trying to implement Wade's old ruling, that he should stress the duty of the Chinese authorities to enable missionaries to settle peaceably in the interior and was at the same time authorizing him to withhold passports for dangerous areas where the situation was genuinely beyond the control of the Chinese authorities. O'Conor can have sent out no general instructions on these lines, for in 1895 Tratman at Chungking complained that Wade's ruling had not been cancelled but was evidently not being observed. A game with such indeterminate rules could be played with success only when British and Chinese officials were sensible and firm and when missionaries were tactful and ready to co-operate with officials. The rules were changed in 1896 by MacDonald, who with vigorous insensitivity told the Foreign Office that in his opinion missionaries had a treaty right to buy property in all parts of China.[75]

Protestant missionaries of all creeds and from all countries were lumped together in the Chinese mind and shared the credit or discredit for each other's proceedings, but they were naturally of diverse character and British missionaries were not cut to a standard pattern. For example, in Formosa there was the Revd George Mackay, an indefatigable and much-respected member of the Canadian Presbyterian Mission who married a local Chinese farmer's daughter and whose numerous children were photographed wearing tartan, and there was the Revd Mr Junor, a newcomer of only three years' residence in China, who plagued Consul Watters at all hours, shook a large stick under his nose, and complained of him to the China-coast press, the Legation, the Foreign Office, and the Canadian government. In central China there was the Revd Griffith John of the London Missionary Society, also greatly respected, a pillar of Welsh Nonconformity who had preached his first sermon at the age of 14. At Foochow there was Archdeacon Wolfe, an honest and choleric Ulsterman who did not love Roman Catholics. In the Amoy district there was the Revd Mr Gregory, a Presbyterian, who whipped a magistrate out of his own yamen, was found to be insane, and was hastily shipped home. In

the Kiukiang district G. Brown took steps, with all possible tact and privacy, to restore to her relatives at home a female member of the Plymouth Brethren who was suffering mild erotic mania at her solitary station in the interior. Among the not insignificant roll of those who turned from missionary labours to worldly activities there was Robert White, a medical missionary and at one time Chinkiang's only doctor, who abandoned mission and medicine for whisky, cards, and such irregular ways that his very pious wife was driven home, and whose financial dealings were extremely shady.[76] Nevertheless among all this diversity traces of some common tendency towards dogmatic beliefs, intensely held, do seem apparent. In 1868 a Protestant sermon at Ningpo identifying Napoleon III, the Pope, or the Tsar as the Anti-Christ led to an official French complaint. In 1877 Adkins at Newchwang contemplated drastic action to prevent further attacks on Roman Catholicism by the Revd J. Ross, who tolerated no creed except that of the United Presbyterian Church of Scotland and who listened to no consular advice. When Raab, in charge of the Chinkiang consulate, died in very distressing circumstances in 1898 the local missionaries one and all pleaded conscientious objections to this or that portion of the Anglican burial service, which consequently had to be read over the grave by Raab's successor. There was also a lunatic fringe. Baber reported in 1878 that a lone Plymouth Brother had made his way through west China to the border of Tibet, which he tried to enter: 'being however a tall man with reddish hair and blue eyes, and speaking about 5 words of Tibetan with a strong Scots accent' his nationality was surmised and he was ejected by the frontier guards. The Legation agreed with Baber that such purposeless and hopeless raids were objectionable.[77]

The Times said in 1869 that missionaries generally were not very well educated and not quite gentlemen.[78] This was an understatement of the position in China. In the 1870s Margary, the nephew of a well-connected Anglican clergyman, praised some of the missionaries around Chefoo as charming men of great culture, education, and sociability,[79] but poor education and backgrounds far below gentility were frequent, notably in the China Inland Mission. Some missionaries could not spell,[80] and entries in consular marriage registers showing that the fathers of two missionary bridegrooms and their missionary brides had respectively been a dairyman, an iron-moulder, a farmer, and a warehouseman

are not untypical of parental occupations shown in other similar entries.[81] Social origins were in themselves obviously irrelevant to missionary work, but intellectual poverty must have made it harder to master so demanding a language and to come to terms with so alien a culture. In 1879 Wade, after affirming his belief in the superiority of civilization based on Christianity and the Bible, said with feeling 'we require, in a word, if we would Christianise China, more ability, more learning, more patience and more charity than, in my experience, we can in general be allowed to possess'. No doubt it was the tradesman and artisan background of so many missionaries that prompted C.T. Gardner in his 1886 Amoy trade report to suggest that as many British missionaries, especially those connected with the China Inland Mission, were acquainted with trade, some of them might with advantage to British trade and without detriment to their spiritual work act as commercial travellers; 'being ostensibly engaged in trade, they would be less liable to suspicion and dislike than if only engaged in proselytisation, the motive for which the Chinese find it difficult to understand'. The suggestion was a strange one even for Gardner, whose invariably good intentions veered erratically throughout his career between sense and nonsense. It was much odder that the hard and efficient B. Brenan should in his overall survey of British trade in China likewise have advocated participation in trade as a means of dispelling Chinese suspicion of missionary motives. The hardest words about the type of missionary sent out came from Bourne. He deplored the apparent mania in Europe for sending out uneducated and impulsive young men and letting them rush up-country; the religious fervour which was their only recommendation soon evaporated in the dry, matter-of-fact, apathetic Chinese environment; some lost their mental balance and many more their nerve; as successive ministers and consuls had vainly advised, only men of high training and strong character should be sent out. His views, though expressed from Canton in 1893, were doubtless based on earlier experience in Szechwan, where he had been equally critical of French priests. He called them well-informed, unscrupulous, and more French than missionary.[82]

The consular officers who sought redress for acts of violence against missionaries deplored the missionary tactlessness or obstinacy which often caused the violence. They spent much energy, with little success, in seeking to dissuade missionaries from banning

convert subscriptions to the festivities, temple-based and therefore condemned as idolatrous, which periodically enlivened the monotony of Chinese life. Some sensible missionaries agreed that converts should subscribe an equivalent sum to community charities, others were unyielding.[83] Gardner sent some cautionary suggestions from Hankow in 1891. The Foreign Office, which considered the suggestions very able and pertinent, passed them to the Archbishop of Canterbury for transmission to missionary societies and the Archbishop gratefully acknowledged them as very salutary, but the elementary nature of the sensible suggestions indicates how much avoidable trouble insensitive missionaries created for consular officers, for foreign communities, for themselves, and for their cause. 'As a rule', Gardner wrote, 'the elder missionaries of all denominations are moderate and temperate', but he recommended that zeal should be tempered with more discretion, that heathen prejudices and superstitions should be attacked with courtesy and without violence, that missionaries should not meddle in money disputes between converts and non-converts, that the outward appearance of Christian buildings should have regard to Chinese ideas, and that there should be less reticence about what went on in orphanages and schools.[84] Gardner was by no means the only officer to see that the tightly closed doors of some Roman Catholic establishments might breed dangerous rumours. Holland, for example, voiced that fear at a time of tension in 1895 at Ichang, where the convent was entered only by the port doctor or an occasional foreign lady. Gardner was unusual only in doing something about it. The mother superior of a Hankow convent accepted Gardner's advice, conveyed through his wife, to open the convent's orphanage to periodic inspection, Gardner arranged for the intendant to visit it, accompanied him, and considered the effect most happy.[85] Female missionaries were of particular consular concern. Hurst said that when travelling alone in the interior they were protected by the supercilious Chinese contempt for womankind, and the general though not unanimous consular opinion was that in doing so they did not expose themselves to much risk, although they were bound to be considered immoral women.[86] On the other hand C.F.R. Allen pointed out that being bigger than Chinese women they risked being taken for men masquerading as women. There was a case in point in the Amoy district in 1895. A young woman, living alone in the interior, came away following rumours

that she was a man in disguise seducing her schoolgirls. Her mission head, whom Gardner considered a bigot and not quite sane, tried to send her back, but Gardner refused a passport.[87]

Consular officers were ready enough to praise or blame individual missionaries but were for the most part discreetly silent about the desirability or otherwise of there being a missionary presence at all. Oxenham and Bourne were two who broke the silence. Oxenham clearly took to China. On reaching Hankow from Peking in the 1860s after a six-week overland journey during which he had been stoned several times he thought the foreign houses stiff and formal 'after dear, dirty, tumble-down China', and after a winter journey in Manchuria in the 1870s he suggested that brigandage in contemporary China was less prevalent than it had been in Europe fifty years earlier.[88] In his 1884 Chinkiang trade report he said that the Chinese, who considered that they had more to teach than to learn, by no means appreciated missionary labours; the money spent on missionaries in China would be better spent in London or Africa; and if there had to be missionaries they should not be teachers of dogma but missionaries of science, medicine, engineering, political freedom, and progress, who might make China's dry bones live and might make the Chinese bless the foreigner's advent instead of, as at present, coupling opium and missionaries together as twin plagues.[89] The flaw in Oxenham's argument was that an alien doctrine of political freedom and progress was even more socially and politically disruptive than an alien religious doctrine. The possibly small number of missionaries who thought it incumbent on themselves to spread both doctrines at once necessarily increased the hostility of the ruling class towards Christian missions. If as a British consular officer Bourne could describe K'ang Yu-wei as a visionary, unfit to lead in troubled times, who had been given crude ideas and very foolish advice by the Revd Timothy Richard in Peking, and could call that well-known British missionary an intriguer,[90] it is easy to imagine the intense suspicion with which the Chinese establishment must have viewed Richard. Bourne's objections to missionaries were on a less elevated plane than those of Oxenham. In 1895 he condemned missionaries in the interior as being in practice subject to no law and to no foreign public opinion and as irritating the Chinese by ridiculous talk and conduct; their present excessive freedom to reside in the interior, where their presence threatened constant

disagreements with the Chinese, had not been intended by the treaty makers and should be curtailed; there was plenty of work for them in the treaty ports and Hong Kong; it was only the glamour of martyrdom and adventure that took them into the interior, 'at the expense of constant danger to solid interests'.[91]

Every local disagreement with the Chinese about British treaty rights, whether relating to trade, taxation, opium, missionaries, or any other issue, involved consular negotiation, friendly or unfriendly, fruitful or frustrating, with Chinese officials who were in general tenaciously conservative.

Knowledge of the West or of its languages spread only slowly even at the larger treaty ports. Two of the earliest Chinese with a good knowledge of Britain to make a quite untypical appearance were Dr Wong Fun and Captain Lu Buah (Lü Wen-ching). Dr Wong, who had taken an Edinburgh medical degree, became medical officer to the Canton consulate in 1867 on D.B. Robertson's recommendation. Complete with queue, fan, long silk gown, and, one would like to think, good Scots accent he attended among others Canton's foreign ladies in their confinements.[92] Lu Buah's story began when Winchester, going on home leave in 1852, took with him 'a young Chinese lad' to help look after his baby. At his own expense Winchester had the lad educated in Scotland, and in due course the servant was metamorphosed into Captain Lu Buah, successively commander of various small Chinese naval vessels, assistant harbour-master at Chefoo, and Canton river police officer. He cannot have had disagreeable memories of Winchester and Scotland, for he was profuse in offers to loan his steam launch to consular officers and in other civilities and was popular among foreigners. His career was chequered. He survived being cashiered twice but in 1903, no longer 'a young Chinese lad' but 'old Captain Lu Buah', he was cashiered a third time and was heard of no more.[93] Western influence showed itself less pleasantly but relatively early in a narrow commercial circle at Shanghai. Winchester in 1867 noted that most Shanghai foreigners believed trade better done without a knowledge of Chinese than with it, and in 1879 W.C. Hillier said that the same attitude had led to the emergence among Chinese brokers and the like of very distasteful swaggering airs which would never have been tolerated in Chinese society but which were put on to suit the imagined taste of foreigners. These types were not confined to Shanghai. In 1894

J.W. Jamieson accused the treaty port Chinaman of being a very objectionable hybrid who abandoned Chinese politeness and honour and substituted the West's worst characteristics.[94] Senior official circles were far more conservative. The first heralds of change were the overseas or Hong Kong Chinese occasionally employed by provincial authorities as English-speakers. Usually they were mere interpreters or translators, but in 1876 a Penang Chinese appeared in a minor official position at Foochow and in 1880 a very amiable and friendly gunboat captain educated in Hong Kong appeared at Wenchow.[95] More perceptible Western impact showed itself sporadically in the last two decades or so of the century. In 1878 an intendant in central China who had briefly visited London repaid Foreign Office attentions to him there by great courtesy towards foreign visitors. In 1880 the Canton viceroy remarked that the Afghans seemed to give the British as much trouble as the Cantonese gave him. In 1890 at Swatow the foreign deputy (a buffer between foreign consuls and provincial government) had been educated in the United States, was a club member, and played billiards well; in 1891 the prefect investigating a Wuhu riot spoke fluent English; in 1895 at Shanghai the intendant countered complaints of minor insults to foreigners by mentioning that when in company with French friends he had been mobbed in the streets of Versailles. At Wuhu in 1898 the local life-style of Li Hung-chang's eldest son, whose father's power presumably made it safe for the son to disregard tradition, was a still more striking portent of change. He spoke excellent English, lived in a finely furnished European-type house with electric lighting and comfortable armchairs and sofas, and entertained consul and Customs commissioner to tea in front of a good fire.[96]

These phenomena among officials were reported because they were unexpected. For similar reasons the earlier efforts of an enlightened official, Ting Jih-ch'ang, to put his relations with British officials on an easy footing had been reported. During the Taiping rebellion Ting, a protégé of Li Hung-chang, rose rapidly without obtaining a degree in the examinations and when a young intendant in the Shanghai area had considerable British contacts, impressing Winchester as consul with his good sense and competence and F.E. Harvey as vice-consul with his subtlety and wiliness. He was a provincial governor before he was 45 and was considered one of China's ablest and most energetic men. After

having left office, in accordance with custom, to mourn his mother's death he was summoned in 1875 for an audience in Peking, where W.S.F. Mayers, the Chinese secretary, who had previously met him, called. Ting received him with great cordiality as an old acquaintance and spoke very freely; at the centre were insincerity and inertia, in the provinces corruption and inefficiency; geomantic objections to mining operations and to telegraphs were ridiculous; for urging civil and military reforms he was abused as a traitor; and for lack of an examination degree he was treated as a nobody. He was appointed governor of Fukien, and Pedder, who called in 1877, was charmed by his friendly, unassuming manner and his perfect frankness in discussing business. More than that, Ting asked Pedder to tell the consuls in Formosa, which at that time was administered from Fukien, that Ting would be pleased to make their acquaintance, that they could depend on being received with the consideration due to them as the officers of another state, and that he would put them up in his own yamen. C. Alabaster called later that year and was equally charmed. Ting was ill, and Alabaster, who had known him in Shanghai, was ushered into his private apartments, where he found Ting, in extreme dishabille, huddled up in an easy chair and expressing the liveliest satisfaction at seeing Alabaster again. Ting's extreme friendliness made the meeting more like 'that of two old and intimate friends than an interview between a comparatively unimportant foreign official and a high officer of a proud, shy and exclusive nationality. Having had a real liking for him when we had met on more equal terms years before, there was nothing affected on my part', but although Alabaster had one or two warm friends among Chinese officials he had not been prepared for such effusive friendliness, which he did not know whether to consider real or affected. Ting's efforts to modernize in Fukien were thwarted by the viceroy and by subordinates and within a year he resigned in disgust and died in retirement.[97] If his friendliness was genuine it did credit to his heart and if affected credit to his head.

For the rest Chinese officials remained in the traditional pattern. That is not to say that they all behaved in the same way. They varied from the able to the incompetent, the reasonable to the unreasonable, the courteous to the rude, the vigorous to the indolent, the clean-handed to the venal. Consular officers were not given to venality, but in other respects the Chinese officials with

whom they dealt doubtless detected similar variations. Relationships between the two sets of officials varied correspondingly. The only safe generalization is that however unsatisfactory relationships at times were in the provinces they were worse in the capital. In Peking officials long repelled every foreign attempt to meet them socially; even in the 1880s no respectable Chinese wished to be seen in public speaking to a foreigner, and it was a recognized financial advantage of the Chinese secretary's post that in the absence of social intercourse no expenditure on official entertaining was required.[98] In the provinces things were much better. On the British side respect and even liking were far from uncommon and perhaps Chinese had similar feelings, though they would have put their careers at risk by admitting it. Nevertheless Bourne was probably not speaking for himself alone when he said in 1890[99] that the Chinese had so strong an antipathy to foreigners that it was very difficult to get on really good terms with them, and E.D.H. Fraser complained in 1899[100] of a 'type of mandarin often encountered, the bluff noisy official who professes to the foreigner to be free from Chinese prejudices and eager for reform, while among his own people he poses as an expert on managing the troublesome European'. In 1865 the Foreign Office had told Alcock that consuls should seek an easy and familiar relationship and should do their best to break down the barriers imposed by different customs and habits of thinking.[101] Some progress was made thereafter, but there was still a long way to go.

8
THE OLD CONSULATES

CANTON'S importance for foreign trade faded. Chinese merchants preferred to buy foreign goods at Hong Kong, which as a free port acted as a bonded warehouse, and to supply the inland market by native craft direct from there.[1] The consulate's political significance was however vastly increased by the severance of the ties formerly linking the governor of Hong Kong, in his concurrent capacity as chief superintendent of trade, with the Foreign Office. The governor's links in Whitehall were now exclusively with the Colonial Office, and the consul became the intermediary between the colonial government and the Canton viceroy. Although the Chinese in Hong Kong and their neighbours in Kwangtung, the province out of which the colony had been carved, were indistinguishable, their respective administrators were so far apart in their concepts of administration that they had difficulty in understanding each other's rights, interests, problems, and susceptibilities. There was perennial friction over issues large and small, notably smuggling and the presence in the one territory of persons wanted in the other territory for piracy, murder, kidnapping, robbery, theft, debt, and the like. The consul's role as intermediary was difficult, delicate, and unrewarding, and involved a heavy work-load. In the years 1886–9 over a thousand despatches were exchanged with Hong Kong, several times more than the number exchanged with the Legation, and over two thousand with the viceroy.[2] Although Wade in 1873 considered the work at Canton lighter than at Shanghai he considered the responsibility heavier, and he forecast, correctly as far as the nineteenth century was concerned, that the Canton post would always be more important politically.[3]

Canton's foreign residents were no longer confined to a ghetto by the Chinese, but most of them elected to confine themselves in the self-created ghetto of Shameen, a reclaimed sandbank in the river

about half a mile long and two hundred yards wide. It was divided into a British concession and a much smaller French concession. In 1885 some fifteen of the eighty British lots were still undeveloped and the French concession was an open space which provided a cricket pitch. No Chinese other than servants, guards, and police were allowed to live there. The whole little oasis of sleepy, orderly calm was separated only by a narrow creek from the noisy throb of Cantonese life, and in particular from some gigantic three-storey brothels just across the creek.[4] The British consulate was on Shameen and the consulate's subordinate staff lived there, but in order to demonstrate that the right of entry into the city had indeed been won a residence inside the city was leased for the consul himself. For some fifteen years after the allies had handed the city's administration back to the Chinese D.B. Robertson occupied in lonely state part of the Manchu general's former yamen. Here he simmered, as he put it, in a stew-pan of a climate,[5] and from here he exercised a personal influence which no later consul in China ever approached.

The yamen possessed a five-acre park with high boundary walls, lofty trees, a herd of deer, and the graves of Robertson's cats and dogs. The beautiful park was one of the sights for foreigners visiting Canton, but a man living alone in this stately home needed to be exceptionally self-sufficient. Robertson was cut off from such evening relaxation as Shameen society had to offer. At sunset the city gates were shut and the street barricades closed, silence falling over the city until dawn, and although Robertson insisted in principle on the right to have the city gates opened for him on demand the right was in practice too bothersome to exercise. In the daytime he rode or walked, believing in air and exercise in all weathers and despising people who were frightened of getting wet, but for weeks and months he never left the yamen after dark, when reading or writing became his sole resource. From time to time he had to visit Hong Kong, but he preferred his picturesque mouldering old yamen and the quiet of its park to Hong Kong's glare and heat. He had a bedroom and study at the consulate, 3 miles away by chair through narrow, crowded streets, but how often he went there is not stated.[6] Amid this extraordinary and depressing monotony Robertson preserved his mental powers, kept abreast of European politics, and studied the Chinese officials, from viceroys to magistrates, with whom he was in constant contact. Passages in

his private letters to Hammond, some of which Hammond laid before the Foreign Secretary and the Prime Minister,[7] show that he studied them to good effect. Residence in the city, he wrote, afforded opportunities of intimacy with the highest officials, 'and more reasonable and sagacious men I have seldom if ever met'; once their confidence was gained they would frankly explain their difficulties in making changes; people who accused such men of mere obstructionism had never witnessed, as he had, a mob sacking a yamen; they felt that the empire's integrity depended on change being gradual and not hasty, and pressure to modernize made them suspicious; 'faults they have and very great ones — but they are the faults chiefly of a proud and sensitive people' unwilling to show openly their inward realization that their ancient civilization was paling before a newer one; 'there is a great deal to be done with these people if you keep on good terms with them'.[8] In official despatches he praised different viceroys not only for expected qualities such as energy and cleverness but also for less expected ones such as simplicity, enlightenment, plain speaking, honesty, and truthfulness, and he mentioned their courtesy, friendliness, and personal kindnesses to him.[9] How he communicated with all these officials is nowhere stated. Although Hance knew Robertson well his allegation that like Hance himself Robertson had never learned Chinese is demonstrably wrong but does at least suggest that Robertson did not speak the language fluently.[10] On the other hand he can hardly have summoned the consulate interpreter into the city for every formal or informal meeting.

At least once Robertson was hoodwinked by one of the officials of whom he thought so highly. He believed he had secured from a viceroy the immediate disgrace of a magistrate who had had 500 strokes administered to a Chinese boatman for bringing a proper complaint to the consulate, treatment which left the boatman in a precarious state in a missionary hospital. Five years later, however, as if to prove his dictum that 'with the Chinese there is always a reserve somewhere and when you think you see the end of an affair you suddenly discover it is only the beginning turned round', he discovered that the magistrate was pursuing a successful career elsewhere.[11] Conversely his trust and liking did not stop him from taking a soberly critical view of the Chinese state. Having as he said stood sole deep in blood (probably at Amoy), trying to stop the slaughter going on around him, he considered that in dealing with

rebellions the Chinese government was the most oppressive in the world, and he was tempted to describe the empire's constitution as an armed neutrality between court, officials, and people.[12] Nor did they stop him from establishing through W.S.F. Mayers, the Canton interpreter, a system of espionage to obtain information. From 1860 a Chinese protégé of Parkes, Feng Yuan, was paid from Secret Service funds to provide copies of yamen documents. Feng, who had relatives in the yamens, visited Mayers on alternate mornings in the guise of a teacher and handed over documents which Mayers burned after use. By these means Robertson heard of the receipt by the yamens of every important document and generally obtained its contents. With surpassing effrontery Mayers obtained for Feng a warrant entitling him to draw a small monthly sum out of customs receipts, an unearned privilege from which according to Mayers many hangers-on of official personages benefited but which was not intended to benefit the undercover agents of foreign powers, and whenever the customs official responsible for issuing warrants changed Mayers asked the new incumbent to renew Feng's warrant. Long after Robertson and Mayers were in their graves, at least up to 1899, either a now aged Feng or a successor continued the espionage. The information obtained was considered worth that obtained at all the other consulates put together, and for that reason a junior capable of understanding the documents without the help of the consulate's Chinese staff was regularly posted to Canton. A few years after Robertson's initiative the Legation similarly found a silver key to Peking's secret archives. Alcock admitted the usefulness of spending Secret Service money for the purpose but deplored as morally odious the whole system of bribery for treachery and breach of confidence. Robertson apparently had had no such qualms.[13]

Robertson believed that China should be treated as an equal and that those who complained of her obstructing so-called progress and civilization might modify their opinions if they looked at the question from her point of view. He spoke to his contacts plainly, frankly, and with goodwill. He assured one viceroy, who had expressed the hope that allowance would be made for the inexperience of a newcomer who had never previously met foreigners, that there would be no difficulty in their dealings, for he would always discuss matters amicably and admit when he was wrong; he told a second that he was always pleased to give advice whenever

requested but cared little if, as generally happened, it was not followed, since he preferred the Chinese to arrive at their own conclusions; he told a third, with whom he was taking up strongly a case where the Chinese were indisputably in the wrong, that he was not threatening a man for whom he had the highest regard but was warning him of what might happen.[14] His attitude went down well, and his advice was sought by one viceroy, whom he regarded as an old friend of broad and liberal views and whose death saddened him, on all manner of foreign problems, such as the Macao coolie traffic. Nowhere on earth, in Robertson's opinion, had more tears been shed than at Macao, that sink of iniquity and shame to Christian nations, and he did his best to expose the traffic; but he advised against rash assertion of Chinese rights against the Portuguese, and it was on his advice that the viceroy, instead of executing a captured Portuguese kidnapper, sent the man to the governor of Macao with a warning that unless kidnapping stopped those caught would be dealt with as slave-traders.[15]

Not only the Chinese brought their problems to Robertson. It was to him rather than to a French consul on the verge of insanity that the French bishop turned about a female convert condemned to death for extracting children's eyes and brains during baptism. Calling on the governor the same day Robertson said that, as the governor knew, a confession under torture was worthless and the charge was all nonsense; the affair had been got up by some subordinate who wanted to make his name; execution would bring a hornets' nest round the governor's ears and he would probably regret it all his life, and he had better send the woman back to the bishop and have nothing more to do with the matter. The governor did so and the bishop, content to get her back, said nothing about her beating and torture, 'which was not much after all'. It was to Robertson that the Prussians turned about the destruction of some Prussian mission chapels. Robertson told the viceroy that although the missionaries had no business to be where they were they had been allowed to stay there for eight years; the failure of Chinese authorities elsewhere to repress anti-missionary violence had ended in the central government losing face and a local repetition of this was to be avoided; the people must not be allowed to take the law into their own hands, and although it was none of his business he considered that the right course was to check violence at once and then to enquire who was wrong. The viceroy agreed, the ringleaders

were arrested, and the chapels were restored, but Robertson told
the missionaries that he had acted solely to get things settled and
had no sympathy with them, and he asked how they would feel if
they found a Roman Catholic priest preaching against their religion
and trying to convert their children, just the position into which
they were putting the Chinese. He reported with satisfaction that
the missionaries left him with small comfort. It was Robertson who
took the initiative after a Manilaman employed in a British establishment at Whampoa had shot a Chinese employee dead, telling
the viceroy 'that he had better leave the matter in my hands and
thus avoid any complications that may arise. To this he agreed with
the expression of his thanks'. He approached the Spanish minister,
who happened to be at Macao, and at the minister's request ap-
peased the dead man's family with a compassionate gift. He acted
similarly when a British naval lieutenant from Hong Kong accidentally killed a Chinese while out shooting in China and was detained
by the victim's fellow villagers. He advised the lieutenant's commanding officer to go immediately to the village with an interpreter
and, as the villagers concerned were a notoriously bad set, with an
armed party, and to offer a money settlement. The widow accepted
the money and the lieutenant was released. Robertson informed the
viceroy privately of the incident and trusted that as the matter had
been settled to the people's satisfaction there would be no need to
take further steps. The viceroy replied that Robertson would no
doubt see that justice was done, and as no complaint had been
lodged Robertson let the matter rest there, although he viewed it
with regret and dissatisfaction.[16] On the other hand when a coolie
murdered his Indian employer he wrote 'of course I shall have a
public execution for the benefit of servants generally' and he got the
Chinese to carry out the execution, which was watched by most of
Canton's foreign residents, at the scene of the crime.[17]

Robertson was extremely outspoken to missionaries and about
missionaries. In 1862 he issued passports for the interior to two
missionaries but prohibited their entry into a disturbed district
which they were desirous of visiting. They went straight there, were
stripped of everything by robbers, and were sent back to Canton by
helpful Chinese officials. Robertson told them that if they had got
through they would doubtless have triumphantly proved that the
consul's warning was all moonshine and his orders of no consequence, instead of which they had broken their word and had

made a nuisance of themselves. He suspended their passports. To
Bruce, who approved very highly of his action, he complained that
devout subscribers to missions gloried in any mishap which might
befall the 'Pioneers of Reformation' in such imprudent missionary
raids and regarded it as a sacrifice in the great cause of 'Divine
Truth'.[18] In 1870 an immense sensation was caused among foreigners at Canton, as elsewhere in China, by news of a very grave
mob attack on French Roman Catholics at Tientsin, the so-called
Tientsin Massacre. Robertson immediately put the violence down
to Catholic imprudence, an opinion which the Foreign Office drew
to the Prime Minister's attention; the Catholics, like the Protestants,
were so utterly lacking in regard for Chinese feelings that the comparative immunity hitherto of both groups surprised him; he utterly
refused to believe in official complicity; 'that the local officers were
frightened, and unable, as usual, to control the mob is about the
truth'. Chinese protection was in his view the only resource of the
defenceless Canton foreigners against a riot, and in a despatch
he expressed full confidence in the willingness and power of the
Canton authorities to preserve peace, although in a private letter he
admitted that the lower classes in an excitable population could
easily get in a blaze. He dissuaded the French consul from bringing
up French troops, told British residents not to show nervousness,
and told the viceroy that he would take no protective steps without
the viceroy's full concurrence. Finally he told a leading Chinese
merchant that he desired to live in peace with all men, as his record
showed, but that if the people wanted a row he was not inclined to
stand any nonsense, and that the gentry and wealthy merchants,
who would suffer most in a disturbance, shared his interest in
peace. He invited the merchant to think this over, and two days
later the trading guilds formed themselves into a committee of
public safety and denounced evil reports against foreigners. Nothing
happened except that a little later a mob burned down a chapel and
house belonging to Protestant converts in a neighbouring town and
beat the Chinese preachers. Robertson went to see the viceroy not
to demand restitution but to confer on the course to be followed
and demurred to the viceroy's proposal to arrest the ringleaders; it
was certainly necessary to show that such disturbances could not
occur with impunity, otherwise they would spread to Canton and
there would be a sea of difficulties, but in the present state of public
feeling he strongly recommended an amicable compromise; he

therefore submitted for the viceroy's consideration that the town elders might be called together and induced to rebuild the premises and to promise that there would be no further outrages. The viceroy accepted the recommendation, and settlement on the lines suggested was reached. Robertson wrote to inform the viceroy of his inexpressible pleasure at a settlement proving the desire for justice and goodwill of the viceroy, to whose wise and far-seeing policy was due the perfect harmony at Canton. The missionary responsible for the chapel received a less agreeable letter; opening the chapel in a turbulent place at a time of strong anti-missionary feeling had been ill-judged and the regrettable occurrence had therefore not been surprising; no claim for pecuniary compensation could be entertained; 'regarding persecution, I do not see how it can be avoided in a country where the religious tenets of the people are diametrically opposed to those of Christianity, and indeed when the latter are considered as subversive of the ancient faith and institutions of the empire'. In reporting the viceroy's opinion that missionary acts would sooner or later cause a war and that they perpetually disturbed friendly relations between China and foreign powers Robertson said he had long entertained the same view; over the previous ten years commercial issues had not once jeopardized relations but peace had three or four times been threatened by the missionary question; he believed a religious war with China to be not far distant, a grave consideration little heeded by those whose one fixed idea was the propagation of Christianity, *coûte que coûte*, each after his own formula.[19]

Despite his opinions Robertson seems to have kept on surprisingly good terms with British missionaries. At a meeting in 1872 he promised them his best assistance provided they exercised the discretion which was the best way of advancing their work, and in his official account of the meeting he commended all of them as gentlemen of high character whose management of their difficult and often dangerous task was in all respects praiseworthy. Writing privately to Hammond not long afterwards he claimed that he and the missionaries, who although sometimes lacking in discretion were good people in their way, got on well together, for he believed they understood he did all he could for them.[20]

Robertson was no more inclined to stand nonsense from Hong Kong than he was from the Cantonese population. He considered it was the colony's duty not to be an offence to China. At one time he

put to Hong Kong the unwelcome argument that armed colonial
police who were to his great displeasure capturing alleged pirates in
Chinese waters were not only guilty of an indefensible infringement
of China's rights but were also themselves at risk of being defined as
pirates. 'I care very little for the opinion of the governor of Hong
Kong or his subjects', he wrote to Hammond at another time. 'I
know the position better than they do. I am not going to jeopardise
friendly relations with the Chinese to suit their book'.[21] Robertson
had to fight off Hong Kong pretensions to deal with the Chinese
authorities direct,[22] and indeed despite Colonial Office instructions
in 1865 that Hong Kong should communicate with the Chinese
authorities only through the Legation or the consulate,[23] governors
frustrated by their dependence on a consular officer ranking much
below them kept trying long after Robertson's time to ignore or
circumvent the instructions.[24] In Robertson's view colonial people,
inexperienced in foreign relations, failed to see the difference between governing and negotiating; their legalism was not suited to
China, where it was personal influence and prestige that counted;
they were strangely ignorant about the rank and status of Chinese
officials; and Governor MacDonnell's views about China and the
tone of his communications left Robertson in no doubt that the
colony's dealings with the Chinese should be channelled through
the consul, whose influence and prestige would otherwise suffer
severely.[25] In 1867 Alcock wrote officially to MacDonnell, whom
he privately described as incapable of decently civil official intercourse and as coarse, bumptious, and exceptionally uncouth and
uncourteous, that it was in his view exclusively for the Foreign
Secretary to confirm, question, or censure diplomatic or consular
acts and that as minister he had approved all the actions by Robertson which had been so freely criticized by the governor. Mac-
Donnell was thereupon instructed by the Colonial Office that
consuls were liable to censure only from their own superiors, but
two years later Robertson was, according to Alcock, still being
treated like a lackey and scolded in the language of a fishwife and
was having to be periodically rescued by the Legation from a storm
of invective and censure. A Legation minute alleged that the very
word 'mandarin' appeared so seriously to affect MacDonnell's
nervous system as to render him incapable of considering anything
calmly, and accused him of having made Hong Kong a nuisance to
the Chinese authorities and a general scandal.[26] Robertson once,

under great provocation, lost his temper with MacDonnell, the most difficult man with whom he had ever dealt, but being convinced that collisions between governor and consul were contrary to the public interest supported him when he believed him to be in the right. He managed to maintain a friendly social tone, but was thankful when MacDonnell was replaced by a more sensible and agreeable governor, Kennedy, who expressed very warm appreciation of Robertson's zeal and discretion, and then by Governor Pope Hennessy, whose views on China seemed to Robertson broader than those of his predecessors. Nevertheless he looked forward with pleasurable anticipation to seeing Hong Kong disappear below the horizon when he went on home leave, and in 1877 wrote that nothing would induce him to relive his struggle over the previous six years to preserve the peace between the colony and the Canton authorities.[27]

In spite of golden opinions at the Legation and the Foreign Office, promotion eluded Robertson. His hope of succeeding Alcock in Japan was dashed by the appointment there in 1865 of his former subordinate Parkes. He saw all prospect of advancement gone and wrote to Alcock 'no man has given less trouble to minister or Foreign Office than I have, and my reward is — being passed over'. He contemplated retirement, but the Order of the Bath, an honour which Alcock had failed to procure for him but which the Belgian royal family successfully solicited on his behalf in return for unspecified services, reconciled him to his position. In 1869 Alcock suggested that on his own retirement Robertson would be the best chargé d'affaires should Wade decide to retire instead of returning from home leave, but Wade did not retire and Robertson remained at Canton, a withered figure dressed on formal occasions all in black, down to black silk gloves, even in that climate.[28] He was sustained by the dread of having nothing to do in retirement and by a grey realism. In countries where life was uncertain he thought it just as well, he wrote to Hammond, not to marry (he was a widower) and to save a good deal of trouble to all parties by leaving as little behind as possible; sometimes he wearied of local politics, 'but I suppose the time comes when we get weary of everything, even of ourselves'; he had saved very little money, having always kept an establishment worthy of his position, 'for I never could see that we were sent out here to make a good thing of it'.[29] During nearly thirty-five years of service he was in England for only

eighteen months or so in all,[30] so in the flesh Hammond and he
were almost strangers, but even after Hammond's retirement as
an elderly man the other elderly man in Canton kept up a flow
of unreserved letters, still signing himself 'Yours faithfully and
obediently', and he corresponded too with Hammond's wife and
daughter. In 1877 he wrote that his health was wrecked by recent
typhoid, that he had given up hope of promotion, and that
ambition was dying out.[31] The Foreign Office chose that belated
juncture to offer him Shanghai, and as they wanted him there and
knew he preferred Canton they baited the hook by offering the then
rare rank of consul-general as a personal compliment.[32] He accepted but before he could take up the appointment ill-health drove
him home and into retirement. He was delighted to be awarded a
KCMG on top of an earlier knighthood, settled in the heart of
London, and soon died. He had had a pension which he described
as very handsome and ample for his requirements, but when his
only child, a rising member of the Japan service, died suddenly in
his prime a few years later only the liberality of Yokohama residents provided the widow with an annuity of about £160.[33] It
was not only the working class who were insecure in Victorian
days.

As successor at Canton Wade selected the amiable and conscientious A.R. Hewlett, in the belief that it would be next to impossible
for any colonial government to quarrel with him. Wade had
underestimated the tensions inherent in the relationship with Hong
Kong. Governor Pope Hennessy was irked by Hewlett's refusal to
take up purely Chinese cases referred to him by Hong Kong, and
Hewlett complained of the governor's reluctance to act in accord
with a consul on whose services the colony made such heavy and
frequent demands. Within four years Hewlett went home with
what was evidently a nervous breakdown. He was away for twenty-
two months and got back in such bad shape that after only a
fortnight he was ordered home again by the Canton doctor. He
retired and settled in Geneva, and as he acted at various times as
consul there Switzerland presumably restored his equilibrium.[34]
The debate about the next appointment was curious. In recommending Hewlett's appointment Wade had called C. Alabaster,
who had also been in the running, an ambitious, irascible intriguer
of boundless self-esteem who might disregard instructions, who
would have misunderstandings with Hong Kong, and who was 'the

man I would not send to Canton'. The Foreign Office for their part held the settled opinion that Alabaster was a dangerous firebrand, and the recommendation now made by O'Conor, the chargé d'affaires, that Alabaster should be appointed was not at all welcome. O'Conor told them that Alabaster had given him the impression of being about the best senior and 'considering how things were carried on in the last few years of [Wade's] reign I don't think much value need be attached to his opinion'; Frater, who had just gone to Canton as acting consul, had done well elsewhere but to judge from his private letters was not a gentleman, and Canton required a gentleman. O'Conor did not explain why Canton required gentility, a point which Wade had likewise made earlier on, but no doubt the real or imagined tastes of Hong Kong governors were the explanation. In fact in point of gentility there was little to choose between Alabaster, the son of a straw-hat maker, and Frater, the son of Aberdeen's assistant city chamberlain, but O'Conor was evidently unaware of this.

To escape from Alabaster the Foreign Office suggested R.J. Forrest as an alternative, but he did not wish to leave Amoy, where he and his wife had greatly improved the consulate, and declined Canton. Currie, the permanent under-secretary, accepted that it was an inconvenient precedent to interfere with the Legation's responsibility for China appointments, but to avoid Alabaster he was prepared not only to risk the precedent but also to reverse his own recently expressed views and a long-standing and carefully considered Foreign Office attitude. His mind turned to Hance.[35] Hance and his botany had been buried at Whampoa for almost a quarter of a century. In 1861 he had opted for the vice-consulship at Whampoa in preference to the Canton vice-consulship because at Whampoa the infamous *Alligator* offered family accommodation not available at Canton. In 1865 he moved into a spacious vice-consulate at last built on shore, and there he stayed, with less and less to do and getting harder and harder up. The replacement of sailing-ships by vessels whose steam power enabled them to make their way up to Canton progressively decreased the work at Whampoa, essentially an anchorage for sailing-ships, and the size of his family progressively increased. The death of his first wife left him with six surviving children to educate at home and with next to nothing to live on himself, and after a still-birth his second wife brought him first one more child and then twins.[36] He had gone

home once as a bachelor, being shipwrecked on the way, and was never during his forty-two years of service able to afford a second leave. He was already 33 when after ten years' service under the Colonial Office in Hong Kong he transferred in 1854 to the China service. He learned no Chinese, and by the time he was senior enough to be considered for a consulship this ignorance had become a bar to the promotion. In 1876 Wade twice urged that as Hance had not passed through the student interpreter grade and unlike the student interpreters had been given no chance of learning Chinese his hard and conscientious work over many years might properly be rewarded with the Ningpo consulship. On the advice of the permanent under-secretary, Tenterden, the Foreign Secretary twice refused. The reasons Tenterden gave him were, given the exceptional circumstances, not unduly convincing. His unexpressed reason for being so hard-hearted may well have been to avoid any precedent which might give an opening in the Far Eastern services for the political patronage appointments which plagued the general consular service. When a not dissimilar case cropped up in the Japan service in 1881 Tenterden, in a minute not addressed to ministers, stated that the student interpreter system depended on no one being introduced into the service over the heads of men who had entered as student interpreters and on no one who had not acquired the language being promoted to an independent post, two principles to which he had stuck through thick and thin and to which he would continue to stick.[37] Subsequent to the adverse decision in 1876 Hance, with apparent lack of logic, was brought up from Whampoa to act as Canton consul during the long gaps caused by Robertson's retirement and Hewlett's collapses.

In all he was acting consul for four years and his performance, particularly during the difficult and dangerous time of the Logan riot, met with approval. Further, in spite of the language barrier he got on well with Viceroy Liu Kun-i. The viceroy, a connoisseur of flowers, appreciated Hance's botanical knowledge, Hance found Liu simple and frank, they took a liking to each other, and on being summoned to Peking Liu went out of his way to praise Hance to Wade.[38] Nevertheless when Hance applied to succeed Hewlett as substantive consul O'Conor said that in view of the 1876 decision he could not support the application, and in London Currie minuted that the promotion was undesirable. Now, only two or three months after so minuting, Currie ate his words, and the

Foreign Office telegraphed that in spite of earlier decisions against Hance they preferred to economize by closing Whampoa down and appointing Hance to Canton. They did not gain their point. O'Conor replied that Hance was in bad health, had married a half-caste who led him a life, drank, 'though not enough to be of consequence at a small port', and was quite out of the question. The Foreign Office saved face by responding that they were not unmindful of Alabaster's claims but wished to examine the recommendation further, and then they capitulated and appointed Alabaster.[39]

Hance's failure to get the Canton post made no real difference to him, for he died the following year at Amoy, where in spite of all his alleged disqualifications O'Conor had sent him as acting consul, and the Whampoa vice-consulate was closed three years later.[40] On the other hand getting the post was a final turning-point in Alabaster's eventful career. In his four and a half years at Canton he successfully dealt with the usual frictions between Hong Kong and the Canton authorities, was on tolerable terms with both, and kept things generally quiet. By the time ill-health forced him to take the first home leave in twenty years and to retire he was in high favour with the Foreign Office which had struggled against his appointment. They made him a consul-general, a distinction which had eluded all his Canton predecessors. They heeded his immodest representation that as every community where he had been consul had looked on him as one of the best men it had ever had the CMG proposed would be inadequate recognition and they procured a KCMG instead, at the time a very rare honour for a China consul. From retirement he sent the Foreign Office long communications about China, one of which they considered so able that it was circulated to the Cabinet. On his sudden death he left only £319, and as a final and signal mark of favour they secured a civil list pension for his widow.[41] A final touch in the Canton comedy of errors was that O'Conor as minister recommended to succeed Alabaster the very Frater whom as chargé d'affaires he had suspected of being socially unsuitable. He withdrew the recommendation on learning that Frater had cancer.[42]

On Robertson's departure the Foreign Office were on Wade's recommendation minded to close the yamen and then, perhaps on Robertson's advice, changed their minds. Hewlett resided there and they unsuccessfully tried to make his successors do so. The

successors moved on to Shameen, and the yamen was abandoned
first to a succession of consulate juniors, and then to colonial
service cadets learning Cantonese, before being handed back to the
Chinese in 1928.[43] Whether or not the move out of the city, and the
consequent loss of physical contiguity, had anything to do with it,
consular relations with viceroys went steadily downhill, and the
intimate relationship of Robertson's day was replaced by at best
distant coolness, and at worst contemptuous dislike, on the British
side. Consular relations with Hong Kong were not easy either.
Without giving prior notice to Hance as acting consul Pope Hennessy came to Canton to call on the viceroy and while there ignored
Hance's existence, for which the Colonial Office at the Foreign
Office's instigation reproved him,[44] and in 1894 B. Brenan was
most incensed by Governor Robinson's attitude during an outbreak
of plague in Canton and Hong Kong which killed some 50,000
people. By giving permission only grudgingly and with bad grace
for the Hong Kong sick to return to China the Hong Kong authorities had, in Brenan's view, missed the opportunity of meeting
the Canton authorities' reasonable wishes and of removing the
common people's fears and suspicions; the attitude in Hong Kong
seemed to be that any deference to Chinese sentiment was a
reflection on Western medical science, which in statistical terms had
been no more successful than Chinese medicine in curing patients,
and that any concession to Chinese prejudice was an abandonment
of British sovereign rights; and as usual the Hong Kong press had
stigmatized any tenderness towards Chinese feeling or religious
conviction as selling the British birthright in Hong Kong to the
Chinese. The Legation's view was that Brenan's efforts had been
largely conducive to improving a very critical situation, but it is
unlikely that either governor or viceroy was equally appreciative.[45] The verdict on that viceroy on his departure was that he
lacked patriotism, a sense of justice, or the curiosity of an active
mind and was unusually selfish and greedy. The next one, old,
decrepit, and nearly blind, brushed aside Brenan's representations
about two assaults on shooting parties from Hong Kong by declaring that such little incidents occurred daily in each of the
hundred and more districts within his jurisdiction and that he could
not attend to such trivialities, and E.D.H. Fraser while in acting
charge said that he was inclined to regard everything except money
as of little importance and that he delegated all foreign questions to

a systematically rude and disobliging subordinate. The viceroy, too, could be rude. At official meetings he twice referred to Hart, the inspector-general of Customs, as 'that creature' (*tung-hsi*) and for good measure accused Hart of pocketing Customs revenue, and he told the next acting consul, Mansfield, in a tone discourteous enough for further discussion to be judged useless, that the minister could give Mansfield any orders he liked but that that did not concern the viceroy.[46] All this was a sad contrast to the relations Robertson had once enjoyed, but Robertson would have recognized Fraser's criticism of the Hong Kong authorities as being prompt to press their own demands on a provincial government almost invariably ready to meet them but as being disinclined to show any reciprocity.[47] Canton was always an exceptionally trying post.

Amoy kept exceptionally free from serious disturbances. During the Boxer outbreak an able and energetic intendant kept the whole consular district quiet,[48] and at other times of international or internal tension the storms broke elsewhere and passed the port by. It prospered as the centre for trade with Formosa until Formosa became Japanese and the trade was diverted into Japanese channels.[49] In the mid-1880s, when 80 per cent of the port's commerce was British,[50] the resident foreign community, numbering close on three hundred, was larger than that at Canton and had trebled in size in twenty years.[51] An unusually detailed description of the community's life on the one and a half square miles of Kulangsu was given in 1878. About half the residents, and two-thirds of the firms, were British. There were over 80 bachelors and widowers as against just over 50 married men, but 13 spinsters and 2 widows were available. The *Amoy Gazette* appeared every day, European stores could be bought locally, Kulangsu produced its own ice and aerated waters, and a supply of pure milk was planned. The new club provided a fair library, foreign and China-coast newspapers, two billiard-tables, a racquet court, a small theatre, a bar for drinks and oysters, and a nightly table d'hôte dinner. There was cricket, tennis, sailing, and bathing, there was an annual two-day race-meeting on the Amoy side of the harbour, and geese, duck, teal, and snipe afforded excellent shooting.[52] There was big game too. Many years before, Swinhoe, out shooting small birds, had unexpectedly been asked by villagers to deal with a tiger. He loaded up with hollow metal buttons off their jackets, followed the tiger into a dilapidated temple, and fired. He finished up, winded, at the

bottom of a precipice, the tiger having vanished. At the beginning of the 1890s better prepared sportsmen shot some twenty-five tigers in the immediate vicinity of Amoy, and an intendant with whom R.J. Forrest was on very friendly terms asked him informally for foreign help in shooting more.[53] The fly in the ointment for foreigners was that Kulangsu was not a settlement or a concession. Administrative arrangements for policing, for public works, and for public health were so deficient in China that in self-defence treaty port foreigners tried to fill the gaps, and consuls, who were as much affected by the deficiencies as were other foreigners, were rarely backward in supporting community pretensions. C. Alabaster, R.J. Forrest, and C.T. Gardner all came forward with proposals for foreign-led reform and improvement,[54] but the Chinese, who had learned by experience that in such matters foreigners given an inch soon took an ell, would have none of it.

An unceasing flood of voluntary emigrants seeking a livelihood in the Straits Settlements and to a lesser extent in other territories crowded on to coolie ships leaving Amoy. The consulate reported in 1883 that since 1877 over 167,000 had left, nearly 140,000 of them in British vessels.[55] Britain took the lead in legal regulation of the carrying trade. British vessels engaged in it were required under the Chinese Passenger Ships Act and under colonial ordinances to avoid overloading, to provide adequate latrines, and so on. To enforce the requirements the Amoy consul became, ex officio, the emigration officer provided for under British law, as did the consul at Swatow, the only other port with similar numbers of emigrants.[56] A sharp consular watch was kept to prevent additional passengers being illicitly taken on board after clearance had been given, but in 1880 one vessel was known to have taken on board nearly 1,000 extra men outside the harbour and was reported to have reached Singapore so crowded that there was no room to sit down.[57] The same year a firm which was wholly or partially owned by Straits Chinese and which had been systematically evading its legal obligations[58] was fined the enormous sum of £5,000 by H.A. Giles, who as a result was sued in the Shanghai Supreme Court for repayment of the money and damages. Giles was a quarrelsome man. His career was littered with silly official quarrels, and in private life he broke off relations with three of his own sons.[59] At Amoy he ran true to form. He quarrelled with the Customs commissioner and with his United States colleague, and Wade had

to make excuses to the admiral for Giles' correspondence with the navy.[60] In this instance, however, his heart was in the right place, even if the Law Officers advised that on technical grounds the fine must be returned. The foreign and Chinese communities at Amoy thanked him effusively for preventing overcrowding, the suits against him were withdrawn, and the plaintiffs paid his court costs.[61]

The emigration had a secondary effect. China considered persons of Chinese race, wherever or whenever born, to be Chinese nationals. British law considered persons born in a British possession to be British, and if not so born they could be naturalized. Straits Chinese of the second and later generations, and naturalized ones of the first generation, were thus dual nationals. Some of them claimed consular registration and extraterritorial status when in China. In 1872 the Law Officers misguidedly advised that such persons owed no allegiance to China and were entitled to British protection. The Foreign Office did not adopt the sounder view expressed in 1879 by Pauncefote, then their legal under-secretary, that international law could not support the claims, neither did they unreservedly endorse the claims. From at least 1887 onwards the curious compromise position was taken that Straits Chinese would be treated in China as British subjects only if their parents too were British by birth or naturalization.[62] Another compromise, an abortive one, was to rule that only persons whose dress enabled them to be readily distinguishable from ordinary Chinese should be registered. Legation circulars of 1868 and 1877 reiterated earlier rulings to that effect, and though the rule had long been a dead letter it was not formally withdrawn until 1904.[63] At first some consular officers applied the dress rule strictly. Indeed Robertson at Canton went further and replied to the 1877 circular that he had invariably refused registration, conceiving that the British government did not intend one man to 'have two nationalities to serve and avail him as circumstances required'. Others tried to interpret the rule. In 1884 Sinclair at Foochow favoured Straits Chinese taking to black frock-coats, and in 1885 Hance asked from Canton whether he should register a Singapore Chinese who had written 'I have dressed myself a foreign straw hat, a front buttons short jackets, trousers and foreign shoes and socks'.[64] Amoy was the main centre for returned Straits Chinese. Forrest in 1889 said that for years they had given the consulate very little trouble, but most

Amoy consuls took a less favourable view. In effect the consuls at Amoy decided *ad hoc* who to register and what degree of protection to afford. Pedder had unrivalled local experience. He spent nearly all his thirty years in the service at Amoy, about half of them as acting or substantive consul. In his opinion in 1873 the overwhelming majority of Straits Chinese were Chinese to the core and shammed being British subjects only to set the Chinese authorities at naught; 'I look on them, in fact, as Chinese malcontents protected by us'.[65] This opinion did not stop him from acting promptly and resolutely on learning one winter's afternoon in 1866 that a registered Straits Chinese had been arrested in a district city some 17 miles up river and was being beaten. Pedder immediately left for the scene, arriving by boat soon after dark and slipping through a postern gate just before the magistrate, who had sent a message that he would receive Pedder, could shut all the city gates to prevent his entry. Once at the magistrate's yamen Pedder desired the presence of the commandant, in whose hands the prisoner was. The commandant, a rather sullen but resolute-looking man, arrived attended by several hundred soldiers who crowded the hall to within a few feet of Pedder. The manner of commandant and soldiers was at first rather evil, but the prisoner was eventually brought in, having been so severely beaten that he could not stand, and handed over to Pedder's custody. Orders had been given for further beatings that evening and next morning, so Pedder was pleased to have saved the prisoner two floggings. The man bore a good character, and the Amoy intendant, 'a thoroughly good officer', told Pedder that he believed the man had been falsely accused after refusing a squeeze to some understrapper. Pedder's action, which seems to have been firm and courteous, was entirely approved by Alcock.[66]

Pedder said his missionaries were with one possible exception so prudent and circumspect that there was little trouble. He himself was prudent and circumspect in deciding whether to take up cases of convert persecution but pursued glaring cases with determination. In one of the worst it took well over a year's apparently hopeless negotiations with evanescent prefects and intendants, and finally the intervention of a viceroy whose action Pedder called just and resolute, for a magistrate who had savagely beaten and plundered converts to be ordered to make financial restitution and for his underlings to be flogged and put in cangues. Characteristi-

cally Pedder reported to the Legation only after he had settled the case. Rather less characteristically Alcock, while expressing pleasure that justice had been done, warned that no attempt to extend a protectorate over Chinese converts would be sanctioned by the British government. C. Alabaster, considered by the Foreign Office so dangerously fiery, was equally circumspect in Amoy missionary cases. In 1878 he wrote to a mission head who was having some trouble that even the most cautious consular interference increased ill-will and at best secured a sullen acquiescence, whereas a conciliatory and forgiving missionary attitude led to cordiality and friendship, and that the less the treaties were quoted and real or fancied rights claimed the better it was for the Christian cause which both he and the mission head had at heart.[67]

Amoy was not a post of political importance and consular relations with the Chinese authorities were confined to parochial issues. Inwardly consuls often lost patience. For example, Alabaster reported in 1876 that an intendant was perfectly aware of the utter falsity of a series of statements advanced by him and that it was difficult to deal with someone so utterly and unblushingly mendacious.[68] However, outward decorum was for the most part preserved on both sides. Some personal relations were positively friendly. In 1867 Swinhoe expressed private affection and esteem for an intelligent, able, willing, and courteous intendant, and in 1870 Pedder wrote that over the years there had been considerable personal friendliness between himself and local officials, many of whom he had found very likeable men though by British standards infamously bad officials. From the Chinese side came two daring gestures of social politeness, both reported as path-breaking and unique, towards consuls' wives. In 1878 an intendant, hearing that the China-bred Mrs Alabaster spoke Chinese, asked to be introduced and brought his children to call on her. In 1887 another intendant asked for two fans to be painted for him by Mrs C.F.R. Allen, who painted prettily, and sent through her husband his thanks for her gracious transformation of two worthless fans into most valuable objects which all his friends envied. Soon afterwards he arranged a very pleasant picnic for eighteen official and non-official foreigners, including Mrs Allen and other wives. On transfer to Kiukiang Allen found relations with Chinese officials there most harmonious but confined to business, whereas at Amoy he had been on terms of private friendship with the intendant.[69] All in

all Amoy was a happy port, although by the end of the century the long shadow of Japan was falling over it and the rest of Fukien.[70]

Foochow's foreign residents were only slightly fewer than Amoy's,[71] but it was a less happy port. Its import trade was always negligible, and although in 1885 the trade in British hands was still greater than at any port except Shanghai, world demand for China teas was diminishing and Foochow, hugging nostalgic memories of golden days when fortunes had been quickly made and as quickly lost by tea-men living splendidly in palatial mansions, was entering a long decline.[72] Some 10 miles down river at Pagoda Island there was a small satellite community and a vice-consul, subordinate to the Foochow consul and with a role similar to that of the Whampoa vice-consul. Pagoda Island was the highest point which could conveniently be reached by foreign vessels coming up river. The vice-consul's function was to control British shipping and to repress disorders among the crews, for which purposes he was provided with a constable and a gaol, and like his Whampoa colleague he was condemned to an isolated and solitary life. In the days of sail the anchorage was full of ships which lay there for months and ship's chandlers, storekeepers, boarding-houses, and two doctors were kept busy, but as steamers, staying only a couple of days and bringing no local trade, replaced sailing vessels the community's life ebbed away. By the early 1880s the vice-consul had for company only a doctor, a trader, two surveyors, an engineer, a schoolmaster, a harbour-master, and a few tide-waiters, and by the turn of the century the only residents were the vice-consulate and Customs staff, a doctor, and a pilot or two. Soon afterwards Brady on taking over the Foochow consulate represented that a posting to Pagoda Island, where the vice-consul had nothing to do, simply threatened moral deterioration. At his suggestion the vice-consular post was abolished and the local doctor, Myers, was put in charge of constable and gaol as consular agent.[73] He remained in charge, latterly with the courtesy title of vice-consul, until his death in 1920. There had been two examples of strange vice-consular behaviour at the post in the recent past, and Brady very likely had them in mind. In 1891 a questionable report from a most unreliable source reached Foochow that Chinese conspirators were plotting to seize the Chinese war vessels at the anchorage. Out of the blue the Legation received a telegram from Hausser, who had taken charge of the vice-consulate five months before, saying that his life was in

imminent danger from conspirators and asking for immediate transfer. The mystified Legation authorized G. Phillips, the Foochow consul, to transfer Hausser and he was moved at once. He then gave a sensational explanation. He had accidentally discovered indications that as part of the plot parties of disbanded soldiers were arriving at the island, 'the numbers so arriving being indicated by secret signals which I heard and found placed in the vice-consulate garden during the night and saw removed at earliest daybreak' by his servants, five of whom he now believed to have been implicated in the plot. He had reported the servants to the Chinese authorities, who after examining three of them had taken preventive action to make the plotters' objectives safe against attack. The plotters had obviously regarded him as responsible for the thwarting of their plans, to his certain knowledge the vice-consulate had been constantly watched until he left it, and if an armed guard had not at his request been posted there by a British naval officer he was firmly convinced that 'these lines would never have been written'. Phillips, who started by thinking Hausser had greatly exaggerated the danger, ended by more than half believing that a servant had really been in a treasonable conspiracy, but Hausser's later history makes it clear that his suspicions and fears at Pagoda Island were figments of his imagination and that his wretched servants had been subjected for no reason at all to the brutalities of Chinese officials on the scent of treason.[74] Then in 1900 Werner was most severely reprimanded for what Mac-Donald called a phenomenally foolish quarrel with a Dr Underwood, Myers' predecessor. Werner defended himself by one of the character attacks typical of him; Underwood was notoriously bitter and eccentric, had quarrelled with every vice-consul, and was the author of endless ill-natured statements about Werner. At Foochow Playfair said that Underwood was popular and a good fellow and that Werner's probably ingrained attitude of intense distrust had been fostered by Pagoda Island's solitude.[75] This was probably a correct diagnosis. Pagoda Island can hardly be blamed for the peculiarities of Hausser and Werner, but it gave them every chance to develop.

At Foochow itself the consulate from 1861 to 1886 was in the charge of Sinclair, incompetent, stupid, and spiteful. No other port was unfortunate enough to be saddled with such a consul for a quarter of a century on end. It would be difficult to find anything he

did right and tedious to detail all he did wrong. When in charge of
Ningpo he had been disliked by the British merchants there,[a] and
there is no reason to believe he was any more popular with the
Foochow merchants. He was on bad terms with the Foochow
missionaries.[76] His relations with the Chinese were unsatisfactory,[77] and so were his relations with colleagues and superiors.
After his retirement he was remembered in the service for quarrelling with all his subordinates and refusing them sight of Legation
correspondence, which he kept under lock and key. Alcock instructed him to refrain from requiring one subordinate to address
him in terms of servile deference, an instruction in which the
Foreign Office entirely concurred.[78] Further bitter complaints from
other subordinates about offensive and unreasonable treatment
came to Wade, who sent Sinclair an undeservedly tactful rebuke
and who received an absurd rejoinder docketed in the Legation 'Mr
Sinclair writes himself down an ass'.[79] He himself was an awkward
and disloyal subordinate. 'We know that consular servants are not
considered by the Corps Diplomatique', he wrote to one chargé
d'affaires, and a second was told that the terms of a reprimand
addressed to Sinclair by the chargé sounded more like a magistrate
upbraiding a police court prisoner than one gentleman addressing
another. To Wade, who during a visit to Foochow had settled
one of Sinclair's disputes with the Chinese, he expressed sore disappointment that Wade's hasty and imperfect settlement had not
met the excessively moderate conditions for settlement which Sinclair had laid down, and a few months later, no doubt in revenge,
he formally accused Wade of leaving Foochow despatches unanswered and of considering commercial disputes unworthy of
notice, a complaint the Foreign Office took very seriously.[80]

The last phase of Sinclair's career shows both the Foreign Office's
reluctance to act drastically against senior incompetents and the
great but not absolutely overriding weight given to seniority when
promotion was in question. In 1879 Sinclair applied on grounds of
seniority for Shanghai, which had been vacant for a little time.
Without Sinclair's knowledge Wade had recommended him for
Shanghai when the vacancy first occurred, although as long ago
as 1870 he had hoped for Sinclair's retirement. While on home
leave he discussed China staffing with the Foreign Office and as a
result withdrew his recommendation. Instead he recommended P.J.
Hughes, considerably junior, and condemned Sinclair as a most

urbane but essentially wrong-headed man of very limited capacity, handicapped by an un-English upbringing in Belgium, and as a man whose retirement would benefit the service. Wade's initial recommendation of a man of whose capacity he had so low an opinion and whose retirement he had long desired can be explained only on the count of seniority, and his reference to urbanity cannot be explained at all. When the Foreign Office considered the Hughes recommendation Pauncefote, who from earlier service in Hong Kong should have known something about Sinclair, saw no sufficient reason for passing over a man whose seniority gave him the first entitlement to the post. Overruling Pauncefote's views Tenterden rejected Sinclair in spite of seniority; 'whatever may be [Sinclair's] merits as regards urbanity he has given constant trouble and is quarrelsome especially with missionaries — probably arising to some extent from the impatience of official old age' (Tenterden was only in his mid-forties).[81] During the Peking interregnum between Wade leaving and Parkes taking over, the chargé d'affaires wrote privately to a Foreign Office official in 1882 that although much of the current trouble at Foochow arose from Wade's neglect of business Sinclair was a deplorable consul; if he could do the wrong thing he always did it, and his long-winded and senseless despatches irritated the Chinese. Later that year a Foreign Office minute described Sinclair as a very incompetent consul and past his work. In 1883 Wade in retirement overcame his inability to put pen to paper for long enough to record for Parkes' benefit his belief that nothing would go well at Foochow so long as so singularly incompetent a man remained there and his regret at not having himself recommended Sinclair's removal. For all that Sinclair remained at Foochow, and in 1884, hearing that Hughes at Shanghai had been promoted to consul-general, he represented to Parkes and to the Foreign Office that he too should be promoted to consul-general; he said he had little doubt that the Foreign Office, in accordance with its traditions in China, had offered Shanghai to him as the senior China consul and that Wade had ill-naturedly withheld the offer from him.[82] In 1886, at the age of 68, he decided to retire, and he drew a comfortably large pension for eleven years. After his departure there was an immediate improvement at Foochow. Watters, the next man in charge, who as a junior had caused a stir in the British community by saying that he knew some Chinese whose word he would prefer to an Englishman's oath,

soon called his relations with the Chinese authorities friendly. In 1890 the authorities were not on good terms with the Russian consul, with whom they were quarrelling about calls, or with the French and American consuls, neither of whom spoke Chinese, but Phillips' way of conducting business pleased them so much that at their instigation the central government offered him a Chinese decoration. He declined it in accordance with British practice but in Chinese style, expressing himself as gratified but surprised beyond measure, since his services had been exceedingly small.[83]

The missionary troubles which had flourished under Sinclair's ineptitude however continued, and missionary cases were eventually averaging one new case a week.[84] In 1892 the Church Missionary Society ran into various troubles in Kienning prefecture. A mission doctor was in much danger when a dispensary was attacked, a magistrate had to rescue two Zenana Society ladies trying despite ominous signs to establish a new station, and the person and room of a clergyman who had started building before his title deeds were in order were drenched in liquid nightsoil. Hurst, still an assistant but acting as consul, said that he and the Chinese authorities had difficulty in restraining their respective flocks, over-zealous young missionaries and an excited anti-foreign population, and that the interests of British merchants suffered if the consul's time was largely occupied with missionaries, whose aims could not be advanced by constant friction. 'Why some members of your mission are intent on forcing their way into a hornets' nest while the rest of the province is open to them I fail to understand', he wrote to Archdeacon Wolfe, the senior mission representative, urging tact, discretion, and a temporary suspension of activities in the prefecture. The archdeacon's authority was however limited. At least one missionary insisted on wearing Chinese clothes, which the archdeacon considered an unwise practice, and the Zenana Society ladies were beyond his control.[85] In the second half of the decade C.F.R. Allen believed many of the most experienced local missionaries to share his view that the want of discipline and organization in the Zenana Society made it a danger and an obstacle to the spread of Christianity; sixty-six unmarried missionary ladies of the Church Missionary and Zenana Societies were 'rather a responsibility for an unfortunate consul. I cannot but think that more advance would be made by a smaller number, and that such an army is more calculated to excite opposi-

tion than to win converts'.[86] In 1895 there were terrible doings
in the undistinguished city of Kutien. The events there were rather
too much for Mansfield, the officiating consul, whose reputation
cannot have been enhanced. In January, shortly after taking over,
he dismissed as sensational and exaggerated the warnings received
from Stewart, a Kutien missionary, about the rising influence of a
local vegetarian sect or secret society. By April he was warning the
viceroy that the sect though not anti-Christian was anti-dynastic,
but the viceroy took no action against it. In August the sect murdered Stewart and British women and children at Kutien. Mansfield
was instructed to proceed there, to hold an inquiry, and to insist on
the summary execution of the principals, but was told not to take
with him the armed naval escort whose impressive presence would
in his view have had a lastingly beneficial effect. He telegraphed
back to ask whether all the hundred odd assailants were principals,
and received the tetchy reply that a barbarous holocaust was not
wanted. The Chinese told him that all present at the massacre were
liable to the death penalty, asked how many heads the British
demanded, and became progressively less ready to take the heads
off. Mansfield, representing the future danger of not inflicting
exemplary punishment, advocated a visit to the viceroy by the
British admiral and a hint of direct action; 'our position is becoming intolerable, long-suffering as we have learned to be, and
unless our government is able bring about some radical change, the
outlook for the future is indeed a gloomy one'. O'Conor minuted
with displeasure that all this was out of place and that what was
wanted was a statement of the circumstances of the case. In the end
Mansfield secured the execution by instalments of twenty-odd
assailants. To avoid being hoodwinked by the substitution of innocent men for the guilty he had reluctantly decided to be present
at the examination of the accused under torture, insisting however
that the torture should not be excessive; 'the Chinese authorities
thoroughly understand that we do not approve of torture but that
we were determined to see justice done and therefore interfered as
little as possible with their procedure'. O'Conor informed the
Foreign Office of this semi-officially, commenting that had he been
in Mansfield's place he would not have reported what he had done
and that Mansfield would have been better advised not to consent
to torture under any circumstances and had been told not to do so
again.[87] If any China consular officer was subsequently present at

an examination under torture he said nothing about it.

Consular relations with the Foochow authorities in the later 1890s were not ideal, Carles complaining of discourtesy and trickery, and E.D.H. Fraser of systematic procrastination and obstruction. During the Boxer troubles relations were however model. Chinese officials were determined to prevent disorder at any cost and Playfair, who trusted them, was most tactful. There was in consequence no disturbance of any sort.[88] Considering how much missionary trouble there had been this was a notable achievement.

Ningpo's foreign ruffianism took a little time to die out after the Taiping turmoil,[89] but after that the port was extremely quiet, and peace was troubled chiefly by occasional missionary aberrations. Following one of these in 1875 R.J. Forrest, while recognizing that the peaceful and quiet efforts of many excellent clergymen of various denominations did a vast amount of good, called for some check on the China Inland Mission's utter want of discretion. Wade told the Foreign Office that the mission drove him almost to despair; though thoroughly earnest and most self-denying in things temporal it was always in scrapes. At the Foreign Office Tenterden suggested that Wade should be authorized to warn the mission that indiscretions could not be countenanced and that unless the missionaries conducted themselves with better judgement their passports for travel in the interior would be withdrawn. The minute by the Foreign Secretary, Derby, showed how carefully politicians were having to tread in missionary matters. He quite agreed with Tenterden, but instructed him to word the warning civilly; 'it is just the sort of case to get discussed and the papers may be called for one day'.[90] The port's foreign trade simply expired, and by the end of the century its shipping was practically confined to one Chinese and one British steamer.[91] There was less and less for the consul to do. In the 1880s and 1890s it was not unusual for the consulate to receive from the Legation only one despatch, or perhaps not even that, in twelve months,[92] and in 1890 H.A. Giles, busy on his *magnum opus*, the first adequate Chinese–English dictionary, sent the Legation nothing but four routine returns and the mandatory annual trade report.[93] Relations with the Chinese authorities and the local people were almost uniformly good.[94] In the 1890s Playfair, who said the local officials were beyond all praise, invited the provincial commander-in-chief and the intendant to the consulate's

Christmas Eve children's party, complete with Christmas tree, and his guests 'seemed highly interested and pleased; the idea of taking so much trouble to entertain children appeared to them novel and admirable'.[95]

Though Ningpo was a dull post officially, and though malaria and dysentery were too common for it to be a healthy one,[a] it ceased to be an uncomfortable one after the dreadful old consulate had been replaced by a commodious and handsome brick house, with arcaded verandas running right round both stories and with a fine garden running down to the river.[a] Indeed, the weekend routine followed in the early 1880s by C.F.R. Allen and his wife suggests an agreeable existence. Accompanied by cook and house-boy they went aboard their houseboat nearly every Saturday evening unless the weather was unduly wet or cold. Through the night hired boatmen rowed the houseboat up canals or with the aid of ropes and capstans got it over the numerous sloping stone or brick em-bankments which were the local versions of canal locks. The Allens slept in spite of noise and bumping and woke the next morning to find the houseboat moored on the edge of the neighbouring hill country. Sundays were spent walking over the hills, collecting flowers and ferns, and enjoying the firs, bamboos, and running streams which contrasted so pleasantly with the stagnant ponds and paddy-fields of the plain. On Sunday evening they went on board again and were taken back to Ningpo. At times Allen varied the routine by a day's shooting in the hills, usually returning with a bag of pheasant, wild duck, teal, and snipe.[a] The bag made a useful change of diet, for the Allens had given up buying meat locally after discovering that cattle for foreigners' consumption were slaughtered in the same slaughterhouses as diseased buffaloes and donkeys, and that 'by the side of the joints intended for our eating were caldrons, in which offal and putrid meat were boiled down for grease'.[96] Instead, the daily steamers from Shanghai brought them down Australian corned beef and north China mutton.[a]

Shanghai dominated China's import and export trade, it was a major shipping port, it became a manufacturing centre, and most leading treaty port businessmen lived there. The interna-tional settlement, whose area was greatly extended in 1899, held a quarter of a million Chinese even before the extension.[97] Its foreign community enjoyed piped water, gas, electric street-lighting, and macadamized roads, and in 1877 supported over thirty foreign

prostitutes.[98] The staff of the consulate, which included specialist shipping and land registries, was much larger than that of any other consulate in China. Some of its work was unusually disagreeable. Spence said in 1880 that in the shipping office there were always between thirty and sixty seamen loafing about or brawling in the passage or offices, and that he had had time and again to defend himself from drunken assaults and had been at risk of injury.[99] Much worse was the duty not infrequently falling on the consul, in his capacity of sheriff, of attending the execution of British subjects condemned to death by the Supreme Court. Medhurst witnessed an execution at 5.30 one morning in 1869, charging in his accounts the cost of erecting and dismantling the gallows, of a coffin, of extra food and beer for forty-four days for the prisoner, and of a cash bonus and suit of clothes for the executioner.[100] In 1871 Markham, the acting consul, formally reported to Wade that he had witnessed the execution of a prisoner the death sentence on whom Wade had felt reluctantly obliged to confirm. In a private letter to Wade Markham said that on being informed that the sentence had been confirmed and the execution date fixed the prisoner had replied he deserved it and did not wish to live a day longer, and that he had gone through the ordeal most admirably, with a prayer on his lips as the bolt was drawn.[101] Few candidates sitting the entrance examination can have visualized that examination success might involve such duties. In general the consulate's work centred round the complexities and disputes of Shanghai's business life, on the management of the international settlement and of its Chinese population by the elected representatives of the predominantly British oligarchy, and on relations with other treaty power consuls. Either the consulate had less to do with Chinese officials and missionaries than other consulates or it reported about them less, and during the long interval between the Taipings and the Boxers it was for the most part surprisingly remote from outside political developments. Medhurst wrote from Shanghai in 1876 that he could provide only meagre political information from a centre which was essentially commercial.[102]

Although no increased expenditure was in question the Foreign Office turned an obstinately deaf ear to repeated pleas, made from the consulate and backed by the Legation, that the post should be raised to a consulate-general, so as to put incumbents on an equal footing with foreign colleagues whose posts had been so raised and

to give them due standing with naval officers and Chinese authorities. Parkes complained that in spite of his KCB he had as a mere consul to wait on every post-captain who entered the port. The Foreign Office, on receiving Winchester's plea, thought that the higher rank, which would upset D.B. Robertson and Medhurst, was unnecessary, as 'no one who knows anything of Mr. Winchester will believe him likely to play second fiddle in any case'. They disingenuously replied that his proceedings were so satisfactory, and the respect and esteem of all classes in Shanghai so well deserved, that they had no desire to alter his position. Medhurst's plea, made at a time when Wade described Shanghai as swarming with consuls-general, raised Foreign Office fears that the higher rank would enable a man who favoured a gun-boat policy to thwart Wade's pacific intentions. A first plea by P.J. Hughes, the next incumbent, was likewise unsuccessful. He tried again on the Belgian consulate being raised to a consulate-general. It took Wade in his retirement a year to summon up the energy to express agreement with Hughes, and in 1884 the Foreign Office at last conceded the point.[103]

A Foreign Office aberration followed. In 1877 Currie, then a rising senior clerk, had suggested that to save money the office of consul at Shanghai should be amalgamated with that of chief judge. Pauncefote was then the legal assistant under-secretary. When attorney-general at Hong Kong at a humbler stage of his career he had himself unsuccessfully applied to become chief judge,[104] something which Currie is unlikely to have known, and he objected forcefully. Tenterden as permanent under-secretary supported him and the matter was dropped.[105] In 1890, however, Tenterden was dead, Pauncefote was in Washington, and Currie was permanent under-secretary. Currie reopened the matter and avoided more inconvenient legal objections by keeping the papers away from Davidson, the Foreign Office legal adviser. Davidson, a man of forthright minutes, testily recorded fifteen years later that the very unfortunate step of amalgamation had been taken without his knowledge and had been contrary to everything he had written before or since. Unhampered by adverse legal advice and brushing aside the chief judge's views in China Currie pushed through the appointment of Hannen, an assistant Supreme Court judge, to the amalgamated post in 1891. He regretted that money had been wasted for years by failure to amalgamate earlier; he looked

forward to a day when a legally trained consul could be appointed
to the amalgamated post; what was needed was 'to promote British
trade and administer consular jurisdiction, not to set up caricatures
of British courts of law'. As should have been foreseen the amalgamation did not work. Everyone except the Treasury disliked it, and
in 1893 Hannen himself said that reversion to the old system would
please everybody. In 1896 B. Brenan did not mince matters in his
report on British trade in China; the two offices obviously needed
to be separated, for a consul-general must to some extent be partisan
and proceed in a way unbecoming in an officer holding high judicial
office; in practice the consul-general now performed the functions
of chief judge and his subordinate consul those of consul-general;
the usefulness of both would be increased if the *de jure* position
were made to correspond with the *de facto* position. MacDonald
endorsed Brenan's views, Currie was safely out of the way in
Constantinople, and the posts were separated again.[106]

On Parkes' promotion from consul at Shanghai to minister
to Japan he was succeeded at Shanghai by Winchester in 1865.
Winchester had been transferred from China to a consulate in Japan
and had given the Foreign Office satisfaction while temporarily
chargé d'affaires there, and during the interregnum at Peking
between Bruce and Alcock they rewarded him with the Shanghai
appointment. Alcock later said he would have preferred the
appointment of Medhurst.[107] Medhurst himself was so aggrieved
at not being appointed that he applied to retire on a pension, an
application which the Foreign Office countered by stating that his
resignation would be regretted but that they would have to inform
the Treasury that he had resigned without adequate motives, in
other words, that he would get no pension.[108] It was as well for
Medhurst that his application was rejected, and that he did not
pursue his alternative idea of cutting the service altogether and
becoming Protector of Chinese in the Netherlands East Indies.[109]
Only three years later he became officiating consul on Winchester's
departure on home leave, and he became substantive consul when
Winchester failed to return. Winchester was firm and tactful in
dealing with the international settlement's restive municipal council
and with the Chinese authorities, but his health was poor. He had
once been described as small and perky,[a] now he was small and
portly.[110] Alcock's answer to a Foreign Office query about the cost
of punkah coolies at Shanghai was that during the summer heat a

punkah might well be a necessity for 'a man of such full habit of body'. Winchester's eyesight was failing, he lost his wife in 1867, and he decided to go.[111] His colleagues had considered him a wide-awake man and were surprised to hear that the widower had engaged himself at home to an enormous and reputedly well-to-do widow who turned out not to have a farthing, to be heavily in debt, and to be on intimate terms with someone else, and that he had had to pay hundreds of pounds to avoid a breach of promise action.[a]

Winchester's incumbency was marred by a scandal at the consulate. At the beginning of 1866 he described the senior assistant, C.T. Jones, as zealous, obliging, faithful, and skilful, in the middle of the year he reported irregularities in Jones' accounts, and by the end of the year his investigations showed that Jones had for years been misappropriating fees and other moneys passing through his hands.[112] The current system of accounting for fees was grossly unsatisfactory. Fees, said a report made that year, were usually collected by assistants who at some ports used them at once for private purposes, the amounts being subsequently charged against their salaries, and the fee chest was usually looked upon as a convenience in which money might be represented either by memoranda or by cash. Fee stamps, affixed and cancelled when a fee was paid, were not introduced until 1885. The wonder is that more people were not tempted.[113] The Foreign Office dismissed Jones and on their instructions he was tried at Shanghai for embezzlement. The jury failed to agree, one of its members standing out against conviction. Winchester termed this a palpable miscarriage of justice. The Foreign Office called for a retrial, but Alcock accepted the chief judge's view, with which Winchester agreed, that as no Shanghai jury would convict a further prosecution was inexpedient, and a *nolle prosequi* was entered. Bankruptcy proceedings were equally unsatisfactory. The court required Jones to set aside a third of his future earnings or income, or subsequently acquired property, to discharge his debts, but the next year he refused to produce his accounts, and an execution on his property recovered only a small sum. This involuntary repayment was the only one he ever made against defalcations amounting to $8,650. He brazenly remained in Shanghai until he left for England in 1871. On his mother's death in 1897, when he was in Australia, he succeeded to a considerable sum, but his interest in it had been assigned to others in 1863, so that the creditors under the bankruptcy order were excluded from

any benefit. The upshot was thus that Jones escaped unpunished and without making restitution. The Foreign Office had been warned by Wade in 1863 that Jones had at one time always been in debt and that there was talk in Shanghai about his speculations, but they seem to have ignored the warning. Their own inaction did not now stop them from casting severe blame on Markham, who had been temporarily in charge at one time, on Parkes, and on Winchester for inadequate supervision. They were particularly and justifiably incensed by Jones' statement that the financial difficulties leading to his embezzlement had been caused by his ownership of a Shanghai newspaper, and they professed inability to understand how this speculative activity, certainly one of the most objectionable in which a consular officer could indulge, could have been a matter of common notoriety in Shanghai without being reported to them. They announced that if Jones' assets were insufficient to cover his defalcations the peccant consuls would have to make the amount good in the proportions for which they were respectively responsible. This threat hung over Markham, Parkes, and Winchester for eighteen months, until the Treasury, advised by a kindly official solicitor who felt unable to report affirmatively that any of the three were liable to make the defalcations good from their private means, decided that they need not do so.[114]

Medhurst was not one of those in whose eyes the foreigner was always right and the Chinese always wrong. In 1876 he ascribed increasing anti-foreign manifestations in the countryside partly to a foreign tendency 'to forget that the natives possess feelings and rights which need to be respected'.[115] He always had, however, a sovereign contempt for Chinese officials, and in dealing with them preferred a bludgeon to a rapier. He was not capable of the sensitivity shown by C. Alabaster when temporarily in charge in 1872 during Medhurst's absence. A magistrate had been ordered by his superiors to call on Alabaster and apologize for mishandling a case. Not wishing to humiliate further a man whom he had known for years and for whose energy and ability he had considerable respect, Alabaster called first and asked that the matter should be forgotten and that they should remain good friends. The magistrate insisted on calling to apologize, but relations reverted to their former most friendly footing and Wade congratulated Alabaster on his behaviour.[116] Alabaster was unpredictable. In another mood he called Chinese officials clever and somewhat ill-conditioned chil-

dren, who should be treated as gently as possible and without anger but whose shrieks and yells should be utterly disregarded.[117] In his better moods he was much superior to Medhurst, who at Shanghai continued his reliance on a somewhat brutal forcefulness. Winchester had hardly gone before a mob attacked members of the China Inland Mission at a town near Chinkiang and sacked their house. Medhurst, who was concurrently in charge of Chinkiang, promptly proceeded up river and, supported by a British warship, threatened to take over pending the completion of negotiations a fine new steamer belonging to the Nanking viceroy. The viceroy caved in, a prefect and a magistrate were dismissed, and the missionaries were restored to their house. The Foreign Office were highly critical. They considered that once the immediate emergency had passed and the missionaries' safety had been ensured redress should have been sought from the central government instead of naval assistance being invoked to bring pressure to bear on the provincial authorities; consuls and naval officers could not be left to decide what redress was due or whether it should be obtained by coercion. Alcock, who had fully supported Medhurst, was so impenitent that he suggested Medhurst should have the Order of the Bath, which was naturally not forthcoming.[118] In 1874 Medhurst was uncharacteristically restrained and was still not right. There was a serious riot in the French concession at Shanghai. Medhurst was against calling out the international settlement volunteers to disperse the mob and favoured offensive action only if the international settlement were threatened. He was outvoted in the consular body and the volunteers, apparently accompanied by Medhurst and the other consuls, marched to the scene of the riot, where they fortunately found that the rioters had already dispersed. Wade disclaimed any wish to censure Medhurst but told him that dispersion of riots, which always compromised the safety of the whole community, was a foremost obligation, and that risk was not increased but greatly diminished by promptly manifesting an intention to stop such outrages. The Foreign Office approved Wade's views. In 1875 braves (the foreigners' name for soldiers, who customarily wore a chest badge bearing the character for 'brave') caused a disturbance at the Chinkiang consulate. Medhurst, again backed by a warship, once more went up river and, as the Chinkiang intendant trifled with him, went on to Nanking. This time he had received from Wade instructions that force was not to

be used or threatened and that the warship's function was merely to give weight to his mission. The acting viceroy, who may well have interpreted the appearance of a warship somewhat differently, took prompt action against the ringleaders, but Medhurst had regretfully to report that although he had satisfied himself that they really had been flogged, the flogging had been administered in a yamen and not, as he had tried to ensure, at the consulate gates.[119] This was his last major clash with the Chinese authorities. He retired in 1877 with a knighthood and a service of plate from Shanghai's foreign community. In retirement he was used at Alcock's instance to organize Chinese immigration into Borneo, which he did not do well, he failed in an attempt to recruit Chinese porters for Stanley in the Congo, and in keeping with his choleric temperament he died on a Boxing Day of apoplexy.[120]

Hughes and Hannen, grey figures compared with their colourful predecessors, headed the Shanghai consulate for the best part of the next twenty years. G. Jamieson replaced Hannen as consul-general in 1897. The contemporary Foreign Office regarded him as exceptionally able and zealous, but to modern eyes he seems a short-sighted imperialist, whole-heartedly backing British commercial interests without much regard to the longer-term implications of doing so.[121] He went on home leave, B. Brenan taking acting charge, and in 1899 unexpectedly retired on health grounds, to devote himself profitably to British mining and commercial interests in China. Brenan then received the substantive appointment. He was a fierce, energetic, and most intelligent official who commended himself to the treaty port mentality by prowess as a horseman and athlete.[122] His career had hitherto been uniformly and deservedly successful, but fortune was about to desert him and to smile instead on P.L. Warren. Brenan stayed at Shanghai until the substantive appointment was safely in his pocket, a customary precaution, and then after being out in China for nine years went on leave in May 1899.[123] In his absence Warren was brought down from Hankow to officiate. Accordingly it was Warren and not Brenan who was in charge when in 1900 Shanghai briefly became a post of extreme political importance. During the first half of June the Boxer threat to the Peking legations became acute. In a momentous telegram to the Foreign Office Warren on 14 June expressed his conviction that if assured of British backing the powerful Hankow and Nanking viceroys would do their utmost to preserve

peace in their districts and that an early understanding with them was essential. Salisbury, the Foreign Secretary, immediately telegraphed a message for them. With the assistance of E.D.H. Fraser at Hankow and Sundius at Nanking, Warren reached an understanding with the viceroys that so long as they preserved peace there would be no armed foreign intervention in their districts. Throughout most of China this invaluable understanding, with which other viceroys and governors associated themselves, saved foreigners from murder and Chinese from the ravages of foreign troops bent on revenge and loot. Until the legations were relieved and communications with the British Legation were restored in September the Foreign Office treated Warren virtually as a temporary minister, and made sure that Tower, the incoming secretary of Legation who inopportunely reached Shanghai, did not get in his way.[124] Salisbury thought Warren insufficiently cool,[125] but a fairer comment came from a Foreign Office official years later, when Warren was retiring under something of a cloud[126] after mismanaging an item of business: 'It was a very difficult time and he never lost his head'.[127] After the Legation had started functioning again Warren remained in *de facto* charge of Shanghai. The hapless Brenan, returning to his post, was instructed before leaving England to efface himself on arrival or to take a holiday in Japan. Brenan praised the great delicacy with which Warren behaved in such an awkward situation but could not stand the humiliating position in which through no fault of his own he found himself. A medical certificate spoke of the failure of his nervous system. He decided to retire, feeling increasingly that 'I not only have lost interest in my work but that it is positively distasteful to me. It is not laziness — it is a sort of nervous irritation which makes me hate the sight of any intruders in my office or of a business letter'. He left China resenting the local belief that he was not much thought of and that retirement had been forced on him. He vainly asked for the KCMG which Warren soon obtained.[128] In retirement he participated profitably, like G. Jamieson, in British commercial interests in China, interested himself in Sino-British cultural relations,[129] and in a large and cheerless Kensington house filled with Chinese porcelain terrified young relatives by his severe grandeur.[a]

NEW CONSULATES SOUTH
OF THE YANGTZE

THE second peace settlement provided for two more treaty ports in
Kwangtung: Chaochow, up river from Swatow, and Kiungchow on
the island of Hainan.

The Swatow area was exceptionally lawless, clan fights abound-
ing in turbulent villages over which official control was nominal. It
had been the illicit resort of foreign ships trafficking in opium and
kidnapped coolies, and the population was extremely hostile to
foreigners. Chaochow was 35 miles inland up a fast, broad, shallow
river.[1] Its people had no wish whatever for a treaty port. On arrival
in 1860 Caine's immediate objective was therefore to establish
himself at Swatow rather than at Chaochow, although even in 1898
the former could still be described as a small village with no
resident official of standing.[2] Caine started by settling temporarily
on Double Island, which was 5 miles nearer to the open sea than
Swatow and where a few other foreigners were living. Almost at
once a foreigner's house was attacked at night, an engineer off a
British warship was murdered on leaving a brothel on the island,
major or minor attacks were made on foreigners landing at
Swatow, and Caine asked for rifles and cutlasses. It was nine
months before he dared land at Swatow to call on a visiting Chinese
official, and three years before he dared move the consulate to the
side of the harbour opposite Swatow.[3] For the defence of the
consulate he obtained from Hong Kong a 12-pound howitzer with
ammunition and relied on the constable, an ex-artillery man, to
train the consulate gigmen in its use. He explained that this was
a deterrent which he did not expect to use, and Wade, though
enjoining every precaution against accident, gave his approval.[4]
There were two makeshift and insecure cells in the basement of the
consulate, and Caine and his family found it disagreeable to have

prisoners shouting, screaming, and trying to break out at all hours of the day and night.[5] His attempts to lease an area of land for British occupation, in other words to establish a concession, were fruitless.[6]

On Caine's first attempt to reach Chaochow an immense stone, dropped from a bridge just outside the city, went through the deck and bottom of one of the boats provided by the intendant for the journey, and he took the hint and turned back. After five years he did get there, but the visit was not a success. The intendant received him most courteously but very early the next day, fearing or pretending to fear trouble, asked him to leave and provided an escort which saw him safely back to his boat through a hostile and very dense mob. Cooper, in acting charge during Caine's home leave, managed to stay in the city for ten days, well protected by Chinese guards, but was asked not to press to reside there immediately. He sensibly suggested to the Legation that as a location for the consulate Swatow, which had a large steamer traffic and a resident foreign community of ninety, half of them British, was preferable to Chaochow, which had no attractions for British merchants, and which indeed in unfavourable conditions was a wearisome twenty-four hours away.[7] The Legation were however determined that Chaochow should be opened in accordance with the treaty provision.[8] Before Caine, back from leave, handed over to C. Alabaster in 1868 some sort of consular quarters had been obtained in the city and Caine considered that no trouble from the locals was now to be feared. Alabaster lost no time in paying a visit. He encountered no trouble, and for the first time spent twenty-four hours in a Chinese city without being called a devil, but he greatly doubted whether foreign residence was safe or desirable in a city where the mandarins exercised no real authority, generally lived in fear and trembling, and trusted to intrigue rather than force to carry out their ordinances. He was apprehensive that an irascible foreigner getting into a dispute might be murdered. Coming from so forceful a man as Alabaster this was strong advice, but Alcock's view was that failure to achieve the opening of the port after so many years might be interpreted as weakness. In accordance with Alcock's instructions Alabaster declared Chaochow open to British residence and trade and informed the intendant that either the consul or an assistant would reside there permanently. The Foreign Office promptly decided that no separate consular

establishment was needed at Chaochow and that periodic visits by the Swatow consul would meet all needs. The point of principle had been carried, and virtually nothing more was heard of Chaochow as a treaty port. Premises there were retained as lodgings for the consuls when calling on intendants at least up to 1911, but the consulate remained firmly at Swatow.[9]

Initially local lawlessness seems to have induced in the consulate and British navy a readiness to resort to force. Within a month of the establishment of the consulate on Double Island Alabaster, then the consulate interpreter, accompanied a naval vessel to a village where a kidnapped French missionary had been held to ransom. A Chinese official was supposed to have been present but went off elsewhere, the village was nevertheless bombarded, and a large landing party fired some houses, released some prisoners, recovered the ransom, and handed over four pirates to the Chinese authorities. The next year three naval vessels, accompanied by Cooper, attacked another pirate village at the request of the Chinese authorities, burned it, and killed well over a hundred pirates. Bruce approved the first action but reacted to the second with instructions that attacks on villages at the instance of the Chinese authorities were to be avoided. Twice in 1867 Cooper called in the navy. Determined to show that the British were not involved in the profitable business of kidnapping coolies, who were fetching $100 a head in Macao, he got the navy to seize a Chinese boat as it left the port limits. Twenty-four kidnapped coolies were released, but in reporting his action Cooper said that since he was aware that he had exceeded his province he could hardly hope for unqualified approval. The Foreign Office advised the Admiralty to leave action against suspect Chinese vessels to the Chinese, a course which they must have known meant giving kidnappers a free hand, but at least they did not reprimand Cooper. His next request to the navy was also in a good cause and also dubious. A village normally engaged in blackmailing sugar exporters had carried off a retired Singapore merchant formerly registered at the consulate as a British subject. The Chinese authorities were trying to deal with the matter and Cooper asked that a gunboat should second their efforts by anchoring near the village for a day or two. The villagers defied the gunboat and proclaimed their readiness to fight, their guns were silenced by a few shots, and the merchant, emaciated to a degree after four months of systematic starvation, was rescued.[10] Cooper

attributed to his activity against pirates and kidnappers an attack on his house. In the summer of 1867 Mrs Cooper had given birth to a son in the terror occasioned by a very violent typhoon which made the whole house shake. One midnight in December, when she had not fully recovered, some twenty armed men with flaming torches used a bag of gunpowder to blow open one of the house doors. There was no one in the house except the Coopers, their two children, and two amahs (nurses). Cooper met them at the door of the bedroom, struck aside the spears aimed at him, and fired at the two foremost men. He hit them and the attack was abandoned, but Mrs Cooper, who as a child in India had been terrified by Indian nurses' stories of thugs, was in a state of nervous prostration and on medical advice was sent home. Cooper's father wrote to the Foreign Office that such cool courage and indomitable pluck had been worthy of the Victoria Cross, but Cooper himself seems to have reported the affair to the Legation only when asked months later why his wife had had to return to England.[11]

No sooner had Alabaster taken over as acting consul than a rapid succession of forceful actions met with a mixed reception even from so vigorous a minister as Alcock and with unmixed Foreign Office disapproval. The navy rejected his application for action against a semi-piratical village where the Chinese employees of a British subject had been robbed and he was told by Alcock that such naval expeditions inland were too hazardous. Difficulties having arisen over a missionary lease in a nearby city Alabaster pulled up in his gig, saw the magistrate, and persuaded him to issue a proclamation. The two men went to the spot and posted it, a tremendous, very dense, and somewhat threatening mob assembled, and only with difficulty could the magistrate get back to his yamen with Alabaster, who believed he might have been torn to pieces but for the magistrate's admirable conduct. The next day, however, the elders gave an assurance that there would be no more trouble and the missionaries were left in quiet possession. Alcock, though warning Alabaster against hazardous personal interventions in the interior, congratulated him on the courage and firmness which had brought success, but a Foreign Office minute said that great discretion and forbearance were needed at Swatow and that unless Alabaster could be induced to moderate his zeal and propensity to violence the sooner he was removed the better.[12] Worse was to come. Without provocation villagers attacked the crew of HMS

Cockchafer up river from Swatow and seriously injured several men. Alabaster asked the admiral to send a force large enough to obtain satisfaction without bloodshed. At the same time D.B. Robertson at Canton asked the viceroy to depute officers to arrest the ringleaders and to co-operate with a naval force from Hong Kong, to which the viceroy agreed. Without waiting for any Chinese official to arrive Commodore Jones went into action and destroyed three villages with considerable loss of life. At Jones' request Alabaster accompanied him, his later defence for having done so being that in his subordinate position he could not have withheld co-operation from a punitive expedition which he had been told had been agreed between admiral and viceroy. Robertson had no answer to the viceroy's complaints and was much embarrassed. Writing privately to Hammond he condemned the navy for burning, killing, and destroying as though they had been in an enemy country and deplored the apparent lack of British good faith. Before Foreign Office reactions to this naval escapade reached China Alabaster made more trouble for himself by reporting that he had been up to Chaochow in his gig, unarmed and unescorted, had passed the villages without disturbance, had done business with the intendant, had walked unattended through the city with far greater comfort than a Chinese could have done in Regent Street, and had returned safely from a trip which local foreign opinion had thought risky but which had demonstrated that Chaochow was now truly open. Alcock accepted Alabaster's reasons for accompanying Jones and told the Foreign Office that Alabaster was to be congratulated on the success of his Chaochow trip, though Alcock would not himself have proceeded in that way.[13]

In due course comprehensive Foreign Office disapproval of his conduct reached Alabaster. He was blamed for letting *Cockchafer* get herself into trouble; the collision with the villagers might have been anticipated by the commonest foresight and Alabaster should have remonstrated with her commander, for 'it is one of the essential duties of H.M. consular officers to discountenance and discourage any measures, on the part whether of private individuals or of H.M.'s naval forces, calculated to lead to a breach of the peace'. He was blamed for not distancing himself from Jones; 'if a naval officer thinks it his duty to have recourse to such measures he must be allowed to do so on his own responsibility, but a consul should not, except in great extremity, make himself party to such

measures. His duty is to moderate, not to sanction violence'. His application to the navy about redress for the robbery had been entirely improper and had shown great lack of judgement. The visit to Chaochow had been wrong too.[14]

Alabaster represented that such stinging rebukes were undeserved; he was living among semi-savages in dealing with whom a moment's hesitation or fear broke the charm, he had been trying to do his duty, and as actions to which in Swatow he saw no alternative met with disapproval he asked for transfer to a more settled post, such as Shanghai, or for home leave. In forwarding Alabaster's representations Alcock drew attention to the exceptional difficulties and dangers at Swatow, where the authorities were totally incapable of maintaining order among China's most lawless and turbulent population; it would be fatal if profoundly discouraged consuls made no effort to avert calamity; sudden dangers and emergencies had to be met; any other principle would lead to discreditable pusillanimity, more dangerous than occasional errors of judgement or even excess of zeal; considering how few people liked responsibility and how unwilling most people were to accept avoidable responsibility he could not help feeling that the danger in China lay more in the direction of inactivity. Neither this powerful statement of Alcock's philosophy nor Alabaster's representations moved the Foreign Office, where minutes referring to 'such an injudicious, hotheaded public servant as Mr. Alabaster' concluded that 'Mr. Alabaster's explanation does not remove unfavourable impressions of his proceedings'. The sequel to so much Foreign Office condemnation of Alabaster seems wholly inexplicable. Less than three weeks after sending his previous despatch Alcock sent another recommending that Alabaster, whose substantive rank was still that of interpreter, should be promoted to vice-consul at Shanghai, and the Foreign Office acted accordingly. In another sequel the following year Cooper demonstrated that the Chaochow visit had not been unduly rash by repeating it, enjoying an exceedingly pleasant social lunch with the intendant, and strolling about the town for some days without meeting annoyance.[15]

Suddenly everything changed at Swatow. The viceroy appointed a general, Fang Yao, to pacify the area. R.J. Forrest, who took charge of the consulate in 1872, considered that the British naval action in the *Cockchafer* affair had pointed the way to this initiative by showing how easily a robbers' nest could be subdued and

had therefore been a major blessing to China. The Foreign Office allowed this opinion, so contrary to their own view of the affair, to be published in Forrest's trade report, and were later told by Wade that the naval action had undoubtedly been beneficial in the immediate vicinity. Whether or not the British action had anything to do with his appointment General Fang, in appearance a mild-mannered little man, was ruthlessly effective. One of his alleged techniques was to surround a village at night and to slaughter all the inhabitants, and he himself acknowledged that he had struck off many thousand heads. He worked so fast that, according to the consulate, foreigners could by 1872 visit anywhere within three days' journey of Swatow as safely as they could visit places round Shanghai, and by 1887 it was said that travellers anywhere in the consular district would rarely meet with anything but a friendly reception.[16] The results achieved were so welcome that there was little consular disposition to cavil at Fang's methods. In 1876 Watters, in acting charge at Swatow, did object to Fang's execution of a coolie broker whom Watters believed to have been falsely accused of kidnapping. Watters asked D.B. Robertson to make representations to the Canton viceroy about Fang's military despotism. Robertson would have none of it. Fang, he replied to Watters, had doubtless not restored order 'without an expenditure of life, such as in western countries would be denounced as butchery', but his methods of suppressing wholesale murder and robbery among a population which was half-civilized and wholly savage in disposition must not be too closely criticized; without his iron rule the people could not be restrained; perhaps the broker had been unjustly beheaded, but Fang certainly knew perfectly well what went on in the coolie business; as Chinese officials went Fang was courteous, and Watters would not find him unreasonably deaf to representations that emigration beneficial to the Chinese state and to individual Chinese might be injured by too great a severity. Wade, while not doubting that Fang was chargeable with acts of most ruthless barbarity, agreed with Robertson, and added that a British complaint against an official to his superiors was too commonly the best service that could be rendered to the official. Consular respect for Fang's work continued to the end. When he died in 1891 the consul of the day, Frater, feared that unless he had an energetic successor turbulence would probably reappear, and the fear was justified. In 1897 Mansfield considered that action as

vigorous as Fang's had been was needed to deal with a revival of clan fights, and in 1898 Goffe said that after a drought the whole area had been very disturbed for months and that Swatow itself had been at the mercy of armed thieves.[17]

Thanks to Fang consular life at Swatow had by the early 1870s become pleasant. The consulate was a fine building with a magnificent garden,[a] Double Island was an agreeable weekend resort, much cricket was played, in the brief cold weather geese, duck, and teal were plentiful, and there was a community of about 140 residents, some 50 of whom were British and some 70 German or American. Forrest can be glimpsed off duty in the recollections of a Customs commissioner published half a century later. He detested clambering into uniform for naval visits, and the community enjoyed tricking him into uniform one April Fool's day by a concerted report of an admiral's imminent arrival. The description of him as an excellent shot in spite of trembling hands due to many years in China failed to mention that this apparently elderly gentleman was about 40 years old. If Forrest was like the rest of the community he had a substantial meal at noon, dined late in a white mess-jacket, lived largely off tinned food, and drank beer, sherry, or claret and soda with meals and whisky soda after them.[18]

Swatow's increasing trade was in Chinese hands.[19] The predominant foreign interest lay in shipping abroad hundreds of thousands of voluntary emigrants driven overseas by the pressure of over-population. Emigration relieved the district of surplus mouths and benefited it by the resulting remittances from overseas, and was so important to receiving territories that in 1889 the Straits Settlements thanked Frater for great assistance in maintaining the system by which their labour was chiefly supplied.[20] Kidnapping and indenture abuses were fresh in consular memory. For that reason Watters in 1875 refused to encourage British participation in the shipment of coolies to the Dutch in Sumatra. Robertson took the same line at Canton, and both refusals were fully approved by Wade. Similarly Frater refused in 1890 to assist the shipment of coolies to British North Borneo. Squeeze and other impositions on defenceless voluntary emigrants were more difficult to detect and check, but G. Phillips had some success, doubtless ephemeral, against such malpractices in 1883.[21] Any consul, however humane and conscientious, was to some extent torn between two conflicting duties, that of seeing that British ships observed rules against

overcrowding and that of securing a due share of the lucrative carrying trade for British shipping. In 1872 Stronach admitted that in order to allow British ships some share in the traffic to Singapore the consulate had for years been permitting breaches of the Chinese Passenger Ships Act and that in continuing this inherited practice he had been acting indefensibly. In 1874 Forrest exploded in an indignant memorandum. British ships, he said, were never used if it was possible to find others, which were virtually under no restraint and packed their coolies like herrings in a barrel; the excellent United States law was not enforced; the German regulations were enforced by a merchant vice-consul who was junior partner of the man conducting most of the passenger traffic and doubling as consul for Norway and Denmark, neither of which countries had any regulations; the Customs allowed the grossest overcrowding and neglected the need for boats and life-saving gear; and Singapore permitted disgracefully overcrowded ships to bring returning emigrants back from the Straits. In 1877 it was still his opinion that hardly a single non-British ship sailed without carrying substantially more than the permitted number, and he knew that in spite of all the consulate's precautions British ships were not always innocent. In 1880 the usually inert Gregory in a rare spasm of activity asked the Straits Settlements to prevent clandestine overloading by checking vessels on arrival. In 1885 Phillips complained that the less onerous requirements applicable to German ships placed British ones at a disadvantage.[22] The cessation thereafter of this flow of criticism perhaps implies improvement. Phillips also complained that those without personal experience could not conceive how nauseating an emigration officer's duties were, that after boarding vessels he had often found on his clothes the most disgusting vermin (doubtless lice), and that his assistant G. Brown had been at great risk from the cholera which had recently been raging among the ships in port. Brown, who while doing the same work at Amoy had described it as neither light nor pleasant, spent almost all his time on emigration at Swatow, and the constable, a trustworthy man who spoke the peculiar local dialect, did nothing else.[23]

British subjects of Chinese race gave the consulate less work than at Amoy, but C.M. Ford had one very unsatisfactory experience. A Singapore man registered at the consulate was arrested and flogged by the intendant in 1897 and was released in a piteous condition, hardly able to walk and with a large open wound on the hip. Asked

by MacDonald what reparation should be demanded from the Tsungli Yamen Ford replied that although the intendant had previously been most reasonable and had probably acted through ignorance he should be dismissed and substantial compensation should be paid to the man. The intendant was not dismissed and at the end of the following year Ford gave the same man three months for keeping a gambling house and began to have very grave doubts about his British status. On release from prison the man could not give security for good behaviour, a deportation order was made against him, and he thereupon admitted that he had been born in China and had obtained his Singapore passport by fraud. Whether Ford expressed any regrets to the intendant does not appear.[24]

The consulate's business was as a rule uneventful, said a Swatow quarterly report in 1900. The service took in its stride occurrences which might in other countries have caused a stir, a similar Swatow report in 1898 mentioning only casually that passengers on a ship with cholera on board had had to be allowed to land after they had threatened, if not landed, to kill all the foreigners on board. Nevertheless the post does seem, after General Fang's appointment, to have been a tolerably quiet one. Information of general or political interest could not be obtained in the absence of any resident senior Chinese official. It took so long to travel to those officials with whom the consulate conducted correspondence that personal intercourse was barely possible. In 1887 the nearest of the four district magistrates with whom the consulate dealt came to Swatow not infrequently and then sometimes lunched with the consul, but in 1895 all four magistrates were described as being more or less inaccessible and therefore immune from consular intrusion, and in 1898 a brief initial call on the intendant at Chaochow took Playfair twenty four hours.[25]

Whatever wild dreams of foreign trade may have inspired the demand for Kiungchow to be opened, a more realistic assessment of Kiungchow's potential as a treaty port followed. Bruce did not urge the Chinese to take administrative steps to open the port, and in an 1869 convention which was never ratified and whose provisions accordingly lapsed Alcock negotiated the substitution of Wenchow for Kiungchow. In 1872 the United States minister, urged on by an American merchant, began to press for action and the Chinese established a Customs post there. Wade was mildly in favour of the port's opening, and D.B. Robertson sent B. Brenan from Canton to

make a reconnaissance. Brenan visited Kiungchow itself, a prefectural city 3½ miles from the coast, and the little walled town of
Hoihow which served as its port, and reported adversely; Kiungchow had hardly any shops worth mentioning; Hoihow, which
scarcely deserved the name of port, was accessible to flat-bottomed
sampans for only twelve hours out of the twenty-four; vessels
drawing more than 10 feet could not come in closer than 3 miles
away, and the anchorage was shallow, difficult of approach, and
apparently very dangerous in a gale; and there seemed to be no
suitable consular accommodation at Hoihow, where he correctly
assumed that the consulate would need to be located (although
formally styled the Kiungchow consulate the post was commonly
known as Hoihow). Robertson added equally discouragingly that as
the Chinese controlled only the shore belt of Hainan, the centre of
which was covered by impenetrable forest and peopled by independent savages, trade prospects seemed unpromising. The American
merchant who had been urging the port's opening then committed
suicide and everyone else lost interest for a time. Nothing more was
done until in 1876 Wade sent R.J. Forrest there to act as Robertson's
vice-consul, giving instructions that as the port was on probation no
settlement or concession should be established.[26]

The Chinese first provided Forrest with a single room, which they
would not allow him to extend or alter, in a fort. Then he rented
what alternative accommodation he could. It was excruciatingly
unsuitable even for temporary use but continued to be occupied for
many years (only in 1901 was a purpose-built consulate on a new
site at last achieved). Howard, visiting Hoihow as secretary of
Legation in 1889, marvelled how anyone could be willing to live
in 'such an apartment' for even double pay. It was a former rope
warehouse, 180 feet long and 30 feet broad, comprising 3 small
courts and 3 roofed enclosures, in the third of which an upper floor
or garret had been erected for the consul. This room originally
served as office, dining-room, sitting-room, and reception room,
with a partition, economically deprived of half its due height,
dividing part of it off into a bedroom. Later another partition
was added, and three rooms, 'which most resemble loose boxes',
resulted. The garret was not provided with venetian blinds or
verandas, it was like a drying kiln in hot weather, and in the wet
season its walls streamed. The space below, dark, damp, and
mouldy, was long occupied by the constable as well as by Chinese

servants. The landlord spent on the structure only the minimum necessary to keep it standing, the rotting tiles continually fell in showers of white dust, and the beams were being consumed by white ants and dry rot. To the east the consulate adjoined two Chinese houses occupied by several poor families. They emptied all their dirty water and filth into their courtyard just below a window of the consul's room; the courtyard, which men, women, and children used as an open latrine, served as a piggery with four or five large pigs; and in the summer heat the smell was often unbearable and made eating or sleeping impossible. To the west the consulate adjoined a native inn whose guests often kept up a din day and night, all their noises being distinctly heard in the consul's room through a very thin wall. Such was Her Britannic Majesty's consulate at Hoihow.[27] Frater, posted to Hoihow from leave and not realizing how unsuitable the accommodation was for a married man, arrived there with his wife and consequently had to be transferred elsewhere after six months. E.F. Bennett, a useless malcontent, took his wife there to save money and then constantly lodged complaints which were countered by an Office of Works offer to sanction any small improvements in accommodation which they acknowledged to be 'limited and rather rough'. In 1896 O'Brien-Butler, ordered to Hoihow from Chinkiang, replied, perhaps innocently and perhaps tongue in cheek, that he was just getting married and asked whether it was a suitable post for a wife. The Legation response has not been traced, but he did not escape the posting and the bride went too. As she gave birth to two daughters at Hoihow one can only hope that at this final stage before the new consulate was at last completed something had been done to improve conditions. Otherwise the post was filled by bachelors. All were no doubt reluctant victims. Johnson, receiving with blank dismay orders to return there, protested that having spent five years in that wretched Chinese hovel he thought he had been passed through the fire enough; even though he was unmarried, health at his age (44) should be a consideration; until a proper consulate was built the post would be better filled by a young, strong junior. His appeal had some effect. He did have to go back to Hoihow but was quickly moved on to Kiukiang.[28]

Walsham reported that Hoihow was the unhealthiest post in China and O'Conor that it was perhaps the least desirable one. It was of extremely little use. There was hardly any British trade. In

the mid-1880s, there were twenty-two foreign residents, ten of
them British. There was one German firm and four bogus British
firms, actually Chinese-owned, which were dealing in opium and
were given no support by the consulate. The port was so insignificant that in the 1890s it was left unvisited for nearly three years by
a British warship.[29] Excitements were rare. In 1881 J. Scott was
called out to rescue a Chinese woman who was being maltreated by
a British subject in the Customs named Harrison. At Harrison's
house he found him standing over the woman, who was bound
hand and foot with her person exposed to the thighs. On being
directed to release her Harrison turned in a most violent and
threatening manner on Scott, who seeing that he was mad with
drink and knowing him to be capable of anything in that condition,
retreated for assistance. He returned with another Customs officer.
While the latter held Harrison Scott released the woman, who ran
away, but not before Harrison had managed to kick her several
times and to strike Scott a sharp blow. Harrison was such a violent
man that a Customs doctor who had been in the house most of the
time had not dared to intervene, so in rescuing the woman Scott
had acted with some courage as well as with coolness. After that,
however, he was at a loss. He did not feel he could conscientiously
expose the constable to the physical risks of trying to apprehend
Harrison, and if Harrison were apprehended there was nowhere to
lock him up. He could only appeal to the Legation, and as the
telegraph had not reached Hainan he could do so only by despatch.
Wade asked the navy to assist in bringing Harrison to justice, but
it was two months before a warship arrived, and by that time
Harrison, who had been dismissed from the Customs, had moved
to Hong Kong, where the governor was advised that he could not
act against him. In 1893 there was an emergency of another sort. A
rusty horse pistol which the consulate writer was firing exploded
and blew off a large part of the writer's hand. M.F.A. Fraser and
two British residents applied a tourniquet until three hours later a
doctor arrived from Kiungchow to amputate. With the patient in a
long cane chair Fraser administered as economically as possible
Hoihow's scanty supply of chloroform while the other two Good
Samaritans acted as dressers, but the chloroform ran out and before
the wound had been stitched the writer came round. For want of
other material Fraser described the incident in much needless detail
in his next quarterly report.[30]

In 1876 an Anglo-Chinese convention provided for the opening of Pakhoi, on the Kwangtung coast facing Hainan, and Wenchow, 18 miles up river on the Chekiang coast. In 1897 another Anglo-Chinese convention provided for the opening of Samshui, at the confluence in Kwangtung of the North and West rivers, and Wuchow, further up the West river at another confluence in Kwangsi. Wuchow was not a success and the other three ports were of no more use than Hoihow, or less.

In the unfounded belief that Pakhoi could become one of south China's leading ports the otherwise admirable D.B. Robertson fought for years, unfortunately with eventual success, for its opening. In 1877 A.S. Harvey, who opened the consulate, described Pakhoi as much smaller than Hoihow, without a single handsome or even decent public building, and as surrounded by barren red soil, and it was later described as little more than a considerable fishing village. In C.F.R. Allen's opinion some small town on the coast between Bombay and Karachi might as reasonably be expected to serve as Delhi's shipping port as Pakhoi with its poor inland communications might be expected to serve the landlocked provinces of western China. He also said that in the recent past Pakhoi had been a haunt of pirates, that a deputy sent there in 1869 on customs matters had had his head cut off, and that although the inhabitants could no longer justifiably be called pirates and robbers they were notorious for petty thieving. The low standard of civilization struck even Chinese from other provinces, according to E.L.B. Allen; gang robbery seemed to him abnormally prevalent, and during a trip 50 miles into the interior in 1890 he had found all the villages in one valley heavily fortified. Posted back to Pakhoi in 1896 he said that if Pakhoi had that year had a monotonous record of piracy, which was in the local blood, and of robberies of every kind, the turbulence and disturbance were even worse in adjacent districts.[31] British trade remained obstinately non-existent, and in the mid-1880s there were only eleven foreign residents.[32] Initially it was believed that British trade would flourish if only an unholy combination among Chinese merchants to keep all the port's trade in Chinese hands could be overcome and if only officials could be prevented from ignoring or circumventing transit pass rights. In 1879 Wade reacted to Stronach's nil return of foreign trade at Pakhoi by expressing the conviction that the port was of very great importance to British trade and that the existence of artificial im-

pediments to trade made the presence of a consul all the more
essential. In reality Pakhoi's unfavourable geographical location
was a far greater impediment than any artificial ones. Hopes of
trade first faded and then expired. B.C.G. Scott reported that
Pakhoi's trade in 1892 was entirely to and from Hong Kong but
was carried in non-British bottoms and that the Chinese had practically the entire control of the carrying and all other trades; it was
notorious that no foreigner had ever been able to make a profit for
long, and the only foreign firm now operating did a trifling business
in kerosene and matches. In 1899 the red ensign was seen in the
harbour for the first time in nearly four years, and in 1900 Savage
described British interests as virtually nil.[33]

Harvey had hardly opened the consulate before he went out of
his mind. On a visit to Hong Kong he ran down naked to a hotel
dining-room where some ladies were breakfasting, and he handed
the consulate papers over for transmission to Robertson only when
the Hong Kong police were called in. He wrote to Robertson that
he had yielded because the policeman had been three times as
strong and twice as heavy as he, but he believed that if he had killed
the constable every judge in England would have held him
innocent, and as for being medically certified unfit for duty he had
never in his life experienced such exuberance of health and such a
flow of animal spirits. After detention in the Hong Kong hospital's
lunatic department he was sent to a brother in the Indian medical
service, who telegraphed two months later that a perfect recovery
had been made. His father, shocked to read in a local paper at
Aberdeen, where he was a medical professor at the university,
that his son was ill, asked the Foreign Office for information. The
Foreign Office wrote without expressing regret or sympathy, 'I am
in reply to acquaint you that...your son has become insane' and
would be sent home, but did in a later letter unbend enough to
express pleasure at the recovery. Wade, in London on home leave,
met Harvey there. He praised him as an able and well-educated
officer against whom there was nothing to be said except that he
had been deranged once before in 1867, but feared that it would
not take much excitement to disturb his equilibrium, and therefore
with exceeding regret recommended his removal on a pension. The
Foreign Office rejected the father's plea that as the trouble had been
due to an affair of the heart, one and the same affair on both
occasions, their decision to act on Wade's recommendation should

be reconsidered. There was a relatively happy ending. Harvey does not seem to have married the lady in question or any other lady, but he was called to the bar, practised on the Oxford circuit, kept up his Chinese, and shortly after the turn of the century reappeared in China for some years as a professor at Peking University, where he was said to have been much liked by the students.[34] Two years after Harvey's breakdown Stronach also got into a queer state at Pakhoi. He reported that the man who had been foremost in the murder of the deputy in 1869 was heading an anti-foreign conspiracy, named the exact date on which the plotters would rise, and in case he too was murdered sent Wade a list of property in the consulate. No similar warning reached Peking from the Pakhoi Customs. Wade told the Foreign Office that while he did not venture to affirm that Stronach had no sufficient reasons for his suspicions he had reason to believe Stronach unduly alarmed.[35] There was no rising on the date named or on any other date, and in fact Pakhoi always remained singularly free of Chinese attacks on foreigners.

There was no official of standing at Pakhoi, and personal contact with the district magistrate or prefect, both 22 miles away, or with the intendant, six days' journey away, was virtually impossible. Such business as the consulate did have with them was perforce dealt with by despatch. This was not the way to get results in China, where the bureaucracy were past masters in the art of protracted and meaningless correspondence, and in 1881 the exasperated C.M. Ford wrote that the authorities regarded a consul 'as a mere dummy, with no particular duties to perform, except, perhaps, writing for his own amusement despatches of which no notice need be taken'. The atmosphere was different on the rare occasions when personal contact could be made. In 1883 Playfair was ordered to a departmental city 130 miles away in connection with a transit pass dispute. There he saw for himself that the magistrate was a genial old nonentity and that the man behind the trouble was a young deputy, exceedingly voluble, marvellously well-informed about events in the outside world, including Gambetta's flight from Paris during the Prussian siege, intelligent, astute, and not very congenial. He believed that in face-to-face discussion he had been able to settle the matter and expressed appreciation of the extreme kindness and attention, going much beyond the more or less obligatory official courtesies, which all officials had shown him during his ten days away from Pakhoi; 'there was a genial and

hearty unofficial welcome extended to me which I cannot pass over in silence'. As the mob in the departmental city had been so unruly that while there he had been a prisoner in his lodgings this seems a generous acknowledgement on Playfair's part.[36]

Although decent accommodation was provided sooner than at Hoihow the first consulate at Pakhoi rivalled Hoihow's horrors. Playfair described it in 1882. It was on the sea-shore, at the bottom of a slope, and was built on porous sand overlying thick clay, and therefore got the full benefit of the drainage from the slope above. It was surrounded on three sides by Chinese houses, and on two sides were a row of privies, the effluvia from which during a hot night, particularly after rain, were indescribable. The outpourings from an adjacent house passed underneath it, and its own drains were most primitive and inefficient. A Customs medical officer said that the site of the house was sodden with excrement, that the most noxious gases must constantly be rising into the house, that Playfair's impaired health resulted from these conditions, and that it was dangerous for Playfair or any successor to live in it. It was also very hot in hot weather and very cold in cold weather. A site for a new consulate was acquired outside the town, the land round Pakhoi being so poor that twenty-one acres were bought for about £80, and pending completion of the building C.F.R. Allen, who arrived in 1884, moved with his wife and at least one child into a five-roomed mat and plaster bungalow, also outside the town. Although the bungalow looked more like a cowshed than a house the Allens considered the healthier surroundings a wonderful improvement. Mrs Allen's confinement in August, a month in which 51 inches of rain fell, must however have contrasted strangely with her three previous confinements in London and Shanghai, and looking after the baby in a bitterly cold January and February, during which the family suffered a good deal, must have been attended with difficulties. Allen was transferred just before the completion of the consulate, but his successor was delighted with what he believed to be the strongest foreign building in China, constructed of granite, brick, tiles, and cement, and therefore indestructible either by fire or by white ants.[37]

In 1887 France, in pursuit of her territorial ambitions in south and west China, opened a consular establishment at Pakhoi covering Hoihow as well, and towards the end of the century both British consulates became ineffectual political listening-posts and

reported on French intentions. In 1897 the Foreign Office sought the Legation's views on supposed French designs on Pakhoi. The Legation referred the query to E.L.B. Allen at Pakhoi and were told by him that unless France embarked on appropriation of Chinese territory on a larger scale the local French would regard French acquisition of Pakhoi as an absurdity. During 1898 W.H. Wilkinson sent lengthy abstracts from the Tongking press to the Legation, who read them with great interest and copied them in part to the Foreign Office, but this was insufficient occupation for the restlessly active Wilkinson, who in renewing an earlier application for home leave said that although his physical health was excellent Pakhoi's lonely life was producing increasing depression and loss of energy. No one can have found much to do at the post. Even the Boxer troubles did not disturb it in 1900. At the end of them Savage reported that the three months which had been so eventful elsewhere had passed in the greatest quiet and monotony at Pakhoi.[38]

Wenchow lay in a small plain intersected by canals and had excellent inland water communications. According to Everard in 1880 it had once been a major trading centre but was now sunk in hopeless apathy, only the ruins of palatial houses, broad and exceptionally clean streets, and innumerable commemorative stone archways remaining as testimony of former greatness. The sunken cheeks, sickly complexion, and lustreless eyes of most people in the streets, he said, showed the frightful extent of opium smoking, and Parker a little later believed some 30 per cent of males to be addicts and another 30 per cent to be occasional smokers. No foreign trade developed. In 1894 Mansfield reported that after two firms trying out the new port had left in 1878 no foreigners had attempted to develop trade.[39] Including women and children there were usually less than twenty residents,[40] nearly all officials or missionaries and mostly British. Communications with the outside world were miserable, and a message to or from Ningpo, the nearest treaty port, took six days by courier. Communications by sea in the early 1880s consisted of a single Chinese wooden steamer running three times a month between Shanghai, Ningpo, and Wenchow. In the early 1890s a decrepit converted warship, owned by a Chinese shipping company, was on the run. Bringing M.F.A. Fraser to take over from Mansfield she broke down several times between Ningpo and Wenchow and her lifeboats were as suspect as her engines and rudder, but as she was close to land and the sea was like a millpond

Fraser was more anxious about the safety of his gear than about his own safety. Mansfield, leaving in her on her next trip, had more cause for alarm. Her rudder broke down 35 miles out with a typhoon coming on, and when the captain tried to get back to Wenchow her engines broke down too. She was caught in the typhoon and drifted towards rocks with her anchors dragging. Mansfield equipped himself with a lifebelt and believed that his last hour had probably come, but he eventually got back to Wenchow in a Chinese gunboat and waited for the next steamer.[41]

C. Alabaster opened the consulate in 1877. Accommodation was rented in a temple on an island in the middle of a river a mile or so wide. The river ran fast through many shoals, and crossing between island and city was dangerous at times. Drinking-water and provisions had to be ferried across. Local provisions were limited, as mutton or goat was never obtainable and beef only when a bullock died of disease or in an accident. The island was too small for proper exercise, but in compensation the temple was breezy, quiet, and very private, and entirely lacked the unhygienic surroundings of the original Hoihow and Pakhoi consulates.[42] The defect lay in the accommodation, consisting of three low-pitched rooms to which the Office of Works later added two temporary rooms. The Legation said in 1887 that the quarters were of the most miserable description, Hosie, the 1889 occupant, said that every other British resident lived in an infinitely better foreign-style house, and in 1891 Hurst, expecting to be joined that year by a wife who was far from strong, said that the partitions between rooms were full of rat holes, that the floors shook when walked on, that only two cold and draughty rooms were habitable in winter, and that the uprights supporting the roof had been so weakened by white ants as to threaten collapse of the whole building in a strong blow. Even the new consulate provided shortly afterwards was notoriously uncomfortable and unhealthy. Water streamed from the walls and ran down the staircase, and as there were no windows at the back no through current of air could be obtained when the temperature was 100° in the shade. After the consulate had been closed Mortimore saw no prospect of letting the house; consuls might have been compelled to live in it but in his opinion no foreigner would take it rent-free.[43]

Unlike Pakhoi Wenchow boasted several senior officials. The 1880 incumbents described by Everard exemplified the variety of

the superficially uniform bureaucracy. A very friendly intendant, reputed to be perfectly clean-handed, was a distinguished literatus; so was the prefect, who had something wrong with his throat and could speak only in a whisper; the magistrate had bought his rank; and the brigadier, said to monopolize most of the port's trade, was illiterate (and, if he was the same brigadier who had previously been mentioned, an ex-pirate). Over the years the officials were usually easy to get on with. In 1884 Parker reported very friendly relations and frequent amicable dinners with them. The people too had been unusually courteous and even friendly when the port was opened.[44] Yet only two months after his previous despatch Parker had to report that a serious anti-foreign riot had blown up one night. Everything foreign in the city was annihilated except for two horses which managed to struggle out of the fires. The magistrate's yamen sheltered missionaries overnight. Some Customs staff armed with guns and pistols escaped over the city wall and made their way to the consulate. There the small party of half a dozen or so at first agreed that if the mob also crossed the river Parker should advance unarmed to parley but that if violence were attempted the party would defend themselves to the last. All except Parker then had second thoughts and went down river by boat. Parker stayed on alone, put on his uniform, and took his seat outside the consulate. No howling mob arrived. Instead an hour later a military officer with fifty men arrived to protect the consulate and the danger was over. The next day Parker received innumerable calls, the river party returned, Parker agreed on behalf of all nationalities the compensation to be paid, and a month later foreigners could again walk freely all over the city. Parkes congratulated Parker on his conduct, courage, and judgement, and on his signal success in settling the incident locally.[45]

Charge of any consulate, however little work it might offer, was welcome to assistants who got extra pay while acting as consuls, and for that reason Hosie regretted the end of his acting tenure of Wenchow, although he had had nothing much to deal with beyond occasional convert incidents. In such matters it was difficult for Chinese officials to act incisively even when they wished to do so, and in 1890 a magistrate who in response to Hosie's pressure went in person to the scene of an incident had to take refuge from a mob in the house of the very ringleader he had gone to arrest. In 1895 Fox encountered more convert troubles and was dissatisfied with

the attitude of both the missionaries and the Chinese officials. He was stoned by a mob in his houseboat, other foreigners were stoned in the countryside and hooted in Wenchow streets, and he feared that a normally peaceful and law-abiding people might be worked up into a general crusade against converts and perhaps against foreigners.[46] During the Boxer troubles his forebodings came close to being realized, and Wenchow shared with Chungking the regrettable distinction of being the only treaty ports from which there was a mass exodus of foreigners. The Peking legations were already under siege when O'Brien-Butler reached Wenchow to take over the consulate after an interregnum. The foreign community had taken refuge on the island, having no confidence in the intendant, regarded as a doddering old opium-smoker, or in the prefect and general, both regarded as ferociously anti-foreign. He evacuated the community and himself as Boxer advance guards reached the city, and reported his action from the safety of Shanghai thirteen days after having taken charge at Wenchow. The prefect was fined $5,000 as the man mainly responsible for Boxer attacks on converts and on mission property, but there was an unexpected later twist to that story. In 1908 Mortimore reported that the prefect had just been reappointed to his old Wenchow post, that in other posts he had meanwhile gained missionary goodwill, that he was contemplating sending his son to a missionary college, and that his grandson was engaged to the half-caste daughter of a Tientsin Scot. Mortimore commented that the prefect's ideas had probably changed. At the end of 1900, when order had been restored, the Legation decided that British interests at Wenchow were not important enough to require the permanent presence of a consul and that monthly visits by the Ningpo consul would suffice. Wenchow never again had a resident consul.[47]

It could obviously have done without a resident consul long before, for during the period in which it did have one it survived without noticeable difficulty two consuls, Stronach and Ayrton, each there for three years in the late 1880s and late 1890s respectively, who were sunk in the hopeless apathy that Everard had detected in the city itself. Neither of them did anything whatever. Stronach, described by O'Conor as a useless officer but harmless at a port with so little trade, was stirred into animation only when the commander of a visiting German gunboat omitted to call on him, though he was in charge of German interests, but did call on the

German assistant in charge of the Customs. The first Mrs Stronach had been the widow of a China Inland Mission missionary, and the second wife seems to have been strait-laced too, for the German assistant, living openly with a Chinese concubine, 'whose clothes, hung up to air or dry, it is impossible to avoid seeing while passing his quarters' had never been invited to meet her. The assistant, Stronach believed, had retaliated by engineering the slight. At the end of his three years Stronach applied to retire on health grounds, and the Foreign Office, who had heard with disapproval that he had become something of a religious enthusiast, did not stand in the way.[48]

Ayrton's previous career had at post after post been notable only for idleness and negligence. As a student interpreter he had preferred drinking to learning Chinese or riding. The Hong Kong postmaster-general complained of his scandalous delay in accounting for money received as post office agent at Hankow and elsewhere, and in transmitting the complaint to Walsham the governor of Hong Kong said that Ayrton would have been dismissed had he been a colonial service officer. He was transferred from Kiukiang under a cloud for failing to forward his consular accounts, and the Danish minister in London complained to the Foreign Office about his neglect of a piece of Danish business at Kiukiang. After failing at Newchwang to forward accounts or to report on a brutal assault on a missionary he was cautioned by Walsham for persistent neglect of his duties. At Tamsui the Foreign Office demanded an overdue trade report immediately.[49] During his first eighteen months at Wenchow, his next post, the Foreign Office heard from his London tailor about an unpaid bill but the Legation received nothing beyond two trifling returns, and those only in response to Legation reminders. The silence continued in spite of MacDonald's threats to report him to the Foreign Office, and probably only his wife's death in childbirth saved him from overdue disciplinary action.[50] Then he submitted an application, the acceptance of which MacDonald strongly recommended, to retire on health grounds, but there was a hitch. In the absence of medical evidence that incapacity was permanent the Treasury in a formal letter declined to award a pension, suggesting instead extended home leave followed by further medical examination. A Foreign Office minute, exclaiming at the true Treasury spirit, pointed out that to retain a man quite incapable of performing his functions would detract from service efficiency. The Foreign Secretary agreed, and

some informal expostulation must have been addressed to the
Treasury, for only eleven days later they followed up with a semi-
official letter in quite a different tone. They suggested that a more
suitable medical certificate should be obtained in China or that
Ayrton should be seen in London by the Treasury medical adviser,
who, they said, 'is a very sensible person and can read between the
lines as well as his neighbours'. With most unwonted alacrity
Aryton procured a further medical certificate from Wenchow. It
was very suitable indeed. It spoke of chronic degeneration of spleen
and liver, probable fatty degeneration of the heart, anaemia, much
nervous debilitation, marked loss of mental vigour, weakness of
memory, and some degree of paralysis agitans in hands and arms. A
pension was awarded and within four years Ayrton was dead.[51]

The Legation demonstrated their opinion of Wenchow as a post
by the successor they found for Ayrton. E.L.B. Allen, who had been
useless at Newchwang, was known to have become incapable of
performing his most ordinary duties, so he was inflicted on
Wenchow. He had hardly arrived before he furnished a medical
certificate that he was mentally and physically incapable of work.
He followed Ayrton into retirement.[52]

Samshui made a most unfavourable impression on E.D.H. Fraser
when he made a preliminary inspection from Canton and on Brady
when he opened a houseboat consulate there at the end of 1897.
The new treaty port was a wretched little place, three-quarters of a
mile back from the river, with some 4,000 inhabitants. The only
sign of life seen by Fraser at an exceptionally tumbledown magistrate's yamen was a dozen malefactors lounging about its gate
loaded with fetters, there was little business, and the few shops
were of the meanest kind. Hokow, Samshui's riverside port, consisted of one indescribably dirty street along which fifty or sixty
shanties straggled and which was flooded annually.[53] Brady, who
was accompanied by his wife and perhaps by his 7-year-old son, got
away after not much more than a year, determined never to expose
his wife to a repetition of their Samshui experiences.[54] His successor Fox brought with him the wife he had married two and a
half years before. She was the daughter of an American Yangtze
skipper, a good background for roughing it at Samshui, but she
did not stay the course. After a year Fox went down with severe
typhoid, she nursed him, caught it, and died, and Fox was left with
an infant son and was transferred. At Hokow he had erected a

matshed office, agreeably cool in summer but chilly in winter, as for fear of fire no stove could be lit, and had purchased a consulate site there. The site had only been flooded once in twelve months, and then only 2 feet deep, so he considered that when raised 2 or 3 feet and bunded it should be quite satisfactory and was annoyed by belated Office of Works doubts about its suitability.[55] After Fox came Little. He was disgusted. The foreign community consisted of four Customs officials, three of whom were tide-waiters, days passed without his speaking to anyone except his servants, his living accommodation was a 40-foot-long houseboat shared with the boatman and his family, and for a time he had to beg drinking-water from passing steamers and use soda-water even for tea, soup, and cooking. To escape from the houseboat he built himself a four-roomed wooden bungalow raised on stilts 7½ feet above the ground and found it a vast improvement, though during a flood it stood in 5 feet of water and both the bungalow and the land on which it stood were at risk of being washed away. He fell out with the Office of Works over his building operations. Against their advice he had built the bungalow on the consulate site. They decided to sell the site and required the unwilling Little to remove the bungalow. The Legation supported them in that demand, but not in a further outrageous demand that Little should pay ground rent retrospectively for the period during which the bungalow had stood on the land.[56] Fox had deluded himself with the hope that Samshui would become the great distributing centre for the produce of the West and North rivers. Seeing that the two best British steamers on the river had been sold Little took the more realistic view that local trade was not on a large enough scale for foreign-officered steamers to run profitably. He was the last British consular officer at the port. Just four years after Brady's opening of the consulate the Foreign Office accepted the Legation's recommendation that it should be suspended.[57]

J.W. Jamieson was temporarily detached from the Canton consulate to open Wuchow, also in 1897. He found a city of some 40,000 friendly inhabitants. It consisted mainly of mean streets in which exceedingly fat pigs outnumbered the dogs and was subject to flooding from a river capable of rising 60 feet in a week. It was however full of temples, and a charming old prefect helped him to find in one of the temples a single, large, lofty room to serve as office and living quarters, accommodation which he found ex-

tremely picturesque even if the stagnant fishponds surrounding it
bred mosquitoes and threatened malaria. The authorities provided
a guard of five soldiers, to whom he gave a monthly gratuity. The
temple was a popular resort for the city's idlers, they assumed a
continued right of access to Jamieson's room, whose doors had no
locks, and the soldiers performed an essential function in evicting
intruders. Jamieson soon saw that as a distributing centre for
foreign imports Wuchow's position would always be secondary,
that trade would remain largely in Chinese hands, and that the only
opening for foreigners was as shipping and forwarding agents.[58]
He was then replaced by Hosie, who had been acting consul
at Newchwang. MacDonald had offered Hosie promotion to the
substantive rank of consul at Wuchow or Samshui, or at new posts
in remote Yunnan. He had replied that he would prefer a post
suitable for a wife and family, MacDonald had said that he could
not comply, and Hosie had opted for Wuchow, either because he
considered Wuchow less unsuitable than the others or because ten
years earlier he had argued for the opening of the West river to
trade.[59] In personal terms the appointment was not a success. On
arrival he was unable to rent a house offering any approach to
comfort even for himself, let alone for his family. He sent the family
home and within three months was struck down by malaria,
followed by rheumatism and dysentery. A year later he was posted
back to Newchwang and brought his family out again. Within
twelve months he was asked to open Nanking, but in the absence
of an assurance that a consulate would at once be built declined,
saying that he knew from very bitter experience at Wuchow and
elsewhere how altogether unsuitable for married officers Chinese
housing was in climates like that of the Yangtze and West rivers.
Hosie had been raised on a failing Aberdeenshire farm, had worked
his way with scanty resources through a Scottish university, and
had an iron constitution, so this was not the opinion of a pampered
middle-class hypochondriac. Hosie's permanent contribution to
consular life at Wuchow was his choice of a site for the consulate.
The past tradition at river ports had been to select close to the river
bank a site which often needed to be filled and bunded before
building and which still remained at risk of flooding. Hosie selected
a 300-foot-high hill, at the top of which a consular bungalow was
later built with very many steps winding up to it from the office at
the foot.[60] Occupants knew only too well exactly how many steps

there were, but lived far above any possible flood and had a fine view.[a]

Hausser was the next officer to spend much time at Wuchow. Before he arrived a temporary incumbent had been warned by the Customs doctor that the temple quarters were most unhealthy and a temple priest and temple servant had both died of plague. He had therefore transferred the consular residence and consular office to two houseboats, and left Hausser this accommodation.[61] It was grossly, if not criminally, insensitive to post Hausser to a lonely port where the accommodation was so uncomfortable and where, according to one of his successors, 'the climate was abominable, decent food almost impossible to obtain, and owing to the number of robbers and pirates life was far too disagreeably exciting',[a] for Hausser was already mentally unbalanced. He had been attached to a Burma-China boundary commission whose job it was to delimit the shadowy frontier between upper Burma and China, and by the beginning of 1898 had persuaded himself, just as he had at Pagoda Island, that there was a plot against his life. He fancied he had more than once overheard his Chinese writer inciting his Chinese servants to assassinate him and he formally charged the writer with incitement to murder. The writer was discharged for want of evidence and arrangements were made to return him from Burma to Shanghai, but the maligned man died on the way at Rangoon. Hausser alarmed the Burma party on the commission by firing two shots at a sentry they had posted near his tent to reassure him. He explained that he had mistaken the sentry for a person who had allegedly been trying to enter his tent. Towards the end of the year a doctor in upper Burma wrote to Mrs Hausser in London, who copied the letter to MacDonald, that her husband was distorting the most innocent everyday activities into proofs of a conspiracy against his life and that unless transferred to a part of China far away from the frontier he would develop very grave mental disease. MacDonald replied that at the end of the commission's work her husband would be given leave or sent to a civilized treaty port. When Hausser's precautions, which included hiring a European as a personal bodyguard, threatened to delay the commission's work the lieutenant-governor of Burma ran out of patience; he felt unable to anticipate with any confidence what Hausser might do next and trusted that a more suitable officer might relieve him. The request for a replacement ground its way through the India and Foreign

Offices to the chargé d'affaires at Peking, who said he was sending a replacement and would try to find a suitable post for Hausser on his return to China.[62] Almost incredibly he considered Wuchow suitable. Hausser was left there for nearly three years, sharing with wife and children, including a new baby, the very scanty accommodation and the insanitary conditions which he later claimed had considerably impaired his health. He left his family for even the shortest journey only with reluctance, and was described by a visiting secretary of Legation as 'silent and depressed, his face being strongly marked by melancholy, even resignation'. The sequel was extraordinary. Instead of becoming certifiable or committing suicide he performed with normal competence at Amoy and Swatow, and in recognition of long and meritorious services would have been promoted in 1911 to be consul-general at Mukden had not cataracts obliged him to retire instead.[63]

Another post in what was geographically part of China was briefly staffed from the China service. After China's recognition of Portuguese sovereignty over Macao in 1887 vice-consuls under the orders of the Canton consul were for some years stationed there. In 1897 B. Brenan at Canton represented that a China officer was wasted at Macao, where there was no Chinese work, no judicial work, and practically no work of any sort, and he recommended that money should be saved by appointing a British merchant as vice-consul. The recommendation was acted upon.[64] By then, however, two successive acting vice-consuls had made fools of themselves in Macao. Werner foreshadowed the rest of his career by quarrelling first with the Portuguese chief justice and then with a local resident who had ventured to disagree with him about the method of calling annual general meetings of a cemetery trust fund. On instructions from MacDonald he apologized to the resident, but did so with very bad grace. Goffe, as a member of the Foreigners Lawn Tennis Club, for which Portuguese were not eligible, received a club circular proposing a series of teas to which any Europeans would be invited. He scribbled on the circular the counter-suggestion, which got into the press and caused much offence, that any Europeans bar Portuguese should be invited. He said he had written this thoughtlessly 'simply because they play so badly and spoil the game' but he was transferred and told he was lucky not to be reported to the Foreign Secretary.[65]

NEW CONSULATES
IN CENTRAL CHINA

THE peace settlement provided for three more treaty ports on the Yangtze, at Chinkiang, Kiukiang, and Hankow. All three were chosen for their good water communications. Chinkiang lies at the mouth of the Grand Canal, Kiukiang not far from a major confluence, and Hankow, one of the trio of Wuhan cities (the others being Wuchang and Hanyang), at another major confluence. Before the consulates were opened in 1861 Parkes in a brisk trip up river earmarked at each of them an area outside the city walls for a British concession.

At Chinkiang Adkins (for whose time there see Chapter 6) was replaced by F.E. Harvey in 1865. Bruce, who had a very high opinion of Harvey, had promised to recommend him for Canton if, as was then thought likely, D.B. Robertson retired. Robertson did not retire and, after consulting the outgoing Bruce, Wade as chargé d'affaires inexplicably recommended Harvey only for Chinkiang, which Harvey called an insignificant hole and where in Adkins' ruined temple he claimed to be the worst-housed officer in China. After taking over in Peking Alcock remarked that the appointment utterly wasted an officer who, if he had an atrabilious facility for affronting people, was very able and efficient. Within two years Harvey's health finally broke and at 42 he retired.[1] He lost all his money in the collapse of a leading British firm in China[a] and his death in 1884 left his widow without provision. In 1867 Bruce in a letter to Hammond had most warmly praised Harvey's services. The popular clamour got up by missionaries and smugglers in favour of the Taipings had, he said, 'deterred more than one consul from acting with vigour in carrying out our policy of putting them down', but Harvey's vigour, decision, and ability at Ningpo had been largely instrumental in removing the Taiping obstacle to

China's tranquillity and to good British relations with the Chinese government. The widow sent in a copy of this letter in appealing unsuccessfully in 1902 for a pension. She renewed her appeal in 1910, a quarter of a century after Harvey's death; she had supported herself until prevented by illness and was now in a cottage in Birmingham, living among the poor and subsisting on a small allowance which barely sufficed for the commonest necessities and which might be withdrawn at any moment. On being turned down again she threatened to publicize her plight in the press, but the Foreign Office heared from her no more.[2]

Harvey left with a low opinion of Chinese officials as a class; political and financial administration in the provinces was not proceeding in the right direction, or in any direction whatever; nothing had been learned from the Taiping rebellion and nothing forgotten; except in rare cases egotism, peculation, indifference, indolence, ignorance, and fraud reigned supreme behind pompous decorum. He had however had good relations with individual officials at Chinkiang. He had been very friendly with a first intendant, whose policy was to refuse everything possible and to humbug the foreigner but whose demeanour was so benign and unctuous and whose smiles were so placid that it was impossible to get angry with him or to make him angry. The next intendant was a courteous and simple old man in his dotage who had completely lost his memory. Under him business was left to a good-natured, indolent young man who preferred pleasure to work and who on private visits to Harvey would pour out feelingly over meals about the hardships of working under so severe a taskmaster as Li Hung-chang.[3] Whether relations were good or bad there was very little to do at Chinkiang, and on Harvey's departure Alcock suggested that in the absence of trade the consulate could be entirely or virtually closed. Hammond minuted against closing it entirely, but also against stationing at Chinkiang a junior who would be ruined by idleness and probably thoroughly demoralized. The decision reached was to make Medhurst at Shanghai concurrently Chinkiang consul and to station a junior under him at Chinkiang. While there in that capacity C.F.R. Allen displeased Medhurst. Medhurst reported indignantly that the Chinese had taken the extraordinary liberty of beheading three men on a vacant British-owned plot of land only just outside the concession and immediately under the consulate's front windows (the consulate was at the edge of the

concession), no doubt to humiliate and annoy concession residents; he had protested strongly against the impropriety and discourtesy and had expressed unmixed astonishment and regret at so extraordinary a proceeding; Allen had successfully remonstrated against an attempt to behead the men on the concession bund, and if he had protested decidedly and in person against the equally objectionable location then selected the men would probably have been beheaded elsewhere. Wade entirely approved Medhurst's views and action.[4]

In 1877 Chinkiang had revived sufficiently for the consulate's independent status to be restored. There were then 42 non-missionary residents, of whom 31 were British, 7 foreign firms, of which 6 were British, and a fluctuating number of Roman Catholic and Protestant missionaries. There was an influx of Protestant missionaries in the 1880s, but the overall number of residents did not greatly increase.[5] This small community sustained over the years so unique a level of personal feuding, and so unique an incapacity to run the concession properly, that Chinkiang was an uneasy consul's post. In 1864, when Chinkiang was still so ruinous that apart from the consulate staff on the island all foreigners were living on hulks in the river, Bruce had doubted the wisdom of a concession on Parkes' site. He did not apparently fear that concessions might be disagreeable to the Chinese, but he understood the home government to be not very favourably disposed towards them and his own experience had been that they created jealousies and gave rise to pretensions on the part of other powers. He therefore favoured foreigners buying land wherever it suited them at Chinkiang and the abandonment of the concession project; if, however, all the foreigners did collect in one quarter an administrative body to deal with roads and so on must be formed on the Shanghai model in order to relieve consuls of this additional responsibility and to leave them free for their proper duties.[6]

Bruce's dislike of concessions was well-founded, but concessions remained at Chinkiang and elsewhere, and at Chinkiang and elsewhere the landrenters (holders of concession leases from the Crown) elected administrative bodies. These bodies, whose functions were confined to concession areas but which were misleadingly styled municipal councils, steadily acquired or usurped functions and powers going much beyond the limits envisaged by Bruce. At Chinkiang the concession was an oblong piece of land along the river, 440 yards long and 250 yards deep, with a bund

and 2 or 3 streets. In a bustling British concession such as that at Tientsin an indefensibly oligarchic constitution might in practice produce tolerably efficient administration. Not so at Chinkiang. The concession became a discreditable anomaly. The prohibition of subletting to Chinese fell into abeyance, in the early 1890s there were less than 40 foreign residents in the concession but over 1,400 Chinese, most of the concession houses had been built for Chinese needs and were unsuitable for foreigners, and some were used as brothels, gaming-houses, or opium dens.[7] The municipal council was for years a farcical scandal and a headache to a succession of consuls. Bean, a British merchant who held several of the nineteen concession leases and who was chairman and treasurer of the council in 1879, physically assaulted H.J. Allen in the club when the latter as consul asked to examine the council's books before approving its accounts. Bullock, replacing Allen later that year, reported that as the landrenters always displayed the greatest readiness to tax everything except their own land, raising funds for proper concession administration was very difficult, and the next year he reported a state of bankruptcy.[8] In 1882 the council, of which an American was chairman, Bean treasurer, and Duff, another British merchant, secretary, seized Chinese boats in an attempt to enforce a licence fee of 50¢ on cargo boats using the bund. Boatmen and Chinese authorities complained. H.B. Bristow, transferred to Chinkiang as acting consul so that he could rest after a very strenuous time at Tientsin, told the council that both the fee and the method of enforcement were illegal, but he found that the boatmen could sue the council through the council secretary only in the Supreme Court at Shanghai and that, as the chairman was not British, legal action against the members of the council would present difficulties. He managed to satisfy the Chinese authorities, who fortunately showed great moderation in the dispute. Then Bean as treasurer refused to receive from Duff as secretary letters which he considered impertinent, and the result was a council whose members would not meet or speak to one another. It might naturally be supposed, said Bristow, that the three men had been unfortunately chosen, but in fact they had been thought to be the only three men with a chance of election who were likely to work harmoniously together, and the only other person willing to serve and likely to be elected was not on speaking terms with either Bean or Duff.[9] In 1886 the council, again under Bean's chairmanship,

formally complained that the current consul, Oxenham, tried to thwart all the council's attempts to manage the concession satisfactorily. Oxenham described Bean as a coarse, cantankerous, uneducated man of low tastes and malignant disposition who had insulted practically every consul and Customs commissioner serving at the port, and his description of the other council members was not flattering. Although Oxenham at first carefully kept clear of Bean he had to fine him for brutally assaulting Duff while Duff was walking with his wife in the hills, and he said he intended to go on struggling against the factious, disorderly, and unscrupulous community. In 1887, a relatively quiet year, the council secretary successfully sued Duff for libel, and the case had to be heard by the assistant judge from Shanghai as Oxenham, being a witness, could not hear it. The next year Bean was elected chairman at a meeting which Duff would not attend, Duff was elected chairman at a meeting Bean would not attend, and Oxenham was confronted by two chairmen, two treasurers, and two secretaries. The rivals could not reach agreement about payments from the municipal account, only on Oxenham's intervention were wages paid, and litigation in the provincial court and an appeal to the Supreme Court were needed before order was restored. The community remained unpleasant. 'This place is full of animosities and spite' said Carles in 1894. 'The community is not socially attractive, I fancy rather below the average of outport communities' said Willis in 1900.[10]

In 1889, very soon after Mansfield had taken over from Oxenham, a trifling incident involving one of the municipal council's Sikh policemen blew up in a few hours into a major riot. At about this period the employment of Sikhs as police in concessions and at Shanghai had become common. It was believed that in any crisis they would be less susceptible to Chinese intimidation than locally recruited Chinese policemen, but in the opinion of one British admiral they were on the contrary a danger, as they despised and ill-treated the Chinese and were hated and feared by them.[11] It was alleged that a Sikh had struck a Chinese, the police compound just below the consulate was attacked, and the Sikhs had to escape out of a back window. Mansfield asked the Chinese authorities for assistance and telegraphed to Shanghai that there was a serious riot and that a gunboat was needed immediately. A few Chinese police from the Chinese city came and did nothing, Chinese soldiers came with fixed bayonets and spears but

only blew their trumpets, and a Chinese official came and had to retreat before the mob, which climbed over the consulate wall. Mrs Mansfield got up from her sick-bed and, escorted by two male foreigners, left by the consulate's back door with her children and with the wife and child of a United States consular officer. She tried to get out of the side gate but was driven back by a shower of stones. Mansfield left by the back door and joined his wife as the mob, armed with sticks and stones, poured into the house. With much difficulty the party broke down enough of the 7-foot rear wall of the compound for the women and children to get over, and after a circuitous walk reached the river and a steamer, on which they and the rest of the community sought safety for the night. The consulate and two missionary houses were burned down and the United States consulate was wrecked. The next morning large numbers of troops restored order, though not before soldiers had been seen completing the looting of the United States consulate and carrying off the British consulate's safe, and to Mansfield's annoyance a telegram arrived from Shanghai saying that a gunboat was getting ready to leave for Chinkiang but that further information was required. He and his family, he said, had barely escaped with their lives and had lost everything except the clothes they stood up in. His wife did not recover from the experience. She suffered for three years from nervous disorders and then succumbed to a form of paralysis which Mansfield believed to have been brought on by shock.[12]

At the end of the century Chinkiang was a busy port of call for Yangtze steamers but little trade was left in foreign hands, and the typical foreign merchant there was employed taking out bogus transit passes for Chinese. It had become an increasingly important Protestant missionary centre, but missionary troubles were few. The statement by Willis in 1900 that he was leading a rather lazy life does not suggest a busy post, and relations with Chinese officials were not difficult. Hopkins said in 1890, for example, that his relations were uniformly good; the intendant, who ran to five or six concubines as well as a wife, had such agreeable manners that meetings with him were a pleasant duty, though he was not a pliant man in business; the magistrate was scholarly, intelligent, and energetic; and the courteous general was cordial which, as the general was the person to whom Hopkins would have to apply in any emergency, was especially pleasing. The consulate rebuilt after the

riot was a good house and stood in a good garden, in which E.L.B. Allen disposed of the maddening noise of cicadas by shooting them with a pistol. Pheasant and snipe shooting were excellent and there was plenty of wild pig, though going after them on foot was a hazardous sport.[13] All in all Chinkiang would have been a pleasant enough post had the community been more congenial.

Although Kiukiang had been so completely destroyed during the Taiping rebellion that at the beginning of the 1880s three-quarters of the city had still not been rebuilt there was enough vigour left in local life for P.J. Hughes to say that opening the consulate had often endangered his own life. In his first two months there were numerous incidents. When he and the captain of the warship which had brought him to Kiukiang went with prefect, magistrate, and brigadier to settle the exact boundaries of Parkes' concession site a crowd fearing arbitrary eviction of the area's occupants started throwing stones. The party began by walking slowly and quietly away, although all of them were hit more or less severely by brickbats, but as the assault became more savage they had to run for it. The next month Hughes, sub-prefect, and magistrate were again assaulted by a mob, and in rapid succession a British doctor walking with Hughes, Hughes' Indian servant, and a consulate servant were attacked.[14] There was a lull until after some months Hughes went home sick and R.J. Forrest took over. There were three incidents in Forrest's first month. Braves broke open the consulate gates and assaulted the servants; braves from sixty-five warboats invaded the settlement and broke open every foreign house; and braves boarded a houseboat in which Forrest was sailing with three British companions and dragged the Chinese boatman into a yamen. Forrest and one companion followed. They found themselves surrounded by several hundred braves who refused egress, Forrest asked for the headman, the headman appeared, and Forrest remonstrated with him. The headman said he knew nothing of foreign-devil consuls but would punish the party for passing that point in the river, and on Forrest taking hold of the boatman to prevent him being forced to his knees he struck Forrest over the hand and 'told his soldiers to bring a knife and kill the foreign devil, meaning me'. Forrest and his companion got away uninjured, but the companion had been much pulled about. The following spring Forrest called in a nine-man naval landing party who at bayonet point drove back an immense crowd using

stones and bricks in an attempt to prevent British use of part of the
concession area, and was told by Bruce to call in force only where
British lives or property were endangered by riots, to cultivate a
good understanding with authorities and people, and to impress the
need for this on the British community. In 1863 Hughes returned
from leave with a bride who had to accommodate herself to a port
which was still tense. At midday and within sight of the consulate
disorderly braves with spears and matchlocks pursued the constable, a man of quiet demeanour, and he escaped death only by
leaping a wall. All foreigners went out armed. Some were disposed
to use their revolvers too readily, and Hughes issued a notification that the braves' rudeness and violence should only make the
community more careful in refraining from aggressive acts and
in firing only when life was endangered or a dwelling attacked,
and that persons acting otherwise might be brought to trial or
deported.[15]

From this point onwards Kiukiang began to settle down. All
Brady's recollections of his time there in the 1880s were pleasant.[16]
When, however, the 30-year-old Baber, in acting charge in 1872,
was ordered to the provincial capital of Nanchang after a visiting
missionary had encountered trouble there, his own visit was an
alarming experience. Baber was a talented and engagingly eccentric
man who kept cool in danger.[17] He disliked paperwork but was a
charming versifier[18] and did not banish humour from his official
prose. In appearance he was tall, thin, and bony, was described
after his death by a friendly Frenchman as looking vaguely like Don
Quixote, and had a reddish moustache, a colour guaranteed to
startle Chinese.[19] He arrived at Nanchang by boat and anchored
near the city gate. By 9 a.m. a large crowd had assembled and
stones and clods of earth fell on the boat with increasing and
alarming frequency and force. It became impossible to remain in-
active so he got out and ascended the bank, intending to go to the
magistrate's yamen and demand assistance. To his great astonishment he saw a bevy of uniformed officials, including the magistrate,
not a hundred yards away, gazing with an unconcerned and con-
templative air and giving not the slightest indication of wishing
to repress the outrage. They said the mob was too large for effective
interference and advised immediate return to Kiukiang. Baber said
that as they would not help he would apply to the governor and,
bidding them a polite farewell, for their urbanity had been as

unquestionable as their incapacity, he proceeded under a volley of stones at a pace which he strove to make as little hasty as the circumstances permitted, with the mob close on his heels making a deafening uproar. Fortunately the mob's ammunition gave out. He got to the governor's yamen and was congratulating himself on arriving safely when the gatekeepers started shutting the doors. He forced his way through just in time, and the gatekeepers were unsuccessful in their attempts to expel him. This, said Baber, was certainly very undignified, but he had no alternative; it would have been extreme folly to have stayed outside or tried to return. He arranged his clothes and sent a card in to the governor, who after some demur received him in a most courteous and friendly way and discussed the missionary incident at length. Baber took his leave at about noon. He borrowed a two-bearer chair and the governor of his own accord sent a dozen or so runners with him. The whole exterior court of the yamen was densely filled with a howling mob, containing as before a large proportion of well-dressed persons, there was a storm of stones, and the chair was tossed on the heads and shoulders of the mob. The runners behaved admirably and the damaged chair and its occupant struggled onwards, runners and mob exchanging blows with promiscuous freedom and stones and brickbats still flying. Once across the court progress was easier, as in the narrow streets the mob could be prevented from pressing too closely. Baber reached the river, thanked his escort, and went off to his boat, heartily felicitating himself on returning from so dangerous an adventure with nothing worse than a few trivial contusions. On reading Baber's account Hammond minuted that Baber deserved the highest commendation. Wade was convinced that the assaults had been officially orchestrated to prove the unwisdom of a foreigner entering Nanchang but that warning had been given for the demonstration not to go beyond a certain point, or Baber would hardly have escaped with his life. Wade got little satisfaction out of the Tsungli Yamen. In such cases, he said, justice was simply unobtainable without local action more stringent than would be acceptable to public opinion at home and hence to the British government; he was in any case opposed to such action, partly because so long as the British put forward the arm of power the central government would not assert its own authority and partly because other powers might act similarly and go much further than the British.[20] A curious feature of the affair is that the Nanchang

governor was the very Liu Kun-i who at the end of his life combined
with Chang Chih-tung to keep foreigners safe from Boxers in the
Yangtze valley and thereby earned so much foreign respect and
gratitude.

At first trade was good at Kiukiang, but by 1869 it was already
losing ground and for a time the post was, like Chinkiang,
downgraded to a vice-consulate. Hughes reported that most import
trade was in the hands of Chinese, who preferred to buy direct from
importers at Shanghai, and that a similar trend was apparent in
exports; 'the days of large communities at minor ports, which have
little or no direct trade with England, are passing away'. C.F.R.
Allen, who served at Kiukiang several times, charted its decline.
When he was first there in 1865 every large firm had a branch there
and trade went on all the year round. In 1875 the large firms had all
gone and the concession was inhabited by steamer agents and
missionaries. In 1887 he thought he scented coming improvement,
but returning yet again in 1889 he concluded that unless something unexpected happened Kiukiang would go on in its old way,
supporting three steamer agents throughout the year and half a
dozen tea-buyers during the three months of the tea season.[21] In the
1880s there were under fifty foreign residents, about half of them
British.[22] Kiukiang as a nineteenth-century treaty port was happy
in having little history. The concession, more or less the same size as
the Chinkiang concession, was tolerably managed, it gave rise to
only minor incidents with the Chinese,[23] and although there were
occasional fears of more substantial trouble the trouble did not
materialize.[24] In the 1890s Brady had difficulties with both Chinese
and foreigners. In the hill country near the city the summer resort of
Kuling, over 3,000 feet above sea-level and soon to be much
frequented by foreigners escaping the heat of the Yangtze valley,
began to emerge.[25] A British missionary, the Revd E.S. Little,
acquired a tract of land at Kuling and disposed of lots to other
foreigners. He was an unscrupulous man with a chequered career.
Having failed the Far Eastern entrance examination in which his
younger brother was later successful he joined the Methodist Epis-
copalian Mission, which he afterwards abandoned for a financially
rewarding business career in China.[26] During his business phase
consular and Legation comments on his character and proceedings
were venomous,[27] and his bad reputation with British officials
cannot have been helpful to his consular brother. How he en-

gineered his acquisition of the tract of land is not clear, but it would have been in character for his methods to have been dubious. The local gentry disliked the foreign incursion and egged villagers on to burn down some of the new buildings. Brady had to deal with an intendant who though very friendly was weak and apathetic and with a grotesquely unsuitable young magistrate who had just purchased his rank and who had had no previous official experience, but he managed to settle the dispute. Nearly thirty years later Brady's obituary said that Kuling, in establishing which he had played an active and decisive part, was an enduring monument to his memory, but at the time the Legation were less appreciative, and the chargé d'affaires minuted on the thirty or so double pages in which Brady reported success: 'Terrible person! We must I suppose approve him as he asks. (He says that he wishes to avoid an unnecessarily long report!!!)'. Brady was given no hint of this adverse reception, receiving instead a reply commending his zeal and ability in bringing a troublesome and protracted case to so satisfactory a conclusion.[28] He was not yet finished with Kuling. The next year Little and some other missionaries raided a gambling den in a nearby village, burned it down, and handed some of the gamblers over to the authorities. Brady wrote to Little that he could not conceive of any extenuation of conduct which seemed to him little short of criminal and which by goading local people into resentment might have had terrible consequences. Brady was not a weak man, but a consul of an earlier generation would probably have acted against Little in the provincial court and had he failed to do so would probably have been instructed by the Legation to act. Now the Legation merely concurred in Brady's rebuke.[29] In the twentieth century the presence of large numbers of foreigners at Kuling during the summer months substantially added to the Kiukiang consulate's responsibilities in times of trouble.

Unlike Chinkiang and Kiukiang, Hankow was a highly successful treaty port. Paying his initial call on the viceroy, Gingell, who opened the consulate, was received with great courtesy and was provided with accommodation in a yamen and with a guard at its entrance to control the curious crowds, but bellicose braves soon threatened foreigners. Within twelve months he was urging the need for the constant presence of a gunboat; whenever a gunboat was not present there were disturbances; one gunboat had only just left and already braves had severely wounded one British subject,

pelted three others with stones, and fired at another. Shortly afterwards braves made an unprovoked attack on yet another; they
bound him, tried to drag him through the streets with a rope round
his neck, and severely beat and kicked him. Gingell called in a
gunboat and the braves' boat was burned. Bruce, who considered
that retaliatory destruction of property set a bad example, did not
approve, and an unfounded rumour that braves had been burned to
death caused ill-feeling for years. A fire-eating communication
which could hardly have been to Bruce's taste was delivered by a
naval officer in Gingell's presence from the British admiral to the
viceroy. It demanded that braves should be kept out of Hankow,
threatened that unless the viceroy implemented his instructions
from Peking a British force might be sent to make him prisoner and
take him to Peking, and warned that a tenth part of the British
forces engaged against the Taipings in the Shanghai area would
amply suffice to bring the viceroy to a sense of his duty. In a long
and reasoned reply the viceroy, who Gingell felt sure was much
offended, temperately said that he would disregard many expressions which were not such as should have been used. Bruce disapproved of further violent proceedings when Gingell called in the
navy to stop illegal taxation of British goods, but in 1863, asking
whether Gingell could defer the immediate sick-leave which a medical certificate had most strongly urged, spoke flatteringly of his
ability and success in a post of great importance. Gingell stuck by
his application for leave but before it was granted was suddenly
taken ill with symptoms which can be interpreted as indicating
cholera and died in agony within twenty-four hours. Bruce regretted this serious loss to the public service and praised the great
judgement, firmness, and good sense shown by Gingell.[30] The post
of great importance was left in the charge of the consulate's idle and
incompetent assistant Webster for well over a year. He imposed a
fine of $500 and a sentence of deportation on a doctor who, for no
better reason than irritation at a noisy Chinese crowd, had fired
three revolver shots from his house and fatally wounded a Chinese.
When Wade as chargé d'affaires prised a long overdue report on the
case out of Webster he had no doubt that trial in Hong Kong for
homicide would have been appropriate, and he ordered Webster
to Amoy in disgrace. Webster countered by renewing an application for home leave, which was granted, and after unaccountably
delaying his departure for months left for home. Two and a half

years later he was still drawing pay in London and the Foreign Office told him to return to China at once on pain of dismissal.[31] He dared not leave his lodgings for fear of his creditors laying hold of him, had no money for his passage back, and accordingly did not return.[a] He was dismissed, was made bankrupt, was reputed two years later to be cutting a dash in London on nothing whatever,[a] and when looking for a job in 1879 vainly asked the Foreign Office to confirm that before retiring he had always given his superiors satisfaction.[32] W.E. King replaced him at Hankow for just long enough to incur Wade's displeasure for taking an attitude which at a later date would have been considered entirely correct. The Chinese authorities sought British and French naval assistance against mutinous braves 17 miles from Hankow who threatened to pillage the city. Although the French consul was prepared to meet the request King's view was that the British gunboat should not give supporting fire to loyal troops unless British interests were being endangered. The mutineers moved in a different direction without attacking the city, but Wade said that a sack of Hankow would have been very dangerous to the British concession, that in such circumstances safety was best secured by demonstrating readiness to support the authorities in the interests of law and order, and that he would have been better pleased had King given the same unreserved support as the French.[33]

It was not far short of two years after Gingell's death before a senior consul, in the person of Medhurst, disappointed by his failure to obtain Shanghai, took over Hankow and new consulate premises. Looking back twenty years later on what he called the old gunboat days C.F.R. Allen, the consulate junior of the time, described Hankow's foreigners of that period as living in a sort of chronic state of petty war with the natives. He himself, visiting with a clergyman the future treaty port of Yochow, was suddenly stoned in the streets by respectably dressed people and the two men had to run for their lives. They took refuge in a house and from there were escorted to the prefect's yamen, which for hours was besieged by a mob. After dark they climbed over the back wall in disguise and were escorted in closed chairs to their boats. Medhurst blamed the attack on a menacing visit paid by the French consul in a gunboat eighteen months before, but a fortnight later he joined the French consul in demanding instant and condign redress for another incident in which two Frenchmen with a dog were seriously

assaulted after a dogfight, one being marched through the streets with bound hands. Both consuls called on the intendant with escorts. Both attended the trial of some of the assailants, who 'confessed after the application of a few of the least objectionable of the incentives to confession which are usually resorted to in Chinese courts'. The sentences on the assailants were very severe, the lightest being 500 strokes with an inch-wide bamboo followed by the cangue. The Foreign Office approved generally but regretted Medhurst's presence at the infliction of torture, however light, considering it highly objectionable that in any circumstances whatever a British officer should countenance by his presence the use of torture or the barbarous punishments common in China.[34]

In 1866 the local Chinese were greatly alarmed by the advance of some of the ferocious rebels or bandits known as Nienfei, and Medhurst and the French consul decided to reconnoitre. The two consuls, the commanders of the two gunboats, and Allen went down the river, landed with a small party of bluejackets, and made for a burning village. On the way they met eight mounted men armed with lances, their saddles apparently laden with bundles and bags. A bluejacket fired without orders. The loads tumbled off and turned out to be women and girls, who on finding themselves free gave a sickly smile of satisfaction and disappeared. The villagers' gratitude was boundless, and so was Medhurst's disgust at authorities too idle or timid to prevent eight mounted men from keeping in abject terror the whole of a large and heavily populated valley in which there were considerable numbers of soldiers. He reported the position to the viceroy, intimating that he would hold the viceroy responsible for any injury to British interests arising from such apathy and incapacity. He reached the conclusion that the available foreign gunboats and a body of foreign volunteers would ensure the foreign community's safety, but at a meeting of British subjects to discuss the situation he castigated Chinese mandarins from the highest to the lowest as conceited, corrupt, effete, incapable, and lacking any particle of energy, power, or wit. Alcock entirely approved Medhurst's steps to protect British subjects but strongly disapproved of his old friend's language at the meeting. The mandarins, said Alcock, were too often as described but it could only do harm to hold them up to scorn to foreigners already disposed to set them at naught; any foreign authority would think the terms used most offensive if applied to itself; and the Chinese daily multiplied

means of finding out what foreigners did and said. He added that it was not for Medhurst to hold the viceroy responsible, a form of words which was irritating and had never done any good. Despatches to and from Peking were still frequently taking six to eight weeks, and the rebuke crossed with two more reports from Medhurst; Chinese troops sent against the Nienfei had been marched through the concession, had broken some windows, had pelted the inmates of other houses, had foully abused every foreigner they met, and had assaulted two French sailors; and in an extreme measure the viceroy had personally taken the field against the Nienfei, in other words, he had left his Wuchang yamen, had crossed the river to Hankow, and had established himself in one of its most comfortable temples, an energetic move to which the rumoured Nienfei retreat would probably be attributed.[35]

In 1867 Medhurst took a short leave and the consulate's interpreter, Gibson, was left in charge. The son of a small Galloway farmer[36] he had in the Scots tradition taken an Edinburgh degree and had qualified as a barrister. After entry into the service he had started well and had impressed the youthful Satow, not an easy man to impress,[37] but then he brought disaster on himself. When temporarily in charge at Tientsin in 1863 he was told to attach himself to a high Manchu official who with the assistance of British officers was operating against the nearby Nienfei. The intention was that he should act as interpreter only. Whether the intention was clearly expressed cannot be determined, as private letters of instruction from Bruce and Wade have not been preserved. Gibson, whose head had in Wade's opinion been turned by the part he had taken in the 1860 campaign, did not confine himself to interpreting, put himself in charge of a body of 200 Mongol and Chinese cavalry, charged and routed 800 mounted Nienfei, and was severely wounded in the head by a spear. Bruce first told Gibson how much he regretted this result of ardour in the field and then reproved him for having to the great inconvenience of the public service exposed himself to risk.[38] The head wound permanently affected Gibson's mind. Adkins commented on the deterioration in Gibson's private correspondence, once a model of neatness and full of humour but now a dirty and meaningless scrawl,[a] Wade said that Gibson's mind had been at least temporarily shaken, and when Gibson returned to China from home leave in 1867 (with a bride who promptly died) Alcock much regretted that a man who gave

very palpable signs of an unsound brain had come out again. For
safety Alcock put him with Medhurst. In Medhurst's absence
Gibson had to deal in court with the failure of a British firm which
owed huge amounts to Chinese merchants, and claimed that every
unprejudiced person in Hankow approved his settlement of a very
difficult case. Medhurst on his return expressed the hope that
Gibson's handling would be favoured with Alcock's marked approval. Instead of approval Alcock sent blistering criticism. In
private letters to Hammond he said that in a scandalous swin-
dle British authorities had been made to look like accomplices
and that Gibson was being transferred to Taiwan 'where if not
very useful there is so little doing that he cannot well do any
mischief', a forecast which proved notably wide of the mark. The
Foreign Secretary gave instructions for Gibson to receive a strong
warning.[39]

Minor attacks on foreigners seem to have died away rather more
slowly at Hankow than at some other ports. In 1875 C. Alabaster,
temporarily in charge, reported that though even ladies could now
go freely about in the concession and in the Hankow suburbs visits
to Hanyang or Wuchang were still risky; two Englishmen had just
been assaulted without provocation in Wuchang, and in Hanyang
he himself had been followed by a yelling crowd of stone-throwing
students, had been hit several times, and had been lucky to escape
serious injury. In 1879, returning as the substantive consul, he
found that foreigners walking in Wuchang no longer risked insult,
and in 1882 he implied that casual assaults had become rare by
commenting, when a missionary in the street was hit on the head
from behind for no apparent reason, that some years before such
incidents had been common enough. In 1888 C.F.R. Allen was not
unduly excited by some recent stone-throwing incidents, one of
which involved a tennis party on the consulate lawn. According to
him there were two classes of offender. The first class consisted of
rowdies, principally coolies and boatmen off work and idlers of all
kinds, who considered Westerners fair game and thought it good
fun to throw stones when they could do so without being caught.
This class was annoying but not nearly so dangerous as the students, the second class of offender. He took the incidents up with
the viceroy, but he did not employ Medhurst's tactics of menacingly
demanding instant and condign redress. He had no wish, Allen
said, to blame officials, who had always laudably desired to sup-

press disorder and protect foreigners, but more important than suppression was that goodwill rather than ill will should be cultivated; things had much improved and still further improvement might be secured by impressing on gentry and elders that throwing stones, following foreigners in crowds, yelling at them, and insulting them should cease. Thereafter the tendency to treat foreigners as targets seems to have abated, and perhaps to have ceased, and increasing readiness among officials to accept foreigners as fairly normal human beings was shown by an unprecedented step in 1896, when Carles was consul. A very friendly governor, concurrently acting viceroy, responded to a wish expressed by Mrs Carles to meet the ladies of his family 'by asking us informally to luncheon. The ladies with whom Mrs. Carles and our little girl took their meal readily accepted an invitation to return the visit and the governor's favourite wife with his son and his wife and his own grandson at their own desire lunched with us at the same table. How great this innovation was is perhaps best seen in the fact that neither of the ladies had previously been allowed to cross to this side of the river'.[40]

Hankow had a substantial foreign community. In 1881 British residents, who predominated, numbered over a hundred. Merchants far outnumbered missionaries.[41] In the 1870s Alabaster was impressed by the concession's magnificent bund, flanked by palaces, and its general air of money and prosperity.[a] The social life of club, outdoor games, and race meetings was in full swing. Alabaster, no great hand at games or sport, noted in his diary immediately after taking over that the role of judge at a race meeting had fallen to him as consul and that he had been astonished to find judging easy, quickness and confidence being as usual sufficient, and he also noted his ignominious defeat at croquet.[a] In the 1880s every room in the concession was occupied during the tea season by tea tasters, brokers, and bank and insurance agents, and as a fine new consulate provided no quarters for juniors they had to keep moving round and to rely on friends' hospitality.[42] In the 1890s the concession had been completely outgrown. An extension doubled its size,[43] and there were French, German, Japanese, and Russian concessions as well. Parkes' selection of the original concession site, twice the size of those at Chinkiang and Kiukiang, showed him at his best and at his worst. The site was admirably suited for commerce, but its use by the British involved the eviction of no less than

7,000 Chinese. It fell to Gingell, who wished Parkes had chosen a site with fewer Chinese residents, to settle compensation for eviction, and although he eventually believed that all concerned considered the compensation handsome the settlement gave him much trouble. Thereafter the existence of the concession seems to have been only a minor irritant to the Chinese during the nineteenth century. In 1889 C.F.R. Allen diagnosed the nature of the irritant. The concession, he said, provided the Chinese with a sort of park where they could stroll on the broad, tree-shaded bund and could get away from their filthy narrow lanes, but the efforts of the municipal council police to preserve good order among the strollers were, according to him, much resented. The police force, which in 1875 had consisted of 1 European and 16 Chinese, numbered 2 Europeans and 40 Chinese in 1891, and a superintendent and 3 other Europeans, a Sikh sergeant, 15 Sikh constables, 3 Chinese sergeants, and 28 Chinese constables in 1895. Allen considered the constables, who were only ignorant coolies, far too ready to strike a blow when a civil word would have done; admittedly the police were much tried by the very boorish and ill-behaved locals, but exaggerated stories of their roughness militated against good feeling; the trouble was partly due to the council chairman, who had been in Hankow since the old days 'and who, not appreciating that things had changed, thought the police quite justified in using batons or canes to enforce municipal regulations'. No doubt for similar reasons it was C.T. Gardner's practice in 1891 to hear all complaints against the police and to procure immediate dismissal for any grave offence.[44] Dubious police behaviour did not deter an intendant who had been summoned to Peking and knew he would be disgraced from asking Alabaster's permission in 1882 to lease a concession house for his family, whom he wished by this means to protect. Alabaster did not want to create a precedent which might lead to the concession being overrun by Chinese or to imply that the family were not fit to live in the concession, and compromised by agreeing to a temporary lease.[45] This is a very early, possibly the first, instance of a prominent Chinese seeking sanctuary in a foreign concession, a practice which became almost routine in troubled future times.

C.T. Gardner, who became consul in 1889, was unlucky to be removed from the post under a cloud. He was a well-intentioned and devoted officer who, on the verge of retirement, said that for

thirty-seven years he had found interest and pleasure in performing his duties, one of the most agreeable of which had been to advance British trade,[46] but his judgement was unreliable and he was excitable. As a junior at Newchwang and again at Chinkiang he twice got himself into trouble with Wade, whose verdict was that he was a trifle cracked but that the Chinese liked him. At Newchwang he had buckled on two revolvers, fired warning shots, and arrested and handed over to the Chinese authorities two blood-stained Chinese whom he suspected of having wounded Austrian sailors. T.T. Meadows, his consul, called this action prompt and vigorous, Wade said it deserved the strongest reprobation, and the Foreign Office threatened dismissal if it were repeated. At Chinkiang Wade censured him very severely for expressing general political opinions which it was not for a junior to express. As consul at Chefoo he was again rebuked by Wade for want of coolness in a dispute with a Russian neighbour about the smell from the Russian's cowshed. As consul at Ichang he included in one report a section on local vegetable produce. Kew botanic gardens said that he seemed grossly ignorant of botany and to have been utterly bamboozled by some incompetent charlatan, and the discovery that the section had been bosh strengthened the long-held suspicion of a senior Foreign Office clerk that Gardner himself was a charlatan.[47] At Hankow Gardner became much concerned by mounting anti-foreign feeling in the consular district. In 1890 a missionary doctor was beaten in a particularly deliberate and humiliating way, and in mid-1891 two foreigners were murdered. Gardner, probably with good reason, attributed much of the anti-foreignism to the circulation of inflammatory pamphlets printed in Hunan. After the murders Gardner informed the Legation that when he had the opportunity he proposed to proceed by gunboat to Changsha, the Hunan capital, to impress on the governor personally the need to destroy the printing presses and the blocks, and he suggested that the Tsungli Yamen should inform the governor of the coming visit. At the Legation Walsham in his usual way left the despatch unanswered. Later in the year Gardner wrote privately to the Foreign Office that he had always been opposed to a gunboat policy but believed that a peaceful demonstration of strength in Hunan would encourage the Chinese authorities to act against the propagandists. Sanderson, the assistant under-secretary concerned, minuted that the letter was worth reading, and Salisbury, the

Foreign Secretary, initialled it with apparent approval.[48] In mid-1892 Gardner informed Walsham that he expected to be well-received in Changsha if he now went there in a gunboat. Walsham again failed to reply, which enabled him to tell the Foreign Office later that he had neither encouraged nor sanctioned the visit. In August the gunboat was put at Gardner's disposal, and almost simultaneously the Hunan governor was removed. Gardner agreed to a request from the viceroy to defer his visit but did not agree to give it up altogether. The proposed visit leaked out in the Shanghai press, the Tsungli Yamen told the Chinese minister in London to protest and to ask for Gardner's removal, the Foreign Office told Walsham not to sanction the visit without reference home and called for a report, and Walsham for the first time told Gardner that he could not approve the visit. On reading Gardner's report Sanderson said that although Gardner's proposal and correspondence had been injudicious there was nothing partaking of a threat, that the Chinese minister would withdraw the request for his removal, and that Gardner could then at the first opportunity be moved to a post where the strain would be less and replaced at Hankow by someone of more solid judgement. The new Foreign Secretary, Rosebery, minuted that he could not approve Gardner's conduct, which did not seem creditable to his common sense. The Chinese minister withdrew his request, blaming the Shanghai press for having misrepresented the facts, and Gardner was transferred to Amoy.[49] Gardner had not been clear-headed and had been sufficiently overwrought to describe himself as broken down by overwork, but Walsham was much more blameworthy and was not blamed. As for putting Gardner under less strain, he had not been a year at Amoy before being ordered to take acting charge at Seoul, where he and his wife were assaulted without provocation by Japanese soldiers. The final word on the Changsha visit can be left to O'Conor, on taking over from Walsham: 'I regret that a gunboat did not go there — perhaps if the matter had been handled very quietly it might have been possible'.[50] On the other hand O'Conor, who in his earlier spell as chargé d'affaires had been justifiably sceptical of a report from Gardner about the strength and state of training of Chinese forces in Manchuria, warned the Foreign Office privately that some of Gardner's despatches were inaccurate and sensational claptrap.[51]

The 1876 Anglo-Chinese convention provided for the opening of

Ichang, where the Yangtze debouches from the formidable gorges obstructing water communications between west and central China, and Wuhu, at a confluence lower down the river between Kiukiang and Nanking.

At the end of 1876 W.E. King reached Hankow under orders to proceed to Ichang and to secure land for a concession, with a cautious proviso that this was subject to the home government deciding to lease land for that purpose. HMS *Kestrel*, which was due to take him on from Hankow, had to wait until the river rose in February and even so, after grounding seventeen times, gave up 40 miles from Ichang. King and his assistant Johnson, now in a small houseboat, were kindly helped to Ichang by a Chinese government steamer but were reduced to such a state of destitution that King, being ashamed to be seen in such a state, refused a call from the viceroy, who happened to pass. A concession site on the river-front was quickly selected and a lease drafted, but putting up boundary stones was not so easy. A deputy who had arranged to meet King at a temple for that purpose failed to turn up and a hostile demonstration swept King and a British companion into the temple, where a number of Chinese held the door of a small room while outside it the mob howled and roared. Across the river the new Customs commissioner and one of his staff were attacked but escaped by flight. The next day King tried again with the intendant. A mob of two or three thousand, egged on by an old crone, resorted to mud and brickbats. The party retreated into the temple, where the previous day's scene was re-enacted for three or four hours. King, who said his life had twice been in great danger, got back to Hankow after five weeks' absence, returned to Ichang with Johnson and a constable, and opened the consulate on three junks. He was vastly annoyed by the offensive impertinence of children and others, and found their shouts, derisive hurrahs, and obscene jocosities an intolerable nuisance. It did not stop at obscene jocosities, for Johnson and a Customs officer while walking in the country were followed for a mile or so by six men who threw stones large enough to maim or kill, though as the assailants were so few the two foreigners were able to avoid the missiles. King was frustrated, writing that the Customs commissioner 'is not needed here, as indeed may be said of myself and everyone at the port...there is no trade, nothing is bought, nothing sold'. During the low-water season no merchant or naval vessel could yet

navigate that stretch of the river, and as King would therefore have been left unprotected, exposed to hardship on his boat, and without means of obtaining foreign commodities, he was withdrawn in the autumn. He went home, and retired on a medical certificate. What he thought on learning that the home government had set their face against an Ichang concession can only be imagined.[52]

Next spring Watters arrived from Hankow in a native boat. Before the year was out his assistant, Crawford, had become ill, had been transferred to Shanghai, had gone mad, and after jumping overboard on the voyage to Hong Kong had returned to England in the care of an attendant. Treasury rigidity cost Crawford the small pension which ten years' service would have given him for the remaining twenty-three years of his life. While on leave at home and still incapable of managing his affairs he sent in his resignation two months before his ten years were up. The Foreign Office, misapprehending his pension entitlement, transmitted it to the Treasury, and the Treasury refused to allow it to be withdrawn and resubmitted two months later.[53] The erudite Watters had brought with him many books, including much in Sanskrit and German,[54] and gave no sign of finding two years at Ichang with minimal official duties disagreeable. He leased a consulate site and moved into one of the dilapidated buildings on it, though even the Office of Works called the buildings scarcely fit for European occupation. Unlike King he found the local people generally friendly, stones were very rarely thrown, almost the only persons to use the expression 'foreign devil' were the Szechwanese boatmen, and they did so only when they were well out in the river.[55] His successor Spence went further, saying that he mixed freely with all classes and met with no incivility, much kindness, and a friendliness quite novel to him. He liked the delightful countryside and the quiet, studious Church of Scotland missionaries who were the only foreign residents besides himself and the Customs staff, but so active a man could not put up with the idleness. He applied for home leave, backing the application with a list of ailments, but with alacrity accepted as an alternative to leave a temporary emergency transfer to Chungking, still further up the Yangtze. On return to Ichang he renewed the application, but on being offered a posting to Shanghai replied that he had no desire whatever for leave so long as he was required in an active capacity. Another reason for his wish to leave Ichang was his deplorable accommodation there. According to him

he was living in something more like a cowhouse than a consulate, surrounded by filth and noisome stench in an exceedingly dirty city. Being told that what had been good enough for Watters was good enough for him did not, he remarked, confer immunity from the illnesses which bad housing constantly inflicted on him and on the whole little community.[56] C.T. Gardner, his replacement, after getting safely away from Ichang said that in his juniors' opinion he had shamefully neglected his duty by not succumbing to the accommodation, which while he was still there he described to the Legation. The consular premises consisted of four sheds once used for storing cotton. The shed nearest the street was the servants' living quarters, kitchen, and lavatory. Through it was the approach to the second shed, the consul's living quarters. It was ruinous and unsafe, the floor was below ground level, one of the four compartments into which it was divided was so dark that candles were necessary in the daytime, Spence's request for proper doors and windows had been rejected by the Office of Works, there was no privacy, and a tool shed on the other side of the compound was the consul's lavatory. At his own expense Gardner built himself a boat which for months he used as residence and office, and a few days after he moved into it the roof of his shed fell in. The Legation urged the need for proper accommodation, and a minute in the Foreign Office, to whom Gardner had shrewdly copied his description, declared that the quarters were clearly totally unsuitable for European habitation. Four years later the Treasury were in correspondence with the Foreign Office about new accommodation, seven years later they agreed to the purchase of a site, ten years later a new consulate was completed, and thirteen years later the consul of the day pleaded for the acquisition of a neighbouring garden over which the contents of cesspools were daily emptied 14 yards from the dining-room windows.[57]

Gardner, who perforce left wife and daughter in Shanghai, suffered from lack of society, recreation, and exercise. He had so little to do that correspondence with the Legation almost ceased, and after his departure in 1884 Parkes decided that the consulate's duties were so light, even though steamers were now running to Ichang in the winter, that the Hankow consulate could take them on.[58] This arrangement might have lasted for some time had Parkes not needed a consul's post obscure enough for Gregory, a tubby, sloppily dressed little man who was well enough liked personally[59]

but who was an exceedingly ineffectual consul. In 1870 Wade, whose judgement of consular officers was often erratic, had expressed a very high opinion of him, but by 1879 was in a more realistic mood doubtful whether he was equal to his duties as Swatow consul: 'Mr. Gregory is a kindly and benevolent man, with the best dispositions, but nervous, and in manner and appearance so eccentric as to excite remark'. Parkes first found an excuse to keep him away from Swatow on return from a home leave and to send him to Formosa, and then, as he was not considered to have shown proper diligence there, sent him to Ichang. Gregory registered a mild protest at being in effect demoted twice in twelve months, correctly deducing that his services were lightly esteemed, and amiably continued as before, submitting one of his annual trade reports exactly a year late. Possible steam navigation of the gorges was then being actively canvassed. Its leading British advocate, finding no support at Ichang, suggested to the Legation that charming though Gregory was in his private capacity he would do well to display a little more energy in public, and the Shanghai press referred to him as Ichang's dummy British representative. O'Conor toyed with the idea of forcing him into retirement by reducing Ichang to a vice-consulate under Hankow but left too soon to carry this through. Gregory remained at Ichang for four years until he retired at 60, a rare nineteenth-century example of retirement in good health. He went back to his home town in Wiltshire, abandoned celibacy and married a widow, frequented the British Museum reading-room, and died at 86 so unobtrusively that the annual Foreign Office lists kept him alive until the Second World War, when the entry for a man who would by then have been 111 years old was silently removed.[60]

At the beginning of the 1890s Ichang was busier, with four British steamers running from Hankow. The riverside boat population objected to the effects of their wash and pelted them when they came within range. Ichang was also less peaceful. Gregory's successor Everard encountered a steady unrest which had previously been unknown and which he attributed to the vile Hunan pamphlets. His coolness, pluck, and discretion were praised by a visiting bigwig who saw him deal in 1891 with what the bigwig, new to China, called a mob and Everard called an excited crowd. Graffiti calling for all foreigners to be killed followed, and just when everything seemed to have subsided a sudden riot destroyed

missionary properties. The mob did not tackle the Customs, whose entrance was guarded by the commissioner and his staff armed with rifles and fixed bayonets, and perhaps this show of force protected the neighbouring consulate, which was not attacked though Everard expected the mob to burst in at any moment. The magistrate, assisted by the brigadier, risked his own life to get missionaries through a raging mob to the safety of a steamer and no foreigners were killed, but in ruined compounds Everard detected evidence of intense hatred, every foreign article having been smashed into ten thousand pieces rather than looted. Placards threatening death to prefect, magistrate, converts, and foreigners kept appearing, one being posted on the consulate door, and he began to find the constant threat of murder intolerable.[61] The area once earmarked by King for a concession had by now been almost entirely absorbed by foreigners and with its two-storied buildings presented a thoroughly foreign appearance, and Everard suggested that it should be turned into a formal foreign settlement, in the absence of which foreigners were unable to maintain peace and good order. He thus unconsciously emphasized the total change which had crept over the concept of concessions and settlements. Their original purpose had been to overcome Chinese obstacles in the way of foreigners obtaining houses and business premises, now they were valued as a means of maintaining order and elementary hygiene and of undertaking public works. Nothing came of his suggestion, but on taking over after Everard's retirement Brady set his mind on public works. He decided that in the absence of a formal settlement he must proceed with extreme caution and in co-operation with the Chinese authorities, and aimed at a main drain into the river, other public works, and possibly a police force wearing the intendant's uniform but paid for by a public improvements committee. He had considerable success during his brief tenure. Before he left, bunding, no inconsiderable task on a waterfront along which the river level varied 40 feet between high and low water, was being completed, trees were being planted along the new bund, and standard lamps like those at Shanghai had been ordered. Road-making continued under the next consul, Holland, but cooking- and drinking-water, heavily polluted by the enormous boat population, still came from the river. During Holland's time the community were made uneasy by anti-foreign outbreaks up the river in Szechwan and down the river at Shasi, and

in 1895 there was an understandable outbreak when a stray shot
fired by a Chinese servant on a gunboat shooting-range killed a
Chinese official. Holland went to the spot with Chinese officials, a
mob stoned them, in a general *sauve qui peut* the officials tried to
protect the British by surrounding them and pushing through the
mob, Holland and two others got separated and had to fight their
own way through, being hit by stones, and Holland was defensive
in reporting to the Legation that a naval landing party had had to
restore order. In spite of such alarms and incidents Ichang consuls
remained underemployed. Brady was delighted to be transferred to
Kiukiang, and after six years at Ichang Holland was pleading for a
more active post.[62]

Wuhu was an even sleepier post. In 1897 British steamers were
making extensive use of Wuhu, paying twenty-three calls in one
quarter, but most residents were missionaries and foreign merchants had very little to do with Wuhu's increasing trade. In 1890
the one bona-fide merchant, an apparently respectable and trustworthy Austrian whom Everard had thought a welcome contrast
to hitherto very indifferent European merchants, suddenly fled,
probably making for Korea in disguise, and left massive debts
behind. There was a foreign element, largely Jewish, in the local
opium trade, but it cannot have been a social asset to the community. Most of these Jews, said B.C.G. Scott in the mid-1880s,
claimed British nationality owing to birth in India but had a very
imperfect knowledge of English, and a frequent lack of correctness
in their dealings made great caution necessary in taking up their
cases. Johnson, who did take up the Chinese closure of one Al-
lahabad man's hong, wrote to the intendant that it was the most
extraordinary outrage he had ever heard of during the whole period
of the intercourse between foreigners and Chinese, and was
reproved by the Legation for unnecessarily strong language.[63] In
two whole years in the 1880s only one despatch was sent to the
Legation and not a single one was received from the Legation.[64]
The only major break in the port's quietness came in 1891. Inflamed by rumours of kidnapping, a mob several thousand strong
suddenly attacked and burned down the Jesuit mission, which
adjoined the consulate, while C.M. Ford and the constable watched
from the consulate veranda. Ten months before, Ford had married
in England B.C.G. Scott's 39-year-old sister and she was now
pregnant, though in describing the riot Ford did not see fit to

mention her condition to the Legation. When a few hundred people broke into the consulate compound Ford 'thought it prudent to go in and shut all windows and venetians, my wife being meantime quietly on the upper floor making some little preparations in case we had to make our escape'. The consulate was not the major target of the rioters, who confined themselves to throwing stones through the windows. At dusk Chinese staff of the Customs contacted the Fords, dressed them in Chinese clothes, and got them away. Mrs Ford and other women spent the night on a hulk, protected by Ford and Customs outdoor staff. The Chinese authorities intervened to save the consulate and the Customs buildings, and after two or three weeks the tension was over.[65] The riot did not affect Ford's relations with local Chinese officials. The following year he described the intendant, who was about to become minister to the United States, as particularly straightforward, business-like, and pleasantly mannered; the succeeding intendant he described as very old and feeble but a most amiable gentleman; and some time later he called his relations with all leading officials exceptionally friendly. He did however take with noticeable seriousness a subsequent renewed allegation of Jesuit kidnapping.[66]

The five years ending with 1900 produced yet another five consulates, at Soochow and Hangchow on the southern stretch of the Grand Canal, at Shasi on the Yangtze, 80 miles as the crow flies below Ichang, at Yochow, near the confluence of Hunan's main river with the Yangtze, and at Nanking. The first three cities became treaty ports under the Sino-Japanese treaty of 1895. O'Conor cannot have had a high opinion of their prospects, for he arranged for consulates at them to be opened by assistants subordinate to nearby existing consulates. As he might have foreseen mere assistants-in-charge cut little ice with Chinese officials, and before Shasi had been opened MacDonald decided that while remaining subordinate the Soochow and Hangchow officers already at their posts should be designated acting consuls. In 1901 Soochow was suspended, and although Hangchow became a full consulate it was never important. At both ports the Japanese, having taken the lead in defining with the Chinese areas for foreign settlements, tried to reserve for Japanese nationals the best locations in the settlements, a portent of future Japanese attitudes in China.[67] The Shasi consulate was short-lived. Clennell arrived in 1897 towards the end of so fearful an epidemic, which he suggested might have killed some

17,000 people, that he could hardly walk in the streets without coming on corpses. In his absence at Shanghai for dental treatment the next year the Customs staff escaped with little more than their lives and their clothes from an anti-foreign riot. Clennell had been living on a junk, which he considered detracted from his consular dignity but which he had loyally illuminated for the Diamond Jubilee. The junk was moved out of harm's way by a resourceful servant who before moving it put his master's cat and two dogs safely on board, and despite Legation instructions to run no risks Clennell returned at once to ensure the safety of government property on the junk. In an admirably full trade report he concluded that foreign trade was likely to remain insignificant, and before the year was out suggested that the opening of the port had probably been a mistake and that the consulate might not be worth maintaining. The Legation responded by making the Ichang consulate responsible for Shasi and transferring Clennell, who got some benefit from the Shasi posting by marrying the sister of one of the Customs staff involved in the riot. No one else ever served at Shasi and the post was formally suspended in 1901.[68] Yochow was opened to foreign trade in response to British pressure. At the end of 1899 the Customs opened an office and a consulate site was selected. An assistant, Sundius, was promoted to be consul but officiated at Nanking instead of taking up his new Yochow post, at which E.F. Bennett may have briefly officiated in his place. In 1901 the Foreign Office told the Treasury that as a treaty port Yochow hampered foreign trade rather than facilitated it, and this obscurest of consulates disappeared.[69] The opening of Nanking was envisaged by the Sino-French treaty of 1858 but was effected only in 1899. Sundius opened the consulate in March 1900.[70] This was most fortunate timing. It meant that at the height of the Boxer troubles there was a British official on the spot to deal with Liu Kun-i, the Nanking viceroy. Sundius got on to terms with Liu by comparing symptoms of the piles from which both men suffered and by suggesting remedies,[a] and warmly acknowledged Liu's protection of foreigners on the lower Yangtze. On the verge of premature retirement a decade or so later Sundius disclaimed any distinguished service but wistfully said that he did think a little of the 1900 kudos might have come his way. In a semi-official letter P.L. Warren at Shanghai, better placed than anyone to know what happened on the Yangtze at that critical time, spoke most apprecia-

tively of Sundius' contribution, in another semi-official letter Satow said that Sundius had done well, and it does indeed seem as though he may have deserved more credit than he got in public.[71]

NORTH CHINA AND KOREA

THREE consulates in the north, at Tientsin, Chefoo, and New-chwang, resulted from the second peace settlement. The last two were established not at the places named in the settlement but at nearby places found on investigation to be more suitable.

Tientsin became a major centre of foreign trade, but it took off slowly. Although in 1867 there were over a hundred foreign residents the two biggest British firms in China had abandoned the port after trying it out, and the treaty port directory of that date said that the native city contained little of interest and was seldom visited, that the summer stench from its surrounding ditch was overpowering, that the effluvia from suburban soap-boiling were indescribably sickening, and that cholera, typhus, and smallpox abounded. In 1870 Wade still ranked Tientsin only fifth in order of treaty port importance.[1] Mongan, who opened the consulate in 1860, had none of the difficulties encountered elsewhere in taking over the concession site which Parkes had selected outside the city, for British troops had not yet left Tientsin. Mongan remained an uninspired but competent consul there for seventeen years, broken by close on five years' absence on two home leaves.[2] In 1877 he went home on sick-leave, lost his wife, was appointed to succeed D.B. Robertson at Canton, and after being given two leave extensions submitted an application to retire on health grounds. The next day Alcock, who had been retired for years, called at the Foreign Office to say that Mongan had become insane but was threatening to return to China at once with a Belgian mistress, that he had with great difficulty been persuaded by friends to sign the application, and that it should be accepted immediately before he changed his mind. The Foreign Office sent off their acceptance of the application that day, and Mongan died eighteen months later.[3]

During Mongan's incumbency a vice-consulate, standing in the

same relationship to the Tientsin consulate as the Whampoa and Pagoda Island vice-consulates stood to the Canton and Foochow consulates, functioned at Taku, 50 miles away at the mouth of the river on which Tientsin stood. It must have had strong claims to being China's dreariest consular post. Whampoa and Pagoda Island at least lay in pretty countryside. Taku, a settlement of junkmen and fishermen, lay among a desolation of mudflats mostly covered by water at high tide. The vice-consul's accommodation, almost wholly Chinese in construction, was surrounded by Chinese mud huts and was in 1872 described as very old and decaying and requiring replacement by a substantial and cheerful residence. The vice-consulate's function was to deal with sailing-ships, which unlike steamers could not get up the river to Tientsin. The post mouldered on, with less and less to do as steam replaced sail, until it was abolished in 1877.[4]

W.H. Lay was in acting charge at Tientsin, in Mongan's absence on home leave, at the time of the 'Tientsin massacre' in 1870. It was rumoured that children were being kidnapped and murdered in Roman Catholic institutions. In a resulting riot the French consul, a dozen or so priests and nuns, and some others were done to death. Lay refused to leave the consulate. Wade attributed the community's security to his firmness, and the Foreign Office said his conduct was beyond all praise. Most foreign women sought safety on board a steamship but Mrs Lay stuck by her husband, though for a week she did not dare undress. In the afternoon of the sixth day news of the outbreak reached Medhurst at Shanghai direct from Tientsin. He arranged for a British gunboat and a British steamship carrying fifteen police to leave for Tientsin that day, an action of which the Foreign Office entirely approved, but two and a half months later he had still heard nothing officially from the Legation about the outbreak or subsequent developments. The absence of information was typical. The next year a private letter from the Shanghai consulate said that Medhurst never heard from Wade,[a] and D.B. Robertson said in 1873 that he heard from Wade on political matters only on the infrequent occasions when they related to Canton. Lay was instructed to act temporarily as French consul and in that capacity had to examine the mutilated bodies of riot victims, the sight and dreadful stench making him sick and faint, and to negotiate with the Chinese authorities about the execution of convicted rioters, locally regarded as martyrs. Only

the urbanity of a Chinese brigadier saved him from another major incident the following year. A British naval officer, one of a naval party riding fast through Tientsin, accidentally struck the brigadier's face with his whip and was pulled to the ground by the brigadier's guard. In Lay's opinion the whole party would have been very seriously hurt or killed by the mob had the brigadier himself not rescued them. Lay arranged for the officer to call to apologize. The brigadier received him very courteously, advised him of the need for care, declared the matter closed, and shook hands. In recognition of his Tientsin services Lay was promoted to be consul at Chefoo, but the continuous tension had told on both him and his wife. She had to go home, suffering from ailments caused by fright and intense excitement, and she later claimed that the Tientsin strain had laid the seeds of the malady of which her husband died at Chefoo.[5]

The conduct of Howlett, the consulate assistant, at the time of the massacre was a good deal less admirable. Howlett had taken to the bottle. Mongan had married his sister in 1864, so in 1865 Wade had posted Howlett to Tientsin in the hope that under his brother-in-law's eye he might reform. Instead he got worse, and during the crisis was confined to his room all but helpless, his sole ailment according to his doctor being intemperance. He was sent home on a discreetly worded medical certificate, and having induced Lay to make a belated formal complaint Wade recommended Howlett's removal from the service. The Foreign Office decided that he should be told the charge before being dismissed but apparently failed to catch him before his return to China and he reappeared at Shanghai. From there C. Alabaster soon afterwards informed Wade in a private letter that Howlett had been seized with paralysis from drinking and had been advised by Alabaster to resign. In forwarding the resignation officially to Wade Alabaster wrote 'as when able to perform [his] duties he has always proved himself efficient and zealous, I trust that you may see fit to recommend his application for a retiring allowance'. Wade, while making all allowance for reluctance to injure a colleague, was much displeased by Alabaster's rejection of a suggestion that this passage should be deleted from his despatch. There was the same notable discrepancy at Shanghai as there had been at Tientsin between the doctor's official medical certificate and his private advice to the consulate. The certificate referred to general debility, hypertrophy of the liver,

valvular disease of the heart, and unfitness for further service. Privately the doctor said that Howlett's brain was steeped in alcohol and that he had been unable to stop him drinking. All this information was made available to the Foreign Office, but Howlett avoided dismissal and was allowed to resign, though without a pension.[6]

For many years after the massacre the Tientsin community escaped major disturbance and prospered, and the British concession was outgrown. In 1897, by which time there was twice as much British-owned land outside the concession as in it, H.B. Bristow, then the consul, secured Chinese agreement to the municipal council extending their sanitary and police powers over an adjoining area, half of which was already in British ownership but which lacked elementary sanitary controls. The previous year Bristow had seen close to the back of one of the area's foreign residences a grave from which dogs had pulled a corpse and eaten half a leg, and the next day the body had disappeared and three dogs lying nearby were so gorged that they could not move.[7] As the community grew the consulate's work, but not its staff, kept increasing. Bristow complained that although consular work had enormously increased, as semi-diplomatic work had done, the staff had meanwhile been so much reduced that for years all inessential work had been cut out and there had been no trade report for the previous two years. The Legation and Foreign Office, he said, might not realize that he could hardly do any work during the office hours of ten to four; a constant stream of callers came about such matters as contracts, claims against the Chinese government, the illegal detention of foreign goods, Customs difficulties, bank loans, and land, shipping, and railway questions; he frequently had to visit Chinese officials, the nearest of whom was half an hour away; collision cases might take days; he and an inexperienced assistant had recently spent three days over a collision case in which seven lives had been lost and meanwhile the other work of the office had had to be carried out by a corporal of marines loaned by the navy.[8]

The semi-diplomatic work to which he referred did not arise from the normal functions of the consulate, which was too close to the Legation to have much scope for independent initiatives, but was Legation work, devolved on the Tientsin consul as the Legation's agent. For a quarter of a century Li Hung-chang, the

most important subject in China, was viceroy of the province in
which Tientsin stood and spent eight months of each year at
Tientsin. He and the Legation used successive consuls as a channel
of communication on political issues unconnected with the consulate's ordinary responsibilities. Acute Sino-Russian tension over
Chinese Turkistan gave Bristow, when acting consul from 1879 to
1881, so much trying and responsible work that for months he
seldom had more than three or four hours' sleep. During Sino-
French tension in 1883 B. Brenan kept the Legation constantly
informed in private correspondence (which has not survived) of Li's
views on French proceedings.[9] Asking in 1886 for more pay Brenan
said that in such a centre of intrigue and activity he could keep
the Legation informed only by being in contact with Li and his
entourage, which meant fostering good relations in a hundred little
ways, most of which cost money; 'the time has not yet come when
social intercourse with Chinese is in itself a pleasure and the consul
here in trying to increase his circle of Chinese acquaintances acts
merely from a sense of duty'.[10] Recurring references to Li's cordial
manner at interviews suggest that he normally went out of his way
to be agreeable in these contacts.[11] The only complaint on that
score came from H.A. Giles, who as a junior assistant aged 26 was
sent by Mongan with a message. Li received him in the coldest
possible way, directing him to a seat on the other side of the room,
replying to his opening set phrases only by a slight inclination of the
head, and angrily using impolite language when the message was
delivered. Very probably, though Giles did not offer this explanation, this was merely the reaction of a high official who had lost
face by having to receive someone so far his inferior in rank.[12]
Besides Li's usual cordiality his readiness to experiment with
foreign ways was another point in his favour in consular eyes. In
1872, in the company of other senior officials and five consuls, he
was drawn through the British concession in an omnibus attached
to a steam traction-engine. In 1885 he rode in a four-horse English
landau, which Brenan likened to the lord-lieutenant of Ireland
processing through Dublin on an elephant. On his seventieth birth-
day in 1892 he invited some ninety foreigners, including women,
and twenty Chinese to a banquet at which Chinese and foreign
dishes were served alternately, the menu was in French, and his
15-year-old son responded in English to Brenan's toast.[13] Nevertheless expressions of personal liking for Li were conspicuously

lacking. Recalling in retirement his days as Chinese secretary Jordan described Li as intensely conceited, speaking a villainous dialect, and being altogether a difficult person to handle. Bristow liked him no better. On Bristow's impending departure from Tientsin becoming known Li, asking through the Tsungli Yamen whether Bristow could not be left at Tientsin, said that his relations with him had been as friendly as they had been with Brenan. MacDonald drew Foreign Office attention to such an uncommon manifestation of friendly Chinese feeling towards a foreign official but did not add that the feeling was not reciprocated. Bristow regarded Li as morally contemptible. The frivolity of many of Li's questions at the height of the Sino-Japanese war drove him to despair, making money seemed to him the only thing which Li took seriously, and he accused Li of subordinating China's interests to questions of personal face. By this time Bristow was very disillusioned about China generally. Asked in 1895 by a modern-minded Chinese whether he saw any hope of China turning over a new leaf he said that as far as he could judge after nearly thirty years in the country there was no hope whatever, to which the Chinese replied that that was exactly his own opinion.[14]

Tientsin's peaceful progress was savagely interrupted in mid-1900, when Carles was consul. Boxers entered the city and were joined by the local soldiery. The foreign concessions came under such heavy attack that a consular officer's brother-in-law made preparations to shoot his young wife if the defence failed.[a] The concessions were able to hold out only because of the chance presence of 1,700 Russian troops who reached Tientsin too late to join an expedition vainly trying under a British admiral to get through to Peking and to the beleaguered legations. A foreign relief force fought its way up to Tientsin from the coast and into the concessions, but they remained under considerable fire until three weeks later the Chinese city was stormed and taken. Carles wrote that the community owed their lives to the Russians, who had fought most bravely but who after the relief force's arrival had been barbarously butchering innocent Chinese and clearing the country-side of all life wherever they marched. He collapsed from overwork and anxiety less than a month after the legations had been relieved, went home sick, and retired. The Foreign Office showed their opinion of criticisms of his behaviour at Tientsin by procuring for him a CMG.[15] Campbell, though not in the best of shape, took

over from him. He had volunteered while on leave to accompany
the admiral's expedition. While acting as an interpreter he put
himself within 100 yards of a Chinese gun and many Chinese rifle-
men in an attempt to parley and escaped unhurt from the heavy
fire opened on him, but on his return to Tientsin a bullet hit him, he
was in hospital for two months with violent blood-poisoning, from
the effects of which he never fully recovered, and he was lame for
months.[16]

On account of its poor communications with the hinterland Chefoo was not a great commercial success, and in 1891 there were
effectively only four foreign mercantile firms, three of them British.
It prospered however in other ways. It had its share of China's
usual diseases but the climate suited Europeans, and it was described as the Brighton of China. In the 1890s C.F.R. Allen wrote of
its schools, hotels, and lodging-houses, of constant visits by foreign
warships, and of foreign ministers residing there in the summer to
avoid Peking's heat, and in a despatch which mentioned a new
foreign cemetery and very heavy cholera deaths among Chinese he
claimed that Chefoo showed immense advance as a sanatorium.[17]

M.C. Morrison opened the consulate in 1861 and busied himself
quarrelling with the local French representatives. Bruce, Alcock,
and Wade all thought well of him as a man and badly of him as
a consul, and there was much relief when after years of peculiar
behaviour he decided to go home, where he retired on health
grounds and quickly died.[18] Morrison's lasting memorial at Chefoo
was a negative one, the absence of a concession. He agreed a site
with the Chinese but spent so much time quarrelling about it with
the French that Bruce had time to decide against unnecessarily
increasing the number of points which, in China's disturbed state,
might require to be defended and to rule against a Chefoo concession. British consuls and their foreign colleagues repeatedly tried
in the later nineteenth century to secure a formally defined foreign
settlement area and regulations for its governance, but they were
not successful.[19]

At the time of Morrison's departure Chefoo's future looked so
unpromising that the sleepy consulate was temporarily reduced to a
vice-consulate. Sleepy though Chefoo was C. Alabaster as acting
vice-consul twice had occasion to display his usual readiness to cut
Gordian knots. The French captain of a Siamese vessel, assaulted by
the non-French mate, complained to Alabaster in the latter's

concurrent capacity of French consul. As French consul Alabaster asked the intendant to try the case, on the grounds that the vessel was Siamese and that Siam had no extraterritorial rights. Then the mate turned out to have been born in England, so Alabaster as British consul became inclined to claim jurisdiction. The United States consul claimed jurisdiction in the belief that the mate had become an American citizen. The intendant would not give up his claim to jurisdiction over a Siamese ship. At Alabaster's suggestion all three officials agreed to try the case jointly, a doubtless illegal solution which Alcock approved. The second case was more serious. Two Chinese were severely beaten for leasing property to a British missionary and were then further examined by the intendant in Alabaster's presence. Embarrassed by Alabaster's questioning the intendant affected to fly into a rage and bounced out of the room. Alabaster found out that on the intendant's orders the men were to be removed in the small hours to a safe enough distance from foreigners for them to be punished again. Asked to counter-mand his orders the intendant regretted his inability to do so as the men had already been moved. Alabaster went quietly to the police magistrate's yamen, ascertained that the men were still there, and took them away over only faint objections, informing the intendant of his action by a letter sent in before daylight. The intendant called in state to profess great sorrow at the misunderstanding, Alabaster readily accepted the apologies, and the friendliest relations were restored, but Alabaster's expectations of a compromise solution were dashed by the intendant's sudden replacement. Alcock, who took the case up strongly in Peking, was not willing to censure Alabaster, saying that his irregular act had been the only way of preventing wrong and perhaps of saving the men's lives.[20]

Quietness continued after full consulate status had been restored, but in 1874 there was a manslaughter case which was grossly mishandled. Villagers had impeded the construction of a Customs lighthouse and in a scuffle an artificer named Fawcett shot and killed one of them. W.H. Lay, the consul, was poor at Chinese, he by now had an incurable disease of unspecified character, and if Cooper, the consulate interpreter, is to be credited, he had become an alcoholic.[21] How much Chinese Cooper knew, and how com-petent he was, is doubtful, as Wade and Parkes in their respective periods as minister expressed disconcertingly dissimilar opinions and coincided only in calling him zealous. Wade called him medio-

crity itself and alleged that he had a remarkable inaptitude for the language, and the Foreign Office classed him among the so-called interpreters who could not interpret. Parkes praised his considerable knowledge of Chinese and tactful handling of Chinese authorities, and unsuccessfully recommended a personal increase in pay in recognition of long and meritorious services.[22] What is certain is that Cooper was not on good terms with Lay and, pleading unfamiliarity with the local dialect, declined to interpret in court. Lay's committal proceedings were a disaster, and a suggestion by the intendant, who was present, that Lay should throw Fawcett on the floor and flog him into a confession did not advance matters. Lay discharged Fawcett for lack of evidence, the Chinese officials present were so indignant that for a time they physically prevented Lay from leaving the courtroom, and the chief judge, who said Lay had turned the proceedings into a formal farce, had Fawcett re-arrested and tried him. Wade was dissatisfied with the verdict of not guilty which the jury took only a few minutes to bring in, but was much more dissatisfied with the earlier handling of the case by the consulate, which he roundly criticized.[23] The removal of Lay from his post in the public interest was however not for a moment considered, and in mentioning to the Foreign Office Lay's mishandling of a subsequent civil action between two British subjects Wade seemed to think it an adequate explanation that ill-health made Lay hardly equal to his judicial duties. Lay remained at his post until he died in 1876, aged 40, leaving under £800 to support a widow, who soon followed him to the grave at 35, and seven surviving children.[24] Five or so years later the community were putting up with an even less effective consul. McClatchie, one of Parkes' nephews, was suffering from a complication of disorders any one of which might have ended fatally, and after a couple of years the excitement of a minor dispute brought on a heart attack which carried him off at 36. He had been neglecting his duties wholesale. His first despatch to the Legation in the calendar year preceding his death had been sent in late September, he submitted no trade reports, and two colleagues successively sent by the Legation to help him get his accounts off failed to unravel or extract them. After his death it emerged that he had kept no cash book and had drawn on one common fund for public and private expenditure. Defalcation does not seem to have been suspected, but the timing of McClatchie's death, a few months before Parkes took over the

Legation, must have avoided embarrassment for the uncle.[25]

By treaty port standards Chefoo was normally a peaceful place, but as China tried to create a modern fleet in the north and as international rivalries and tensions mounted the consulate ceased to be a political backwater. When H.B. Bristow was consul in 1886 the British admiral sailed to Port Arthur to call on the Manchu prince nominally responsible for the fleet, which in reality was the creation of Li Hung-chang. In discussing with Li the protocol for the admiral's call on the prince Bristow perceived that the Chinese did not want the admiral to watch the fleet manoeuvres in case mistakes were made, and he therefore said that the admiral hoped he would not be thought discourteous if owing to urgent business elsewhere he sailed immediately after calling. Li, previously rather reserved, broke into smiles, insisted on Bristow taking wine with him, and shook his hand with somewhat embarrassing warmth, and the official call became a great success. To Bristow's astonishment the prince called for a group photograph, all formality vanished, the prince, the Manchu general, and Li talked and joked freely, and Li nudged Bristow to call his attention to such satisfactory proceedings. The Legation were apparently shocked, for in forwarding Bristow's report to the Foreign Office they partially deleted his description of the informality.[26]

In 1889 Bristow feared an attack on the foreign residential area by mutinous troops, but nothing happened. Similarly during the Sino-Japanese war C.F.R. Allen was uneasy, the cause of unease being not so much the probable behaviour of Japanese troops attacking the town but the probable behaviour of Chinese troops defending it, but the Japanese contented themselves with taking Weihaiwei and left Chefoo alone.[27] The growth of the Boxer movement in Shantung was more alarming. The movement was either encouraged or was not repressed by two successive provincial governors who were arch-conservatives and who were removed in response to Western pressure. The two reactionaries were followed by Yuan Shih-k'ai, later president of republican China. He took strong measures against Boxers, but had hardly assumed office before they murdered a British missionary at the beginning of 1900. Campbell, the vice-consul at Shanghai, had known and liked Yuan in Korea. Presumably for that reason it was not the acting consul but Campbell who was sent to Tsinan, the provincial capital and the governor's seat, to see that justice was done on the male-

factors. Campbell reported that Yuan, whom he knew to be quick-tempered and as obstinate as a mule, received him with his usual bonhomie, urged him with friendly insistence to occupy the official quarters prepared for him, and on Campbell declining to put him to so much trouble hinted with a laugh that Campbell probably preferred to stay with the missionaries because he could hear things there, to which Campbell replied that Yuan had hit it exactly. Campbell presided jointly with the provincial judge at the trial of eighteen accused men, took charge of the trial when the provincial judge's handling did not please him, examined the accused, and satisfied himself that many of them were innocent. The punishments recommended for the guilty by the provincial judge were relatively lenient. Campbell went over his head to Yuan, secured Yuan's agreement to one of the two principals being beheaded and the other being strangled, was present when at least one of the executions was carried out, and was praised by MacDonald for energy, tact, and judgement.[28]

T.T. Meadows arrived at Newchwang in 1861 to open a consulate whose jurisdiction covered the whole of Manchuria. Finding that foreign shipping could not reach Newchwang, 40 miles up river from the mouth of the Liao river, he established the consulate lower down, 13 miles from the mouth. It always remained there, though it was misleadingly called the Newchwang consulate. Its situation, surrounded by mudbanks, salt-marsh, and bare salty plains, appeared to Meadows most uninviting, and the 1867 treaty port directory called the place dreary in the extreme, standing on a muddy river which was closed by ice from mid-November to the end of March and which ran through a plain of mud, being characterized by unusual filth and squalor and being built of mud. A later incumbent however spoke of beautiful scenery in the nearby hills and of a splendid climate, less cold than Canada in winter, where the European could enjoy sunny days, cloudless skies, and as much vigour as at home.[29]

Within ten days of arriving Meadows settled the site for a riverfront British concession and divided it into lots. This was the only British concession for the siting of which Parkes was not responsible and it was a total failure. When a consulate was built it was built elsewhere, the concession was not laid out, only a few lots were leased, and the river, which was half a mile broad and sometimes ran at 9 knots, kept washing bits of it away. In the twentieth

century only four lots remained as an almost forgotten relic of imperialism, the rest having disappeared into the river.[30] Meadows himself moved into a temple which remained in consular occupation until the new consulate was built in the early 1870s.[31] The treaty port directory said that the temple was somewhat better than the other primitive foreign residences, Alcock said that it was unfit for stabling European horses, and Meadows said that it had its inconveniences. The bedroom, sitting-room, dining-room, and drawing-room were all separated from each other by open court-yards which Meadows had to traverse in all weathers, and his servants were so far away that to summon them he employed a small ship's bell, a large gong, and a somewhat smaller gong. Both dining-room and drawing-room were reduced in size, and rather disfigured, by the presence in an alcove of a god which he considered it would have been tactless to remove. In the winter he had to heat his stove red-hot, and wear furs, in order to be able to write, and a successor objected to the luxuriant growth of herbage on the dining-room floor and walls in the hot weather. Meadows put in European windows, doors, and fireplaces, and round the grounds he built a 6-foot mud wall, in the interests of privacy and as a protection against the local habit of relieving nature under the nearest blank wall. He kept six large dogs ready to attack any stranger and an abundance of weapons, ranging from a 32-pounder, rifles, smooth-bore guns, and pistols to spears used in his tiger, bear, and wolf hunts. The consul's appearance matched the peculiarity of the consulate. Always tall with long arms and sinewy hands he was now gaunt, his head was closely shaved, he wore immense Chinese spectacles on a large nose, and his clothing was 'of that character which tells of no age or nation'.[32]

At the start it was hardly a lucky consulate. Meadows' original assistant, Davenport, got so wet one night on the deck of the warship which brought Meadows and him to Newchwang that he was seized with spasmodic stricture of the bladder and would have died in intense suffering but for the presence of a naval surgeon, and immediately after arrival he was severely injured while trying to rescue a Chinese woman from Chinese assailants. Goddard, another assistant, was fortunate that a naval surgeon was in the port when he broke his arm in a fall on ice, but the surgeon had gone when Meadows' horse fell and he too injured his arm. It was left to Davenport and the United States merchant consul to examine

Meadows' injury and to decide that the arm was neither broken nor dislocated. Then while riding from Newchwang to Peking Meadows dismounted, his pony shook itself, and a revolver in a saddle holster went off and broke his thigh. It took eleven days for a doctor to reach him from Tientsin and set the bone, he was carried to Tientsin in a box-bed serving as a litter, and he could not resume his post for six months.[33]

Meadows was becoming increasingly odd and solitary. He did not give a warm welcome to the wife and sister-in-law of a new constable. 'I interfere so little with the extra-official life of those officially under me', he told the Legation after the women had been there for some fifteen months, 'that although inhabiting the same group of buildings I have scarcely seen and have never spoken to either'. The Legation also learned from him that he and his assistants usually communicated by reciprocally stating on slips of paper what would otherwise be stated orally.[34] This remoteness no doubt accounted for his failure to notice the habits of one of his later assistants, Beatty, until Platt, one of the port's leading British merchants, protested to him about them. Beatty, it seems, smoked opium with his servants and liked describing in company the distasteful details of his homosexual relations with them. Once alerted Meadows' reaction was characteristic, for he must have been the only Victorian servant of the Foreign Office to have included four-letter words in an official despatch. Equally characteristic was Alcock's reaction, preserved in his draft of a despatch to the Foreign Office. He transmitted Meadows' report with extreme repugnance and regret; 'I would willingly spare Your Lordship or anyone else the odious task I have been compelled myself to perform of going through these voluminous papers in all their filthy details, and as I cannot bring myself to pass them through the Chancellerie [sic] to be copied I send the originals'. He suggested that as the charges against Beatty were not actually proven the interests of the service, and perhaps of justice, might be secured by allowing Beatty to retire. The Foreign Office were so scandalized that the signed fair copy of Alcock's draft is not to be found in its expected place in their archives and may not have been allowed to survive at all. They instructed Alcock to call forthwith for Beatty's resignation and to dismiss him immediately should he even hesitate about resigning. Whether he resigned or was dismissed is not clear. Being unable to find work in China he asked Alcock for a ticket

to Australia. Alcock provided the ticket on condition that libel proceedings which Beatty had instituted against Meadows were dropped, believing that this would save legal expenses and probable further annoyance from Beatty's continued presence in China.[35]

In 1868 the number of Newchwang residents had risen to eighty, of whom twenty were pilots. The British predominated, Americans coming next.[36] Meadows' despatches do not give a flattering picture of the community. In a brawl between a German tide-waiter and a British pilot the pilot bit off part of the German's nose and his own nose was also bitten, either by the German or by another tide-waiter's dog. There were only six married men, and two-thirds of the unmarried men had Chinese concubines, who figured largely in civil and criminal cases in the British consular court. Concubines were so normal that the written contract of an American merchant's British employee provided for the employee's concubine to receive board, lodging, and medical attendance on the firm's premises. During the employee's absence on the firm's business the American, who had a concubine of his own, tried to have relations with the employee's concubine and the contract was produced as evidence in the resulting suit in the United States consular court. Meadows much disapproved of the behaviour of Customs Commissioner MacPherson, whose position in the port he considered second only to his own. Outside the consulate gate MacPherson and another resident, both drunk, got into a deep muddy puddle 'where they rolled about for some time, plastering each other's faces with mud and laughing idiotically at the feat. They then sank into apparent unconsciousness', and MacPherson's servants were summoned to carry him home. Drunk again, MacPherson got into the house of the absent Platt and tried to force his attentions on Platt's Cantonese concubine, or to rape her. A substantial payment by MacPherson bought off any complaint by the concubine and Platt did not want to make enemies by lodging a charge, so, mindful of instructions that consuls should support the Customs, Meadows in his judicial capacity let the matter rest. In his capacity as consul he felt unable to let it remain unnoticed; few bachelors at treaty ports were disposed to be over-prudish about concubines; 'Mr MacPherson might have had 2 or 3 such in his own house, and might have visited at night those of every other British resident of the place, so long as the women themselves were consenting parties' without official or personal relations with Meadows being affected;

but Meadows felt bound to cease cultivating private intercourse with a man whose conduct was so scandalous.[37]

Alarming reports flowed in from Meadows about a local breakdown of Chinese law and order.[38] Alcock, disclaiming any wish to reflect on Meadows' undoubted conscientiousness and truthfulness or on his admitted moral and intellectual attainments, warned the Foreign Office that forcibly and ably though Meadows expressed himself he was apt to give local circumstances a magnitude and importance they would not possess in other eyes. The warning was justified, but banditry was certainly so rife that most wayfarers went armed with sword, spear, or gun. Meadows had much to say about Newchwang gangsters known as sword-racks. He learned that a sword-rack chief had announced in one of the brothels which served as local clubhouses an intention of assassinating first Meadows and then the remaining foreigners, and according to his account three leading officials to whom he mentioned this threat all declared that the chief must be put to death, intimated that it would be quite proper for Meadows to shoot the chief himself, and evidently preferred that solution. It was presumably owing to the disturbed state of the countryside that when travelling to try an alleged homicide case at the scene of the incident, a week's journey away, he was accompanied not only by the accused, 2 assessors, the constable, the assistant constable, and the writer but also by 3 consulate messengers, 11 private servants, 7 riding-horses, and 18 small carts. The party was so strong and well-armed, and attack was therefore so unlikely, that the Chinese authorities provided a series of escorts which relied on the party for safety.[39]

While the port was iced up in winter the navy in the early days usually left an armed guard,[40] but Meadows was concerned to increase the community's own capacity to repel violence. He drilled twenty-four volunteer residents in the manual of platoon exercise, teaching himself his business as an officer as he went along and like all the volunteers participating in target shooting without distinction of social footing. In one of his wildest moments he proposed to the Legation that the Chinese government should authorize him to raise, at their expense and in their service, a troop of 100 horse which he would employ against all who defied the imperial authority.[41] In vast journeys through Manchuria he travelled heavily armed and his behaviour in his travels led to strong Tsungli Yamen

complaints. The Foreign Office issued a rebuke; his suitability for his responsible post had begun to be doubted; he should maintain friendly relations and not take things into his own hands; consuls, whose duty it was to prevent British acts of violence against Chinese, must set an example of respect for Chinese laws, customs, or even prejudices. For once Meadows did not argue and accepted the rebuke, but his superiors remained anxious. In 1866 Hammond minuted that Meadows was clever but had as little judgement and tact as could well be found, and that he really dreaded what he would do.[42] In 1868 Meadows removed the problem by dying suddenly at his post. Alcock's comment was that the poor fellow had gone to his rest, with all his impracticable zeal for the public interest. The Foreign Office minuted that a clever though at times too energetic a servant had been lost and that the salary of the Newchwang post could now be reduced.[43]

After Meadows' death banditry, though endemic in winter, ceased to be such a major concern.[44] In 1871 Adkins, who had started a nine-year tenure of the Newchwang post the previous year and who was suffering such deep depression that on medical advice he took a three-month winter trip into unknown parts of northern Manchuria to examine trade routes, assured Wade that the journey would be free from any danger other than the ordinary risks of travel. During the winter of 1885 C.T. Gardner in a journey of 460 miles saw not a single armed man except uniformed soldiers, whereas twenty years before he never met an unarmed man, and he met with unvarying politeness from manly, honest fellows who only needed soap to be quite agreeable people among whom to sojourn. Even in peaceful conditions, however, the consular traveller in Manchuria had to be hardy. Chinese travel was normally arduous and exhausting, but cold was an additional discomfort in Manchuria, where travelling was done in winter. When the ground thawed, or in the rainy season, horses often suffocated or drowned in quagmires, and the roads were suitable for carts only when the country was ice-bound. Adkins was spitting blood by the time he got to Kirin, and on the way to Kirin in 1896 Hosie recorded 66° of frost. Gardner started out at 4 or 5 a.m. for up to fourteen hours on the road, dismounting every so often for ice to be knocked off the horses' feet. He made himself still more uncomfortable by standing on his dignity. He went in first to a wayside hut for his midday meal of frozen meat and then waited

outside in the cold while the men ate their meal inside, not caring to forfeit their respect by allowing them to eat in his presence.[45]

So quiet did the consulate become that for a period of years in the 1880s and early 1890s its numbered despatches to the Legation rarely reached double figures in any one year, and in 1892 only two were sent.[46] Military operations in Manchuria during the Sino-Japanese war jolted the consulate out of its torpor. In 1894 Bullock sent over eighty despatches and Hosie sent nearly as many in 1895.[47] Bullock's main concern was the safety of missionaries, nearly all of whom he tactfully persuaded to withdraw. One was murdered by Chinese troops. In his pursuit of the case Bullock demonstrated consular absorption of Chinese concepts, in this instance the concept that decapitation, which left the body muti-lated, was much worse than strangulation, which left the body in one piece. He angrily protested to the governor, who he understood to have agreed to behead the main culprit, on hearing the man had merely been strangled, and he told the Legation that the punishment was unquestionably insufficient. Newchwang fell to the Japanese without resistance and they remained in occupation for some nine months.[48] With the return of peace the consulate reverted briefly to its old ways and in 1897 only six despatches went to the Legation.[49] The port was however moving into a different world. By the end of the century it was connected by rail both with Tientsin and with Dairen and its physical isolation by land had ended.[50] In 1900 the Russians used the Boxer troubles as an excuse for taking effective control over all Manchuria, and at Newchwang Fulford found them more troublesome than Hosie had found the Japanese.[51] From then on consuls at Newchwang, and at other posts subsequently opened in Manchuria, fought a long-drawn but losing battle against British interests being squeezed out of Manchuria by Russia and Japan.

The two posts in Korea, the consulate-general at Seoul and the vice-consulate at Chemulpo, were staffed from China from the mid-1880s until 1902, after which they were with occasional exceptions staffed from the Japan service. Both posts were almost entirely political. The consulate-general, which was filled successively by three former Chinese secretaries, Baber, W.C. Hillier, and Jordan, was for a time a plum China service post.[52] It would be outside the scope of the present book to enter into the tortuous violence of politics in Korea, where China's claims to suzerainty conflicted

with Russian and Japanese territorial ambitions, but the effect of Korea postings on the careers of some China officers calls for mention.

Baber was perhaps being kicked upstairs when sent from Peking to Seoul as acting consul-general in 1885. He disliked the Peking climate and was not cut out for the Chinese secretary's work. Other Chinese secretaries slaved away at their desks, whereas according to O'Conor Baber never put pen to paper.[53] Seoul was much better suited to his idiosyncratic style. He established such good relations with the Chinese resident, Yuan Shih-k'ai, that for hours the two men would lie gossiping in front of a roaring fire and smoking innumerable cigarettes, a habit which Yuan learned from Baber. Then Baber fell ill. He suffered from chronic malaria and rheumatism, but this illness, medically ascribed largely to defective accommodation, may have been something new, for a French source put his later death down to a disease contracted in Korea.[54] The United States chargé d'affaires in Seoul wrote to Parker, the acting vice-consul at Chemulpo, that Baber was greatly changed, very thin and forgetful but not seriously affected in his mind. Parker reported that according to the consulate-general doctor, Baber had been seeing double and walking about all night with a gun on the look-out for thieves; that he had been coaxed away to Chemulpo in the charge of the doctor, who did not consider his condition bad enough to warrant removal against his will; and that he had been got away from there to Chefoo on the high road to derangement but in time to prevent any further encroachment on his reason. Baber went home on sick-leave on various gloomy medical certificates, but whether his mental stability was ever affected seems very doubtful. Later Legation archives provide no clues, for at the end of his leave he was seconded to the Indian service as a deputy commissioner in upper Burma and died there in 1890 without returning to China.[55] What is indisputable is that Parker himself was in an abnormal mental state.

Pending the arrival from Foochow of Watters, who had been instructed to take over Seoul temporarily, Parker on Baber's departure moved, with or without instructions, to Seoul. From papers there he discovered that his suitability to take acting charge of Seoul had been doubted by Baber,[56] and at the Legation Walsham received a barrage of cryptic telegrams about the alleged misdeeds of Baber. Parker requested that in view of painful

disclosures Watters' arrival should be delayed, thus saving a great public scandal and Baber's honour; Baber, unsound in mind or false, had placed numerous untruths on official record, cruelly humbugging Walsham, Parker, and many others; Watters might be an accomplice and had long ago been declared by the Foreign Secretary unfit for responsible duties; Baber had written telegrams and memoranda on tiger skins and porcelain; Baber had wanted to keep Parker away from Seoul for fear that Baber's blunders would be detected by a man too truthful to conceal them; Baber had at all his posts shown symptoms of mania by violent acts. Walsham's demand that an explanation of the allusions to Baber should at once be accurately and briefly telegraphed received the succinct but unenlightening reply 'Briefly and accurately deranged forgiven'. Parker was ordered away from Korea to Shanghai, where the consul-general soon described him as very penitent. He received an enormously long reprimand from Walsham,[57] but within three years was promoted vice-consul and a year later was promoted consul at Hoihow, both promotions being on Walsham's recommendation.[58] He detested Hoihow and at times behaved somewhat eccentrically there.[59] On home leave in 1895 he asked not to be sent back to Hoihow, but the Foreign Office, where he had the reputation of being rather mad and often troublesome, knew that O'Conor preferred to keep him at a distance from Peking and were unsympathetic. To avoid more of Hoihow he opted to retire on health grounds, and five years into retirement was still continuing vain efforts to get Walsham's reprimand withdrawn. He long held a fairly nominal chair of Chinese at Manchester.[60]

Joly, like Baber, was a victim of Korean accommodation. He died of a chill caught in his unheated Chemulpo bedroom. He was still not yet a substantive vice-consul and had for years been supporting his mother, herself the widow of a vice-consul in the Levant. Consequently he left his widow and three young children almost entirely without provision. The Foreign Office could of course do nothing for them, but the Tsungli Yamen sent them £140 in recognition of Joly's services to Chinese in Chemulpo and Mrs Joly found work as teacher of the Korean crown prince.[61] When grown up the two sons entered the well-paid Customs in China and the daughter married the no doubt well-paid employee of an oil company in the Far East, but on the widow's death in China thirty years later her estate there was valued at less than £100.[62] For

Jordan, on the other hand, appointment to Korea opened the way upwards.

Although Jordan was unquestionably a man of outstanding ability and high character he had more than his share of the luck without which no official can rise to the top. At first luck ran steadily against him. After attending Bangor Endowed School[a] he did well in classics at the Queen's University, and for unknown reasons set his sights on the Japan service. Writing to the Foreign Office at the age of 21 in a not unduly literate hand or style he said he wished to compete for a Japan place but could not go on preparing for the examination for more than another year, and he therefore asked whether there would be another entrance examination within that period. A typically unhelpful and curt reply said that the date of the next examination was not known. Undiscouraged he waited almost two years for the next examination. He came second to another Irishman who took the only Japan place, and he had to settle for China. In his first four years he was seriously ill three times. Illnesses at Peking lost him three months' language study, and a decision to bring forward the second-year language examination left him insufficient time to make up the lost ground. Instead of coming top in the examination, as Wade thought he would otherwise almost certainly have done, he was beaten into second place by his contemporary Bourne, who thereby became his senior. The Legation sympathetically said that in a service where all future promotion was governed by seniority this was a most serious misfortune.[63] So it proved to be. Bourne was promoted second assistant in 1880. In 1883 Jordan sought similar promotion so that he could go on leave without the humiliation of returning home in the same rank and at the same salary as when he had left, but although he had done well as acting consul at Hoihow, where he was again seriously ill, he went home unpromoted as a student interpreter after eight years' service. Only after his return as a married man in 1885 did he become a second assistant, five and a half years later than Bourne.[64] Thereafter his luck changed and fortune consistently smiled on him. The post of Legation accountant fell vacant on the death of a man from outside the service who had held it for many years. The Legation recommended a named first assistant to fill it. The Foreign Office unexpectedly ruled that it should instead be filled by a second assistant with an allowance, a ruling which made Jordan eligible. O'Conor wished to avoid fre-

quent changes of accountant, and Jordan volunteered to accept the post for a minimum of five years.[65] It was a boring job, but Jordan's object in volunteering[a] was to escape a possible further posting to anywhere as uncongenial as Hoihow. The result was that Jordan was on the spot in Peking when staff changes in the Chinese secretariat occurred. Within a year he had moved sideways into the secretariat as acting assistant Chinese secretary. He gave so much satisfaction, and there were so many other changes in the secretariat, that by 1891 he was Chinese secretary.[66] Then glaucoma forced W.C. Hillier, the consul-general at Seoul, into retirement in his prime. O'Conor and MacDonald both considered Jordan the most suitable successor, but the much senior B. Brenan had claims which could not be overlooked. Brenan declined Seoul, and with Hillier and Brenan both out of the way Jordan received the appointment in 1896, thus rising from student interpreter to consul-general in eleven years. The crucial step in his career followed. In 1898 it was decided that the Seoul post should be independent of the Peking Legation and that Jordan needed to have the right of audience with the Korean monarch. A consular officer could not claim the right, so Jordan was first made chargé d'affaires and then minister resident.[67] By mere chance he had left the consular service behind him and entered the diplomatic service. The tightening Japanese grip on Korea, which was losing its independence, led to the closure of the Seoul Legation in 1906. The new diplomatist was left without a post. By a final extraordinary stroke of luck Satow was just vacating the Peking Legation. Against Satow's advice Jordan was appointed his successor.[68] He held the post for fourteen years with so much distinction that he achieved the exceptional honour of membership of the Privy Council.

WESTERN AND
SOUTH-WESTERN CHINA

THE provinces of Szechwan, Kweichow, and Yunnan in the west and south-west of China long remained virtually unknown to the British. In an attempt to lift the veil the Indian government in 1874 sent a mission from Bhamo in upper Burma into Yunnan to explore routes between the two countries. Passports for the mission, which with its armed escort numbered nearly 200 persons, had been obtained from the Tsungli Yamen by Wade, but in the Yunnan borderland the mission met armed resistance and had to retire. With the Yamen's agreement Margary, a second assistant, had been sent overland right across China to join the mission as interpreter. He was murdered in the borderland. The despatch of the mission was ill-judged. Even in ordinary times China exercised only a wavering control over her unsinicized border tribes, and a Muslim rebellion in Yunnan lasting nearly twenty years and costing many millions of lives had only just been put down in a sea of blood. It is difficult to disagree with D.B. Robertson's comment to Hammond from Canton that the British had invited attack by unwisely attempting the passage of a frontier so recently the seat of war, that the whole affair had been a most unnecessary imbroglio, that there would be a fuss were an armed party to be marched across France or Germany, and that the ways of the Indian government passed all comprehension. Nevertheless, to settle what became known as the Margary affair China had to meet British demands on a variety of wholly unrelated issues.[1]

Margary had had a great deal of difficulty in getting into the service. He failed the entrance examination three times owing to bad spelling. In acceding to B.C.G. Scott's request for a third nomination after he had twice failed the examination the Foreign Office had very recently noted unenthusiastically that a third

chance though not prohibited was not usual. After his third failure Margary asked whether as his other marks had been good he could be given an appointment if he were able to pass a special spelling test to be set for him by the Civil Service Commission or whether alternatively he could be nominated to compete a fourth time. The Foreign Office received his pleas more sympathetically, no doubt because he was related to the political under-secretary. Hammond recommended the special test, the Foreign Secretary preferred to give yet another nomination, and this time Margary did succeed.[2] In 1871 he distinguished himself at Kelung by gallantry in saving lives at sea during a typhoon and although for some time Wade forgot to report this the omission was repaired and Margary was awarded the Albert Medal (equivalent to the modern George Medal).[3] Now he was a friendly, uncomplicated young man of 28. He left Shanghai in August 1874 and reached Bhamo in January 1875. He travelled by boat until the end of October and then by chair and on horseback, maintaining his spirits and enthusiasm in spite of indigestion, fever, dysentery, pleurisy, rheumatism, very bad neuralgia, and toothache. For the most part he was treated with great courtesy by officials. Many of them he found most congenial; 'by being daily thrown into the very midst of their private life [I] have learned more in this trip than I could have done at the ports in any number of years'; he was proud to think how much good his contacts along the route had done towards establishing amicable relations. He was treated with particular courtesy in Yunnan, met the mission at Bhamo, returned with it across the frontier, went forward unaccompanied except by personal servants to look into rumours of a coming attack on the mission, and was murdered with nearly all his servants. Who murdered him, and who instigated the murder, is unknown to this day. Wade intuitively blamed the acting viceroy of Yunnan and demanded his personal punishment, a demand which was not met. Twenty years later Li Hung-chang in a conversation with O'Conor said he had no doubt that the acting viceroy had connived at the murder and probably instigated it. The statement could safely be made as by that time the acting viceroy was dead, but why Li chose to make it, whether he believed it to be true, and whether he was in a position to know the truth are matters for speculation.[4] All that can be said with certainty is that the murder deprived China of an unusually sympathetic consular official and that Margary was a sad

loss to the service. Margary's ailing father died the following year, leaving a widow with a very small income on which to support three surviving sons and nine entirely dependent daughters, and a huge indemnity of £10,000 paid by the Chinese government was put in trust for the family's benefit. Margary was commemorated on the Shanghai bund by a 37-foot-high memorial, described as a neat and graceful structure after the Gothic style, and was given a place in the *Dictionary of National Biography*. In the twentieth century the register of Brighton College, where he and his brothers had been educated, included some biographical information about the unremarkable brothers and none about the consular officer, whose posthumous celebrity had apparently escaped the college's memory.[5]

In settling the Margary affair Wade, who in 1871 had deplored the prevailing sad ignorance about west China, extracted Chinese agreement to the stationing of a consular agent in the Szechwanese city of Chungking on the upper Yangtze, but accepted a Chinese proviso that Chungking should at present not be opened to foreign trade. It was not opened until 1891. Pending the opening the main consular functions at Chungking were to see that the treaty provisions about transit passes were observed and by extensive travel to find out as much as possible about west China and its resources.[6] It was a post for the hardy. It was difficult to reach, once there life was comfortless, and there was appreciable risk. The journey by junk to Chungking was hazardous. Getting a junk through rapids, whirlpools, and against the current required great skill and also required haulage by trackers. No slave, said Bourne, ever did such inhuman work as the trackers, and yet he found them the most merry, good-natured creatures, with a quick sense of humour and of the ridiculous.[7] Fatal accidents were frequent, and the time taken for the journey was unpredictable. In 1881 it took Spence fifty-eight days from Ichang. He was held up by floods, once for twelve days and once for seven days, two men were drowned when a junk in company with him was in a collision, the steersman of his own junk was washed overboard in a whirlpool and was 'of course' drowned, and when safer water was reached two sweeps broke, tow-ropes broke repeatedly, and finally the junk hit a rock and sank, luckily in shallow water. In 1883 C.T. Gardner, the Ichang consul, decided to see for himself whether steamers could get through and his zeal nearly cost him his life. His boat upset in a

rapid and was dashed to pieces in a moment. He lost bedding, clothing, stores, gun, and the quinine he was taking against ague but was saved from drowning by a Chinese lifeboat which took him back to Ichang after a kindly official had loaned money, clothing, and bedding. In 1890 Fulford temporarily abandoned the attempt to reach Chungking after being turned back twice. The introduction of steamers did not eliminate hazards. The German steamer carrying Wilton to Chungking in 1900 hit a rock and within half an hour disappeared in 23 fathoms with all Wilton's effects, and he had to turn back to Shanghai to refit. Nothing could be taken for granted on the journey. In 1918 Toller and his family were safely transported to Chungking by gunboat, but as there was no prospect of a steamer that year their 128 cases of furniture had to be shipped in 2 junks without insurance against damage being obtainable. The family lived in almost intolerable conditions until the furniture arrived three months later, and practically all of it was either damaged or ruined.[8]

Chungking did not inspire consular affection. It lay on a rocky promontory running down to the confluence of the Yangtze with a tributary, and consequently was wrapped in damp grey mist for most of the year. In the summer the sun did get through and Chungking was then much too hot. The damp air, the water carriers, and what Tratman discreetly called the vile local habits combined to make the crowded streets, only a few feet wide, perpetually slippery and filthy. The rat population was enormous. The Yangtze, running fast between walls of rock, was dangerous. Few of those who fell into its sinister eddies got out alive. During the winter it was some 300 yards wide and 30 feet deep, and during the summer floods it could with unbelievable rapidity rise 90 feet or more and double its width.[9] Initially there was a complete lack of company or recreation. Parker said in 1881 that in nine months he had in all spent at most twenty-four hours in European company. Coming towards the end of nearly four years there Cockburn in 1890 spoke of an unspeakably dreary life of solitude in a most depressing climate. In 1898 Litton, in only his second year at Chungking, began applying for home leave or for a transfer away from a post which in his opinion was one of the East's most depressing stations.[10] Although a consulate site had recently been acquired the consulate had not been built. Litton, who said that all other foreign residents now had reasonably clean and sanitary

dwellings, complained that the existing consulate was a dark, dilapidated Chinese house in the filthiest quarter of one of China's filthiest towns, that it had for neighbours coolies, pedlars, and women of the lowest class, and that a new consulate could have been built for half the amount paid in exorbitant rents. Passing through in 1905 Campbell thought Chungking the most disagreeable Chinese city he had ever seen, 'a dripping, mouldy, crass antheap' where everything was damp and draggled. In 1913 W.R. Brown wrote from the consulate that without exception every officer stationed there had made every effort to escape as soon as possible; the permanent winter cloud filled the most sanguine with despair; the blazing summer sun drew out each smell from incredibly filthy streets and blended it into one indescribable whole; outside society and amusement were unobtainable; and only an officer with inward resources could hope to remain there without mental impairment.[11] To make things worse supplies which foreigners considered necessities could not be bought locally in the nineteenth century. In 1882 the tinned and bottled stores which Spence took up with him for a short stay included jam, marmalade, butter, coffee beans, baking and curry powder, two casks of Appollinaris water, and nine dozen bottles of wine and spirits, and the Legation certified that the cost of shipment was a perfectly reasonable expense. In the late 1890s newcomers still usually brought up six months' supplies, which had to be expensively packed in tin-lined cases and could not be insured in transit.[12] Medical attention, the greatest need, was a month's journey away in 1887, but in 1892 the Treasury, assured that in parts of China the climate was unusually healthy and invigorating, jibbed at designating Chungking an unhealthy post for pension purposes unless they were given direct evidence that Chungking's climate was exceptionally injurious to men of ordinarily vigorous constitution. They were persuaded to give way.[13]

Roman Catholics were strongly represented locally. They and their converts, and latterly the increasing number of Protestant missionaries and their converts, were objects of a suspicion which extended to foreigners generally. Baber, who in 1877 became the first consular officer at Chungking, travelled extensively and intrepidly when outside the city but inside it was extremely discreet, hardly ever going out and always doing so in an official chair. He thus avoided trouble. His successor Parker was less discreet and

walked out twice daily for exercise.[14] The result was rumours that he had killed a child or alternatively had caused a drought by an act of impiety. A threatening mob of some 2,000 people gathered outside his house and stove in the gate with a coffin. In trying to escape over a wall he fell off, spraining both ankles. The magistrate, to whom he had sent, arrived in time to save him, but Parker was understandably shaken. His lengthy account of the riot was none too coherent, he noticed himself growing so morbidly suspicious and nervous that he feared for his mental equilibrium, he felt obliged to go down river without waiting for his relief to arrive, and although a sensible doctor certified that an immediate and complete break from China would put him to rights the Foreign Office were told that he had been very seriously affected morally by the riot. He went on home leave. On taking over, his successor Spence paid tribute to Parker's friendly intimacy with officials and with some of the gentry and neighbours, but he was warned that Parker's frequent walks had been injudicious.[15] Nothing untoward happened to Spence or to the next officer, Hosie, but in 1886 Bourne met a riot in which with one exception every foreign residence in the city was looted or destroyed, as were the houses of converts. Gardner at Hankow forwarded to the Legation a despatch he received from Bourne. It was written on two small pieces of paper in a firm and rapid but minute hand and was sent from the Chungking intendant's yamen, where Bourne had taken refuge. Hearing of a riot against China Inland Mission members Bourne had gone to the yamen to ask for protection, and for his return journey was escorted by a guard of some forty men under an officer. The guard were no match for the mob. Bourne's chair was smashed with huge stones which hurt him badly on an arm and a leg, a stick hit him on the temple, and for half an hour he expected to be murdered at any minute. The magistrate arrived and got Bourne into a small room where he lay until evening. His servants, whom he described as very plucky, rushed him out to another refuge, and from there he was escorted back to the yamen at the dead of night. His clear and matter-of-fact despatch ended 'The affair looks now as bad as it can be and I am very doubtful whether I shall ever write another letter'. His retrospective opinion was that foreigners had escaped with their lives only because the Margary affair had shown how expensive and troublesome it was to murder them, and that had he remained in his house he would have been

1a Sir Rutherford Alcock, KCB (1809–97), minister to China, 1865–70 (by permission of the Mansell Collection)

1b Sir Thomas Wade, GCMG, KCB (1818–95), minister to China, 1871–82 (by permission of the *Illustrated London News*)

2a Sir Harry Parkes, GCMG, KCB (1828−85), minister to China, 1883−5 (by permission of the BBC Hulton Picture Library)

2b Sir John Jordan, GCMG, GCIE, KCB (1852−1925), minister to China, 1906−20 (by permission of the Mansell Collection)

3 Newchwang consulate, 1910, showing the gaol at the rear (by permission of Mrs N. Newman)

4 Nanking consulate, 1911 (by permission of Mrs N. Newman)

5 Foochow consulate, 1910 (by permission of Mrs N. Newman)

6 Nanking consulate, 1900. British deputation thanking Viceroy Liu Kun-i for his actions during the Boxer outbreak. *Standing*: second from left, A.J. Sundius, consul, Nanking. *Seated*: left to right, intendant; Vice-Admiral Sir Edward Seymour, commander-in-chief; Viceroy Liu Kun-i; P.L. Warren, Shanghai consulate-general; Captain J. Jellicoe (later Admiral of the Fleet Lord Jellicoe) (by permission of Mr Pelham Warren)

7 Amoy consulate, Coronation Day, 1911. Consul A.J. Sundius (seated sixth from left) 'entertained the Consular Body, a few prominent British citizens and the Chinese local authorities to a sumptuous lunch, after which a group photograph was taken...' (Amoy despatch of 18 July 1911) (Crown copyright)

8 Foochow, First World War period. F.E. Wilkinson (left), consul, and W.W. Myers (right), vice-consul (local and personal rank) at Pagoda Island (by permission of Mrs N. Newman)

murdered, for being ignorant of the extent of the riot he would probably have shot some of the first comers. He put the immediate cause of the outbreak down to American missionary imprudence in placing a new building where to Chinese eyes it was very objectionable, and the underlying cause to extraordinarily high rice prices and to the resulting wish to pillage. Men, he said, naturally preferred breaking the law and possibly being punished to observing the law and certainly starving, a position in which any man would turn robber. Except the clothes he was wearing he lost everything, to the value of 6,000 taels, and thanks to Walsham's instructions to compromise on claims did not secure full compensation. He spent seven months cooped up in a series of yamens, restricted to Chinese clothes, books, food, and medicines, suffering from lack of exercise, and getting in recompense unusual opportunities for seeing things from a Chinese point of view. At the time of the riot he had been active in securing the safety of British and American missionaries, but he cautiously rented a house away from them and near the Chinese brigadier when the Chinese at last judged it safe for him to move out of the yamens. Unlike Parker, however, he was not shaken. Before leaving on transfer he recommended that Chinese permission should be sought for a consular officer wearing Chinese dress and trusting entirely to Chinese protection to enquire in Tibet about trade possibilities; the risk of the officer coming to grief, which would afford an excellent pretext for insisting on the immediate reception of a British mission in Tibet, would have to be accepted; and he volunteered for the task.[16] His offer was not taken up.

In 1895, when Tratman was acting consul, there was a major anti-Christian riot in the provincial capital, Chengtu, 300 miles away. Although missionaries were in great danger none were killed, but every mission property was razed to the ground, and attacks on other Szechwan mission stations followed. Tratman ascribed the absence of trouble in Chungking entirely to the watchfulness and decisiveness of a well-disposed intendant who had spent eight years in Europe and two in Japan and with whom he was in almost daily consultation, and he was much distressed that the intendant went mad under the strain. His description of Chungking officials with whom he dealt showed a China uncertainly poised between the old world and the new. The insane intendant was replaced first by an obstructive reactionary and then by an active, liberal-minded man

who had had much to do with foreigners at Shanghai and who took the greatest pains to make foreigners comfortable when he entertained them; a prefect who had been a useless encumbrance for years was replaced by another who asked whether one travelled by rail from England to the United States and whether India was coterminous with England; and the capable and respected magistrate, the same man who had saved Bourne from the mob, was genuinely friendly and called personally on every foreign resident. During the troubles Tratman made no distinction of nationality in giving whatever assistance he could, being the only consul in the province and regarding himself as in practice representing all countries. O'Conor praised his coolness and judgement under very difficult circumstances, and throughout his incumbency he seems to have been sensible, conscientious, and hard-working.[17] Chungking, however, finished him. In applying for two extensions of his subsequent home leave he said that his four years there had seriously affected his mental and bodily health; the indescribably filthy surroundings of a consulate shut in on all sides by low-class Chinese dwellings, the fierce steamy summer heats, and the almost complete isolation tried the stoutest constitution; and he had had two attacks of cholera. He got back to China from home leave a changed man. Satow saw in him only an incorrigibly lazy consul. In 1906, having completed his next tour of duty, he applied to retire at the age of 48. The application mentioned physical troubles, but the nub lay in his statement that 'during recent years I have found myself increasingly unable to face responsibility and work. My nerve in fact is gone'. He lived on until 1945 with his pension of £600 odd, shielded from the worst effects of inflation by some private means.[18]

The opening of Chungking to foreign trade did not bring an influx of foreign merchants. In 1897 there was only 1 resident British merchant and 3 Chinese representatives of British firms in Shanghai, and of the 240 British subjects resident in west and south-west China 232 were Protestant missionaries and their families. The opening did however mean that the consul was needed in his office daily and was no longer free to travel in the area of nearly half a million square miles, extending from Yunnan in the south-west to Kansu in the north-west, for which he was responsible. In 1897 MacDonald therefore selected Litton as Tratman's assistant so that travelling might be resumed.[19] Litton,

an obsessive and enterprising traveller, was a brash Irish Etonian who had come into the service through a back door. He took a First at Oxford, entered the Straits Settlements service, and was sent to Canton to learn Cantonese. He travelled in little-known parts of Kwangtung, found promotion prospects very bad when he got back to Singapore, and applied to transfer to the China service. B. Brenan at Canton warmly supported the application, describing Litton to the Legation as a man who liked the Chinese and made friends with them, as a particularly pleasant fellow, and as a thorough gentleman. The China service was short of men and the transfer went through. Litton spent ten months in Peking adding spoken Mandarin to his previous knowledge of the Cantonese and Hakka dialects and of the written language and was straightaway sent to Chungking.[20] On Tratman's departure less than a year later MacDonald left Litton, not yet 30 and with negligible consular experience, in charge and then allowed him to proceed to the neighbouring province of Kweichow to deal with the murder of a British missionary. Litton was too raw for the assignment. He did secure the execution, 'a most ghastly spectacle', of two of the murderers, but the British demand for the arrest and execution of the alleged ringleader, T'an Tzu-ch'eng, was not met, even though Litton did not scruple to threaten the governor, in his opinion an anti-foreign dotard, with dire personal consequences were T'an not apprehended. There was confusion and disagreement between Litton and MacDonald. MacDonald told the Foreign Office semi-officially that Litton's reports had been wild, alarming, and sent by a man who had lost his head, and he reprimanded Litton for their improper and disrespectful tone. T'an remained at liberty, Mac-Donald after again reprimanding Litton went home on leave, and Litton applied for sick-leave.[21] Considering the views which MacDonald had expressed the chargé d'affaires' reactions to the application were most odd. He gave Litton the choice of going at once on leave or of at once taking charge of the Ssumao consulate (see pp. 316–18). Litton chose Ssumao and before taking up the new post provided further evidence of wildness by volunteering the highest admiration for the gallant way in which a Captain Pottinger, seconded by the War Office to survey in Yunnan for a British company, had carried on his work in the face of Chinese attacks. So contrary an opinion of Pottinger's behaviour was held by the Legation and by the Foreign Office that the War Office were told

Pottinger was unfit to be further employed in China.[22] As for T'an, the Chungking consulate never succeeded in handling the case satisfactorily. After Litton had gone T'an was at last arrested, but three years later a subsequent governor of Kweichow informed Wilton, the acting consul, that T'an had not plotted the murder and should be punished only for failing to protect the missionary, and without informing the Legation Wilton acquiesced. Another two years went by, and yet another governor informed the consulate, of which Russell was then in charge, that T'an would be released from prison as part of a general amnesty for criminals. Russell likewise acquiesced but did inform the Legation, who were much put out to discover belatedly T'an's inadequate punishment.[23]

Arrangements for the Chungking consulate in MacDonald's day continued to be unsatisfactory. Litton's successor M.F.A. Fraser, always peculiar, had become very peculiar indeed. During the siege of the legations he evacuated the whole British community down river, an action criticized in China. The Foreign Office took the view that although he was a foolish and tiresome person the action had been properly taken, but in all other respects his performance during the crisis met with a chorus of unqualified official disapproval. To the permanent under-secretary he was an ass whose shrieks for gunboats which he should have known could not reach Chungking had been very discreditable, and a minute from lower down the hierarchy despondently noted the arrival of more of his silly despatches. A 140-page despatch reporting to the Legation how colossal his work had been and how successfully he had carried it out was minuted 'he is evidently mad'. Satow said that he was as mad as a March hare and unfit for any responsible post, and trusted that there would be no difficulty about his retirement.[24] There was a difficulty. Fraser had no wish to retire and at 50 was in such good shape that it was very rare indeed for him to need a doctor or medicine, but his reluctance to leave was unavailing, the Treasury medical adviser must have read between the lines, and into retirement Fraser went. He died, an old bachelor, thirty years later, peculiar to the end. Expressing a hope that the teaching of Latin by the Continental pronunciation would be assisted and that his books on the Jewish question would be studied, he bequeathed much of his estate to his solicitor's Cambridge college, with which he himself had had no connection whatever.[25]

The travels of the early Chungking consular agents were

enormous and fruitful. Baber received the coveted Gold Medal of
the Royal Geographical Society, Parker claimed to have averaged
25 miles a day, mostly on foot, for at least six months, Hosie in his
three years travelled over 5,000 miles. Most of the travelling was
done on foot or on horseback. A sedan-chair, the bearers of which
were in difficult mountain country helped by additional men
hauling on traces, was according to Baber an essential mark of
respectability but did not actually have to be used. He described the
misery of mapping the day's journey by flickering rushlight in a
single room without doors or windows, huddled in dripping clothes
amid blinding smoke over a brushwood fire and fortified only by a
meal of potatoes and maize, but he was the fortunate possessor of a
keen sense of humour. He had the inspired notion of travelling with
pet monkeys, whose greater peculiarity diverted popular attention
from his own lesser peculiarity, and he took in his stride the theft of
all his money while he slept in the wilds.[26] He was destitute, he
cheerfully told the Legation: '2 servants, 10 coolies and myself are
banqueting by the bounty of the hostess on eggs and onions, a
simple but nutritious fare which the fact that I cannot pay for it
renders curiously succulent', and as the local authorities a day's
journey away 'have not done anything to assist me I propose to stay
here until they do'. Interim relief came from a friendly rhubarb
merchant who lent 10 taels and from a tribal chief who sent 2 taels,
after a fortnight a courier returned from Chengtu with 50 taels
from the intendant, and but for fear of injuring the intendant Baber
would have asked for him to be officially thanked for such
handsome behaviour. No sooner had his funds been replenished
than he went down with severe fever but by sticking it he managed
to average 4 miles a day for four days until the fever left him and
then got over a snowy 13,000-foot pass.[27] Not all the travellers'
reports were intended for the public eye. Bourne travelled in
Szechwan, Kweichow, and Yunnan to assess the probable effect on
British trade of a recent Sino-French treaty and in a confidential
section of his report sharply criticized the French, who among other
things he accused of being feared and distrusted and of destroying
confidence in the security of property by constantly demanding new
girls in an area where girls were usually sold.[28] Most of the reports
were however published, but they were buried in blue books or in
learned or semi-learned journals. Hosie alone found a commercial
publisher for some account of his journeyings. Baber's report on the

white wax insect was particularly badly treated. Written in 1879, it
was not sent home by the Legation until 1884 and did not appear
in print until 1893, three years after his death, in a publication
repugnantly entitled *Kew Bulletin of Miscellaneous Information*,
Kew botanic gardens expressing to the Foreign Office regret at a
delay 'due to the slender means of publication at our disposal'.[29]
Reprints of some reports would probably be of interest to modern
travellers, whether foreign or Chinese, along the same routes.

Two consulates, at Tengyueh and Ssumao, were opened in the
remoter parts of Yunnan in the last years of the century. The
opening of the Tengyueh consulate stemmed from an Anglo-
Chinese convention of 1894 about Burma. In 1895 O'Conor, who
did not expect that any immediate influx of British traders would
require a consul to reside at Tengyueh throughout the year, recommended that one of the younger and more active members of the
service should be appointed and should travel widely in the district to obtain commercial information. He may or may not have
realized that serious travel was ruled out by incessant monsoon rain
between May and October and was practicable only in the dry
season. Hausser, who in no way fitted O'Conor's specification, was
appointed in 1897 to open the post but was diverted to the
Burma-China boundary commission, from which he had to be
removed before ever getting to Tengyueh. The consulate was not
actually opened until J.W. Jamieson, who had already opened
Wuchow and Ssumao, arrived in 1899. It was unlike any other post
in China. Whatever function O'Conor may have foreseen for it its
primary functions ultimately became to facilitate a primitive trade
between Burma and China carried on by caravans of pack animals
and to help settle disputes along a border both sides of which were
largely inhabited by a variety of tribes such as peaceful Shan, less
peaceful Kachin, and head-hunting Wa. In view of these functions
the Indian government met half the cost of maintaining the
consulate. At this period Tengyueh had only 1,400 or so inhabitants. The area within the city walls had not been rebuilt since
the devastation during the Muslim rebellion in Yunnan, and the
suburbs had been almost totally destroyed in a recent fire. Jamieson
first occupied a granary whose walls were tumbling down, whose
doors were lacking, and whose roof leaked like a sieve, not very
agreeable at 5,400 feet above sea-level, and whose only latrine for
the consul and his Chinese staff was a field. Next he moved into an

old yamen and put the skilled Chinese carpenter whom he had providently brought with him to making repairs, alterations, and office furniture.[30]

Jamieson, who at this time had been only thirteen years in the service, later became one of the best-known characters on the China coast. Behind his back he was universally known as 'Monkey Jamieson', a nickname given him in the Peking students' mess on account of a long upper lip, but whether in his heyday many people ventured to call him 'Monkey' to his face may be doubted. He was a formidable, domineering creature. Well-read and a good linguist who spoke excellent German and good French as well as both Mandarin and Cantonese, he was also, at least in his later years, a notoriously deep drinker. Although his drinking did not commend him to the Legation or to the Foreign Office, treaty port society admired an able and incisive consul-general who walked to the club of an evening but not infrequently needed to be carried home in a sedan-chair.[a] He was always set on running affairs as he thought best without bothering unduly on whose toes he trod. The toes at Tengyueh were primarily those of British officials in Burma. He had already crossed swords with them while working with the boundary commission. Being a believer in courtesy and fair dealing, he reported, it was at times difficult indeed for him to acquiesce in the treatment of the Chinese commissioner, 'such a dear old boy — one of nature's perfect gentlemen', by Scott, the commissioner from Burma; Scott's rudeness was almost unbearable when, as was only too often the case, he chose to be in a bad humour; Scott's attitude in the delimitation of the frontier was all take and no give; Indian officials, accustomed to subordinates and to subject races, could hardly treat with equals, which at least in theory the Chinese were; but after Jamieson had had a royal row with Scott the atmosphere had been considerably cleared. At the consulate he assumed that he stood in the same relationship to Burma as the Canton consul did to Hong Kong and nominally suggested, and in effect demanded, that all Burma's correspondence with Chinese officials should be routed through the consulate. On subsequently discovering a Chinese messenger carrying despatches from Burma through Tengyueh to the Yunnan viceroy he read the Burma authorities a lecture; the address on the cover indicated that the sender was superior in rank to the recipient; no one in Yunnan could read letters in English; letters in Chinese were likely to give offence by breaches of epis-

tolary etiquette, the observance of which was no triviality but essential to friendly intercourse; correspondence should therefore pass exclusively through the consulate.[31] He also acted to prevent misbehaviour by some British travellers in Yunnan, fearing that the behaviour of persons who seemed to believe themselves in a savage country where they were freed from all restraint might extend to the British name in Yunnan the same odium which French misconduct had attracted. He reached Tengyueh too late to catch a party of hooligans on bicycles or another British traveller who knocked off his pony every Chinese who did not at once dismount on meeting him, but he drafted regulations intended to prevent any recurrence. Four months after reaching Tengyueh he left it for good on promotion to the newly created post of commercial attaché to the Legation. He claimed that during his brief tenure officials, gentry, and people had been made to realize that opposition to the consulate was futile, that he could now walk the streets without an escort and without insult or cries of 'kill the foreign devil', and that he had got officials to show some energy in dealing with Burma cases. On the other hand all his eleven despatches to the Burma government remained unanswered.[32]

An 1895 Sino-French convention provided for the opening of Ssumao as a treaty port to serve the trade between Yunnan and Laos in Indo-China. O'Conor, wrongly believing it commercially important as the depot for locally grown tea and politically important as a post from which French designs could be watched, recommended a consulate. No action was taken until the end of 1897, when Jamieson was transferred there from Wuchow. The tedious journey from Haiphong involved four different boats, a mule caravan, and a chair, and took him seven weeks. He described as very uncivil his treatment at a prefectural city along the way, and some people would have used a stronger adjective. He went for a walk to inspect the shops and was immediately surrounded by a large crowd shouting 'kill, kill' with great energy. At first he took no notice, but as the crowd got bigger and he happened to pass the prefect's yamen he went in to ask for a guard to escort him back to his inn. He was taken aback on entry to discover that a military examination had just been going on, and he was hailed with repeated and perfectly deafening shouts of 'kill'. Not having with him one of the red cards obligatory for official calls he had much difficulty in conveying a message to the prefect that he wished to see

him. After a considerable time the prefect decided to see him and then had the mob cleared. Not on his own account but for the benefit of future travellers he lodged a complaint with the governor. On reaching Ssumao in the back of beyond he rapidly convinced himself that the consulate was a waste of money and of a consular officer; he could see no prospect of trade at Ssumao, where the local Chinese traders were not real merchants but men of small capital or successful pedlars; no British subjects were ever likely to come there. Ssumao was also, though Jamieson did not stress this aspect unduly, excruciatingly inconvenient. A Hong Kong cheque could not be sold there, and he managed to buy silver along the way only because a Customs commissioner was a personal friend. The silver then had to be packed for mule transport. It was unsafe to travel alone with so much silver and the departure of the next caravan therefore had to be awaited, and as no safe could be transported to Ssumao Jamieson on getting his silver there had to dig a dry well, line it with cement, and deposit in it the silver and valuable papers.[33]

Jamieson urged that the consulate should be transferred to the provincial capital at Yunnanfu; commercially this was the centre on which all caravan routes converged; politically a consulate there would show the French that Britain did not mean to be shut out of that part of Yunnan and would stiffen the Chinese against France; Britain needed to strengthen her position in a province contiguous to Szechwan, which in any partition of China should certainly be within the British sphere of influence. Before leaving Ssumao to open the Tengyueh consulate Jamieson submitted views, which the Legation considered very able, about French intentions in south-west China. He was scathing about the French authorities in Tongking; they were most grossly ignorant about China and had most exaggerated ideas about Yunnan's wealth; civil officials were of such poor quality that a senior one had recently been a third-class Customs tide-waiter in China; the military seemed to be a law unto themselves and to have the most inordinate contempt for the civil arm; only lack of money prevented Tongking 'from annexing everything in sight — including Hainan — on her own initiative without reference to the home government'; though French consular officials were of a much superior type to the colonial ones the views of his French consular colleague at Ssumao on the interpretation of treaties filled him with much astonishment.[34]

Litton, coming to replace Jamieson, took so circuitous a route that
he was travelling for close on four months. On arrival at Ssumao he
gave no sign of being abashed by his lack of success at his previous
post and reported so racily that the Legation blue-pencilled at least
one despatch before sending it on to the Foreign Office. Among
other fatuous excisions the words here shown italicized were deleted from a passage describing French railway projects in Yunnan
and the simultaneous presence of three separate French missions,
all 'more or less hostile to each other, *but they all spend a lot of
money, wear uniform, blow trumpets* and have trouble with the
people'. Litton's opinion of Ssumao was no better than Jamieson's
had been. In a trade report which was pungent enough to need
considerable editing before publication and interesting enough for
the Foreign Secretary to be advised to read it he said that the town if
in Kwangtung would rank only as a large village, that its communications were execrable, that all conditions for a flourishing
commerce were conspicuous by their absence, and that as a political listening-post it was equally useless.[35] Litton's stay at the
Ssumao consulate was extremely brief. Some three months after
taking charge of it he was working with the boundary commission on the Burma frontier, where he was nearly killed. A Burma
civil official, an army doctor, and Litton, accompanied only by a
Chinese soldier, were attacked by Wa tribesmen with stones and
crossbows. Litton was knocked unconscious by stones. When he
came to, the other two British were apparently dead and Wa were
hacking at their heads 25 yards away. He shot one man who came
towards him with a sword and the others left him alone. He had
only a faint recollection of staggering back with the Chinese soldier
to the Sikh guard 3½ miles away. He said that he owed his life
partly to the Chinese soldier, who although wounded several times
had behaved splendidly and had been suitably rewarded, and that
neither the Chinese members of the commission nor the Chinese
government should be blamed for murders which could not possibly have been foreseen. Litton seems to have gone on home leave
soon afterwards and after him no member of the service was
stationed at Ssumao.[36]

FORMOSA

THE island whose Chinese name is Taiwan was christened Formosa ('the verdant isle') by the early Portuguese explorers. The Portuguese name, universally used by Westerners until recent times, is retained here to distinguish between references to the island and references to the consulate at the city of Taiwan (later renamed Tainan) in the south of the island. Few parts of the world have changed faster than Formosa. In the 1860s it was still a raw frontier area administered as part of Fukien. Much of the mountainous interior was the home of unsubjugated aboriginal tribes outside Chinese control. Fever abounded, and the island became notorious among foreigners for unhealthiness.[1]

In 1861 Swinhoe and his assistant Braune were taken by gunboat across the Formosa channel from Amoy to open the consular establishment at Taiwan. During a rough four-day passage their baggage, unprotected on deck, was all either spoiled or ruined by water. Among other things Swinhoe lost 10 shirts and 6 nightshirts and Braune 20 rather cheaper shirts and 6 pairs of white trousers. Swinhoe had been sent as vice-consul, but as the intendant thought it beneath his dignity to deal with a vice-consul Swinhoe conferred on himself what he termed the brevet rank of acting consul. As trade prospects at Taiwan seemed negligible he obtained Bruce's authority to move to Tamsui in the north of the island. Whether Swinhoe knew it or not before moving there, Tamsui was nothing but an anchorage and a straggling fishing village near a river-mouth. Before leaving for Tamsui he applied for home leave, claiming that Taiwan had reduced him to a wreck, and after waiting for some months for a reply sent a further despatch in 1862 to say that he was handing over to Braune and catching the next mail to England. The Legation docketed the despatch 'Announcing his intention of taking (French) leave of absence', but the Foreign

Office, where Hammond regarded Swinhoe as very deserving, accepted his excuses for returning without permission and granted a year's sick-leave. While on leave he recommended aboriginal territory on Formosa's inhospitable east coast as suitable for a British convict station; the rocky shore in front and the savages in the mountains behind would cut off all hope of escape, and mining and logging would afford abundance of work.[2]

Braune had to deal with actions by the British navy which Hammond considered very violent and improper and which the Admiralty conceded had shown excess of zeal,[3] with obstreperous British subjects and obstreperous Chinese coolies, and with the looting of wrecked British vessels and the murder of one of their masters.[4] His conduct was approved, but before twelve months were out he submitted a vain appeal to be given home leave or at least to be sent elsewhere for part of the summer, saying that his health was utterly failing and that he could not bear Tamsui, where he was single-handed, had no one to consult, and constantly felt insecure.[5] Swinhoe's return in 1864 released him at last, but he got no further towards England than the mainland side of the Formosa channel. There he had a heart attack which made him dread the onward voyage so much that instead of proceeding he went to Peking for a change of climate and died suddenly of another heart attack. He was 26 and it was not three years since he had first landed in Formosa in good health.[6] Swinhoe, though he could little afford a separate home establishment for wife and child, had decided against bringing them back to what he called Tamsui's solitary confinement, with its riots and its low, damp, and badly ventilated consular hovels that in England would scarcely have been fit for cattle. On his first day back he endorsed Braune's recommendation of a move back to Taiwan, where Braune had believed that contact with the highest authorities in Formosa might perhaps permit settlement of cases which at Tamsui were merely ignored by the local sub-prefect. Swinhoe followed up by inveighing against Tamsui's continuous rain, fog, damp, and monotony. He was authorized to leave Gregory, Braune's replacement, in charge of Tamsui and to move himself back to the south, not to Taiwan itself but to Takow, some 25 miles away.[7] Takow, at this period much used by vessels trading with Taiwan, was a dirty little place with a shallow anchorage from which passengers reached shore in tubs on top of bamboo rafts. Swinhoe's self-conferred status of

acting consul was now regularized by promotion to the rank of
consul, and the consulate was soon split between Takow and
Taiwan, the usual arrangement in subsequent years being that
the consul resided at Takow and the assistant, if there was one,
at Taiwan. In 1877 a steam tug was running three times a week
between the two places and there was a telegraph link, but initially
getting from the one to the other was exceedingly tedious, the
journey taking at least twelve hours in normal conditions and up to
seventeen hours in bad weather. In 1866 Watters, the consulate
junior, described the journey, which he had to make much more
often than once a month. He left Takow by water, crossing lagoon,
oyster-beds, and mangrove swamp, and disembarked some way up
river. Then after much haggling he hired a chair and proceeded
along very narrow muddy tracks and over streams which were
forded or crossed by catamaran or bamboo bridge. Along the way
there were set halting places, one of them outstanding for miserable
shelter and noisome entertainment. Once in an emergency he had
to make the journey after a typhoon had rendered the route impracticable for a chair, and had to wade for several miles through
mud and water up to his knees.[8]

Swinhoe, after six months mewed up in a Takow hulk, was
pleased to be able to rent a Chinese house, even though it was
small, low, and extremely damp, and though the owner in-
conveniently insisted on retaining quarters in it for his own use.
Swinhoe and his wife and child, who had now joined him, lived in
the front, Watters in the rear, the servants in the dark godown
below, and the constable in a hut. Mrs Swinhoe made herself useful
as an unpaid consulate copyist but suffered much from the climate
and from being the only European woman in Takow, and a pregnant one at that. She was lucky that at this juncture a missionary doctor, Maxwell, arrived. Previously there had been no
doctor resident in Formosa, and Swinhoe had made various unauthorized visits of considerable length to Amoy to obtain medical
treatment for himself. Although Wade did express surprise at this
behaviour he accepted Swinhoe's explanation. After Mrs Swinhoe's
confinement Maxwell ordered her to Amoy, where her parents
were missionaries, for a change. Swinhoe escorted her over. During
the crossing the ship in which he was travelling had to make for the
Pescadores to shelter from a storm, the same thing happened on the
way back, and the result was that he was once again absent from

his post without permission for about a month. The sea never seems to have been kind to Swinhoe while he was in Formosa. Coming across from Amoy on a visit Mrs Swinhoe's parents lost property, as did Swinhoe, on a schooner which was pirated while becalmed, he lost more property on a ship which was wrecked and plundered and on two ships which foundered in a typhoon, and he very nearly drowned while bathing.[9]

If Swinhoe's truancies escaped censure other actions got him into trouble. His reasons for passing a light sentence on a British gunner who had drawn a knife on a Malay were that the gunner had been drunk, which Swinhoe treated as an extenuating circumstance, and that he was too useful to his employer and for the defence of the small foreign community to be gaoled for more than a few days. Wade did not approve this reasoning, and he returned, to be rewritten in more intelligible English and more respectfully, a despatch reading in part 'you drove me with your peremptory orders into the horns of a dilimma [sic], leaving me but one loop-hole, to escape from which when to maintain my position I attempted, you [word illegible] the step with a burst of disapproval'. Alcock rebuked him for the very objectionable tone of another despatch and told the Foreign Office that the site chosen by Swinhoe for a Takow consulate might make a convenient cemetery but was fit for nothing else.[10] In 1866 Swinhoe was moved to Amoy to officiate during the Amoy incumbent's home leave, and his Takow post was put in charge of a series of acting consuls.

Watters had an unpleasant scene with an intendant who, regardless of the treaties, had prohibited the export of rice in British vessels. Although an infirm old man the intendant flew into a paroxysm of rage, crushed the fan he was holding, screamed 'Who dares to say "cannot" to me in my own yamen?', said that the treaty provisions were the work of persons who knew nothing of Formosa and applied only to the mainland, and declared that if commanded by the emperor to withdraw the prohibition he would disobey the command.[11] Carroll achieved the unique consular distinction of being twice fired on by aborigines. The American barque *Rover* was wrecked in aboriginal territory and Carroll accompanied a British warship in an attempt to rescue the crew, who were eventually presumed to have been murdered. As a landing party which included Carroll were getting out of a ship's boat at the scene of the wreck a sharp volley of musketry and a

shower of arrows came from a dense thicket not 20 yards away. One seaman was wounded, the boat was perforated in several places, and the party retreated to their ship. Then the United States navy decided to force a way through the jungle and inflict punishment on aboriginal villages, and as Carroll knew the exact locality they took him with them. Some 200 men landed, fire was opened from the jungle, the first ball coming close to Carroll, the flag-lieutenant was killed, and the punitive expedition was a complete failure. Carroll's remedy for aboriginal troubles was a simple one; let the cunning head-hunting wretches only be driven off the coast by European rifles and their enemies among the other aborigines would kill them off. Alcock scornfully said that such proceedings would be no less savage than the acts denounced by Carroll, adding that the aborigines' hostility was allegedly due to the treachery and ill-usage they had experienced many years before from foreign sailors, the old, old story of how Europeans started their intercourse with the dark races all over the world. There was a distasteful postscript to the affair. Carroll managed to obtain one victim's remains for the Americans, the United States consul at Amoy was reluctant to reimburse his expenses, and Carroll wished that he had held on to the remains until he had been paid.[12] Adkins was there for only three months. His passage across in a gunboat which ran into a storm and took four and a half days between Amoy and Takow was exceedingly unpleasant. The sea was very high, water pouring through a badly fitted skylight covered his cabin floor 6 inches deep and soaked his bed, he was wet to the skin the whole time, for two days there was nothing to eat but bread, and he was supremely miserable. Once he got there he quite liked Takow, contrary to his expectations. He did not have much in common with the community, but the Customs commissioner was an old friend and they messed together. He rose at 7.30 and breakfasted on fruit with tea or coffee, at 12 he had fish, meat, eggs, and fruit, and dinner at 7 was much the same. Fish was good, semi-tropical fruit was very fair, poultry middling, beef bad, and mutton and game unobtainable. Beer he never touched in such a warm climate and wine only seldom. The local amusements were cards and sailing, but having lost £15 the first time he played cards he decided not to play again and he had always hated sailing. In retrospect he counted himself fortunate to have missed the troubles which mounted after his uneventful stay.[a]

Useful though it was to have a doctor to hand, Maxwell's arrival heralded the beginning of missionary troubles. He and his colleagues disregarded Swinhoe's advice to start by practising quietly at Takow and to defer evangelizing. Their proselytizing efforts in Taiwan started the customary rumours of poisoning and so on. Watters was sent up to Taiwan to look after them and for months was subjected to horrible abuse, or pelted with stones, or had guns fired at him, whenever he appeared on the streets. The missionaries were mobbed and had to retire to Takow. G. Jamieson, who took Adkins' place for four months, encountered anti-missionary riots, a Chinese preacher of good reputation was arrested, and the magistrate asked Jamieson to find out whether the preacher had been distributing poison on his own responsibility or on Maxwell's orders. Although barely four years in the service Jamieson gave the missionaries the sound advice that as popular opinions could not be altered by official mandate they must either live down the rumours or leave Formosa for a district where their labours would be more thankfully received.[13]

In July 1868 Jamieson was replaced by Gibson, who lost no time whatever in disproving Alcock's belief that Formosa was a safe place to which to post a discredited officer. The local situation was deteriorating. A catechist was murdered, converts were in peril of their lives, one British commercial agent, whose behaviour was far from blameless, was stabbed, an armed attack was made, not without provocation, on another, and British trade in camphor was obstructed. A new intendant refused redress. A cool head was needed, instead of which Takow was in the charge of a man whose despatches from there put, as Wade retrospectively said, his sanity in question. Before July was out Gibson, who as well as being acting British consul also represented France, Germany, and Denmark, was protesting to the intendant in the name and by the authority of the Queen, of their Imperial Majesties the French Emperor and the Emperor of north Germany, and of the King of Denmark, and was asking for gunboat protection. In September he and a naval officer accompanied by a twenty-man guard called on the intendant with demands. The intendant flew into a violent passion, struck Gibson twice with his fan, 'hurryed' (sic) off to his private apartments, and did not reappear. Up to this point Alcock approved Gibson's proceedings, but after receiving more wild despatches he instructed Swinhoe in October to break off a special

9 British Legation, Peking, 1892, Lady Walsham's 'At Home'. The lady on the right is emerging from one of Peking's famously uncomfortable springless carts (by permission of the *Illustrated London News*)

10 Shanghai, 1907. Another uncomfortable conveyance, the wheelbarrow, with F.E. Wilkinson's daughters (by permission of Mrs N. Newman)

11 Newchwang, 1910. Mrs F.E. Wilkinson boating with her children on the consulate's private pond, which in winter became the consulate skating-rink (by permission of Mrs N. Newman)

12 Chengtu, 1924. A comfortable conveyance, containing the wife and daughter of acting Vice-Consul Ogden (by permission of Mr B.J.N. Ogden)

13 Chengtu, about 1924, the Anglo-Chinese Club. *Seated*: extreme left, acting Vice-Consul Ogden; second from right, acting Consul-General Combe (by permission of Mr B.J.N. Ogden)

14 Shanghai consulate-general, 1930s. One more consular chore. Acting Consul-General Davidson in front, acting Consul Ogden to his rear (by permission of Mr B.J.N. Ogden)

15 Tientsin, British Concession, 1941. Annual inspection of the British Municipal Emergency Corps (the 'Tientsin Volunteers'). Acting Consul-General Ogden in front, acting Consul W.G.C. Graham to his rear (by permission of Mr B.J.N. Ogden)

16 Chungking, 1943. Signature of the treaty ending British extraterritoriality. *Seated*: left to right, Sir H. Seymour, British ambassador; T.V. Soong, minister for foreign affairs; H. Richardson, Indian agency-general in China. *Standing*: behind the ambassador, G.V. Kitson, Chinese secretary (by permission of Lady Seymour)

enquiry he was making in the Yangtze area and to resume his
Takow post. In November Gibson called in the navy and a
Lieutenant Gurdon with a handful of men stormed Anping, a fort
and fishing village near Taiwan's suburbs. Chinese lives were lost.
The Chinese authorities were told that Anping would be held until
British demands were met. In December Swinhoe arrived but
decided against resuming charge and thereby robbing Gibson of
kudos. Gibson, he considered, was about the best man who had
been in Formosa and his unflinching firmness and high notions of
dignity were just what were needed there. He announced in January
that he himself was leaving to resume his Yangtze enquiry. Meanwhile the commodore at Hong Kong had congratulated Gurdon
on a most brilliant exploit.

This satisfaction was not shared elsewhere. In London the
Admiralty asked whether the Foreign Secretary, Clarendon, approved of these unusual proceedings, which in their view should be
emphatically condemned unless their necessity could be established.
Clarendon replied that his view was wholly unfavourable. He instructed Alcock that Gibson, whose rash and inexcusable action
had shown him wholly unfit to be entrusted with any discretionary
power, was to be removed from Formosa and was not again to be
put in charge of any consulate or vice-consulate, and he hoped that
this decision would serve to warn all consular officers in China that
the government would visit with the severest condemnation wanton
and unsanctioned acts of violence. Alcock in Peking wrote privately
to Hammond that Gibson's measures had been rash and ill-judged;
that he would try to get Gibson home, where he had better be
pensioned off; that Swinhoe's failure to take over had been regrettable; and that the promotion of Gurdon, who deserved to be
broken for his insane conduct and needless sacrifice of life and
property, put the British in a very false position. In official despatches which crossed Clarendon's despatch he expressed great
reluctance to judge harshly juniors who might have erred through
an excess of zeal and impatience; he would defer a final report on
Gibson's responsibility until Gibson had replied to his queries;
Gibson's actions had at least disposed of local difficulties on which
nine months of negotiation and remonstrance had previously been
spent in vain. On receipt of Clarendon's despatch he replied that
although he condemned Gibson's precipitation and had already
relieved him of his Formosa charge, extenuating circumstances

might when known possibly lead to some modification of the censure and that for the time being Gibson had been told only of Clarendon's strong disapproval of his action.[14]

In March Gibson, still unaware of the storm about to break over him, described the present mood of people and officials as conciliatory and peaceable, claimed to be on the best of terms with new mandarins, and forecast that there would be no new cases in the consular district for a very considerable time. In May he heard that he was being transferred to Canton in disgrace, but still maintained that the results of action condemned as a blunder had been good. In June he was relieved by Cooper, who found him looking as gaunt and lean as a half-starved greyhound and found the office in a great muddle, with no cash book kept for six months and the correspondence register as Jamieson had left it, but who nevertheless praised the courage, firmness, judgement, and sense of duty shown by Gibson in an emergency. Gibson did not get to Canton. He arrived in Amoy extremely depressed and mere skin and bone, was too ill to go further, and died there of consumption in July. There were those on the China coast who regarded him as a martyr. A Shanghai newspaper suggested as an inscription on his tomb that he had died a victim of harsh Foreign Office treatment, and a subscription for a memorial was opened by residents of Amoy and Formosa.[15] He died insolvent. A firm of drapers in which his brother was senior partner and at which his late wife had fitted herself out for China on credit could recover little from the estate, and he still owed Adkins £200, which he had borrowed three years before in order to be able to get back to China and had promised to repay in three months.[16] Adkins did not feel disposed to contribute to the memorial, but considered that Gibson had been too loyal to put the blame on Gurdon, where it belonged, and that Clarendon's censure had been unjust. In Galloway Gibson's 80-year-old mother and invalid elder sister, who had been entirely dependent on him, were saved from absolute want only by a small annuity purchased for them by his friends in China.[17]

Gibson's death was not the end of the affair. In December he and Swinhoe had been present in the Chinese court which was trying Chinese accused of anti-foreign or anti-Christian violence. They had pressed for some of the guilty to be flogged and had witnessed one flogging. When one of the accused denied guilt in court they withdrew on the appearance of torturers, who obtained a con-

fession after the man had come to after his first faint and had been tortured a second time. They had pressed the reluctant Chinese commissioner to pass sentence of death on one murderer and had witnessed the execution. Swinhoe reported all this in a despatch copied by Alcock to the Foreign Office. In a private letter to Alcock Hammond, who noted reproachfully that in copying the report Alcock had offered no comment, said that he had never read anything more horrible than a despatch apparently exulting in barbarities of which Swinhoe had been the promoter and to a great degree the witness; the first impulse at the Foreign Office had been to dismiss both men immediately, but it had been thought proper to give them the opportunity of pleading any excuse they might have to offer, though he feared that there was no excuse which would avail them. The official Foreign Office despatch expressed horror at the torture, and grief that Swinhoe and Gibson had stood by to witness severe corporal punishment, and said that the cause of Christianity was not to be promoted by such proceedings in cases of assault upon Christianity. Gibson died before he could enter a defence. Swinhoe was extremely hurt. Torture, he said, was normal in Chinese courts and he could not have stopped ordinary court proceedings, particularly as an immense crowd was present; a consul had no right to interfere with Chinese jurisdiction over Chinese, and no good had been done in the past by protests by Pedder and himself against the flayings, crucifixions, and cutting off of women's breasts that foreigners could not help noticing in their rambles past the Amoy execution ground; it was very hard to be blamed for seeing that outrages were punished; witnessing such atrocities filled him with horror, as it did nearly all Englishmen, but was it always obligatory to express the horror when one reported? 'My mistake I presume was being too frank in my narrative'. Alcock supported Swinhoe vigorously; a consul pressing for a charge to be brought in a Chinese court was in a sense thereby automatically a party to torture, whether personally present or absent; if there was objection to this the search for justice for injury to foreigners could be abandoned; Swinhoe, placed in a situation from which there was no unexceptionable issue, had tried to discharge a painful duty conscientiously and for the public good. Clarendon was not convinced. He regretted Swinhoe's active and personal part in the punishment of the malefactors; acquittal for want of evidence would have been better than a British failure to

intervene to prevent torture; no consular officer in China should countenance any acts by the Chinese authorities incompatible with humanity and abhorrent to the British nation's feelings; he would however not pursue the matter because Swinhoe's position had been novel and full of difficulty. Elevated though these sentiments were they were precious little use to consular officers trying to do their duty amid the harshness of contemporary China. Rather oddly, this half-hearted exculpation had been preceded in the previous month by another Foreign Office despatch expressing high appreciation of Swinhoe's attention and diligence in his Yangtze enquiry.[18] The two despatches virtually marked the end of Swinhoe's active career. He went home sick for two years, on getting back begged off a return to Formosa on health grounds, and had two paralytic strokes at Ningpo. In 1873 he at last ceased to be titular consul at Taiwan on appointment to Ningpo, had a third stroke, again went home sick, retired in 1875 without returning, and died in 1877 of syphilis, a condition which none of the numerous medical certificates he had produced during his career seems to have mentioned.[19] Before his death his contributions to zoological knowledge from China had been recognized by election to the Royal Society and modern China is interested in him as a zoologist, but he was not much of a consular officer.

For Cooper nothing was right about Takow. His complaints were legion. He and his family had a dreadful crossing and were disgusted by the wretched consulate; foreign trade was conducted by mere agents of Amoy firms, the partners in which preferred paying the agents high salaries to facing an unhealthy climate, rough living, and bad food themselves; the agents recruited by one Amoy firm from advocates' offices in Edinburgh had little pretensions to accomplishment or much refinement; there was not a single resident British merchant; the mandarins were obstructive; nearly all cargo was carried in German bottoms; and a costly consulate was being maintained to protect half a dozen traders and two missionaries. He claimed that his letters to the intendant were moderate yet decided, but their tone was in fact so angry and offensive that Wade strongly criticized it. Fever drove him out after seven months, and he went home on sick-leave in such a fearful condition that he was taken off the ship at Hong Kong so that he could die more tranquilly on land. He survived, but he was not a good advertisement for Takow.[20]

A.R. Hewlett, his successor, acted against the misbehaviour of British traders. Three of them, accompanied by four Malays, all armed, went to villages to which British-owned camphor plundered from a wrecked junk had been removed and 'advised' two suspected ringleaders to return to Takow with them. Hewlett was sure that the party did not appreciate the illegality of their proceedings (a telling indication of attitudes in Formosa), but he arrested the party and fined the most culpable. There was a local sensation. Decades later Pickering, who had been a third mate and a Customs tide-waiter before trading in Formosa and participating in this misbehaviour and who later became Protector of Chinese in the Straits Settlements and a CMG, indignantly recalled in his reminiscences how European 'gentlemen' (sic) who lived on terms of daily intimacy with the consul had been marched through the streets by the consular constable. The salutary effect was ruined by the chief judge, who to the great annoyance of Hewlett and Wade quashed the convictions on appeal. Wade saw great danger in the chief judge's apparent doctrine that as the Chinese responded so tardily to appeals for justice allowances should be made for British who took the law into their own hands, and he assured Hewlett of his support should his consular authority be set at naught.[21] Nothing so drastic was necessary, and for years after Hewlett's departure in 1871 the consulate's history was as uneventful as it had previously been eventful. In 1876 Watters, back at Takow, reported a continuance of the usual dull monotony and remarked 'it is seldom indeed that any event transpires here of much importance either to us or to the Chinese'. A new consulate was built at Takow in 1878, but the Takow anchorage fell out of favour with trading steamers, who preferred the open roadstead at Anping, even though during the south-west monsoon it was most difficult and dangerous to get across the bar and unloading a cargo might take weeks. In 1895 the only non-consular British residents at Takow were a doctor, a Customs officer, and their families, but Takow kept its consulate.[22]

In 1884 the French instituted a naval blockade of Formosa. Their actions, which Spence called most cruel and revoltingly brutal, caused considerable tension between the Chinese and foreign residents, and he had much difficulty in procuring from the intendant, who was subsequently most helpful, a proclamation dissociating other foreigners from the French. Many in the British

community left, but Spence saw the remainder safely through and was warmly praised by the Legation.[23] His other main preoccupation while in acting charge was obtaining compensation for the looting of a wrecked British vessel. His predecessor Gregory had queered the pitch by total inertia. Spence persevered and at length extracted the intendant's agreement to $10,000 compensation. At that point news came like a thunderclap that the intendant was condemned to strangulation for embezzlement. All his property was confiscated 'and his wives and families [were] turned into the street'. Spence had to start all over again with a new intendant, and after negotiations had degenerated into 'haggling of a commonplace and undignified nature' had to settle for $9,000. Some eighteen months later the former intendant was sighted by chance travelling comfortably in a Shanghai-bound steamer with family and servants into the exile into which the death penalty had been commuted and under the escort of two officers one of whom was his personal friend, and his partial reinstatement on reaching exile in Manchuria was expected.[24] From 1886 to 1893 P.L. Warren was consul. He had been a junior at the post for three years, for two spells, each of about a year, he had subsequently been acting consul, his wife had died there,[25] and in all he spent about a quarter of his forty-three years of service at this one petty consulate, a strange prelude to the distinguished final stages of his career. Formosa was changing. It became a province independent of Fukien, and the innovatory Liu Ming-ch'uan, appointed governor after peace with France had been restored, established himself in the north, away from Taiwan, where the intendant ceased to be the island's senior official. Warren was not impressed by the results in the south; Liu confined his attention to the north; the intendant's instructions were ignored by district magistrates; bribery and corruption flourished to an extent previously unknown even in Formosa; brigandage was rife; and no sooner did a Chinese merchant become largely indebted to a foreigner than he was officially declared to have become bankrupt, or to have left the island, or to have died. However, before leaving Warren reported very satisfactory relations with the Chinese authorities[26] and in recognition of his consistent efforts to further their commercial and social interests the foreign community as a whole, knowing him to be a keen shot, gave him a gun as a parting present and pleasingly said that they had been able to see that duty, not ambition, had ever been the

guiding influence on his life.[a] The Legation were so appreciative of
his ability and zeal in the Formosan backwater that he was promoted to Hankow, which led in turn to Shanghai.[27]

Hurst was consul at the time of the Sino-Japanese war. Troops
were brought over from the mainland to defend the island, and
troops commanded by an illiterate ex-brigand general came to
Taiwan. Hurst described them as a fine body of men but turbulent,
ill-disciplined, and very anti-foreign. There were constant insults
and some assaults. An ineffectual resistance movement to the
formal cession of Formosa to Japan in June 1895 made things
worse. In the north Japan landed troops at once and instantly
crushed opposition but as the weather was unfavourable for
operations against Taiwan they were delayed until October. The
intendant and all leading officials left and until the Japanese arrived
the ex-brigand was local dictator. At first very suspicious of British
naval movements he became not unfriendly and on the Japanese
navy's approach tolerated Hurst's advice to surrender, though in
fact he fled and his troops surrendered without fighting. O'Conor
thought Hurst and the British navy unmindful at times of China's
status as a belligerent and in one minute accused them of shameful
bullying, but his final verdict was that Hurst had done well during
very critical months when his own life had been in some danger and
that his handling of the ex-brigand had largely contributed to the
safety of British subjects.[28] Hurst, wrongly believing that he might
be compulsorily transferred to the Japan service, from which the
Formosa consulates were staffed after 1895, entered a strong objection. He believed his prospects in the China service better, but he
also objected to serving in a country where extraterritoriality was
being abolished and where 'the status of a consul will be merely one
of a commercial character', evidence of the standing China service
belief that extraterritoriality made their functions more interesting
and responsible than those of consular officers elsewhere.[29]

The consulate staff in all these years had rarely ventured into the
territory of the aborigines. The general foreign opinion, according
to Sundius in 1894, was that any discreet and well-behaved
European would be safe among them and that their raids on
Chinese were merely repaying unpardonable Chinese misbehaviour
towards them. Perkins' personal experience in the same period was
that a visitor who had the sense to treat them as brothers was
received most hospitably and eagerly invited to take part in war

dances. Bullock in 1873 had been more dubious. After a fortnight among what he called the civilized aborigines he and two companions made a three-day trip to a village of wild aborigines. They were given a friendly but not cordial reception and caused considerable dissatisfaction by the attention they unthinkingly paid to the skulls on display. Twenty-five of these, of which four were not yet bleached, were set out in front of one house. They were accompanied out of the territory by a gradually increasing number of armed men dressed for war who showed neither hostility nor friendliness and who left them after they had passed the last of the village's clearings. Bullock's party were uncertain whether this was a head-hunting expedition whose path happened to coincide with theirs or whether they were being watched out of the territory.[30]

In the north of the island there was more than one change of mind about the Tamsui post's status. After Swinhoe had moved back south it was at times an independent vice-consulate and at times a subordinate limb of the southern post, but as an exchange of letters between the two posts took about three weeks and the couriers were at risk of being attacked and robbed the latter arrangement was inconvenient. Even when it was independent as a vice-consulate the judicial powers exercisable by acting incumbents were dubious, and it came to notice in 1875 that although H.J. Allen had for two years been trying civil and criminal cases at Tamsui he had no legal power to hold a court. Finally the post became a full consulate in 1877.[31] Its lowly status in the late 1860s had not prevented it from acquiring a still more lowly satellite 35 miles along the coast at Kelung, a port to which foreign shipping was attracted by the availability of local coal. Alcock considered that if British ships frequented Kelung an assistant under Tamsui's orders was needed there. Accordingly in 1869 the Customs staff and the single merchant house which had previously constituted the exclusively male community were joined by McClatchie, who lived and worked in a wretched Chinese hut. The monotony of the community's life was broken only by a few ships loading coal for Shanghai and by the arrival from Australia of a fiancée whose position became most unpleasant when she found that the Tamsui vice-consul had no marriage warrant and could not unite her in matrimony. The Kelung branch office was closed in 1871, but its reopening was being considered four years later and even in 1890 the eventual building of a Kelung consulate had not been finally

ruled out. After 1871 Kelung's consular needs were met by occasional visits from Tamsui, the journey by boat and chair through
rapids and along mountain paths taking twelve to sixteen hours up
river and ten hours down river. In 1883 Frater's visits became
socially embarrassing. Hitherto the consul had been the guest of the
Customs assistant, but now the Customs house was in the charge of
a mere tide surveyor. Frater did not think that the consul should
place himself under an obligation to a man of that standing by
asking for quarters, but there was no other place for the consul to
go.[32]

Tamsui in its early days was not a desirable post. Gregory, not a
man given to complaints, said in 1866 in applying from there for a
first home leave after twelve years' service that his years there had
been peculiarly depressing. His depression is not surprising. After
visiting Tamsui Alcock described him as wretchedly housed in a
little temple in a back street, and a report laid before Parliament
expressed wonder that any Englishman could have occupied for a
week the accommodation which Gregory had been occupying for
years. It was no doubt to cheer himself up that he imported a
harmonium. In 1870 Wade said that the port had the double
disadvantage of coming little to Foreign Office attention and of
having a worse reputation for ill-health than any other port.[33]
Tamsui was not even the local centre for foreign trade. All the
port's foreign business was done some miles further up the river at
Twatutia, another insignificant village, but the Chinese contended
that foreigners were not entitled to own land either there or
at neighbouring Banka (otherwise Bangka).[34] Incessant disputes
arose from the Chinese desire to channel the important camphor
trade through a monopoly and the British desire to trade in
camphor freely.[35] Disputes on this or any other subject were
difficult to settle while the nearest responsible Chinese official, a
sub-prefect, was nearly 40 miles away and his superiors, the prefect
and intendant, were some 200 miles away, and this remained the
position until in the late 1870s a prefecture and a district magistracy
were established at Banka, renamed Taipeh.[36] A good consulate
site, including an historically interesting seventeenth-century Dutch
fort, was acquired at Tamsui, but the consul's house built on the
site in 1876 was defective and very unhealthy.[37]

Yet worse, there was among foreigners a restless frontier spirit,
exemplified by the disparate careers of two British subjects. Horn,

registered at the consulate in the artisan class, was married to a woman from an assimilated aboriginal tribe in the plains. He described himself as a contractor but was made bankrupt over a contract at Kelung. An even less successful venture, surprisingly undertaken in partnership with the merchant consul for the Hanse towns, was to lease two valleys from independent aborigines. Raiding head-hunters wounded him in the foot, the Tsungli Yamen protested against his activities, and Alcock instructed Gregory to give the venture no support. Horn sailed away from his valleys with over thirty motley companions, their vessel capsized, those who reached land were held to ransom by the aborigines, and Horn and half the company drowned.[38] Dodd, a merchant, lasted much longer. For two decades or so he brought his troubles to consular officers or gave them trouble by his actions, the consular reaction varying with the characters of the consular officers in charge at the time. In 1867, then in his late twenties, he purchased the rights in a wrecked Dutch barque. It was plundered, and failing to get satisfaction from Gregory he appealed to a Lieutenant Luard, whose gunboat was in port. Luard made house searches, recovered some property, and destroyed two houses belonging to leading robbers. Gregory told Luard that his proceedings had undermined local goodwill, the authority of Chinese officials, and the vice-consulate's influence; Alcock had to offer compensation to the Tsungli Yamen; the commander-in-chief severely censured Luard; but Dodd had got some of his property back. In 1868 two of Dodd's British employees going to take possession of rented Banka premises were assaulted by a mob armed with guns, knives, spears, bamboos, and huge stones. A musket blow sent one of them into a cesspit, both were robbed, and they only just escaped with their lives to a yamen, where they were given an escort back. By deferring presentation of demands until a British warship was in port, Holt at the consulate obtained satisfaction and was commended by Alcock for judgement and firmness. In 1885 Dodd formally complained that Frater had not taken seriously enough threats to Dodd's firm and had insulted Dodd. To the Legation Frater said that no one in the firm had ever been in the slightest danger and called Dodd a fussy, excitable, obstinate, and somewhat self-important man. To Dodd he wrote 'your letter is of such a character that I decline to keep it in my archives. There is a proper way of saying even disagreeable words, and your letter has passed that limit. If I failed in

courtesy I had no intention of doing so. You ought to know that I
am a man of peace with all men. Yours truly.' In 1886 the right to
occupy some Twatutia premises was in dispute between Dodd and
an influential Chinese of senior official status. Dodd went to the
premises with his employees and started pitching into the street all
the belongings of the Chinese. The Chinese seized Dodd by the
throat and called to his servants to secure him. Dodd, who was
extremely powerful, held him off with one hand, three of Dodd's
foreign employees rushed in, and one threatened to blow out the
brains of the Chinese. H.A. Giles, the acting consul, made Dodd
give up his claim to the premises and managed to pacify the very
angry Chinese authorities. How much longer Tamsui suffered from
Dodd's vagaries has not been ascertained, but unlike Horn he left
Formosa alive and was worth the best part of £10,000 when he
died in Wales in 1907.[39]

Like Spence in the south Frater had difficulties during the Sino-
French hostilities of the 1880s, but he was more troubled by French
military operations than by Chinese xenophobia. Although in the
countryside there were initial rumours that the Chinese authorities
had beheaded Frater and there were mob attacks on chapels,
compensation for which was negotiated by Frater with tact and
success, the behaviour of well-disciplined mainland troops towards
foreigners at Tamsui and Kelung was excellent, Frater kept on good
terms with their general and with the other Chinese authorities, and
the Tamsui people continued very friendly. On the other hand a
French bombardment scored direct hits on the consular compound,
all foreign women and children had to leave, and Mrs Frater was
stranded in Amoy for seven months. French landing parties were
beaten back at Tamsui and when he called on the Chinese general,
Frater saw with disgust eight of their heads displayed on a tree. He
wrote to the general that the West regarded such barbarity with
displeasure, that the French would become doubly incensed, and
that public notices offering large rewards for French heads might
tempt the people to cut off the wrong heads. Rewards for heads
were a time-honoured Chinese custom, so it was broadminded and
conciliatory of the general to reply that in deference to Frater's
views he would forbid the cutting off of heads and would recall the
notices. At the instance of a French family the Foreign Secretary
later instructed Frater to try to recover the remains of a French
naval officer. Accompanied by the consulate doctor Frater went to

Taipeh, identified the officer's almost bare skull from among other French heads, and pending knowledge of the family's wishes buried it in the consular compound. Throughout months of tension Frater remained cool and efficient, and the minister, the Foreign Office, and the commander-in-chief all paid him well-deserved compliments.[40]

However unsuccessful Liu Ming-ch'uan may have been in governing southern Formosa he effected great changes in the north. A cable was laid between Tamsui and the mainland. Taipeh was lighted by electricity. A steam sawmill, an arsenal, a steam-roller, even a railway between Taipeh and Kelung were among the modern wonders to be seen, and his children were taught English. W.H. Wilkinson, who admittedly was only very briefly at Tamsui, thought Liu a wonderful man. Bourne too seems to have been favourably impressed and was quickly on very friendly terms with him. Liu was so ready to seek and take Bourne's advice on Western technology that on Bourne's departure in 1889 after a mere fifteen months the whole foreign community, which was almost entirely British, asked the Foreign Office to send him back to them. He was not sent back, but this made little difference. In 1891 Liu met the usual fate of nineteenth-century Chinese innovators and was dismissed, and innovation in Formosa ceased until the island's cession to Japan.[41] At the time of the cession there was mutiny, looting, and eventually anarchy round Tamsui but a conspicuous absence of anti-foreign manifestations. Hopkins was congratulated on his able and efficient protection of British interests while in charge during a trying and critical position.[42]

MANAGEMENT OF THE SERVICE

THROUGHOUT the nineteenth century the method by which men were recruited into the service remained unsatisfactory.

In 1874 Wade blamed the Civil Service Commission for admitting many entrants who besides other shortcomings lacked linguistic ability.[1] The entrance examination barely tested it. French and at times German were included but were taken almost as dead languages. In 1872 Johnson had got in without the Commission noticing that he had a painful stammer.[2] In 1887 the Commission suggested that a certain proficiency in speaking the languages might be required, but it seems that even after that candidates could opt out of orals.[3] Although a handful of nineteenth-century officers were good scholars[4] or fine speakers[5] the average standard in Chinese was low, whether through lack of aptitude or lack of application. The statement made in 1890 by Howard, recently secretary of Legation in Peking, that a great many consuls knew half a dozen Chinese dialects was rubbish.[6] To encourage application after the initial period in Peking two subsequent interpretorial examinations were at Wade's suggestion introduced in 1878. The concept, interpretorial allowances for those who passed and no promotion for those who failed, was sound, but the application was not. After ploughing two men in their senior interpretorial orals in 1900 B. Brenan said that very probably no one had ever been ploughed before (this seems to have been a slight exaggeration) and that in examining juniors, most of whom had a vocabulary of about 500 words, other consuls probably looked on the examination as a matter of form.[7]

The rest of the examination was equally unsatisfactory as a test of other potential. It fell into two parts. The first part consisted of papers in handwriting and orthography, in arithmetic and in English composition. In handwriting and orthography candidates

had to write out in a fair hand, correcting mistakes of spelling and grammar, passages such as 'The faite of the infortunet royal familley, after this difeet, was sufficiantley singuler to diserve ricording...' Although the other two papers were little more demanding fifteen out of thirty-five candidates in November 1873 failed the first part and were therefore barred from proceeding to the second part, consisting of précis, geography, Euclid, Latin, French, German, and mercantile and criminal law, all easy papers.

Open competition much increased the number of candidates. At most three candidates, in practice often fewer, competed for each place under limited competition, whereas in the November 1873 open competition the thirty-five candidates competed for three places.[8] Stiff competition in an elementary examination let in the crammers. Scoones, the famous London crammers, concentrated on prestigious branches of the public service but occasionally crammed Far Eastern service candidates whose parents were prosperous.[9] Most coaching for student interpreterships was done by a humbler establishment, the civil service department at King's College, London. Year after year a puff in the college calendar stated that clerkships in the lower division of the civil service offered a fairly remunerative base from which the studious and able could with good prospects of success prepare themselves at the department's evening classes to sit for posts as assistant tax surveyors, superior clerks in the India Office, or student interpreters. The puff added half-heartedly that even posts in the first division of the civil service, though mostly gained by university men, were by no means impossible for lower-division clerks coached in the department. The department crammed so successfully for student interpreterships that over half the China service entrants from 1888 to 1907 had been coached there. The small number of persons entering at the minimum age of 18 suggests that some form of cramming was usually necessary.[10] An additional advantage of crammers was that they made it their business to find out in advance when entrance examinations, the incidence of which was quite irregular, were likely to be held.[11] Once it had been decided to hold an examination the Civil Service Commission advertised the fact widely in the press and the Foreign Office informed universities, but the notice given was far too short to permit subsequent reading up for the examination.[12]

From the introduction of open competition to the end of the

century a substantial proportion of entrants were plebeian. Fathers included three drapers, two merchants' clerks, two small farmers, a bootmaker, a pensioned coastguard, a railway storekeeper, a tailor, a valet, and a licensed victualler.[13] The type of recruit was viewed with mounting dissatisfaction. The dissatisfaction was by no means entirely a matter of social snobbery. The Foreign Office official who in 1890 minuted that Wilton, Goffe, and Fox seemed entrants of unusually good stamp[14] was a shrewd judge, for Wilton ended with a KCMG and the other two with KBEs, but snobbery did not come into the judgement. Wilton's father was a foreign-born Singapore merchant,[15] Goffe was the son of a small master plumber,[16] and Fox as a schoolboy had a marked Cockney accent.[a] Certainly when in 1896 Jordan started considerable debate by a memorandum deploring falling standards among entrants he was deploring falling intellectual standards, not falling social standards, something which would not have greatly concerned a man who himself came of Ulster farming stock. As Chinese secretary he had been superintending entrants' Chinese studies and he was not satisfied with the entrants. He advocated urgent changes in the entrance examination. The examination, he said, was so elementary that after two or three tries men from the crammers eventually passed and defied competition from those whose education had been more liberal; the former recruitment from the Scottish and Irish universities had been squeezed out by the crammers' products. Both Jordan's predecessor and his successor in the secretariat agreed that the standard needed to be raised. The Civil Service Commission commented that the existing age limits of 18 to 24 mixed men and boys, that the minimum age should be raised, and that the examination, which they called an uneasy compromise between the liberal and the commercial, should be recast. Proposals on the lines of the Commission's views were put to the Foreign Secretary, Salisbury, who could hardly have been more unhelpful. He was against raising the minimum age; he was against Latin and Greek, though he knew this was a minority opinion and that 'for many years to come men will be prepared for political duties in China and Japan by deciphering the choruses of corrupt Greek plays'; his school years had been entirely wasted and 'I should have known more and been healthier if I had never been to school at all'. Officials attempting to get round this Delphic obstructionism submitted revised proposals. This time they were told that the class

with some knowledge of Latin and Greek 'is much more agreeable in manner, and somewhat more trustworthy, than the class whose education has not been carried so far. But the latter class possess distinctly more energy, and more knowledge of business. Both classes have their advantages, but I doubt whether it is wise to aim at the entire exclusion of either'. For the time being officials gave up. The examination was not recast, the age limits so casually laid down by Russell in 1862 remained in force, and the crammers went on cramming. During the debate no one seems to have pointed out that the London location of the most successful crammers worked against potential competitors who lived far away from London.[17]

Recruits entered a close service, numbering sixty or so for most of the period and seventy-six in 1901, which suffered from a permanent promotion blockage. Both in 1889 and in 1893 at least one first assistant had entered twenty years previously, and it was recognized that for juniors the service had lost its attractions.[18] Promotion, except in occasional cases of extreme merit or demerit, went entirely by seniority, and occurred only when death or infirmity created a vacancy. In 1870 Foreign Office minutes said that Alcock had allowed incompetents to creep up by seniority into responsible positions and that it was quite hopeless to expect a service conducted on principles of mere seniority to be of a really high class, but these were rare glimpses of good sense, and promotion by seniority became if anything even more strongly entrenched.[19] Juniors had always been badly paid. In 1867 Watters, a second assistant in his fourth year of service, had after meeting outgoings for mess, servants, teacher, and miscellaneous domestic expenses $2 a month left over for medicine, clothing, and any other essential needs. He could afford no sort of amusement, had had to sell his watch, bed, and nearly all his furniture, and was a few score dollars in debt; surely, he exclaimed, the government never intended to bring a young man to China and leave him in such poverty.[20] These miserable salaries became even less easy to bear as promotion prospects got worse and worse. The abolition of the grades of interpreter in 1877 and of third assistant in 1880 meant that a first assistant could hope for no promotion until he at last achieved commissioned rank and that the entrant who had once after five or six years been able to go home as a third assistant on £300 might after seven or eight years still have to go home, if he could afford his share of the passage money, as a student interpreter

on his starting salary of £200. The abolition of the two grades, and reductions in consuls' salaries, were penalties inflicted on the service by a protracted struggle between Treasury and Foreign Office. The Treasury sensed that the service could be run more economically but did not have enough information to be able to prove it. They could do little more than oppose any overall increase in cost. Their attitude meant that as more treaty ports were opened the additional salaries for the resulting new senior posts had to be squeezed out of a more or less static overall budget.[21] Hammond was very conscious that juniors were paid too little. He told a Parliamentary select committee in 1871 that he could not understand how they could exist on their remuneration. He fought on unsuccessfully and relieved his feelings by minuting that one Treasury refusal of a trifling pay increase was a notable instance of parsimony and folly. Successors fared no better. There were further despondent Foreign Office minutes in 1882. One minute foresaw that though something should be done for the service it would not be possible to raise salaries without cutting the number of posts. Another, in which the Foreign Secretary concurred, said that it would be a great mistake to go on scraping salaries but did not suggest how this might be prevented. The despondency was justified, for the Treasury stuck to their tactics and in 1884 refused to sanction a consular establishment in Korea until the considerable reductions of which the diplomatic and consular estimates seemed to them capable had been effected.[22]

Matrimony was a costly enterprise. In 1893 nine out of nineteen assistants were married,[23] which given the ages of assistants at that time is not in itself a surprising proportion, but how they managed financially is not easy to understand. Marriage almost inevitably meant maintaining at some time a separate establishment at home for wife or children or both. Illness might send them home, or an officer might be posted somewhere unsuitable for a family, and it was generally accepted that for reasons both of health and of education children should be sent home at least by the age of 10.[24] In 1870 Fittock had for nine years been spending between £200 and £250 annually to maintain and educate his three eldest children in England, and in 1900 W.H. Wilkinson was spending well over half his pay for similar purposes.[25] Temporary summer separations might be necessary. As opportunities for avoiding the worst summer heats developed officers who could afford it sent children,

and perhaps wives too, away to coolness while they themselves sweltered at their posts.[26] A British nurse or British governess might be needed.[27] On top of the expenses of marriage came the pangs of separations, which disrupted family life to an extent that today seems intolerable and which at the time were felt keenly enough for Jordan to write that nothing the East could offer compensated for separation from one's children. Cooper, unable to afford to retire, spent years missing his wife, whose health forbade a return to China.[28] P.L. Warren was on home leave in 1881 when the wife he had married six years before had her fourth child in England. At the end of 1882 husband and wife went back to China taking the baby girl and leaving a son and two other daughters behind with their widowed grandmother. The wife died some twelve months later. By the time that Warren next came home the son was at a preparatory school. Sent by the school to meet his father at a railway station he waited on the platform wondering what his father looked like. After that leave he and his three sisters were grown up before they saw their father again.[a] One officer declared that he might be able to afford the doubtful luxury of struggling on with a wife and children but could not contemplate leaving a widow and children to struggle on by themselves.[29] This sentiment was only too realistic. Two unavailing appeals to the Foreign Office for financial help show to what despairing depths dependants were still liable to sink. In 1880, soon after Middleton's death at 38, an unmarried sister wrote that she had been very ill and that her money had all gone, but if she were enabled to tide over until she had regained strength she could accept an engagement as companion to a lady in Clapham, provided, that was, that the lady could wait for her. In 1915 a spinster daughter of Swinhoe wrote nearly forty years after his death that his widow had recently died in great poverty after a long and terrible illness; two daughters had been trying to struggle on by taking lodgers, but the other daughter had been very ill for months and was awaiting an operation; both women were in terrible straits; 'a few pounds would indeed be most acceptable'.[30]

Fares to and from home remained cripplingly expensive, particularly for men with families. Letters written to his family by Adkins as he returned to China in 1867 show that the journeys at that date were in addition tiring, tedious, and uncomfortable even for a bachelor. He travelled overland from Calais to Brindisi, a route still used thirty years later. From Paris he reached the foot of

the Alps by train, crossed them by diligence, and went on by train to Brindisi, a very hard and fatiguing journey of bad meals and of wretched nights in trains and station waiting-rooms. On the fairly comfortable steamer leaving Brindisi for Alexandria the passengers, nearly all Italians, Greeks, and Egyptians, varied from the fat and dirty to the very fat and very dirty. At Alexandria he narrowly escaped being quarantined and the train to Cairo was so full that he had to travel second class. He could only get a bed on the floor in the hotel at Suez, where to the unkind amusement of other passengers it seemed at first that there might be no room for him on a steamer full to overflowing. The shipping company agent turned out to be concurrently British consul and did wonders for a brother officer, giving him an officer's cabin rather bigger than the ordinary cabins into which four passengers were packed, and the unkind amusement turned to envy. The passengers were the usual mixed lot, the young married couple and the young lady going out on spec perhaps predominating, and their manners and selfish, greedy jostling for places at the main table sickened Adkins, who quietly found himself a place elsewhere. There were a great many children on board with whom the heat disagreed so much that they yelled incessantly, the steamer was slow and not very clean, her engines shook so much that it was difficult to write, there were no books on board, and at times he felt almost worn out with ennui. From Singapore to Hong Kong he was in an overloaded ship which rolled and pitched madly and in which the food was very bad. From Calais to Hong Kong took him about seven weeks.[a] In 1864 C.T. Jones had taken 136 days from England to Shanghai, but that had been an exceptionally slow passage.[31]

Foreign Office and Legation had little idea how to cure the promotion blockage. This is not surprising, for the same trouble afflicted the diplomatic service, nearly a third of the entrants to which in the half century from 1851 onwards resigned before reaching a post of responsibility, presumably because they had failed to reach one.[32] Frustrated junior diplomatists, recruited from the higher reaches of society, could afford to resign. Juniors in the China service, in which private means were very rare, could not afford that luxury, and their experience was that their training fitted them only for careers in China and that after some years it was too late to seek employment elsewhere.[33] The fundamental problem, imbalance between the numbers of senior and junior

posts, was not tackled. O'Conor and Currie in the 1880s both mooted a reduction in the number of juniors, but instead an over-large intake at the bottom continued and the imbalance got worse. In 1889 there were 22 commissioned officers, of whom 2 were vice-consuls, as opposed to 22 assistants and 16 student interpreters. Then the single year 1898 saw 15 student interpreters recruited. Consequently in 1901 there were 27 commissioned officers, again including 2 vice-consuls, as opposed to 23 assistants and 26 student interpreters.[34] The enforced retirement of useless seniors would have had only a marginal and temporary effect on the blockage but might have given juniors some encouragement, but in spite of occasional Legation suggestions nothing decisive was done.[35] The Foreign Office went no further than giving the unwanted strong encouragement, very occasionally so strong that it amounted to an ultimatum,[36] to apply to retire early on health grounds.

Spence, considered by O'Conor one of the best men in the service, expressed his frustration when tendering his resignation at the age of 37. He had been offered a six-year engagement by China's leading British firm, who were looking for a representative to negotiate with the Chinese for them. In applying for a pension Spence said he was still a poorly paid first assistant without pro-motion prospects for years; he seemed destined to spend his best years in places where the petty nature of British interests, the con-stant sense of stagnation, mean and squalid surroundings, and bad accommodation made an active, useful, and happy life impos-sible; and he could now serve British interests better than he could hope to do as assistant or acting consul at small ports. O'Conor was encouraging and the Foreign Office co-operative. They suggested to the Treasury, who they knew would not agree to a pension, that Spence should be placed *en disponibilité*, that is, that he should retain his position in the service and his eventual pension rights but should receive no pay. The Treasury agreed, but this early and interesting experiment in loaning an official to business ended inconclusively. Suffering in Peking from malaria and what was probably sprue Spence ignored medical advice to leave at once for home. He stayed on in order to conclude his current negotiations with the Chinese and went home only to die.[37] What prospects he would have had in the service if he had lived to return to it cannot be guessed. The only other similar experiment came in the 1890s, when Bourne was given extended leave to take

charge of a chamber of commerce mission enquiring into the cotton textile trade in China. He received a substantial payment from the chamber on top of his leave pay and returned to the service at the end of the mission.[38]

Singularly few officers sought to better themselves by leaving the service of their own volition. J.A.T. Meadows was alone in becoming a self-employed merchant. McL. Brown, W.T. Lay, McKean, and O'Brien left to join the Customs. Abdy and Douglas left the East for good. Abdy unexpectedly came into money or prospects very soon after entry, resigned, and after inheriting a baronetcy and an estate attracted attention by his matrimonial affairs.[39] Douglas had had enough of China after a spell at Taku. He entered the British Museum library, in his numerous writings exhibited no great admiration for the Foreign Office, and was knighted.[40] Dennys, a rolling stone, became at first a journalist in Hong Kong and then an official in British south-east Asia.[41] Cooper after nearly seven years in the service and Carroll after four years were offered official posts outside the service but Bruce declined to accept either resignation; 'the public has a moral claim on the services of those who have been sent out and maintained as students, which cannot, without impropriety, be ignored by them'. The remarkable doctrine that permission to resign could be withheld still had more than half a century of life before it. In 1917 a junior, George, decided it was his duty to enlist and tendered his resignation. The head of the consular department said that in his opinion the Foreign Office claim to a right to refuse resignations was all bluff and a consular officer could call their bluff, snap his fingers at them, and leave whenever he pleased, and the legal adviser was disposed to agree. Nevertheless the Foreign Office, politely expressing appreciation of George's motives, refused to accept his resignation, and George did not call the bluff any more than Cooper and Carroll had done.[42]

O'Conor, who expressed great respect for the service, said pithily that it needed 'fewer men, more work, quicker promotion and higher pay'.[43] Probably few examination candidates realized that the service they were seeking to enter offered underemployment, slow promotion, and bad pay. The strangely varied motives which brought young men into it in more modern times are still in part remembered. They ranged from a spirit of adventure through a wish for respectable and steady employment to such unexpected

reasons as a desire to get a maximum distance away from parents. The doubtless equally mixed motives of most Victorian entrants are no longer known, though family connections with the East sufficiently explain some candidatures. The motives of three Victorian entrants, Bourne, J. Scott, and Tours, have been handed down. Bourne, the son of a deceased clergyman who had left a widow and six children in reduced circumstances, was working as a supplementary War Office clerk at £110 a year, was advised that pay and prospects were better in China, and proceeded to cram at the civil service department.[a] J. Scott, who was the son of a small Aberdeenshire farmer and knew nothing whatever about China, had recently graduated from Aberdeen University and was tutoring in the Borders when a newspaper announcement of a forthcoming examination caught his eye[a] (at Peking the written English of the Aberdeen graduate was found much below standard and he was highly commended for indomitable efforts to improve it).[44] Tours was the eldest of the five sons of a Dutch musician long resident in England. The father was in poor health and in order to help support the family the son needed quick employment, even at the cost of leaving a fiancée behind in England.[a] Each of the three young men, all of whom did well in the service, was thus thinking primarily of employment and pay. China was not in itself their goal, and indeed Tours first opted for Siam and then changed his mind. This was no doubt a common enough attitude. Entrants included an abnormally high proportion of men whose fathers were already dead.[45] Being fatherless tended to imply a need to earn as soon as possible, and here with the cachet of an appointment under government was a job obtainable through an examination which could be taken young and without a university education. The importance of the cachet should not be underestimated. Becoming an official was viewed with approval by relatives[a] and conveyed immediate status.

For their part the Foreign Office gave candidates practically no information. After a Japan entrant had before even reaching Japan accepted £1,000 a year to edit a Shanghai newspaper successful candidates were required to furnish a bond to repay the cost of their passage if they resigned or were dismissed within five years of appointment, and after another Japan entrant was found to be married they were required to be unmarried and to remain so for two years. They had to be British by birth and, if not born within the United Kingdom or if born there of parents not so born, had to

obtain the Foreign Secretary's permission to compete.[46] Obtaining permission was a mere formality. Tours' father had never bothered to naturalize himself, but the Foreign Office did not take up his obliging offer to do so if necessary. Wilton was born in Singapore of a Danish father and Dutch mother, though both were at some stage naturalized, and competed without seeking permission. When he had passed, the omission came out. The Foreign Office considered his excuses for the omission lame, but they gave retrospective permission, and all the indications are that they would unhesitatingly have given permission had it been requested at the right time.[47] Candidates were told these conditions and requirements and what their starting salary would be. They were also told that they would have to learn Chinese, Japanese, or Siamese. They seem to have been told nothing else. Baber, volunteering when on leave in 1888 to give an entrant lunch and useful hints about life in Peking, said that when he had himself gone out in the 1860s he had sadly felt the lack of such information. In the twentieth century a document was at last prepared giving entrants hints about clothing and so on, but it was revised too infrequently to be a reliable guide.[48] In Baber's day entrants were not spoon-fed in other ways either. His near contemporary G. Jamieson on first appointment reached Shanghai after Tientsin had been iced up for the winter, so he was despatched by gunboat to Chefoo. There M.C. Morrison put him into a mule-litter with money for the sixteen-day journey overland to Peking and a missionary lent him an invaluable sheepskin coat and a servant who turned out to be a rascal. Owing to heavy snow he had not got half-way after twenty days and money was running out. Having been advised by Morrison to apply to an intendant if in trouble he used his smattering of Chinese to discover there was an intendant at the provincial capital and got to the intendant's yamen accompanied by half the city's riff-raff. Yamen underlings tried to fob him off, he staged a sit-down strike and, as a result, was sent on to the magistrate. The magistrate received him courteously and lent him 30 taels, which saw him through until he reached Peking a week later.[49] A month's solitary and freezing travel through a by no means always peaceful or friendly countryside whose language and customs were unknown was a fairly testing overture to a career in China.

Following representations by Alcock the entrants' quarters in the Peking students' mess were provided with beds, chests of drawers,

wash-stands, and cane-bottomed office chairs. By the 1890s the
bolsters and pillows which had been in continuous use for over
twenty years were candidates for replacement, the only furniture
provided was apparently a bed, two chairs, and a table, and the
common-room was in a state of total neglect.[50] The privilege of
furnished accommodation, however spartan and dilapidated, was
strictly confined to the mess. It was self-evident that public money
would be saved if private furniture were not being constantly
moved from post to post, and that consular officers would be saved
financial losses from damage to furniture in transit, losses so heavy
that the service reckoned three transfers as bad as a fire.[51] Nonetheless decades of representations by Legation and Foreign Office
failed to secure the furnishing of accommodation against payment
of a furniture rental by the occupants. Though the Office of
Works maintained that the initial cost of part furnishing and the
need to increase their Shanghai staff were insuperable difficulties
their real objection was that the cost of transporting furniture fell
on the Foreign Office vote and that the capital cost of furnishing,
put in 1893 at £16,000, would fall on their vote.[52] In 1919 the
Treasury agreed that the Office of Works should furnish. Until then
taxpayers and consular officers went on wasting money. The more
than $2,000 spent on transporting 115 cases of Fox's furniture
from Peking to Yunnanfu in 1913 would have furnished the
consulate, and a great number of his effects were badly damaged
during the journey. Most officers of any period would have
endorsed Pauncefote's 1882 opinion: 'The Office of Works sours
the existence of our officials in China and I wish it could be
abolished as far as China is concerned. I suppose we must continue
to groan under the system'.[53]

Whereas the Foreign Office kept control over public expenditure
on the service firmly in their own hands they would seem, to judge
from the official files, to have left career management and China
appointments almost entirely to the Legation, rarely questioning
Legation recommendations and hardly ever insisting on their views.
Certainly after Hammond's death the Foreign Office at times
seemed quite out of touch, so much so that when in 1898 P.L.
Warren, one of the leading seniors and long a widower, wrote to
them from a leave address his signature rang no bell and the reply
was addressed to Mrs P.L. Warren.[54] It may however be that at
times the Foreign Office were more closely involved in career

management than the official files show. It is well-known that the famous Barrington, who with one three-year gap was private secretary from 1885 to 1905, acted almost as a one-man personnel department for the diplomatic service, whose members courted his favour. It is not so well-known that private secretary activities extended to the China service (and doubtless to other consular services too). Private secretaries covered their traces by leaving no papers. A minute at the time of Warren's retirement by Barrington's successor Tyrrell, stating that Warren had in his experience been one of the most unsatisfactory consular officers with whom he had had to deal,[55] seems almost the only indication that Tyrrell had ever had any dealings with the China service. Barrington left a few more traces, not enough to show what he did but enough to suggest that he may have done a good deal. In 1901 it was to Barrington that confidential thumb-nail sketches of consular officers, including juniors, were sent after the secretary of Legation had toured the consulates. It was Barrington who minuted in the same year that Perkins, a first assistant on home leave after ten years' service, had a very unsavoury reputation, that although enquiries into his conduct two years previously had not revealed enough to justify dismissal there would in all probability be a disagreeable scandal if he remained, and that it was most desirable to get rid of him. It was Barrington who then induced Perkins to apply on health grounds to retire on a pension, but he acted so discreetly that eight years later a Foreign Office official could find no papers which would inform him what the real complaint against Perkins had been. These and other shadowy indications suggest that Barrington was someone with whom the China service may, like the diplomatic service, have had to reckon. He had the reputation of being a fair man. He was evidently kindly too, for in promising Satow in 1904 to do his best to rid China of some undesirables the chief clerk said that Barrington's soft heart was among the many obstacles in the way. Barrington was however also known as a snob and as a stickler for sartorial correctness, and neither trait can have made him the ideal man to sit in judgement on China officers.[56]

For some thirty years from the 1860s onwards the Foreign Office battled with the Treasury over free medical attention, which for a long time was provided at some consulates and not at others. In 1868 the practice of paying a subscription to doctors from public funds seemed to the Treasury very objectionable, and they refused

to agree to the practice being extended to three of the ports then
open. Alcock protested that it was a positive economy to pay
doctors to preserve officers as healthy public servants. A Foreign
Office minute on his despatch had no doubt that he was right,
but 'the Treasury have queer notions of economy'.[57] In 1874 the
Treasury sanctioned expenditure not exceeding a total of £1,200,
but they had not thrown in the sponge. In 1888 they tried to make
an increase in consuls' pay conditional on free medical attendance
being confined to constables, distressed British subjects, and the
like, everyone else paying for their own medical attention, a course
which they reproachfully said they had often urged. Although the
Foreign Office insisted that second assistants and below should get
free attendance they were minded to acquiesce in others paying,
and the situation was retrieved only by O'Conor declaring that he
could not conscientiously concur. In 1896 a Treasury letter to
the Foreign Office, admitting that Treasury views had been unanimously rejected by the best judges in and out of China, conceded
the principle of free attendance for all officers and their families.
The letter was a striking departure from the stilted phrases in
which the Treasury were wont to reject, without deigning to enter
into discussion, proposals for expenditure on the service. It was
reasoned, reasonable, and pleasantly worded, and yet it revealed
that after all these years of argument the Treasury in their Whitehall seclusion still had no inkling of what life in China was like.
During those years few had left the rank of second assistant behind
without having been seriously ill, many had left it with constitutions so undermined that only early retirement or death awaited
them, and seven student interpreters or junior assistants had died of
disease. The Treasury letter, regretfully recalling the 1888 Foreign
Office stand over second assistants, described them as 'youthful
bachelors, who have not been long enough in China to be much
affected by the climate and who, if they live prudently, need have
little to do with doctors'.[58] Doctors under contract were a great
boon provided they were professionally tolerable, but treaty port
practitioners were a mixed bag, witness Pedder's welcome in 1877
for the fit of delirium tremens which conveniently removed from
Foochow a particularly unsatisfactory consulate doctor.[59] Nursing
was often a matter of self-help. Although a nurse was brought up
from Hong Kong in 1876 when a student interpreter, Taylor,
caught typhoid at Canton, his contemporary J. Scott was in con-

stant attendance as well as the nurse until Taylor died. At Amoy in 1895 a second assistant, H.F. King, so ill that he was delirious for most of a week, was nursed during the day by his consul, C.T. Gardner, and the constable, and at night other volunteers from the community took over. At Chinkiang in 1898 no nurse could be procured from Shanghai for Raab, who had smallpox, and he died in the care of his devoted houseboy, of the constable, and of relays of coolies engaged for the purpose.[60] Dental treatment was a problem. A consulate doctor might stop or pull an offending tooth,[61] but it seems that in the 1890s Shanghai was the only treaty port in the Yangtze area to boast a dentist, and consuls up the river were not always given prompt permission to leave their posts for dental treatment at Shanghai.[62]

The Chinese secretary occupied a key post which Wade in 1881 called more important than any consulate.[63] By definition he had to know the written and spoken language well and therefore had to be selected from the consular service, but his duties were diplomatic. As no one in the Tsungli Yamen understood any foreign language he was the minister's indispensable channel of communication with the Yamen, translating the Legation's communications, many originally drafted by him in English, into Chinese and the Yamen's into English, and he acted as the minister's interpreter or representative at interminable meetings with the Yamen. When the minister did not have a China background the Chinese secretary was necessarily his chief adviser on the ever-increasing complexities of the extraterritorial system and on Chinese psychology and etiquette. A hard-working man of ability and character was favourably placed to rival or usurp the influence with the minister of the Legation's career diplomatic staff, who lacked his expertise.[64] The Foreign Office were in a quandary. The Legation could not do without the Chinese secretary, but the Foreign Office distrusted the undue influence of experts. Tenterden minuted in 1874 as permanent under-secretary that in his view it was not 'at all a good plan to place our Eastern Missions entirely in the hands of Orientalists'.[65] Further, diplomatists were one thing and consular officers another. Even the Tsungli Yamen quickly learned to regard consuls as an inferior species. The diplomatic service did not need to learn this. In evidence to a royal commission Howard expressed very clearly its innate sense of superiority: 'As a rule in the consular service a man wants a salary to live upon. We [diplomatists], as a

rule, do not. I, at all events, did not go into the diplomatic service to make it a trade and to live upon my salary'.[66] Even in the twentieth century a young Legation diplomatist regretted that his sister, who had become engaged to an unexceptionable student interpreter, was 'going to marry outside the family'.[a] The Foreign Office therefore did not know what status should be enjoyed by the outstandingly able W.S.F. Mayers, who became Chinese secretary in 1871, any more than they knew what to do with his near contemporary Satow, who was also outstandingly able and became Japanese secretary in Japan.

Mayers spoke several European languages well, knew both Mandarin and Cantonese, and had a working knowledge of Korean. His Chinese was so good that Wade, a hypercritical judge, considered him equal to any written or oral negotiation, and said that although he was a fiery little being his manner with the Chinese, to whom he was acceptable, was excellent. He was a dedicated public servant who turned down most advantageous offers of employment from the Customs and from the Shang-hai municipal council, and Li Hung-chang was understood to be willing to pay £12,000 a year for his services. He was an immense worker, who deplored student interpreters wasting time on billiards and bowls, 'commonly known as recreation', and in the midst of his heavy official duties wrote reference books of lasting value to sinologues. By 1875 he and Satow were described to the Foreign Office as the mainstays of their respective Legations, but their official futures were most uncertain. When Mayers was first appointed Chinese secretary Wade had been against his having a diplomatic commission. Hammond had agreed; young diplomatists in the Legation, who should be encouraged to take an interest in China, would be discouraged were they to be in an inferior position to 'one who in his origins and previous service had merely been a consular officer'; Mayers should wear a consular uniform, not a diplomatic one. Then Wade changed his mind and at his instance the Foreign Office more than once considered his suggestions that Mayers should be brought into the diplomatic service. Currie, then an assistant under-secretary of state, recommended that Mayers and Satow should be made local second secretaries, thus entitling them to the social position and uniform of diplomatists so long as they held their posts, but that they should have no claim to promotion in the diplomatic service. Tenterden and the Foreign

Secretary concurred, and when Wade tried a last time Tenterden was crushing: 'It would never do to hold out hopes to Mr Mayers of succeeding Sir T. Wade for which in my opinion he would be quite unfit'. (Tenterden's adverse opinion was probably mere prejudice. Still maintaining after Mayers' death that it was most inexpedient to give the linguists diplomatic status he quite wrongly blamed Mayers, who he acknowledged had been indefatigable, for the interminable length to which of late years all Chinese questions had been dragged out.)[67] The correspondence and minuting about Mayers rested with Tenterden's adverse opinion. Early in 1878 Mayers left Peking on a medical certificate stating that for twelve months he had been suffering from insomnia, lassitude, and incapacity for sustained mental exertion, the result mainly of overwork of the brain. He got no further than Shanghai, where he died of typhus (probably the Legation's usual typhoid). The Legation said that the loss of a man of such exceptional talent would be very severely felt, a royal bounty grant was made to the widow, and Li Hung-chang and Ting Jih-ch'ang both contributed to a fund for educating his children.[68] There was never any question in the future of a Chinese secretary being given substantive diplomatic rank. Until the end of the nineteenth century even the local rank of second secretary was an honour reserved for an exceptionally deserving incumbent, but in the twentieth century the local rank of first secretary, latterly of counsellor, went automatically to the head of the secretariat.[69]

In running the service the Foreign Office were extremely conservative. Systematic inspections of consulates at fixed intervals do not seem to have been considered for a moment, and an inspection by Howard in 1889, the first for twenty years and the last until the twentieth century, was put in hand only in response to Treasury pressure for a review of the service.[70] Characteristically the Foreign Office received unfavourably Alcock's recommendation in 1866 that as a means of checking dissipation and idleness among entrants they should be on probation for their first three years. With lunatic logic officials and Foreign Secretary agreed that while the habits of intemperance of some juniors were very lamentable the loss of student interpreters whose passages out and whose education in China had cost so much could not be afforded. This attitude was later slightly modified, but only in cases of failure to learn Chinese. Two 1872 entrants were threatened with dismissal

for what Wade called their simply disgraceful lack of zeal in their Chinese studies and avoided dismissal by mending their ways, but in 1883 G.V. Fittock, charged with failing to apply himself to his studies even to a minimum degree, had to resign in order to forestall dismissal.[71]

Over the years some changes were made but they were not fundamental. Perhaps the most important were the arrangements introduced in the 1880s enabling officers to be given extensions of home leave to read for the bar.[72] Legal training was useful at some major ports and some officers had a particular interest in their judicial functions. Others, it is clear, applied to read for the bar mainly because it meant a longer period at home, a reason which became more cogent after the happy days of at least one extension of home leave being granted semi-automatically were brought to an end in 1889. Such motives did not escape notice, and by no means everyone who applied to read for the bar was allowed to do so.[73] Senior consuls were much less often left for many years at the same port than they had been, a change which may perhaps have been due to accident rather than to design but which was consistent with the later official view[74] that shorter tenures were preferable. Towards the end of the century the Foreign Office finally abandoned their objections to consuls-general, and Canton, Hankow, and Tientsin were all raised to consulates-general to keep level with a Portuguese, a Belgian, and a French consulate-general respectively.[75] Office procedures changed as little as service organization. Cyphers and typewriters were the main innovations, though it was not until the twentieth century that the flood of cypher telegrams became a plague and that despatches had to be hammered out with a dozen carbon copies.

Cyphers made a modest entry, the initial distribution of cypher books in the 1870s including only the leading consulates. Telegrams were so expensive that they were most sparingly employed. Not until the beginning of the twentieth century did consulates begin to need a telegraphic address. They were given the ill-judged instruction to register it as 'Breasts' (presumably a syncopation of 'British eastern establishments'), but the address was quickly condemned as not all suitable and 'Britain' was substituted. The cyphers were issued for the personal use of consuls, a restriction long taken literally. In 1889 C.F.R. Allen reported that no one other than himself had had access to the cypher he held at Han-

kow.[76] In 1898 B.C.G. Scott was equally punctilious in allowing no one access at Tientsin. This got F.E. Wilkinson, the second assistant there, into hot water. Scott fell ill while the vice-consul was away, and Wilkinson was in charge when it was reported that the emperor had been murdered and that foreigners in Peking were in danger. He telegraphed accordingly to MacDonald, who was taking the sea air further up the coast. MacDonald telegraphed to the British admiral requesting him to come immediately and made hotfoot for Tientsin. It was then learned that the emperor had merely been seized by the empress dowager and that Peking foreigners were not in danger. Wilkinson was instructed to telegraph urgently to the admiral cancelling the request, and being unacquainted with the cyphers he used one not held by the admiral. The receipt of an urgent but undecypherable telegram made the admiral fear the worst and at the cost of 2,000 tons of coal and of 4 broken-down warships he pressed on to Taku, where there was not a soul to welcome him and where no one had heard of the startling events in Peking. Relations between admiral and minister were temporarily strained, but they composed their differences by tearing Wilkinson to pieces. Then a leading British newspaper glowingly praised admiral and minister for having nipped anti-foreign trouble in the bud by bringing up the fleet and soon afterwards Wilkinson received very unexpected promotion. Late in life he put the story down for his family under the title 'How History is Made'.[a] Instructions issued by the ever-efficient Satow that juniors were to be trained in the use of cyphers removed the risk of a repetition of similar incidents. Consuls who for one reason or another found themselves without cyphers had occasional recourse to Latin. In imperial China *clavibus zeroque arreptis* was no doubt baffling enough to be secure, but *vidi judicem provincialum qui telegraphabit praefecto* seems less so.[77] Typewriters were first mentioned in 1895. Demonstrating the new appliances by a typed despatch Shanghai assured the Legation that typed work was more legible and neater, that the proper manipulation was easily acquired, and that a little practice soon ensured far greater rapidity than a pen could give. The next year the Legation possessed a typewriter, by 1905 two student interpreters were doing all the Legation typing, and by 1906 the Foreign Office considered a typewriter an absolute necessity in every properly conducted office.[78]

Whitehall cannot escape responsibility for the contribution made

by low pay, slow promotion, loneliness at one-man posts, and bad
accommodation to the physical and mental, and sometimes moral,
deterioration too often apparent.

Physical health was almost universally unsatisfactory. Of those
who survived long enough to retire on a pension very few indeed
did so in robust health. Constitutions were undermined by the
twin scourges of chronic malaria, which left sufferers 'shrunken,
wizened, cachetic, leather-skinned', and of intestinal disease.[79]
Nearly everyone retired early on a medical certificate. Some did
so unwillingly. Others once entitled to a full pension did so with
alacrity. The notional additional pensionable years earned by
service at posts officially designated as unhealthy meant that on a
medical certificate a full pension could be obtained after twenty-
seven years' service. The Treasury disliked unduly free use of
certificates in such circumstances.[80] At the age of 47 and with just
under twenty-seven years' service H.A. Giles applied to retire on the
strength of a certificate which, although no one seems to have
noticed, had probably been issued by one of his deceased wife's
relatives. In his case the Treasury suggested, as they not infrequently did, employment in a healthy country as an alternative
to retirement. The Foreign Office had in the past always declined
to consider that solution, but on this occasion did minute that it
would be a good thing if such employment could be managed;
'these early pensions make a considerable scandal whether justifi-
able or not when the recipient lives on as sometimes happens up to
80 or so'. This was a prescient minute, as Giles lived to 89, but he
was not transferred to a healthy country and got his pension.[81]
Later the Foreign Office very cautiously experimented with occasional transfers into the general service[82] but found the results unsatisfactory. They concluded that training in the Far Eastern and
Levant services did not equip men for duties in the general service,
that in any case the general service had too few salubrious posts to
accommodate those of its own officers whose health had been
impaired by bad climates, and that the experiments could not be
repeated.[83] There was an undoubted element of bogusness about
some certificates,[84] but when it was desired to be rid of the persons
submitting them the Foreign Office were happy enough to turn a
blind eye in the hope that the Treasury would not cavil. At times
the production of a dubious certificate was encouraged. In 1890
even the permanent under-secretary, Currie, openly did so. He

suggested that P.J. Hughes, whose continued presence as consul-general at Shanghai impeded Currie's pet scheme for amalgamating the posts of chief judge and consul-general, might be able to 'cook up an illness'.[85] To defend themselves the Treasury appointed a medical adviser to whom applications to retire early on medical certificates were referred, but at first he almost invariably confirmed that the officers concerned were indeed not fit for further service in China.[86]

Mental trouble was far too common. Life in China may not have been the prime cause for the derangement of Crawford and A.S. Harvey. It cannot be blamed for the peculiarities of Neale and Peachey, who were both so patently odd when they entered as student interpreters that the former was quickly dismissed and the latter was quickly allowed to resign.[87] Life in China must however certainly be blamed for the remarkable frequency with which men ceased to be able to face work or responsibility. Mention has been made of the lamentable mental state in which Wade and W.S.F. Mayers, two exceptionally able men, finished their careers. There were many like them. Each of the six competent men successively commissioned as consuls at Tientsin in the nineteenth century ended with what would nowadays probably be called a nervous breakdown or came close to having one. Before he went mad on home leave from Tientsin Mongan was described by a doctor as suffering from depression in a high degree. A Tientsin doctor described Davenport before his retirement as suffering from frequent attacks of great nervous depression. B. Brenan's aversion to work at his later Shanghai post was entirely out of character. In applying to retire H.B. Bristow wrote from Tientsin that any press of work brought on almost intolerable depression and that he feared he might break down in a crisis. After transfer to Canton B.C.G. Scott begged to be allowed home without delay, as his work had become very distasteful and irksome, worried him, and made him nervous, and although he was physically sound he had an extreme desire to get away from China and retire. Carles collapsed so completely at Tientsin under the Boxer strain that absolute cessation of work was medically ordered.[88]

Self-inflicted incapacity was far too common too. Drink was the usual cause. 'When a junior in China begins to go downhill', said an 1870 Foreign Office minute, 'debt, drink and disgrace soon hurry him to the bottom'.[89] Like Egan, Howlett, and Lowder, Payne and

Murray were victims of the bottle. Payne was so busy drinking himself to death when sent home in disgrace that it was doubtful whether he would reach home alive. After delirium tremens Murray went home at 33 with a weak heart and an infected lung. Wade attributed the downfall of a man who had once been most promising to his company having been so agreeable. The Foreign Office seem to have been reluctant to proceed to extremes with Murray and wrote to him that his return to China could not be sanctioned unless medical examination showed that his habits had changed and that his health had improved. He died within the month.[90] The other four were all allowed to avoid dismissal by resigning. Applications for pensions sent to the Treasury by the Foreign Office were required to be accompanied by a certificate that the applicant's duties had been discharged with diligence and fidelity. On compassionate grounds Alcock had no objection to Payne getting a small pension, but regarded the facts as precluding him from furnishing such a certificate. Payne accordingly got no pension. Howlett was similarly refused a pension. Egan and Lowder had not served long enough to be eligible for one.[91] The requirement remained in force but became a fiction. In 1905 E.F. Bennett, who was addicted to morphia and had persistently neglected his duties, was forcefully induced to apply to retire on a pension. The head of the consular department persuaded a doubtful superior that the certificate must be given in order to avoid the difficulty and perhaps scandal that would otherwise be involved in getting rid of Bennett; 'we have had to have recourse to the same pious fraud in other cases'. The certificate went to the Treasury with other documents making it clear that the certificate was meaningless. The Treasury nonetheless agreed to a pension, though as Bennett's incapacity was due to causes within his own control not at the full rate.[92]

There were other black sheep. Misappropriation of public money was an unforgivable crime, and Caine, less fortunate than C.T. Jones, went to prison for it.

Caine's personal finances had got into a desperate state. By the failure of a China firm he had lost whatever money he had, and by 1870 he had a wife and nine children, debts believed by a colleague to amount to some £5,000, and no income beyond his pay. The Foreign Office had a low opinion of him. His statements about the amount of public money lost when his Swatow consulate was

robbed in 1864 had been unsatisfactory. They knew him as a man who tried to charge every petty item of household expenditure to the public and as a man whose bills in England were unpaid.[93] In China he was less out of favour. Although he had neglected to learn Chinese both Alcock and Wade considered him a reasonably satisfactory consul. In 1868 Alcock moved him from Swatow to act at the much better paid Hankow consulate while Medhurst, the Hankow consul, acted at Shanghai, and in 1870, when Medhurst was given the substantive Shanghai appointment, Wade recommended Caine for the substantive Hankow appointment. The Foreign Office took the almost unprecedented step of rejecting the recommendation, being of the opinion that Caine's only possible claim to the promotion was the insufficient one of mere seniority, and preferred P.J. Hughes, who Wade had to concede had higher qualifications. Wade was reduced to despair about Caine, who he said would have to take his boys away from school unless promoted, and asked for Caine's Swatow pay to be increased. The Foreign Office refused.[94] In 1872 Hughes returned from home leave to take over Hankow. Caine's creditors demanded to be paid before he left Hankow for Newchwang, of which he was instructed to take temporary charge. To meet their demands he withdrew over $9,000 from the Hankow consulate's funds, reporting at once that he had taken a liberty which he trusted would after twenty-two years' faithful service not be disapproved and offering repayment by instalments. He was suspended and reacted by applying for a pension. Hammond informed Mrs Caine in England that proceedings would be instituted; 'I regret much to be the channel of what must to you be so painful a communication'. Evidence formally justifying the issue of a warrant took an unconscionable time to procure, and meanwhile Caine left China to seek employment in Australia, borrowing more money to get his family from England to Australia. A few months later he reappeared in Shanghai in custody, having borrowed yet more money to bring his whole family with him from Australia, and was tried. The chief judge, who had feared that as in the Jones case a conviction might not be obtained, refused to accept the jury's first verdict that in taking the money there had been no fraudulent intent, succeeded in obtaining a verdict of guilty with a strong recommendation to mercy, passed a sentence of two years, seemed rather satisfied that his handling of the case had made him unpopular locally, and in

recollections published after his death shed some crocodile tears over what he retrospectively called a cruel prosecution. The Treasury expressed satisfaction that the delinquent had been satisfactorily brought to justice.[95] Caine had to be hospitalized almost at once, and it was not long before doctors certified that his life was in danger and that the depression caused by imprisonment was lessening his chances of recovery. Medhurst telegraphed from the consulate for instructions and was told by the Foreign Office to act as humanity dictated provided that any other prisoner similarly situated would be treated in exactly the same way. In the chief judge's absence Medhurst and the assistant judge considered further medical advice and the remainder of the sentence was remitted. Medhurst, who did not often lack confidence, reported that his proceedings had caused him much anxiety and somewhat nervously hoped for Foreign Office approval. His nervousness was justified. The permanent under-secretary thought the remission hurried and the Foreign Secretary added the words 'it is impossible to imagine a case in which less indulgence was due to the offender' to a reply which, instead of approving Medhurst's proceedings, said that in the peculiar circumstances they were not disapproved. By dying within a month Caine demonstrated that the remission had not been improperly hurried. His widow and eight surviving children under 15 were left almost destitute but a charity concert provided for their passages home. In all, the Shanghai and Hankow communities contributed 6,000 taels for the family's benefit, a sum ironically more or less equivalent to the amount misappropriated. One of Caine's brothers gave up a good position at home and returned to the army in India so that he could help support the family. The widow, who died in poverty nearly half a century later, never ceased to believe her husband a victim of injustice, and her hand must surely be seen in a marriage announcement in *The Times* in 1900 which defiantly described the bridegroom's father as 'sometime H.B.M. Consul at Hankow'.[96]

There may have been a third case of defalcation later. In 1896 Carles reported from Hankow that a student interpreter, Allan, was drinking heavily, was head over heels in debt, and had been required to resign from the club, and that failing prompt dismissal a criminal prosecution and a prison sentence were to be feared. He alleged that some fees had not been paid in or accounted for. Allan was dismissed but for unexplained reasons prosecution was not

considered. The usual practice in the past had been to avoid scandal by getting disgraced officers out of China as soon as possible, at the cost of paying their passages. On this occasion the Legation were on the contrary instructed by telegram not to pay Allan's passage, but in transmission the negative was omitted and the Legation provided Allan with a ticket to New Zealand. Thus the four officers who had committed or been accused of criminal offences,[97] Beatty, C.T. Jones, Caine, and Allan, all left China for Australia or New Zealand, evidently still accepted bolt-holes.

In the immediate aftermath of the Caine affair J.P.M. Fraser was treated with an abrupt harshness quite uncharacteristic of Foreign Office management. On the day Wade reported Caine's death he launched an attack on Fraser, whom little more than two years previously he had described as a good assistant though one who had neglected his Chinese studies, for idleness, dissipation, and neglect of the Chinese studies which were the essential condition of his employment; although Wade had never seen Fraser really drunk his hard drinking absorbed all his means and he was perpetually in debt. The permanent under-secretary could not recall any instance in China of a man with thirteen years' service being dismissed except for positive crime but saw no alternative to dismissal in a so evidently irreclaimable case of idleness, extravagance, and dissipation which set an injurious example. The Foreign Secretary agreed and Fraser was dismissed without being offered the option of resignation. Fraser complained with justification that others who had behaved worse had been allowed to resign and that his exact contemporary Goddard had even been allowed a pension. Officially Goddard had retired on account of very severe depression and melancholy, but, as Fraser implied, the real trouble was almost certainly drink. The complaint, however justified, was brushed aside and Fraser remained dismissed and unpensioned.[98] In 1876, with the Caine affair receding into the past, Foreign Office management reverted to normal. Wade recommended pensioning off Carroll, a vice-consul with eighteen years' service known to the Foreign Office as one of the regular shufflers in China. Wade had censured Carroll three times that year for quarrelling with colleagues and with the navy and said he could not support Carroll's application for promotion and would have recommended dismissal had Carroll been in normal health and not under threat of apoplexy. The same permanent under-secretary who had been so fierce

to Fraser now said that although Carroll had shown much ill-temper, had used very improper language, and was unfit for promotion, and although the service would be well quit of him, insufficient cause for dismissal had been shown and evidence of ill-health was insufficient to satisfy the Treasury. The Foreign Secretary, who did not consider the charges against Carroll very grave, decided that action should be confined to refusing promotion on health grounds and that the decision should be conveyed in mild terms. As it happened the Foreign Office were wasting their time in even considering the matter, for Carroll was carried off by apoplexy within two months of Wade's recommendation being sent to London.[99]

Part III
China's Collapse and Resurgence

THE LAST DAYS OF THE MANCHUS

AFTER the beleaguered legations had been relieved in August 1900 there were long negotiations among the treaty power ministers at Peking about the penalties to be inflicted on China. MacDonald was no longer in Peking to argue the British case. In a move which had been planned earlier[1] and did not signify dissatisfaction with his performance he had been transferred to Japan and replaced by Satow. The ministers eventually formulated the victors' terms in the lengthy instrument known as the Final Protocol of Peking, which Chinese plenipotentiaries perforce signed. The terms were harsh and the financial indemnity included claims for military expenses which Satow called exorbitant and unjust.[2] E.D.H. Fraser, who had at Hankow worked with Viceroy Chang Chih-tung for local peace, commented that the indemnity would for the most part have to be met by increased taxation in the trouble-free provinces, which would make foreigners more hated than ever.[3] The terms included the establishment of an extraterritorial legation quarter in Peking guarded by foreign troops and the replacement of the Tsungli Yamen by a fully fledged Ministry of Foreign Affairs. When the Final Protocol had been signed the empress dowager returned to Peking and agreed to some reforms, including the abolition of the antiquated literary examinations as a channel of entry into state service. Discredited though she was she retained her grasp on power until her death in 1908. Her captive the emperor predeceased her by one day, which no one has ever believed a natural coincidence, and on her orders an infant emperor succeeded under a feeble regent. Regent, emperor, and dynasty were swept away in 1911 by risings. China had had enough of the alien dynasty which had failed to preserve her from foreign aggression. In remote and backward Pakhoi Fletcher in 1907 detected everywhere an electric feeling of dissatisfaction, a heath fire smouldering in men's hearts,

a Tientsin despatch of 1909 compared China with France at the beginning of the French Revolution, and from Canton in 1910 strong and widespread anti-dynastic feeling and rampant sedition were reported.[4]

Meanwhile China was prostrate. Russia had used the Boxer troubles as an excuse to move into Manchuria and had no intention of moving out again. Her ambitions there clashed with those of Japan. In 1904 the two powers went to war on Manchurian soil, paying no regard to it being Chinese territory. Japan won. She took over the Liaotung peninsula and Dairen, but Russia was left in control of the so-called Chinese Eastern Railway which she had driven straight across northern Manchuria and which gave her a much more direct route to Vladivostok than the circuitous route through Russian territory. In 1907 the two former enemies reached a *modus vivendi*. They agreed that northern Manchuria and Outer Mongolia should be within the Russian sphere of influence and that southern Manchuria and Korea should be within the Japanese sphere. In their respective spheres both powers systematically impeded the commerce of other foreign countries. Chinese administration of Manchuria was on sufferance, and it was well understood that no Chinese action seriously threatening Russian or Japanese interests there would be tolerated. Elsewhere in China other powers continued their economic aggression, quarrelling between themselves over rights to build railways, to open mines, and to make loans on advantageous terms. In the atmosphere prevailing immediately after the signature of the Final Protocol Britain was for the last time associated with the establishment of a new foreign-controlled enclave in Chinese territory. China, hoping to ward off Japanese designs on Amoy,[5] conceded that Kulangsu should be administered by its foreign residents. The form of administration adopted, an international settlement on the Shanghai model, was far too cumbersome for so small a foreign community, which came to regret Kulangsu's changed status. By 1930 the British residents were almost unanimously in favour of giving up an international settlement which functioned so badly,[6] but fears that this would have implications for the future of Shanghai prevented action. China screwed up her courage to resist the diplomatic body's pressure for an international settlement at Chefoo, and Brady, the consul there in 1909, was unlike many of his predecessors opposed to such a settlement. He wisely foresaw

that its establishment would cause endless annoyance and friction to the detriment of much more important interests, and said that the main trouble at such a peaceful port was caused by drunken foreign sailors, who could be dealt with by other means.[7]

China was now in an intellectual ferment, particularly marked among students. There was a deep division of opinion about what should replace the dynasty. Conservative Chinese tradition called for a strong leader. Radicals, whose numbers were swelled by the flood of 'returned students' coming back from Japan and to a lesser extent from the West, tended to favour an elective parliamentary system or even social reform. Not every returned student spent his time abroad with unremitting seriousness. A 23-year-old who came back to Amoy with an Edinburgh engineering degree had seduced his Edinburgh landlady's daughter and left her with a child, had left large debts in Edinburgh, had had two lady friends in Essex, and denied an alleged marriage in London.[8] Nonetheless most returned students brought back with them alien concepts, exciting and explosive even when only partially digested. Newspapers and modern-style schools spread the new ideas. In 1906 Tours reported as an example of the new patriotic spirit fostered by modern education that when he protested against bodies of armed Chinese troops passing through the Chinkiang concession without permission one local school countered with a protest against foreign permission being required for a march over Chinese soil.[9] One of the earliest consular officers to draw attention to the long-term significance of the ferment was Flaherty. He wrote from Tientsin in 1909, a few months before appendicitis robbed the service of an able junior, that although the local people remained the same nameless herd with no political rights beyond paying taxes the newspapers were bringing wider horizons; as Western ideas about the rights of the individual gained ground they would modify or overthrow patriarchal methods of government; and Tientsin people were well qualified by energy and intelligence to take a foremost place in the inevitable advance towards more wholesome conditions in China.[10] Most officers of that time, though they welcomed the increasing emancipation of women,[11] paid relatively little attention to the ferment and when they mentioned it were usually dismissive. Three typically slighting references came in 1908. Harding dismissed the Kwangsi newspaper as being of the usual Chinese stamp, hopelessly ignorant, violently anti-foreign, and printing any-

thing, true or false, which would help to make it pay; O'Brien-Butler described an Amoy intendant as a most amiable gentleman but badly infected with the 'China for the Chinese' craze; and Pitzipios ascribed to the 'sovereign rights microbe' the objections of an otherwise agreeable Chinkiang intendant to the Shanghai hunt meeting near Chinkiang.[12] The reason for such myopia was no doubt that consular officers were normally in touch only with decorous officials and did not hear the opinions of other classes.

For years the retribution exacted for Boxer excesses inspired respect for the persons of foreign merchant and missionary, and consular responsibilities were correspondingly lightened. On the other hand a post-Boxer influx of Indians brought new responsibilities. The China service, unacquainted with India or Indian languages, was not equipped to deal with the influx and disliked it. From Tientsin, where the influx was particularly marked, Hopkins reported in 1903 that several hundred Indians, many allegedly known in India as bad characters, were employed in the city and up-country as watchmen and escortmen in Chinese establishments, and Flaherty in 1905 described the Sikhs who made up most of the local Indian community as tall, powerful, forbidding-looking, and disreputable, notorious for usury at iniquitous rates, and varying the monotony of disputes with Chinese by quarrelling among themselves. In 1907 the increasing Indian community at Hankow seemed to E.D.H. Fraser to menace British relations with Chinese officials and people; many failed to register and the 90-odd who had registered were all named Singh; and 'the reckless disregard of truth common to the parties and their witnesses' made it difficult to deal with the frequent charges and countercharges of assault and robbery among feuding Sikhs.[13] This last aspect of Indian life in China was a perennial source of consular annoyance. Every consul was anxious wherever possible to avoid time-consuming formal court proceedings and the Chinese avoidance of them except as a desperate last resort was as welcome as the Indian taste for litigation was unwelcome.

To most British officials in China the Indians probably seemed second-class British subjects. Certainly at Canton in 1904 the trial and execution of an Indian for murder were handled in a way which would never have been tolerated had the man been white. The chief judge took the case. The trial lasted a day and a half, and the bill for the white five-man jury's expenses included 2 bottles of

champagne, 2 bottles of claret, 1 bottle of sherry, 1 bottle of port, 20 whiskies and soda, 5 brandies, and 32 cigars. The Foreign Office passed the bill but asked that such charges should be kept much lower and ruled that in future charges for cigars must be excluded. The well-fortified jury brought in a verdict of guilty and the chief judge sentenced the prisoner to be taken back to the consular gaol and hanged there. Having passed sentence the chief judge left Canton so quickly that Campbell, the acting consul-general, had no opportunity of discussing with him the obvious objections to carrying it out. The consular compound was a crowded one, accommodating the offices, the residences of the consul-general, vice-consul, and two assistants, and the quarters of the constable and of thirty or so Chinese servants. The gaol, which had barely been used for years, was merely a single room 13 feet high, to which two small lavatories were attached, on the ground floor of the constable's quarters. Mrs Campell was not at Canton. The vice-consul sent his wife to Hong Kong, by the most careful discretion and secrecy Campbell avoided a public objection by Shameen residents, and a Hong Kong prison warder acted as executioner for a fee of $70. The constable's sitting-room and veranda were used for the execution, the man being hanged in one of the gaol lavatories through a trap made in the veranda. At the time there was no constable, but in reporting the circumstances Campbell said that there was now a married one, who 'might have legitimate objections to his family remaining in the house while an execution was being carried out in the sitting room and verandah'. The Foreign Office were shocked to hear of 'sights and scenes unfit for delicately nurtured ladies or indeed for any woman' and by the lack of propriety and seemliness, and Satow recommended that any future executions in China should be carried out at Shanghai. The only redeeming feature was that before his execution the condemned man confessed not only to the murder for which he had been tried but also to another murder which had escaped notice, so at least he had not been unjustly convicted.[14]

There was the usual sufficiency of white British undesirables. By and large they had ceased to be violent and an alleged murder of a Chinese by a British subject was now regarded as an exceptional occurrence,[15] but they were still crooked. As far up the Yangtze as Chungking *lie hong* continued to flourish.[16] In 1901 Sundius deplored the appearance at Nanking of some of the second-rate

foreigners, unfortunately mostly British, who for payment took out
transit passes to cover Chinese-owned goods; it was humiliating to
have to argue with the Chinese over transit passes which he knew
and they knew to have been fraudulently obtained but the fraudu-
lence of which he could not prove.[17] Some years later Pitzipios went
into some detail about three so-called merchants, all British, at
Chinkiang. One man lending his name to Chinese had while at
Canton been the object of constant consular vigilance, had been
discharged from the Customs for suspected dishonesty, and had
narrowly escaped conviction for a jewel robbery at Shanghai. A
former resident who, presumably owing to his intemperate habits, had failed as a Shanghai auctioneer had marked his return to
business in Chinkiang by applying for seventy-nine transit passes.
The hopelessly insolvent inspector of the concession's police force
tried to set up an 18-year-old half-caste son, who spoke the local
dialect like a native, as a commission agent for Chinese; then he lost
his position as inspector, a post which he had held for many years
although practically everyone in the port had an unfavourable
opinion of him, and was declared bankrupt; and immediately
afterwards, while still an undischarged bankrupt, he set up as an
auctioneer and commission agent and ran two *lie hong*.[18]

In the south British abuses were rampant on the West river.
In 1904 Fox at Wuchow reluctantly recognized most of the so-
called British firms trading locally, usually headed by a Eurasian
or Indian, as otherwise other nations would have offered the
protection of their flags. An epidemic of West river piracy made the
flag abuses particularly undesirable, as most of the vessels on which
the pirates preyed flew the British flag. An intendant suggested to
F.E. Wilkinson, Fox's successor, that a guard of six Chinese soldiers
should be placed on each vessel, a remedy which all interested
parties rejected as worse than the disease.[19] On leaving his post the
intendant asked Wilkinson to provide three bluejackets, or failing
that the consular constable, as a guard on the vessel in which he
was travelling, and when asked why he did not take six Chinese
guards explained that he was now talking to Wilkinson man to man
and not as an official.[a] In 1907 Hosie travelled to Wuchow in a
steamer all the officers of which carried revolvers and Winchester
repeating-rifles and went to bed with them. Hosie took a stricter
view of flag abuses than Fox had done. It was an open secret, he
said, that hundreds of foreign-flag steamers plying from Canton,

many of them British, had nothing foreign about them except their flags, and although it was argued that British prestige would suffer if the British flag were withdrawn and other flags were adopted British prestige was never built up on what was tantamount to fraud. It does not appear that Hosie's views led to action, and there was much truth in Wilkinson's opinion that if Chinese officials stopped squeezing Chinese vessels the abuses would automatically end; 'it is to get protection against the extortion of their own officials that Chinese merchants are obliged to incur the expense of placing their vessels under a foreign flag'.[20] Flag abuses long continued. In 1921 over 5 tons of opium were found on a Chinese-owned vessel flying the French flag on the Yangtze, and the Legation commented that the French flag scandal was assuming incredible dimensions.[21]

It is to be feared that at all periods the unavowed attitude towards missionaries of Foreign Office, Legation, and consulates may not have been far removed from that expressed in two re-publican-era minutes. In 1926 a Foreign Office under-secretary minuted 'all these missionaries are an infernal nuisance', and in 1930 Teichman as Chinese counsellor minuted that women missionaries had been 'an infernal nuisance for years'.[22] During the Manchu twilight such profane sentiments were probably less strongly felt, for the missionary troubles coming to consuls were less frequent and less serious than they had been in the past or would be in the future. Carnegie, the secretary of Legation in 1905, found on visiting the principal ports that there were few important missionary cases in hand and that missionaries were now giving little or no trouble to British consuls, and believed the principal reason to be that 'a much better class of man' was now being sent out.[23] However, some unsuitable Protestant missionaries, not necessarily British, certainly remained. In 1907 Fox learned with surprise that most American and Canadian missionaries carried firearms in the interior of Szechwan; he saw no serious objections provided that the weapons were concealed and produced only in extreme peril, but he greatly regretted the behaviour of one American missionary who went openly armed and had discharged his revolver when a mule-train failed to make room for him quickly enough. In 1909 reputable British and American missionaries combined to represent to Barr at Ningpo the risks of an outbreak from the irresponsible activities of the Dowseyite Mission, and Barr

alleged that the mission's founder was a bigamist and outlaw and that its headquarters in the United States had been officially confiscated.[24] Friction between Protestants and Roman Catholics continued to plague consuls. In 1908 Twyman was so struck by a Canadian Methodist pastor and a French priest being on such friendly terms in one Szechwan town as to consult each other about difficulties that he drew their unusual relations to the Legation's attention. Animus occasionally reached extraordinary peaks. In 1910 J.L. Smith reported from Chungking that a priest in Szechwan was selling for next to nothing a pamphlet which accused Luther of having kidnapped women and Calvin of having been as incestuous as the brute creation and which alleged that according to Protestant theology defiling 100,000 women in a day was not to be feared provided one firmly believed in Jesus. The French legation took steps to secure the priest's removal from China.[25] Occasionally there were still serious missionary incidents of the old type. In a riot in Hunan province in 1902 two China Inland Mission members were murdered on suspicion of causing cholera by poisoning wells. They contributed to their own deaths by twice refusing offers of refuge in a yamen and by insisting that they should be protected in their own premises, but the Foreign Office endorsed the immediate demands of E.D.H. Fraser at Hankow that prefect and magistrate should be banished, that two military officials who had failed to intervene should be executed, and that £10,000 compensation should be paid. Seven men, including at least one of the military officials, were executed in the presence of consular assistants, and although the mission refused to receive the compensation the Chinese duly paid it.[26] As part of the settlement the Chinese were required to erect a stone memorial tablet recording the crime and the punishments inflicted. In 1926 the tablet was deliberately mutilated or destroyed on the orders of a Chinese general. The Legation accepted the view of the assistant Chinese secretary, who minuted that in the altered conditions of 1926 such an inscription could only cause bad feeling.[27] The minute was written only four years after Fraser, the prime mover in the original settlement, had died in harness at Shanghai, evidence of the speed with which attitudes had changed.

During the subsequent years of warlords and anti-British agitation the service looked back on the last years of the Manchus as a golden age.[a] Outside some perennially troubled areas a

tolerable degree of law and order was maintained in the country-side, and whether for business or pleasure, the latter usually meaning shooting trips, the foreigner could travel in it safely.[28] Many Chinese officials who in public business with consuls thought it their duty to be obstructive and dilatory laid themselves out to be personally friendly and obliging. In 1901 W.H. Wilkinson much appreciated the attentions shown him when he called from Ningpo on an incoming governor at Hangchow. The treasurer, who had invited Wilkinson to be his guest, put him up in a yamen guest-room furnished with foreign lamps and carpet, placed at his disposal a sedan-chair, a pony, an English-speaking houseboy, a cook, and an interpreter, and was a most considerate and kindly host. After the first formal reception he and Wilkinson talked without ceremony, both laying aside their official hats and Wilkinson laying aside his sword. The governor received him with much distinction, the guard presenting arms as Wilkinson's chair passed. The judge showed all the *bonhomie* of a Manchu official away from Peking's restraints and prejudices. The intendant, a gentle scholarly old man, was an old acquaintance who took both Wilkinson's hands and led him to a kiosk in his yamen's private garden. The salt commissioner received him in his yamen in a bungalow furnished in the foreign style, and while the two men partook of the usual collation the commissioner's numerous children, and apparently some of their mothers, looked on through a glass door.[29] It must be confessed that not all such friendly advances were met with understanding on the British side. At this period every Chinese of standing adopted in addition to his for-mal name a *hao*, a sort of nickname by which his friends addressed him. In 1908 an elderly prefect at Chinkiang made the pleasant suggestion to the consul, Pitzipios, and to the Customs commis-sioner that all three men should drop formality and address each other by their *hao* and he invested the two foreigners with *hao* which he considered appropriate. While Pitzipios believed the old gentleman's suggestion to have been thoroughly sincere he found the occurrence somewhat embarrassing and promptly forgot his newly acquired *hao*.[30]

Consular life was becoming much less physically uncomfortable. At established ports decent accommodation in good compounds was normal. In 1909 water was still laid on at only two or three posts, but that aid to gracious living, the water-closet, was ap-

proaching, a sewerage scheme in the Legation being completed in 1915.[31] Electricity was coming in, and the Canton and Hankow consular compounds had electric lights and ceiling fans by 1907.[32] In Shanghai there were motor cars, witness the destruction in a 1905 Shanghai riot of Pitzipios' de Dion Bouton.[33] Some officers had taken to moving with pianos, even grand pianos.[34] For a brief but happy period, ended by the First World War and the Bolshevik revolution, London could be reached in tolerable comfort from Shanghai across Siberia in fifteen days.[35]

The difference in living conditions between the larger treaty ports, more exposed to Western influence, and the smaller ones was accentuated. Western influence was strong at Tientsin. Its local government had been in the hands of the foreign military commanders for two years after its capture in 1900.[36] The original British and French concessions had been greatly extended and German, Japanese, and Russian concessions, even Austrian, Belgian, and Italian concessions, had been added. In reports in 1905 and 1909 Flaherty recorded remarkable changes in the native city. Broad, clean carriage roads were kept well repaired by steamrollers, Chinese officials and merchants drove along them in foreign carriages drawn by foreign horses, clerks and even skilled workmen bicycled to work at a rather reckless speed, every yamen and every important shop had electric light and a telephone, the shops were filled with European and Japanese goods, women and little girls frequented the theatres, restaurants provided table-cloths and napkins, admittedly dirty, and foreign gloves and stockings were sometimes added to Chinese dress. Least progress, he said, had been made in administration, which remained incoherent, wasteful, and ineffective and changed with every change of viceroy, and there was still a need for permanent and reliable government servants, for modern education, and for uniformity in laws, money, and weights and measures, but time could be expected to soften the crude blend between China and Europe which characterized Tientsin. In 1910 Fulford, the consul-general, successfully applied for a carriage allowance, the use of sedan-chairs having entirely ceased at Tientsin.[37] In 1908 Little described a different world at Ichang. There were no roads, no wheeled vehicles, no municipal government, no street-lighting, no police, no fire brigade, no places of amusement, no social intercourse with the natives, 'no shops as we know them... no pretty girls to look at'. The foreign community of sixty

to seventy men, women, and children, well over half of them British, consisted entirely of missionaries apart from the British and German consuls, the Customs staff, and three shipping agents. In place of Tientsin's numerous recreational facilities the community had nothing beyond a small recreation ground and the Customs club. Tennis, bridge, and walking were about the only local amusements. There was good shooting, including tiger, leopard, pig, wild cat, wild goat, and several sorts of deer, but it was two or three days' journey away and involved great hardship in very difficult country. The only traces of Western influence mentioned by Little were two establishments, much frequented by Chinese, which served meals in foreign style.[38] Later such contrasts became if anything even more marked. In 1916 Peking's roads were so improved that the Legation messengers were using bicycles instead of horses, and heads of mission were changing their carriages for motor cars, while at Shanghai an acting consul with wife and children could run a decent house and garden with a staff of eight.[39] A decade later at Chengtu a junior was still carried in a sedan-chair, which he modified so that the right-hand arm-rest would hold a beer glass and the left-hand one a beer bottle and so that a case of beer could be carried under the seat. An unmarried man, he lived in a miserable little three-roomed house. To run it he needed over a dozen servants, including four chair-bearers, two water-carriers, and a gateman.[a] At the beginning of the 1930s a junior was knocked down and killed by a Shanghai taxi, while at Chinkiang, not far up the river, official calls were still paid in a chair.[a]

At many posts work was very light. In 1903 Willis said that his main objection to Swatow was his underemployment, 'but that is the case almost everywhere', and in 1906 O'Brien-Butler at Amoy, where he presumably considered himself fully occupied, said that at some consulates a forenoon's work was more than sufficient to dispose of the day's business. Some once busy ports were in full decline. At others where trade was growing rapidly, such as Swatow and Kiukiang, shipping was the only foreign interest to benefit, the trade itself being largely in Chinese hands. At Swatow the very large quantities of merchandise imported passed straight into Chinese hands and only two or three foreign firms were engaged in local trade of any importance. Apart from Russians in the tea trade and missionaries the sole foreign residents remaining

at Kiukiang in 1904 were the staff of the British consulate and of the Customs, one mercantile assistant, two hulk keepers, and a doctor.[40]

Predictable routine was never central to consular life in China, where the unexpected, and sometimes the alarming, was liable to crop up without warning, but in the dying days of the Manchu dynasty work at most of the posts established in the nineteenth century, whether they were busy or sleepy, came closer to routine than before or after. There was however little routine in E.D.H. Fraser's relations at Hankow with Chang Chih-tung, in the relations at Canton between consuls-general on the one hand and viceroys and Hong Kong governors on the other hand, or in the work of the Tengyueh consulate.

After the deaths of Li Hung-chang and Liu Kun-i, Chang Chih-tung was unquestionably the most eminent Chinese subject of the Manchus. As acting consul-general at Hankow during the Boxer troubles Fraser had established so productive a relationship with Chang that Satow recommended Fraser for the substantive appointment when Warren's promotion to Shanghai left Hankow vacant. Fraser had reached the rank of consul only two years previously and was not much more than 40, but Satow told the Foreign Office that in his view a markedly efficient man on the spot known to be superior to others of the same standing should be given preference. At the Foreign Office a terse marginal comment in red ink said 'Certainly' and Fraser was appointed.[41] He was an Aberdonian who had failed the examination for the Indian civil service before sitting for the Far Eastern services.[a] His father, an army officer in India, was then already dead and the family can have had little money, for an obituary which called Fraser a studious, earnest man, reserved and retiring, said that hardness of circumstance in youth had framed his character.[42] Unusually good at Chinese, he could personally draft in Chinese some of his official communications,[a] and he was a stickler for Chinese epistolary etiquette.[43] He was a devoted family man, had a strong sense of duty, was tall and lean, and had a fine presence.[a] China had undermined his health and at Hankow he followed an extraordinary regime. He announced that the state of his health precluded summer residence there, and his practice was to move to Kuling's coolness for nearly three months a year. He visited Hankow for some days at the beginning of each month to make sure all was

in order, and at Kuling daily received and answered reports from the consulate-general. In any emergency he was twenty-four hours away from his post, but he was in such high favour with the Legation, where Satow and Jordan in turn both called him the best man in service, that no one seems to have queried such a peculiar way of running an office.[44] At Hankow he was used by Satow as a channel for confidential political communications with Chang in the same way as previous ministers had used the Tientsin consuls for communication with Li Hung-chang.

Chang's personality was complex and at least to foreigners unpredictable. As F.E. Wilkinson discovered to his discomfort Chang was capable of quirky humour. On Liu Kun-i's death Chang was temporarily moved from Hankow to act as viceroy at Nanking, where Wilkinson, a young assistant with little more than ten years' service, was in acting charge. Bent, diminutive, and renowned for his aversion to calling on consuls,[45] the old statesman called on Wilkinson. Hardly had he taken his seat, and hardly had the obligatory cups of tea been placed in front of both men, than Wilkinson absent-mindedly took a sip from his cup, the host's conventional signal that a call had lasted long enough. The great man thought it an excellent joke to rise obediently, to prepare to take his leave, and to spend some time allowing himself to be persuaded to resume his seat.[a] Whether because this performance tickled him, or because he took a liking to his youthful host, Chang thereafter showed Wilkinson his most agreeable side and was always ready to see him.[46] Wilkinson's verdict, which by no means all foreign consuls would have endorsed, was that although Chang 'could be a very superior person when he chose, he was on the whole easy to get on with, though difficult to get anything out of, and far more accessible than most viceroys'.[a] During the Boxer crisis Fraser had taken to Chang and believed the feeling mutual. Certainly in the immediately following years Chang showed great trust in the discretion of Fraser, who was amazed by such frank criticism of China's leaders, and expressed to him such exceedingly dangerous views as a hope that the empress dowager might be induced gradually to restore power to the emperor. Fraser described Chang to the Legation as a Chinese hating equally the Manchus who preyed on his country and the foreign powers who supported the Manchus in order to absorb Chinese territory, as a man dreaming of a court purged of eunuchs and greedy placemen and of a govern-

ment cautiously undertaking imperative reforms, and as a man despairing of China's future under her present government. Chang urged Fraser to defer a planned home leave, on the grounds that his absence would be detrimental to the vastly important interests of both Britain and China. Fraser undertook to leave the decision to Satow in a reply that was so Chinese in style as to suggest that it was drafted in Chinese.

I am deeply sensible of the great honour conferred on me by the terms in which this request is couched; but I must protest against the exceedingly high estimate put by Your Excellency on such services as my very ordinary abilities, joined to an earnest desire to promote the interests of our two countries, have enabled me to render. The trifling success which has at times attended my efforts is entirely due to the confidence reposed in me by Your Excellency and His Majesty's Minister; and I have been constantly ashamed of the want of skill and suavity which must have proved irksome to Your Excellency. I should not dare to prefer my personal feeling to public duty.

Satow decided that the leave should be taken. On Fraser's return his opinion of Chang became less favourable and the relationship gradually declined into coolness. At first the viceroy was still very cordial in personal relations, supplying a secret telegraph code for confidential communications with him and through his confidential secretary frequently consulting Fraser, but to Fraser, who was fobbed off with nothing but fair words, he now seemed old and timid, and primarily concerned to finish a long career without being denounced or at least without being degraded. Then he became more difficult of access, his response to letters and telegrams became very slow, at rare interviews he was more garrulous than ever, and his subordinates complained of wasting hours waiting to see him after being summoned. For years he had feared transfer to Peking and in spite of his objections to foreign interference in Chinese affairs had not been above seeking through Fraser the Legation's intervention to prevent it. In 1907 the dreaded transfer came. By that time he had politely but firmly shut his doors on Fraser on pleas of ill-health.[47]

At Canton B.C.G. Scott had during the Boxer crisis been the only member of the consular body to enjoy the intimate confidence of Li Hung-chang, the viceroy, a personal friend from former years, and Scott's personal kindness and courtesy made him popular in the

foreign community. He was not, however, popular with Governor Blake at Hong Kong, who in 1901 accused him to the Colonial Office of lack of co-operation and inertia. On hearing this Lansdowne, the Foreign Secretary, minuted that if there were a doubt about Scott, which he thought there must be, Scott had better be moved, and after visiting Canton from the Legation, Tower in effect agreed with Blake. The charge of inertia may well have been justified, for Scott was longing to retire and to make way for a younger and fresher man, and his only doubt was whether his medical certificate would be acceptable. The certificate was indeed most unconvincing. It mentioned nothing worse than muscular rheumatism, a chronically inflamed foot, and a constant sore throat, but it was made to pass muster and Scott entered a quarter of a century's retirement.[48] The charge of lack of co-operation, on the other hand, may merely signify that Scott, like other Canton incumbents, did not always consider Hong Kong's proposals expedient.[49]

Filling the Canton vacancy was once again an odd business. Satow intended to recommend Mansfield but accepted the suggestion made by Mansfield, who wanted to take home leave first, that his junior J. Scott would be a suitable man to act meanwhile. In spite of the earlier theory that for Canton a gentleman was required, Scott, who had a broad Aberdeen accent and the roughest of manners, gave so much satisfaction that in 1902, before Mansfield got back, Satow telegraphed to Scott an offer of the substantive appointment. Scott was so taken aback that he decyphered the telegram twice to make sure he had decyphered it correctly. He withdrew his recent application, backed by a strong medical certificate, to retire and accepted the offer. Mansfield was understandably aggrieved and the CMG given to him that year was presumably a sop to his feelings, for he had done nothing particular to earn it.[50] Scott may well have lived to regret that ambition had tempted him. In 1903 he went home sick, telling Satow that he had had his day and would be glad to retire at the end of his leave. Instead he obtained a leave extension and reappeared at Canton at the end of 1904, but before 1905 was out he felt it his duty to make way for an abler and more active man and submitted a renewed application to retire on health grounds and a medical certificate referring to a recurrence of neurasthenia. As with his namesake B.C.G. Scott the demanding Canton post seems to have

been too much for him.[51] Satow by now hoped that Mansfield would retire too, but as he did not he had to be appointed in Scott's place. He did not fill it with much success and soon retired, having at one point described his work as heart-breaking.[52]

J. Scott and Mansfield both had a trying time with the Chinese authorities. At first all went well for Scott. There was a viceroy who insisted on all questions, whether purely Chinese or international, being dealt with fairly, there was an enlightened prefect with a thorough knowledge of English, and there were other intelligent and sensible officials. Relations were most friendly and cordial until Ts'en Ch'un-hsüan took over as viceroy in 1903. Scott's first impressions were unfavourable; 'he is short and squat of stature, active and alert...and the impression he makes on me is that he is equal to any act of treachery and capable of gross cruelty'. Scott's second impressions two months later were no more favourable; word had gone out from Ts'en's yamen to obstruct foreigners; every local official friendly or obliging towards them had been degraded or ruined; and one of Ts'en's recently appointed interpreters had formerly been given a life sentence in Hong Kong for blackmailing Chinese residents on behalf of the Chinese authorities.[53] Ts'en seems to have been more like a republican warlord than a high imperial official. Although not a habitual toper he was a formidable drinker. F.E. Wilkinson, in charge at Wuchow, where Ts'en had come to suppress a rebellion, was invited to a meal. Wilkinson, who disliked alcohol and hardly ever touched it, and Ts'en himself were the only survivors, the viceroy having drunk his other ten guests under the table.[a] According to Wilkinson Ts'en and all his staff after the execution of a leading rebel sipped the man's blood.[54] Immediately before his Canton appointment Ts'en had been acting viceroy in Szechwan. There Hosie at Chengtu had given him credit for restoring order by drastic measures and for walking in the streets like an ordinary Chinese gentleman, without pomp or display, and Rose, who had been at Chungking at the time, looked back nostalgically at a fierce old man who had been a first-class official and infinitely preferable to the lying, dishonest, and wholly self-seeking intriguers from whom Rose was then suffering in Yunnan. Fox in 1907 regretted that Ts'en's reappointment to Chengtu had been cancelled and said that he would rather deal with a strong bad man than a weak good man. At Canton, however, neither Scott nor Mansfield found a good word to say for him.

Jordan, who thought Ts'en one of the worst characters in China, probably hit the nail on the head in a private letter to the Foreign Office, giving his opinion that the only way of getting on with such men was to trust to personal intercourse rather than to correspondence, 'and some consuls do not much care for this'. On Ts'en's departure after three and a half years at Canton Mansfield sent a summing-up; he had been arbitrary and arrogant to a degree; he had uniformly countered representations against his high-handed actions by alleging that established regulations, the product of his imaginative brain, precluded action or by alleging that the matter was entirely an internal Chinese affair. After Ts'en had gone things were little better, and Mansfield described a subsequent acting viceroy as rabidly anti-foreign and quite lacking the politeness almost always shown by the most hostile officials.[55]

In 1903 the question of protecting in China Hong Kong-born Chinese was raised by the Colonial Office with the Foreign Office, who minuted that one of the most thorny and intricate problems the Foreign Office had ever tried to solve was being revived. Satow favoured protection and it was ruled that Chinese born in British colonies, including Hong Kong, should be registered and protected as British subjects on production of a certificate confirming that they had previously been residing in a British colony for three consecutive years. Jordan in due course expressed the view that the ruling had been mistaken and it was criticized by consuls, but it was a long time before the British finally conceded that while these dual nationals were in China their Chinese nationality was the master nationality and that jurisdiction lay with China. The ruling's effect was to put Hong Kong more than ever at the centre of the work of the Canton consulate-general, which reluctantly set about protecting persons 'who would only get what they deserved if they were left to bear the consequences of their own conduct'. In 1908 Fox, acting as consul-general, wrote that he had no very important cases pending with the Chinese authorities but that the staff's time was fully taken up by pursuing Hong Kong's judgement debtors, acting as bill collectors for the Hong Kong business community, serving as an enquiry bureau for the colonial government, who were currently taking a close interest in Chinese affairs, and generally attending to Hong Kong's wants; he supposed that that was what the office was there for.[56]

J. Scott, Mansfield, and Fox seem to have had reasonably smooth

relations with Hong Kong, but successive governors repeatedly tried to bypass them. Reporting to the Foreign Office in 1905 Governor Nathan's wish to make Viceroy Ts'en's acquaintance at Canton Satow said that Governor Blake's reception when he had called on the viceroy at Canton had not been such as to encourage a repetition and that he did not consider it convenient for governor and viceroy to discuss matters of business; the consul-general was the natural medium of communication between the two, and in the long run it would be better not to depart from this rule. Governor Lugard evidently soon departed from it, for in 1908 he was instructed to consult Jordan before visiting Canton again and Jordan was instructed to refer to the Foreign Office if in doubt about the opportuneness of such a visit.[57] In 1909 J.W. Jamieson, who had been away from consulate work for some years, first as commercial attaché and then on well-paid secondment to South Africa as superintendent of the Chinese labour employed in gold mining, was appointed consul-general at the early age of 42. Hosie and Fulford had successively declined Canton, and coming down the seniority list to the next suitable candidate Jordan recommended that Jamieson should not be allowed to decline. There is nothing to suggest that Jamieson did have to be bullied into accepting the post with which he was to be so long associated.[58] Throughout their respective careers both Lugard and Jamieson much disliked not getting their own way, and within a few months the fur began to fly. While Jamieson was visiting Hong Kong, leaving the acting vice-consul, L. Giles, in charge, Canton saw an outbreak between Chinese soldiers and Chinese police. Jamieson was nettled by Lugard's complaint that Hong Kong had not been promptly informed by Giles, who had not considered the outbreak significant, and came vigorously to Giles' support. In a despatch to Lugard in which decorum of phrasing was more marked than decorum of content he told His Excellency that his dissatisfaction would undoubtedly have been justified had the outbreak had the serious importance for Hong Kong which His Excellency was inclined to attach to it; Jamieson however took the view that the incident had had no political significance, and being on the spot and therefore perhaps more closely in touch he might claim to be better placed to gauge the situation. Lugard took his complaint to the Colonial Office, who passed it to the Foreign Office. The Foreign Office saw no reason to suppose that Jamieson had in any way failed in his

duty but laid down that Jamieson should give Hong Kong early and full information of any important events at Canton.[59] This still left it to Jamieson to decide what events were or were not important. In this case Lugard had probably been in the right.

In 1911 Lugard put himself entirely in the wrong. Through his officials he engaged in direct negotiations with the Chinese authorities about extradition and police measures. Jamieson first heard of the negotiations through the press. Officially he told Jordan that he had been extremely embarrassed and that while in accordance with Jordan's injunction to maintain friendly relations with Lugard he had refrained from official protest, he had sent strong private remonstrances and had received very inadequate explanations in reply. Privately he told Jordan that his temper had been sorely tried and that the morbid craving of colonial governors for being on friendly terms with viceroys needed to be curbed. Jordan informed Lugard that he took serious exception to what had occurred. In reply Lugard expressed much regret for what he described, improbably, as an accidental oversight, and hypocritically said that his relations with Jamieson had always been cordial. In fact he had privately informed the chargé d'affaires some time before that Jamieson habitually drank too much and had been quite drunk at a colleague's house, a piece of underhandedness of which Jamieson would not have been capable.[60] Jamieson's masterful temperament made him an uncomfortable subordinate, colleague, or superior, but he was a straightforward man. Towards the end of the year the Foreign Office received through the Colonial Office a sweeping Hong Kong allegation that Jamieson had acted contrary to the views of previous consuls-general at Canton, of the minister, of Hong Kong, and of the home government by concurring in some opium regulations made by the Kwangtung authorities. The allegation came from May, administering Hong Kong in one of Lugard's absences, but Jamieson believed Lugard the true author of the charge and when May later became governor of Hong Kong Jamieson and he were on excellent terms. Whether or not this was another example of underhandedness on Lugard's part the Foreign Office satisfied themselves and the Colonial Office that the charge was baseless and were much annoyed that it had been made.[61]

Tengyueh, left vacant for nearly two years, was reopened towards the end of 1901 by Litton at the end of his leave. It was at Tengyueh that he was to make his name, but this time he stayed for

only a few months before being moved temporarily to Yunnanfu until W.H. Wilkinson, who was greatly delayed by bereavement, by illness, and by the monsoon, could take over there. Wilkinson's appointment to Yunnanfu was peculiar. Satow had wrongly understood the Foreign Office to have agreed to it being a consul-general's post, and offered Wilkinson appointment on promotion. The Foreign Office agreed to honour Satow's offer, but there was no treaty right to a consular establishment at Yunnanfu, which was not a treaty port. Wilkinson therefore settled himself at the provincial capital in the strange guise of consul-general at Ssumao. After two or three years the Chinese accepted reality and started to address Wilkinson as consul-general for Yunnan and the Ssumao fiction was abandoned.[62] While Litton was at Yunnanfu Mackinnon, an officer with only seven years' service, acted at Tengyueh. He was a particularly black sheep. For nearly a year he did absolutely nothing at Tengyueh. The archives were a total blank, and he explained the absence of any accounts by alleging that he had sent off the accounts and that they had been lost in transmission. He was transferred under a cloud, was found to be an opium addict and heavily in debt, and in 1906 anticipated dismissal by resigning.[63]

On Wilkinson's arrival at Yunnanfu Litton returned to Tengyueh. He was as energetic as Mackinnon had been idle, and as there were only three other European residents, all in the Customs, he was unhampered by routine and was free to throw himself into multifarious activities. He did battle against exactions on trade. Likening local conditions to the age in Europe when a robber baron in every valley extorted what he could he counted twenty-one tax barriers on one principal trade route and thirteen on another; 'each official makes his own rules for his own tax barrier and they are such rules that if they were carried out it would be impossible to transport any merchandise anywhere'. He took part in the annual frontier meetings at which officials from Burma and China haggled over the compensation due from their respective sides for tribal raids across the border. He studied Chinese rule, or misrule, in the Shan states whose day-to-day government was left in the hands of their *sawbwas* (chieftains), he studied the relations between the *sawbwas* and the Kachin tribesmen nominally subject to them, and he was authorized by Satow to intervene with discretion where misrule in the states threatened frontier security. Above all

he travelled arduously through the virtually unadministered and almost unknown tribal areas along the undelimited border with Burma. Long journeys, each of many weeks, took him through wild country with few and primitive inhabitants. After a very difficult ascent he might camp at 11,500 feet on a waterless pasture and the next day toil up to the Yangtze-Mekong divide at 13,000 feet and then down, excessively steeply, to the Mekong 7,000 feet below; he might haul himself up by shrubs and roots to nearly 10,000 feet along a slippery track; he might trudge all day in snow and sleet through a foot of slush; he might spend a month in wet clothes; a mule might have to be sent 20 miles or more to obtain supplies of food. The journeys were not free from more direct hazards. In one mood he considered, having one day met two bands of robbers who had shown him little but their heels, that a well-armed and prudent European probably ran little risk of attack; in another mood he feared his throat might be cut.[64] The verve of his reports still occasionally brought out the Legation's blue pencil. The Foreign Office were not allowed to see a passage about the Kachin reading 'Free love prevails among these nasty people...no disgrace attaches to their fugitive amours', though they were inconsistently allowed to read of unnatural vices, on which Litton thought it indecent to expatiate, prevailing in lamaseries in Tibetan areas. The Legation eventually gave up trying to restrain Litton's pen. The draft of a Legation despatch informing him that one report had been read with interest warned that it contained much that was unsuitable for forwarding to the Foreign Secretary and that a certain reticence in criticizing the action of superior authorities was always recommendable, but the warning was deleted before the despatch was issued. Whether originating from Tengyueh or from Yunnanfu Litton's despatches were full of brisk and usually derogatory observations about Chinese officialdom. A fair specimen is his statement that the modern-style schools in Yunnanfu were in the charge of three officials whose proper place was the mummy case in a museum of antiquities.[65] His reporting was not notably balanced but was extremely readable.

In 1905 Satow recommended Litton's appointment as substantive Tengyueh consul. He justified such a departure from 'the ordinary practice of promotion by seniority' by referring to Litton's distinguished service and to his special aptitude for the post. He was correspondingly irked to receive Litton's request to be allowed

to decline promotion over the heads of colleagues, wondered whether Litton was a little off his head, and in effect recommended that he should be promoted willy-nilly. The Foreign Office sent Litton his commission. By the time they received his reply again declining he was dead and, minuting that no action was required, they firmly put him down in the records as having been Tengyueh consul.[66] Meanwhile Litton had applied for home leave on the grounds that his travels through difficult and sometimes dangerous country for the past four years had been very laborious, that he had increasing difficulty in performing his duties, and that he was suffering from increasing deafness. He completed one more major journey to the upper Salween, through country which he called inhospitable, unhealthy, difficult, and barbarous but unforgettably beautiful. Traversing Lisu territory he found nearly all the villages were at war with one another, he had to quieten one bullying Lisu by demonstrating on a boulder the powers of his Winchester carbine, and he considered the crossbows and poisoned arrows without which no male Lisu left his hut such diabolical weapons that any traveller quarrelling with a bellicose or tipsy Lisu would do well to shoot first. Then in 1906, at the age of 36, he was found dead in his sedan-chair during a short routine journey. The immediate cause of death was said to be erysipelas, but Ottewill, who was due to relieve Litton and arrived after his death, put it down to the continual excessive strain of travelling and working late into the night on reports. Litton had private means, and besides remembering in his will relatives at home he bequeathed a substantial sum to a Chinese woman in Hong Kong.[67]

The best of Litton's immediate successors was Rose. He admired Litton's work but himself had a different approach. Litton had accused the Burma authorities of taking too seriously the threat from a contemptibly incompetent China and had sneered at comic-opera troops, made up of beggars, loafers, and dead-beats, who were far more dangerous to local chickens than to the enemy. Rose accused the Burma authorities of still regarding China as a country despicable as an enemy and unworthy to be a friend, and of being unable to believe in a new China, new politics, and a new spirit. To him the Chinese force at a border post seemed composed of men of fine physique, well-fed, well-paid, well-equipped, and well-armed, under a keen little officer. His sympathetic approach did not prevent him from energetically supporting British interests or from

noticing less agreeable aspects of Chinese life. He wrote semi-officially to Jordan that returning from a morning ride he had thought nothing of four bodies lying in the grass but had then glimpsed a wooden cross from which another body hung; 'I had had the misfortune to meet a crucifixion before breakfast once before so quickly backed my horse into a thicket and hurried home'.[68]

Rose had a happy touch with Chinese. At this stage of his career he was able to say that during travels through many provinces he had never once met a discourteous word or unfriendly action from the people, a statement which speaks volumes for his own tact and manners. He enjoyed Tengyueh, liking the genial hospitality and antiquated courtesy which old-fashioned Chinese gentlemen sometimes offered him in their homes. Two or three times a week in the rainy season he and the British Customs commissioner led their respective staffs to play a sort of baseball against each other. Great crowds watched, even officials forgot themselves sufficiently to shout 'Run' with much enthusiasm, and the garrison threatened to challenge the foreign-led teams. He appreciated the frontier meetings, where buffaloes and babies might be court exhibits, where a lovelorn damsel might offer to commit suicide in court unless allowed to leave with her sweetheart, and where a Kachin who having dined too well had broken his arm in a fall down a precipice might win a suit for damages against his host. On an earlier appointment to Chungking he had travelled there overland from Peking, and although no one could have rivalled Litton he travelled strenuously in the Tengyueh consular district and still had enough gusto to go on home leave through India and central Asia. He improved and furnished the cold and bleak Chinese house serving as a consulate, made himself a photographic dark-room, and kept a pointer and a red setter for the shooting which was his great solace in Tengyueh's solitude. He left useful advice for successors; the frontier meetings were by way of becoming social occasions, attended on the British side by ladies, and a dinner-jacket for the evenings and decent jungle clothes for the daytime were needed; for travelling canvas boots with rope soles were recommended, also a supply of medicines, the distribution of which was regarded as an inalienable right in tribal territory; 'quinine, epsom salts, castor oil, boracic acid, iodine and elliman's embrocation will cure most ills'. One of his last acts was to acquire a site for a proper consulate.[69]

Rose wrote with tolerant affection of an intendant who must have been one of China's odder officials. He was a slack old man, full of memories of beloved Peking, who had 'a horror of all responsibility and an unfulfilled longing for a bower of peach-blossom and a flute'. On Rose telling him that he really must go to a frontier meeting he burst into tears and accused Rose of brutality for suggesting such a thing to a man with domestic difficulties. He would plead with Rose to make some preposterous proposal so that he could gain credit by rejecting it. Rose described the pleadings as Gilbertian but some years later he himself lapsed into advice which may have reflected these strange conversations at Tengyueh. A genial old Ningpo official confided that he was hauled over the coals if foreign cases remained unsettled and would be dismissed as unnecessary if there were no such cases, and Rose 'urged on him the advantages of a few innocuous cases which would merely involve amicable local discussion and a policy of mutual compromise'. At length the Tengyueh intendant fell ill. He was induced to see the consulate's Indian hospital assistant, and a failing heart, a diseased lung, and virulent malaria were diagnosed. Quite aggrieved that having his temperature taken did not lead to improvement he refused a further visit. Instead he relied on prescriptions from the city temple obtained by a priest shaking a tube of spills, and he proceeded to die, leaving everything in his yamen in a hopeless muddle. The people, who were much attached to him, chiefly, Rose thought, because he left them to their own devices and was known to be completely honest, mourned him greatly. Rose had found him a very genial colleague with whom social relations had always been most pleasing, but as 'he had had a rooted objection to any sort of work' and had done none at all since assuming office Rose thought his death likely to remove a stumbling-block in frontier politics. He was rapidly disillusioned. The new intendant, capable and in-dependent but untruthful, unreasonable, quite surprisingly unscru-pulous, and most discourteous, soon asked the Ministry of Foreign Affairs for Rose's removal. Rose was hurt. No one, he said, could reasonably contend that he had been an unfriendly consul, and almost every previous official had gone out of his way to show personal consideration even when official relations had been at their thorniest. The ministry did not transmit the request to the Legation, and after protracted efforts the Legation got the in-tendant removed.[70]

Before the fall of the dynasty seven new China service posts were opened, at Kongmoon in the West river delta, at Changsha south of Yochow on the Hsiang river, at Tsinan in Shantung, at Mukden, Antung, and Harbin in Manchuria, and at Chengtu in Szechwan. In addition a consulate was established at Kashgar in remote Sinkiang (Chinese Turkistan). Since 1889 the Indian government had wished to establish a consulate there but in the absence of Chinese agreement had hitherto had to content themselves with posting an officer of indeterminate status at Kashgar. The post was staffed and run by India and did not come under the Legation. The standard journey time from Peking to landlocked Kashgar was four months and a China service junior attached to the post in 1918 at India's request took seven and a half months.[71]

Kongmoon, opened in 1904, was an utter failure and merely served to inflict discomfort on its incumbents Fox and Werner, who were there only briefly, and on Tebbitt, who was there longer. Tebbitt took over from Werner a boat which provided a room for an office and a room for the consul and which was also occupied by the writer, the office messenger, and the boatman's family. Apart from Customs staff no other foreigners lived locally, and the Chinese town was 4 miles away and the magistrate 10 miles away. Tebbitt should never have been sent to such a post. He had contracted tuberculosis at his previous post, had spent his recent home leave in a sanatorium, and was accompanied back to China by a kindly aunt who came to look after him if he fell ill again. He had no work to relieve the tedium. Carnegie, visiting Kongmoon in 1905, said that the houseboat was very cramped and miserable and that Tebbitt did not look very well but that his aunt, a youngish woman, seemed quite happy and contented although neither Tebbitt nor she ever left the place. He thought it unnecessary to have an officer permanently at Kongmoon and the consulate was closed. No more is heard of that unsung heroine, the aunt.[72]

Changsha, as Hunan's provincial capital, was far more worthy of a consulate. It had many wealthy inhabitants and Flaherty, who opened the consulate in 1905, had hardly arrived before the governor gave him an elaborate lunch at which Chinese and foreign dishes alternated and wines were so recklessly served that brandy and curaçao were being poured wholesale into large glasses. He liked the Hunanese but had reservations about the disaffected and anti-Manchu student class, for many of the Japan-returned students

seemed to him ill-mannered, offensive, and full of revolutionary ideas. Nor was he enamoured of Changsha's constant gloom. The rambling houses, separated from each other by massive walls 30 or 40 feet high which cut off light and air, were forbidding, the streets were too narrow for any wheeled vehicles except diminutive wheelbarrows, and the skies were leaden. He started off in a cramped and very noisy houseboat whose gangplank was so dangerous for visiting officials that he thought it a powerful inducement for them to find him a residence. They did find him one in the city, but it was decaying and unhygienic. He left Changsha within a year, having developed consumption. His three immediate successors likewise failed to stand up to the post.[73] After less than eighteen months the next acting consul, B. Giles, had a severe attack of nervous prostration, from which two years later he had not completely recovered.[74] M. Hughes lasted even less long. He had entered the Siam service but soon had 'a violent attack of Siamese fever at Bangkok which brought on a fit of suicidal mania. While suffering from this he attempted to cut his throat'. The attempt was dismissed by the doctors as merely a phase of the disease, but they advised against return to Siam, 'as the climate evidently does not suit him', and he was transferred to the China service. First reports there were not unduly favourable, but at Foochow in 1904 Brady, a sensible judge, considered him one of the most capable and trustworthy juniors, with an unusual amount of common sense. From Foochow he was transferred to Hoihow, where almost without warning he was afflicted by intense depression. He was given home leave, promoted consul, and sent to Changsha. After a few months the local doctor telegraphed that Hughes was suffering from delusions and needed strict surveillance and special treatment. He was got to Shanghai, where he severely injured himself in a suicide attempt induced by religious melancholia and where shipping companies made difficulties about making room for him and his attendants on a home-bound ship. He was pensioned off and recovered sufficiently to be called to the bar, to return to Shanghai, to serve in France with the Chinese Labour Corps during the First World War, and to live on into his sixties.[75]

Next came W.M. Hewlett, with the wife whom he had brought out to China and married at Shanghai two and a half years previously and their baby. Fox, somewhat older and with only too much experience of living conditions at new ports, feared that the

less experienced Hewletts had unfavourable first impressions of Changsha and that Mrs Hewlett was inclined to be hypersensitive about dirt, damp, and drains.[76] In his maturity Hewlett was renowned as a temperamental man of often irrational likes, dislikes, and feuds,[77] at one moment all enthusiasm, at another crying with vexation.[a] He was neither universally popular in the service[a] nor intellectually outstanding, but he was a devoted public servant. He was always intent on achieving close working relations with the Chinese, on whose actions and attitudes he tended, to the disapproval of some colleagues, to place the most favourable possible construction, and his unconventional methods not infrequently succeeded where more orthodox ones failed. As a young man at Changsha he was already trying out unorthodoxy. He set about cultivating the local gentry, to whom he suggested monthly discussions, and he tried over *crème de menthe* and cigarettes to mollify representatives of craftsmen's guilds who were angered by non-Hunanese being employed to construct foreign buildings, including a consulate on the island where the Customs staff had established themselves. In both cases he thought he had been successful and found later that he had not been. Violent changes of mood were already in evidence. Having moved out of the city into a temporary consulate he professed that he and his wife were most awfully happy at such a fine port and that his little son was the picture of health. By the next year he had become despondent; no official except the governor was trying to check the anti-foreign and anti-treaty feeling exemplified by a well-dressed passer-by who had said 'Kill' in Hewlett's ear in the street; he considered the situation very dangerous. His fears were justified. In a major disturbance orchestrated by the gentry all mission and Customs buildings were totally destroyed, though when the consular gateman remonstrated against damage to the dwelling of so good a man as Hewlett the consulate was left alone. Hewlett got all the foreign community, who expressed warm appreciation of his leadership, safely on board a foreign steamship and then boarded it himself. During the crisis he behaved with good sense and moderation but after it was judged so close to collapse that he was moved briefly to Hankow and then sent home. He had been barely two years in Changsha.[78]

The consulate at Tsinan, the provincial capital of Shantung, was intended as an observation post from which German designs in Shantung could be observed and Clennell, who opened it in 1906,

was told by Satow not to expect much regular consular work. Chinese officials, doubtless looking for a counterweight to German influence, made much of him on his arrival. To his astonishment he was welcomed by 'God Save the King' at the dinner to which the governor immediately invited him and 'Rule Britannia' was played as he sat down. Nevertheless Clennell found it a frustrating post and was not sorry to leave.[79] His immediate successors did not achieve much more at a consulate which was more or less superfluous so long as a central authority in Peking maintained real control over the province. Later, when Shantung was largely independent, Tsinan came into its own.

In a semi-official letter to the Foreign Office in 1904 Satow said he supposed the intended establishment of a consulate-general at Mukden and of a consulate at Antung, neither of which was likely to be of much use commercially, was meant to demonstrate goodwill towards the United States. His uncertainty suggests that he may not have been consulted by the Foreign Office before the decision to establish the posts was reached. The implementation of the decision was delayed, no doubt owing to the Russo-Japanese war. Antung, on the Korean border, was not opened until 1908, and then only as a vice-consulate, proved useless, and had a very short life. Savage was commissioned as vice-consul, but as he was going home on leave Russell opened it as acting vice-consul. He made one month-long journey of 600 miles on horseback, subsisting on maize cake, beancurd, pork, beans, and a heavy sort of sodden pancake, a diet he called unappetizing and best avoided, and he reported that the local Japanese lower classes were badly behaved and bullying, even foreigners being far from immune. Then recurrent dysentery, said to be very probably due to Antung conditions, sent him home. Having in his first few years experienced both Chungking and Antung he applied for a transfer into the general service, saying that his coming marriage was conditional on his obtaining an appointment outside China and that few would venture to take a refined English girl to the conditions at remote consulates in outlandish Chinese places. The application was rejected, a medical certificate sufficient to satisfy the Treasury was produced, and Russell retired on a pension of just over £3 a week. He was fit enough for active service throughout the First World War, in which he was decorated, and did sufficiently well in later life to appear in *Who's Who*.[80] His place in the

wretched hut at Antung was taken by Savage, who with nothing to do was bored to distraction. Some eighteen months after the consulate had been opened Savage was withdrawn and it was closed for good.[81]

Mukden, essentially a political post, was opened by Fulford in 1906. Jordan told a later incumbent in 1911 that while there would be little consular work, there would be lots of political questions and that the principal duties would be to keep in close touch with the Chinese authorities and to follow all developments in Manchuria. Fulford and his successor Willis encountered the accommodation difficulties customary at new posts. Willis, who at great cost had to leave wife and children at Newchwang, first had prostitutes on one side and a barracks on the other, then he was lodged in a decaying temple, then he had two rooms in a Chinese house. The provision of decent accommodation was however now taking much less long, and in about three years he moved into a large new house in a large new compound outside the Chinese city. He found Mukden alarmingly costly. He had to furnish the large house, Mukden's position as a railway junction meant that he had to entertain a stream of visitors furnished with letters of introduction, and the cost of living was high.[82]

Harbin, where a consulate was opened in 1910, had a savagely cold winter lasting for over half the year and had the reputation of being the most expensive place in the Far East. It was unlike anywhere else in China. It was the Russian headquarters of the Chinese Eastern Railway and had been the Russian army base in the Russo-Japanese war. Alongside an insignificant riverine Chinese town containing 'impassible roads, dilapidated dwellings and an indescribably squalid population' the Russians were building a modern European city with a Russian population of some 30,000, broad avenues, imposing government offices, tree-filled parks, well-stocked shops, factories, and churches with onion domes. It was essential to keep up with the Russians, and the tone of Russian society was extravagant. It was Willis who had suggested that developing British interests in northern Manchuria required a consulate at Harbin, but when the suggestion was accepted and he was formally commissioned as consul he begged in the strongest terms not actually to be sent there, pleading that it would be ruinous for a married man with a family, and when he did get there continued in the same vein.[83] The style of Harbin life in tsarist days

can be judged from what it was like much later, when the now stateless Russian community, much swollen by White Russian refugees from Siberia, was falling into ever more desperate poverty. In the early 1930s Moss was present at a banquet prepared for distinguished foreign visitors by the authorities, who employed White Russian chefs. A table at least 100 feet long groaned under three huge sturgeons baked whole, boars' heads, whole deer complete with their horns, and pheasants, geese, wild duck, and a variety of other fowl all carrying their full plumage, which when lifted off revealed beautifully carved meat. He felt himself transported out of China into Europe's Middle Ages.[a] At roughly the same period a United States consular officer was called out by a former tsarist officer for allegedly insulting a woman, and his refusal of the challenge made his social position so untenable that he had to be transferred.[a]

The consulate-general at Chengtu was another political post. The main object in establishing it was to obtain readier access to the viceroy of Szechwan and so to counter French designs in that province. It was also the natural post at which to obtain information about Tibet and Chinese activities there. Hosie opened the office in 1902, after losing most of his effects when his boat was wrecked above Chungking. In a three-month journey, the only major journey undertaken by any Chengtu consul-general of the period, he followed the route to Lhasa as far as Batang, the furthest point in that direction yet reached by a consular officer, and at far-away Tengyueh rumours reached Litton that a strange traveller of enormous wealth, venerable aspect, and imposing person, whom he tentatively identified as Hosie, had appeared at Batang with a large retinue. Chinese objections to a consular establishment at a city which was not a treaty port were met by arrangements analogous to those at Yunnanfu, and it was agreed that while Hosie would in practice reside at Chengtu he would be formally appointed consul-general at Chungking (the Chungking post, temporarily demoted to a vice-consulate, continued to have a separate existence in the charge of a series of bachelors). From 1903 the titular French consul at Chungking also resided at Chengtu.[84] Chengtu was a fine city enclosed by walls 18 miles long. Hosie thought it finer even than Peking, but he was lonely there and spoke of a depressing climate which tended to make young men old before their time. It was so exceptionally remote that it was the only post besides

Kashgar to which Satow telegraphed news that the Japanese had destroyed the Russian fleet in 1905, and until the telegram arrived the French consul had been spreading news of a Russian victory.[85] For the first incumbents appointment disrupted family life. Hosie left his wife in England and got back just in time to see her die of cancer. Campbell, who agreed to replace him only on the understanding that he would not be left there long, left his wife and baby in Shanghai. He said on reaching Chengtu that he was thankful to have done so; the river journey was difficult and dangerous and the nakedness of the crews made it extremely disagreeable for a European woman; and the Chinese house he occupied would have been quite unsuitable. The next man, Goffe, on Campbell's advice left his wife behind. Fox succeeded Goffe. Whereas the three previous incumbents had left behind wives well used to China Fox brought with him a second wife whom he had recently married at home. She was very proud to be the first consular wife to penetrate so far into the interior but she had a weak chest. He dared not keep her over the summer in such unhealthy accommodation and having sent her home at great expense pleaded to be transferred himself.[86]

Disregarding an appreciable number of Japanese there were in 1907, during Fox's incumbency, about 120 foreigners in Chengtu. Over half were British, and apart from a mercantile agent and a teacher the British colony consisted entirely of missionary families. The numerous Canadian Methodist and American missionaries lived well. Fox contrasted his own poor quarters with their spacious compounds, comfortable houses, tennis-courts, and trim gardens. He disapproved of their life-style. In his view their constant comings and goings on furlough, to the mountains for the summer, to attend conferences, or to escort their families to the coast went far to justify the charge that they did not take their work seriously. He disapproved of their tendency to neglect preaching and even medical work for the more attractive and less burdensome task of providing Western education, and he considered the China Inland Mission, whose methods were more similar to those of the Roman Catholics and who likewise played no part in secular education, to be the most successful Protestant organization in west China. During a later tour of duty at Chengtu Fox described the ever-growing number of Canadian missionaries as generally enthusiastic, kindly, fairly energetic, of splendid physique but not of high intellectual standards, believers in making themselves

comfortable and immoderately opposed to wine and tobacco. He was not alone in criticizing the Canadian and American missionaries in Szechwan. W.R. Brown at Chungking described them as lower middle class and absurdly vehement in their objections to tobacco, and Mrs Mead, later the second consular wife to reach Chengtu, disliked attending the innumerable At Homes of missionary ladies with whose living standards she could not afford to keep up.[a] According to Fox the local Roman Catholic priests, all of whom were French, regarded all the Protestant missionaries, but particularly the Canadians and Americans, as people who had come to China mainly to live comfortably.[87]

After Fox came the unmarried Twyman. In less than a year he had to be hurriedly sent home on sick-leave, as he was medically certified to be suffering from nervous depression and he himself feared a total breakdown imminent. The widower W.H. Wilkinson, who replaced him in 1909, lasted better, although he inveighed against living in the heart of the city in an airless, drainless, rat-ridden shanty surrounded on all sides by other shanties and their primitive privies.[88] As he was to show when the Manchus were overthrown and revolution came to Chengtu he was a courageous man, but he was also an ambitious one whose judgement was defective and who wrote too much. His wild and wholly indefensible treatment of one unfortunate British subject indicates why Satow called him a clever ass and why Jordan said that although he was clever he was not gifted with wisdom or a sense of proportion. In 1911 a Chinese student arrived in Chengtu accompanied by a respectable London girl whom he had married in England and by their two children, and they all moved in to live with the Chinese wife he had previously married. Wilkinson's attitude was that the Englishwoman's position was degrading to her and damaging to British prestige, that her virtual prostitution to a Chinese was humiliating to local Englishwomen, that she should be deported, and that if she would not abandon the children they should be deported too. The student apparently had some minor official post. The Chinese authorities looked into the matter, no doubt at Wilkinson's instance, decided that he had been guilty of bigamy (as opposed to taking a concubine in the normal way), and transferred him at a very much reduced salary to the west of the province. As the Englishwoman, left behind in Chengtu, still resisted Wilkinson's pressure to leave he suggested in effect that she might be kid-

napped; she could be inveigled on some pretext into a covered chair with drawn curtains and then rushed on to a boat and taken to the coast in the charge of some missionary couple. At the Legation Hosie minuted with vast indignation. Wilkinson, he said, had done everything in his power to wreck an innocent woman's life; he had separated her from her children's father and had impoverished him and thereby her; under English law it was not a punishable offence to live with a man, even a married man and a Chinese, and it was her affair if she chose to do so; Wilkinson's suggestion to her that she was a prostitute and that English prostitutes were not allowed to remain in China was unworthy of an official in his position or in any position; and Wilkinson's other suggestion that the man should divorce his lawful wife and marry the Englishwoman was disgraceful. Officially the Legation confined themselves to telling Wilkinson that to remove the woman in a covered chair without her consent would be a most improper proceeding which might involve him in serious trouble.

In 1915 J.L. Smith, then in charge at Chengtu, provided a tragic postscript. The woman was said to have cut herself off from foreigners, to be very unhappy, and to be drinking, and her husband was said to be gambling and in debt. She had apparently adapted to Chinese life sufficiently to develop into a classic Chinese termagant, for she flew into a rage with her husband, seized a whip, and ordered him to kneel before her. There was a general family scuffle, she emerged from the house scratched and bleeding and for two hours wandered round Chengtu's streets followed by her husband begging her to go home. Smith considered that while this behaviour would be trivial in the lower quarters of a European city, in remote Chengtu it brought all foreign women into disrepute.[89]

CHAOS AND WARLORDS

AN anti-Manchu rising at Wuchang in October 1911 led to similar risings elsewhere. To restore order the court called Yuan Shih-k'ai back from the retirement to which he had been relegated on the empress dowager's death. He had his own ambitions. He secured the infant emperor's abdication and the Manchu dynasty was replaced by a Chinese republic in which he was the most powerful man. His power base was a disciplined northern army which he had created and in which the leading generals were his henchmen. The only immediate challenge to the conservative Yuan came from the incoherent radical forces behind the risings. The radicals, the most prominent among whom was the Cantonese Sun Yat-sen, were influenced by foreign ideas and vaguely stood for political, social, and economic reform. They lacked effective leadership, clear policies, and a military power base. Yuan outgunned them in the field and outmanoeuvred them in an ineffective parliament which he eventually dissolved, and the assassination of more than one radical leader was laid at his door.[1] Though confusion and local feuding continued in some parts of China he established his overall control as president of the republic. Then he took the traditional decision to found a new dynasty. He misjudged the country's mood. Generals rebelled, he had to cancel his planned investiture as emperor, and he died disconsolate in the middle of 1916. There was no one of large enough stature to take his place. China dissolved into a chaos of civil wars and was carved up between rival warlords. The 'rule of avoidance' prohibiting an official from holding office in his native province had vanished with the empire and local militarists struggled for local power. Despite a mounting nationalism among the educated the warlords' primary or sole concern was with their own interests. They incessantly fought each other to enlarge or defend their territories and incessantly formed

and re-formed alliances with each other and against each other, and their relative strengths and the extent of their territories kept changing kaleidoscopically. The country groaned under extortionate taxation which enriched parasitic warlords and paid their ragged, undisciplined troops.

The position of consuls changed. Clarendon in his desire to prevent consular wars had laid down in the nineteenth century that redress for grievances which could not be peacefully settled by consuls must be sought from the central government by the Legation. The doctrine had never been entirely appropriate for dealings with a country which Satow described as a congeries of satrapies.[2] When satrapies subject to ultimate control from the centre were replaced by local regimes which at best took little notice of a shadowy central government and at worst might challenge its legitimacy or even be in armed conflict with it, the doctrine became meaningless. Local officials did not care a rap about futile consular threats to refer disputes to the Legation, said Teichman as acting Chinese secretary in 1923.[3] What could not be settled locally could usually not be settled at all. In meeting the frequent emergencies caused by civil wars and local changes of regime consuls had to act first and report afterwards, and they were in a more responsible and independent position than at any time since the chief superintendent of trade had moved from Hong Kong and become the minister at Peking.

Consuls had to adjust to the disappearance of the old, highly literate officials, with their formal dignity and courtesies, and to the emergence of a new generation of office-holders. They often viewed without enthusiasm young men peddling panaceas for China's ills but lacking experience of public business and frequently lacking even potential administrative ability, and preferred experienced conservatives like Yuan Shih-k'ai, whatever the latter's faults and limitations. The Foreign Office said that Sun Yat-sen was probably an unscrupulous visionary and J.W. Jamieson that he was a political adventurer slightly tinged with madness. Willis, who was on very good terms with the Mukden viceroy at the time of the revolution, said that he much preferred men of the viceroy's stamp to the modern product and that he had no great admiration for the English-speaking gang. H. Porter had no opinion of what he called the usual run of unkempt Japan-returned students, Savage spoke of leadership by hot-headed, half-educated students with whom solid

Chinese of age and experience would have nothing to do.[4] Among
the conservatives power for the most part fell into the hands of
provincial military governors (tuchün) who had had a regular
career in the imperial army or who had made their own often
disreputable way to the top. F.E. Wilkinson left descriptions of
both these types. At Foochow he dealt for years with a burly
military governor who had been a soldier all his life, who like most
Chinese generals of his age group had had hardly any education,
and who was extremely hospitable, friendly, and pleasant.[a] From
Foochow he moved to Mukden, where his dealings were with the
opium-smoking warlord Chang Tso-lin. Under the empire Chang
had successively been a soldier, a deserter, and a bandit chief, and
on abjuring banditry had been made first a colonel and then a
general. At the time of the revolution he commanded the Mukden
garrison. This opening enabled him to become Manchuria's warlord, and he maintained himself as such until the Japanese army
grew weary of him and arranged his assassination. Returning
Wilkinson's first call he dismounted from a horse, a servant
emerging from a car hooked a breastplate of decorations on to
his chest, and he was then ready to shake hands. 'He was a small,
delicate looking man', said Wilkinson, 'of the type of the old
viceroys rather than the modern tuchün. Although quite uneducated and in some ways very ignorant he had great natural ability
and was extraordinarily astute'.[a] Coales' impression of Chang was
not dissimilar; Chang's quiet demeanour was more reminiscent
of a literatus than of an ex-brigand, he was quick to apprehend
and to decide, and was 'a Chinese official with whom it would be
refreshing to deal were he not totally unscrupulous'.[5] Then there
was a miscellany of minor upstarts. At Tengyueh C.D. Smith was
not taken with the first new leader to emerge; previously a small
merchant, he had no great education or refinement and no
particular abilities, and he dressed like a fairly well-to-do coolie; in
his suspiciousness, obstinacy, and incompetence he resembled the
old-style official but he lacked the dignified urbanity characterizing
the best class of Chinese manners. Twyman at Chinkiang doubted
the complete sanity of a strange, gaunt quondam salt-smuggler,
now a ruthless prefect with a most exaggerated sense of power.
Hewlett at Ichang described another new prefect as a semi-educated
and brutally cruel underling of repulsive appearance. Less unpleas-
ing were the Wuchow officials of 1915, who Kirke said were

extremely courteous and dealt promptly with minor matters which he raised.

They are all typical officials of a small Chinese city. They seldom leave their residences and their interest in, and knowledge of, public affairs which do not affect them personally appears to be quite negligible. Surrounded by a crowd of gaping underlings and half a dozen ruffians armed with rifles, they receive their visitors with the greatest urbanity in what are, I think, the darkest, most tumble-down and most squalid yamens I have ever seen.[6]

The dress of officials altered too. Gone were the pleasing robes of imperial China, and bowler hats became *de rigueur*. In 1918 Kirke described the appearance of the Kiukiang intendant on official visits. He wore a bowler with an unusually wide brim, a frock-coat of unprecedented cut, elastic-sided boots with no elastic left, trousers several inches too long, and two black ties, one a bow and the other a knot, to accompany a soft linen collar part of which always overlaid his coat collar. His hair was rather long and he called to mind a caricature of a dissenting minister.[7] On occasion official behaviour also altered for the worse. According to W.R. Brown sailors from the United States fleet on shore at Chefoo had no alternatives to pernicious alcoholic compounds and brothels of unspeakable squalor and filth, and had turned the summer and autumn of 1920 into a nightmare by their lurid language, drunken brawls, crude familiarities, and offers of personal violence. That winter a foreign believer in Sino-foreign co-operation proposed at a dinner attended by the principal Chinese and foreign officials and merchants the provision of a recreation ground. The proposal was acclaimed by all except the intendant,

who, his habitual deceit for once dissolved by immense draughts of brandy and port mixed, staggered to his feet and refused to be connected with the scheme or anything else in which foreigners had a hand. No Chinese present would interpret his speech and he stood swaying on his feet until a swift indisposition overcame him and he was hurried from the room to return a pallid wreck two hours later and explain that nothing was nearer to his heart than the scheme of his honourable friends whom he would support to the extent of his power.

The next day he bought a plot in the middle of the proposed site, other Chinese gentlemen present at the dinner did the same, the price of the site quadrupled, and in searching for another site the

proposers of the scheme decided to dispense with Chinese assistance.[8]

A republican administration replaced an imperial administration smoothly enough at some ports, where no disturbances affected foreigners. Ningpo, Wuhu, and Hangchow were examples of cities taken over without bloodshed. The insurgents did not lose a man in taking Ichang, though they celebrated victory by killing some Manchu women and smearing their blood on yamen doors to bring the new administration good luck. At Changsha the initial coup was bloodless, and a proclamation issued after a subsequent mutiny stated that if any foreigners were accidentally or intentionally killed not only the soldier responsible but his whole section would be executed. At Amoy Sundius had little more to do than see to the personal safety of a Manchu intendant. At Foochow the Manchu general and Manchu soldiers were executed and the viceroy committed suicide, but armed conflict was brief.[9] Some normally uneventful ports were on the other hand thrown into confusion. Chefoo fell bloodlessly, but the subsequent vagaries in the foreign quarter of some 4,000 largely unpaid troops under three different commanders alarmed the more nervous foreign women and gave Porter, the acting consul, a good deal of concern.[10] Swatow offered no resistance to several hundred revolutionaries armed with bombs and other weapons who came by ship from Hong Kong to take over the town, but then insurrectionary factions quarrelled among themselves. Tours would not allow a British ship to land a second revolutionary force to whom the dominant local insurgents were hostile. The force was put ashore 90 miles away, marched overland, and took the town in a fight during which the combatants seemed to him anxious to discharge as many cartridges as possible in any direction in the shortest possible time and during which foreign buildings were considerably damaged by gun and rifle fire. Jordan commented that a quiet treaty port had had a rather unpleasant experience. A third and stronger force arrived and after a month's negotiations paid the second force $70,000 to leave. Order was restored by drastic methods, but Tours, who thought the arrangements too makeshift to endure, considered the new officials at least as corrupt as their imperial predecessors.[11]

It was very rare for anything, good or bad, to happen at Pakhoi. There had been a flutter of excitement in 1907. The threat that a local rebellion might reach Pakhoi at that time had prompted the

normally valetudinarian Savage to a stout declaration that if it came to fighting he expected to give a good account of himself; 'I have not some skill in the use of firearms for nothing'. The threat blew over, Pakhoi remained as uneventful as ever, and Savage had no opportunity to prove himself as a marksman.[12] Now the revolution suddenly gave Moss, the assistant in charge there, some lively weeks. Imperial officials fled, and local soldiers after murdering their officers policed the town in a manner which Moss compared with wolves herding sheep. The chamber of commerce tried to maintain order, organized their own police force, and ordered some executions. Their new police ate the victims' livers, got out of hand, blackmailed, plundered, and killed. Although the chamber's leaders, with whom Moss conferred almost daily, were genuinely anxious to protect foreign life and property the presence of a helpful German gunboat seemed to him the best protection against the constant danger that a mob might pillage and burn the town. At the nearby prefectural city the honest and popular prefect cut off the queue which to republicans was a hated symbol of submission to Manchu rule, reached the consulate disguised as a coolie, and was sent on to Hong Kong. Through a thoroughly disturbed countryside Moss set out to bring in an outlying missionary. They missed each other but the missionary got to Pakhoi without suffering anything worse than robbery and Moss got safely back. A general from Canton reached Pakhoi with republican troops who attacked some of the local soldiers in a guardhouse next door to the consulate. Moss watched the fighting from the top of the consulate, over which bullets were freely flying and which was occasionally hit. Most of the men under attack fled but two got into the consulate compound and begged on their knees for protection. One hid in the stable and Moss just had time to lock the other in the gaol before he turned to eject the first pursuers as they entered the consulate gate. Most of the staff were terrified but the head messenger and the groom stood by him and he persuaded a corporal who spoke Mandarin that the consulate should not be entered. The two fugitives made good their escape, apologies were tendered by the general in person, and consular life returned to normal.[13]

In Szechwan the birth of the republic was accompanied by an extreme confusion which foreshadowed decades of disorder in the province. Provincial independence was declared. An incoming viceroy was killed by his own men on his way to Chengtu and his

head was brought to Chungking in a kerosene tin and paraded round the city. The incumbent viceroy was killed too and a variety of republican military governments sprang up. W.R. Brown, in charge at Chungking, said that these governments had nothing in common except jealousy and dissension, Teichman, W.H. Wilkinson's assistant at Chengtu, that they had nothing in common except lack of funds. Brown wrote of some cities being in the hands of robber bands and of other cities being beset by them, of bandits infesting every road, of a total lack of patriotism, of a universal scramble for place, of power exercised tyrannically by men blind to everything except their private interests. Teichman wrote of such utter chaos that one hardly dared take a ride outside Chengtu in case there should be a *coup d'état* and the city gates closed; living in Chengtu was bad enough in times of peace, 'under the sort of reign of terror we have been having for the last few weeks it is about the limit...altogether I am heartily fed up with Szechwan'. Wilkinson could not at first discover amid the looting and arson whether there was a government in Chengtu and feared that if troops and mob got out of hand, as they seemed perilously close to doing, he and Teichman were lost; the telegraph wires had been down for weeks, there was no mail, and there was no place of refuge or possibility of naval aid. British subjects were evacuated from the province but Wilkinson decided to stay on and Teichman volunteered to stay too. For many nights both men thought it prudent to sleep in their clothes, and although neither came to any harm Teichman's health suffered so much that after some months he had to go home on sick-leave. Jordan commended their decision to remain as requiring after three months of strain and anxiety no ordinary courage and determination. In 1913 Brown described recent fighting in Chungking between troops from Chengtu, 'an amiable but rough set of brigands', and troops from Kweichow as the worst of his many trying and dangerous experiences in the city; mediation by himself and the French vice-consul had resulted in the Chengtu forces leaving the city and had saved it from being pillaged and burned to the ground, but the mediation had been a delicate operation in which the slightest indiscretion or hesitation would have been fatal to both men; 'I can hardly understand now how we managed to get back alive'.[14] The nature of the subsequent consular experience at Chungking was sufficiently indicated by Archer, who in one quarter of 1923 logged siege conditions for eight days in the first month, for

six days in the second month, and for two separate periods of six and seven days respectively in the third month. The generals, he said, were changing sides almost from day to day.[15]

Goffe and F.E. Wilkinson were caught up in fighting at Han-kow and Nanking respectively. Inside the service, in which he was remembered for bullying subordinates, Goffe was so little liked that when he died in retirement not one of its members attended the funeral. Outside it his style can be judged from his report from a later post that he had addressed a missionary as 'an impertinent hound — an expression quite inadequate to describe him or my feelings'.[16] He was however intelligent and efficient. In 1910 he summed up the current Chinese attitude towards foreigners very well. More or less acute anti-foreign feeling would remain, he said, until China was strong enough to resist aggression and to treat with foreign powers on equal terms; the dividing line between anti-foreignism and patriotism was very fine; a reform movement in China must aim at removing the conditions which enabled foreigners to occupy their present position and to that extent was essentially and inevitably anti-foreign. Just before the October rising at Wuchang in 1911 he gave notice that the local troops were seriously disaffected and he asked for a warship, characteristically doing so in terms which annoyed the admiral. When the rising occurred he again acted competently and, again characteristically, combined doing so with complaints that he was having a very strenuous time with too little sleep, that life in China was not peaceful enough, and that he did not think his pay included that sort of thing. For a month the British concession was practically in the middle of a battlefield between defending republicans and attacking imperialists and was continually hit by shells and bullets. Goffe, however, saw the courage and enthusiasm of the republicans and the spirit and discipline of the imperialist troops as signs of a new spirit in China.[17]

At Nanking the viceroy had been expected to hand the city over but the Manchu general and Chang Hsün, a Chinese general so conservative that for years after the revolution he refused to cut his queue, decided otherwise. The republicans attacked. Republicans in the city were summarily dealt with and, said Wilkinson, absence of a queue or possession of money, particularly the latter, was regarded as proof positive of republicanism. He saw forty heads impaled round Chang's yamen and there were similar sights in

numerous other places. Chang was cordial when Wilkinson called but did not impress. He was dressed in ordinary Chinese clothes and looked like a very second-rate shopkeeper, with a yamen to match and disreputable soldiers and coolies hanging around, and he obviously could not read the despatch which Wilkinson handed to him. British women and children were evacuated from the city at once, nearly all the British men who originally stayed to protect their property gradually faded away, and when the British, American, and German admirals refused their consuls further protection in the city the American and German consuls withdrew. Wilkinson considered that a consulate which was British government property would best be protected by his continued occupation and stayed on. Only repeated warnings from the republicans outside the city that in view of their impending attack he should leave made him decide that it was politic to go, and even then he considered he could have stayed without serious risk. Nanking surrendered a week or so later and the same day he went back to the consulate, which he found intact. On his way to it he was the unwilling witness of many gruesome incidents, and he did not echo Goffe's sentiments about a new spirit in China. Some months later unpaid troops mutinied one night, firing kept everyone awake, and a row of houses opposite the consulate was pillaged. Wilkinson thereupon sent his wife and five children home, saying with moderation that in recent months conditions for women and children at Nanking had been somewhat trying.[18]

At Shanghai republicans took over the Chinese city without disorder and with what E.D.H. Fraser judged to be the practically unanimous support of the inhabitants. Fraser had previously requested the presence of the largest warship, or warships, available, in order to overawe hotheads, but he stood out against the British admiral's suggestion that an international force should occupy the international settlement, an action which in his view would have confirmed suspicions that foreigners were on the imperialist side and might easily have turned the rising into an antiforeign movement. He kept in close contact with the protracted negotiations in Shanghai between radical representatives and Yuan Shih-k'ai's emissaries, urging on both sides the need for the agreement which they eventually reached.[19]

At Canton things did not go so smoothly for J.W. Jamieson. First he had to give the fleeing viceroy refuge and get him away to Hong

Kong. Then the situation became so tense that for months Shameen was defended by troops from Hong Kong. Immediately before 500 tourists from an American liner arrived, troops under one of Canton's most desperate ex-robber chiefs ate the hearts and livers of prisoners shot as suspected imperialists, a so-called people's army dismembered suspects alive at one of the city gates, and the local Chinese press deplored the bad effect such doings must have on foreign opinion. Soon afterwards the ex-robber chief was to the general satisfaction arrested and shot and the people's army was defeated by regular troops and disbanded, giving rise to hopes that Shameen would be less under threat.[20] Jamieson however became embroiled in a violent quarrel with the new radical authorities, whom he dismissed as a collection of young nonentities unworthy to be called a government. As the police were shooting practically everyone arrested in the city, even for minor offences, he had suspended the practice of handing over to them for punishment Chinese committing offences on Shameen. A Chinese servant on Shameen attacked his German employer, was tried instead in the consular court, and was sentenced to three months' hard labour and fifty strokes. Jamieson's motives in sparing the man probable execution in the city were understandable but the proceedings were indefensible. A Chinese official protested in language so strong that Jamieson broke off relations. The Chinese would not yield and an impasse was reached. The dispute was referred to Peking, and the Ministry of Foreign Affairs asked for Jamieson's transfer. Jordan, who had difficulty in devising a face-saving peace formula, told Jamieson that the incident had been unfortunate and after its settlement minuted that the wearisome affair should not be reported to the Foreign Office. Jamieson had not been at his best in this matter. He was, however, little abashed, and continued in his customary style, telling Jordan that as Kwangtung would in future probably be governed by Cantonese it was likely that governors of Hong Kong would be unable to resist the temptation to interfere.[21]

In mid-1913 a widespread radical rebellion against Yuan Shih-k'ai quickly collapsed, but not before another consul, Tours, had lived through another siege of Nanking. The city was taken and thoroughly looted by the troops of Chang Hsün, who had gone over to Yuan. Shells dropped in the consular compound and Tours was commended for the zeal and energy he had shown while in constant danger from gun and rifle fire and while seriously unwell.

A few weeks later the victorious Chang invited Tours and other Nanking foreigners to a reception. No longer dressed like a shop-keeper but wearing a sky-blue uniform, Chang walked round in a highly festive mood with a magnum of Mumm's extra dry champagne in each hand, filling glasses and drinking toasts. Many foreigners fiercely criticized Chang's rule at Nanking. Tours did not believe the condemnation justified. His successor B. Giles on the other hand said that Chang's troops established a reign of terror (a frequently recurring expression in this period) wherever they were stationed.[22] Twyman, the consul at Chinkiang, certainly had an unpleasant experience with them. An angry and very menacing group of Chang's men made for the concession. Backed up by a solitary foreign merchant Twyman went to stop them. He came within an ace of being shot but kept cool and held them off until one of their officers came panting up and got them under control. When they were safely out of sight Twyman permitted himself a 'Whew!' and a wipe of his forehead but made no other comment.[23]

Shortly before the abortive radical rebellion Jordan, giving E.D.H. Fraser political guidance, said that the British wished Chinese of all parties to sink their differences and to work together to develop the country, and he expressed his personal conviction that the Chinese nation's common sense would carry it through all difficulties. The outbreak of the rebellion did not indicate much readiness to sink differences, in coming years belief in the national common sense became hard to sustain, and by 1919 Jordan, who liked the country and its people, was minuting in a still sympathetic but saddened tone 'It is easy to abuse Chinese but placed in their position how many of us would escape censure!'[24] After the collapse of the rebellion there were however still superficially encouraging signs. By the end of 1913 the republican government headed by Yuan as president had been recognized by all the treaty powers, in most parts of China a semblance of normality was returning, and Yuan looked increasingly firm in the saddle. It was not until his attempt to make himself emperor that the illusory character of the encouraging signs became fully apparent, and meanwhile the next major shock wave to hit the service came not from internal Chinese developments but from the outbreak of the First World War in Europe.

Until China decided in 1917 that a declaration of war on the central powers would be in her interest she was a neutral, and her

neutrality raised awkward problems. Awareness of the common culture shared by Europeans and Americans was sharpened by living in China, the treaty port instinct and tradition was for them all to stand together in times of stress, and there was a network of intermarriage between nationalities.[25] In the rift now opened personal friends became official enemies without ceasing to be neighbours. Consular officers varied in their personal reactions. In 1915 a despatch from H.F. King at Kiukiang referred to Germans as 'these beastly people' but Toller at Pakhoi considered that the French vice-consul and French schoolmaster had acted in the worst taste by hanging and burning the Kaiser in effigy, and soon after the outbreak of war Clennell at Newchwang said that the behaviour of the German vice-consul, whom he had encountered two or three times, had been everything he could have asked from a gentleman and a friend. Anomalies abounded. J.L. Smith, drawing up contingency plans for protecting Ichang foreigners in any emergency, let the five German residents know that if they wished they could be included in the scheme, and when a crisis threatened at Swatow the German consul said that British subjects would be welcome to use the German consulate as their assembly point. With the approval of both the British and German Legations the German senior consul at Chefoo conveyed to Jordan as dean of the Peking diplomatic body the collective views of the consular body, including those of the acting British consul, Combe. Jordan told Combe that consular bodies should use the pre-war machinery, that the various heads of mission in Peking had tacitly accepted this, and that Combe should try to restrain a French colleague who had been minded to object.

At Canton Germans remained in the British concession and very large British interests remained in the German concessions at Tientsin and Hankow. The tone of the German-owned newspaper at Hankow remained remarkably mild, as its circulation depended largely on subscribers in the interior, most of whom were British. The combined finesse of the diplomatic body was baffled by the existence of the legation quarter, and until China declared war armed and uniformed troops who in other parts of the world would have been busily killing each other continued jointly to guard the quarter against the theoretical danger of Chinese attack.[26] As the war went on feelings rose, and the wounds it inflicted on Western solidarity were slow to heal. In 1922 F.E. Wilkinson at Mukden

advised the newly arrived German consul-general not to call on
British residents and saw little chance of his being elected to the
club. In reporting this Wilkinson said that he saw little hope for
world peace so long as Germans were treated as pariahs, that
he intended to make himself unpopular by inviting his German
colleague to an official dinner, and that he regretted the British
community's attitude.[27]

So long as China remained a neutral consular officers were not
allowed to join up. At the outbreak of war H. Porter was at home
with nine months' leave in hand and sought permission to do. Some
Foreign Office minutes implied that the war would be over before
the leave expired and favoured permission being given. Caution
prevailed, and it was decided that men who were very expensively
trained experts should not be released. The decision was very ill-
received by some men eager to do their bit, for it was evidently
difficult to feel that official work in China contributed much to
the allied cause. Even Jordan, then in his sixties, broke out 'I
sometimes wish I were younger and able to make munitions or do
something useful instead of spinning ropes of sand in China'.
Despite the decision against volunteering, the service, recruitment
into which was suspended throughout the war, became increasingly
short-handed, a situation made worse after China's declaration of
war by the release of half a dozen or so younger men to officer the
Chinese Labour Corps recruited for work behind the lines in
Europe. Short-handedness in conjunction with restrictions on travel
by women and children disrupted home leaves.[28] F.E. Wilkinson
did not see his children for eight years,[a] and it took nearly twenty
years to get the leave roster back to normal, just in time for it to be
disrupted again by the next world war.[a] Absence of home leave
added to pressures on physical and mental health.

The long-term effects of the war on the foreign position in China
were profound. On China's declaration of war Germany and
Austria-Hungary automatically lost their extraterritorial rights, the
Bolsheviks later surrendered theirs, leaving a stateless, impoverished, and defenceless White Russian community marooned in
China, and the implications were not lost on a China whose major
foreign policy objective was to get rid of the unequal treaties and
extraterritoriality. At the end of the war Germany was prostrate
and Austria-Hungary dismembered, Russia was in turmoil, and the
strength and will-power of Britain and France were sapped. The

obstacles in the way of Japan's ambitions were thus greatly reduced. She had made a move in 1914 by capturing Tsingtao from the Germans and taking over German rights in Shantung and, according to J.T. Pratt at Tsinan, flooding a once peaceful province with drugs, arms, and brigands.[29] Before the end of 1914 Pratt reported that the Japanese military in Shantung treated Japanese civilians, including the Japanese consul, with high-handed contempt and that Britain could evidently expect nothing from her Japanese ally except a contemptuous and discourteous disregard of British interests. He was told by Jordan that local British grievances must be subordinated to wider national interests and, in effect, that Britain did not at present have the strength to resist.[30] After some years Japan deferred her designs on Shantung, and the history of the British consular post established at Tsingtao, which Japan allowed China to repossess, was agreeably uneventful, but Britain never recovered the strength to resist Japan effectively in Shantung or anywhere else in China.

At the end of 1915 internal events in China came back to the fore. A successful rising against Yuan Shih-k'ai began in Yunnan and swiftly spread. First British assessments of the situation were strikingly wrong. Jordan instructed Goffe at Yunnanfu to impress on the local leaders of the rising that their course was utterly hopeless and that no foreign power would give support or sympathy. Goffe, who had given advance warning of the rising as correctly as he had given warning of the 1911 Wuchang rising, was now equally adrift. He told Jordan that the movement had little or no public support, that recruits were not coming in, and that ammunition was short. As usual he took the opportunity to complain; Yunnanfu lacked everything that made life worth living; 'riots, revolution and rebellion seem to follow me about, and I think it would pay the British government to pension me off; I would go cheap, as I have lost my faith in the Chinese and am thoroughly sick of the country. Life is getting altogether too strenuous in China'. Whether misled by Goffe or by his own relations with Yuan, Jordan deluded himself into the belief that the Yunnanese leaders were showing signs of regretting their foolish enterprise and that other provinces showed no signs of joining them, and some months later was still calling them a 'gang of agitators and reformers'.[31] From this point onwards the opinions of the most experienced observers about the probable course of Chinese

politics were for years little more use than fortune-tellers' predictions would have been. Lung Chi-kuang, the military governor of Kwangtung, gave an assurance in very strong language to J.W. Jamieson that he would at all hazards adhere to the central government and four days afterwards declared his independence. Jamieson had to express extreme regret at having given an erroneous impression of Lung's intentions and was completely at a loss to understand his change of front.[32] Before long the Legation were not infrequently telling the Foreign Office that the position in one or another province was confused and obscure and transmitting without further comment reports from the consuls concerned, and the consuls were not infrequently confessing their inability to make head or tail of events. By the beginning of 1925 the Foreign Office, usually so practical and clear-headed even when wrong, were reduced to imbecility by the chaos. Noting the alarming frequency of high-handed and illegal Chinese actions they suggested that as foreign treaty rights were known only to a small number of Chinese civil officials who were apt in civil wars to be replaced by military officers, the Ministry of Foreign Affairs might be induced to distribute to the civil arm a number of memoranda setting out the principal treaty rights, so that any endangered civil authority might bring copies of the memoranda to the urgent attention of military commanders. Legation minutes contained such adjectives as futile and absurd, but a polite reply was sent that the proposal was open to objections.[33]

Consular officers who tried to mediate in the incessant civil wars did so either in the narrower interests of foreign communities or in the broader interests of suffering Chinese civilians. Sometimes they took the initiative and volunteered an offer of mediation. In 1916 J.W. Jamieson proposed a temporary suspension of hostilities to Ts'en Ch'un-hsüan, who was advancing to attack Canton, and was sarcastically snubbed. Ts'en replied that he was extremely obliged, and that as Jamieson was on such friendly terms with the covetous and cruel Canton commander the Cantonese would be inexpressibly grateful if Jamieson would urge the commander to repent and leave, whereupon hostilities would cease. So unhelpful a response to an offer of mediation was unusual. Sometimes consular mediation was requested by one or other opposing faction. Mediation attempts were as often as not attended by personal hazard. In 1921, for example, J.L. Smith and his Japanese colleague, constituting the

Ichang consular body, were being rowed back across the Yangtze on their return from a truce mission undertaken at the request of one warring group. Half way across the river they came under shell fire. The shells came progressively closer, and as they reached the opposite bank two final shells, which failed to burst, landed within 20 or 30 feet. The consular body ran along the bank, pursued by a few bullets, and recovered breath behind a house.[34]

Mediation went badly wrong at Tengyueh in 1926, when Harding was in charge. Several hundred bandits allied to a local General Yang entered Tengyueh, whose terrified inhabitants started collecting money and supplies for them. The illiterate 25-year-old bandit chief called on Harding accompanied by twenty or so truculent-looking men who sat, and spat, on the drawing-room floor. Harding, who spoke Chinese exceedingly well[a] and whose penchant for the coarsest Chinese language[a] may have been helpful in such company, found him pleasant and thought he could detect the qualities of decision, ruthlessness, pluck, bravado, and *bonhomie* which enabled him to dominate a band of hardened outlaws. The call went off well enough, apart from the visitors' onslaught on Harding's stock of Grand Marnier, which by an unfortunate mistake his nervous staff produced for them. Harding returned the call and two days later the chief, accompanied as before, called again and asked Harding to mediate between the bandits and approaching provincial government troops under a General Ch'en. After the request had been endorsed by Yang as the bandits' nominal superior Harding set off with bandit representatives and other negotiators, unsure whether he would be allowed to mediate or would himself be carried off into the hills by the bandits, by whom he was closely supervised 'even in my most private moments'. *En route* to Ch'en he spent a very uncomfortable and entirely sleepless night in a village of ten houses already occupied by 300 of Yang's men. He met Ch'en and negotiated a settlement under which Yang's men and the bandits would quit Tengyueh and would under Ch'en's orders proceed to fight other bandits. On Ch'en's arrival at Tengyueh Harding introduced Yang to Ch'en, who received Yang in the most friendly way. The grateful inhabitants of Tengyueh undertook to erect a memorial stone to commemorate Harding's service, and he reported his proceedings with elation. Despite the settlement the bandits continued their depredations in nearby villages. Yang became nervous. Harding sought and

obtained confirmation that Ch'en guaranteed Yang's personal safety and on the strength of this Yang abandoned plans to move into Burma. A few days later Ch'en seized and executed Yang, whose heart was cut out and probably eaten, and a large number of his men. The local magistrate broke the news to Harding as Harding was waiting for Ch'en to come to lunch. Harding in a fury struck the magistrate, who responded in kind. His second report to the Legation, sent eleven days after the first one, was on a different note. He expressed his deep regret to the Legation at having lost his composure but said that as in his view relations between any British officer and persons guilty of so gross a breach of faith were undesirable he was leaving Tengyueh for Burma to await instructions. The Foreign Office minutes on the two despatches were understanding. Toller of the China service, who was temporarily serving in the Foreign Office, said that Harding might well have been unable to avoid getting dragged in at the beginning and that consuls had no instructions how to deal with an occupation by bandits; he had probably been mistaken in not getting out when the original settlement became invalid and probably no one had ever had any intention of keeping the promises given, but unorthodox methods had saved Tengyueh from the sack. Another official minuted that although in the calm atmosphere of Whitehall Harding's departure seemed quite wrong things had looked different to a man whose nerves after months of exceptional strain had been affected by revolting brutality and treachery; 'although technically to blame I don't think we can blame him'. Harding was sent on home leave.[35] Yunnan was not his lucky province. In the 1930s he came back there as Yunnanfu consul-general, flew into another passion on finding American-led Chinese boy scouts trespassing on consulate property, and struck them.[a] The Ministry of Foreign Affairs complained[a] and he went into retirement in Tahiti.

The Chinese authorities instigated no attacks on consular officers, whom they were on the contrary usually most anxious to protect, but hazards from undisciplined and trigger-happy soldiers and from bandits became normal. S.W. Smith's encounter with soldiers at Wuchow in 1919 was reported in more detail than most. As he passed the office on an evening walk with his family the constable rushed out to say that soldiers who had been interfering with the wife of a consulate gigman were trying to shoot him for intervening. A group of soldiers including a sergeant followed and

as far as their incomprehensible dialect could be understood demanded $80. On being refused they bound both men's arms behind their backs, beat them with rifle butts, marched them to a sampan, where they were unbound, and took them to the yamen of the defence commissioner, who was astounded to see the consul in such a position. The consulate messenger had tried to reason with the soldiers and had been severely beaten for his pains, the writer had headed for the magistrate, and a neighbouring cottager had provided various people with sampan money so that they could inform other foreigners. As a result the British gunboat was alerted and after three hours its commander marched into the yamen with an armed guard of five sailors and escorted consul and constable back. Smith was shaken. He finished a long telegraphic report by saying that he and his wife and children, who he said had suffered severe shock from witnessing the incident, and the constable and his wife must leave China immediately, that it would probably be inadvisable for them ever to return, and that at least £20,000 compensation should be paid to him and £5,000 to the constable. Jordan deduced from this that Smith was hardly in a state to handle the matter and ordered J.W. Jamieson to come from Canton to settle it, which he did with speed. The sergeant was shot, sentences on the other soldiers were commuted to imprisonment, ample formal apologies were made, and $10,000 compensation was paid. To avoid any suspicion that a consular officer was getting more than reimbursement of direct expenses Jordan ruled that half the $10,000 should go to local mission hospitals. The writer and messenger got a year's pay each and the cottager was handsomely rewarded. Smith got $2,500 because leave to England was required, but realizing in a calmer mood that immediate departure would not look well he volunteered to stay for some months and in the end stayed for another year.[36] In 1921 H. Porter at Harbin reported encounters with both soldiers and bandits in a single four-week period. First he and his wife were travelling in a motor boat close to the city when four shots, one of which went through the cabin, were fired at them at close range from a junk apparently manned by soldiers. Then they, a friend, and two Chinese mechanics were travelling in a borrowed motor boat on which sixteen mounted bandits opened fire. A volley of twenty or so shots disabled the engine, and the party had to stand on the bank under levelled rifles and watch their boat being looted. The bandits debated whether to take the for-

eigners for ransom but were dissuaded by one of the mechanics, who had the presence of mind to say that the foreigners were minor employees of a Harbin newspaper and were not worth holding. No consular officer came closer than that to being carried off by bandits, which was an experience much better avoided. A 50-year-old British subject in perfect health was carried off in Yunnan while travelling in an area he had been advised to avoid. A month later he escaped, but by then had lost 2 stone and was suffering from very acute gastritis, very severe dysentery, very severe malaria, a severe tooth abscess, and inflammation of the prostate.[37]

Battles for possession of territory were a much greater hazard to consular officers than the occasional deliberate attacks by soldiers or bandits. Some ports fared better than others. Tientsin was relatively undisturbed, whereas at Canton disturbances were incessant and in a ten-year period eight different leaders controlled Swatow.[38] Most officers were at one time or another at considerable personal risk during such conflicts, and some stormy petrels were for ever in the thick of things. Given the perpetual references to bullets flying and shells falling and to rioting, looting, and arson by victorious or fleeing troops it is astonishing that the only serious casualty was E.S. Bennett. Accompanying the military attaché to the scene of hostilities outside Peking he was hit in the head by a ricocheting bullet not aimed at him, never fully recovered, and had to be prematurely retired some years later.[39] Responsibility for the safety of British subjects, and often of other foreigners, during fighting was an onerous task which told on some men. In 1918 Savage with apparent competence brought his flock safely through the second major disturbance at Changsha in six months and said that 'as usual, the women showed up well', one of them having actually smiled when a bullet came dangerously close. He emerged however with a catalogue of personal woes. During the first crisis he had more than once felt within measurable distance of hysteria and his much younger United States colleague, a very sound man, had been on the verge of breakdown. During the second crisis continuous rifle fire had deprived him of sleep and he had suffered from a bad liver attack, he badly needed to get to an oculist, a dentist, a tailor, and a bootmaker, his health would not stand much more of these perpetual excitements and alarms, he was in his fourth year at a post notoriously bad for the nerves, and he would be glad to see the last of it.[40]

Labour troubles in the form of strikes, boycotts, and riots became troublesome in the 1920s. The usual consular reaction was to blame agitators. Combe and Goffe were more perceptive. After a battle between rival sets of coolies in the Kiukiang concession in 1920 Combe pushed through a scheme, which was unwelcome to the British shipping companies but got at the root of the trouble, whereby coolies were licensed and casual labour was abolished. At Hankow in 1923 the concession's police superintendent was among those badly hurt during a strike in British factories. Goffe said that the labour movement was there to stay and should not be dismissed as resulting from Bolshevik agitation; it was an expression of labour's legitimate demands in a world-wide social upheaval; no one knowing the harshness of life for Chinese labourers could resent the activities of any union trying to ameliorate their condition, and raising Chinese standards of life and pay would incidentally benefit British workmen. Three weeks later he reported, without overtly contrasting foreign and Chinese methods of dealing with strikers, the breaking of a railway strike by the Chinese authorities; the head of the union had been decapitated on a station platform, a local lawyer prominent in the union and an engine-driver had been executed too, a large number of other strikers had allegedly been killed when troops opened fire on them, and as a result normal working on the railway had been resumed.[41]

An account of how consulates throughout China were affected by the rise and fall of major and minor warlords would be tediously crammed with forgotten warlord names, with transient warlord victories and defeats, and with sordid and incomprehensible warlord intrigues. Two consular posts in Szechwan, a province in which the evils of warlordism reached their chaotic peak, will serve as extreme examples.

To the existing Szechwan posts at Chengtu and Chungking a third even more remote post, Tachienlu, was for political reasons added in 1913. Tachienlu lay nearly 10,000 feet above sea-level in Szechwan's mountainous and ethnically Tibetan western marches. It was some twelve days' journey westward from Chengtu.[42] In their dying years the Manchu dynasty found the energy to push westwards through the marches, which were brought under tighter and more direct control, and into Tibet proper, where an imperial commissioner was installed at Lhasa. On the fall of the dynasty the Chinese were expelled from Tibet, which recovered its previous *de*

facto independence. In 1913 Chinese, Tibetan, and British plenipotentiaries met in India to discuss Tibet's status and the boundary
between Tibet and the marches. During the negotiations the Indian
government wished to be kept informed of any Chinese activity in
the marches and L.M. King was sent there, ostensibly as an
assistant attached to the Chengtu consulate-general but with secret
instructions to proceed west, to make his headquarters at Tachienlu
or as near to it as the Chinese would allow, and to report any
Chinese troop movements. He was warned to avoid friction with
the Chinese authorities and to exercise the greatest tact and discretion. Originally a mere trade emporium, Tachienlu had now
become the seat of the Szechwan frontier commissioner responsible
for the marches. King duly established himself there and estimated
it to contain a resident population of 1,600 families, half of them
ethnically Chinese and half ethnically Tibetan, and a floating
population of some 5,000 tea coolies and yak-drivers.[43]

King, the son of a Customs commissioner, was not of a retiring
nature. He had just published anonymously in London an extraordinarily foolish book about China which correctly claimed that
the author had spent two-thirds of his life in China but did not
mention that the author was still in his mid-twenties. It accused the
Chinaman of being uncivilized, intellectually warped, physically
inferior, yellow, and unwashed, and contained the assertion, which
later events were to make ironic, that Far Eastern women were
unattractive. His performance at Tachienlu was infinitely better
than might have been expected from the author of such a book. He
was received with the greatest courtesy and in the first few months
his only difficulties were the mechanics of travel in the marches. All
food had to be carried, as very little could be procured along the
way, and on his first journey of nearly 400 miles in the intense
winter cold he was accompanied by a writer, 3 personal servants, 2
interpreters, and a 5-man escort, all riding ponies, by 5 pony
drivers, by 22 yaks, and by 24 porters. He himself rode a pony,
with a mule as a spare mount. The pace of the cortège was governed
by the yaks, which moved about as fast as a browsing cow, and on
the first day out it took eight hours to do less than 14 miles. In 1914
Jordan intended to withdraw him, but the Indian government
represented that withdrawal would mean the loss of their only
reliable source of information and might be interpreted as a British
loss of interest in proceedings in the marches. The Foreign Office

decided against withdrawal and paid King compliments which Jordan considered well deserved.[44] In 1915 Tachienlu was threatened with the sack by an advancing body of rebels or mutineers. The border commissioner appealed to King to intervene and King, accompanied by two missionaries and some Chinese merchants, went to and fro negotiating. At one point he was fired on at point-blank range by nervous town outposts, who missed. At another point the negotiators were detained by the rebels. Some of the rebels advocated immediate execution of the whole party but were silenced on King bringing to the rebel chief's notice 'the inadvisability of allowing the expression of such opinions'. At Chengtu the Chinese authorities, who feared King might be held to ransom, disapproved of King's initiative, so did the consul-general, and so did Jordan. Although negotiations were satisfactorily concluded and in the view of the Tachienlu missionaries only King's daring and effective intervention had saved the town from total destruction, Jordan told the Foreign Office that great courage and energy had been shown but that the grave risk incurred was not justified even by success; he proposed to warn King against any future intervention in internal disputes, not only because of the personal risk but also because the British government might become involved in a difficult situation not directly concerning them. Foreign Office minutes, while agreeing that there would have been serious trouble had King lost his life, praised his success and courage, which it was considered must have raised British prestige, and when towards the end of the year failing health required his transfer the Foreign Office expressed warm approval of his proceedings at Tachienlu.[45]

The Indian government still urged the need for a British representative in the marches, so Coales was sent. He reached Tachienlu with 67 baggage coolies and 17 chair coolies and illustrated the inconvenience of China's monetary system for travellers in the interior by expending nearly 800,000 copper cash in travelling by land through Szechwan to get to his post, the apparently astronomical sum being in fact equivalent to only a few hundred dollars.[46] Though not constitutionally robust Coales was an enthusiast for rough travel. In 1910 he had spent eight months of his home leave returning to England through central Asia, now in a four-month winter journey from Tachienlu he penetrated much further westward than King had done, and when he went on home

leave in 1917 he was bitterly disappointed that the Foreign Office, mindful of Russian susceptibilities, ruled against travelling via Lhasa.[47] He was replaced by Teichman, another enthusiastic traveller who had already made enormous journeys in north-west China.[48] Now in his early thirties, he was the son of a very prosperous German merchant settled in England and was a gruff, determined man with a kind heart, an iron constitution, unlimited energy, and a great deal of common sense. Throughout his career he was renowned for the infamous English accent and the complete absence of tones which marked his spoken Chinese,[a] and while in the marches he made only limited progress in Tibetan.[49] The Chinese forces on the western border of the marches had attacked Tibet, had been soundly beaten, and had been driven back eastwards far beyond their original positions. Teichman moved west from Tachienlu and in accordance with Legation instructions sent in May 1918 set about negotiating a truce on the basis of the new positions held by both sides. From then on defective communications kept him out of touch with the Legation. Legation instructions telegraphed in August to abandon his negotiations and to return to Tachienlu did not get through. Not until late November did he realize that there was a Legation question mark over his activities, and a fortnight after the armistice ending the First World War he was still hoping that hostilities in Europe might soon cease. In February 1919 he got back to Tachienlu. He had travelled thousands of miles through country so forbidding that in one six-day period he had crossed four passes at heights between 14,000 and 16,000 feet, he had personally beaten off at least two bandit attacks, although handicapped by the undefined status of the Tachienlu post he had negotiated a truce on the lines of his original instructions and had negotiated the release of prisoners, he had apparently had the confidence of both sides, and he had been entirely on his own. Jordan summoned him to Peking as acting assistant Chinese secretary so that he could participate in discussions aimed at inducing the Chinese government to confirm the truce. King was sent back to Tachienlu to try to keep the peace between the two sides, and Teichman spent the rest of his career in the secretariat.[50]

In 1921 King described his manner of life. His barn-like and very meagrely furnished rooms were full of icy draughts, the country round the town was too mountainous for riding or walking, there

were no other recreations, and his principal social contact was a semi-insane frontier commissioner (Teichman agreed that he was not mentally normal) who flogged and shot as he pleased but who after long acquaintance regarded King as a friend. When he called on the commissioner a mounted messenger went ahead carrying his card, and he followed with a mounted groom in front and another behind. When he called on the Tibetans on the other side of the border he was accompanied by half a dozen or so mounted and armed grooms, who served as a protection against bandits during the day or two he spent crossing no man's land, and the Tibetans received him with military pomp and ceremony. He declared himself happy enough to stay at a post which with all its disadvantages brought a measure of limelight, whereas elsewhere an officer of his seniority would be a nonentity, but he represented that as the breakdown of central authority had made his personal influence the only restraint on the now independent commissioner and on the Tibetans he should be given a consul's status. The Foreign Office responded by making him an honorary consul. The Legation realized that King was being left too long in so trying a post but political reasons against making a change prevailed until late 1922, when it was decided that the Chengtu post could carry out the Tachienlu duties.[51] Pending the arrival at Chengtu of a substantive replacement for W.M. Hewlett, the outgoing incumbent, King was ordered to take temporary charge there. Before leaving Tachienlu King sent Hewlett the advance formal notice required before any consulate marriage that on arrival he intended that Hewlett should marry him to a Tibetan. Hewlett's reaction was outrageous. Whether he disapproved of any marriage to a Tibetan, or of marriage to a Tibetan who had already given King a daughter and was again pregnant, he tore the notice up.[a] When King got there the two men quarrelled furiously, and Hewlett left after handing over to a still unmarried King. Ogden, an assistant posted to Chengtu, arrived to find office work more or less suspended in favour of heated exchanges between King and the Legation. King reputedly replied to one Legation letter that its frankness enabled him to enquire with equal frankness what could have induced the sender to marry his own wife. The Legation eventually instructed Ogden to take charge as acting consul-general and to forbid his superior King access to the office.[a] In his acting capacity Ogden had authority to perform marriages and he fixed a date to marry King. The date proved ill-

chosen. The previous day a siege of Chengtu suddenly began, on the wedding morn two shells passed within a few feet of Ogden in his bedroom and landed close by, and the marriage formalities were punctuated by a shell landing in the next compound and by other bumps and bangs.[a] The happy couple then left, never to return.

King was called on to resign, a medical certificate was faked up, the Treasury were with some difficulty persuaded to accept it, and he retired on a small pension. His domestic life in England must have been strange. He spoke very little Tibetan, his wife spoke very little English, and although a book which he published under her name alleged that both of them spoke Chinese fluently and communicated in that language Ogden's testimony was that at the time of the marriage she knew only a minimum of Chinese. Whatever her private virtues may have been her linguistic deficiencies alone would have ruled her out as the wife of a treaty port consul. In 1925 King applied through the Foreign Office for employment as an intelligence officer in central Asia. J.T. Pratt, then working in the Foreign Office, minuted that although King's marriage, the sole reason for requesting his resignation, had unfitted him for ordinary consular duties he had been very harshly treated, that the Legation were very largely to blame for having kept him so long in the remoteness of the marches, that he had been considered very able, and that in central Asia his wife would be an asset. Other minutes were likewise sympathetic, but no offer of employment could be procured. In 1929 a Labour administration was in office and on the grounds that Labour were against racial discrimination a prominent Labour politician backed King's application to Henderson, the Foreign Secretary, to be reinstated. Officials convinced Henderson that the application should be turned down and in a letter to his party colleague he stated confidentially that even before King's marriage the Foreign Office had doubted whether it would be wise for King to continue in the service. If this was not a plain lie it was extremely disingenuous, for the only thing that could have been held against King before he married his Tibetan was that he was already living with her. Mrs King died a few months after this application had been turned down, and King tried again through another Labour member of Parliament. This time the reply had the effrontery to say that in previous discussions of the case the question of the Tibetan wife had received undue prominence. Thereafter King seems to have

given up. He remarried and on his own death left his second wife practically nothing.[52] After King no consular officer resided at Tachienlu. For some years the Chengtu staff visited it during the summer and during the rest of the year a Chinese writer and an English-speaking Tibetan employee kept the Chengtu office in touch with developments.[a] Then the post lapsed entirely. Its probably very interesting archives were lost to bandits in 1924.[53]

At Chengtu itself progress back to normality was made so long as Yuan Shih-k'ai's hold on power was undisputed, despite much banditry in the countryside. A tiny group of less than a dozen, including J.L. Smith as acting consul-general and his assistant Mead, constituted the non-missionary element in the foreign community. It ran to a tennis club,[54] it gave regular dinner parties,[a] and it indulged in the treaty port obsession with status. At one of her dinners Mrs Mead was worried about the postal commissioner, who appeared to be indisposed during the meal and left as soon as it was finished, but she later learned that he had merely been registering offence at having been incorrectly seated.[a] On the fringe of the group was an extremely undesirable and extremely awkward British ex-missionary who dabbled in shady and unsuccessful business ventures. Smith had encountered him at Chungking some years before and Smith's complete nervous breakdown there had been largely ascribed to the ex-missionary's truculence. From Chengtu the ex-missionary anonymously attacked Smith and Mead in the Shanghai press as 'the dilettante consul' (Smith left a collection of Tibetan Lamaist objects of worship to the Victoria and Albert Museum) and 'an academic debutant' (Mead had taken a First at Cambridge), and his claims, complaints, and threats of proceedings were such a worry to Smith, so unduly conscientious that he was always going back to the office to make sure he had really locked the safe,[a] that there were fears of another breakdown. Then the Yunnan rising against Yuan brought Smith larger worries. Yunnan forces advanced on Chengtu, emergent Szechwanese warlords jockeyed for position, Smith and his French colleague tried unsuccessfully to mediate, and before Smith was relieved in September 1916 Chengtu changed hands at least three times.[55]

During a working wartime home leave Fox, who was commissioned as Chengtu consul-general, was usefully employed in preventing trading with the enemy. He expressed extreme reluctance to return for a third term at his titular post, which he

represented was remote, unhealthy, and out of the question for a wife at present being treated in a sanatorium for lung disease, so W.M. Hewlett was moved from Ichang up to Chengtu to act as consul-general. Shortage of money and wartime service exigencies had ruled out his taking his own considerably overdue home leave, but he had sent his wife, three children, and a governess back to England earlier in the year and was therefore temporarily free of family ties. Apart from a short home leave in 1919 he stayed in Chengtu until the end of 1922 amid incessant civil wars or threats of civil war. His responsibilities were heavy and he had no assistant. He described the condition of his house, whose floors were rotten and many of whose rooms had lost their straw and paper ceilings, as appalling and scandalous. He began a long sacrifice of normal family life, the family being together for only eighteen months in the next thirteen years.[56] In compensation he made his name at Chengtu.

So rife was banditry that on his way to Chengtu from Chungking the Chinese authorities provided him with a military escort of two lieutenants, whom he tipped $5 each, and sixty men, whom he tipped $1 each. The year 1917 began peacefully for him and in April he reported that the preceding quarter had been singularly uneventful. The very next day hostilities broke out between Yunnanese forces holding part of the city and Szechwanese forces holding another part of it, while Kweichow forces remained neutral. Casualties among the combatants did not exceed 200 but there were some 3,000 civilian casualties. Trying to mediate, Hewlett and the French consul took Szechwanese terms to Yunnanese headquarters. There they got cut off by renewed firing. The Yunnanese commander, his staff, and the two consuls got what sleep they could in a single room, with coverings borrowed from soldiers, and shelling and rifle fire made it necessary to change rooms three times in the night. The following morning the consuls had difficulty in leaving. The cease-fire which was sounded before their first attempt to leave served only as a signal for increased firing. At the second attempt they got out safely and continued negotiations. In the street containing the consulate-general the opposing forces were a mere 100 yards or so apart and Hewlett had to walk between them every time he went out, but both sides treated him very courteously. The mediation succeeded and a truce was arranged, Yunnanese and Szechwanese both agreeing to quit

the city and to leave the Kweichow forces in possession. In August it was the turn of the Kweichow and Szechwan forces to fight. Hewlett was woken by a terrific fusillade and throughout the day the consulate-general was incessantly hit. The Kweichow men fell back, burning street after street with much loss of civilian life. Hewlett replied to repeated civilian appeals for his intervention that he would act only at the request of the combatants, who made no such request. The Kweichow forces eventually agreed to leave the city and were overwhelmed as soon as they got outside it. The destruction and desolation appalled Hewlett, who estimated that an eighth of China's finest city had disappeared.

A Szechwanese, Liu Tsun-hou, was left in possession, but his position was weaker than it looked. When he was attacked in 1918 he was deserted by everyone except two right-hand men and about fifty soldiers. He pleaded with Hewlett, whom he had asked to call, to arrange for a week's respite and was urged by Hewlett to face facts and to leave at once. Later that day he fled through a hole in the city wall behind his headquarters while 700 wounded soldiers wrecked his offices. The incoming general confessed to Hewlett that the Kweichow troops with him were rather a problem and that he would prefer a Yunnanese contingent not to arrive. The incumbent police commissioner, who had had ambitions of his own, asked Hewlett to call the same day. He was so agitated that he burst into tears and Hewlett left him sobbing convulsively, but he recovered sufficiently to threaten to blow any attacker to pieces and thus to secure his confirmation as police commissioner. In the nick of time before Liu's flight Hewlett settled an Indian's claim for some $4,400 compensation for losses incurred during the 1917 fighting. In response to his incessant pressure over many months he was successively offered 300 taels, $1,000, $3,000, and $3,600. Hewlett settled for the last sum on condition of immediate payment. The treasurer was ordered to make the payment but refused to make it. Hewlett declined a luncheon invitation from Liu, giving the failure to pay as his reason. The next day the treasurer paid $2,000 and said he had no more money, but thanks to the good offices of a Chinese bank manager the balance was paid in a few more days. Less than a fortnight later Liu fled. If payment had not by then been made the wearisome negotiations would have started again from scratch. Hewlett called it a typical case, settled only through his personal relations with Liu and with other leading

officials. The next warlord, Hsiung K'o-wu, was driven out by
Yunnanese in the middle of 1920, and Chengtu was garrisoned by
what Hewlett called a horde of organized brigands drawn from the
worst classes. This was the ninth change of government in four
years, and another promptly followed with the return of forces
under Liu and Hsiung, now acting in co-operation. Hewlett
watched the attack from the outlook on top of his house until he
came under fire; 'after about 6 shots had been fired, and being
satisfied that they were in fact aimed directly at the outlook, I
descended'. Liu called on Hewlett, the meeting was hearty, and the
two men spoke of their last meeting, two and a half years earlier,
just before Liu's flight. Within six months Liu had been ousted
again.

Throughout all these changes Hewlett cultivated good personal
relations with as many generals and other prominent Chinese as he
could, in the conviction that on a personal basis he could get things
done which he would not get done by official approaches. He
conceded that it was wrong in principle for the maintenance of
British rights to depend on his personal influence and regretted that
the influence often had to be acquired by social eccentricity and by
a greater expenditure of nervous energy than anyone who had not
served in the interior since 1911 could conceive. He saw with
disgust and indignation the sufferings of the common people caused
by the selfish personal ambitions and moral degradation of military adventurers and at the same time sedulously cultivated the
adventurers' society without being apparently conscious of any
great contradiction. He saw, or persuaded himself that he saw, a
better private side in men whose public actions were contemptible.
He had for example the lowest opinion of Liu as a public man, but
in private found in him a friendly and polite, if unduly suave, man
who in other circumstances would merely have been a good
companion of the jolly schoolboy type.

His policy paid off, and at the Legation a minute by Teichman
contrasted the success achieved by Hewlett's 'wonderful personal
influence over all these wretched people' with the failure of Eastes,
who while acting during Hewlett's home leave had taken a stiff
correct attitude, had fulminated about referring issues to the
Legation, and had effected nothing. The same minute threw light
on Hewlett's mysterious reference to social eccentricity by remark-
ing admiringly on 'his willingness to drink champagne, beer,

liqueurs, wine etc. and drink them all under the table'.[57] A warlord dining with one of Hewlett's successors pointed out to the vice-consul an elderly rug on the floor and recalled that the last time he had dined in the house Hewlett had been on all fours on the rug, pretending to be a bear and bitting at the warlord's legs.[a] The consulate-general's writer explained to the same vice-consul Hewlett's technique for disposing of minor incidents, such as a missionary in trouble in the interior. Hewlett would telephone the warlord of the day and after enquiring after his hang-over and so forth would say that some vague unconfirmed story had come to his ears about some missionary or other being in trouble at a place he believed was called so-and-so, that there was probably nothing in the story but that it would be kind of the warlord to make enquiries; upon which the missionary's troubles would cease.[a] Hewlett combined these informalities with keeping up appearances in public. On official calls he was preceded by a messenger bearing his card. Then came two runners wearing the consular uniform which Hewlett had designed (if it was night-time they carried large paper lanterns on which the Chinese characters for 'British consul-general' were written).[a] Behind them came the consul-general himself, carried in his chair by four uniformed chair-men.[58]

No successor at Chengtu matched Hewlett's performance.

THE TWENTIETH-CENTURY SERVICE

WITH the new century came a greater official readiness to concede that the efficiency of the service and the conditions for its officers were not necessarily ideal, but few radical changes were made except in recruitment.

In 1907 the Foreign Office chief clerk alleged that the officers currently in China would in the home civil service be mere second-division clerks on £350 or so a year. This was the grossest exaggeration, but there had by then for some years been a consensus that 'a better type of man' was needed not only in China but in all the consular services. What type of man would be better was a matter on which opinion was much divided and on which there was much muddled thinking. Some favoured public-school men, an expression evidently used as a synonym for gentlemen, others favoured university graduates, whether gentlemen or not, yet others favoured men, described as coming from a lower social class, who had been intimate in their home life with business matters or who had been put into business houses at the age of 18. From the debate emerged a decision that in the Far Eastern entrance examination limited competition should be substituted for open competition. The reasonable and desirable aim of the substitution was to eliminate candidates who, though they might after due cramming succeed in a written examination, lacked the personal qualities enabling them to represent their country worthily, but some at least of those advocating limited competition came close to implying that the personal qualities desired went hand in hand with gentility. The examination and the age limits for sitting it at first remained unchanged, but after 1904 only those who were recommended by members of Parliament, aristocrats, schools, universities, admirals, generals, and the like and who then survived an interview before a Foreign Office selection board were nominated by the Foreign Secretary as eligible to compete. The Foreign Office made this change

without running into criticism, but in 1908 Barrington, although himself strongly in favour of limited competition, warned that an outcry in the new House of Commons was probable if a similar change then under consideration for the Levant service, the only service under the Foreign Office entry into which was still by open competition, were carried into effect. Nevertheless the Levant service also went over to limited competition.[1] The selection board was a stiffer hurdle than the recommendation, which was readily obtainable, but the board was considered by the Foreign Office after some years' experience of its operation a not altogether satisfactory instrument for assessing such desirable qualities as tact, discretion, powers of observation, judgement, and personal address.[2] No China entrant is known to have described his appearance before the board. Reader Bullard, an eminent Levant service officer from a humble background, thought he had been lucky to get in just before the introduction of limited competition,[a] and one gentlemanly but indigent Levant service entrant wryly recalled being asked at his interview whether he hunted or shot and what his clubs were. A Levant service belief that the board was snobbish is evidently implied, but the facts from the China service do not support the charge. During the five years for which the 1905 system lasted the social mix among the twenty China entrants does not seem to have differed from the earlier mix. Close on half of them crammed at the unpretentious King's College civil service department, and at least a quarter came from backgrounds well removed from gentility.[3] The nomination given to R.S. Pratt is noteworthy. He came of a family which had long been connected with India and into which Indian blood had entered. The Indian blood showed in some members of the family.[a] It was easily noticeable[a] in an elder brother, J.T. Pratt, who had already entered the China service, and in another brother who was not considered bright enough to attempt the examination[4] but who as Boris Karloff made his name in horror films. It was far more noticeable in R.S. Pratt. As a young man he was good-looking, but so swarthy and Indian in appearance that he startled the students' mess on his arrival in Peking.[a] Both consular brothers were extremely sensitive about their heritage and it was a handicap to them in China.[a] When acting consul-general in Shanghai J.T. Pratt was said to have encountered some colour feeling among the British community and behind his back the Chinese staff called him the black consul, while at a port at which R.S. Pratt was consul a

leading British subject used to think it witty to invite him to perform the Indian rope trick.[a] Against the background of such oafish
contemporary prejudices the board deserves some credit for accepting R.S. Pratt's candidature. As was to be expected the number
of candidates sharply declined with the introduction of limited
competition, 53 candidates competing for 4 Far Eastern places in
the last year of open competition and 41 candidates for 10 places in
the first year of limited competition.[5] On the other hand Jordan
considered that there was a marked improvement in the standard of
China entrants.[6]

Soon the examination itself was changed. Jordan reiterated his
1896 plea for better educated recruits and recommended that in
order to attract university graduates the Far Eastern entrance examinations should be brought into line with the examinations for
other more prestigious services. With Lord Salisbury out of the
way there was no longer any opposition. The Civil Service Commission advised that university candidates would best be attracted
by holding the entrance examinations simultaneously with the examinations held annually for entry into the home and Indian civil
services and into other services and by adopting with any necessary
modifications the same scheme of examination. The advice was
accepted and the new system was put into effect in 1910. The
principal modification for Far Eastern service candidates was that
they took considerably fewer papers than candidates for the top-
grade services. Age limits of over 21 and under 24 were the same
for all candidates. So were the papers. They were far more demanding than those set for the old examination, in which a
China entrant had not long before obtained over half-marks in one
subject after three weeks' reading. Jordan described the papers
which a new entrant brought out with him as awful and said that
he himself would not get 5 per cent in any of them.[7] The disappearance of the wretched old examination, casually and ama-
teurishly devised fifty years before, only marginally altered in
subsequent years and held at irregular and unpredictable intervals,
and its replacement by a well-devised examination held at the same
time each year might have been expected to encourage candidatures. The reverse was the case, and the number of Far Eastern
service candidates plummeted. The first two examinations in 1910
and 1911 did not produce enough successful candidates to fill all
the vacancies, and two China places had to be filled by appointing

men who had narrowly missed Foreign Office and general consular service places. In 1912 the last three China vacancies were filled by men whose marks were far below an acceptable standard and who received appointments only because the Foreign Office and Civil Service Commission had between them failed to stipulate that candidates not reaching a given overall number of marks would be failed. The worst performer among the three got 301 marks, as against the 1,750-odd marks of the top candidate, and did not last long at Peking. The 1913 examination produced only just enough successful candidates to fill Far Eastern vacancies, and at the end of their first year both the China recruits were accused by the Legation of having an inadequate conception of work.[8] There were a few good recruits under the 1910 system, but the overall result of its introduction was most disappointing. The Foreign Office were mystified by the dearth of candidates, as was Jordan, and they tried rather inexpertly to puff the advantages of the Far Eastern services through university appointment boards.[9]

In the immediate aftermath of the First World War all consular service appointments were made by competitive selection by a board consisting of officials and businessmen.[10] The board were markedly successful in selecting recruits for the Levant service.[a] They were markedly unsuccessful in selecting China recruits,[11] a number of whom, scarred by their war experiences, came to grief in ways over which it is kindest to draw a veil. The Civil Service Commission written examinations were resumed in 1921. The examination for the Far Eastern services was combined with that for the general and Levant consular services. Consular candidates were now required to take the same number of papers as candidates for the diplomatic service and for the home and Indian civil services, and consular candidates could compete for entry into these other services as well as for entry into the consular services.[12] The nomination system was dropped for all services under the Foreign Office,[13] but although examinations included a dreaded viva voce ordeal the Foreign Office still insisted on consular candidates being interviewed by a preliminary selection board before being allowed to sit. What standards were applied by the board, which was not entirely composed of officials, has not been ascertained, but appearance before it was no formality. In 1922 only 24 out of 36 persons interviewed were passed as suitable to sit, in 1930 17 out of 20, in 1931 34 out of 42.[14]

The results of the 1921 changes were as disappointing as those of the 1910 changes had been. In 1927 a Foreign Office official wrote that for reasons neither the Foreign Office nor the Civil Service Commission could explain there had for years been a horrible lack of recruits for all the consular services. On the 1930 examination results becoming known he asserted that the number of qualified candidates that year had considerably exceeded consular vacancies, but he spoke too soon. The first nine qualified candidates opted for the general consular service or home civil service and the next three for the Levant service. Two out of the next six declined a Far Eastern appointment and two went to China and two to Japan. For the single Siam vacancy four qualified candidates were left. One failed his medical, one was believed certain to turn Siam down, and the other two had done so badly in their vivas, a good performance in which was considered very important, that it was decided to leave the vacancy unfilled.[15] The Far Eastern services were the worst affected by the 1921 changes. Their situation had been radically altered. Previously candidates for the Far Eastern services had sat an examination in the hope that success would take them to China or Japan rather than Siam. Now candidates usually sat the combined consular examination in the hope that success would take them anywhere but the Far East, and apart from occasional exceptions the Far Eastern services received reluctant, or at best unenthusiastic, recruits. The candidates who passed highest almost invariably opted for the general service and the next on the list for the Levant service, leaving the Far Eastern services with those who had passed too low to have any other choice. It was noted in Whitehall in 1926, and again in 1934, that the China service, once a *corps d'élite*, was regularly getting men from the bottom of the examination barrel. The only crumb of comfort offered by one Foreign Office minute was the suggestion that in China the bottom men might be as useful as their brainier competitors.[16] As no selection board, viva voce, or written examination could establish the presence or absence in candidates of two qualities highly desirable in China, a modicum of physical courage and a good sense of humour, there may occasionally have been a slight element of truth in the suggestion. The difficulty in getting recruits for China was so acute that in 1927 a reversion to the old-style recruitment of young men of 18 or 19 straight from school was mooted, but this was not pursued.[17]

The China service might have been expected to have attractions. The Siam service remained an unpopular backwater, and consular work in Japan, where extraterritoriality had been abolished, had ceased to be semi-political and had become so routine as to be barely distinguishable from work in the general service. Continued extraterritoriality in China gave the China service a superior status. In 1926 Macleay as minister at Peking said that neither the general nor the Japan service could be compared with a service whose officers, particularly at the large ports, had 'duties of the greatest consequence and responsibility — more often than the heads of many diplomatic posts'. A Legation committee said in 1928 that the service's status, duties, and responsibilities resembled those of other consular services only in name and that much, if not most, of senior officers' work was political and diplomatic in character.[18] Probably there was no single cause for the service's failure to attract. China may simply have seemed too far away and uncomfortable. On the other hand Palairet, chargé d'affaires in 1925, said that as the Customs had a waiting-list of British candidates for recruitment the chaos in China could hardly be the main objection to the China service, and he put part of the blame on the ever-soaring cost of living. In this he was not alone. Jordan in his later years as minister constantly and with increasing vehemence represented that owing primarily to unfavourable exchange rates officers were in the direst financial straits and could barely afford home leave, one consul in 1920 was known to have only one suit of clothes, and associations representing British traders in China formally voiced dissatisfaction at the entire inadequacy of consular pay, which they called a public scandal.[19] Then there was a widespread feeling in the service in the mid-1920s, an exceptionally troubled period in China, that it had been let down at home, and it was not agreeable for men carrying out the home government's often unwelcome instructions to be accused by reactionary British businessmen of being spineless, lazy, defeatist, and anxious only to liquidate British responsibilities in China.[20] Palairet and others put the main blame, however, on the notorious promotion blockage, which became so bad that Affleck, a competent 1902 entrant, was promoted consul-general only at the age of 56.

Although the primary cause of the blockage was the imbalanced staff structure produced by the inordinate number of juniors recruited around the turn of the century there were still unen-

lightened voices urging that the mistake should be repeated. In the early 1920s the Foreign Office relieved the staff shortage by sending out to China a number of clerical officers seconded from the home civil service but they disparagingly called this useful and indeed overdue innovation an expedient.[21] Clerical officers enterprising enough to volunteer for secondment to unknown China tended almost by definition to be of above average quality. One of them, Pelham, attracted attention by starting to learn Chinese, was allowed to take the student interpreters' language course at Peking, and on completing it creditably became a fully fledged member of the China service.[a] The Foreign Office shut that door to promotion behind Pelham,[22] but others among the clerical officers deservedly rose to heights which they would have been most unlikely to have reached had they stayed at home.[a] Valuable though they were the clerical officers were initially viewed with suspicion in some quarters, and the British community at Hankow had difficulty in deciding whether the first clerical officer sent there should or should not be invited to dinner.[a] As late as 1927, when the service numbered about eighty officers, the then minister, Lampson, was contending that the clerical officers' posts would be better filled by student interpreters recruited from among intelligent and physically fit young men of the public-school type.[23]

If, however, the introduction of clerical officers prevented the structural imbalance from increasing it did nothing to reduce the existing imbalance, and advances in tropical medicine made the promotion blockage worse. Seniors in better health than their predecessors stayed on longer. They were frequently past their official best and stood in the way of more vigorous juniors. Jordan, arguing for earlier retirement in appropriate cases, said it was incontrovertible that in China the ability and mental and physical energy of many officers, especially those who had long served at outports, became sapped after twenty-five years or so; 'they become a dead weight with which it is a false economy to burden the state, to which the termination of their employment is an unmistakeable advantage'. The impediment lay in the superannuation acts. No amount of notional pensionable years added for unhealthy service gave an entitlement to retire a day before 60 unless ill-health was medically certified, so that at least in theory the privilege of added years was, as Jordan put it, robbed of all its advantages 'except for those whose state of health makes it improbable that they will enjoy

their pension for any length of time'.[24] In practice the inconsistency of Treasury reactions to medical certificates made applications to retire early on medical grounds something of a lottery. In 1907 Hopkins, who at the age of 53 applied to retire in such excellent health that he lived to 97, told the Legation semi-officially that he could furnish only a weak certificate but had brought into it everything of which he could think; of course bad health was not the reason he wanted to retire but after thirty-four years' service he thought himself entitled to go. He got his pension, but in 1912 the Treasury were very awkward over Sundius, who unlike Hopkins was really in poor health at the age of 48. He said that although he was suffering from no particular disease he had a chronic cough, the slightest physical exertion tired him, and for two years he had been practically living on boiled milk and Sanatogen as his digestion could no longer cope with old buffalo and goat masquerading as beef and mutton, with stringy tasteless fowl, or with sawdust bread and formalin-treated butter; he did not think himself likely to make particularly old bones (in fact he died at 59); he thought it not unreasonable to wish to pass his last few years at home; and he was 'quite prepared to forego without a single regret the privilege of seeing another native of this favoured land [China] during the term of my natural life'. His medical certificate said that further residence in China would be very prejudicial and even dangerous to his life, but the Treasury maintained that as it did not say he was actually incapable of discharging his duties it did not satisfy superannuation act requirements. The Foreign Office replied that if a pension could not be awarded in such circumstances amending legislation was needed, further medical certificates were produced, the Treasury backed down, and Sundius was pensioned.[25]

In 1912 and 1919 Foreign Office committees recommended lowering the retiring age for consular officers with unhealthy service. Although the statutory provisions remained unaltered for years, administrative action seems gradually to have gone a long way towards lowering the age in practice, for in 1928 the Foreign Office, who the previous year had expressed the unprecedented view that 'on almost every point on which we approach them nowadays the Treasury show an entirely reasonable spirit', indicated to the Legation that there was at present every disposition to facilitate retirements rather than to block them.[26] When legislation was at last passed reducing the retirement age to 55 it

continued to be supplemented by administrative action. In the
1930s an oral assurance was given to at least one entrant that for
pension purposes ergophobia would after the age of 50 be treated
as an incurable disease.[a] Administrative action which could be used
in consular officers' favour could also be used against them. At the
time Jordan was arguing in favour of retirement before 60 the
theoretical position was that an officer of good conduct could if he
chose stay on to 65. The practice was different. When nearing 60
Playfair, O'Brien-Butler, and W.H. Wilkinson were all considered
past their work and it was agreed that their retirement would
benefit efficiency. The Foreign Office decided that Playfair should
be called upon to retire at 60, though as he spontaneously decided
to go at that age this did not have to be done. Jordan recommended
that the other two should be told that they would be granted their
pensions at 60.[27] This was probably done in the case of O'Brien-
Butler, who went quietly, and was certainly done in the case of
W.H. Wilkinson, who did not retire from Hankow at all quietly.
He denied a charge, which sixty years later his then assistant at
Hankow still considered most unfair,[a] that he had failed to protect
British Yangtze shipping. He protested that as he had not finished
educating his children he had intended to stay until 65 and that as
he was being constrained to forego that right he should receive an
enhanced pension or, which he would prefer, some mark of public
recognition. He bombarded everyone with despatches and private
letters and printed and circulated the correspondence. A member of
Parliament took the case up, asked for a KCMG, which was
refused, and then put down a Parliamentary question. A minute
noted that the Foreign Office had committed themselves to the
difficult proposition that Wilkinson had not been called upon to retire in the general interests of the service but had been called upon
to retire in connection with the reorganization of the service, and
therefore recommended that the reply to the question should be as
little argumentative as possible. On that confused note Wilkinson's
attempt to obtain a larger pension or an honour died away.[28]

   Besides the voluntary or involuntary retirements of seniors who
had shot their bolts there was substantial wastage from other
causes. Some very young men still had to be invalided out and there
was still an abnormal proportion of early deaths. Slow promotion
and low pay induced at least eight useful men to resign[29] in the
hope, usually fulfilled, of doing better in other employment, and

two juniors[30] disliked life in China so much that they resigned. The bottle continued its ravages. Carvill, an 1894 entrant, managed in his first two years to be reproved by one minister and by a chargé d'affaires, and to be threatened with dismissal by a second minister, for unseemly and disorderly behaviour, extravagance, indebtedness, and neglect of his Chinese studies. He was not without ability and at one subsequent post was called a hard and willing worker, but at 30 he was finished and the Foreign Office had difficulty in getting him even a reduced-rate pension. He died in his bed in London some years later and the body was not found for weeks. The coroner's formal verdict was death from natural causes, but there was a hint of suicide.[31] The conduct of Keown, who entered in 1910 under the supposed safeguards of limited competition, was even less satisfactory. He drank, frequented low prostitutes, got into debt, and was suspended from the Tientsin club. When he went home on his first leave Jordan strongly recommended acceptance of the resignation he had been told to tender; repeated warnings had failed to induce him to abandon habits of intemperance and 'past experience has shown that the chance of reform in China of a man of Mr. Keown's habit is infinitesimal'. The Foreign Office were at first unusually stern and were minded to dismiss him, perhaps because his behaviour at Tientsin had become a public scandal, but then decided that his future career must not be ruined and permitted resignation.[32] Seniors as well as juniors succumbed to the bottle. In 1910 Max Müller as chargé d'affaires alleged in a semi-official letter that he had had to put Hosie under surveillance in hospital with a mild attack of delirium tremens.[33] Max Müller had a venomous pen[34] and his allegation about so distinguished a member of the service may have been exaggerated or even untrue, but however that may be there were glaring subsequent examples of seniors being incapacitated or undermined by drink, and there were discreet resignations and pensions.[a] Some of these seniors may from the start have been weaker vessels, like the juniors Carvill and Keown, but at least part of the trouble was probably due to the incessant tensions of the republican era. The tensions told in other ways too. In 1923 C.D. Smith was certified insane after telegraphing from Kiukiang that he could stand his responsibilities no longer and had thrown the office keys down the well.[a] In the same year E.A.H. Sly was in acting charge of Chinkiang. There was a guest for lunch and Mrs Sly called up to her husband that the meal was

waiting. He called back that he was coming, there was a heavy thud, and he was found to have cut his throat.[a] In the period 1897–1920 there were under ninety entrants. Five of them committed suicide and at one time or another an appreciable proportion of the remainder were said to be suffering from nervous breakdowns or nervous strain. In 1926, for example, six breakdowns from over-work or nerves had occurred in the last two years.[35] It was not without cause that Blackburn, himself eminently sane, later wrote 'China is a country which is liable to get on people's nerves'.[36] Entrants on reaching Peking were regaled with assurances, the exaggeration of which concealed an element of truth, that on past form one out of every four would die young, one would take to drink, and one would go mad, and that only the fourth would survive to become a consul-general.[a]

A provision in the 1887 superannuation act enabled men who could not discharge their duties efficiently to be pensioned off before 60 even if in good health, but a stigma was cast on those so removed.[37] The Foreign Office much preferred to use, or abuse, the medical certificate system, as they demonstrated when getting rid of Higgs in 1913 and and Byrne in 1919. Their attitude towards Higgs exemplified their customary solicitude for undeserving employees. Higgs preferred the club to work, he was dunned for debt by Chinese, and he kept failing to produce consular accounts. After reminders that the Ningpo accounts were overdue had been ignored for nearly a year Jordan persuaded the Foreign Office that Higgs was hopeless and incorrigible and that he set a bad example. At the age of 39 he was told to resign and was also told, apparently as a matter of routine, to obtain a medical certificate for pension purposes. The decision to proceed to extremes with this encum-brance to the service had not been reached unanimously in the Foreign Office, where one kindly minute had contended that 'there seems to be a recognised form of constitutional slackness which creeps over many of our consuls in the Far East, the result of climate, want of leave etc., and Mr. Higgs does not seem to suffer from it in a more pronounced form than several others'. Now further kindly minutes maintained that his neglect of duty had undoubtedly been due to inability to take leave and that the Foreign Office must do their best to get him a pension. The Foreign Office set about the task with a zeal and ingenuity worthy of a better cause. Higgs, accompanied by a wife and two children, came home

with medical certificates which included references to heart and liver trouble. Jordan, completing a standard form which required him to state among other things whether incapacity was due to excess, wrote that in his opinion heart and liver would have been in better condition had liquor and tobacco been more temperately used, but yet another kindly Foreign Office minute was of the opinion that in the Far Eastern services drinking and smoking too much should not be judged too hardly. After a first examination of Higgs the Treasury medical adviser declined to countersign the certificate. Only after he had examined Higgs again were the Foreign Office ready to approach the Treasury. They stated that the medical adviser's report was very unpromising; they did not consider that Higgs' health and powers of work would improve enough to justify his retention; such cases occurred from time to time as the result of residence in China; the Foreign Secretary wished to have only mentally and physically fit officers in China, whose growing importance made an efficient consular staff essential there. They misleadingly added that Higgs' case was similar to that of Sundius. Possibly dispirited by their lack of success over Sundius the Treasury accepted that the superannuation act requirement was satisfied, and a final Foreign Office minute noted, without overt jubilation, that there was now no question of having to remove Higgs under the 1887 act. Higgs retired on his small pension, was predeceased by his wife, and on his death left £34.[38]

Byrne's case was much more awkward. His actions as a junior assessor in court at Shanghai had been criticized locally. E.D.H. Fraser, the consul-general, at first ascribed this to the self-importance, tactlessness, and hasty temperament of a personally unpopular man, but then learned that the Chinese believed Byrne to have been taking bribes channelled through his houseboy and that several reputable British lawyers credited the allegation. Whatever the faults of the service corruption was unknown and unthinkable, and there was consternation. The houseboy, who was believed to have protection in very high Chinese quarters, fled and could not be brought to trial. Though Jordan thought the inconclusive evidence against Byrne supported rather than controverted the allegation he was advised that the evidence did not justify prosecution. He therefore favoured a full public inquiry, and the Foreign Office instructed him that pending such an inquiry Byrne should not be

permitted to resign and should not be given the home leave for which application had been made on health grounds. However, in the light of subsequent medical advice that Byrne's reason might be affected unless he were given the leave Jordan felt obliged to grant it. He did so with the gravest reluctance, as granting leave in effect meant dropping the matter. His suspicions remained and he was convinced that Byrne's return to China, where he could never again command confidence in the community, would be contrary to the public interest. He told Byrne that he had recommended to the Foreign Office that he should retire, and he told the Foreign Office that he considered retirement essential. Byrne thus arrived in England under suspicion but possibly innocent. He was prepared to retire, but the Treasury medical adviser would not countersign a medical certificate mentioning only neurasthenia, a complaint from which in his opinion a young man of Byrne's age (he was 35) usually recovered. The Foreign Office found themselves in the ridiculous position of having to ask the possibly innocent man whom they were forcing to retire whether he would object to the use of the 1887 act. The situation was saved by a slightly stronger medical certificate which the medical adviser, with whom someone may perhaps have had a word, countersigned. After retiring Byrne seems to have qualified as a doctor and to have practised in Ireland.[39]

The 1887 act provision was actually applied to the China service only twice, to remove Werner in 1914 and to remove Fletcher in 1918. Werner was a byword throughout China for maniacal quarrelsomeness. As consul at Foochow, his last post, he was not on speaking terms with eight of the thirty-five men who belonged to the club and his relationship with many of its other members was strained. He sent Jordan a despatch with sixty-two enclosures complaining about the United States consul and copied it to the United States minister. He quarrelled with successive assistants and abused them wildly to the Legation. Harding, for example, was rude, hot-headed, undisciplined, insubordinate, insolent to both Werner and his wife, had socialistic tendencies, and tried to make Werner a laughing-stock in the community's eyes.[40] The story went that the despairing Legation sent Blackburn to Foochow as an assistant with whom it would be impossible to quarrel and in less than no time were told that Blackburn had been peeping at Mrs Werner while she undressed.[a] At last Werner overstepped all limits. In the club he and his wife, respectively armed with a whip and a

stick, assaulted a Customs assistant who had given some trifling provocation. He was sent home on leave to be retired. He furnished a medical certificate that he was quite fit and that during the previous five years his health had been very good, so recourse to the 1887 act was inevitable. In seeking Treasury sanction to apply it the Foreign Office said that although it was doubtful whether Werner could be considered insane in the legal sense his condition bordered on insanity, but they did not explain why a man in that condition had not been removed earlier, as he most undoubtedly should have been. Werner asked that the published Foreign Office list should record as his reason for retirement his unwillingness to serve longer under so unjust a minister as Jordan.[41] He took himself back to China and settled in Peking, where years later his adopted daughter became the victim of a horrible and unsolved sex murder. He lived on long enough to be interned by the Japanese during the Second World War, and his doubtless quite unfounded belief that a fellow internee was the murderer added to the strains of internment camp life.[a]

Fletcher, who was highly promising and although only a second assistant had been in acting charge of Hoihow, was granted home leave in 1908 after nearly seven years in China. He went no further than Hong Kong and enquiries revealed that he was living there with a Chinese wife. He explained that he liked the Chinese, that life in China suited him, that he had lost touch with home, and that by his marriage he was irrevocably committing himself to China. J.A.T. Meadows might well have said the same about his marriage to a Chinese half a century earlier. Neither chief superintendent, minister, nor Foreign Office had displayed unease about Meadows' marriage while he was in the service, nor had the marriage stopped him from later becoming a leading and respected merchant in the mainly British community at Tientsin. Fifty more years into the twentieth century and such marriages would again be acceptable, but Fletcher married at the wrong time. Jordan told the Foreign Office that the marriage was an unfortunate example of the way in which lonely and remote posts tended to produce even in strong characters a degree of degeneration, that by his marriage Fletcher had lost caste in the eyes of the British in China, and that his usefulness would be very seriously impaired. Jordan suggested a warning to the China service that the Foreign Secretary's permission was required for marriages to Chinese. The Foreign Office saw objec-

tion to that wording but issued a confidential circular. It strongly reprobated marriages to Chinese as detrimental to the public interest; career prospects must be affected; clearly no consul with a Chinese wife could be appointed to any large commercial centre; in some cases dismissal might be necessary. Unlike Mrs Meadows, Mrs Fletcher was not illiterate and Fletcher claimed that she came of a respectable though impoverished family, but her relatives were not well viewed. Fox said that Fletcher's brother-in-law was unprepossessing, J.W. Jamieson that Fletcher's Chinese entourage was pretty poisonous, and Jordan that Fletcher's domestic arrangements put him on terms of equality and familiarity with Chinese in menial positions. Despite so much disapproval Fletcher in 1911 received a normal promotion to first assistant and was subsequently in acting charge of three posts. He was acknowledged to be a hard and conscientious worker and he sent some good reports, but in 1918, when he was in charge of Hoihow for a second time, the crash came. He requested immediate transfer for fear of assassination by a Chinese gang whom he had detected in a murder. According to his account he had while travelling to Hoihow on a French-flag vessel which carried no European officers discovered the presence on board of a kidnapped girl destined for a Hoihow brothel. The crew had learned of his knowledge, and he had overheard them talking of an intended murder which would cover their tracks. Misled by the words for 'he' and 'she' being identical in Chinese he had believed himself the intended victim and had put himself into a posture of defence in his cabin, but instead the girl had been murdered and her dismembered body thrown into the sea. On reaching Hoihow he had reported the crime to the French consul, and in revenge the gang had more than once plotted against his life. This uncorroborated story was so extraordinary that Jordan was not unnaturally incredulous and put it down to a temporarily disordered imagination. He was confirmed in his view that Fletcher's marriage had made him unsuitable for a senior post in the service. He told the Foreign Office that Fletcher could evidently not again be sent to any responsible or independent post, and while regretting so sad an ending to a once highly promising career recommended that he should be pensioned off forthwith. Fletcher made no difficulty about tendering his resignation, and why the 1887 act was used is not clear. He remained in China and died fifteen years later. In 1920 the French authorities in Indo-

China declared that his story about the murder had been almost entirely confirmed by witnesses who had been on board the vessel, that two Chinese who had admitted attacking the girl had been condemned to death, and that Fletcher had rendered a signal service to justice, but Fletcher was left in his retirement.[42]

The service had no doubt always had its views about the suitability or otherwise of the wives imported into it by its members, but evidence is scanty. For unspecified reasons Jordan strongly disapproved of Higgs' marriage in 1906 to a widow in Shanghai and said that ever since Higgs had been little good.[43] In 1907 Fulford commented from Mukden that not all the Newchwang community were likely to appreciate society being led by the local American merchant's daughter whom Tebbitt had just married at Newchwang, but he did not explain whether the objection was to her personality, her background, or her nationality.[44] Marrying into missionary families was not well thought of. In 1910 W.H. Wilkinson at Chengtu hurried his assistant Toller away from the city in a bid to prevent him from marrying a missionary widow,[a] and in 1922 Ogden was warned that his intention of marrying a missionary's daughter was ill-advised.[a] Neither man was deterred and both lived happily ever after.[a] By 1919 the Foreign Office were overtly interested in the suitability of consular wives. A Foreign Office committee which sat that year was told that wives of the right sort could play a large part in helping their husbands and that in the Levant service there had of recent years been far too much marrying of foreigners, often of the Levantine type,[45] and there are indications thereafter that the Foreign Office liked to have information about wives and in particular whether they were British by birth.[46] There were eminently helpful wives. Hosie's first wife drew the maps accompanying the reports of his travels, and Ogden in a privately printed memoir commemorated his wife's contribution to his eventful career.[47] During an emergency at Changsha Burdett and his wife would lie together in their double bed decyphering the urgent telegrams received during the night, and when Pearl Harbour caught Burdett incapacitated by serious illness it was his wife who burned the Chefoo cyphers and war contingency plans under the noses of the Japanese.[a] Equally there were wives, best forgotten, who impeded or ruined their husbands' careers.[a]

Widows continued to be left in indigence. The position in which

E.D.H. Fraser's sudden death as consul-general at Shanghai left his family was not the worst case, but on account of his pre-eminent position it shocked the service. In early life he had burdened himself financially by helping his step-mother pay off the debts of her cashiered son,[a] and the calls made on him by his own relatives had made saving impossible. In 1910 he had applied from Hankow to retire on health grounds and was much troubled to receive instead the offer of Shanghai, a post which was uncongenial to him but which Jordan was convinced no one else in the service would fill anything like as well. His health was so poor that the Treasury would not allow him to opt into newly introduced superannuation arrangements which would have provided the family with a small lump sum on his death. He believed he would live longer at home, and felt that acceptance of Shanghai meant sacrificing the claims of his family to the claims of public duty. His wife insisted that duty to the service must come first, and he accepted Shanghai.[48] He probably lasted longer there than he had expected, but when eleven years later he died at his post, after an incumbency so distinguished that the leading local paper, not given to praising the service, declared that Shanghai would not look upon his like again, his original fears for his family were realized. He had not finished educating his children, whose education had to be broken off, and the Foreign Office, who were not successful in obtaining a civil list pension for the widow, expected her to be dependent on charity. Lady Fraser, however, struck a modern note and within six months got herself a position at an Eastbourne girls' school.[49]

The service continued to be administered by the ministers at Peking. In 1917 the Foreign Office consular department opted out of comment on a China consul's memorandum on China service organization on the grounds that the department had practically nothing to do with the service.[50] At the end of the First World War a Department of Overseas Trade, answerable jointly to the Foreign Office and to the Board of Trade, was established. It was given responsibility for all the consular services and administrative control of the consular department,[51] but it was a long time before there was much impact on China service administration. In 1922 a Peking recommendation that certain consuls should be passed over for promotion elicited in the Foreign Office only the comment that in such cases the minister's recommendations were invariably accepted. The annual reports on consuls which the Legation had in

1916 been instructed to furnish must in these circumstances surely have been so much waste paper.[52] In 1927 the consular department were still stating that the China service was administered from Peking subject to only nominal Foreign Office approval.[53] The Department of Overseas Trade and the consular department had an uphill struggle even to induce China officers to call during home leaves, and Teichman retired in 1936, after years as the Legation's right-hand man, without having made himself known in the consular department. It was probably not until the 1930s that Peking's recommendations about appointments ceased to be automatically accepted.[54]

Satow (1900–6) and Jordan (1906–20), the first two ministers appointed in the twentieth century, had both been promoted into the diplomatic service from a Far Eastern consular service. Their consular background was both advantageous and disadvantageous for China officers serving under them. The advantage was that they had both had first-hand experience of consular life, and Jordan indeed knew most members of the service personally. The disadvantage was that in their official youth they had lived hard and in a more modern world expected men to go on living hard. The Foreign Office retrospectively considered Little's abominable living conditions at Samshui to have been rather a scandal, but Satow's comment was that Little had had to put up with the conditions for only two years.[55] Jordan, who had waited eight years for his first home leave and nearly as long for his second, objected to a proposal that juniors should get leave every three years, and he flatly turned down an application for an adequate married quarters rent allowance from an assistant who had married at the age of 27, which Jordan considered unreasonably young.[56]

Satow, his fiery youth behind him, had turned into an efficient, wary, discreet, and impeccably groomed diplomatist. Unlike Jordan[57] he was a most methodical paper worker, so much so that alone among the ministers he preserved for posterity, neatly filed, the private correspondence between himself and members of the service. His discretion could verge on deviousness. Having removed Ker from the post of assistant Chinese secretary he drew attention in an official despatch to Ker's zeal and efficiency and to MacDonald's high appreciation of Ker's services, whereas a semi-official letter had previously given notice that he intended to replace little Ker, whose only virtue was some knowledge of the

language, who was intellectually a child, and who was quite inadequate for a post which needed some character and ability.[58] Satow had been trained in Japan under Parkes, with whom he did not hit it off but from whom he acquired the habit of driving himself and subordinates hard.[59] He was not impressed by the China service. Promotion strictly by seniority seemed to him to have induced an all too apparent lack of emulation and in appropriate cases he favoured promotion by merit, an attitude which the Foreign Office endorsed.[60] Jordan was generally admired as an able, just, and straightforward chief. Having been bred in the service Jordan had views about its organizational defects. Besides trying to secure reform of the entrance examination, the removal of dead wood and of undesirables, the lowering of the retiring age, the improvement of pay, and the closure of minor posts, he set about improving the flow of information from the Legation to the consulates. How necessary this was can be judged from Clennell's statement, after receiving a first batch of Legation information slips at Tsinan in 1907, that hitherto he had frequently been ignorant of the whereabouts of half or more of the men in the service.[61]

The next two ministers, Alston and Macleay, were run-of-the-mill career diplomatists who left no great mark on the China service. Lampson, another career diplomatist who took over in 1926, was an able, energetic, domineering prima donna, characteristics which later led to his elevation to the peerage. So lordly was his lack of interest in small fry that a new entrant after months in Peking found himself being introduced to his own chief by the Japanese minister.[a] Lampson's ability was recognized in the service, but as a man he was little liked.[a] He was notoriously tight-fisted,[a] and the jovial and far from teetotal encounters with which he usefully lubricated relations with the Chinese[a] were not felt to square with his fulminations against consular drunkenness.[62] Those most resentful of his lack of consideration and of sensitivity in his dealings with them[63] might have been surprised to learn how strongly he kept representing to Whitehall that the tumultuous conditions in China imposed an almost intolerable strain on the service.[64] He was not a sophisticated administrator. His ideas did not go much beyond placing great emphasis on promotion by merit rather than by seniority, and Whitehall was probably right in considering that he was disposed to go too far in that direction.[65]

The ministers relied heavily on the Chinese secretary. On leaving

Peking Satow said that he had regarded the secretary of Legation and the Chinese secretary as his twin advisers, and that Campbell as Chinese secretary had drafted far the larger part of the Legation's official and semi-official correspondence with the Chinese. Jordan subsequently recalled that as Chinese secretary he had done the same under O'Conor and that under MacDonald Cockburn had perhaps done even more of the drafting.[66] This did not suit the subordinate diplomatic staff. By 1909 diplomatists at Peking and Tokyo were complaining privately to the Foreign Office that the ministers left too much of the missions' work to the Chinese and Japanese secretaries, and when Max Müller was sent to Peking as counsellor a Foreign Office official asked him to look into the complaints. In private correspondence with the Foreign Office Max Müller accused Campbell, whom he characteristically chose to call a consular interpreter, of keeping all the interesting work away from the diplomatic staff and of treating them with disdain, and said that the interpreters had become much too powerful and that the position of the Legation's diplomatic staff was all wrong. A Foreign Office voice warned that Campbell was a very good man and that Max Müller, who was clever but thought a good deal of himself, would probably want to boss Campbell completely, but the warning was ignored, and although Max Müller was told to be most tactful in handling the situation his views were approved. On becoming chargé d'affaires the next year Max Müller handled the situation with such total and offensive tactlessness that Campbell, who was in bad health and probably touchy, retired in dudgeon.[67]

Max Müller offered F.E. Wilkinson the post. Wilkinson, refusing the offer because his Chinese was not good enough, refused it in terms which showed what a prize the post was considered. He said he knew only too well that this was the parting of the ways for him and that by not accepting he was giving up his ambitions and the best chance of his life. In a sense events proved him right. He served for another eighteen years with courage, competence, political acumen, and good sense, but although he ended as a trusted consul-general the valuable work of his later years was not recognized by any honour.[68] Nothing was altered by Campbell's retirement. His successors were at least as influential in the Legation as he and his predecessors had been, and the position of the Legation's diplomatic staff remained much as before. In 1938 Clark Kerr as ambassador to China even suggested to the Foreign Office that

Blackburn's competence as Chinese counsellor made the diplomatic counsellor superfluous and that the latter could be withdrawn, a suggestion which the Foreign Office turned down as contrary to the interests of the diplomatic service.[69] These problems were solely due to the ever more archaic caste distinction, latterly known to consular officers as 'the gulf' and as unhappily obvious to the Levant service as to the China service, between the diplomatic service and the consular services.[70] Caste feelings prejudicial to the public interest were not new in China, for in the 1860s Wade as Chinese secretary had not taken kindly to the secretary of Legation's frequently expressed opinion that consular interpreters should be kept in their places,[71] but the archives somehow convey the impression that consciousness of the gulf gradually became stronger on both sides. A private document points in the same direction. In the 1920s Turner became consul and accountant at Peking, a post which involved responsibility, 'under the minister and Chinese secretary', for arranging all consular moves and transfers.[72] Turner does not seem to have been filled with unbounded admiration for his diplomatic colleagues in the Legation. He composed and circulated to consular intimates an imaginary exchange of despatches and telegrams between fictitious Legation staff and a fictitious consul at a fictitious consular backwater. The scenario was some preposterous incident which had suddenly disturbed the forgotten consulate's slumbers. Imbecility and unhelpfulness were the hallmarks of the diplomatists' minutes and communications, one Legation telegram reading 'no objection to course proposed provided no objection', and the story ended with a shower of honours for the diplomatists and the consul's transfer in disgrace to an even worse post.[73] On the surface it was a cheerful *jeu d'esprit* but the underlying sentiments were less comfortable.

The pool of those linguistically qualified to be considered for the Chinese secretaryship was small in 1900 and got steadily smaller.[74] The merest handful of twentieth-century entrants learned enough written Chinese to read for pleasure,[a] and the average standard of spoken Chinese was almost certainly even lower than in the nineteenth century. Although modern-minded Chinese had begun to associate with foreigners, opportunities for conversation in Chinese with educated Chinese paradoxically diminished. For some odd reason the increasing number of Chinese who spoke English well, and of others who spoke it indifferently, took it amiss if

foreigners spoke Chinese with them,[a] and the official interviews which had once been in Chinese were now often conducted in English.[75] Jordan, himself an admirable speaker, tried to improve the teaching of student interpreters by sending them for their first year to a Peking language school run by Protestant missions and having them taught by the Legation's teachers only in their second year.[76] This move was not a success. The school's prayers, hymn-singing, heartiness, and volley-ball were uncongenial, the budding missionaries were on the whole not very bright, and in vocabulary 'the archangel Gabriel' was learned before 'British Legation'.[a] Attendance at the school was later much shortened and finally eliminated altogether.[a] With or without attendance at the mission school fluent and cultured spoken Chinese, one of the service's basic needs, was rarely achieved,[a] perhaps largely because the right lead was not always given to juniors. As a junior at Shanghai in the early republic Prideaux-Brune, a future Chinese counsellor, set about making Chinese friends as a relief from the monotony of local British society, but if not actively discouraged from this course equally received no encouragement,[a] and in Lampson's day[a] one student interpreter was rebuked for spending too much time exploring Peking and not enough time at the club or on the hockey pitch.[a]

The diagnoses made by ministers of the service's ailments were supplemented by amateurish Legation inspections of consulates. As in the nineteenth century inspections took place only rarely and at irregular intervals. An inspection by Tower in 1901 came twelve years after Howard's previous inspection. Briefed by Satow to consider whether some consulates should be closed Tower concluded that although Wade and Parkes had recommended a consulate at each port it was not in the public interest that trained men should spend the best part of their lives in the complete idleness and often extremely bad sanitary conditions of minor ports. This was a sound statement of principle, but his specific recommendations, which except for his Wenchow recommendation were all accepted, were half-hearted. He recommended only the closure of the obviously useless posts at Samshui, Shasi, Soochow, and Yochow, and the definitive closure of Wenchow (which continued its shadowy existence until 1922), the amalgamation of Hoihow and Pakhoi under a consul at Hoihow and an assistant at Pakhoi, and the withdrawal of the Pagoda Island vice-consul.[77] The Foreign Office

had asked that Tower should in addition report confidentially on all the officers he met. His confidential report went semi-officially to the private secretary, Barrington. Tower barely knew the people he described, and besides being inevitably superficial his descriptions were not always in the best taste. Barrington learned for example that Flaherty was uncouth in speech and appearance, that H.E. Sly looked Jewish, that Holland was famous for misadventures in seeking marriage through matrimonial agencies, and that M. Hughes was universally known as 'Pink Mary'. This was not a very useful or creditable contribution to staff management.[78]

Tower's successor Carnegie had little to say after touring the principal ports in 1905.[79] It was presumably this tour which stimulated Little into an acid recommendation from Ningpo in 1906 that inspection should be periodic and much more thorough, for 'a few hours' visit to a port by a person without special knowledge and a chat with the consul is not calculated to lead to any satisfactory result'. Little submitted his own views on what was wrong with the organization and administration of the service. Instead of being part of a team each consulate, he said, was a largely independent and separate unit left uninformed of developments elsewhere. Improved communications and the concentration of trade in a few big centres at the expense of dwindling outport communities had made small consulates out of date, and the policy of establishing consulates at new ports before local commerce had developed was equally out of date. Small consulates were responsible for most of the service's shortcomings. Their closure would stop men wasting their lives at ports where 'dreary environment, loneliness, absence of the simplest amusements, bad food, trying climate, no opportunity for physical exercise and pretty well every demoralising influence [were] calculated to drive a man to the devil', to unfit him for work, to make him eccentric, and to ruin his health. Available manpower should instead be concentrated in large consulates providing better commercial intelligence. Training and leave arrangements should be improved, uniform office procedures introduced, China officers should be posted to other parts of the world for short spells, and one of them should always be attached to the Foreign Office.[80] Little's analysis and recommendations were much to the point, but they came from the wrong source. He was known to be prickly and embittered. Satow had called him a tiresome grievance-monger, Jordan's opinion was most

unfavourable, he was not in good odour with the Foreign Office, and his opinions were not seriously considered.[81] Any chance they might have had of serious consideration cannot have been increased by his submission the following year of a paper entitled 'Some Facts Descriptive of the Life of Consular Officers in China' which he ventured to suggest should be made accessible to examination candidates. The tone of this effusion can be judged from its opening, which read:

H.B.M.'s consular officers in China probably live under worse conditions than any other body of men in the world. From the age of about 30 for 15 or 20 years most of them are stationed in remote and lonely places where few of the comforts and amenities of life are obtainable. There is no social intercourse with the native inhabitants, and the foreign community is generally limited to a dozen or so missionaries, merchants and Customs officials, of whom not more than 3 or 4 can be counted on for social purposes.[82]

Such inspections as there were continued to be of poor quality. Max Müller attached so little importance to his tour of consulates in 1909 that the need to report on it escaped his memory until 1911. Between the two world wars the Foreign Office introduced inspectors-general of consulates, but the first inspection of China consulates under that system in the mid-1920s was considered in Whitehall to have been very unsatisfactory and inadequate and not to have been worth the expense.[83] None of the inspections explored the causes of unduly frequent transfers. It was exceptional for Harding to suffer five or six transfers, involving 7,000 miles of travel, in just over a year, but Willis' dozen or more postings in a career lasting twenty-five years were not abnormal.[84]

Jordan's views on minor posts were not dissimilar from Little's. He too believed in centralization. He considered that it wasted money to retain consulates at ports where trade had either decayed or showed no strong tendency to expand and that the men in charge, with little scope for their energies or abilities, frequently ran to seed and lost initiative and decision.[85] There were however obstacles in the way of closures. They were unwelcome to commercial interests,[86] they made promotion prospects still worse,[a] and even in Jordan's day some officials may have held the view, certainly expressed after his time, that small posts enabled officers to develop initiative and a sense of responsibility at the right age.[87]

Consequently posts which should have been axed lingered on. In the middle of the First World War for which he had been forbidden to volunteer H. Porter, asking whether there was any chance of his getting a real job, said that with care he could spread out his official duties at Wuhu to fill an hour a day. Wuchow provided a few hours' work a week. There was so little to do at Hangchow that it was combined with Ningpo in 1919, by which time both posts had for many years been regarded as backwaters usually filled by men of indifferent calibre.[88] Yet it was not until the 1920s that Wuhu, Wuchow, and Hangchow were formally closed and that Ningpo was allowed to fade away. The Hoihow-Pakhoi post went too, and Kiukiang and Chinkiang were abolished after the rendition of their respective concessions,[89] but other small posts regrettably remained open.[90]

After the First World War there were a few other organizational changes. The period of service entitling officers to home leave was reduced and salary reductions during home leaves were abolished.[91] The transformation of student interpreters into probationer vice-consuls and of assistants into vice-consuls was merely cosmetic, but the temporary attachment of a succession of China service officers to the Far Eastern department of the Foreign Office was a genuine advance which recognized the peculiarity of the situation in China and the need for expertise in London.[92] This process was taken a step further in 1925, when a senior, J.T. Pratt, was posted to the Foreign Office as an adviser on China. He stayed there, latterly with the rank of an acting counsellor, until he retired in 1938 and his influence on policy-making was strong enough to annoy Lampson, who minuted crossly about 'J.T. Esau'.[93] In general, however, the service, though healthier and much better housed, remained in the 1920s much as it had been in the later nineteenth century.

THE ANTI-BRITISH MOVEMENT

THE province of Kwangtung was the base of the amorphous radical grouping out of which emerged the Kuomintang, China's future government, and in which Sun Yat-sen remained until his death the best-known figure. After the collapse of Yuan Shih-k'ai's power Kwangtung declared itself independent of Peking. For years thereafter it was at best in confusion. At worst it was in anarchy, Canton and its suburbs being occupied at one point in 1923 by seventeen commanders-in-chief and over ninety independent commanders.[1] Power shifted bewilderingly to and fro. At times Sun had to leave Canton for Japan or Shanghai. At others he styled himself Generalissimo or Provisional President of China, declared war on Germany, or tried to campaign against the north.[2] Even when Sun and radical civilians were nominally in charge their control over the military element was shaky. One general supposedly supporting Sun, asked whether he had been appointed to his command by a mandate from Sun, expressed in 'a very colloquial expression' of two words (doubtless coarse) the value he placed on such mandates.[3] The Canton consulate-general had no high opinion of Sun's capacity. At one time they said that as usual he was quite oblivious of the real facts of the situation, at another that he had no real influence on events and that much done in his name was done without his knowledge.[4] The independent governments at Canton were not formally recognized by Britain. British relations with them were in the hands of J.W. Jamieson, who apart from home leaves and a few months during which he officiated at Shanghai was at Canton as consul-general from 1909 to 1926.

Lung Chi-kuang, whose sudden abandonment of Yuan's cause in 1916 had so surprised Jamieson (see p.412), found it wise to remove himself from Canton later that year. Wilton, acting as consul-general during a Jamieson home leave, had described Lung as an

uneducated but remarkably shrewd man whose personal courage
had a considerable admixture of ferocity, Jordan later called him an
ignorant aboriginal freebooter, and Jamieson treated him roughly.
For example, in what he himself described as a 'snorter', Jamieson
reproached Lung for failing to guard the Canton–Kowloon railway
line and gave Lung notice that he would be held strictly responsible
for the derailment and looting of a train by robbers; 'I have no
hesitation in stating that this deplorable incident is directly attributable to the indifference you have seen fit to display towards
repeated warnings on my part'. Nevertheless Jamieson and Lung
got on well together. On the eve of being forced out of Canton
Lung embarrassingly insisted, in spite of Jamieson's protestation
that he was forbidden to accept presents, on sending him two pieces
of porcelain, a bronze, and a panel of marble as a memento of their
friendly public and private relations. As Jamieson suspected that
the porcelain and the bronze were fakes, thought the marble practically without intrinsic value, and knew that continued refusal of
the gifts would cause offence he sought and obtained Jordan's
sanction to accept them.[5]

Jamieson's tone towards Lung's successors remained brusque. In
1918 a military governor, angered by Hong Kong's refusal to
permit the export to him of military material, threatened to seize
every British vessel in port. Jamieson sent an oral response that
'it was immaterial to me what steps His Excellency might take,
and...were he willing to assume the responsibility for embroiling
himself with Great Britain that was his affair'. Indeed, Jamieson
allowed himself considerable freedom of speech even towards the
minister. In a despatch rejecting Jordan's strictures on him for
having facilitated the export of munitions from Hong Kong to
Canton he stated that the strictures could, he felt sure, only have
been dictated by an incomplete appreciation of the local conditions
which in practice compelled the consulate-general and Hong Kong
to deal with the unrecognized southern government as though it
had been recognized by Britain. Jordan overlooked the impertinence and continued to praise Jamieson as an exceptionally able
man who had rendered eminent public service.[6]

On succeeding Jordan Alston was less appreciative. During
Jamieson's home leave in 1920 Goffe officiated at Canton and
criticized Jamieson's high-handed attitude towards the Chinese
authorities. Alston thereupon recommended that Goffe should be

substantively appointed to Canton and that Jamieson should be transferred to Hankow. Although Jamieson, the senior member of the service, was an obvious candidate to succeed at Shanghai whenever E.D.H. Fraser vacated that post, and had been selected by Jordan to officiate there while Fraser had been ill, Alston went on to recommend that Jamieson should be told not to expect appointment to Shanghai at any future date. The recommendations came before Clark, comptroller-general of the Department of Overseas Trade. He knew Jamieson of old as a man who had drawbacks of manner and who obtruded his personality but who was forceful and conspicuously able, he was repelled by Goffe's indictment of a man whose position Goffe was temporarily holding, and he opposed Jamieson being transferred to Hankow as a result of charges from such a quarter. He carried the day. To the annoyance of Alston, who claimed that for many years Legation recommendations had invariably been accepted, Alston's recommendations were rejected. Jamieson escaped with a warning from Clark that he should be less high-handed and that appointment to Shanghai would largely depend on the Legation's subsequent reports.[7] On returning to Canton in 1921 Jamieson carried on as before. In no time he was expressing to the civil governor at Canton deep regret that His Excellency should have given credence to a ridiculous lying report that a named British warship was conveying arms up the West river to rival forces; any intelligent person would know that the vessel's draught prevented her from entering the river; if Canton's agents in Hong Kong disturbed friendly relations by such false reports the Hong Kong government would be asked to deport them immediately.[8]

However brusque the tone of Jamieson's communications with the Chinese authorities he fought a running battle with Stubbs, May's successor as governor of Hong Kong, in the interests of good relations with them. In 1921 Stubbs, in a curt 5½-line despatch, rejected representations made by the Canton government through Jamieson that the Hong Kong activities of one of their opponents should be curtailed. Jamieson angrily told Alston that while professing a wish for friendly relations with the Canton government Stubbs did everything calculated to annoy them and that unless a less contemptuous attitude were adopted British interests would suffer severely, and Alston minuted that Stubbs was incorrigible. In 1922 a seamen's strike lasting nearly two months

crippled Hong Kong. Jamieson was called in to negotiate and claimed to have settled the dispute in two days by appealing to the concepts of abstract right (*li*) and fair dealing to which in his experience nearly all Chinese still responded. He was critical of Hong Kong in this particular case for having underestimated the strikers' strength, and he made more fundamental criticisms. Even more than in mainland China foreigners in Hong Kong, he said, had failed to grasp the nature and extent of changes in republican China, and notably the growth of an exceedingly sensitive spirit of nationalism; the foreigners needed to adapt to a changing China and to cultivate a sympathetic understanding with the people by whom they were surrounded and with whom they traded; instead, apathy and abysmal ignorance of the mainland prevailed at Hong Kong; Stubbs and his colonial secretary, who so regrettably lacked knowledge of the Chinese language and Chinese temperament, were in the hands of advisers who although efficient had trained in the days of imperial China and had not absorbed the atmosphere of the republic.[9] Much of Jamieson's criticism of Hong Kong, whose officials were often startlingly out of touch with mainland affairs, was justified, and he was in advance of many consular contemporaries in preaching the need to adapt. The pity was that he marred his enlightenment by controversy and by disregard for others' feelings. Stubbs told Alston that he would not be sorry to see a change of consul-general, Jamieson's open criticism of Stubbs' actions was common talk, and the bad feeling between the two men was so apparent that the Foreign and Colonial Offices enjoined a spirit of co-operation on both. Jamieson blandly replied that he had consistently worked on those lines and would continue to do so. On E.D.H. Fraser's death in 1922 he did not get the Shanghai appointment. It went to his junior, Barton, who had succeeded Campbell as Chinese secretary. Alston's recommendations about filling the vacancy were contained in private correspondence which is missing.[10]

In 1923 Sun Yat-sen came under the influence of Soviet emissaries, who set about organizing the Kuomintang apparatus on efficient Soviet lines. Stubbs was so disturbed that he proposed a loan to one of Sun's adversaries in order to keep Sun out of power. Jamieson's view was that changing conditions in China could not be ignored or resisted and that Bolshevistic anarchy was more likely to be prevented by wise counsel and sympathetic action; declaring

open war on the Kuomintang by helping their opponents would do infinitely more harm than good; Sun's name was still one to conjure with; although Sun's mental and physical breakdown was frequently reported, appointments recently made by Sun to his government did not 'yet indicate a complete departure from sanity'. He opposed a proposal by Stubbs to use British forces against nests of pirates on the mainland, arguing that an armed landing would be unlikely to commend itself to the British government and would be violently resented by the Chinese, and he opposed a proposal by the governor of Singapore to dissolve the Kuomintang organization there, arguing that in Singapore the Kuomintang would be driven underground and that in China relations with Sun and British interests would both suffer. In each of the two latter cases Macleay, who had replaced Alston, confined himself to endorsing Jamieson's arguments, although the arguments were ones which in normal conditions would have originated from the minister and not from one of his consular subordinates.[11]

Kuomintang extremists continued to strengthen their hold on the party during 1924 while Jamieson was on home leave. B. Giles, in acting charge, said that the military were the real rulers of Canton and were outside any control by civil officials and that Sun's government was a government in name only. Towards the end of the year Sun left Canton, dying soon afterwards, and the extremists had the field to themselves. Jamieson on his return described the Canton government as an entirely irresponsible and arbitrary dictatorship, did not believe that Britain could propitiate the Kuomintang's communist wing or prevent it from capturing the whole party apparatus, and feared forces similar to those which had brought the Bolsheviks to power in Russia. In Peking Macleay shared his fears. He favoured a more or less conservative government backed by Chang Tso-lin, and considered that even a Chang military dictatorship would be 'infinitely preferable to a government formed by extreme Kuomintang elements and directly inspired by the bolsheviks'.[12] Then in 1925 came the 'May Thirtieth incident' at Shanghai. International settlement police fired on students demonstrating against the treatment of Chinese workers in Shanghai's Japanese-owned mills. Some demonstrators were killed. Nothing could have suited the Kuomintang extremists and their Soviet advisers better.[13] A month earlier Ogden, far away in Chengtu, had said that the Chinese while submitting without murmur to

the most revolting and inhuman treatment by their own people
were always ready to agitate over the slightest, or even fancied,
injury done by a foreigner. Whether or not this was a curious
mentality, as Ogden claimed it to be, the Shanghai incident proved
his point.[14] Over much of China there was an immense outcry.
British influence still preponderated in the administration of the
international settlement, 85 per cent of whose foreign staff were
British.[15] The Japanese cause of the demonstration was largely
forgotten and Britain became the main target.[16] Although she was
in reality no longer strong enough to do China much harm, the
legacy of history made her in Chinese eyes the embodiment of
Western aggression. She had taken the lead in opening China and
establishing extraterritoriality, she had more of the offensive treaty
port concessions than any other power, the inspector-general of
Customs was still a British subject, Britain ruled Hong Kong, and
her activities on the Burma frontier and her interest in Tibet were
suspect. There was a flood of anti-British demonstrations, strikes,
and trade boycotts. In Manchuria and north China anti-British
manifestations were kept under firm control by Chang Tso-lin and
others.[17] In Yunnan reactions were muted. From Yunnanfu Tours
reported that the press was full of 'the sort of verbose slush in
which the "educated" Chinese mind loves to wallow', but although
the authorities would not act overtly against inflammatory placards, such as placards which depicted a British policeman at
Shanghai stabbing a Chinese boy asleep in bed, they gradually
pasted them over with official notices, and boycotting local British
trade would according to Tours have been like beating a dead dog.
Visiting two towns in his Tengyueh consular district Harding
believed he had largely dispelled rumours of war between Britain
and China by ostentatiously strolling round the streets and
spending hours, or even days, in the company of officials and gentry
and playing mahjong with them.[18] Practically everywhere except in
the north and in Yunnan, however, consular life in China became at
best tense and at worst hazardous.

At Shanghai itself the incident was followed by a strong show of
foreign force. A few months previously naval landing parties from
foreign warships had protected the port's foreign life and property
from the threat posed by a major civil war.[19] The same course was
now followed. The day after the incident Barton telegraphed a
request for at least three British cruisers, and 2,000 men were

landed from British, Japanese, United States, French, and Italian warships.[20] If Shanghai's importance for many foreign powers thus helped Barton in his efforts to preserve law and order, only his ability and his very forceful character enabled him to overcome the handicaps presented by the settlement's international constitution. He had to work with a body of eighteen consuls, 'not a few of whom are notoriously corrupt' and others among whom lacked knowledge of local conditions or even interest in them. By the end of August it was considered safe to declare an end to the state of emergency in the international settlement and to withdraw the landing parties, but British trade remained affected by an anti-British strike and boycott.[21]

Up the Yangtze there was serious trouble in the Chinkiang, Kiukiang, and Hankow British concessions within a fortnight of the Shanghai incident. At Chinkiang E.G. Jamieson, who at the beginning of the year had been narrowly missed by a bullet through his office window during a civil war, had to deal with a students' protest procession which got out of hand. The concession's police quarters were set on fire and the mob came on yelling and indicating by signs the mutilations they intended to inflict on foreign men and women. They were stopped by the concession police firing over their heads and using rifle butts. With the help of the constable and of a Chinese railway engineer Jamieson got his wife and children and some other women who were sheltering in the consulate into the relative safety of the engineer's house behind the consulate and was ready to order fire to be opened in earnest should there be another determined attack. For four hours, until Chinese troops at last arrived, it was touch and go. Jamieson got all women and children away to Shanghai on the next steamer and was commended by the Foreign Office for his courage and good judgement in most trying and dangerous conditions.[22] At Kiukiang, where Davidson was in charge, a hundred or so demonstrators broke into the consulate and started wrecking it. Davidson's mother and another woman took refuge in a bedroom, whose door resisted efforts to force it. By the time Davidson got there three fires started in the building were well alight, but it was possible to extinguish them. The Japanese consulate was sacked and a Japanese bank burned. The concession police refused to turn out and were dismissed, and it took three hours for the Chinese authorities to send troops. The Legation entirely approved Davidson's conduct.[23] At

Hankow H. Porter called on a naval landing party and the volunteers to defend the concessions against a mob of coolies, and three or four attackers were killed. The Legation entirely approved Porter's action and expressed confidence that he would judiciously mix firmness with conciliation, and the Foreign Office followed up with an expression of high satisfaction.[24]

At Nanking anti-British strikes gave B. Giles so much trouble that at the end of the year he sent a report of fifty pages plus enclosures on Nanking's anti-British movement. It was a very clear report but Macleay minuted irritably that he had no time to read anything so interminable.[25] At Chungking British property was damaged wholesale and the personal bodyguard of a notoriously anti-foreign general invaded and damaged the consulate. Archer moved to a gunboat, where one small cabin served him as bedroom and office, and evacuated British women and children.[26] From Chengtu Affleck reported that ever-present anti-foreign feeling had now become intense, and although excellent order was being kept by Yang Sen, the local warlord, who had arrested two leading agitators and threatened to behead them, things did not promise to be very pleasant for some time to come and tact would be needed to keep the peace in a city where foreigners were entirely dependent on their own resources. He had a low opinion of the student agitators, who in his view were for the most part a lazy collection of ignorant youths glad of any excuse to get away from homework and examinations, whose patriotism was confined to flag-waving, tub-thumping, and using filthy language to foreigners, and whose heads had been swollen by the commotion they had raised throughout the country. Manifestations of a general anti-foreignism continued at Chengtu into 1926. The Japanese consulate was wrecked by a mob, and a Chinese struck off the head of a Canadian woman missionary in the streets, walked on carrying the head, and threw it into a public latrine before being himself shot by police. The Chinese authorities alleged the man had been mad, but as the next day a well-dressed Chinese dragged an American woman missionary from her rickshaw and tried to strangle her Affleck suspected something more sinister.[27] At Ningpo students and roughs destroyed the shop which supplied the foreign community with provisions and a mob then destroyed the junior Customs mess, the Japanese and Russian Customs assistants saving their lives only by hiding in two of the huge jars locally used for water storage.[28]

At Canton the repercussions of the Shanghai incident were disastrous. A monster protest procession along the Shakee bund, across the creek from Shameen's British and French concessions, was arranged for 23 June. Jamieson asked that the procession should be accompanied by troops to ensure that foreigners were not molested, arranged for Shameen's naval and civilian defence forces to keep as far out of sight as possible at their posts, and prohibited other residents from appearing. Accompanied by one or two of the consulate-general staff, two or three naval officers, the police superintendent, and a few unarmed Chinese concession policemen he watched an eminently orderly procession, which included schoolchildren, move along. He was about to return to the office to report by telegram that all had passed off peacefully when first one shot, and then a volley, was fired at Shameen as a group of cadets was processing past. Bullets spattered all around Jamieson and the rest of his party and they beat a hasty retreat. Posts on both concessions returned the fire without being ordered to do so, and it was some ten minutes before cease-fire orders reached all the posts. In the concessions a French non-combatant was killed and a few people were wounded. On the other side of the creek there were heavy casualties, which Jamieson first put at 37 killed and some 80 wounded and the Chinese later put at 52 killed and 117 wounded. Jamieson blamed the majority of these Chinese deaths on firing from the French concession, where he said the French had lost their heads. He absolved the Canton government, and even the main body of the cadets, from intending to start trouble. It was his view, and his successor shared it, that the first shots had been fired by agitators desiring an incident. If that was so the agitators' plan succeeded in full measure. A strike and boycott ensued which crippled Hong Kong.[29]

Two platoons of Indian troops were brought up to Shameen but the Foreign Office were much concerned about the safety of a community which, as they put it, was isolated by 100 miles or so of hostile river and was situated in a large Chinese city where there was a weak and treacherous government, a trained communist army, and an active band of communist agents.[30] Jamieson continued cool and decided. He opposed proposals for a British naval blockade of Canton, which some quarters in Britain, including the King, favoured, or for other forcible action against the Canton government. On the other hand he was ready to accept

the consequences in Canton of closing Kuomintang branches in
Malaya, believing that nothing could make anti-British feeling in
Canton worse than it was and that there would be no attack on
Shameen. Palairet, the chargé d'affaires during Macleay's home
leave, confined himself, as Macleay had earlier done, to agreeing
with Jamieson. He told the Foreign Office that Jamieson's long
experience and local knowledge gave his views on forcible action a
weight necessarily absent from Palairet's own views. On Malaya he
said that Jamieson was the best judge of the position and that he
himself had no observations to offer. Palairet was however less
uncritical of the abrasive, or positively discourteous, tone of Jamieson's correspondence with the Canton authorities. He minuted that
Jamieson's style was a little crude. Garstin, the acting Chinese
secretary, went further, calling some of Jamieson's correspondence
painful.[31]

At the beginning of 1926 the Foreign Office telegraphed to
Macleay, who had resumed charge, that according to Hong Kong
reports Jamieson was virtually out of touch with the Canton
government because he feared assassination if he entered the city.
The telegram expressed great appreciation of his services and
personal courage at this critical time but asked whether his usefulness at Canton had been permanently impaired. O'Malley, a
diplomatist about to join the Legation as counsellor, was instructed
to look into the position on his way out. O'Malley was damning.
He justifiably criticized the tone of Jamieson's correspondence with
the Chinese. He doubted whether the fear of assassination was
well founded, something which as a stranger to China he was
hardly qualified to judge. Then he went on: 'Over and above this
Jamieson is a public and notorious drunkard. He is rarely quite
sober and frequently quite intoxicated from lunch-time onwards'.
He said that his drunkenness exposed Jamieson to the censure of
decent people in Hong Kong and to the jeers of the Chinese, that he
should be replaced, and that Clementi, the new governor of Hong
Kong, was in decided agreement about the need to replace him.
Against O'Malley's savage report, which virtually finished Jamieson's active career, may be set the judgement of T.V. Soong, a
leading member of the Kuomintang. He volunteered to W.M.
Hewlett some years later that he had a very soft corner in his heart
for Jamieson, who had said hard things at times but had always
been straight.[32]

Jamieson was brought home. There he declared that after fifteen years of battling at Canton he had recently completely changed his mind and now saw in the Kuomintang and the Young China movement a democratic, nationalist force which would throw off the suspect Russian connection and might give the great and lovable Chinese race a stable national government, something which unprincipled warlords could never achieve; the Kuomintang should be met not by the use of force but by friendly financial, political, and social overtures. This was not the orthodoxy of the moment, and his declaration was the less palatable for being made without permission at an Institute of International Affairs meeting. A senior Foreign Office official condemned as intolerable Jamieson's habit of discussing official business in public and Macleay condemned the expression of some of his views as undesirable and imprudent. Meanwhile his future was in the balance. He would normally have had to retire the following year on reaching 60. It was considered unfair to retire him early and uneconomic to send him back to China for a year or less, so he was offered three years at Tientsin. He felt his removal from Canton keenly, accepted Tientsin reluctantly, and asked for an honour to save his face. He already had a KCMG and suggested the Order of the Bath. Officials fighting a long battle against drink in the Far Eastern services objected to so notorious an offender being rewarded, the Foreign Secretary called the request a quite intolerable pretension, and Jamieson went to Tientsin without the face-saving honour.[33] His Tientsin period was mere anti-climax. After serving out his three years he settled in London and lived on there, subdued by a stroke but not broken, until the age of 78, while in China an abundance of anecdotes about his former manner of life and behaviour continued to go the rounds.[a] On finding the main gates of a Canton yamen discourteously unopened for his call Jamieson was for example said to have got out of his chair, to have relieved himself on the gates, and to have been borne back to Shameen, which he had barely reached before an agitated yamen secretary arrived with profuse apologies.[a] The story may well have been apocryphal, but it was believed to be true by the later consul-general at Canton who told it.

A British warship brought news of the Shakee bund incident in Canton to R.S. Pratt at Hoihow before the news reached the local Chinese. He got all women and children away the next day but remained much concerned that in any sudden emergency it would

be difficult to get the men away from a port with such irregular communications. Some months later troops of the Canton government took over the town. Although most of the local population remained friendly the attitude of the soldiers and agitators was such that foreigners kept as much as possible off the streets and faced the future in a spirit of hopeless resignation to inevitable humiliations. Pratt was transferred in the following spring and the consulate was left in the charge of the constable, who was later evacuated with all British subjects.[34] At Amoy Hewlett refused either to call in the navy or to evacuate and put his trust in protection by the Chinese authorities, with whom he cultivated the closest personal relations. He even won over the leading student agitator, who in consequence was promptly assassinated for betraying student aims. Hewlett's attitude was much disliked by some of the British community, a leading member of which accused him of gambling with the lives of women and children. He himself was oppressed by the responsibility for their lives which he was assuming by relying on the Chinese authorities, but the gamble, if gamble it was, paid off, and he saw the community safely through demonstrations in the British concession and on Kulangsu, a boycott, and the threat of a strike.[35] At Foochow the Chinese authorities kept the agitators within reasonable bounds and L. Giles deplored the effect on Chinese opinion of foreigners running away from purely imaginary perils, as three English ladies whom he considered timorous had done.[36]

At Swatow Kirke had an exceptionally trying time. Even in 1924 he said that the officials were impossible; at other posts he had through the most trying times maintained a semblance of friendly relations; if some warlords with whom he had dealt were scoundrels they were at least pleasant scoundrels; the Swatow officials on the other hand were a brood of anti-foreign nonentities; all he could do was to try to check the impertinences and anti-foreign inclinations of such a rascally lot, the worst among whom were the foreign affairs commissioner and his staff. (Despite their resounding title, foreign affairs commissioners under the republic resembled their imperial predecessors, the foreign deputies, in being ineffectual buffers interposed between consuls and Chinese authorities.)[37] Then early in 1925 Canton government troops captured Swatow and immediately anti-Christian and anti-imperialist pamphlets were distributed and youthful orators at street corners expounded socialist theories.[38] After the Shanghai and Canton incidents the

anti-foreign propaganda became a flood; Swatow was completely controlled by agitators and union strike-leaders; churches were seized by a so-called Agricultural Society devoted to overthrowing the existing social order and Christianity; the domestic servants of British and Japanese residents were forced to leave, as were office staffs, including the consulate staff; rickshawmen and the crews of launches and sampans were forbidden to accept British or Japanese fares; stores were forbidden to supply food; and there was an open attempt to drive the British from the port. In July Kirke said that British and Japanese were isolated, outlawed, and ostracized; provisions had to be brought from Hong Kong; two of the younger men spent all their days over an oven cooking in the summer heat for everyone and cleaning greasy pots and pans; all water had to be carried from wells and there were other even less agreeable occupations (evidently water-closets had not reached Swatow). He knew that many posts were worse off in terms of actual danger, he did not think violence imminent, he was very fit and not in the least worried by physical hardships and the lack of what were usually regarded as necessities, but he was profoundly irritated by indignities and insults which were bad enough in a country like China for any Englishman but were intolerable treatment for a representative of the British government. Garstin minuted that the Swatow situation brought home to local foreigners their true position in contemporary China; face and prestige were mere phantoms unless based on goodwill and respect, and he feared 'that the general attitude of our nationals to Chinese in the treaty ports entitles them to neither'. In September there was a brief lull when anti-communists suddenly took over and shot the mayor, but in November Chiang Kai-shek re-took control for the Canton government. The anti-British measures were re-introduced. Changing his tune Garstin minuted that the British at Swatow had undergone at the hands of Canton government officials insults and humiliations which a few years previously would have been a *casus belli*. Another Legation minute, noting that the past summer's appalling conditions had returned to Swatow, said that the Legation could not help Kirke. For his part Kirke said that until the affair was over, if it ever was to be over, he was ready and anxious to stay at Swatow under these semi-siege conditions, making occasional sorties when opportunity offered and continuing the protests he had been making for months.[39]

Macleay, thanking Kirke for his courage and patience, asked

whether he would strongly object to the Foreign Secretary's sanction being sought to his withdrawal. Kirke replied that withdrawal
would cause the local authorities little or no embarrassment, would
be regarded as a victory by the unions, and would enhance the
difficulties and anxieties of the British community, and Macleay
dropped the idea. At this point Kirke's reading of the situation, a
reading which was not far wrong, was that there were two elements
in the anti-British agitation, Chinese anti-foreignism and Russian
Bolshevism, each directed against Britain only for expediency and
each using the other for its own ends and having different ultimate
aims. In the spring of 1926 Kirke was assaulted by half a dozen or
more strike pickets while he was removing communist posters from
the consulate's front wall but defended himself so successfully
with a stick that he retired unhurt into the compound, the chance
presence there of other foreigners deterring the pickets from pursuit. Unremitting anti-British agitation continued throughout the
summer but discomforts lessened. In roundabout ways food could
sometimes be bought locally, it was usually possible to hire rick-
shaws and sometimes sampans, and most British households had
acquired White Russian, Eurasian, Indian, or occasionally Chinese
staff, the last however still being at risk. In the late autumn the staff
of some British firms ventured to return, although intimidation of
domestic servants continued. Early in 1927 a local Kuomintang
manifesto stated that the eyeless babies and iron pans, stoves, and
butchers' blocks found in a Foochow missionary establishment
were irrefutable evidence of babies being murdered, but in reply
to Kirke's furious protest the Chinese authorities alleged that the
manifesto was the unauthorized work of a minor official, who had
been dismissed. At last in the spring of 1927 right-wing Kuomintang elements acted against the Swatow communist centres and
union interference with foreigners' staff ceased. The ensuing relative quiet was broken in the autumn, when revolutionaries seized
Swatow and an armed and murderous mob took control. The
revolutionaries maintained their hold for only four days and foreigners were not molested, but going on home leave after three and
a half years at Swatow Kirke left a port at which the situation in the
aftermath of the disturbance was so confused that he had no clear
idea of what was going on or what the outcome was likely to be.[40]
His dogged, angry determination not to be beaten and to stick it out
had already been recognized by a CBE and was now rewarded by

promotion to consul-general at Yunnanfu, but at 52 he looked an old man and, whether or not as a result of her Swatow experiences, his wife died on the voyage home. Even at Yunnanfu, which should have been a quiet post before his retirement, trouble pursued him. During preparations for a civil war an explosion of gunpowder destroyed much of the city and entirely demolished the consulate-general and most of its contents. Kirke laconically reported that he was not seriously hurt and that the cyphers were safe.[41]

In July 1926 the Canton government launched an attack, led by Chiang Kai-shek, towards the north and, unexpectedly, were so successful that they soon moved from Canton to the Yangtze and set themselves up in the Wuhan cities as a nationalist government of China. Consular post after consular post came under their control. Changsha, Hankow, Kiukiang, Ichang, Amoy, Foochow, and Ningpo fell before the end of the year. Everywhere anti-British turmoil accompanied the Kuomintang advance, and by the beginning of 1927 British subjects had been advised to leave the interior of every consular district then under nationalist control.[42]

As though the Shanghai and Canton incidents of 1925 and the anti-British agitation accompanying the nationalist advance were not trouble enough, September 1926 brought a further serious incident at Wanhsien, at the Szechwan end of the Yangtze gorges. Yang Sen, of whom Affleck had spoken so warmly at Chengtu and whose subsequent expulsion from Chengtu Affleck had much regretted, now controlled Wanhsien. He alleged that a British river-steamer was responsible for the drowning of some of his troops. As a means of obtaining compensation he seized two other British river-steamers. HMS *Cockchafer*, the gunboat at Wanhsien, was heavily outnumbered and was impotent. Yang refused to negotiate with anyone but the Chungking consul, Eastes, who accordingly came to Wanhsien. Negotiations broke down. Another gunboat and a river-steamer carrying sixty-odd naval officers and ratings joined *Cockchafer*. The combined force made an unsuccessful attempt to release the two impounded steamers by a surprise attack, lost seven dead, and after shelling Wanhsien and causing considerable loss of life withdrew down river. During the engagement Eastes was on *Cockchafer*. Before the month was out he was certified to be on the verge of a nervous breakdown and was hurriedly replaced, and Yang in further negotiations at Ichang came to terms and released the two steamers. As soon as he heard of the

incident J.F. Brenan, in acting charge at Canton, called it 'a dreadful affair, with a ghastly loss of life, all about nothing', and when Eastes' despatches reached the Foreign Office Toller in the Far Eastern department condemned Eastes' aggressive attitude in negotiating with Yang; 'we have always said that [in this affair] the British authorities went to the extreme limit of conciliation but these reports contain not the least evidence of this'.[43] Eastes was not a smooth negotiator. In the early 1920s his tone during two very difficult years at Amoy had been criticized in the Legation. Teichman had said that Eastes lacked the happy knack of settling cases by tact and personal influence. A despatch reporting that he had exploded in a vigorous oral protest against a damnable outrage on the British flag had attracted the anonymous marginal comment 'quite in the style of the good old days of Sir Harry Parkes'. Macleay had reproved him for unwarrantably harsh and provocative language and on his transfer from Amoy to Ichang at the end of 1923 warned him in a private letter that he tended to be somewhat intemperate and aggressive towards the Chinese. The warning did not deter Eastes from telling Ichang officials that if such a calamity as the abolition of extraterritoriality supervened he would forthwith resign, even at the cost of losing his claim to a pension.[44] From Ichang he moved to Chungking. The six months he spent there before the Wanhsien incident were not calculated to moderate intemperance of language. Just before his arrival the general whose bodyguard had previously invaded the consulate had driven out a rival and taken entire control of the city, and Eastes had to deal with ensuing anti-Christian demonstrations and a serious riot at mission premises. After three months the general, whom he described as a filibusterer commanding 20,000 opium-sodden and ragged but well-armed soldiers, was driven out in five days of hostilities during which foreign buildings were so repeatedly hit by rifle and machine-gun fire that the limitation of foreign casualties to one severe injury seemed to Eastes almost miraculous. He battled against a boycott, against attacks on British property, and against incessant illegal taxation of British goods. For seven days a week he conscientiously but unwisely worked long office hours, normally eleven hours a day and at times much more, a killing routine in Chungking's summer heat.[45] His nerves must have been frayed before he started negotiations with Yang. He was a courageous, conscientious, and honourable public servant, and according to one

colleague[a] a man of much personal charm, but it seems probable that if the negotiations with Yang had been in other hands the Wanhsien incident, which added more fuel to the flames of anti-British agitation, would have been avoided.

The next major incidents on the Yangtze occurred lower down the river. Goffe at Hankow said in July 1926 that should the 'red army' (by which he meant the southern forces) reach the city a very serious situation would be created, and he asked for a large warship. At the Legation Teichman, usually so sensible, thought this unduly alarmist, and O'Malley told the navy that he did not expect the nationalists to cause any serious disturbance at Hankow and that Goffe was sometimes a bit panicky. Nevertheless two cruisers were present when the city fell to the nationalists in September, and Goffe attributed to their presence, and to the presence of a landing force in the British concession for some weeks, the comparative respect with which the concession was initially treated. He suggested that there was nothing to stop the nationalists from overrunning the country and was again regarded as an alarmist. He tried to avoid any action which might give agitators fomenting anti-British feeling a pretext for direct action. During November and December there were constant incidents. At the end of December he regarded the situation as grave. Lampson, who after replacing Macleay had visited Hankow, told him at this point that firmness was the only sound policy and that according to Foreign Office instructions (which it later transpired Lampson had misunderstood) force was to be used without hesitation in defence of British concessions. At the beginning of January a mob attacked the concession. To avoid bloodshed a naval landing party was withdrawn instead of being ordered to fire, and the Chinese took control of the concession.[46]

Lampson was furious. He told the Foreign Office that the deplorable withdrawal had given the position away and that even at the risk of bloodshed sufficient forces should be landed to restore British control. Rear-Admiral Cameron at Hankow defended the decision to withdraw; British subjects had not been under attack; if the mob had been fired on and driven out nationalist troops would have taken the concession with appalling loss of life and the whole of China would have been led to war; resort to force would have been suicidal. Goffe too defended withdrawal as the only possible course. He added that although, given sufficient force, it would

be possible to hold British concessions the resulting strikes and boycotts would strangle the British trade which the concessions were presumably there to foster.[47]

Lampson was humiliatingly rebuffed. The home authorities approved the withdrawal. So did the King, who entirely agreed that the decision by Goffe and Cameron to evacuate without firing a shot had been perfectly right, though he seriously doubted whether a similar course at Shanghai would be wise. Lampson was instructed to thank Goffe and Cameron for their wise and courageous action. He lamely told them that it was now clear that they had acted with conspicuous courage and were free from all blame.[48] In private his opinions were probably unchanged, for during subsequent negotiations with the Chinese about the concession's future administration he minuted 'the Foreign Office are a backboneless set of lubbers'.[49] It is unlikely that these events endeared Goffe to him, and they soon led to Goffe retiring two years prematurely. O'Malley, temporarily detached from the Legation to Hankow, did not get on with Goffe, in whose house he was living. Lampson presented this to the Foreign Office in a manner implying that Goffe was to blame, which given his character may very well have been the case, and the Foreign Secretary, Chamberlain, was displeased. Later in the year Goffe was 'encouraged' to take home leave. Lampson told Chamberlain, with whom he kept up a flow of personal correspondence, that Goffe's return to China was undesirable. Chamberlain was puzzled that the reasons for regarding Goffe as disqualified from further work in China had not been very precisely stated, but Goffe, who successfully bargained for a KBE as the price of going quietly, was sent into reluctant retirement.[50]

At Kiukiang Ogden had been taking precautions ever since the Wanhsien incident and the nationalist capture of Hankow. Thousands of foreigners had sought coolness at Kuling and for all of them, regardless of nationality, he felt himself, as the only nearby official, morally responsible.[a] He checked incipient panic at Kuling, overhauled the defence scheme, and unostentatiously organized a stock of food in the concession. In November 1926 Kiukiang fell to the nationalists, the well-armed and well-disciplined defending troops collapsing like a pricked bubble before a mere handful of ragged boys,[51] and for the rest of the year the community in the concession lived in a state of siege.[a] Ogden evacuated women and children on hearing of the events in the Hankow concession and in

the expectation of an immediate similar attack on the Kiukiang concession telegraphed for instructions. Lampson instructed him to defend the concession by all available means against an attack by a mob, provided the navy were satisfied that they had sufficient force to do so, but not against an attack by troops. The expected attack came from a mob. It broke into the concession. No resistance was offered and male foreigners retired in good order through the hostile mob to the safety of gunboats. Ogden expressed regret for his inability to hold the concession but said that once the Hankow concession had gone the Kiukiang concession was not worth fighting for and that he had decided to get out with the minimum loss of dignity and property and without loss of life.[52] His sensible decision was covered by the approval given to Goffe's decision.

The Kiukiang concession was no real loss. Minor concessions were more trouble than they were worth. In 1922 Clennell at Chinkiang had tentatively suggested that the retention of the concession might no longer serve any useful purpose. The Legation were sufficiently impressed to ask Eastes at Amoy for views on the possible surrender of the Amoy concession as well. Surprisingly for so fiery a defender of extraterritoriality Eastes favoured giving up both the concession and the Kulangsu international settlement. He argued that as both had become targets for anti-British agitation they were a liability for British trade and that action should be taken while it was still possible for dignity to be preserved and for the motive to be construed as generous. The Foreign Office were however against handing back either the Chinkiang or Amoy concessions without seeking a quid pro quo, it was decided that further consideration should be deferred until the political situation in China became more stable, and the minor concessions remained as unnecessary irritants. Even the Hankow concession, once it had gone, was recognized not to have been of major significance. The Foreign Office pointed out that the four largest local British establishments all operated outside it and that the foreign residential areas were largely in the former German and Russian concessions already under Chinese control.[53] When Britain in February 1927 accepted the *faits accomplis* and formally surrendered the Hankow and Kiukiang concessions she thus sustained no great material loss, but by visibly yielding to force had lost much prestige.

From Ichang Blunt reported early in 1927 that the general labour union had called a lightning strike of all Chinese in British

employment, that there had been an orderly but hostile demonstration by some 10,000 people, and that the streets had become unsafe for British subjects. He was irked by 'the constant indignities, impertinences and insults to which the officials and the flag of one of the greatest powers in the world are subjected by coolies, riff-raff, soldiers, students and children'; the consulate's official and domestic staff had unwillingly left; most British subjects were however being visited under cover of darkness by their staff bringing fresh food and 'some compounds are even regularly visited by the sanitary scavenger — a lady who deserves great credit either for her defiance of the union or her devotion to her unpleasant task'.[54] At Chungking it was much worse for R.S. Pratt. Whenever he went on the streets in January soldiers cursed him or cried 'Kill him' and more than once they covered him at short range with their rifles, a situation which drew from Lampson the comment that it was wonderful how consular officers stood up to such conditions and that they could hardly be expected to carry on in them indefinitely. In March Pratt wrote that his situation, at the summit of the noisome city, isolated from other foreigners, was truly horrible and causing acute mental depression. A fortnight later he accompanied a naval lieutenant and seven bluejackets, all unarmed, who went to retrieve cases of naval cigarettes and gin seized by pickets. Coolies carrying off the cases dropped them on the party's approach, but as the party were taking the cases back they were cut off by pickets. They were beaten with spears and prodded with swords, came under a hail of stones and bricks, and had to abandon the cases and run for it. No one suffered more than slight flesh wounds and rather severe bruising, but the Legation called it a narrow escape. Pratt's experiences at Chungking and at previous posts left their mark on him. The following year, when he was aged 45, a confidential report described him as a most efficient and quick worker but as having a marked dislike for China and the Chinese and as longing to retire.[55] It was to no one's advantage that before achieving retirement he was obliged to serve another nine years in a country he had grown to dislike so much.

At Chengtu there was a recrudescence of anti-Christian propaganda. Early in January 1927, on the same day that Lampson instructed Ogden to resist at Kiukiang, he instructed Affleck to withdraw himself and his vice-consul after taking what steps he could for the safety of British subjects. Affleck had for months been

urging missionaries to leave.[56] They had disregarded his advice, partly, perhaps, because the advice came from a professed atheist,[a] partly, perhaps, as Teichman suggested, because their life in Szechwan was so easy and pleasant,[57] and primarily, no doubt, out of devotion to their cause. In the light of the Hankow events a large number, though still a minority, of the missionaries now decided to leave with Affleck. The consulate-general had been holding 20 rifles with bayonets and 10,500 rounds of ammunition, though what good the rifles, the bayonets, and the vast store of ammunition could ever have been expected to be for two British consular officers and the British missionary community is not easy to understand. It was too risky to travel with them, and accordingly one night Affleck and the vice-consul secretly buried the rifle bolts, bayonets, and ammunition under a wooden bathroom floor, leaving the dismantled rifles in a store-room (on the permanent closure of the Chengtu post later on the arms and ammunition were left in the custody of the French consulate and were then stolen, a very valuable haul for the thieves).[58] In inconsequential contrast to so much anti-foreign chaos Combe and Yunnanfu's foreign community, as remote and exposed as the Chengtu community, were meanwhile the local warlord's guests at a friendly, peaceful, and very well-run athletics meeting for 3,000 male and female students.[59]

In March 1927 the nationalists extended their control down the Yangtze to Chinkiang, Nanking, and Shanghai. Then a major split in their ranks halted their advance. Chiang Kai-shek broke with the Kuomintang's Soviet mentors, executed many Chinese communists, and set about establishing himself as leader of a purged Kuomintang whose internal policies were henceforward conservative.

At Chinkiang the British were merely humiliated. It had been decided not to attempt to hold by force a concession described not long afterwards by Teichman as 'a concession of absentee rent-collecting landlords, the *reductio ad absurdum* of the object of holding concessions in China'. The nationalists took the city without fighting, they took the concession over too, most foreign residents left for Shanghai, and those who remained had previously moved on to the river or close enough to it to be protected by foreign warships. W.S. Smith, the acting consul, ruefully quoted as applicable to his own circumstances the remark of Adkins in 1863: 'life on board a hulk at Chinkiang is a most distressing kind of

existence'. He concluded that it was impossible to resume residence in the concession, and indeed before long troops were billeted in the consulate. He was withdrawn to Shanghai to continue his Chinkiang functions from there, and by the end of the year he was enjoying a transfer to Tengyueh, where everything was very peaceful and where officials, merchants, and peasants were markedly cordial towards foreigners.[60]

At Nanking events took a far more serious turn for B. Giles. Lampson had just told the Foreign Office that no one at home could imagine the strain on consular officers who were sitting on a magazine which might explode at any moment.[61] Giles was the unfortunate under whom the magazine exploded. An element among the nationalist force which took Nanking ran amok. At the British consulate-general soldiers shot a British doctor dead on the lawn, shot the British harbour-master dead in the office in front of Mrs Giles, whose head was narrowly missed by two other bullets, wounded an Indian army officer in the arm and leg, and shot Giles himself above the knee. The head messenger bolted the foreign men and women into the strong-room from the outside and while they were hidden there denied to invading soldiers who repeatedly threatened his life that he knew the foreigners' whereabouts. This group of soldiers accepted his statement and left after robbing the safe. The foreign party inadvertently revealed themselves to a subsequent group of soldiers. Giles was convinced that they would all be shot, but a Chinese policeman persuaded the soldiers that there was nothing more to be got out of the party, which he escorted to the consular gatehouse. There they had constantly to explain to other soldiers that they had already been stripped of all their valuables and Giles was in great dread that after killing the men the soldiers would turn to raping the women. After the night had been spent on the gatehouse floor the consulate writer and the messenger came in and were asked to contact the responsible authorities, servants from the Customs club brought in food and drinks, which incongruously included champagne, and in the evening the Chinese equivalent of the Red Cross Society, called in by the messenger, got the party to the bund, where they were taken on to a British warship. The Nanking violence was anti-foreign rather than specifically anti-British. The Japanese and United States consulates were likewise looted, an American missionary was killed in cold blood, and the United States consular staff could make their escape

only when United States warships dropped shells round the building in which the staff had taken refuge. British warships shelled the city too.[62] The outrages of the Chinese troops explain, and probably justify, the shelling, but it caused much local resentment. Even three years later most foreign households at Nanking kept an emergency suitcase ready, one of the British consulate-general's staff was stoned while out riding, and another was dragged from his rickshaw close to the office.[a]

Giles, who was certain that the outrages had been planned from above, suggested that in addition to formal apologies being made and compensation given, the army commander, the divisional generals, and 100 junior officers and men, to be identified by the Chinese as having been responsible, should be executed publicly, preferably on the bund. This suggestion may perhaps be excused as coming from a shaken man, but it is extraordinary that Lampson agreed, merely suggesting as a modification that only a proportion, say one in ten, of the juniors should be publicly executed, the remainder being otherwise punished. The Foreign Office agreed that these measures would be in accordance with Chinese methods and if adopted would be most salutary, but with some appearance of reluctance ruled that any demands made must be consonant with British traditions and acceptable to Western opinion, and that Britain would lay herself open to criticism were she to demand the execution of named individuals before their trial or to specify the number of persons who were to be found guilty and executed. There was a long pause, British tempers cooled, the nationalists having broken with communism were able to blame the incident on communists, and it was settled tamely by an exchange of diplomatic notes.[63] By that time the unwilling Giles had been pressured into producing a medical certificate that the Nanking events coming on top of a disposition to neurasthenia unfitted him for further service and had succumbed to a fatal stroke within a week of being granted a pension. As his death was ascribed to the outrage the Treasury awarded the widow a pension of about £280. This was no princely sum on which to support herself and a completely paralysed son needing a male nurse's care, and it was providential that she had a private income of some hundreds a year.[64] The office messenger fared better. He had added to his services by saving the cyphers. At great risk he returned to the consular offices, saw the cyphers lying about, realized that having come from the safe they

must be precious, told soldiers that his little son liked the foreign books with figures, and was allowed to remove them. Owing to an oversight in the subsequent confusion nothing was done for him for two years, but then the Treasury sanctioned a substantial payment,[65] a whip-round in the service provided a sum handsome enough to keep the frail, elderly man in comfort for the rest of his days,[a] and in a ceremony which must have given him immense face Lampson presented him with a pair of honorific scrolls.[a]

The Nanking violence caused a great stir and Lampson issued sweeping instructions. He ordered the evacuation of the Chungking, Ichang, and Changsha posts, and he instructed all other posts on the Yangtze and south of the Yangtze, Shanghai and Canton alone excepted, to be prepared to evacuate and if necessary to evacuate without consulting him. Although at Hankow the consular staff and the few remaining British males considered it prudent to start sleeping on board a ship, as was already being done at Kiukiang and Chinkiang, none of the officers given discretion to evacuate seems to have thought of doing so and certainly none did so.[66] The Foochow community was more at hazard than most, as in any emergency the navy could not get closer than Pagoda Island, and there had been alarming recent troubles. A Spanish orphanage, American missions, two British hospitals, and a British school had been looted, only outward calm and geniality had saved the British postal commissioner from a severe beating, and perhaps death, at the hands of strikers a few weeks later, and two other British subjects had been in grave danger. Nevertheless Moss said that although life at Foochow was very unpleasant it was right to hold on and that the remaining missionaries, the stuff of which martyrs were made, were most reluctant to abandon the work of three generations of particularly fine British missionaries. He complained only that he was completely in the dark about the British government's intentions towards the nationalist government and asked to be enlightened.[67]

The British government had no intention of allowing Shanghai's international settlement to go the way of the Hankow concession. To secure it against possible attack they sent troops in massive strength, far exceeding the contribution to the settlement's defence made by any of the other powers who shared responsibility for its status.[68] Chamberlain had reservations about Barton as consul-general. He recognized Barton's ability and knowledge but

mistrusted his judgement. In a private letter of March 1927 he instructed Lampson to keep an eye on Barton, who he said had called for troops before any of his consular colleagues had thought it necessary to do so and having got the troops apparently wanted to use them for a policy of force for which Britain had neither the resources nor public approval. In reply Lampson sent soothing assurances that Barton was the best man in the service and had become much more conciliatory in recent years, and a year later, after an extremely delicate and dangerous period for the settlement, told Chamberlain that things at Shanghai were at last moving in the right direction and that for this Barton, who had been given much too little credit at home, was largely responsible.[69] Barton was, however, probably still viewed with suspicion in Whitehall. In 1929 he was promoted into the diplomatic service and appointed minister to Ethiopia. The appointment may have been a reward for his Shanghai services, but the belief in his family was that he was kicked upstairs to what was expected to be a remote backwater,[a] though it turned out to be a crucially important post. While occupying the post Barton, on the very best terms with the emperor, became utterly disgusted with British policy towards Ethiopia,[a] and the Foreign Office may have wished that they had left him in China.

Immediately after the Hankow concession had been overrun the Foreign Office gave full discretion to the men on the spot to hold the Shameen concession at Canton against mob violence or attack by troops for as long as they considered it possible to do so. The concession, in which British subjects numbered no more than 150 or so, was of very little intrinsic importance but was presumably considered too close to Hong Kong for its loss to be accepted with equanimity. The man on the spot in the consulate-general was J.F. Brenan. When J.W. Jamieson went home in the spring of 1926 Brenan, a vice-consul aged just over 40, had in a startling departure from promotion by seniority been sent to take acting charge of this very difficult key post. He had originally got into the China service only by a fluke. When he sat the entrance examination in 1903 there were no China vacancies and he had to accept the Siam service. At the time the intention, which was not carried into effect, was to abolish the Siam service and to distribute its members over the general consular service. Knowing that Brenan had wished to follow his father, a Customs commissioner, out to China the Foreign Office promised Brenan a transfer into the next China

vacancy instead of a transfer into the general service, and after some eighteen pointless months in the Siam service he was duly sent to Peking. Thereafter he had only once been in charge of a consulate, Nanking, and that had been for a mere nine months. There seem to be no papers to show what decided the Legation to send him to Canton over the heads of his seniors. Brenan was at the time serving under Barton at Shanghai, and perhaps Barton recommended him. His performance at Canton gave so much satisfaction that three years after taking over acting charge as a vice-consul he was the substantive consul-general there and was shortly to become consul-general at Shanghai, a meteoric rise.[70]

Brenan, cool in manner and somewhat testy, was masterful, clear-headed, and did not suffer fools gladly.[a] He seems to have viewed the Chinese with sceptical and lucid disillusion and without the liking underlying Jamieson's roughness. In his opinion the way to negotiate with them was to combine an offer of really generous terms with a show of force, neither being much use without the other. A month after taking charge he described his tactics. While maintaining friendly personal relations, avoiding vain threats, and giving assurances that Britain wished to live in peace and not to infringe China's sovereign rights he was making it clear that if British subjects were not protected from outrage and insult he would himself act as far as it lay in his power. He told the Legation, who agreed, that immediate bloodless retaliation against outrage would have nothing but good results. He put theory into practice in August. In a friendly talk over dinner with a leading nationalist he gave warning that if the anti-British boycott continued Britain might be forced to take more active steps to protect the overseas trade on which she depended; the Canton authorities had been left alone so far on account of their insignificance, but were they to become a serious danger political wheels would begin to turn; there were more ways than armed intervention open to Britain; it was open to her to reach understandings with other foreign powers or even with the Canton government's enemies in China; the nationalists would be wise to seek British support rather than British enmity. He followed up by obtaining Foreign Office agreement that the navy should seize and disable the picket boats which were daily enforcing the boycott by firing on boats and junks bound for Hong Kong steamers. He said a few days later that at the first sign of activity by the navy the picket boats had disappeared and the

shooting had stopped; the Chinese were worried, precisely the effect which he had expected; and that it would now be desirable to get the gunboats away again. Although he was convinced that Governor Clementi at Hong Kong was misguided in arguing for the use of substantial force to break the boycott, that its use would play into the hands of the leftists, and that anti-British agitation in south China would subside only when Britain came to terms with the Kuomintang, overtly he tried to leave the Chinese with the opposite impression. He did his best to encourage their fears that the insignificant naval action against the picket boats was the forerunner of large-scale British action against Canton, the base from which the Kuomintang's military drive towards the Yangtze was being mounted. Whether on account of his Macchiavellian manoeuvres or for other reasons the boycott was formally called off within a month.[71] A Foreign Office minute attributed the ending of the boycott in good measure to Brenan and called it a truly remarkable achievement. Clementi, on the other hand, sent a lengthy despatch to the Colonial Office attacking the general weakness of Foreign Office policy and Brenan's weakness in particular. Brenan protested, Lampson, who was later to complain that Clementi had for years been trying to run British policy in China, backed him up, and the Colonial Office agreed that the despatch should not be circulated.[72]

At the end of 1926 Brenan submitted a memorandum on the Kuomintang. Although he had lost no time in deciding that Chiang Kai-shek was a 'mark 1926 warlord', bent on unifying the country by force with himself as supreme ruler, he regarded the Kuomintang as the most effective force in China. With its corruption and incompetence went a modicum of accomplishment and of public spirit he had not noticed elsewhere; it had gone a fair way to including all the educated and articulate part of the nation; it appealed to the idealism of youth, especially as it embraced the theory, soothing to Chinese *amour propre*, that China's ills were due to foreign interference; the foreign mercantile community had very little sympathy for Young China's aspirations, cordially disliked Sun Yat-sen, and were disposed to think in terms of half-baked students, but Britain could not arrest the march of events in China or try to deflect it without seriously risking burnt fingers. Fears of Bolshevization after a Kuomintang victory were in his opinion exaggerated; the Kuomintang had been thrown into Soviet

arms by the hostility of the other powers and would probably split on domestic issues; the menace to foreign trade was less likely to be Bolshevism than China's age-old vices of arrogance, injustice, corruption, and excessive and arbitrary taxation; Britain might do well to take her own line in China, for bungling was inseparable from collective diplomacy and the solidarity of the powers towards China was offensive to the Chinese in theory and non-existent in fact. In mid-1927, after the Hankow, Kiukiang, Chinkiang, and Nanking incidents and after Chiang Kai-shek's action against the left wing Brenan submitted further views, which Lampson commended to the Foreign Office as extremely able. The driving force behind the anti-British movement had, as he saw it, been the discarded Soviet advisers; the usual Chinese self-seeking, personal intrigue, and general incompetence had now destroyed the formidable organization so carefully built up by the Russians; 'the Chinese are so hopelessly incompetent and corrupt that they are incapable of organising anything on a grand scale, whether it be a commercial enterprise, a government or a revolution'. He argued that in present circumstances any further attack on British interests might be effectively countered by stopping all Chinese traffic on Kwangtung's main waterways. It would be possible to go further by destroying the arsenal, the military academy, and the aviation sheds; Kwangtung was always either at war or on the verge of war with its neighbours, and the threat of interference with its military preparations would have a great deterrent effect; such very serious measures could however be justified only by a cause so patently righteous that the Chinese, who knew well enough when they were in the wrong, would recognize it as such. The conciliatory policy previously adopted had been galling to British subjects in south China, 'and to no one more than myself, who has had to put up personally with the consequent Chinese truculence and rudeness' for longer than anyone except Kirke at Swatow, but at least it had proved that Britain did not selfishly oppose a Chinese national revival, and if she retaliated against further attack all decent foreigners and many Chinese could be expected to sympathize. Brenan's expression of views, and their favourable reception, showed how deeply a consular officer could engage, as in the initial treaty port era, in politics and diplomacy.[73]

The year 1927 was a tense one at Canton. After the Hankow incident Brenan warned the Chinese authorities that any attack on

Shameen would be resisted by force and no attack was made. After the Nanking incident the concession was garrisoned by some 200 officers and men who were brought up from Hong Kong with howitzers and machine-guns. Again no attack was made. Canton at this juncture was controlled by Li Chi-shen, a general who was a nominal adherent of the nationalist government but who was prepared to accept only unimportant orders coming from that quarter. In the spring he imitated Chiang Kai-shek by taking successful action against local communists. In the early autumn there were signs of another anti-British boycott. Brenan sent an oral message to Li that conciliatory forbearance in the face of outrage and insult having been tried and found useless a fresh boycott should not be expected to be endured by the British in the same way as they had endured the previous one. In a written communication he professed the friendliest feelings towards Li and his administration but advised him in the gravest terms not to permit a renewed boycott. A few days after these warnings had been sent the boycott scare for a time died away, but everything remained in chaos and a boycott began in earnest at the end of the autumn. Brenan was authorized by the Foreign Office to arrange, should the need arise, for Chinese shipping in Canton waterways to be immobilized by the navy, the course that he had previously recommended. Before the course needed to be adopted Li was expelled by a rival, who closed the boycott down, and early in December Brenan rashly stated that Canton was exceptionally quiet. Three days later communists seized the city in a sudden coup, held it for forty-eight hours, and ordered the extermination of landlords. Hall, the vice-consul, went by launch to evacuate foreigners from a suburb. The launch came under heavy and purposeful rifle fire, its engine was temporarily put out of action, and while it was being repaired Hall and the German consul-general flattened themselves in the bottom of the launch. There were no casualties, although the launch was hit thirteen times, but it was a dangerous trip. The communists were put down with what Brenan called barbaric severity. Hundreds of corpses littered the streets, at least five Russians were publicly executed, and the Soviet consul-general was arrested. Before December was out Li's rival decided that his position at Canton was untenable and removed himself and $2 million, taken from the vaults of the central bank, and Li returned to the city to resume his former position. To Brenan the events demonstrated that while the

people's destiny remained in such hands there was little chance of
stability or unification in south China.[74]

After the communist rising had been put down at Canton anti-
British agitation in the city died out and there was a total volte-face.
Early in 1928 Brenan was practically the guest of honour at a
banquet given by Li, Lampson was most cordially received on a
visit to the city, and a visit by Clementi was made the occasion for
an almost effusive demonstration of pro-British sentiments, with
Union Jacks flown everywhere. By December Brenan was reporting
as a pleasant if precarious change that locally the British were the
blue-eyed boys while French and Americans were having difficulties and that a local Chinese newspaper had praised Clementi for
pioneering reconciliation; 'so much for his daily clamour for war
and his denunciations of myself for mixing water with his wine'.[75]

The same pattern of action against communists and fence-
mending with the British was repeated elsewhere. Throughout the
year relations with Swatow officials were uniformly friendly. On
the suppression of the Shanghai communists anti-foreign agitation ceased to be countenanced there. At Ningpo agitation died
away after sensational executions which were carried out by a
general arriving with twelve executioners and which according to
Prideaux-Brune local Chinese opinion seemed inclined to resent as
anachronistic. After the Chungking post had been re-opened Handley-Derry said that the situation had been completely changed by a
drastic massacre of extremists, and relations with officials were
most cordial. At Hankow H. Porter said that the anti-communist
drive had enormously improved conditions. Similar comments came
from other posts without sympathy for communist victims being
apparent.[76] The communists took to the countryside, where they
survived the numerous campaigns mounted against them by Chiang
Kai-shek, and henceforward consular officers had no direct experience of their behaviour. During a period of extremist control at
Changsha in 1926 a despatch from P.G. Jones which impressed
Teichman had quoted with approval the view of a local West-
ernized Chinese that a time was coming more subversive of the
existing bases of society than the French Revolution,[77] but now the
communists were normally seen as mere bandit nuisances who kept
the countryside in a turmoil and kidnapped or murdered missionaries. This attitude was typified by Martin's 1929 report from
Foochow that of the two principal brigand groups in south Fukien

the communist one was led by Chu Te and Mao Tse-tung. Handley-Derry at Chungking in 1929 and W.M. Hewlett at Hankow in 1932 regarded communist disorders merely as a reflection of misrule and poverty.[78]

Occasionally there were more perceptive consular views. In 1928 L. Giles at Swatow reported that nineteen men and two women executed for a communist plot had sung revolutionary hymns from the prison to the place of execution, where they were shot in the usual barbarous way, one woman needing five shots and both women's bodies being stripped and mutilated after death. He regretted 'that these misguided fanatics are about the only Chinese who have the courage to die for their convictions; for until their opponents are similarly inspired there can be no real hope of salvation for China'.[79] Still more perceptive was a 1930 report from Harding at Changsha on the communists' strategy; they waged a guerilla war, avoiding collisions unless in overwhelming force; they raided insufficiently guarded cities, where they carried out their policy of selective looting, destruction, kidnapping, and money-getting; in response government troops, none of whom showed a fraction of communist courage and determination, moved constantly from city to city, found on arrival that the communists had gone, and could not follow them into the mountains, where all the inhabitants were communist sympathizers.[80] Harding had become a professing Buddhist and vegetarian and his behaviour, both personal and official, was peculiar.[a] Nowhere was he odder than at Changsha. Dinner guests were made to race cockroaches across the table and he retired to bed and left them to their own devices when an alarm clock went off at 10 o'clock,[a] in hot weather he took his trousers off in the office for coolness and received callers without putting them on again,[a] and according to service legend two female missionaries who disregarded his advice to withdraw from a dangerous position were informed that he presumed they wished to be raped.[a] The general official view was that he was an eccentric crank,[81] and his report on communist strategy made no impact.

Though the Soviet advisers had been thrown out and the Chinese communists driven into the wilderness the anti-British movement which they had jointly fostered had been a resounding propaganda success, and had made inevitable a harder British look at treaty rights in China. Views among senior members of the service varied

greatly. Teichman said that it was the foreigner's privileged position which made Chinese anti-foreign, that the British would be anti-foreign were they in the same position, that the conditions under which foreign trade was conducted had to change, and that the change had to be made without undue friction.[82] Garstin, arguing that the Amoy concession should be rendited at once, said that the early British at Amoy had no doubt shown the spirit that had caused so much trouble at Shanghai and that the harvest sown was now being reaped in the shape of anti-British agitation at Amoy.[83] Goffe considered that the treaties had in many respects become morally indefensible and that as many treaty rights had for years been systematically ignored, giving these rights up would not alter anything.[84] The furthest F.E. Wilkinson thought it admissible to go was withdrawing extraterritorial rights from foreigners living outside treaty ports.[85] L. Giles declared that a country in which the military could arrest, imprison, punish, and even execute without paying the slightest regard to legal codes was at present unfit to be granted a surrender of extraterritorial rights.[86] Years later Harding, incensed by reports of lepers in Yunnan being buried alive to get rid of them, was still taking that line and attacking J.S. Pratt for advocating the opposite view in the Foreign Office.[87]

At home, however, the anti-British movement convinced the British government of the need to yield ground on the treaties. They backed down step by step. In 1926 they declared that the treaties were out of date and that China's claim for revision was essentially just. In 1927 they expressed readiness in principle to apply as far as practicable the modern Chinese legal codes in British courts in China, to discuss modifications in the way in which British concessions were administered, to make British subjects liable to pay regular and legal Chinese taxes, and to accept that British missionary, educational, and medical institutions should conform to Chinese laws and that missionary rights to purchase land in the interior should be relinquished.[88] In 1928 they recognized the nationalists, a key item in whose programme was the abolition of all foreign extraterritorial rights, as China's national government. By so doing they implicitly recognized that the unequal treaties would have to go.[89] The only remaining question was when, and on what terms, British rights under the treaties would be surrendered.

EPILOGUE

ALTHOUGH internal Chinese weakness and external Japanese aggression combined to give British extraterritorial rights an unexpectedly long further lease of life the writing on the wall was clear, and the Foreign Office turned towards dismantling the specialist China service whose origins and functions had been rooted in the unequal treaties. The service was not abolished but after 1934 recruitment into it ceased. Instead, an appropriate number of new entrants into the general consular service were posted each year to Peking for the customary language study without being thereby committed to a lifetime in China.[1]

The national government which Britain had recognized exercised only a nominal control over much of the country. Its effective power extended to only a limited number of provinces. Elsewhere virtually independent militarists paid mere lip service to the national government. From time to time this or that province declared itself entirely independent. In further civil wars the victory of Chiang Kai-shek, the leader of the national government, was so little assured that Lampson in 1928 said that if it came to a struggle between Chiang and Feng Yü-hsiang (a genial, burly, and exceptionally treacherous warlord) 'there can be no doubt who will come out on top, for Feng is obviously a big personality whereas I don't believe that Chiang really is'.[2] Apart from communist activities ordinary banditry and local disorders abounded. In 1929 unpaid soldiers at Kiukiang looted a street of shops alongside the former concession, killed the garrison commander's chief of staff and some others, and fled with their loot. No foreigners were molested and Mills, the acting consul, reported 'so comparatively trifling an incident' only because of exaggerated rumours that the whole city had been looted. Lampson commented that in a country where conditions were far removed from those in normal civilized coun-

tries such matters had come to be judged by abnormal standards.[3] There were plenty more incidents, trifling or otherwise, but the saving grace was that as a rule they were no longer deliberately aimed at British targets. In such circumstances Sino-British negotiations about extraterritoriality did not move very fast, and there was a tacit understanding that provocative British assertion of treaty rights and provocative Chinese denial of their validity were both best avoided pending the outcome of diplomatic negotiations, in which the British aim was to get the best possible terms for surrendering rights.[a] Early agreement was reached on some peripheral issues. The Chinkiang concession was formally rendited in 1929.[4] In 1930 the Amoy concession was rendited.[5] So was the unwanted Weihaiwei leasehold, at the cost of establishing a Weihaiwei consulate to keep an eye on British interests in the territory.[6] After China regained her tariff autonomy in 1930 the main outstanding issues were Chinese jurisdiction over British subjects and the safeguarding of British interests in the Shanghai international settlement and in the Tientsin British concession. According to J.T. Pratt, who was handling the issues at the Foreign Office, negotiations were making excellent progress until interrupted by Japanese aggression.[7] In the last years of extraterritoriality a previously unknown degree of cordiality, even of friendliness, agreeably emerged. Chinese dislike and distrust of Britain were so deep-rooted as to be almost instinctive,[8] but the dislike and distrust were progressively pushed into the background by fear and hatred of the Japanese. According to Blunt at Nanking in 1934 he was being invited out by Chinese to five or six meals a week and was having hundreds of Chinese back, whereas in his previous twenty-seven years' service he had probably in all eaten less than twenty meals with Chinese.[9]

The turning-point in Japan's relations with China came in 1928, when against Japanese advice the son of the assassinated Chang Tso-lin threw in his lot, and Manchuria's lot, with the national government. Both F.E. Wilkinson at Mukden and P.G. Jones at Harbin promptly predicted[10] that Japan would act to safeguard interests in Manchuria which she regarded as vital, and so it proved. In 1931 she struck, took over Manchuria, and turned it into a puppet state. From then on there was no turning back. In 1932 she engaged in considerable hostilities with China at Shanghai. Next she extended her military influence into Inner

Mongolia and north China. In 1937 she embarked on what amounted to full-scale war against China and had much initial success. By 1938 most China consulates were in territory controlled by the Japanese military. The threat to British interests in China no longer came from China but from Japan. China consular officers did not speak Japanese, did not understand Japanese ways, and detested the arrogant Japanese military who systematically disregarded all representations about British rights and who delighted in humiliating anyone white. Trying to protect British interests against the Japanese from a position of weakness was a frustrating exercise in futility.

The staff of consulates in Chinese territory controlled by Japan fell into Japanese hands when war between Britain and Japan broke out in 1941. Wearisome months elapsed before they could be exchanged and redeployed elsewhere. In 1943 Britain surrendered her extraterritorial rights to her wartime Chinese ally. Shortly afterwards all members of the former diplomatic and consular services were amalgamated into a new Foreign Service and the China service ceased to exist. At the end of the war in 1946 consulates were re-opened by former China service officers in their new guise as Foreign Service officers. In a civil war ending in 1949 the Chinese communists routed Chiang Kai-shek, who was driven out of the mainland to Formosa, and established themselves as the government of China. Consulates were closed again and former members of the China service were posted all over the globe. Freed from the limitations of a close service more than one rose to the top of the official tree, as some others in earlier generations would doubtless have done had they had similar opportunities.

So ended the tightly knit service, whose members had been proud of its separate identity and of their specialist functions and skills and had been bound together by a strong *esprit de corps*. Despite a not inconsiderable proportion of failures and a scattering of black sheep the majority of the service had been united, too, by an unwritten and nearly always unspoken code of personal conduct, the pillars of which were devotion to duty, integrity over money, and a sense of personal honour.

Devotion to duty seems to have been Alcock's prime motivation, and others were not far behind. In a country where bribes or *douceurs* were normal they were not offered to members of the service,[a] a silent recognition of its integrity. It can be left to Moss to

express the sense of personal honour. Looking back from retirement on his career[a] he took pride in never having received or given an order which had given him moral qualms. That is not a bad thing to be able to say of any career, or of any public service.

APPENDIX I

British Consular Establishments in China

Consular Establishment	Date of First Opening	Name in Pinyin
Amoy	1843	Xiamen
Antung	1908	Andong
Canton	1843	Guangzhou
Changsha	1905	Changsha
Chefoo (established in lieu of Tengchow)	1861	Yantai
Chengtu	1902	Chengdu
Chinkiang	1861	Zhenjiang
Chungking	1877	Chongqing
Foochow	1844	Fuzhou
Hangchow	1896	Hangzhou
Hankow	1861	Hankou
Harbin	1910	Ha'erbin
Hoihow (established in lieu of Kiungchow)	1876	Haikou
Ichang	1877	Yichang
Kashgar	1904 (date at which a consul's commission was issued to an Indian government official already stationed at Kashgar)	Kashi
Keelung	1869	Qilong
Kiukiang	1861	Jiujiang
Kongmoon	1904	Jiangmen
Mukden	1906	Fengtian
Nanking	1900	Nanjing
Newchwang (established at Yingkow)	1861	Yingzi
Ningpo	1844	Ningbo
Pagoda Island	1867	Luoxing
Pakhoi	1877	Beihai

Samshui	1897	Sanshui
Shanghai	1843	Shanghai
Shasi	1897	Shashi
Soochow	1896	Suzhou
Ssumao	1897	Simao
Swatow (established in lieu of Chaochow)	1860	Shantou
Tachienlu	1913	Dajianlu
Taiwan (later, Tainan)	1861	Tainan
Takow	1864	Dagou
Taku	1862	Dagu
Tamsui	1862	Danshui
Tengyueh (otherwise, Momein)	1899	Tengyue
Tientsin	1860	Tianjin
Tsinan	1906	Jinan
Tsingtao	1919 (date at which a career officer took over from a local British merchant previously in charge)	Qingdao
Weihaiwei	1930	Weihaiwei
Wenchow	1877	Wenzhou
Whampoa	1843	Huangpu
Wuchow	1897	Wuzhou
Wuhu	1877	Wuhu
Yochow	1900	Yuezhou
Yunnanfu	1902	Yunnanfu

APPENDIX II

Chronological List of Members of the China Consular Service
(originally styled 'the China Establishment' or 'the Far Eastern Establishment')

Notes: col. (i) Appointments made without competitive examination before 1861 are shown in alphabetical order in each year concerned. Appointments made without competitive examination in 1919 and 1920 are shown in date order of appointment in each year. All other appointments are shown in examination result order.

col. (ii) Where 'London' is shown as the place of residence the London County Council area is denoted, whether before or after the establishment of the London County Council.

cols. (iii) and (iv) Where the month and day of birth are not known the ages given may be a year out. In later years retirements due to age and retirements due to ill-health are rarely distinguishable.

(v) Fuller knowledge would certainly permit additions to the family connections with the East now shown. Marriages mentioned are to British subjects unless otherwise stated.

(i) Name, and age on first appointment	(ii) Father's occupation and place of residence (not necessarily at time of son's appointment)	(iii) Age and rank at time of death in service, retirement, resignation, or dismissal, and any honours	(iv) Age at death after leaving service	(v) Remarks, including known family connections with the East
		1843–60: Appointments by patronage, without examination		
		1843		
1. J. Backhouse 25	Foreign Office official. London.	Retired, ill-health, 37. Vice-consul.	42	Previously in Royal Navy and in a merchant's office.
2. G. Balfour 32	Army captain. Montrose.	Resigned, 35. Consul.	83	Previously captain, Madras army, and staff officer, China, 1840 on. Became a full general and an MP.

(i) Name, and age on first appointment	(ii) Father's occupation and place of residence (not necessarily at time of son's appointment)	(iii) Age and rank at time of death in service, retirement, resignation, or dismissal, and any honours	(iv) Age at death after leaving service	(v) Remarks, including known family connections with the East
3. A. Bird 29	Not known.	Retired, ill-health, 46.	48	Formerly in Bombay. Joined Pottinger's staff, 1840.
4. W. Connor 24	Father, Anthony Connor, 'gentleman'. Occupation and residence not known.	Died, 32. Vice-consul.	—	Arrived Hong Kong, 1842. Married sister of No. 35.
5. A.W. Elmslie 23	'Owner of bank and other shares' (? a merchant). Weston-super-Mare.	Retired, ill-health, 35. Vice-consul.	55	Member of superintendency staff from 1837. Younger brother of No. 6.
6. E. Elmslie 28	As above.	Resigned, ill-health, 28. Treasurer, superintendency.	58	Member of superintendency staff by 1835. 'Of weak mind' in later life. See No. 5.
7. E.F. Giles 15	Landscape painter. Aberdeen.	Died, 21. First assistant.	—	Selected for appointment by Foreign Secretary personally.
8. W.R. Gingell 26	Doctor and landed proprietor. Thornbury, Glos.	Died, 46. Consul.	—	Previously surgeon, Madras army. In China from 1842. Married widow of No. 32.
9. H. Gribble 38	Possibly captain of Indiaman. Near Barnstaple, Devon.	Services not required because provisional appointment not confirmed, 39. Provisional consul.	Over 70.	Previously captain of Indiaman and China merchant. Died between 1878–86. Related to Revd Charles Gribble, chaplain, British Embassy, Constantinople, 1858–78.

No. & Name, Age		Outcome		Notes
10. K.F.A. Gutzlaff 40	Tailor. Pomerania.	Died, 48. Chinese secretary.	—	German. Originally brazier's apprentice, then China missionary. Member of superintendency staff by 1836. Second wife cousin of No. 27.
11. P. Hague 26	Chairman, visiting magistrates, Yorkshire. York.	Retired, ill-health, 38. Vice-consul.	59	Previously nine years in merchants' offices. Married sister of No. 18.
12. F.H. Hale 24	Chaplain, British Embassy, Paris.	Retired, ill-health. Vice-consul.	45	Previously surgeon.
13. F.E. Harvey 17	Consul. Bayonne.	Retired, ill-health, 42. Consul.	56	Previously in a merchant's office.
14. F.L. Hertslet 20	Sub-librarian, Foreign Office. London.	Died, 28. First assistant.	—	Previously employed in Colonial Office and part-time in Foreign Office.
15. R.B. Jackson 35	Not known.	Retired, abolition of office, 43. Consul.	77	First employed in Foreign Office, 1825.
16. A.R. Johnston 29	Chief justice, Ceylon. Latterly of Dumfriesshire.	Retired, abolition of office, 38. Secretary, superintendency.	75	Born Ceylon. Brought to China by his cousin, Chief Superintendent Napier. Member of superintendency staff from 1834. Fellow of Royal Society. Died under the name of Campbell-Johnston.
17. G.T. Lay 43	Not known.	Died, 45. Consul.	—	Formerly Bible Society agent, Macao. Joined Pottinger's staff, 1841. Father of Nos. 46, 51, and 94. Another son in Chinese Customs.

(i) Name, and age on first appointment	(ii) Father's occupation and place of residence (not necessarily at time of son's appointment)	(iii) Age and rank at time of death in service, retirement, resignation, or dismissal, death after leaving service	(iv) Age at death after leaving service	(v) Remarks, including known family connections with the East
18. T.H. Layton 40	Tea-broker. London.	Died, 47. Consul.	—	Formerly East India Company tea-inspector. See No. 11.
19. F.C. Macgregor 60	Not known.	Retired, ill-health, 65. Consul.	93	First employed by Foreign Office, 1813. Born under the name of Coleman.
20. T.T. Meadows 24	Not known.	Died, 49. Consul.	—	Born Northumberland. Younger brother of No. 40.
21. W.H. Medhurst 20	Originally printer, then Congregationalist missionary in China and elsewhere in Far East.	Retired, ill-health, 54. Consul. Knighted.	63	Born Batavia. Member of superintendency staff from 1840. Half-brother to father of No. 68. Sister married No. 70. Second wife was daughter of US consul, Macao.
22. W.S. Meredith 17	'Independent means'. London.	Died, 21. Second assistant.	—	Arrived Hong Kong, 1843. Appointed after arrival.
23. J.R. Morrison 28	Originally last-maker's apprentice, then Congregationalist missionary in China and Chinese secretary, East India Company.	Died, 28. Chinese secretary.	—	Chinese secretary, superintendency, from 1834. Half-brother to Nos. 24 and 41. Nephew in Chinese Customs.
24. M.C. Morrison 15	As above.	Retired, ill-health, 39. Consul.	43	See No. 23. Brother of No. 41.

No. and Name	Age	Father / Origin	Career	Age at death	Notes
25. H. Oakley	25	Clergyman. Dorset.	Retired, ill-health, 38. First assistant.	57	
26. F. Parish	19	Diplomatist.	Transferred to Buenos Aires, 28. Retired, ill-health, 49. Consul (Buenos Aires).	81	Born Buenos Aires. Grandfather in East India Company service. Great-uncle in military escort of Macartney embassy to China. Previously acted as father's secretary in Naples.
27. H.S. Parkes	15	Iron-master. Walsall.	Died, 57. Minister to China. GCMG, KCB.	—	Arrived Macao, 1841. Attached to Pottinger's suite, 1842. See Nos. 10, 103, and 127. Two sisters married China missionaries. Daughter married a leading British merchant in China trade.
28. D.B. Robertson	33	Father Daniel Robertson, 'esquire', occupation not known. Christchurch, Hampshire.	Retired, ill-health, 68. Consul-general. KCMG, Kt., CB.	70	Entered East India Company's mercantile naval service aged 16, later barrister. Employed in Foreign Office from 1842. Brother of No. 38. Another brother in China. Son in Japan consular service.
29. N. (de) St. Croix	42	Father Nicholas (de) St. Croix, occupation not known. London.	Resigned, 47. Consular agent, Whampoa.	81	Formerly captain of an Indiaman. After resignation resident Canton until 1851. Not related to the (de) Ste. (sic) Croix in the Chinese Customs, but one or more nephews, and a great-nephew, were merchants in China.
30. C.A. Sinclair	25	Father Charles Sinclair, 'esquire'. Occupation and residence not known.	Retired, 68. Consul.	79	Related to the Aufrère family of Norfolk.

(i) Name, and age on first appointment	(ii) Father's occupation and place of residence (not necessarily at time of son's appointment)	(iii) Age and rank at time of death in service, retirement, resignation, or dismissal, and any honours	(iv) Age at death after leaving service	(v) Remarks, including known family connections with the East
31. H.C. Sirr 36	Wine merchant and town major. Dublin.	Resigned, 37. Vice-consul.	65	Formerly barrister. First employed in Foreign Office, 1841.
32. G.G. Sullivan 35	Not known.	Died, 44. Consul.	—	Previously a master, Royal Navy. See Nos. 8 and 65.
33. R. Thom 35	Merchant (? coal agent) and a police commissioner. Glasgow.	Died, 39. Consul.	—	From the age of about 14 in business, in Glasgow, Liverpool, Latin America, and from 1834 in China. On Pottinger's staff from 1840.
34. J.T. Walker 27	Attorney and solicitor. Havant, Hampshire.	Died, 36. Vice-consul.	—	
35. E. Warden Age not known.	Captain, Bombay Marine. Latterly of London.	Resigned (?) about 1845, age not known. Fourth assistant.	Not known.	Later shipping agent, Shanghai. See No. 4.
36. C.A. Winchester 23	Advocate. Aberdeen.	Retired, ill-health, 50. Consul.	63	Assistant naval surgeon, 1841. Medical officer, Hong Kong, 1842. Son offered appointment in Chinese Customs.

37. R. Alcock 33	Doctor. Ealing.	*1844* Retired, 62. Minister to China. KCB.	88	Formerly surgeon, employed in Foreign Office from 1840. Second wife widow of Anglican chaplain, Shanghai. Stepfather of No. 106. Another stepson in Chinese Customs. A third stepson in Japan consular service.
38. F. Robertson 23	Father Daniel Robertson (see No. 28).	Died, 27. Third assistant.	—	See No. 28.
39. C.T. Watkins Age not known.	Not known.	Dismissed, 1847, age not known. Third assistant.	Not known.	Already in Hong Kong when appointed.
40. J.A.T. Meadows 28	Not known.	*1845* Resigned, 44. Interpreter.	57	Born Northumberland. See No. 20. Married a Chinese. After resignation became a merchant at Tientsin, where he acted as US vice-consul and consul for various other powers.
41. G.S. Morrison 16	Chinese secretary, East India Company (see No. 23).	*1847* Transferred to Japan consular service, 1858. Retired, ill-health, 31. Consul (Japan).	61	See Nos. 23 and 24.

(i) Name, and age on first appointment	(ii) Father's occupation and place of residence (not necessarily at time of son's appointment)	(iii) Age and rank at time of resignation, or dismissal, death in service, retirement, after leaving service	(iv) Age at death after leaving service	(v) Remarks, including known family connections with the East
42. T.F. Wade 25	Adjutant-general. Ireland.	Retired, 64. Minister to China. GCMG, KCB.	76	Previously army officer in China and interpreter to Hong Kong garrison, 1843; Cantonese interpreter to Hong Kong Supreme Court from 1846. After retirement became professor of Chinese, Cambridge University. Son in Chinese Customs.
43. W.H. Pedder 21	Lieutenant, Royal Navy, and Hong Kong harbour-master.	*1848* Retired, impaired sight, 52. Consul.	73	Married sister of No. 58.
44. J. Bowring 57	Cloth merchant. Exeter.	*1849* Relieved of duties as chief superintendent, 67. Knighted.	80	Previously member of Parliament. Grandson (?) in Chinese Customs.
45. W.H. Fittock 20	Master, Royal Navy. In China, 1840–7, latterly of London.	Retired, ill-health, 45. Consul.	53	Clerk in Hong Kong government offices from 1844. Married daughter of assistant harbour-master, Hong Kong. Father of No. 156.

46. H.N. Lay 17	China consular officer.	Resigned to become inspector of Chinese Customs, 23. Second assistant.	65	Son of No. 17, brother of Nos. 51 and 94. Married daughter of China missionary. Inspector-general of Chinese Customs, 1861–3.
47. W. Woodgate 28	Colonel. Paris.	Died, 37. Registrar, superintendency.	—	Relative of Chief Superintendent Bonham, who recommended his appointment.
1852				
48. G.W. Caine	Lieutenant-governor, Hong Kong.	Dismissed, 40. Consul.	41	Studied Chinese at King's College, London. Clerk in Hong Kong government offices from 1850.
49. J. Markham 17	Lieutenant, Royal Navy. Guernsey.	Died, 36. Consul.	—	Selected for appointment by Foreign Secretary personally. Born Leghorn. Grandfather private secretary to Warren Hastings. Married daughter of marine surveyor, Hong Kong.
50. A.J. Thompson 15	Not known.	Resigned, ill-health, 17. Student interpreter.	Not known.	Selected for appointment by Foreign Secretary personally. An orphan.
1853				
51. W.H. Lay 17	China consular officer.	Died, 40. Consul.	—	Son of No. 17, brother of Nos. 46 and 94. Married daughter of China missionary whose other daughter married No. 58 (see also No. 87). A son in Japan consular service, another sat entrance examination unsuccessfully, a third in Chinese Customs. A daughter married a Japan service consular officer.

(i) Name, and age on first appointment	(ii) Father's occupation and place of residence (not necessarily at time of son's appointment)	(iii) Age and rank at time of resignation, or dismissal, death in service, retirement, after leaving service	(iv) Age at death after leaving service	(v) Remarks, including known family connections with the East
		April–June 1854		
52. W. Gregory 24	Currier. Trowbridge, Wiltshire.	Retired, 60. Consul.	86	Recommended by University College, London. Congregationalist.
53. H.F. Hance 26	Accountant. Devon.	Died, 58. Vice-consul.	—	Clerk in Hong Kong government offices from 1844. Two sons in Chinese Customs.
54. R. Hart 19	Spirit grocer. Co. Antrim.	Resigned to become inspector of Chinese Customs, 23. Second assistant.	76	Recommended by Queen's College, Belfast. Inspector-general of Chinese Customs, 1863–1911.
55. P.J. Hughes 20	Father Thomas Hughes, occupation not known. Newry, Co. Armagh.	Retired, ill-health, 57. Consul-general. Second assistant.	69	Recommended by Queen's College, Galway. Roman Catholic. Brother in Chinese Customs.
56. O.J. Lane 19	Not known.	Killed during hostilities, 21. Second assistant.	—	Previously private secretary to his cousin, No. 44, who recommended his appointment.
57. J. Mongan 23	Father Thomas Mongan, 'gentleman', occupation not known. Dundrum, Dublin.	Retired, ill-health, 49. Consul.	50	Recommended by Queen's College, Cork. Married sister of No. 71.

APPENDIX II

No.	Occupation	Status	Age	Notes
58. R. Swinhoe, 17	Solicitor. India.	Retired, ill-health, 38. Consul.	41	Recommended by King's College, London. Born Calcutta. Brother colonel, India. See Nos. 43 and 51. Fellow of Royal Society.

October 1854

No.	Occupation	Status	Age	Notes
59. C. Bell, 22	'Argentarius' (?silversmith). London, latterly Glasgow.	Resigned, 24. First assistant.	27	Recommended from China class, King's College, London. Died Bangkok.
60. W.M. Cooper, 21	Barrister. London.	Retired, ill-health, 55. Consul.	63	Recommended from China class. Married daughter of army officer, India. Her sister married No. 114.
61. E.F. Forrest, 17	Home Office official. London.	Died, 21. Second assistant.	—	Recommended from China class. Elder brother of No. 78. Another brother in Ceylon. Cousin Anglican chaplain, Shanghai.
62. C.T. Jones, 17	Doctor. Hong Kong.	Dismissed, 29. First assistant.	Not known.	Recommended from China class. Probably married sister of No. 94's wife. Alive in Australia in 1894.
63. T. Adkins, 18	Farmer. Stratford-on-Avon.	Retired, ill-health, 44. Consul.	76	Recommended from China class. Wife's brother in Chinese Customs.
64. C. Alabaster, 16	Straw-hat maker. London.	Retired, ill-health, 54. Consul-general. KCMG.	59	Recommended from China class. Younger brother of No. 67. Married daughter of US surgeon in Chinese Customs. Son attorney-general, Hong Kong. Nephew in Chinese Customs.

(i) Name, and age on first appointment	(ii) Father's occupation and place of residence (not necessarily at time of son's appointment)	(iii) Age and rank at time of death in service, retirement, resignation, or dismissal, and any honours	(iv) Age at death after leaving service	(v) Remarks, including known family connections with the East
65. W.E. King 17	Clergyman. Dorset.	Retired, ill-health, 40. Consul.	79	Recommended from China class. Elder brother a Shanghai merchant who married daughter of No. 32.
66. W.N. Payne 20	Commercial agent. London.	Required to resign, 33.	Not known.	Recommended from China class. Younger brother in Chinese Customs.
		1856		
67. H. Alabaster 19	Straw-hat maker. London.	Transferred to Bangkok, 1857, and resigned from Siam consular service, aged 35. Interpreter (Siam).	48	Recommended from China class. See No. 64. Died Bangkok as 'His Siamese Majesty's Interpreter'. (?) in Chinese Customs.
68. G.C.P. Braune 18	Clergyman. Yorkshire.	Died, 26. Second assistant.	—	Recommended from China class. Father the son of army officer, India. See No. 21.
69. A.A.J. Gower 20	Banker. Leghorn.	Transferred to Japan consular service, 1859. Retired, ill-health, 40. Consul (Japan).	62	Previously private secretary to No. 44, who recommended his appointment. Born and died Leghorn.

No.	Occupation / Origin	Outcome	Age	Remarks
70. C.B. Hillier Age not known.	Not known.	Died, age not known.	—	Previously chief magistrate in Hong Kong, where he had originally arrived as second mate of a merchant ship. See No. 121. Father of No. 121. A second son in Chinese Customs. A third son in a British bank in China married sister of No. 230's wife.
71. H.G. Howlett 18	Farmer. Norfolk.	Required to resign, 34. First assistant.	Not known.	Recommended from China class. See No. 57.
72. J.A. Webster Age not known.	Not known.	Dismissed, 1868, age not known. First assistant.	Not known.	Recommended from China class. Married a Chinese.
73. A. Davenport 20	Clergyman. Gloucestershire.	*1857* Retired, ill-health, 49. Consul.	80	Recommended from China class.
74. J. Gibson 22	Farmer of 100 acres. Kirkcudbrightshire.	Died, 34. Interpreter.	—	Recommended from China class.
75. G. Phillips 21	Master baker. Walmer, Kent.	Retired, ill-health, 55. Consul.	60	Recommended from China class.
76. C. Carroll 21	Colonial produce merchant. London.	*1858* Died, 39. Vice-consul.	—	Recommended from China class. Previously served with Turkish contingent in Crimea, 1855–6, and then in a mercantile house.

(i) Name, and age on first appointment	(ii) Father's occupation and place of residence (not necessarily at time of son's appointment)	(iii) Age and rank at time of resignation, or death in service, retirement, or dismissal, and any honours	(iv) Age at death after leaving service	(v) Remarks, including known family connections with the East
77. R.K. Douglas 19	Clergyman. Devon.	Resigned, 26. First assistant.	74	Recommended from China class. Later became keeper of oriental books and manuscripts, British Museum.
78. R.J. Forrest 22	Home Office official. London.	Retired, ill-health, 57. Consul.	66	Recommended from China class. See No. 61.
79. A.R. Hewlett 20	Surgeon. Harrow.	Retired, ill-health, 47. Consul.	63	Recommended from China class. Uncle of No. 204.
80. H.F.W. Holt 20	Solicitor. London.	Retired, ill-health, 37. Interpreter.	51	Recommended from China class.
81. Revd W.C. Milne 43	First shepherd and carpenter's apprentice, Aberdeenshire, then Congregationalist missionary, Malacca.	Died, 48. Interpreter.	—	London Missionary Society missionary, China, 1839. Application for appointment to China consular service backed by various members of Parliament.
82. J.P.M. Fraser 18	Sheriff substitute, Inverness and Argyllshire. Fort William.	Dismissed, 33. First assistant.	Not known.	Selected for appointment by Foreign Secretary personally.
83. J.B. Goddard 20	Surgeon. Christchurch, Hampshire.	Retired, ill-health, 34. First assistant.	57	Selected for appointment by Foreign Secretary personally.

84. W.S.F. Mayers 19	Chaplain, Marseilles.	Died, 39. Chinese secretary.	—	Selected for appointment by Foreign Secretary personally. Born Tasmania. Father of No. 189. A second son in Chinese Customs.
85. J.T. Middleton 19	Portrait painter. London.	Retired, abolition of office, 37. Vice-consul.	38	Selected for appointment by Foreign Secretary personally.

Note: Nos. 94, 105, and 106 were appointed without initial examination but subject to passing a qualifying examination after appointment; Nos. 178 and 232 transferred from the Siam consular service; No. 188 transferred from a Straits Settlements cadetship.

1861–1909: APPOINTMENTS FOLLOWING COMPETITIVE ENTRANCE EXAMINATIONS FOR THE CHINA, JAPAN, AND SIAM CONSULAR SERVICES (special papers set for these examinations only; age limits in 1861 over 16 and under 26, thereafter over 18 and under 24; limited competition 1861–71, open competition 1872–1904, limited competition 1905–9)

1861 (June examination)

86. J.J.M. Beatty Age not known.	Merchant. Enniskillen, Co. Fermanagh.	Required to resign, 1867. Third assistant.	Not known.	Nominated by Trinity College, Dublin.
87. W.G. Stronach 25	Presbyterian missionary. China.	Retired, ill-health, 52. Consul.	68	Nominated by King's College, London (China class and BA). Cousin of wives of Nos. 51 and 58. First wife a China missionary's widow. Sister married captain of an opium ship.

(i) Name, and age on first appointment	(ii) Father's occupation and place of residence (not necessarily at time of son's resignation, or dismissal, appointment)	(iii) Age and rank at time of death in service, retirement, and any honours	(iv) Age at death after leaving service	(v) Remarks, including known family connections with the East
88. J. McI. Brown 25	Presbyterian minister. Co. Antrim.	Resigned to enter Chinese Customs, 36. Assistant Chinese secretary.	90	Nominated by Queen's College, Belfast.
89. E.D. Jones 23	Clergyman. Cambridge.	Retired, ill-health, 32. First assistant.	44	Nominated by St. John's College, Cambridge (BA).
90. G.P. Thomson 20	Tailor. Aberdeen.	Died, 27. Interpreter.	—	Nominated by Aberdeen University (MA).
91. J.G. Murray 20	Artisan. Stranraer, Wigtownshire.	Died, 33. Interpreter.	—	Nominated by Glasgow University (BA). Younger brother in Chinese Customs.
92. C.T. Gardner 19	Doctor. London.	Retired, ill-health, 57. Consul.	72	Nominated from Foreign Secretary's list when at King's College, London. Brother in India.
93. H.J. Allen 19	Bengal Civil Service. Latterly of Pembrokeshire.	Retired, ill-health, 46. Consul.	80	Nominated by Trinity College, Cambridge. Born India. Brother in Rangoon. Cousin of Nos. 96 and 139.
94. W.T. Lay 21	China consular officer.	*1861 (special entry)* Resigned to enter Chinese Customs, 22. Student interpreter.	77	Son of No. 17. Brother of Nos. 46 and 51. See also No. 62.

1863 (December 1862 examination)

95.	T. Watters 22	Presbyterian minister. Co. Down.	Retired, ill-health, 55. Consul.	60	Nominated by Queen's University, Belfast (MA).
96.	C.F.R. Allen 19	Master of Dulwich College. Latterly of Pembrokeshire.	Retired, ill-health, 54. Consul.	76	Nominated by Cambridge University. Half-brother to father of No. 139. Cousin of No. 93.
97.	N.B. Dennys 23	Chaplain, Gosport Military Prison.	Resigned, 25. Student interpreter.	60	Nominated from Foreign Secretary's list. Previously assistant paymaster, Royal Navy. Younger brother Crown solicitor, Hong Kong. Three uncles in India. Son in Malayan civil service. Died in service of British North Borneo Company.
98.	E. Solbé 20	Clergyman. Uppingham.	Retired, ill-health, 32. Interpreter.	59	Nominated from Foreign Secretary's list. Father formerly chaplain, Smyrna.

1863 (July examination)

99.	A. Frater 22	Assistant city chamberlain. Aberdeen.	Retired, ill-health, 52. Consul.	53	Nominated by Aberdeen University. Previously War Office clerk.
100.	O.A. Vidal 22	Captain, Royal Navy. Worthing.	Transferred to Japan consular service, 1865. Suicide, 26. Student interpreter.	—	Nominated by Oxford University (BA).

(i) Name, and age on first appointment	(ii) Father's occupation and place of residence (not necessarily at time of son's appointment)	(iii) Age and rank at time of death in service, retirement, resignation, or dismissal, after leaving service	(iv) Age at death after leaving service	(v) Remarks, including known family connections with the East
		1864		
101. R.A. Mowat 21	Father Joseph Mowat, probably a commission agent. Edinburgh.	Transferred to Supreme Court, China and Japan, 1868. Retired, ill-health, 54. Judge, Japan.	82	Nominated by London University.
102. G. Jamieson 21	Farmer. Banffshire.	Retired, ill-health, 56. Consul-general. CMG.	77	Nominated by Aberdeen University (MA). Father of No. 228. Brother Presbyterian missionary, China. Daughter married Shanghai exchange broker. After retirement became director, British and Chinese Corporation.
		1865 (April examination)		
103. H.P. McClatchie 18	Chaplain, Hankow.	Died, 36. Consul.	—	Nominated from Foreign Secretary's list. Brother in Japan consular service. Nephew of No. 27. See No. 127.
104. M.J. O'Brien 22	Father Michael O'Brien, occupation not known. Dungarvan, Co. Waterford.	Resigned to enter Chinese Customs, 24. Student interpreter.	Not known.	Nominated by Queen's College, Cork (BA). Resigned from Chinese Customs aged 36. Died after 1882.

		1865 (special entries)		
105. E. Egan 24	Father John Egan, 'esquire', occupation not known. Brighton.	Required to resign, 27. Student interpreter.	Not known.	In Canton when appointed. Previously army ensign in China.
106. W. Lowder 24	Chaplain, Shanghai.	Failed to pass qualifying examination, 25. Student interpreter.	Not known.	Previously temporarily employed in a Japan consulate. After his failure to qualify appointed to Supreme Court, China and Japan, in 1866 and required to resign in 1869. Stepson of No. 37.
		1865 (October examination)		
107. E. McKean 22	Merchant. Co. Armagh.	Resigned to enter Chinese Customs, 29. Second assistant.	85	Nominated by Queen's College, Belfast (BA).
108. A.S. Harvey 21	Professor of medicine. Aberdeen University.	Required to retire, mental derangement, 34. First assistant.	68	Nominated by Aberdeen (?) University (BA). In later life professor of law, Peking University, 1905–9. Brother in India.
109. F.K. Porter 19	Presbyterian minister. Belfast.	Drowned, 23. Third assistant.	—	Nominated from Foreign Secretary's list.
		1866		
110. E.C. Baber 23	Schoolmaster. Rossall.	Died, 47. Consul.	—	Nominated from Foreign Secretary's list.
111. E.L. Oxenham 22	Clergyman and housemaster. Harrow School.	Retired, ill-health, 47. Consul.	52	Nominated from Foreign Secretary's list. Previously clerk in National Debt Office.

(i) Name, and age on first appointment	(ii) Father's occupation and place of residence (not necessarily at time of son's appointment)	(iii) Age and rank at time of death in service, retirement, resignation, or dismissal, after leaving service	(iv) Age at death after leaving service	(v) Remarks, including known family connections with the East
112. B. Brenan 18	Lieutenant-colonel, Imperial Ottoman Army. Laterly of Jersey.	Retired, ill-health, 53. Consul-general. CMG.	79	Nominated from Foreign Secretary's list. Uncle of Nos. 232 and 268. Elder brother in Chinese Customs from 1871. After retirement was Shanghai representative of British and Chinese Corporation.
		1867 (January examination)		
113. A.R. Margary 20	Major-general. Brighton.	Murdered, 28. Second assistant. AM.	—	Nominated from Foreign Secretary's list (an uncle was political under-secretary, Foreign Office). Born India.
114. B.C.G. Scott 20	Solicitor. Aylsham, Norfolk.	Retired, ill-health, 55. Consul-general.	83	Nominated from Foreign Secretary's list. See Nos. 60 and 119.
115. H.A. Giles 21	Clergyman. Oxford.	Retired, ill-health, 47. Consul.	89	? Nominated from Foreign Secretary's list. Father of Nos. 186 and 213. After retirement became professor of Chinese, Cambridge University.

APPENDIX II

No.	Background	Career		Notes
116. W.N. Abdy 22	Baronet. Essex.	Resigned, 23. Student interpreter.	66	Nominated from Foreign Secretary's list (an uncle was a Foreign Office official).
117. P.L. Warren 21	Admiral. Devon.	Retired, 65. Consul-general. KCMG.	78	? Nominated from Foreign Secretary's list. Son in Chinese Customs. One daughter married a Shanghai merchant, another a Shanghai doctor.

1867 (June examination)

No.	Background	Career		Notes
118. H.B. Bristow 18	Inn-keeper. South Lynn, Norfolk.	Retired, ill-health, 48. Consul.	84	Nominated from Foreign Secretary's list. Father of No. 205. A second son in Indian Civil Service. After retirement became representative of Pekin Syndicate.
119. C.M. Ford 20	Merchant. India.	Retired, ill-health, 51. Consul.	71	Nominated by Aberdeen University (MA). Previously preparing for Indian Civil Service examination. Born India. Married No. 114's sister.
120. C.W. Everard 21	Clergyman. Norfolk.	Retired, ill-health, 48. Consul.	79	Nominated from Foreign Secretary's list.

(i) Name, and age on first appointment	(ii) Father's occupation and place of residence (not necessarily at time of son's appointment)	(iii) Age and rank at time of death in service, retirement, or dismissal, and any honours	(iv) Age at death after leaving service	(v) Remarks, including known family connections with the East
		1867 (October examination)		
121. W.C. Hillier 18	China consular officer.	Retired, ill-health, 47. Consul-general. KCMG, CB.	78	Nominated from Foreign Secretary's list. Son of No. 70. Two daughters and two nieces married Tientsin residents. One sister-in-law was daughter of Shanghai barrister, another was sister of No. 230's wife. After retirement became professor of Chinese, King's College, London, and adviser to Chinese government. See No. 146.
122. C.J. Andrews 21	Queen's counsel. Dublin.	Died, 29. Second assistant.	—	Nominated from Foreign Secretary's list.
123. W.R. Carles 19	Clergyman. Warwickshire.	Retired, ill-health, 52. Consul-general. CMG.	80	Nominated by Marlborough College.

		1868		
124. E.H. Parker 19	Surgeon. Liverpool.	Retired, ill-health, 46.	77	Nominated from Foreign Secretary's list. Left school at 15, worked in merchants' offices in Liverpool and London and studied Chinese. ? married a Chinese. After retirement became professor of Chinese, Owens College, Manchester.
125. W.D. Spence 20	Stocking-cotton manufacturer. Huntly, Aberdeenshire.	Died, 42. First assistant.	—	Nominated by Aberdeen University (MA).
126. T.L. Bullock 23	Clergyman. Essex.	Retired, ill-health, 51. Consul.	69	Nominated from Foreign Secretary's list. Son entered general consular service. Daughter married Hong Kong government official. After retirement became professor of Chinese, Oxford University.
127. W.S. Ayrton 19	Commissioner in bankruptcy. Residence not known.	Retired, ill-health, 50. Consul.	52	Nominated from Foreign Secretary's list. Married sister of No. 103 (niece of No. 27).
128. R. Gardner 18	Father Ephraim Gardner, occupation not known. Huntly, Aberdeenshire.	Died, 21. Student interpreter.	—	Nominated from Foreign Secretary's list.
129. J.D. Crawford 19	Resident magistrate, New Zealand.	*1870 (March examination)* Required to resign, mental derangement, 29. Second assistant.	52	Nominated from Foreign Secretary's list.

(i) Name, and age on first appointment	(ii) Father's occupation and place of residence (not necessarily at time of son's resignation, or dismissal, appointment)	(iii) Age and rank at time of death in service, retirement, after dismissal, and any honours	(iv) Age at death after leaving service	(v) Remarks, including known family connections with the East
130. R.W. Mansfield 19	Clergyman. Dorset.	Retired, ill-health, 58. Consul-general. CMG.	70	Nominated from Foreign Secretary's list. Uncle of No. 192. Married daughter of government official, French India. Son (?) in Chinese Customs. A daughter married elder brother of No. 192.
131. W.L.B. Neale Age not known.	Consular officer, later diplomatist.	Dismissed, mental derangement, 1872. Student interpreter.	Not known.	Nominated from Foreign Secretary's list. Father formerly secretary of Legation, Peking.
132. W.H. Young 20	Clergyman. Shrewsbury.	*1870 (May examination)* Died, 22. Student interpreter.	—	Nominated from Foreign Secretary's list.
133. G. Brown 20	Wine and spirit merchant. Rugby.	*1871* Retired, ill-health, 45. Consul.	85	Nominated from Foreign Secretary's list. Daughter after being divorced by Tientsin merchant married No. 171. After retirement became agent-general, Pekin Syndicate.

		1872 (June examination)		
134. G.M.H. Playfair 22	Surgeon-general, India. Originally of St. Andrews, Fife.	Retired, 60. Consul.	67	Grandfather inspector-general of hospitals, India. An uncle consul-general in Algeria, another a member of Parliament. Married daughter of officer of Supreme Court, China and Japan.
135. W. Holland 21	Solicitor. London.	Retired, ill-health, 51. Consul.	72	Son in British bank, China.
136. M.F.A. Fraser 22	Not known.	Required to retire, 51. Consul.	80	
137. R.W. Hurst 23	Grocer. Manchester.	*1872 (July examination)* Retired, ill-health, 51. Consul.	75	
138. O. Johnson 20	Sculptor. London.	Retired, ill-health, 48. Consul.	55	
139. E.L.B. Allen 19	Clergyman. Glamorgan.	Retired, ill-health, 46. Consul.	66	See Nos. 93 and 96. Brother a tea-taster in China.
140. J.A.H. Taylor 22	Clergyman. Stockport, Cheshire.	Died, 26. Third assistant.	—	
141. J. Scott 21	Small farmer. Aberdeenshire.	Retired, ill-health, 55. Consul-general. ISO.	69	Father of No. 274.
142. L.C. Hopkins 19	Average adjuster. London.	*1873* Retired, ill-health, 54. Consul-general. ISO.	97	See No. 217.

(i) Name, and age on first appointment	(ii) Father's occupation and place of residence (not necessarily at time of son's appointment)	(iii) Age and rank at time of death in service, retirement, resignation, or dismissal, and any honours	(iv) Age at death after leaving service	(v) Remarks, including known family connections with the East
143. J.R. Coulthard 19	Draper. Bath.	Retired, ill-health, 45. Vice-consul.	61	Younger brother a China missionary.
144. J.N. Jordan 23	Farmer. Co. Down.	1876 Retired, 68. Minister to China. PC, GCMG, GCIE, KCB.	73	Coached for entrance examination at Civil Service Department, King's College, London. Previously supplementary clerk, War Office. Married daughter of China missionary, another of whose daughters was mother of No. 264 and two of whose sons were respectively a consul-general in Japan and a Chinese Customs officer. A brother in the Chinese police, married daughter of No. 206. Other son in Indian Civil Service.
145. F.S.A. Bourne 21	Clergyman. Norfolk.	Transferred to Supreme Court, China and Japan, 1898. Retired, 61. Assistant judge, China and Korea. Knighted, CMG.	86	
146. H.F. Brady 22	Inspector of Irish fisheries. Dublin.	Retired, ill-health, 54. Consul.	70	Married half-sister of No. 121.

147. A. Hosie 23	Small farmer. Aberdeenshire.	Retired, ill-health, 59. Consul-general. Knighted.	72	Second wife daughter of a China missionary. Brother army doctor, India.
148. W. Warry 23	'Private gentleman'. Sherborne.	*1878* Transferred to Indian Civil Service, 1890. Retired, ill-health, 50.	82	
149. J.N. Tratman 19	Shipowner. Bristol.	Retired, ill-health, 48. Consul.	87	
150. L.W. Henley 22	Silk manufacturer. Derby.	Died, 27. Student interpreter.	—	
151. P.F. Hausser 21	Father Frederick Hausser, professor of music. Residence not known.	Retired, ill-health, 54. Consul-general.	69	
152. E.D.H. Fraser 21	Lieutenant-colonel, India. Latterly of Aberdeen.	*1880* Died, 63. Consul-general. KCMG.	—	Previously failed Indian Civil Service examination. Half-brother army officer, India. Married daughter of Foochow tea-merchant, another of whose daughters married No. 172.
153. H. Cockburn 20	Bengal Civil Service. Latterly of Bedford.	Retired, ill-health, 50. Consul-general. CB.	68	Married daughter of commissioner, Arakan.
154. W.H. Wilkinson 21	Commercial agent. Wolverhampton.	Retired, 60. Consul-general. Knighted.	71	Younger brother solicitor, Hong Kong. A daughter married Hong Kong barrister.

(i) Name, and age on first appointment	(ii) Father's occupation and place of residence (not necessarily at time of son's appointment)	(iii) Age and rank at time of death in service, retirement, resignation, or dismissal, after leaving service, and any honours	(iv) Age at death after leaving service	(v) Remarks, including known family connections with the East
155. H.E. Fulford 20	Clergyman. London, previously of Australia.	Retired, ill-health, 57. Consul-general. CMG.	69 (suicide)	Educated, married, and died in Australia. Previously in mercantile office, London.
156. G.V. Fittock 20	China consular officer.	Required to resign for failure to learn Chinese, 23. Student interpreter.	Not known.	Coached for entrance examination at Civil Service Department. Son of No. 45.
157. P.E. O'Brien-Butler 21	Inland Revenue official. London, originally of Tipperary.	Retired, 60. Consul-general.	95	Married daughter of Chinkiang merchant; one of her sisters married Transvaal emigration agent, Chefoo, and another a US merchant, Shanghai. One of his own daughters married the US consul-general, Hankow, another an employee of a British bank in China.
158. R.H. Mortimore 22	Tanner. Cullompton, Devon.	Retired, ill-health, 55. Consul-general.	69	
159. H.B. Joly 22	Vice-consul, Smyrna.	Died, 40. First assistant.	—	Two sons in Chinese Customs. A daughter married a US merchant, Korea.

		1884		
160. C.W. Campbell 22	Sergeant-major. Enniskillen, Co. Fermanagh.	Retired, ill-health, 49. Chinese secretary. CMG.	65	Previously Lower Division clerk, Science and Art Department. Married daughter of a Shanghai bill-broker.
161. W.B. Fitzgibbon 20	Merchant draper. Tarbert, Co. Kerry.	Died, 31. Second assistant.	—	Younger brother in Chinese Customs.
162. E.T.C. Werner 19	Independent means. Tonbridge.	Compulsorily retired, 49. Consul.	89	Married daughter of British Resident, Nepal.
163. E.F. Bennett 21	Watch manufacturer. Coventry.	Retired, ill-health, 42. Consul.	46	Married Austrian, separated from her husband in the Chinese Customs.
		1886		
164. J.W. Jamieson 18	Merchant. Shanghai.	Retired, 63. Consul-general. KCMG.	78	Born China. Mother a China missionary.
165. A.J. Sundius 21	Stepfather an army tutor and justice of the peace. Folkestone.	Retired, ill-health, 48. Consul.	59	Believed by Foreign Office to be of Swedish extraction.
		1888		
166. G.D. Pitzipios 22	Independent means. London.	Retired, ill-health, 54. Consul.	67	Father Greek by birth, a naturalized British subject.
167. W.J. Clennell 20	Solicitor. London.	Retired, 58. Consul.	61	Coached for entrance examination at Civil Service Department. Married sister of Chinese Customs officer.

(i) Name, and age on first appointment	(ii) Father's occupation and place of residence (not necessarily at time of son's appointment)	(iii) Age and rank at time of death in service, retirement, resignation, or dismissal, after leaving service	(iv) Age at death after leaving service	(v) Remarks, including known family connections with the East
168. E.M.H. Hobart-Hampden 23	Indian Civil Service. Latterly of Clifton.	Transferred to Japan consular service, 1889. Retired, 56. Japanese secretary.	84	Brother in India. Son in Chinese Customs.
169. W.P. Ker 23	Minister, Free Church of Scotland. Aberdeen.	Retired, 62. Consul-general. CMG.	80	
170. H.A. Little 20	'Landowner and agriculturalist'. Dorset.	*1890* Retired, ill-health, 50. Consul.	77	After failing entrance examination elder brother became first a Methodist missionary, and then a merchant, in China.
171. E.C.C. Wilton 20	Merchant. Singapore.	Transferred to Chinese Salt Administration, 1922. Retired, 56. KCMG.	82	Father Danish and mother Dutch by birth, both naturalized British subjects. Born Singapore. See No. 133. After retirement became president of Saar Governing Commission.
172. H. Goffe 20	Master plumber. Cheshunt, Hertfordshire.	Retired, 58. Consul-general. KBE, CMG.	69	See No. 152.

173. H.H. Fox 18	Managing mercantile clerk. London.	Retired, 57. Commercial counsellor. KBE, CMG.	64	First wife daughter of US captain of a Yangtze steamer.
1891				
174. E.F. Allan 23	Tea-dealer. Woodford, Essex.	Dismissed, 28. Student interpreter.	Not known.	Coached for entrance examination at Civil Service Department.
175. R. Willis 23	Clergyman. Somerset.	Retired, ill-health, 48. Consul.	52	
176. B.M.N. Perkins 23	Major-general. Sandown, Isle of Wight.	Required to resign, 33. First assistant.	83	
177. H.F. King 21	Storekeeper, Great Indian Peninsular Railway.	Retired, 61. Consul.	86	Born India. Brother assistant judge, Supreme Court, China. Son in Chinese Customs, and married daughter of French commissioner in that service. Both daughters married British merchants in China.
1893				
178. M. Hughes 23	Royal Irish Constabulary. Wexford.	Retired, ill-health, 40. Consul.	62	Appointed to Siam consular service, 1891. Transferred to China service, 1893.
179. A.M.C. Raab 20	Merchant tailor. London.	Died, 25. Second assistant.	—	Father German, not naturalized. Coached for entrance examination at Civil Service Department. Previously failed Indian Civil Service examination.

(i) Name, and age on first appointment	(ii) Father's occupation and place of residence (not necessarily at time of son's appointment)	(iii) Age and rank at time of death in service, retirement, resignation, or dismissal, and any honours	(iv) Age at death after leaving service	(v) Remarks, including known family connections with the East
180. F.E. Wilkinson 21	General consular service officer. Latterly of Smyrna.	Retired, ill-health, 57. Consul-general. CMG.	78	Born Salonica. Grandfather a Levant merchant. Brother a Straits Settlements cadet, latterly governor of Sierra Leone. Married daughter of a Yangtze pilot. One son in government service, Hong Kong, another in Ceylon. A daughter married a Chinese Customs officer.
181. B.G. Tours 22	Professor of music. London.	Retired, 60. Consul-general. CMG.	74	Father Dutch, not naturalized. Coached for entrance examination at Civil Service Department.
182. H.A. Ottewill 20	Commercial assistant, Calcutta. Latterly of Bedford.	*1894* Retired, 50. Consul.	87	Born Calcutta. Coached for entrance examination at Civil Service Department. Sister married Chinese Customs officer. After retirement served in Department of Overseas Trade.
183. V.L. Savage 21	Sub-inspector of military schools, Aldershot. Latterly of London.	Retired, 53. Consul.	57	

184. H.L. Higgs 20	Corn merchant. Gloucester.	Required to retire, 39. Vice-consul.	55	Married a (? Shanghai) widow. After retirement served in British Military Mission to Siberia.
185. T.G. Carvill 19	Barrister and member of Parliament. London.	Required to retire, 30. First assistant.	38	
186. B. Giles 20	China consular officer.	Retired, ill-health, 53. Consul-general. CMG.	53	Son of No. 115, brother of No. 213. Married daughter of Shanghai merchant.
187. S. Barton 18	Army captain. Devon.	*1895* Transferred to Diplomatic Service, 1929. Retired, 60. Minister to Ethiopia. GBE, KCVO, CMG.	69	Coached for entrance examination at Civil Service Department. Married daughter of leading Shanghai merchant. Elder son failed entrance examination, died Shanghai. Younger son merchant, Hong Kong.
188. G.J.L. Litton 25	Father John Litton, 'esquire', occupation not known. Dublin.	Died, 36. Consul.	—	Appointed Straits Settlements cadet, 1891. Transferred to China service, 1895.
189. S.F. Mayers 22	China consular officer.	Resigned, 36. Vice-consul.	61	Son of No. 84. After resignation joined British and Chinese Corporation and became its chairman. Brother in Chinese Customs.

APPENDIX II

(i) Name, and age on first appointment	(ii) Father's occupation and place of residence (not necessarily at time of son's appointment)	(iii) Age and rank at time of death in service, retirement, or dismissal, resignation, and any honours	(iv) Age at death after leaving service	(v) Remarks, including known family connections with the East
190. L.A.R. Mackinnon 21	Father Thomas Campbell Mackinnon, 'gentleman', occupation not known. Jamaica.	Required to resign, 32. Second assistant.	41	Born Jamaica, as were both his parents. Coached for entrance examination at Civil Service Department. See No. 199. Married daughter of doctor and consular agent, Pagoda Anchorage, whose son entered Chinese Customs and whose other two daughters married Chinese Customs officers.
191. B. Twyman 22	Spinner and weaver. Canterbury.	Died, 42. Consul.	—	Coached for entrance examination at Civil Service Department.
192. D. Oliphant 20	Father Thomas Truman Oliphant of Rossie, occupation not known. St. Andrews, Fife.	*1897* Killed during siege of legations, 24. Second assistant.	—	See No. 130.
193. H.E. Sly 20	Valet. London.	Retired, 49. Consul-general. CMG.		Coached for entrance examination at Civil Service Department. Brother of No. 235. Uncle an office-keeper in Foreign Office.
194. J.L. Smith 20	Tea-planter. Ceylon.	Suicide, 50. Consul.	55	Born Ceylon. Coached for entrance examination at Civil Service Department.

195. W.P. Thomas 19	Cattle-dealer. Shrewsbury.	Required to resign, ill-health, 23. Student interpreter.	62	Died as secretary, Administrative Commission, Diplomatic Quarter, Peking.
196. R.T. Tebbitt 21	Manufacturer. Croydon, latterly Germany.	Died, 36. Vice-consul.	—	Previously second-class clerk, India Office. Coached for entrance examination at Civil Service Department. Married daughter of US merchant, Newchwang.
197. J.T. Pratt 22	Indian Civil Service. Latterly of London.	Retired, 62. KBE, CMG.	94	Coached for entrance examination at Civil Service Department. Brother of No. 233. Two other brothers in Indian Civil Service.
198. L.G.C. Graham 19	Merchant. London.	Transferred to general consular service, 1905, ill-health. Died, 39. Vice-consul.	—	Coached for entrance examination at Civil Service Department. Father of No. 293.
199. G.W.W. Pearson 20	Treasury accountant. London.	Required to retire, 39. Consul.	43	Married sister of No. 190.
200. W.P.M. Russell 23	Chief constable. West Riding, Yorkshire.	Retired, ill-health, 35. First assistant.	76	
201. H. Phillips 19	Major. Reading.	Retired, 62. Consul-general. KCMG, OBE.	79	
202. C.C.A. Kirke 23	Fancy draper and milliner. Leicester.	Retired, 57. Consul-general. CBE.	84	Daughter married a Chinese Customs officer.

(i) Name, and age on first appointment	(ii) Father's occupation and place of residence (not necessarily at time of son's appointment)	(iii) Age and rank at time of death in service, retirement, resignation, or dismissal, after leaving service	(iv) Age at death after leaving service	(v) Remarks, including known family connections with the East
203. A.J. Flaherty 20	Pensioned coastguard. Margate.	Died, 30. First assistant.	—	See No. 79. Coached for entrance examination at Civil Service Department. Son, China merchant, married daughter of construction engineer, China.
204. W.M. Hewlett 22	Master, Chancery Division, Supreme Court. London.	Retired, 59. Consul-general. KCMG.	67	
205. H.H. Bristow 20	China consular officer.	Retired, 55. Consul.	82	Son of No. 118. Married daughter of China missionary.
206. H. Porter 20	Merchant's clerk. London.	Resigned, 49. Consul-general. CMG.	58 (suicide)	Younger brother in Chinese Customs. Married daughter of US missionary, Korea, all of whose other daughters are said to have married consular officers (? in Japan). After resignation became general manager, Pekin Syndicate. See No. 145.
207. C.A.W. Rose 19	Bootmaker. Bedford.	Resigned, 42. Commercial secretary. CIE.	81	After resignation entered London offices of companies trading in China.
208. G.P. Peachey 24 (23 at time of examination)	Barrister. London.	Resigned, 25. Student interpreter.	29	

No.	Name	Age	Occupation	Status		Notes
209.	J.G. Hancock	22	Licensed victualler. London.	Died, 24. Student interpreter.	—	
				1899		
210.	R.G. Drury	21	Architect and surveyor. London.	Died, 22. Student interpreter.	—	Coached for entrance examination at Civil Service Department.
211.	L.H.R. Barr	22	Cabinet manufacturer, London. Latterly of Bedford.	Died, 38. First assistant.	—	Coached for entrance examination at Civil Service Department. Married widowed daughter of a marine surveyor, Amoy.
212.	H. Warren	20	Tea-merchant. Waltham Cross, Hertfordshire.	Killed during siege of legations, 21. Student interpreter.	—	Two brothers connected with tea plantations, India.
213.	L. Giles	21	China consular officer.	Died, 56. Consul-general. CMG.	—	Son of No. 115, brother of No. 186.
214.	W.E. Townsend	20	Hongkong and Shanghai Banking Corporation. New York.	Died, 21. Student interpreter.	—	Born Yokohama. Uncle a leading figure in same bank as father.
				1901		
215.	C.H.M. Bosman	20	Merchant in Eastern trade. Hong Kong, latterly of London.	Died, 21. Student interpreter.	—	Coached for entrance examination at Civil Service Department.
216.	A.G. Major	21	Solicitor. Barrow-in-Furness.	Retired, 60. Consul-general.	60	
217.	H.F. Handley-Derry	20	Public Works Department, India. Latterly of Bournemouth.	Retired, 60. Consul-general. CBE.	87	Coached for entrance examination at Civil Service Department. Married niece (?) of No. 142.

(i) Name, and age on first appointment	(ii) Father's occupation and place of residence (not necessarily at time of son's appointment)	(iii) Age and rank at time of death in service, retirement, resignation, or dismissal, and any honours	(iv) Age at death after leaving service	(v) Remarks, including known family connections with the East
218. C.D. Smith 21	Schoolmaster. Rugby.	Retired, mental derangement, 44. Consul.	81	Coached for entrance examination at Civil Service Department.
219. W.R. Brown 21	Bank manager. London.	Retired, 53. Consul-general. CBE, AM.	86	Coached for entrance examination at Civil Service Department.
220. H.J. Brett 22	County surveyor. Dublin.	Retired, 53. Commercial secretary. CMG.	85	
221. W.J.B. Fletcher 21	Surgeon, Royal Navy. London.	Compulsorily retired, 39. First assistant. CMG.	54	Married a Chinese.
222. A.E. Eastes 23	Surgeon. London.	Retired, 55. Consul-general. CMG.	70	
223. G.A. Combe 23	Hotel owner. Aberdeen.	Retired, 55. Consul-general. CBE.	56	
224. O.R. Coales 20	Tutor. London.	Died, 45. Consul.	—	Coached for entrance examination at Civil Service Department.
225. C.F. Garstin 20	Indian Civil Service. Latterly of London.	Retired, 55. Consul-general. CMG, OBE.	89	Coached for entrance examination at Civil Service Department. Married sister of No. 236.

226. P.G. Jones 24 (23 at time of examination)	Hotel-keeper. Isle of Wight.	Transferred to Supreme Court, China, 1931. Retired, ill-health, 64. Assistant judge. CBE.	67	
227. G.S. Moss 20	Officer of Supreme Court, China and Japan. Japan.	Retired, 56. Consul-general. KBE.	77	Born Japan. Coached for entrance examination at Civil Service Department.
228. E.G. Jamieson 19	China consular officer.	Retired, 58. Consul-general. CBE.	76	Son of No. 102. Born China. Coached for entrance examination at Civil Service Department.
229. L.E. Keyser 23	Merchant. Smyrna.	Resigned, 1904, as student interpreter. Entered general consular service, 1905. Retired, 54. Consul-general.	77	Born Smyrna. Coached for entrance examination at Civil Service Department.
230. H.I. Harding 19	Father Edwin John Harding, 'gentleman'. Occupation and residence not known.	Required to retire, 54. Consul-general.	60	Born Canada. Coached for entrance examination at Civil Service Department. Married daughter of a China Baptist missionary, another of whose daughters married brother of No. 121.
231. J.B. Affleck 21	Chemist. Liverpool.	Retired, 60. Consul-general. CBE.	62	Coached for entrance examination at Civil Service Department. Married widow of a Tientsin accountant.

(i) Name, and age on first appointment	(ii) Father's occupation and place of residence (not necessarily at time of son's appointment)	(iii) Age and rank at time of death in service, retirement, resignation, or dismissal, and any honours	(iv) Age at death after leaving service	(v) Remarks, including known family connections with the East
		1905		
232. J.F. Brenan 20	Chinese Customs commissioner.	Retired, 60. Consul-general. KCMG.	69	Coached for entrance examination at Civil Service Department. Appointed to Siam consular service, 1903. Transferred to China service, 1905. See No. 112. Half brother of No. 268. First wife a cousin of No. 245.
233. R.S. Pratt 23	Indian Civil Service. Latterly of London.	Retired, 54. Consul.	93	Coached for entrance examination at Civil Service Department. See No. 197.
234. A.P. Blunt 22	Major-general. Portsmouth.	Retired, 60. Consul-general. CBE.	62	Coached for entrance examination at Civil Service Department. See No. 193.
235. E.A.H. Sly 21	Valet. London.	Suicide, 39. Vice-consul.	—	
236. L.M. King 20	Chinese Customs commissioner.	Required to retire, 38. Vice-consul.	63	Born China. Mother a China missionary's daughter. Great-uncle in Chinese Customs. Brother a China merchant. See No. 225. Married a Tibetan.

237. W.P.W. Turner 21	Coal agent. London.	Retired, 54. Consul-general. CMG, OBE.	78	Coached for entrance examination at Civil Service Department.
238. A.J. Martin 23	Commercial traveller. ? London.	Died, 58. Consul-general. CBE.	—	Coached for entrance examination at Civil Service Department.

1907 (December 1906 examination)

239. W.S. Toller 22	Grocer. Taunton.	Retired, 57. Consul-general. CMG, OBE.	83	Coached for entrance examination at Civil Service Department. Married widow of China missionary.
240. S.W. Smith 19	Clergyman. Gloucestershire.	Retired, 57. Consul-general.	71	Coached for entrance examination at Civil Service Department.
241. E. Teichman 23	Fur trader. London.	Retired, 52. Chinese counsellor. GCMG, CIE.	59 (murdered in England)	Father German by birth, a naturalized British subject. Married widowed sister of a Shanghai lawyer.

1907 (September examination)

242. G.P. Byrne 23	Commercial traveller. Belfast.	Required to retire, 35. Second assistant.	83	Coached for entrance examination at Civil Service Department.

1908

243. A.D. Blackburn 21	Civil engineer, Public Works Department, India. Latterly of Bedford.	Retired, 56. Chinese counsellor. KCMG, OBE.	82	Married daughter of French inspector-general, Chinese Posts.
244. E.W.P. Mills 23	Army captain. Dorset.	Retired, 57. Consul-general.	62	

(i) Name, and age on first appointment	(ii) Father's occupation and place of residence (not necessarily at time of son's appointment)	(iii) Age and rank at time of death in service, retirement, resignation, or dismissal, after leaving service	(iv) Age at death after leaving service	(v) Remarks, including known family connections with the East
245. A.H. George 22	Brewery chairman. Bristol.	Suicide, 57. Consul-general. KCMG.	—	See No. 232.
246. H.W. Gammon 19	Banker's clerk. London.	Resigned, 25. Second assistant.	Not known.	
247. J.C. Hill 21	Lieutenant, Auxiliary Forces. Isle of Wight.	Died, 46. Vice-consul.	—	Married White Russian in China.
248. S.P. Bryant 22	Shipping agent's manager. London.	Retired, ill-health, 26. Student interpreter.	36	
249. N. Fitzmaurice 21	District medical officer. Sussex.	Retired, 56. Consul-general. CIE.	72	Elder brother in Siam consular service.
250. D.B. Walker 24 (23 at time of examination)	Builder. Edinburgh.	1909 Resigned, 33. Second assistant.	84	After resignation became a merchant in China and India.
251. J.W.O. Davidson 21	Marine engineer. Shanghai.	Retired, 60. Consul-general. CMG, OBE.	84	Born China.

1910–15: Appointments following limited competition entrance examination for China, Japan, and Siam consular services (same examinations as those for the Diplomatic, Indian Civil, Home Civil, and certain other Services, but candidates for the Far Eastern consular services were required to take fewer of the papers; age limits over 21 and under 24)

1910

252. E.W. Mead 23	Solicitor. London.	Seconded to Chinese Salt Administration, 1923. Resigned, 42. Vice-consul.	53	
253. H.D. Keown 23	Father Richard Henry Keown, 'gentleman', occupation not known. Eastbourne, formerly of Castleroe, Co. Londonderry.	Required to resign, 29. Student interpreter.	Not known.	A relative resident at Tientsin.

1911

254. H.I. Prideaux-Brune 24	Clergyman. Gosport.	Retired, 58. Consul-general. KBE, CMG.	93	
255. F.A. Wallis 24 (23 at time of examination)	Fellow, Corpus Christi College, Cambridge.	Retired, 56. Consul.	83	Competed unsuccessfully in 1910 Diplomatic Service entrance examination and on the strength of his results was offered a place in the China service without further examination.

(i) Name, and age on first appointment	(ii) Father's occupation and place of residence (not necessarily at time of son's appointment)	(iii) Age and rank at time of death in service, retirement, resignation, or dismissal, and any honours	(iv) Age at death after leaving service	(v) Remarks, including known family connections with the East
		1912		
256. H.A.F.B. Archer 24	Major. London.	Retired, 59. Consul-general. OBE.	63	Competed unsuccessfully in 1911 general consular service entrance examination and on the strength of his results was offered a place in the China service without further examination. Mother the daughter of army officer, India. Brother in Japan consular service.
257. E.S. Bennett 23	Accountant. Belfast.	Retired, following accidental wound received in Chinese civil war, 43. Second assistant.	About 77.	
258. A.G.N. Ogden 23	Railway auditor, India.	Retired, 59. Consul-general. KBE.	92	Born India. Married daughter of China missionary.
259. A.A.L. Tuson 22	Commissioner, Andaman and Nicobar Islands.	Retired, 55. Consul.	78	Married daughter of Chinese Customs officer.

No. & Name	Age	Background	Career	Age at death	Notes
260. C.E. Whitamore	22	Wesleyan missionary, India.	Retired, 60. Consul-general. OBE.	74	Born India.
261. B.G. Chamberlain	24 (23 at time of examination)	Isinglass merchant. Richmond, Surrey.	Required to resign, 26. Student interpreter. Subsequently vice-consul, Algiers, resigned, 43.	Not known.	
1913					
262. K.W. Tribe	23	Stockbroker. Bristol.	Retired, 55. Consul.	79	Second wife daughter of China missionary.
263. C.R. Lee	23	Clergyman. Worthing.	Retired, 49. Consul.	68	
1915 (October 1914 examination)					
264. J.C. Hutchison	23	Silk and tea merchant. Hong Kong.	Retired, 60. Chargé d'affaires, Peking. KBE.	74	Born Hong Kong. Mother daughter of China missionary (see No. 145). Married daughter of China merchant.
265. W.A. Alexander	22	Baronet. Kent.	Died, 35. Vice-consul.	—	Successful in Diplomatic Service entrance examination but father would not guarantee the £400 p.a. private income then required for Diplomatic Service entrants. Married daughter of Chinese Customs officer.

1919–JULY 1921: EX-SERVICEMEN APPOINTED ON THE RECOMMENDATION OF SELECTION COMMITTEE COMPOSED OF REPRESENTATIVES OF GOVERNMENT DEPARTMENTS AND OF BUSINESS

1919

(i) Name, and age on first appointment	(ii) Father's occupation and place of residence (not necessarily at time of son's appointment)	(iii) Age and rank at time of death in service, retirement, resignation, or dismissal, and any honours	(iv) Age at death after leaving service	(v) Remarks, including known family connections with the East
266. H.N. Steptoe 26	Naval ordnance officer. Portsmouth.	Died, 57. Rank equivalent to that of consul-general (minister to San Salvador).	—	In China before the war. First wife daughter of China missionary.
267. M. Milton 26	Master brewer. Sussex.	Died, 38. Vice-consul.	—	Chinese Customs officer before the war.
268. E.H. Brenan 26	Chinese Customs commissioner.	Resigned, 29. Vice-consul.	About 68.	Born China. Half-brother of No. 232. See No. 112.
269. E.C. Miéville 23	Surveyor. Acton, Middlesex.	Resigned, 31. Vice-consul.	75	Uncle originally in Levant consular service. Retired as assistant private secretary to King George VI.
270. H.J. Macdonald 20	Medical missionary. China.	Retired, mental derangement, 26. Vice-consul.	Not known (died before 1937).	Born China.

271. R.A. Hall 27	Corn merchant. Nottinghamshire.	Retired, 56. Consul-general. CBE.	73	Successful in 1914 Diplomatic Service examination but lacked the necessary private income. Offered a place in China consular service instead, but volunteered for the army before appointment.
272. S.G. Beare 23	Master grocer. London.	Retired, 44. Consul.	62	Employed before the war in Estate Duty Office.
		1920		
273. W.C. Cassels 25	Anglican bishop. China.	Resigned, 37. Vice-consul.	66	Born China. Married sister of Chinese Customs officer. Three sisters missionaries in China. After resignation entered British bank in China.
274. A.L. Scott 23	China consular officer.	Transferred to Home Civil Service, 1948. Consul.	81	Born China. Son of No. 141.
275. S.L. Burdett, MC 23	Solicitor. London.	Retired, 54. Consul-general. CBE.	64	
276. G.A. Herbert, MC 24	Mechanical engineer. Glasgow.	Retired, 48. Consul. OBE.	52	
277. M.R. Montgomrey, MC 22	Tutor. Bournemouth.	Suicide, 31. Vice-consul.	—	

(i) Name, and age on first appointment	(ii) Father's occupation and place of residence (not necessarily at time of son's appointment)	(iii) Age and rank at time of death in service, retirement, resignation, or dismissal, and any honours	(iv) Age at death after leaving service	(v) Remarks, including known family connections with the East
278. D.H. Clarke, DSO, MC 25	Civil engineer. Northumberland.	Resigned, 38. Vice-consul.	78	Born Ceylon.
279. W.V.B. Hughes 25	Clergyman. Cardiff.	Resigned, 37.	76	

AUGUST 1921–34: APPOINTMENTS FOLLOWING OPEN COMPETITION ENTRANCE
EXAMINATIONS FOR CHINA, JAPAN, AND SIAM CONSULAR SERVICES
(same examinations, and same number of papers, as for the
Diplomatic, Indian Civil, and Home Civil Services, for the General
and Levant Consular Services, and for certain other Services. Age
limits over 21 and under 24)

Note: No. 287 did not sit the examination. Those entrants who survived long enough were later all posted away from China as China consulates were closed down wholesale during and after the Second World War, and the amalgamation during the war of the diplomatic and consular services gave them greatly improved career opportunities. Consequently their lives cannot usefully be compared with those of their predecessors. Data about the parentage of China entrants also ceases to be meaningful; from now on study of the class structure of recruitment must include other services recruiting through the uniform examination system. Entries in columns (ii)–(v) are therefore omitted, except for premature deaths, resignations, and retirements.

280. L.H. Lamb 21				

1921 (November examination)

No.	Name		
281.	G.V. Kitson 22		1922
282.	C.A. Hopper 23		Resigned, 26.
283.	G.E. Stockley 23		1924
284.	J.P. Coghill 23		1926
285.	D. Cameron 23		
286.	E.W. Jeffery 23		
287.	G.C. Pelham 27 (promoted from the rank of clerical officer in China)		
288.	A.C.L. Paton 22		Resigned, 23.
289.	R.H. Scott 22		1927

(i) Name, and age on first appointment	(ii) Father's occupation and place of residence (not necessarily at time of son's appointment)	(iii) Age and rank at time of death in service, retirement, resignation, or dismissal, and any honours	(iv) Age at death after leaving service	(v) Remarks, including known family connections with the East
290. J. Dunlop 22				
291. J.P. Price 22				
292. J.A.C. Alexander 22		1928 Retired, 49.		
293. W.G.C. Graham 22		Died following street accident, 27.		
294. M.C. Gillett 21		1929		Son of No. 198.
295. A. Price 23				
296. G.R. Turral 24 (23 at time of examination)		Suicide, 40.		
297. G.W. Aldington 22				

298. D.J.S. Adams
23

1930
Resigned, 25.

299. G.F. Tyrrell
23

Resigned, 43.

300. H. Braham
24
(23 at time of
examination)

1931

301. K. Bumstead
23

302. G.W. Creighton
23

1932
Retired, 42.

303. F.F. Garner
22

304. J.P. Reeves
23

305. I.C. Mackenzie
23

306. H.D. Bryan
21

(i) Name, and age on first appointment	(ii) Father's occupation and place of residence (not necessarily at time of son's appointment)	(iii) Age and rank at time of death in service, retirement, resignation, or dismissal, and any honours	(iv) Age at death after leaving service	(v) Remarks, including known family connections with the East
307. J.F. Brewis 23		1933		
308. E.B. Boothby 23				
309. J.A.M. Marjoribanks 23		1934		

SOURCES AND BIBLIOGRAPHY

Unpublished Sources

The Public Record Office, London

Fire, riot, war, and other hazards have devastated the erstwhile archives of China consulates. Consulate activity is now comprehensively documented only in the archive of the Hong Kong superintendency of trade and Peking diplomatic mission, an archive in which the correspondence between them and the Foreign Office and between them and the consulates is largely preserved. The archive was the principal source used. The main body of it, over 4,000 bound volumes, many of them bulky, forms Public Record Office class FO 228. The two supplementary parts of the archive (FO 676 and 677) are far smaller and less useful. Occasional use was made of Legation miscellanea (FO 233) and of consulate correspondence with the British Supreme Court at Shanghai (FO 656). China probate records (FO 917 and supplementary material in FO 678) and consulate registers of births, deaths, and marriages (in the various Public Record Office classes relating to individual China consulates) provided personal data about consular officers and their families. The fair copies received in London of handwritten despatches from China were often consulted in FO 17 (General Correspondence China) in preference to untidy drafts of the same despatches in FO 228.

For Foreign Office management of the China service before 1905 the principal sources used were those volumes in FO 17 containing domestic correspondence or correspondence with or about consular officers, and from 1905 onwards that part of FO 369 (General Correspondence Consular) relating to the China service.

Occasional use was made of the remainder of FO 17, of China papers in FO 371 (General Correspondence Political) and in Foreign Office confidential print (FO 405 and FO 881), and of scattered papers in other Foreign Office classes mentioned in the notes.

The personal papers of Pottinger, Hammond, Satow, and Jordan (FO

707, FO 391, PRO 30/33, and FO 350 respectively) and the Far Eastern department papers (FO 800/244–8) were consulted, also the less informative Tenterden papers (FO 363) and Bertie, Lansdowne, Langley, Austen Chamberlain, Cadogan, Knatchbull-Hugessen, and Clark Kerr papers (all in FO 800).

All these classes were originally consulted at the Public Record Office's Chancery Lane repository in central London. Their subsequent transfer to the remoter Kew repository ruled out any final checking of references to these classes in the notes. Apologies are offered for any resulting errors in the notes.

Odd copies of Civil Service Commission documents preserved in FO 17 tantalizingly showed that at least at certain periods the commission supplemented publication of the names and marks of successful examination candidates by circulating for confidential official information lists of the names, marks, and last places of education of all candidates. Unfortunately no run of these illuminating lists could be traced in the Public Record Office holding of commission papers.

Census records, England and Wales, provided some personal data.

Neither Treasury nor Board of Trade papers were consulted.

Government Records Held Elsewhere

Personal data were obtained from:

Probate records, England and Wales: Somerset House, London.

Registers of births, deaths, and marriages, England and Wales: St. Catherine's House, London.

Scottish census records and registers of births, deaths, and marriages, Scotland: New Register House, Edinburgh.

Registers of births, deaths, and marriages, Ireland: Oxford House, Belfast, and Custom House, Dublin.

Documents in Other British Repositories

Use was made of the registers of Shanghai baptisms, deaths, and marriages held at Lambeth Palace, London; of private letters home from D.B. Robertson and Crawford in the National Library of Wales (Glansevern MSS 5021–55) and the Berkshire County Record Office (D/EDd) respectively; and of papers concerning G.T. Lay in the Bible Society archive, London.

Access to the Parkes papers in the Cambridge University Library was not obtainable. Bowring was so transient an intruder into the China consular service that his papers in the John Rylands Library, Manchester, were not examined. The Wedgwood Museum, Stoke-on-Trent, were unable to say whether they held among unsorted papers the private letters home from

Mrs C.F.R. Allen, née Wedgwood, which a descendant believed to have been deposited in the museum.

Privately Held Papers and Private Information

Extensive efforts to discover privately held papers of China consular officers led only to a box of Adkins' letters home, to some scrappy diaries of C. Alabaster,* to two unpublished typescripts of more recent personal reminiscences, and to a few brief notes. Distance ruled out use of a massive diary now in New Zealand. The holders of this material do not wish to be identified. Statements deriving from it are marked in the text by an [a].

Caches of other personal papers, including the letters and diaries of consular wives hitherto sadly lacking, no doubt await discovery, but it will be useless to hunt for Alcock's China papers, the destruction of which was ordered in the will of his step-daughter Lady Pelly, or for W.M. Hewlett's diaries, which have also been destroyed.

Information supplied privately by surviving members of the service or by their families is likewise marked in the text by an [a], as are occasional statements based on the author's personal knowledge.

* In July 1987, after the above had been written, Alabaster's diaries were deposited with the School of Oriental and African Studies, London, and when listed they will become available for consultation there.

Published Material

Official Publications

The very numerous nineteenth-century Parliamentary Papers (PP) about China for the most part reproduce, with or without editing, documents to be found in FO 228 or FO 17, and for that reason have not been frequently cited. Where they have been cited the note references are to the continuously paginated volumes of the modern photographic reprints (*Area Studies Series: British Parliamentary Papers: China* (Irish University Press, Shannon, 1971, 42 vols.)).

Other useful PP include:

Report from the Select Committee on Consular Service and Appointments, PP 1857–8, VIII.

Second Report from the Select Committee on Diplomatic and Consular Services, PP 1872, VII.

Correspondence Respecting the Question of Diplomatic and Consular Assistance to British Trade Abroad, PP 1876, LX.

Fourth Report of the Royal Commission on Civil Establishments, PP 1890, XXVII.

Royal Commission on Opium, PP 1894, LX–LXII.

Report of Committee to Consider Organisation of Oriental Studies in
London, PP 1909, XXXV.
Fifth Report of the Royal Commission on the Civil Service, PP 1914–16,
XL.
Annual reports of the Civil Service Commission.

Other published material
Six publications were outstandingly helpful:
  The Foreign Office List and Diplomatic and Consular Handbook
(London, annually) is extremely accurate, and almost indispensable for
dates of death in retirement, but is liable to mislead if its conventions are
not understood. The annual *Lists* do not by themselves constitute a reliable
guide to where a given officer was serving at any given time, for while they
record the posts to which China officers were commissioned and record
acting appointments (temporary appointments at a rank higher than
substantive rank) most nineteenth-century officiating appointments (temporary appointments at a rank no higher than substantive rank) are disregarded, and absences on home leave are invariably disregarded. 'Services
ceased' is a euphemism for dismissal, and 'resigned' or 'retired' are not
infrequently euphemisms for enforced departures.

  D.C.M. Platt, *The Cinderella Service: British Consuls since 1825*
(London, 1971), was the first adequate history of the modern British
consular services. Given the broad scope of a path-breaking book some
errors of detail about the China service were almost inevitable.

  R.A. Jones, *The Nineteenth-Century Foreign Office; an Administrative
History* (London, 1971) and *The British Diplomatic Service 1815–1914*
(Gerrards Cross, Buckinghamshire, 1983), were two other path-breaking
books. Knowledge of the way in which the Foreign Office managed itself
and managed the diplomatic service makes Foreign Office management of
the China service more comprehensible.

  H.B. Morse, *The International Relations of the Chinese Empire*
(Shanghai, Hong Kong, Singapore, and Yokohama, 1910–18, 3 vols.) and
O.E. Clubb, *20th Century China* (New York and London, 1972, second
edition), are two factually reliable accounts of the general background by
authors who knew China well.

  Among the innumerable other books about China during the period of
extraterritoriality those of which only incidental use was made are specified
in the appropriate notes. The surprisingly few found to be of wider use are
listed below. The list includes some newspapers, used primarily but not
exclusively for announcements of births, deaths, and marriages. It excludes
many books by consular officers, particularly sinological works, and nearly
all their contributions to journals.

Alcock, R., *Notes on Medical History and Statistics of the British Legion of Spain*...(London, 1838).

—— *The Capital of the Tycoon*...(London, 1863, 2 vols.).

Allen, B.M., *Sir Ernest Satow. A Memoir* (London, 1933).

Baber, E.C., 'Travels and Researches in the Interior of China', *Royal Geographical Society Supplementary Papers Vol. I* (London, 1886).

Carles, W.R., *Life in Corea* (London, 1888).

Chang Hsin-pao, *Commissioner Lin and the Opium War* (Harvard, 1964).

China as it Really Is: by a Resident in Peking [L.M. King] (London, 1912).

China Mail (Hong Kong).

Chinese Repository (Macao and Canton).

Clennell, W.J., *The Historical Development of Religion in China* (New York, 1917).

Collinge, J.M., *Foreign Office Officials 1780–1970* (London, 1979).

Combe, G.A., *A Tibetan on Tibet* (London, 1926).

Cordier, H., *Bibliotheca Sinica* (Paris, 1904–24, 5 vols., second edition).

Couling, S., *The Encyclopaedia Sinica* (Shanghai, 1917).

Elliston, E.F., *Shantung Road Cemetery Shanghai 1846–1868* (Shanghai, c. 1946).

Endacott, G.B., *A Biographical Sketch Book of Early Hong Kong* (Singapore, 1962).

Fairbank, J.K., *Trade and Diplomacy on the China Coast*...(Stanford, 1969, paperback edition). (Contains some errors of detail about British consular officers.)

—— Bruner, E.F., and Matheson, E.M. (eds.), *The I.G. in Peking: Letters of Robert Hart, Chinese Maritime Customs, 1868–1907* (Cambridge, Mass., 1975, 2 vols.).

Freeman-Mitford, A.B. [later Lord Redesdale], *The Attaché at Peking* (London, 1900).

Gardner, C.T., *Simple Truths: The English Version of a Small Treatise on Political Economy for the Information of Chinamen* (London, 1899, second edition).

Gerson, J.J., *Horatio Nelson Lay and Sino-British Relations* (Harvard, 1972).

Giles, H.A., *A Glossary of Reference on Subjects Connected with the Far East* (Hong Kong, Shanghai, Yokohama, and London, 1878).

—— *A Short History of Koolangsu* (? Amoy, 1878).

Grafftey-Smith, Sir L., *Bright Levant* (London, 1970). (Some comments on the Levant consular service, and on its relations with the diplomatic service, are equally applicable to the China service.)

Hewlett, Sir M., *Forty Years in China* (London, 1943).

Hertslet, Sir E. (ed.), *Treaties, &c., between Great Britain and China; and between China and Foreign Powers*... (London, 1896, 2 vols.).

Hornby, Sir E., *An Autobiography* (London, 1929). (Of doubtful reliability.)

Hosie, A., *Three Years in Western China*...(London, 1900).

—— *Manchuria, Its People, Resources and Recent History* (London, 1901).

—— *On the Trail of the Opium Poppy* (London, 1914).

Hummel, A.W. (ed.), *Eminent Chinese of the Ch'ing Period (1644–1912)* (Washington, 1943–4, 2 vols.).

Hurd, D., *The Arrow War* (London, 1967).

In Memoriam. Walter Ewen Townsend (privately printed, 1901).

Jordan, Sir J., 'Chinese I have Known', *Nineteenth Century*, Dec. 1920.

—— 'China and the Powers', *Central Asian Society Journal*, X, 1923.

The Journey of Augustus Raymond Margary, from Shanghae to Bhamo... (London, 1876).

Kann, E., *The Currencies of China* (Shanghai, 1927).

King, F.H.H., and Clarke, P., *A Research Guide to China-Coast Newspapers 1822–1911* (Harvard, 1965).

King, L.M., *China in Turmoil. Studies in Personality* (London, 1927).

King, P., *In the Chinese Customs Service* (London, 1924).

King's College, London, calendars.

Lane-Poole, S., and Dickens, T.V., *The Life of Sir Harry Parkes* (London, 1894, 2 vols.).

Life's Problems: Essays Moral, Social and Psychological [no author's name: actually by Sir Rutherford Alcock] (London, 1857).

Lo Hui-min (ed.), *The Correspondence of G.E. Morrison* (Cambridge, 1976–8, 2 vols.).

Loch, H.B., *Personal Narrative of Occurrences during Lord Elgin's Second Embassy to China* (London, 1869).

London and China Express (from 1922 onwards *London and China Express and Telegraph*) (London).

MacMurray, J.V.A. (ed.), *Treaties and Agreements with and concerning China* (New York, 1921, 2 vols.).

Mayers, W.[S.] F., Dennys, N.B., and King, C., *The Treaty Ports of China and Japan* (London, 1867).

—— *The Chinese Government*...(Shanghai and London, 1897, third edition revised by G.M.H. Playfair).

Meadows, T.T., *Desultory Notes on the Government and People of China*...(London, 1847).

—— *The Chinese and their Rebellions*...(London, 1856).

Medhurst, W.H., *The Foreigner in Far Cathay* (London, 1872).

Michie, A., *The Englishman in China*...(London, 1900, 2 vols.).

Memoirs of the Life and Labours of Robert Morrison, D.D. [by his widow] (London, 1839, 2 vols.).

North-China Herald (Shanghai).

Ogden, Sir A., *Jessie Vera Ogden* (privately printed, *c.* 1969).

Parker, E.H., *John Chinaman and a Few Others* (London, 1901).

—— *China Past and Present* (London, 1903).

Pearson, J.D. (ed.), *Guide to Manuscripts and Documents in the British Isles relating to the Far East* (Oxford, 1977).

Playfair, G.M.H., *The Cities and Towns of China* (Hong Kong, 1879).

Pratt, Sir J.T., *War and Politics in China* (London, 1943).

Rasmussen, A.H., *China Trader* (London, 1954).

Redesdale, Lord [formerly A.B. Freeman-Mitford], *Memories* (London, 1916, 2 vols.).

Satow, Sir E., *A Diplomat in Japan* (London, 1921).

Swinhoe, R., *Narrative of the North-China Campaign of 1860...* (London, 1861).

Teichman, E., *Travels of a Consular Officer in North-West China* (Cambridge, 1921).

—— *Travels of a Consular Officer in Eastern Tibet* (Cambridge, 1922).

—— *The Consular Officer's Vademecum: Notes on Treaty Interpretation and Precedent and Diplomatic and Consular Procedure in China, compiled for the use of Student Interpreters...* (printed for private circulation only, Tientsin, 1920). (Authoritative.)

—— *Affairs of China* (London, 1938).

T'oung Pao (Leyden).

Toynbee, A.J. (ed.), *Survey of International Affairs, 1926* (Oxford, 1928).

—— *Survey of International Affairs, 1929* (Oxford, 1930).

Tregonning, K.G., *Under Chartered Company Rule (North Borneo 1881–1946)* (Singapore, 1958).

Wehrle, E.R., *Britain, China and the Anti-Missionary Riots, 1891–1900* (Minneapolis, 1966).

Werner, E.T.C., *Autumn Leaves* (Shanghai, Hong Kong, and Singapore, 1928). (Unreliable.)

'*Where Chineses Drive': English Student-Life in Peking by A Student Interpreter* [W.H. Wilkinson] (London, 1885).

Wilkinson, F.E., 'Early Days of the Treaty Port of Foochow', *Foochow Literary Society*, 1918.

Wright, M., *Treasury Control of the Civil Service* (Oxford, 1969).

Wright, S.F., *Hart and the Chinese Customs* (Belfast, 1950).

Wylie, A., *Memorials of Protestant Missionaries to the Chinese* (Shanghai, 1867).

Sources for Appendix II

Data supplementing information from the above sources were obtained from the published and unpublished records of schools, universities, and

the like; from local record offices; from surviving members of the service, from widows, and from descendants; from other kindly helpers; and from various published works of reference. Space does not permit identification of sources in greater detail.

NOTES

REFERENCES are unless otherwise indicated to Public Record Office classes. Numbered despatches are normally identified only by their numbers. Numbered telegrams are identified by numbers prefixed by 'tel.' Unnumbered despatches and telegrams, semi-official letters, and private letters are identified by their dates. Except where otherwise indicated Foreign Office communications are to be understood as addressed to the superintendency or Legation, superintendency and Legation communications as addressed to the Foreign Office, and consulate communications as addressed to the superintendency or Legation. From 1869 onwards Foreign Office and Legation despatches about the management of the China service were marked 'consular' and were consecutively numbered each year in 'consular' series distinct from the consecutively numbered series of political despatches. The 'accounts' series used between Legation and consulates served much the same purpose. Numbered 'consular' and 'accounts' despatches and telegrams are distinguished in the notes by the prefix 'cons.' or 'accts.'.

Other abbreviations used in the notes are:

CSC   Civil Service Commission.
DNB   *Dictionary of National Biography.*
DOT   Department of Overseas Trade.
F.O.   Foreign Office (the form 'FO' is used only for Public Record Office classes).
IUP   *Area Studies Series: British Parliamentary Papers: China* (Irish University Press, Shannon, 1971, 42 vols.).
Leg.   Legation.
PP   Parliamentary Papers.
sup.   superintendency.

For the reasons indicated on p. 545 in the Sources and Bibliography, references are not provided for statements marked [a] in the main text.

Notes to Chapter 1

1. FO 228/26, F.O. 4, 1843.
2. FO 17/564–5, Alcock to Tenterden, 12 Jan. 1871; and FO 17/666, reference to a 'hereditary claim on the Foreign Office', Littleton to Granville, Jan. 1873.
3. FO 17/147, Macgregor to F.O., 24 June 1848.
4. FO 228/36, F.O., 6 Mar. 1844.
5. FO 17/160, Macgregor to Addington, 21 Aug. 1849, Hammond's minute.
6. FO 228/67, sup. 154, 1847.
7. For the appointments of vice-consuls and assistants see FO 17/72; FO 17/74;

and FO 228/27, F.O. 107 and 110, 1843. For Giles' parentage see 1841 census for Bon Accord Street, Aberdeen, his address on appointment, and for the father's relations with Lord Aberdeen see *DNB*, VII, p. 1227.

8. FO 17/58, sup. 58, 1842; FO 707/65, Thom to Pottinger, 12 July 1843; FO 228/46, sup. 175, 1845; and FO 17/103, Johnston to F.O., May 1845.

9. FO 228/26, F.O. 18, 1843; IUP, Vol. 2, p. 35; and FO 228/96, F.O. 120, 1849.

10. FO 228/15, sup. 11 and 13, 1842; and FO 228/82, F.O., 12 July 1848. Still described in 1872 as being of weak mind, see England and Wales probate records, 1873, father's will.

11. FO 228/32, sup. 92, 1844; and FO 17/279, Bonham to Hammond, 10 Jan. 1857.

12. FO 17/69, sup. 118, 1843; and FO 228/91, Shanghai 124, 1848.

13. Chang, *Commissioner Lin*, p. 210.

14. *Chinese Repository*, VIII, pp. 97–8.

15. FO 228/26, F.O. 55, 1843; and FO 228/24, sup. 105, 1843.

16. FO 228/58, F.O. (Palmerston) 17, 1846.

17. Meadows, *Chinese and their Rebellions*, p. 376.

18. FO 228/34, sup. 50, 1844; and FO 228/33, sup. 92, 1844.

19. B. Lubbock, *The Opium Clippers* (Glasgow, 1933), p. 272; and FO 228/33, sup. 92, 1844.

20. FO 707/65, Thom to Pottinger, 29 July 1843; and FO 707/71, Lay to Pottinger, 29 July 1843.

21. FO 228/66, sup. 78, 1847. For the early lives of Medhurst and Parkes see respectively *Journal of the Royal Asiatic Society of Great Britain and Ireland*, Vol. 18, 1886, pp. xxii–xxiii, and Lane-Poole, *Parkes*, Vol. I, pp. 3–14.

22. Meadows, *Desultory Notes*, pp. vii–viii; and FO 17/119, Pottinger to Palmerston, 27 Nov. 1846.

23. FO 17/71, Pottinger to Campbell, 27 Dec. 1843; FO 228/55, sup. 82, 1846; and FO 228/132, sup. 7, 1852.

24. FO 228/42, Ningpo 32, 1844; and FO 17/254, Mrs Spencer to Hammond, 18 Jan. 1856. The introduction to the admiral came through a member of the Aufrère family (National Library of Scotland, Admiral Sir Thomas Cochrane's correspondence and papers, MS 2426 f. 34v.: information kindly supplied by the library), and on his death in 1881 G.A. Aufrère, who had been a witness at Sinclair's London wedding in 1858 (England and Wales marriage registers), left one-third of his substantial estate to Sinclair (England and Wales probate records, 1881). Sinclair's precise relationship to the Aufrères has not been established.

25. FO 17/103, Pottinger to Aberdeen, 17 Nov. 1845.

26. FO 17/71, sup. 170, 1843.

27. FO 228/90, Shanghai 34, 1848.

28. FO 228/166, sup. 204, 1854.

29. FO 228/82, F.O. 124, 1848; and FO 228/93, sup. 79, 1849.

30. FO 228/67, sup. 198, 1847; and 1841 census return for 3 Durham Place, Lambeth.

31. FO 228/34, sup. 90, 1844. The father, whose own father may have been a victualler, had been an attorney before taking orders (information kindly supplied by Dorset County Record Office).

32. FO 228/34, sup. 50, 1844.

33. FO 17/76A, F.O. correspondence with Admiralty, Dec. 1843; FO 228/34, sup. 14, 1844; FO 17/91, Robertson to F.O., 7 Jan. 1844; and FO 228/54, Shanghai 27, 1845.

34. Guildhall Library, London, MS 11, 218, for Macao marriage and birth; and FO 17/91, Layton to F.O., 12 Jan. 1844.

35. FO 228/40, Canton 15, 1844.
36. Lane-Poole, *Parkes*, Vol. I, p. 74; FO 228/34, sup. 75, 1844; FO 228/36, F.O. 74, 1844; and FO 17/306, Sirr to F.O. and F.O. reply, 8 and 20 Oct. 1858.
37. Diary of Captain F.W. Beechey, Book 2 (information kindly supplied by University of British Columbia Library).
38. He quotes Hebrew, Greek (*Chinese Repository*, VII, pp. 257 and 425), and Latin (correspondence with Bible Society in Society's archives, London).
39. FO 228/34, sup. 55, 1844.
40. *Chinese Repository*, VIII, p. 42.
41. Captain F.W. Beechey, *Narrative of a Voyage to the Pacific* . . . (London, 1831, 2 vols.), Vol. I, pp. 213, 315, and 319, and Vol. II, p. 89.
42. Archives of Bible Society, W.A. Garratt to Society, 8 Oct. 1835; and Lay to Society, 11 May 1836.
43. FO 17/51, minutes by Palmerston and Lenox Conyngham, 24 and 30 June 1841; and FO 228/58, F.O., 17 Apr. 1845.
44. Lane-Poole, *Parkes*, Vol. I, p. 24; FO 228/41, Foochow 23 and 24, 1844; and FO 707/65, Thom to Pottinger, 27 Nov. 1843.
45. FO 228/26, F.O. 14, 1843.
46. FO 228/25, sup. 153 and 165, 1843.
47. FO 228/32, sup. 92, 1844; and FO 228/34, sup. 43, 1844.
48. FO 228/36, F.O. 36, 1844. For Alcock's early life see Michie, *Englishman in China*, and for his Peninsular experiences see his *Notes on Medical History*.
49. FO 17/317, sup. 20, 1859. Michie's statement that as commissioner Alcock was unpaid is disproved by FO 228/96, F.O. 112, 1849.
50. FO 228/34, sup. 55, 1844.
51. Wilkinson, *Early Days*.
52. FO 228/41, Foochow 7 and 13, 1844; FO 228/34, sup. 85, 1844; FO 228/44, sup., 7 Feb. 1845; and FO 228/52, Foochow 18, 1845.
53. FO 228/41, Foochow 15, 1844; FO 228/44, sup., 21 Jan. 1845; FO 228/67, sup. 198, 1847; and death certificate, Lambeth registration district, 1848.
54. FO 228/41, Foochow 24, 1844; FO 228/44, sup., 17 Mar. 1845; and FO 228/52, Foochow, 2 Apr., and sup., 10 Apr., 1845.
55. FO 228/44, sup., 15 and 17 Mar., and 27 Apr., 1845; FO 228/50, Amoy 36, 63, 74, and 76, 1845; FO 228/46, sup. 169, 1845; and FO 228/58, F.O., 17 Apr. 1845.
56. W.C. Hunter, *Bits of Old China* (London, 1885), p. 189.
57. FO 228/31, Gribble to Woosnam, 17 Oct. 1843; and FO 707/72, Gribble to Pottinger, 18 Mar. 1844.
58. FO 228/31, Amoy 2, 1843; FO 228/585, Amoy, 8 Sept. 1877; FO 405/68, Amoy 3, 1931; and FO 228/3470, Leg. 17, 1923.
59. FO 228/98, Amoy 5, 1849; FO 228/31, Amoy 15, 1844; and FO 228/166–7, sup. 204, 1854.
60. FO 707/65, Thom to Pottinger, 18 Feb. 1844. Mrs Harriet Gribble was in her mid-thirties (see 1851 census return for 21 Pembridge Villas, Bayswater), Mrs Fanny Sullivan in her early twenties (see Fanny Gingell in 1880 England and Wales death registers).
61. For Gribble at Amoy see FO 228/31 and FO 228/39.
62. FO 228/32, sup. 17, 1844; and FO 228/33, sup. 92, 1844.
63. FO 228/34, sup. 95, 1844; and FO 228/47, F.O. 16, 1845.
64. *DNB*, XVI, p. 226.
65. Archives of Royal Geographic Society, London, Gribble to Society, 17 June 1851.
66. Henry Edward Gribble, member of Law Society Council.

67. Information kindly supplied by Liverpool Record Office; see also W.E. Cheong, *Mandarins and Merchants*...(London and Malmo, 1979), p. 159.
68. *Chinese Repository*, XVI, pp. 242–5.
69. FO 228/25, sup. 154, 1843.
70. T. Watters, *Essays on the Chinese Language* (Shanghai, 1889), p. 99; and FO 228/211, Amoy 52A, 1856.
71. FO 17/58, sup. 58, 1842.
72. FO 228/60, Amoy, 21 Apr. 1846.
73. FO 707/65, Thom to Pottinger, 12 and 25 July, and 3 Sept., 1843.
74. FO 228/31, Ningpo 3, 1843, and 5A, 1844.
75. FO 228/40, Ningpo 32, 1844; and FO 228/118, sup. 34, 1851.
76. FO 228/42, Ningpo 28, 1844; and FO 228/35, sup. 85, 1844.
77. FO 228/31, Ningpo 4, 1844.
78. FO 228/53, Ningpo 18, 1845; and FO 228/45, sup. 150, 1845.
79. FO 707/65, Thom to Pottinger, 13 Apr. 1844.
80. FO 228/31, Ningpo 21, 1844; FO 228/42, Ningpo 29, 1844; and FO 228/53, Ningpo 18, 1845.
81. FO 228/31, Ningpo 20 and 23, 1844; FO 228/42, Ningpo 48 and 57, 1844; FO 228/34, sup. 15, 62, and 87, 1844; and FO 228/44, sup., 10 Jan. and 11 Mar. 1845.
82. FO 228/36, F.O. 75, 1844.
83. FO 228/125, Amoy 1 and 8, 1851; and FO 228/511, Amoy 6, 1872. The Mandarin version of the name is Ch'en Ch'ing-chen.
84. FO 228/454, Leg. to Chefoo 6, 1868.
85. FO 17/626, Leg. 5, 1872.
86. For example, Dr Macartee's reminiscences, *North-China Herald*, 16 Mar. 1869.
87. Sir J.F. Davis, *Chinese Miscellanies* (London, 1865), p. 60.
88. FO 228/44, sup. 48, 1845; and FO 228/47, F.O. 61, 1845.
89. FO 228/63, Ningpo, 14 July 1846; and FO 228/57, sup. 96, 1846.
90. FO 228/57, sup. 147, 1846; FO 17/119, Hammond's minute on Staunton's letter of 10 Dec. 1846; and FO 228/68, F.O. 20, 1847.
91. For Balfour's career before and after his incumbency of the Shanghai consulate see his entries in *DNB* and in Couling's *Encyclopaedia Sinica*.
92. FO 17/58, sup. 55, 1842.
93. For Balfour's dealings with the Chinese authorities see FO 228/31 and FO 228/43.
94. FO 228/34, sup. 85, 1844.
95. FO 228/77, Shanghai 62, 1847.
96. Morse, *International Relations*, Vol. I, pp. 350–1.
97. FO 228/54, Shanghai 21, 23, and 75, 1845; and FO 228/64, Shanghai 17, 1846.
98. FO 228/46, sup. 175, 1845; and FO 228/57, sup. 97 and 114, 1846.
99. FO 17/207, Bowring to Granville, 29 Nov. 1852.

Notes to Chapter 2

1. FO 228/45, sup. 125, 1846.
2. Parker, *China Past and Present*, p. 249.
3. FO 228/247, sup. 161, 1858.
4. For example, FO 17/72, F.O. to Jackson, Dec. 1843.

5. FO 228/34, sup. 3, 1844.
6. FO 228/111, sup. reply to Amoy 11, 1850.
7. FO 228/96, F.O. 2, 1849.
8. FO 228/299, Bruce to Alston, 31 Dec. 1860.
9. FO 228/131, Shanghai 92, 1851.
10. FO 228/102, Foochow 22, 1849: and FO 228/164, sup. 9, 1854.
11. For example, FO 228/45, sup. 125, 1845; and FO 228/265, Amoy 7, 1859.
12. Meadows, *Desultory Notes*; and FO 228/372, Newchwang 21, 1864.
13. Lane-Poole, *Parkes*, Vol. I, p. 169.
14. FO 228/128, Foochow 30 and 31, and sup. 34 to Foochow, 1851; FO 228/185, F.O. 56, 1855; FO 228/133, sup. 25, 1852, and FO 228/138, F.O. 27, 1852; and FO 228/215, Foochow 2 and sup. 6 and 8 to Foochow, 1856.
15. FO 228/183, sup. 353, 1855; and FO 228/208, F.O. 34, 1856.
16. FO 228/216, Foochow 50, 1856.
17. FO 228/289, Foochow 77, 1860.
18. FO 228/260, sup. 14, 1859.
19. FO 228/634, Tamsui 6, 1879, and FO 17/1046, Leg. cons. 13, 1887.
20. Alcock's evidence to Select Committee on Consular Service and Appointments, Q. 1701; and Lane-Poole, *Parkes*, Vol. I, p. 94.
21. For the Foochow calls see FO 228/180, sup. 159, 1855, and FO 228/247–8, sup. 229, 1858.
22. For example, FO 228/1119, Kiukiang 17, 1893; FO 228/1285, Foochow, 6 July 1898; FO 228/408, Foochow 18, 1866; and FO 17/674, Leg. 126, 1874.
23. For example, FO 228/128, Foochow 30, 1851; and FO 228/183, sup. 391, 1855.
24. The reference for this description has been mislaid, but see another description in FO 17/674, Leg. 126, 1874.
25. FO 228/585, Amoy, 8 Sept. 1877.
26. Alcock's evidence to Select Committee on Consular Service and Appointments, Q. 1665; and FO 228/365, Ningpo 39, 1864.
27. For example, FO 228/100, Canton 101, 1849; FO 228/125, Amoy 10 and 12, 1851; and FO 228/496, Tientsin 53, 1870.
28. FO 228/99, Canton 57, 1849.
29. FO 228/134, sup. 90, 1852; and IUP, Vol. 2, p. 439 (Gregory).
30. PRO 30/33/8/22, Brenan to Satow, 21 Nov. 1900.
31. FO 228/285, Amoy 76, 1860; and FO 228/237–9, Ningpo 32, 1857.
32. FO 228/116, Shanghai 13, 1850.
33. FO 228/193, Ningpo 62, 1855; and FO 228/286, Canton 8 and 30, 1860.
34. FO 228/92, sup. 17, 1849.
35. Morse, *International Relations*, Vol. I, p. 392, and FO 228/82, F.O. 60, 1848; and FO 228/134, sup. 56, 1852.
36. FO 228/79, sup. 32, 1848; FO 228/98, Amoy 17 and sup. 4 to Amoy, 1849; FO 228/166–7, sup. 207, 1854; FO 228/203, sup. 302, 1856, and FO 228/229, sup. 366, 1857; and FO 228/265, Amoy 8 and Leg. 5 to Amoy, 1859.
37. FO 228/263, F.O. (Malmesbury to Bruce) 12, 1859; and FO 228/265, Leg. 30 to Foochow, 1859.
38. FO 228/100, sup. 168, 1849; and FO 228/163, sup. 48, 1854.
39. FO 228/134, sup. 89, 1852.
40. FO 228/236, Foochow 63 and sup. 75 to Foochow, 1857.
41. FO 228/245, sup. 19, 1858.
42. FO 228/245–6, sup. 25, 66, and 106, 1858; and FO 228/250, F.O. 41, 1858.
43. FO 228/249, sup. 272, 1858; and FO 228/250, F.O. 118, 1858.
44. FO 228/92, sup. 17, 1849; and FO 228/222, sup. 15, 1857.

45. FO 228/101, sup. 200 and 203, 1849.
46. FO 228/180, sup. 157 and 200, 1855; and FO 228/215, Foochow 32, 1856.
47. FO 228/226, sup. 209, 1857; and FO 228/289, Foochow 96, 1860.
48. FO 228/96, F.O. 38, 1849. For Palmerston's attitude see also FO 228/68, F.O. 119 and 159, 1847.
49. FO 228/68, F.O. 120, 1847; FO 228/92, sup. 17, 1849; and FO 228/96, F.O. 39, 1849.
50. FO 228/246, sup. 94, 103, and 133, 1858.
51. FO 228/133, sup. 22, 1852.
52. FO 228/111, Amoy 39, 1850.
53. FO 228/51, Canton 113, 1845; FO 228/44, sup. 50, 1845; FO 228/61, Canton 15, 1846; FO 228/163, sup. 48, 1854; FO 228/168, F.O. 56, 1854; and Meadows, *Chinese and their Rebellions*, p. 199.
54. FO 228/133, sup. (Bowring) 1, 1852.
55. FO 228/81, sup. 147, 1848, and *China Mail*, 7 Dec. 1848; and FO 228/135, sup. 144, 1852.
56. FO 228/45, sup. 155, 1845; FO 228/63, Foochow 70, 1846; FO 228/81, sup. 122, 1848; FO 228/87, Foochow 52, 1848; and FO 228/215, Foochow 3, 1856.
57. FO 228/75, Ningpo 12 and sup. 23 to Ningpo, 1847.
58. FO 228/71, Amoy 75, 1847; FO 228/79, sup. 50, 1848; and FO 228/82, F.O. 82, 1848.
59. FO 228/76, Shanghai 32, 1847.
60. PRO 30/33/15/1, entry for 22 June 1862.
61. FO 228/87, Foochow 52, 1848.

Notes to Chapter 3

1. FO 228/77, Shanghai 82, 1847.
2. FO 228/166–7, sup. 208, 1854; FO 228/178, sup. 56, 1855; FO 228/181, sup. 233, 1855; and FO 228/184, sup. 372, 1855.
3. FO 228/285, Amoy 52, 1860.
4. For example, FO 228/183, sup. 325, 1855; FO 228/233, Amoy 27, 1857; and FO 228/219, Shanghai 30, 1856.
5. FO 17/302, Alcock to Hammond, 4 Jan. 1858.
6. FO 228/103, Ningpo 33, 1849.
7. FO 228/448, Canton 7, 1868.
8. FO 228/77, Shanghai 62, 1847; FO 228/147, Shanghai 89, 1852; FO 228/161, Shanghai 55, 1853; FO 228/196, Shanghai 53, 1855; FO 228/229, sup. 344, 1857; FO 228/243, Shanghai 143, 1857; FO 226/274, Shanghai (Robertson to Bowring) 49, 1859; and FO 228/292, Shanghai 56, 1860.
9. FO 228/273, Ningpo 4, 1859; FO 228/84, Amoy 4, 1848; FO 228/60, Amoy 59, 1846; FO 228/108, sup. 132, 1850; FO 228/125, Amoy 14 and 42, 1851; FO 228/211, Amoy 38, 39, and 41, 1856; FO 228/251, Amoy 54 and 62, 1858; FO 228/254, Foochow 29, 1858; FO 228/288, Foochow 44, 1860; FO 228/51, Canton 38, 1845; and FO 228/106, sup. 53, 1850.
10. FO 228/60, Amoy 31, 1846; FO 228/70, Amoy 4, 1847; FO 228/111, Amoy 40 and sup. 44 to Amoy, 1850; FO 228/125, Amoy, 15 July 1851, and 55, 1851, and sup. 47 to Amoy, 1851; and FO 228/303, Amoy 39, 1861.
11. FO 228/75, Ningpo 41 and sup. 56, 1847; FO 228/88, Ningpo 5, 1848; FO 228/83, sup. to Waterhouse and Gutsell, 26 Apr. and 21 Aug. 1848; FO 228/255,

Ningpo 35, 1858; and FO 228/263, F.O. (Malmesbury to Bruce) 6, 1859.

12. FO 228/54, Shanghai 8, 1845; FO 228/56, sup. 73, 1846; FO 228/117, Shanghai 64, 1850; FO 228/130, Shanghai 32, 1851; FO 228/146, Shanghai 25, 1852; FO 228/161, Shanghai 53, 1853; and FO 228/196, Shanghai 53, 1855.

13. FO 228/130, Shanghai 12, 1851; and FO 228/196, Shanghai 53, 1855.

14. FO 228/77, Shanghai 62, 1847; FO 228/181, sup. 221, 1855; and FO 228/193–4, Ningpo 83, 1855.

15. FO 228/196, Shanghai 117, 1855; FO 228/405, Amoy, 15 Dec. 1866; and FO 17/449, Leg. 64, 1866.

16. FO 228/35, sup. circular 21 to consuls, 1844; FO 228/132, sup. 35, 1852; and FO 228/263, F.O. (Malmesbury to Bruce) 6, 1859.

17. FO 228/286–7, Canton 4 and 69, 1860.

18. FO 228/103, Ningpo 33, 1849.

19. FO 228/211, Amoy 38, 39, and 41, 1856.

20. FO 228/287, Canton 69, 1860.

21. FO 228/178, sup. 50 and 57, 1855; and FO 228/195, Shanghai 31, 1855.

22. FO 228/188, Amoy 58, 1855.

23. FO 228/251, Amoy 95 and sup. 104 to Amoy, 1858.

24. FO 228/273, Leg. 3 to Ningpo, 1859.

25. FO 228/263, F.O. (Malmesbury to Bruce) 12, 1859; FO 228/273, Leg. 3 to Ningpo, 1859; FO 228/217, Ningpo 46 and sup. 36 to Ningpo, 1856; FO 228/219, Shanghai 28, 1856; and FO 228/103, Ningpo 23 and sup. 20 and 36 to Ningpo, 1849.

26. FO 228/25, sup. 129, 1843; FO 228/141, Amoy 12, 1852; FO 228/53, Ningpo 18, 1845; FO 228/132, sup. 20, 1852; and Hornby, *Autobiography*, p. 255.

27. FO 228/147, Shanghai 77, 1852.

28. FO 228/45, sup. 36 to Shanghai, 1845.

29. FO 228/104, sup. 15 and 33 to Shanghai and Shanghai 29, 1849.

30. FO 228/107, sup. 91, 1850; FO 228/122, sup. 144, 1851; FO 228/191, Foochow 2 and sup. 14 to Foochow, 1855; and FO 228/232, F.O. 126, 1857.

31. FO 228/250, F.O. 109, 1858; and FO 17/312, Leg. 21, 1859, and Hammond's minute thereon.

32. FO 228/289, Foochow 77 and Leg. 53 to Foochow, 1860.

33. Lane-Poole, *Parkes*, Vol. II, p. 356.

34. FO 228/203, sup. 321, 1856.

35. FO 391/2, Alcock to Hammond, 4 July 1868.

36. FO 228/299, Bruce to Alston, 31 Dec. 1860.

37. FO 228/134, sup. 98, 1852.

38. Mui Hoh-Cheung and L.H. Mui (eds.), *William Melrose in China 1845–1855* (Edinburgh, 1973).

39. FO 228/120, sup. 64, 1851.

40. FO 17/237, Meadows to Hammond, 21 Apr. 1855.

41. FO 17/237, Meadows' letter to Hammond ascribes this view to Thom.

42. FO 228/84, Amoy 24 and sup. 16 to Amoy, 1848.

43. FO 228/75, Ningpo 6, 1847; and FO 228/103, Ningpo, 6 Aug. 1849.

44. FO 228/1289, Pakhoi 12, 1898.

45. Fairbank *et al.*, *I.G. in Peking*, Vol. 1, p. 205.

46. FO 228/254, Foochow 95 and 100, 1858.

47. FO 228/125, Amoy 21 and 25, 1851; FO 228/164, sup. 7, 1854; and FO 228/229, sup. 369, 1857.

48. FO 228/114, Foochow 32, 1850.

49. FO 228/87, Foochow 23 and 24, 1848.

50. FO 228/101, Canton 200 and 206, 1849.

51. FO 228/134, sup. 56, 1852.
52. FO 228/204, sup. 375, 1856; and FO 228/217, Ningpo 106, 1856.
53. FO 228/133, sup. 8, 1852; and FO 228/211, Amoy 18, 1856.
54. FO 228/266, Canton (Alcock to Bruce) 1 of May 1859.
55. FO 228/199, sup. 86, 1856; and FO 228/245, sup., 12 Mar. 1858.
56. FO 228/188, Amoy 43, 1855; FO 228/261, sup. 87, 1859; and FO 228/135, sup. 129, 1852.
57. FO 228/138, F.O. 24, 1852.
58. FO 228/199, Shanghai 86, 1856.
59. FO 228/261, sup. 78, 1859; and FO 228/274, Shanghai (Meadows to Bruce) 12, 1859.
60. FO 228/183, sup. 318, 1855.
61. FO 228/285, Amoy 20 and Leg. 19 to Amoy, 1860; and FO 228/247, sup. 153, 1858.
62. FO 228/264, F.O. 54, 1859.
63. FO 228/136, sup. 175 and 177, 1852; FO 228/149, sup. (Bowring) 3 and 19, 1853; FO 228/153, F.O. (Clarendon) 1, 1853; and FO 228/223, sup. 110, 1857.
64. FO 228/84, Amoy 13, 1848; FO 228/93, sup. 103, 1849; FO 228/107, sup. 94, 1850, and FO 228/111, Amoy 29, 1850; FO 228/151–2, sup. 103 and 132, 1853; FO 228/155, Amoy 54, 1853; FO 228/185, F.O. 10, 1855; FO 228/188, Amoy 54, 1855; and FO 228/200, sup. 148, 1856, and FO 228/211, Amoy 21, 1856.
65. FO 228/76, Shanghai 4, 1847; FO 228/90, Shanghai 79, 1848; FO 228/146–7, Shanghai 6 and 77, 1852; FO 228/132, sup. 44, 1852; FO 228/199–200, sup. 66, 132, and 415, 1856.
66. FO 228/178, sup. 81, 1855; and Alcock, *Capital of the Tycoon*, Vol. II, Chapter I.
67. FO 228/57, sup. 157 and 166, 1846; and FO 228/65, sup. 10, 1847.
68. Morse, *International Relations*, Vol. I, pp. 381–4.
69. FO 228/68, F.O. 47, 1847; and FO 228/82, F.O. 1, 1848.
70. FO 228/265, Amoy 7 and Leg. 4 to Amoy, 1859.
71. FO 228/288, Leg. 33 to Foochow, 1860.
72. FO 228/279, F.O. 169, 1860.
73. For example, FO 228/1693, Ichang, 3 Apr. 1908; and FO 228/3283, Ichang, 24 Sept. 1923.
74. FO 228/147, Shanghai 55, 1852.
75. FO 228/224, sup. 149, 1857; and FO 228/145, Ningpo 41, 1852.
76. FO 228/289, Foochow 66 and Leg. 47 to Foochow, 1860.
77. For example, FO 228/161, Shanghai 4, 1853; and FO 228/181, sup. 213, 1855.
78. FO 228/181, sup. 213 and 275, 1855.
79. FO 228/208, F.O. 31, 1856; and FO 228/199, sup. 84, 1856.
80. FO 228/306, Canton 67 and Leg. 38 to Canton, 1861.
81. FO 371/13942, minute by J.T. Pratt on Shanghai Publicity Bureau News Bulletin No. 3 of February 1929.

Notes to Chapter 4

1. FO 228/27, F.O. 107, 1843.
2. Platt, *Cinderella Service*, pp. 21–5.

3. FO 228/66, sup. 139, 1847.
4. FO 228/45, sup. 113, 1845.
5. FO 17/317, sup. 20, 1859; and FO 228/117, Shanghai 46, 1850.
6. Endacott, *Biographical Sketch Book*, p. 88; FO 228/185, F.O. 24, 1855; and FO 228/208, F.O. 66, 1856.
7. FO 17/119, Hammond's minute on Staunton's letter of 10 Dec. 1846.
8. For example, solicitations by Sinclair's aunt (FO 17/238, 18 Jan. 1855); W.E. King's mother (FO 17/364, 6 June 1861); Holt's father (FO 17/512, 5 Aug. 1868); R.J. Forrest's father-in-law (FO 17/539, 15 Apr. 1869); Cooper's uncle (FO 17/527, minutes of November 1869); and Cooper's aunt (FO 17/643, 27 July 1872).
9. FO 228/134, sup. 98, 1852; and FO 228/160, Ningpo 11, 1853.
10. FO 228/68, F.O. 98, 1847; and FO 228/107, sup. 75, 1850.
11. FO 228/150, sup. 31 and 42, 1853; and FO 228/153, F.O. 45, 1853. For Oakley see FO 228/164, sup. 16, 1854; FO 228/201–2, sup. 183, 250, and 255, 1856; and FO 391/1, Alcock to Hammond, 24 Jan. 1866.
12. Alcock's evidence to Select Committee on Consular Service and Appointments, Q. 1760.
13. FO 228/134, sup. 82, 1852; FO 228/138, F.O. (Malmesbury to Bonham) 21, 1852; *The Times* obituary, 3 May 1906; and England and Wales probate records, 1906. See also Hon. N.L. Kay Shuttleworth, *A Life of Sir Woodbine Parish, K.C.H. and Early Days in Argentina* (London, 1910).
14. FO 228/168, F.O. 11, 1854.
15. FO 228/90, Shanghai 34, 1848; and FO 228/166–7, sup. 204, 1854.
16. For example, FO 228/90, sup. 10 to Shanghai, 1848; and FO 228/94, sup. 129, 1849.
17. For example, FO 228/46, sup. 169, 1845; FO 228/50, Amoy 79, 1845; and FO 228/63, Ningpo 18 and 19, 1846.
18. For example, FO 228/150, sup. 70, 1853; FO 228/169, F.O. 120, 1854; FO 228/185, F.O. 44, 1855; and FO 228/297, F.O. 6, 1861.
19. FO 391/2, Alcock to Hammond, 2 Apr. 1869.
20. For example, FO 228/208, F.O. 4, 1856.
21. FO 17/302, Malmesbury's response to Hammond's minute of 16 July 1858.
22. FO 228/263, F.O. (Malmesbury to Bruce) 6, 1859.
23. FO 391/2, Hammond's minute on Alcock's letter of 26 May 1868; and FO 17/528, F.O. minutes on Leg. cons. 78 and cons. 80, 1869.
24. FO 228/55, sup. 82, 1846; FO 228/58, F.O. 18, 1846; FO 228/78, sup. 1, 1848; and FO 228/134, sup. 98, 1852.
25. FO 228/68, F.O. 83, 1847.
26. FO 228/58, F.O., 18 Nov. 1846; FO 228/93, sup. 80, 1849; and FO 228/152, sup., 5 Dec. 1853.
27. FO 228/78, sup. 29, 1848 (Pedder); FO 228/82, F.O. 124, 1848, FO 228/92, sup. 31, 1849, and FO 228/96, F.O. 41, 1849 (Fittock); and FO 228/106, sup. 56, 1850, and FO 228/138, F.O. (Malmesbury to Bowring) 26, 1852 (Caine).
28. FO 228/46, sup. 159, 1845; FO 228/90, Shanghai 34, 1848; FO 228/81, sup. 117, 1848; and FO 228/219, Shanghai 98, 109, and 124, and sup. 103 to Shanghai, 1856.
29. FO 228/92, sup. 31, 1849; FO 228/96, F.O. 41, 1849; and FO 228/109, F.O. 77, 1850.
30. FO 17/222, Hammond's minute of 5 July 1854; and FO 228/201, sup. 172, 1856.
31. FO 228/66, sup. 120, 1847.
32. FO 17/192, Malmesbury's minute on sup. 98, 1852.
33. FO 228/215, Foochow 11, 1856; FO 228/199, sup. 99, 1856; and FO 391/19,

Wade to Hammond, 6 June 1867.
34. FO 228/164–5, sup. 48 and 116, 1854.
35. *North-China Daily News* (Shanghai), 10 Oct. 1871 (reference kindly supplied by Canon G.W. Markham).
36. FO 17/220, Hammond's memorandum of 1 Jan. 1854 and action thereon.
37. FO 228/169, F.O. 67, 1854.
38. Estimates, PP 1854–5, XXXI, Colonial, Consular, and other Foreign Services, pp. 20–1, Hammond to Treasury, 7 Aug. 1854.
39. FO 17/220, Hammond's memorandum of 1 Jan. 1854.
40. FO 228/168, F.O. 5, 1854.
41. FO 228/169, F.O. 145, 1854; FO 228/186, F.O. 196, 1855; FO 228/232, F.O. 138, 1857; and FO 228/250, F.O. 58, 1858.
42. Couling, *Encyclopaedia Sinica*, p. 532; FO 228/183, sup. 320, 1855; FO 228/224, sup. 123, 1857; FO 228/229, sup. 337, 1857; and FO 228/232, F.O. 138, 1857.
43. Wright, *Treasury Control*, Chapter 3.
44. *The Times*, 28 Feb. 1859; and J.E. Hoare, 'Mr. Enslie's Grievances: The Consul, the Ainu and the Bones', *Japan Society of London, Bulletin*, No. 78, Mar. 1976.
45. FO 228/250, F.O. 58 and 72, 1858; and FO 17/307, Hammond's memorandum of 2 Dec. 1858 and Malmesbury's minute thereon.
46. FO 17/321, G. Middleton to Malmesbury, 15 Jan. 1859, marginal minute, and Revd M.J. Mayers to Malmesbury, 12 Feb. 1859.
47. FO 228/263, F.O. (Malmesbury to Bruce) 18, 1859; and FO 228/262, Leg. 35, 1859.
48. Wright, *Treasury Control*, pp. 67–9.
49. FO 17/363, F.O. to CSC, 20 and 30 Mar. 1861.
50. FO 17/363, F.O. to universities and Wellington, 30 Mar. and 20 Apr. 1861, and Jones to Russell, 9 Apr. 1861.
51. CSC Seventh Report, PP 1862, XXI, p. 81; and FO 17/364, CSC to F.O., 22 June 1861.
52. FO 17/363, F.O. to universities, 30 Mar. 1861.
53. FO 17/371, Russell's minute on Leg. 52, 1862; and FO 228/359, F.O. 2, 1864.
54. FO 17/371, Leg. 52, 1862, and Russell's minute thereon.
55. FO 17/617, Bovill to F.O., Nov. 1864, and Mrs Annesley to F.O., Jan. 1865; and FO 17/618, Dawson to F.O., May 1866.
56. FO 17/617, Lord Stratford de Redcliffe to F.O., 1865 (Brenan); FO 17/618, Lord Suffield to F.O., 1866 (Scott); FO 17/620, Lord Leigh to F.O., Sept. 1870 (Brown); and Berkshire Record Office (D/EDd/F21) (Crawford).
57. See FO 17/384–5 and FO 17/617–19.
58. See England and Wales birth registers, 1848, for father's occupation; Bible Society archives, Lay to Society, 9 May 1836, for Lay's King's Lynn address; 1851 census for King's Lynn addresses of Bristow and of Mrs Lay's brother, R. Nelson; and FO 17/619 for recommendation of Bristow to F.O. by Dr Vellère, kindly identified by Harrow local history librarian as principal of a Harrow school.
59. For example, FO 17/618, Hammond's minute of Nov. 1866; and FO 17/619, invitations for Oct. 1867 nominations.
60. FO 17/617, F.O. minute of Feb. 1865.
61. See Appendix II and FO 17/617–19, including tables of examination results; FO 391/1, Alcock to Hammond, 6 Feb. 1864; and FO 17/450, Alcock to Hammond, 6 June 1866.
62. FO 17/362, F.O. to CSC, 20 Mar. 1861.
63. FO 228/298, F.O. 123, 1861; and FO 228/380, F.O. 102, 1865.

64. FO 228/403, F.O. 123, 1866; FO 17/617, minutes by Hammond and Clarendon, 1866; FO 391/2, Alcock to Hammond, 6 July 1868; and FO 17/539, minute, 27 July 1869.

65. FO 17/424, Leg. 28, 1865; FO 391/8, Robertson to Hammond, 10 Aug. 1865; FO 391/2, Alcock to Hammond, 25 May 1868; FO 17/498, Leg. 180, 1868, and minutes thereon; FO 17/508, F.O. to Egan, 12 Sept. 1868; and FO 228/447, F.O. 223, 1868.

66. FO 228/320, Bruce to Lay, 23 Aug. and 13 Oct. 1862; and FO 228/330, Chinkiang 12, 1862.

67. Platt, *Cinderella Service*, p. 27; Wright, *Treasury Control*, p. xxxi; and FO 228/201, sup. 172, 1856.

68. FO 228/161, Shanghai 4, 1853.

69. FO 228/91, Shanghai 120, 1848; FO 228/219, Shanghai 155, 1856; and FO 228/274, Shanghai (Meadows) 44, 1859.

70. FO 228/66, sup. 121, 1847; FO 228/68, F.O. 110, 1847; FO 228/96, F.O. 42, 1849; and FO 228/164, sup. 12, 1854.

71. FO 228/56, sup. 74, 1846; FO 228/81, sup. 143, 1848; FO 228/96, F.O. 24, 1849; FO 228/134, sup. 98, 1852 (Harvey); FO 228/118, sup. 11, 1851; FO 228/123, F.O. 44, 1851; and FO 228/134, sup. 82, 1852 (Parish).

72. FO 228/116, Shanghai 44, 1850.

73. FO 228/134, sup. 98, 1852; FO 228/141, Amoy 32, 1852; and FO 228/211, Amoy 52A, 1856.

74. FO 228/136, sup. 158, 1852, and FO 228/164, sup. 11, 1854 (Lay); FO 17/656, Leg. 227, 1873 (Wade); FO 228/247, sup. 157, 1858 (Swinhoe), and FO 17/596, Swinhoe to F.O., 1871; FO 228/450, Amoy 29, 1868 (Pedder); and FO 228/164, sup. 33, 1854 (J.A.T. Meadows). For T.T. Meadows see his *Desultory Notes*, p. 45.

75. FO 228/56, sup. 74, 1846.

76. Alcock's evidence to Select Committee on Consular Service and Appointments, QQ. 1531–2; FO 228/92, sup. 38, 1849; FO 228/65, sup. 8, 1847; and FO 228/116, Shanghai 44, 1850.

77. FO 228/68, F.O. 111, 1847; and FO 228/78, sup. 1, 1848.

78. FO 228/96, F.O. 42, 1849; FO 228/121, sup. 89, 1851; FO 228/134, sup. 98, 1852; FO 228/169, F.O. 120, 1854; and FO 228/166–7, sup. 201, 1854.

79. Endacott, *Biographical Sketch Book*, p. 35.

80. FO 228/133–4, sup. 13 and 98, 1852; FO 228/166, sup. 154, 1854; FO 228/179, sup. 128, 1855; FO 228/201, sup. 172, 1856; and FO 228/226, sup. 210, 1857.

81. FO 228/55, sup. 17, 34, and 82, 1846; FO 228/58, F.O. (Palmerston) 18, 1846; FO 17/119, Hammond's minute on Pottinger's memorandum of 27 Nov. 1846; FO 228/65, sup. 51, 1847; FO 228/121, sup. 95, 1851; FO 228/123, F.O. 94, 1851; FO 228/132, sup. 7, 1852; FO 17/195, Wade to Malmesbury, 6 Dec. 1852; and FO 228/166, sup. 172, 1854.

82. FO 17/592, Wade to Hammond, 20 Oct. 1871.

83. FO 228/164–6, sup. 82 and 172, 1854; FO 17/224, Hammond's minute of 31 Dec. on sup. 172, 1854; and FO 17/239, Hammond's memorandum of 7 May 1855.

84. FO 228/121, sup. 95, 1851, and FO 228/181, sup. 231, 1855; FO 228/186, F.O. 194, 1855; and FO 228/209, F.O. 161, 1856.

85. FO 228/264, F.O. 24, 1859; FO 228/297, F.O. 11, 1861; FO 228/298, F.O. 144, 1861; and FO 17/537, Wade to Clarendon, 22 Mar. 1869.

86. FO 17/475, Leg. 95, 1867.

87. FO 17/426, Leg., 22 June 1865; and FO 228/381, F.O., 7 Oct. 1865.

88. FO 391/2, Alcock to Hammond, 22 May 1869; FO 17/537, Wade to

Clarendon, 22 Mar. and 10 Apr., and Hammond's minute of 21 Apr., 1869.
89. FO 17/921, Wade to Granville, 13 Jan. 1883; and FO 17/1106, Wade to Sanderson, 5 July 1890.
90. FO 228/262, Leg. 35, 1859; FO 228/264, F.O. 39, 1859; FO 228/226, sup. 210, 1857; and FO 228/232, F.O. 157, 1857.
91. FO 228/263, F.O. (Malmesbury to Bruce) 5, 1859; FO 228/302, Wade to Bruce, 22 June 1861; and FO 228/134, sup. 98, 1852.
92. FO 17/373, Bruce to Hammond, 14 Aug. 1862.
93. PRO 30/33/15/1, entries for 11, 20, and 30 May 1862.
94. FO 228/262, Leg. 35, 1859; and FO 17/394, Leg. 139, 1863.
95. For example, FO 228/116, Shanghai 24, 1850.
96. FO 228/219, Shanghai 176, 1856.
97. FO 17/200, Mrs Sullivan to F.O., 11 and 28 Mar. 1853.
98. IUP, Vol. 2, pp. 408–9 (Pedder, 1869).
99. FO 228/359, F.O. 21, 1864.
100. For losses on salary bills see FO 228/46, sup. 178, 1845; FO 228/51, Canton 85, 1845; FO 228/158, Canton 125, 1853; and FO 228/173, Canton 112, 1854.
101. For example, FO 228/93, sup. 53, 1849.
102. For example, FO 228/213, Canton 88 and 140, 1856; FO 228/76, Shanghai 37, 1847; FO 228/272, Foochow 61, 1859; and FO 228/181, sup. 234, 1855.
103. FO 228/19, sup. 42, 1842; and Endacott, *Biographical Sketch Book*, p. 65.
104. FO 228/285, Amoy 76, 1860; FO 228/279, F.O. 163, 1860; and Hammond's evidence to Select Committee on Diplomatic and Consular Services, Q. 1780. For Hammond's opinion of medical certificates see FO 17/562, his minute on Carroll's letter of 20 Sept. 1870.
105. FO 228/152, sup. 143, 1853; FO 228/169, F.O., 5 Sept. 1854; FO 228/185, F.O., 29 Apr. 1855; FO 228/208, F.O. 99, 1856 (Meadows); FO 17/903, Leg. cons. 11, 1882; and FO 17/938 and FO 17/962, Baber to F.O., 19 June and 17 Dec. 1883, and 27 June and 20 Dec. 1884.
106. For example, FO 17/278, Medhurst to Hammond, 20 July and 22 Oct. 1857 (travel); and FO 17/133, Medhurst to Addington, 20 Feb. 1847, and FO 17/182, Gingell to Addington, 23 Apr. 1851 (levees).
107. FO 17/182, Jackson to Addington, 9 Jan. 1851.
108. FO 228/135, sup. 108, 1852; FO 228/181, sup. 234, 1855; FO 228/202, sup. 289, 1856; FO 228/247–8, sup. 212, 1858; and FO 228/310, Shanghai 8, 1861.
109. FO 228/298, F.O. 161, 1861.
110. FO 228/168, F.O. 11, 1854.
111. FO 228/405, Amoy, 8 Dec. 1866; and FO 17/538, Winchester's comments of 24 Feb. 1869 on Treasury report.
112. FO 228/168, F.O. 11, 1854.
113. FO 228/324, Canton 84, 1862; FO 228/224, sup. 123, 1857, and FO 17/652, Leg. 13, 1873; FO 228/222, sup. 20, 1857; FO 17/564–5, Mrs Layton to Clarendon, 4 June 1870; and FO 228/122, sup. 122, 1851, and FO 228/132, sup. 33, 1852.
114. FO 228/57, sup. 109, 1846; FO 228/102, Foochow 19, 1849; FO 228/114, Foochow 32, 1850; FO 228/104, Shanghai 74, 1849; and FO 228/150, sup. 46, 1853.
115. FO 228/549, F.O. circular 57, 1875.
116. For their health see FO 228/149, sup. (Bonham) 5, 1853; FO 228/190, Canton 101 and 105, 1855; FO 228/160, Ningpo 10, 1853; and FO 228/150, sup. 40, 1853. For pensions see *Foreign Office Lists*. For Hague's children see *China Mail*, birth announcements (at least 8 between 1845 and 1856), and 1861 census, Acomb, York.
117. FO 17/69, sup. 116, 1843.

118. FO 17/843, G. Jamieson to Tenterden, 23 June 1880, and Treasury to F.O., 31 Aug. 1880.
119. FO 369/2190, gratuity to Milton's widow, 1931; FO 228/55, sup. 54, 1846; and FO 369/1774, Leg. cons. 308, 1922, and F.O. letter to No. 10, Downing Street, arising therefrom.
120. FO 17/279, Bonham to Hammond, 10 Jan. 1857 (Mrs Hillier); FO 678/1903, letters of administration to Mrs Lay; FO 228/107, sup. 87, 1850 (Mrs Layton); FO 228/149, sup. 27, 1853, and FO 678/2050, Sullivan's will (Mrs Sullivan); England and Wales marriage registers, 1850, and birth registers (W.W.C. Connor), 1851, and FO 228/120, sup. 42 and 62, 1851 (Mrs Connor); and FO 228/55, sup. 54, 1846, and FO 228/107, sup. 87, 1850 (widows' passages).
121. FO 17/119, Hammond's minute on Staunton's letter of 10 Dec. 1846.
122. FO 17/619, application for nomination for son from Mrs Marshall-Hole (formerly Mrs Hillier), 1867; England and Wales marriage registers, 1860 (Mrs Connor); FO 228/93, sup. 80, 1849, and England and Wales probate records, 1882 (Mrs Lay); FO 17/564–5, Mrs Layton to F.O., 4 June 1870; and FO 228/163, sup. 14, 1854, and FO 228/379, F.O. 48, 1865 (Mrs Gingell).
123. FO 228/45, sup. 85 and 125, 1845; and FO 228/55, sup. 30, 1846. For lack of free quarters for some juniors see FO 228/92, sup. 31, 1849; FO 228/180, sup. 160, 1855; FO 228/217, Ningpo 9, 1856; and FO 228/237, Ningpo 9, 1857.
124. FO 228/151, sup. 76, 1853; and FO 228/274, Shanghai 22, 1859.
125. FO 228/358, Leg., 10 Nov. 1864.
126. FO 228/251, Amoy 11, 1858; FO 228/304, Amoy 41 and 45, 1861; and FO 228/322, Amoy 29, 1862.
127. FO 228/63, Ningpo 24, 1846; FO 228/103, Ningpo 35 and sup. 47 to Ningpo, 1849; FO 228/237–9, Ningpo 35, 1857; FO 228/1287, Ningpo, 1 Apr. 1898; and FO 228/250, F.O. 94, 1858.
128. FO 228/230, sup. 386, 1857; FO 228/247–8, sup. 206, 1858; and FO 228/250, F.O. 93, 1858.
129. FO 228/304, Amoy 41 and 42, 1861; FO 228/274, Shanghai (Meadows) 43 and 48, 1859; FO 228/237–9, Ningpo 35, 1857; FO 228/223, sup. 62, 1857; and FO 228/232, F.O. 98, 1857.
130. For example, FO 228/113, sup. 134 and 141 to Canton, 1850; and FO 228/142, Canton 25, 32, and 35, and sup. 34 and 39 to Canton, 1852.
131. FO 228/263, F.O. (Malmesbury to Bruce) 6, 1859.
132. FO 228/80, sup. 83, 1848; FO 228/104, Shanghai 37, 1849; FO 228/265, Leg. 28 to Canton, 1859; FO 228/191, Foochow 67, 1855; and FO 228/264, F.O. 87, 1859.
133. FO 228/261, sup. 83, 1859; FO 228/151, sup. 76, 1853; and FO 228/44, sup. 1, 1845.
134. See Appendix II.
135. Parker, China Past and Present, p. 168; and Mayers et al., Treaty Ports, pp. 395–9.
136. FO 228/50, Amoy 47, 1845; FO 17/478, Leg. 168, 1867; and Mayers et al., Treaty Ports, p. 396.
137. FO 228/120, sup. 70, 1851; and FO 228/93, sup. 79, 1849.
138. FO 228/78, sup. 29, 1848; FO 228/149, sup. (Bowring) 17, 1853; FO 228/233, Amoy 15 and 16, 1857; FO 228/362, Amoy 39, 1864; and FO 391/19, Wade to Hammond, 18 July 1871.
139. FO 17/786, Pedder to F.O., 1 May 1878.
140. FO 228/160, Ningpo 41, 1853; and FO 228/80, sup. 72, 1848.
141. For example, FO 228/87, Foochow 4, 1848; and FO 228/247–8, sup. 232, 1858.
142. Lane-Poole, Parkes, Vol. I, p. 170.

143. For example, FO 391/19, Wade to Hammond, 22 Dec. 1869 (T.T. Meadows); and Parker, *John Chinaman*, p. 175 (Hance).
144. FO 228/211, Amoy 52A, 1856; and Mayers *et al.*, *Treaty Ports*, pp. 264–9.
145. FO 228/89, Shanghai 21, 1848; and Mayers *et al.*, *Treaty Ports*, pp. 255 and 283.
146. Mayers *et al.*, *Treaty Ports*, p. 403.
147. For the Chinese marriages see FO 656/44, Tientsin 7 to Supreme Court, 1875, and FO 666/2, birth of Webster's son, 24 Feb. 1865. The other data derive from official archives, from marriage registers, and from press announcements.
148. For his father-in-law D.J. Macgowan see Fairbank *et al.*, *I.G. in Peking*, Vol. 2, p. 942; FO 17/533, Robertson to Hammond, 3 Apr. 1869; FO 228/770, Wenchow 16, 1884; and FO 228/1062, Wenchow accts. 4, 1891.
149. For example, FO 228/141, Amoy 50, 1852; FO 228/150, sup. 70, 1853; and FO 228/253, Canton 70, 1858.
150. First wife: England and Wales marriage registers, 1847, and Elliston, *Shantung Road Cemetery*, for her death in Dec. 1848. Second wife: *China Mail* announcements of marriage in Feb. 1854 and death in Feb. 1855.
151. FO 678/2810 and 1841 census, Colkirk, Norfolk, for age at death of first wife; FO 663/89 for age at death of second wife.
152. FO 228/50, Amoy 50, 1845; FO 228/1050, Chinkiang accts. 6, 1890; and FO 228/999, Swatow accts. 6, 1883.
153. FO 228/183, sup. 329, 1855; FO 228/204, sup. 364, 1856; and FO 228/412, Shanghai 42, 1866.
154. FO 228/533, Ningpo, 13 July 1874.
155. FO 391/2, Alcock to Hammond, 25 May 1868; and FO 17/538, Alcock to Hammond, 18 July 1868.
156. FO 228/152, sup. 146, 1853; FO 228/165, sup. 115, 1854; FO 228/169, F.O. 184, 1854; FO 228/178, sup. 70, 1855; and FO 228/208, F.O. 4, 1856.
157. FO 17/373, Bruce to Hammond, 14 Aug. 1862.
158. For Mrs Meadows see FO 917/166, probate J.A.T. Meadows; FO 228/617, Tientsin, 16 Feb. 1878; FO 656/44, correspondence 1875–7 between Tientsin and Supreme Court; FO 228/766, Tientsin 33, 1894; and FO 917/545, administration of son's estate, 1903.

Notes to Chapter 5

1. FO 228/90, Shanghai 36, 1848; FO 228/39, Amoy, July 1844; FO 228/155, Amoy 13, 1853; and FO 228/106, sup. 53, 1850.
2. FO 228/169, F.O. 92, 1854; and FO 391/1, Alcock to Hammond, 20 Oct. 1854.
3. FO 228/78, sup. 42, 1848.
4. FO 17/160, Bowring, 7 July 1849, and other letters to Palmerston.
5. FO 228/106, sup. 53 and 55, 1850.
6. W.R. Costin, *Great Britain and China 1833–1860* (Oxford, 1937), p. 152.
7. FO 228/123, F.O. 120, 1851.
8. FO 228/133, sup. (Bowring) 1, 1852; FO 228/138, F.O. (Malmesbury to Bowring) 18 and 28, 1852; FO 17/207, Bowring to Granville, Nov. 1852; FO 228/153, F.O., 20 Jan. 1853; FO 228/149, sup. (Bonham) 1, 1853; and FO 228/156, Canton 39, 1853.
9. Fairbank, *Trade and Diplomacy*, p. 278.

10. W.G. Beasley, *Great Britain and the Opening of Japan 1834–1858* (London, 1951), p. 96; and G.F. Bartle, 'Bowring and the Arrow War', *Bulletin of the John Rylands Library*, 43 (1961), p. 312.

11. FO 228/165, sup. 128, 1854; FO 228/172, Canton 87, 1854; FO 228/179, sup. 130, 1855; FO 228/182, sup. 297, 1855; and FO 228/212–13, Canton 18, 37, and 73, 1856.

12. For example, FO 228/144, Foochow 31, 1852.

13. FO 17/302, Alcock to Hammond, 4 Jan. 1858.

14. Royal Commission on Opium, Vol. 1, Q. 1291.

15. FO 228/205, sup. 403, 1856.

16. Lane-Poole, *Parkes*, Vol. I, p. 262.

17. FO 228/222, sup. 14, 1857.

18. Hurd, *Arrow War*, p. 75; and FO 228/231–2, F.O. 72, 104, 105, 106, and 190, 1857.

19. FO 228/227, sup. 296, 1857; FO 228/230, sup. 397, 1857; and FO 228/263, F.O. (Malmesbury to Bruce) 1 and 3, 1859.

20. FO 228/232, F.O. 88, 1857; Hurd, *Arrow War*, pp. 116 and 125; and Lane-Poole, *Parkes*, Vol. I, p. 370.

21. Morse, *International Relations*, Vol. I, pp. 505–6; FO 228/261, sup. 89, 1859; FO 228/245, sup. 73, 1858; and FO 228/264, F.O. 82, 1859.

22. FO 228/259, Canton to Elgin, 23 Feb. 1858; FO 228/245–6, sup. 56, 61, and 87, 1858; and FO 228/252, Canton 55, 1858.

23. FO 228/173, Canton 97, 1854.

24. FO 228/247–8, sup. 202 and 213, 1858; FO 228/250, F.O. 98, 1858; Hurd, *Arrow War*, p. 105; FO 228/259, Alcock to Elgin, 7 Sept. 1858; FO 228/249, sup. 291, 1858; and FO 228/253, Canton 158, 1858.

25. IUP, Vol. 33, pp. 474–81.

26. FO 228/261, sup. 89, 1859; FO 228/266, Canton 7, 1859; FO 228/246, sup. 120, 1858; FO 228/287, Canton 93 and 94, 1860; and FO 228/306, Canton 71, 1861.

27. FO 228/123, F.O. 24, 1851; FO 228/120, sup. 51 and 107, 1851; and FO 228/132, sup. 22, 1852.

28. FO 228/428, Canton 5, 1867; FO 228/252, Canton 104, 1858; FO 17/555, Leg. cons. 48, 1870; Mayers *et al.*, *Treaty Ports*, pp. 127 and 282; and FO 228/120, sup. 64, 1851.

29. FO 228/67, sup. 221, 1847; and FO 228/112, sup. 41, 1850.

30. FO 228/100, sup. 106 and 111 to Canton, and Canton 139, 1849; FO 228/123, F.O. 24, 1851; FO 228/127, Canton 95 and sup. 67 to Canton, 1851; FO 228/134, sup. 86, 1852; and FO 228/224, sup. 149, 1857.

31. FO 228/80, sup. 71, 1848; and FO 228/121, sup. 79, 1851.

32. FO 228/150, sup. 60, 1853; and FO 228/153, F.O. 59, 1853.

33. FO 228/158, Canton 140, 1853.

34. FO 228/113, Canton 165 and sup. 135 to Canton, 1850.

35. FO 228/99, Canton 12 and 15, 1849; FO 228/119, sup. 25, 1851; and FO 228/123, F.O. 51, 1851.

36. FO 228/81, sup. 121 and 125, 1848; and FO 228/113, Canton 170 and sup. 139 to Canton, 1850.

37. FO 228/123, F.O. 25, 1851; FO 228/122, sup. 127, 1851; FO 228/133, sup. (Bowring) 6, 1852; and FO 228/245, sup. 79, 1858.

38. FO 228/157, Canton 103, 1853; FO 228/149, sup. (Bonham) 15, 1853; and FO 228/163, sup. 20, 1854.

39. FO 228/164, sup. 2, 1854.

40. FO 228/172–3, Canton 30, 97, and 146, 1854; FO 228/169, F.O. 86, 1854;

and FO 228/223, sup. 60, 1857.
41. FO 228/230, sup. 432, 1857; FO 228/246–9, sup. 112 and 202, 1858, and 1 Nov. 1858; FO 228/253, Canton 134, 1858; FO 667/14, *The Hongkong Directory with a List of Foreign Residents in China* (Hong Kong, 1859); FO 228/292, Shanghai 89, 1860; and Elliston, *Shantung Road Cemetery*.
42. FO 228/113, Canton 167, 1850; FO 228/105, sup. 24, 1850; FO 228/149, sup. 15, 1853; FO 228/164, sup. 2, 1854; and England and Wales probate records, 1861.
43. FO 228/173, Canton 77, 1854.
44. FO 228/260, sup. 2, 8, and 21, 1859; and FO 228/363, Canton 15, 1864.
45. England and Wales marriage registers, 1850; *China Mail*, birth announcement, July 1851; and Elliston, *Shantung Road Cemetery*.
46. FO 228/254, Foochow 40, 1858; FO 228/246, sup. 130, 1858; FO 17/305, F.O. memorandum on sup. 130, 1858, and Hammond to Caldecott Smith, 22 July 1858; and FO 17/302, Caine to Coles, 21 May, and Hammond to Malmesbury, 16 July, 1858.
47. FO 228/149, sup. 15, 1853; FO 228/208, F.O. 25, 1856; and FO 228/286, Canton 2, 1860.
48. FO 228/120, sup. 64, 1851; and FO 228/233, Amoy 3, 1857.
49. Lane-Poole, *Parkes*, Vol. I, p. 149; FO 228/132, sup. 39, 1852; FO 228/138, F.O. (Malmesbury to Bowring) 39, 1852; FO 228/179, sup. 122, 1855; FO 228/585, Leg. 8 to Amoy, 1877; and FO 228/3182, Clive's tel. 10 from Amoy to Leg. and Barton's minute on Amoy 21, 1922.
50. FO 228/83, Amoy 54, 1848; FO 228/151, sup. 103 and 105, 1853; and FO 228/155, Amoy 60, 81, 85, 93, and 98, and sup. 62 to Amoy, 1853.
51. FO 228/224, sup. 139, 1857.
52. For example, FO 228/211, Amoy 34, 42, and 43, 1856; and FO 228/249, sup. 272, 1858.
53. FO 228/469, Amoy 16, 1869.
54. FO 228/211, Amoy 51, 1856.
55. FO 228/188, Amoy 43, 1855; FO 228/179, sup. 120, 1855; and IUP, Vol. 3, pp. 400–1.
56. FO 17/478, sup. 175, 1867; Fairbank, *Trade and Diplomacy*, pp. 291–3; and FO 228/62, Foochow 7 and 45, 1846.
57. FO 228/52, Foochow 33 and 36, 1845; FO 228/45, sup. 125, 150, and 155, 1845; and Lane-Poole, *Parkes*, Vol. I, pp. 108 and 118.
58. FO 228/62, Foochow 10, 14, 16, and 22, 1846.
59. FO 17/317, sup. 20, 1859.
60. FO 228/74, Foochow 40, 1847; FO 228/87, Foochow 3, 1848; and FO 228/63, Foochow 68, 1846.
61. FO 228/34, sup. 55, 1844; FO 228/45, sup. 86, 1845; FO 228/74, Foochow 48, 1847; FO 228/87, Foochow 20 and 24 Jan. 1848; FO 228/78, sup. 39, 1848; FO 228/82, F.O. 39, 1848; FO 228/81, sup. 137, 1848; FO 228/92, sup. 3, 1849; and FO 228/94, sup. 130, 1849.
62. FO 228/81, sup. 142, 1848; FO 228/106, sup. 46, 1850; FO 228/109, F.O. 73 and 77, 1850; FO 228/120, sup. 49, 1851; and *Foreign Office Lists*.
63. FO 228/102, Foochow 3, 1849, and Jackson to Bonham, 28 May 1849; and FO 228/114, Foochow 25, 1850.
64. FO 228/151, sup. 122, 1853; and Wilkinson, *Early Days*.
65. FO 228/191, Foochow 32, 1855; FO 228/236, Foochow 7, 1857; and FO 228/245, sup. 20, 1858.
66. Wilkinson, *Early Days*.
67. FO 228/203, sup. 302, 1856; FO 228/236, Foochow 20 and sup. 22, 1857;

and FO 228/229–30, sup. 366, 420, and 425, 1857.

68. Wilkinson, *Early Days*.

69. FO 228/128, Foochow 6 and 34, 1851; Wilkinson, *Early Days*; FO 228/260, sup. 14, 1859; FO 228/289, Leg. 53 to Foochow, 1860; FO 228/180, Foochow 160, 1855; and FO 228/265, Leg. 28 to Foochow, 1859. For the retention of the old consulate see, for example, FO 228/385, Leg. 7 and 11 to Foochow and Foochow 15, 1865, and FO 17/1047, Leg. cons. 90, 1887.

70. FO 228/115, Ningpo 22, 1850; FO 228/109, F.O. 73 and 77, 1850; and FO 228/120, sup. 49, 1851.

71. For similar rackets at Foochow see FO 228/87, and at Shanghai see FO 228/104, Shanghai, 28 June 1849.

72. FO 228/103, Ningpo 18, 1849; and England and Wales probate records, 1887.

73. FO 17/69, sup. 118, 1843; Fairbank, *Trade and Diplomacy*, pp. 163 and 333; and G.F. Davidson, *Trade and Travel in the Far East or Recollections of Twenty One Years passed in Java, Singapore, Australia and China* (London, 1846). For W. Davidson's age see FO 228/120, sup. 64, 1851, and England and Wales probate records, 1887.

74. FO 228/103, Ningpo 13, 1849.

75. FO 228/115, Ningpo 52, 1850; and FO 228/129, Ningpo 18, 21, 23, 42, and 46, 1851.

76. FO 228/160, Ningpo 45, 1853; FO 228/164, sup. 110 and 125, 1854; and FO 228/175, Ningpo 19, 20, 29, and 31, 1854.

77. FO 228/180, sup. 183, 1855; and FO 228/193–4, Ningpo 27, 1855.

78. FO 228/178, sup. 84, 1855.

79. FO 228/180, sup. 183, 1855.

80. FO 17/237, T.T. Meadows to Hammond, 21 Apr. 1855, and F.O. docket thereon; FO 656/44, Tientsin 7 to Supreme Court, 1875; and FO 228/186, F.O. 177, 1855.

81. FO 228/193–4, Ningpo 87, 121, and 123, 1855; FO 228/184, sup. 404, 1855; FO 228/217, Ningpo 9, 1856; FO 228/198, sup. 54, 1856; FO 228/208–9, F.O. 53, 102, and 222, 1856; FO 228/205, sup. 411, 1856; FO 228/222, sup. 33, 1857; FO 228/247, sup. 167, 1858; FO 228/250, F.O. 96, 1858; FO 228/260, sup. (Caine) 4 and 17, 1858; and FO 228/273, Leg. 22 to Shanghai, 1859.

82. FO 228/310, Leg. 2 to Shanghai and Shanghai 8, 1861; FO 228/297–8, F.O. 47 and 99, 1861; FO 17/451, Leg. 32, 1866; and FO 17/552, Leg. 108, 1870. For consular appointments see FO 228/460, Tientsin 38, 1868; FO 228/526, Tientsin 6, 1873; and FO 17/653, Leg. 91, 1873.

83. FO 228/193–4, Ningpo 34, 46, 54, and 62, 1855; FO 228/217–18, Ningpo 52 and 114, 1856; and FO 228/237, Ningpo 6, 1857.

84. FO 228/230, sup. 380, 1857.

85. FO 228/237, Ningpo 19, 1857.

86. A British Resident [John Scarth], *Twelve Years in China* (Edinburgh, 1860), p. 265.

87. FO 228/227, sup. 270, 1857; FO 228/230, sup. 380, 1857; FO 228/246, sup. 135, 1858; and FO 228/237–9, Ningpo 32 and 92, and sup. 91 to Ningpo, 1857.

88. FO 228/228–30, sup. 334, 343, and 380, 1857; FO 228/232, F.O. 236, 1857; FO 228/237–9, Ningpo 85, 1857; and FO 228/250, F.O. (Clarendon) 25, 1858.

89. FO 228/237–9, Ningpo 107 and sup. 110 to Ningpo, 1857.

90. FO 228/255, Ningpo 54, 1858; FO 228/245, sup. 19, 1858; FO 228/247–9, sup. 250 and 295, 1858; FO 228/272, Ningpo 3, 1859; FO 228/290, Leg. 16 and 21 to Ningpo, and Ningpo 37, 42, and 43, 1860; and FO 228/308, Ningpo 24, 25, 28, 29, and 35, 1861.

91. FO 17/312, Leg. 21, 1859.
92. FO 228/58, F.O. 10, 1846.
93. FO 17/103, F.O. to Johnston, 26 May 1845; FO 228/47, F.O. 75, 1845; FO 228/82, F.O. 28, 1848; FO 228/132, sup. 25, 1852; FO 228/134, sup. 70, 1852; and FO 17/223, F.O. to Johnston, 30 Dec. 1854. See also *DNB*, X, p. 941, and England and Wales probate records.
94. FO 228/78, sup. 60, 1848; FO 228/79, sup. 3, 7, 14, 15, and 20, 1848; FO 228/90, Shanghai, 25 Apr. 1848; and FO 17/317, sup. 20, 1859.
95. FO 228/82, F.O. 60, 1848.
96. FO 228/96, F.O. 102, 1849; FO 228/105, sup. 19, 1850; and FO 228/109, F.O. 34, 1850.
97. FO 228/105, sup. 32, 1850; FO 228/117, Shanghai 74, 1850, and marginalia thereon; FO 228/109, F.O. 50, 1850; and FO 228/113, Canton 169 and sup. 138 to Canton, 1850.
98. FO 228/117, Shanghai 67A, 67B, and 80, 1850.
99. FO 228/108, sup. 127, 1850; and FO 228/123, F.O. 21, 1851.
100. FO 228/65, sup. 39, 1847; FO 228/92, sup. 38, 1849; FO 228/135, sup. 113, 1852; FO 17/206, minute on Alcock's letter of 19 Mar. 1853 to Clarendon; FO 17/501, minute on Alcock's despatch of 4 Dec. 1868; Redesdale, *Memories*, Vol. 1, p. 358; *London and China Express*, supplement, 27 Nov. 1918, B. Brenan's recollections; and *The Times*, 13 Sept. 1886.
101. FO 228/152, sup. 130, 1853.
102. FO 228/92, sup. 17, 1849; FO 228/106, sup. 46, 1850; FO 228/117, Shanghai 62, 1850; FO 228/134, sup. 56, 1852; FO 17/206, Alcock to Clarendon, 19 Mar. 1853; and FO 228/181, sup. 234, 1855.
103. Morse, *International Relations*, Vol. I, pp. 346–9; and FO 228/274, Shanghai 44, 1859.
104. FO 17/219, Alcock to Hammond, 13 Apr. 1854; FO 228/149, sup. 30, 1853; FO 228/163, sup. 6, 1854; FO 228/164, sup. 6 and 8, 1854; and FO 228/169, F.O. 71, 1854.
105. Morse, *International Relations*, Vol. I, p. 463; and Alcock, *Capital of the Tycoon*, Vol. I, p. 37.
106. FO 228/131, Shanghai 92, 1851; and FO 228/146, Shanghai 4, 1852.
107. Morse, *International Relations*, Vol. I, pp. 352–3.
108. Morse, *International Relations*, Vol. II, pp. 22–4.
109. FO 228/182, sup. 303, 1855; and FO 228/195, Shanghai 21 and 29, 1855.
110. Fairbank *et al.*, *I.G. in Peking*, Vol. 2, p. 845; and England and Wales probate records, 1898.
111. FO 17/206, Alcock to Clarendon, 19 Mar. 1853, and minutes thereon; FO 391/1, Alcock to Hammond, 5 May 1854 and 17 and 21 Jan. 1857; FO 228/183, sup. 321, 1855; and FO 228/185–6, F.O. 19 and 239, 1855.
112. FO 228/117, Shanghai 67A and 67B, 1850; and FO 228/77, Shanghai 87, 1847.
113. FO 228/196, Shanghai 118, 1855; FO 228/219, Shanghai 61 and 111, 1856; and FO 228/222, sup. 15, 1857.
114. FO 228/163, sup. 6, 1854; and FO 228/164, sup. 19, 1854.
115. FO 228/147, Shanghai 89, 1852; and FO 228/161, Shanghai 4, 1853.
116. FO 228/205, sup. 395, 1856; FO 228/219, Shanghai 12, 1856; FO 228/224, sup. 122 and 126, 1857; FO 228/232, F.O. 143, 1857; and FO 233/98, memorandum of February 1883.
117. FO 228/272, Foochow 70 and 76, 1859; and FO 228/265, Leg. 11 to Foochow, 1859.
118. FO 228/281, Bruce to Elgin, 31 Aug. 1860.

Notes to Chapter 6

1. FO 228/206, sup. 423, 1856; FO 228/237, Ningpo 20, 1857; and FO 228/227, sup. 302, 1857.
2. FO 228/205, sup. 373, 1856; FO 228/226, sup. 227, 1857; FO 228/245, sup. 8, 1858; and Morse, *International Relations*, Vol. I, p. 591.
3. FO 228/149, sup. 17, 1853.
4. Morse, *International Relations*, Vol. I, p. 591.
5. FO 228/290, Leg. 43 to Ningpo, 1860.
6. FO 17/360, minute of 18 Jan. 1862.
7. Meadows, *Chinese and their Rebellions*, p. 324.
8. FO 228/196, Shanghai 118, 1855.
9. J.S. Gregory, *Great Britain and the Taipings* (London, 1969), pp. 171 *et seq.*
10. FO 228/169, F.O. 133, 1854.
11. FO 228/311, Shanghai 85, 1861.
12. FO 17/423, Leg. 8, 1865.
13. FO 228/326, Ningpo 20, 21, and 22, 1862.
14. FO 228/362, Amoy 32, 1864; and FO 17/425, Leg. 70, 1865.
15. IUP, Vol. 32, p. 153.
16. For Parkes' experiences see Loch, *Personal Narrative*.
17. FO 17/381, Treasury to F.O., 14 Apr. 1862.
18. Loch, *Personal Narrative*, pp. 47–8.
19. FO 228/247, sup. 207, 1858.
20. FO 228/302, Wade to Bruce, 11 Jan. 1861.
21. Banno Masataka, *China and the West 1858–1861: The Origins of the Tsungli Yamen* (Harvard, 1964), p. 333.
22. FO 228/313, Chinkiang 4 and 8, 1861; and FO 228/314, Kiukiang 4, 1861.
23. FO 228/360, F.O. 157, 1864.
24. FO 228/391, Adkins to Wade, 10 Jan. 1865; and FO 228/426, F.O. 125, 1867.
25. FO 391/2, Alcock to Hammond, 22 May 1869.
26. FO 17/813, Leg. 20, 1879; FO 17/820, F.O. to Treasury, 30 Dec. 1879; and long obituary in *Evesham Journal*, 28 Dec. 1912, short one in *The Times*, 30 Dec. 1912.
27. PRO 30/33/15/1, entry for 17 Feb. 1862.
28. Werner, *Autumn Leaves*, p. 550.
29. FO 228/226, sup. 210, 1857.
30. FO 228/247–8, sup. 147, 219, and 221, 1858.
31. *The Doctrine of the Chi or Occasional Papers on Chinese Philosophy* (Amoy, 1876: not seen).
32. FO 17/1138, Alabaster to Sanderson, 31 Jan. 1892.
33. FO 228/286, Canton 1, 1860; FO 228/285, Amoy 57, 1860; FO 228/293, Swatow 7, 9, and 25, 1860; FO 17/528, Leg. cons. 41, 1869, and FO 228/302, Wade to Bruce, 20 Feb. 1861.
34. FO 228/328–9, Shanghai 119 and 185, 1862; and FO 228/347, Shanghai 46, 1863.
35. FO 17/528, Leg. cons. 41, 1869.
36. FO 228/347, Shanghai 9, 46, and 60, 1863; and FO 17/1138, Alabaster to Sanderson, 31 Jan. 1892.
37. FO 228/325, Foochow 24 and Leg. 17 and 21 to Foochow, 1862; FO 17/375, Bruce to Russell, 11 Dec. 1862; and FO 17/411, Bruce to Russell, 9 Dec. 1864.
38. FO 228/299, Bruce to Alston, 31 Dec. 1860.

Notes to Chapter 7

1. FO 228/408, Foochow 45, 1866.
2. FO 17/411, Bruce to Russell, 9 Dec. 1864; FO 228/381, Russell to Alcock, 26 Sept. 1865; and FO 228/1295, Leg. 72, 1899.
3. Jordan, *China and the Powers*.
4. F.O. Confidential: Handbooks Prepared under the Direction of the Historical Section of the F.O., No. 67, China (March 1919), final para.
5. FO 17/584, Leg. 87, 1871; FO 17/924, Leg. 129, 1883, and FO 17/952, Leg. 211, 1884; and FO 228/779, Leg. 97, 1885.
6. FO 228/1201, Tientsin 7, 1895.
7. FO 228/1293, Shanghai 59, 1898; and FO 228/1282, Canton, 7 Oct. 1898.
8. IUP, Vol. 10, p. 446.
9. FO 228/520, F.O. 95, 1873.
10. IUP, Vol. 20, p. 205.
11. FO 17/538, Treasury report on China consulates, 4 Feb. 1869; and IUP, Vol. 2, pp. 239–44.
12. FO 228/487–8, F.O. (Clarendon) 68 and F.O. (Granville) 83, 1870; FO 17/635, Leg. cons. separate 3, 1872; FO 17/666, Treasury to F.O., 28 Jan. 1873, F.O. minute; and FO 17/652, Leg. 13, 1873.
13. FO 17/476, Leg. 117, 1867; and IUP, Vol. 2, pp. 248–62, Leg., 29 Oct. 1869.
14. FO 17/550, Leg. (to Granville) 12, 1870; FO 228/533, Ningpo 4, 1874; FO 228/1022, Wuhu accts. 5, 1886; FO 228/1108, Ichang accts. 12, 1893; Meadows, *Chinese and their Rebellions*, p. 581; and FO 228/395, Newchwang 19, 1865.
15. FO 228/533, Ningpo 22, 1874.
16. FO 228/358, Leg. 31, 1864.
17. FO 228/604, F.O. 51, 1878.
18. FO 228/1255, Leg. tel. to Shanghai, 28 Jan. 1897.
19. FO 17/475, Leg. 67, 1867; and Jordan, *China and the Powers*.
20. FO 228/401, F.O. 17, 1866; and FO 228/807, Taiwan 9, 1885.
21. FO 228/836, Shanghai 47, 1886, and FO 17/1138, Alabaster to Sanderson, 31 Jan. 1892.
22. FO 228/495, Leg. 9 to Taiwan, 1870; FO 228/702, Hoihow 21, 1882; and FO 228/757, Ningpo 26, 1884.
23. FO 228/865, Newchwang 1, 1888; and FO 228/1164, Tainan 35, 1894.
24. For example, FO 228/1228, Newchwang 8, 1896, and FO 228/1206, Leg. 229, 1896; and FO 228/1252, Ningpo 10, 16, and 17, 1897.
25. For example, FO 228/832, Hoihow 20, 1886.
26. FO 17/1041, Leg. 15, 1887; FO 228/440, Taiwan 24, 1867; and FO 228/837, Taiwan 14, 1886.
27. FO 228/1170, Leg. 29, 1895; and FO 228/1177, F.O. 79, 1895.
28. For example, FO 228/645, Amoy 31, 1880; FO 228/1248, Amoy 13 and Leg. 1 to Amoy, 1897; and FO 228/1950, Shanghai 268, 1915.
29. FO 17/635, Leg. cons., 1 May 1872.
30. For an example of delicacy see FO 17/508, Wade to Hammond, 18 June 1868.
31. FO 228/925, Wade to Tung Hsün, 13 Feb. 1865.
32. FO 17/654, Leg. 126, 1873; and FO 17/719, Leg. 22, 1876.
33. FO 391/12, Robertson to Hammond, July 1876; Redesdale, *Memories*, Vol. 1, p. 358; and *DNB*, XXII, p. 30. For Borneo see Tregonning, *Under Chartered Company Rule*.
34. FO 17/923, Wade to F.O., 25 June 1883, and FO 17/1084, Wade to F.O., 21 Jan. 1884; FO 17/905, Spence to F.O., 8 Feb. 1882, and FO 17/904, F.O. minutes

on Foochow 11 to F.O., 1882; FO 17/597, Sandford to F.O., 12 May 1871, and FO 17/897, Grosvenor to F.O., 13 and 19 Sept. 1882; FO 17/938, Spence to F.O., 23 Jan. 1883, F.O. minute; FO 17/929, F.O. to Wade, 6 Nov. 1883, and FO 17/1307, F.O. minute on draft of 11 Dec. 1883; and FO 17/1057, F.O. minutes on Legge's letter of 1 Mar. 1887 and Wade's memorandum relating thereto.

35. Lane-Poole, *Parkes*, Vol. II, pp. 416 and 420; FO 391/2, Alcock to Hammond, 18 Apr. 1868; FO 363/1, Kennedy to Tenterden, 30 Oct. 1879; and FO 228/779, Leg. 123, 1885.

36. Hewlett, *Forty Years in China*, p. 6, seems to imply a personal choice by Salisbury.

37. FO 228/1059, F.O., 12 Nov. 1891. For Salisbury's low opinion of Walsham see Wehrle, *Anti-Missionary Riots*, p. 31.

38. For example, FO 228/848, Walsham's rebuke regarding C.F.R. Allen's correspondence with Singapore, 1887; and FO 17/1087, Leg. cons. 13, 1889, and FO 228/1044, Amoy accts. 5, 1889.

39. FO 83/1486, MacDonald to Campbell, 8 Feb. 1898.

40. FO 17/1421, Leg. cons. 56, 1900; FO 369/1886, Phillips' Chefoo report, 9 Dec. 1926, Crowe's minute; and FO 228/1979, Chengtu tel. 62, 1916, Jordan's minute.

41. PRO 30/33/8/1, Mansfield to Satow, 1 Nov. 1900, Satow's minute.

42. Morse, *International Relations*, Vol. III, p. 280.

43. *In Memoriam. Walter Ewen Townsend*, under date of 28 Aug. 1900.

44. FO 800/163, MacDonald to Bertie, 4 Sept. 1900.

45. IUP, Vol. 2, pp. 159–202.

46. FO 97/555, Leg. tel. 4, 1891, Sanderson's minute; and FO 233/96, Winchester to Alcock, 1 Apr. 1868, and FO 17/1518, Bertie's minute, July 1895.

47. FO 17/583, Leg. 34, 1871; and FO 228/525, Leg. 5 to Kiukiang, 1873.

48. FO 228/1694, Tientsin 9, 1908, and Jordan's minute thereon; and FO 369/1775, Supreme Court 20 to F.O., 1922, F.O. minute.

49. FO 17/1116, Leg. cons. 32, 1891.

50. FO 233/96, Winchester to Alcock, 1 Apr. 1868; FO 228/514, Shanghai 1, 1872; FO 228/632, Shanghai 12, 1879; FO 228/636, Tientsin 17, 1879, and FO 228/663, Tientsin 56, 1880; FO 17/1016, Chefoo 131, 1886; and FO 228/1358, Samshui, 26 May 1900.

51. FO 17/924, Leg. 120, 1883; FO 228/722, Canton 19 and 25, 1883, and tel., 28 Sept. 1883; FO 17/926, Leg. 57, 1883, and Pauncefote's minute thereon; and FO 228/737, F.O. 58, 1884.

52. FO 228/3980, Shanghai 15, 1929; and FO 676/249, Shanghai 65, 1936.

53. A. Sargent, *Anglo-Chinese Commerce and Diplomacy* (Oxford, 1907), p. 314.

54. FO 228/890, Kiukiang 5, 1890; FO 228/1225, Chungking, 1 Aug. 1896; FO 228/1820, F.O. 50, 1912; PRO 30/33/9/10, Hosie to Satow, 20 Aug. 1905; and FO 350/1, Campbell to Jordan, 22 Sept. 1911.

55. FO 228/428, Canton 16 and Leg. 12 to Canton, 1867; FO 228/414, Chefoo 4, 1866; FO 228/622, F.O. memorandum, Oct. 1879; IUP, Vol. 10, p. 446; and FO 17/635, Leg. cons. separate 3, 1872.

56. IUP, Vol. 13, p. 421.

57. Correspondence respecting the Question of Diplomatic and Consular Assistance to British Trade Abroad, PP 1886, LX.

58. FO 228/835, Pakhoi 16 and Swatow 20, 1886; FO 17/1033, Spence to Currie, 8 Dec. 1886; and FO 228/850, Chefoo 15, 1887.

59. IUP, Vol. 20, pp. 193–264; FO 228/1265, MacDonald tel. to Bertie, 10 Aug. 1898; FO 881/7205, Cockburn to Villiers, 14 Feb. 1897; and FO 228/1190, Canton, 14 Jan. 1895.

60. FO 228/599, Wuhu 10, 1877.
61. FO 17/1015, Leg. 77, 1886.
62. See, for example, FO 228/515, Kiukiang 22, 1872, and FO 228/709, Hoihow 4, 1883.
63. IUP, Vol. 20, p. 212.
64. FO 228/726, Hankow 6, 8, and 40, and Leg. 4 to Hankow, 1883.
65. IUP, Vol. 2, p. 330, and FO 228/1340, F.O. 148, 1900; and FO 228/507, India to Leg., 28 Apr. 1871.
66. IUP, Vol. 12, p. 672; FO 228/718, F.O. 145, 1883; Royal Commission on Opium, Vol. 5, evidence of Ford and other China consular officers; FO 228/788, Amoy 15, 1885; FO 228/781, Leg. 410, 1885; and FO 228/1189, Amoy, 9 Mar. 1895.
67. FO 17/672, Leg. 21, 1874; FO 228/626, Chefoo 4, 1879; and FO 228/687, Tientsin 19, 1881.
68. Morse, *International Relations*, Vol. I, pp. 565–6; FO 17/583 and 17/589, Leg. 16 and 263, 1871; and Wehrle, *Anti-Missionary Riots*, p. 12.
69. FO 228/865, Pakhoi 8, 1888; and FO 228/534, Canton 11, 1874.
70. See, for example, FO 228/1284, Chungking, 1 Feb. 1898.
71. FO 228/1363, Ningpo, 30 Dec. 1899.
72. IUP, Vol. 8, p. 534; FO 228/726, Hankow 22, 1883; FO 228/1022, Hankow accts. 12, 1885; and FO 228/533, Ningpo 23, 1874.
73. FO 228/362, Leg. 11 to Amoy, 1864; IUP, Vol. 29, p. 157; FO 228/500, F.O. 36, 1871; FO 391/10–11, Robertson to Hammond, 19 July and 3 Dec. 1870 and 14 Jan. 1873; FO 17/683, Robertson to Hammond, 20 Jan. 1874; and FO 228/846, Currie to Walsham, 10 Dec. 1887.
74. FO 228/833, Kiukiang 10 and Leg. 3 to Kiukiang, 1886; and FO 228/892, Wuhu 1, 1890.
75. FO 228/1084, Chungking 10, Foochow 18, 19, 21, and 23, and Leg. 6 to Foochow, all of 1892; FO 228/1115, Chungking 29, 1893; FO 228/1193, Chungking, 1 May 1895; and FO 228/1262, Leg. 45, 1898.
76. FO 228/616, Tamsui, 8 Aug. 1878, FO 228/713, Tamsui 5, 1883, and G.L. Mackay, *From Far Formosa* (Edinburgh and London, 1896); FO 228/686, Tamsui 10, 1881; FO 228/1118, Hankow 5, 1893, and R.W. Thompson, *Griffith John, the Story of Fifty Years in China* (London, 1907, second edition), p. 9; FO 228/642, Wade to F.O. from Hong Kong 9, 1879, and FO 228/1254, Foochow, 4 Jan. 1897; FO 228/1113, Amoy 5, 1893; FO 228/1157, Kiukiang 4, 1894; and FO 228/829, Chinkiang, 3 Aug. and 1 Nov. 1886.
77. FO 228/450, Ningpo 23, 1868; FO 228/597, Newchwang 15, 1877; FO 228/1287, Chinkiang 9, 1898; and FO 17/779, Leg. 28, 1878.
78. *The Times*, 10 Mar. 1869, p. 8 (quoted by R.W. Thompson, *Griffith John*, p. 245).
79. *The Journey of Augustus Raymond Margary*, p. 71.
80. See, for example, FO 228/431, Ningpo 20, 1867; and FO 228/1190, Canton 17, 1895.
81. FO 664/8, Chengtu marriages, 1911; and FO 228/1276, Hankow 1, 1898.
82. FO 228/642, F.O. 74, 1880 (Wade); IUP, Vol. 20, p. 121 (Gardner), and p. 260 (Brenan); and FO 228/1114, Canton 38, 1893, and FO 228/850, Chungking, 7 Feb. 1887 (Bourne).
83. For example, FO 228/512, Canton 40, 1872; FO 228/848, Amoy, 17 Jan. 1887; FO 228/1127, Wenchow 6, 1893; and FO 228/1167, Wenchow 7, 1894.
84. FO 17/1122, F.O. to Archbishop, and FO 17/1124, Archbishop to F.O., both Dec. 1891.
85. FO 228/1195, Ichang 8, 1895; and FO 228/1085, Hankow 8, 1892.

86. FO 228/1164, Tainan 9, 1894. For some other opinions see FO 228/1159, Newchwang 4, 1894; FO 228/1163, Swatow 5, 1894; and FO 228/1167, Wenchow 8, 1894.
87. FO 228/1225, Foochow 3, 1896; and FO 228/1189, Amoy, 19 Aug. 1895.
88. *North-China Herald*, 1 June 1872; and FO 228/617, Newchwang 1, 1878.
89. FO 228/792, Chinkiang 11, 1885.
90. FO 228/1293, Shanghai 59, 1898.
91. FO 228/1190, Canton 22, 1895.
92. FO 17/474, Leg. 37, 1867; and Parker, *John Chinaman*, p. 219.
93. FO 17/219, Winchester to Addington, 21 Jan. 1854; FO 228/722, Canton 42, 1883; FO 228/1116, Chefoo 17, 1893; FO 228/1546, Canton 12, 1904; FO 228/701, Ningpo 2, 1882; and FO 228/765, Tamsui 16, 1884.
94. FO 228/432, Shanghai 7, 1867; FO 228/632, Shanghai 12, 1879; and FO 228/1161, Shanghai, 6 Jan. 1894.
95. FO 228/568, Foochow 58, 1876; and FO 228/664, Wenchow 7, 1880.
96. FO 228/612, Ichang 2, 1878; FO 228/647, Canton 30, 1880; FO 228/891, Swatow, 29 Aug. 1890; FO 228/1069, Wuhu 13, 1891; FO 228/1198, Shanghai, 30 Mar. 1895; and FO 228/1290, Wuhu, 21 Apr. 1898.
97. FO 228/389, Shanghai 80, 1865; FO 17/452, Leg. 52, 1866; FO 233/35, interviews, 20 and 21 Apr. 1875; FO 17/753, Wade to F.O., 20 Feb. 1877; FO 228/584, Amoy 30, 1877; and Hummel, *Eminent Chinese*, Vol. II, pp. 721–2.
98. FO 17/952, Leg. 316, 1884; Jordan, *Chinese I have Known*; and IUP, Vol. 2, p. 111.
99. Fourth Report of Royal Commission on Civil Establishments, Q. 29,956.
100. FO 228/1324, Foochow 16, 1899.
101. FO 228/381, Russell to Alcock, 26 Sept. 1865.

Notes to Chapter 8

1. IUP, Vol. 10, p. 317; FO 228/503, Canton 35, 1871; and FO 228/825, Canton 9, 1886.
2. FO 228/607, Canton, 31 Oct. 1878; and FO 17/1093, Howard to Walsham, 31 Dec. 1889.
3. FO 17/652, Leg. 26, 1873.
4. FO 228/789, Canton, 18 Sept. 1885; and FO 228/875, Canton 20, 1889.
5. FO 228/320, Bruce to Robertson, 8 Oct. 1862; Mayers *et al.*, *Treaty Ports*, p. 169; and FO 17/427, Robertson to Alcock, 27 May 1865.
6. Mayers *et al.*, *Treaty Ports*, p. 169; Parker, *John Chinaman*, p. 221; National Library of Wales, Glansevern MSS 5029; FO 391/12, Robertson to Hammond, 13 July 1876; and FO 17/497, Leg. 132, 1868.
7. For example, FO 391/8, Robertson to Hammond, 29 Mar. 1864; and FO 391/10, Robertson to Hammond, 12 July 1870.
8. FO 391/8–10, Robertson to Hammond, 27 Apr. and 6 July 1869 and 19 Mar. 1870.
9. FO 228/324, Canton 107, 1862; FO 228/344, Canton 5 and 62, 1863; FO 228/383, Canton 5, 1865; FO 228/429, Canton 54 and 80, 1867; FO 228/470, Canton 9, 1869; and FO 228/552, Canton 38, 1875.
10. For the allegation see FO 17/989, Leg. 64, 1885. For its disproof see FO 228/134, sup. 55 and 98, 1852, and National Library of Wales, Glansevern MSS 5041.

11. FO 228/324, Canton 72, 1862; FO 391/10, Robertson to Hammond, 6 Feb. 1871; and FO 228/428, Canton 41, 1867.

12. FO 391/11, Robertson to Hammond, 23 Oct. 1872; and FO 228/429, Canton 80, 1867.

13. FO 391/9, Robertson to Hammond, 15 Sept. 1871; FO 17/584, Leg. 114, 1871; FO 228/503, Canton 21, 1871; FO 228/344, Canton 20, 1863; FO 228/1321, Canton, 7 Apr. 1899; FO 17/835, Leg. 40, 1880; FO 228/971, Canton accts. 14, 1880, and accts. 3, 1881; and FO 391/2, Alcock to Hammond, 7 May 1869.

14. FO 391/8–10, Robertson to Hammond, 10 July 1867, 14 Apr. 1869, and 8 Jan. 1870; FO 228/344, Canton 12, 1863; and FO 228/428, Canton 40, 1867.

15. FO 391/8 and 12, Robertson to Hammond, 24 Oct. 1868 and 24 Sept. 1874; FO 228/512, Canton 23, 1872; FO 228/522, Canton 12, 1873; and FO 228/534, Canton 14 and 19, 1874.

16. FO 391/8 and 10, Robertson to Hammond, 31 Aug. 1869 and 19 Mar. 1870; FO 228/428, Canton 13, 1867; and FO 228/566, Canton 48, 1876.

17. FO 391/8, Robertson to Alcock, 2 Feb. 1868; and FO 228/448, Canton 14, 1868.

18. FO 228/324, Canton 112, 1862, and Bruce's minute thereon.

19. FO 391/10, Robertson to Hammond, 12, 19, and 26 July, 26 Nov., and 3 Dec. 1870; FO 228/490, Canton 33 and 40, 1870; IUP, Vol. 29, pp. 468, 472, 487, and 490; and FO 228/503, Canton 14, 1871.

20. FO 228/512, Canton 18, 1872; and FO 391/11, Robertson to Hammond, 14 Jan. 1873.

21. FO 391/12, Robertson to Hammond, 20 Aug. 1874 and 6 Oct. 1877; and FO 228/448–9, Canton 56 and 71, 1868, and FO 228/512, Canton 13, 1872.

22. FO 17/427, Robertson to Alcock, 27 May 1865; and FO 228/383, Canton 28, 1865.

23. FO 228/380, F.O. 174, 1865.

24. For example, FO 228/624, Canton, 18 Feb. 1879; FO 228/1569, Leg. 154, 1905; FO 228/1677, F.O. 79, 1908; and FO 228/1797, Leg. tel. 5 to Canton, 1911, Canton tel. and letter, 9 June 1911, and FO 228/1785, Lugard to Jordan, 10 July 1911.

25. FO 391/9, Robertson to Hammond, 8 Sept. 1866; and FO 228/449, Canton 89, 1868.

26. FO 391/2, Alcock to Hammond, 3 and 17 July 1869; FO 17/475, Leg. 89, 1867; FO 228/426, F.O. 167, 1867; and FO 228/467, F.O. 158, 1869, Leg. minute.

27. FO 391/8, 11, and 12, Robertson to Hammond, 6 July and 3 Aug. 1869, 19 Sept. 1872, 11 June, 20 Aug., and 14 Oct. 1874, and 27 Feb. and 6 Oct. 1877; and FO 17/656, Leg. 224, 1873.

28. FO 17/427, Robertson to Alcock, 27 May 1865; FO 391/1, Alcock to Hammond, 13 Jan. 1865; FO 391/8, Robertson to Hammond, 25 Sept. and 13 Dec. 1865; FO 391/2, Alcock to Hammond, 22 May 1869; and D. Boulger, The Life of Sir Halliday Macartney, K.C.M.G. (London, 1908), p. 272.

29. FO 391/8 and 12, Robertson to Hammond, 30 Oct. 1862 and 8 July 1875; and FO 17/533, Robertson to Hammond, 3 Apr. 1869.

30. FO 17/820, Robertson to Villiers, 1879.

31. FO 391/12, Robertson to Hammond, 28 June and 12 July 1877, and other letters during Hammond's retirement; and FO 228/586, Canton 5, 1877.

32. FO 17/767, Tenterden's minute, Oct. 1877; FO 391/12, Robertson to Hammond, 17 Oct. 1877; and FO 17/965, Wade to Granville, 12 Jan. 1884.

33. FO 391/12, Robertson to Hammond, 8 July 1875, 23 and 30 Oct. 1877, and 6 May and 21 Aug. 1879; and FO 46/382, Trench cons. 10, 1888, and 24 Apr. 1888.

34. FO 17/813, Leg. cons. 47, 1879; FO 228/672, Canton 7, 1881; FO 17/930,

Leg. cons. 62, 1883; FO 228/1020, Watters to Leg., 10 June 1885; FO 17/989, Leg. cons. 42, 1885; FO 17/999, Fayrer to F.O., 1 Dec. 1885; and *Foreign Office Lists*.
35. FO 17/813, Leg. cons. 47, 1879; FO 17/1084, Leg. cons. 70 and tel., 15 Dec., with F.O. minutes on both, F.O. tel., 17 Dec., and O'Conor to Currie, 22 Dec., all of 1885; and FO 17/1145, Connemara to Sanderson, 2 Feb. 1892.
36. FO 228/305, Canton 16 and 24, 1861; FO 228/383, Canton 14, 1865; FO 228/428, Canton 5, 1867, and FO 17/989, Leg. cons. 45, 1885; FO 228/512, Canton 32, 1872; *London and China Express* birth announcements, 1876 and 1878; and FO 228/646, Canton 1, 1880.
37. FO 17/989, Leg. cons. 64, 1885, and E. Bretschneider, *History of European Botanical Discoveries in China* (London, 1898, 2 vols.), Vol. II, p. 632; FO 17/729–30, Leg. cons. 19 and 59, 1876, and F.O. minutes on both; and FO 363/1, Tokyo, 28 Sept. 1881, Tenterden's minute.
38. FO 17/989, Leg. cons. 64, 1885; FO 228/624, Canton, 18 Feb. 1879; FO 17/831, Leg. 99, 1880, and FO 228/673, Canton 18, 1881; Parker, *John Chinaman*, pp. 174 and 188; and FO 228/720, F.O. 65 and 126, 1883.
39. FO 17/989, Leg. cons. 64, 1885, and F.O. minute thereon; and FO 17/1084, F.O. tel., 17 Dec., Leg. tel., 18 Dec., O'Conor to Currie, 22 Dec., and F.O. minute thereon, F.O. cons. 69 and 70, all of 1885, and Leg. cons. 45, 1886.
40. FO 228/824, Amoy 49, 1886; FO 17/1024, Leg. cons. 92, 1886; FO 17/1084, Leg. cons. 25, 1887; FO 17/1087, F.O. tel. 19, 1889; and FO 17/1106, Office of Works to F.O., 4 June 1890.
41. FO 17/1141, Alabaster to F.O., 1892; FO 17/1116, F.O. cons. 28, 1891; FO 17/1138, Alabaster to Sanderson, 31 Jan. 1892, F.O. minutes on Alabaster's memorandum of 7 Feb. 1892, and FO 228/1077, F.O. 46, 1892; FO 228/1178, Wylde to O'Conor, 11 July 1895; England and Wales probate records, 1898; and *Foreign Office Lists*.
42. FO 17/1161, Leg. cons. 5 and 13, 1893; and FO 17/1163, Frater to F.O., 22 July 1893.
43. FO 17/767, Tenterden's minute, Oct. 1877; FO 17/820, F.O. minute, 10 May 1879; FO 228/646, Canton 6, 1880; FO 17/1045, F.O. cons. 9, 1887; FO 17/1047, Leg. cons. 90, 1887; FO 228/745, Canton 80, 1884; Parker, *John Chinaman*, p. 148; FO 17/1490, Leg. cons. 63 (section on consular buildings), 1901; and FO 228/3826, Canton 38, 1928.
44. FO 228/624, Canton, 18 Feb. 1879; and FO 228/672, Canton 7, 1881.
45. FO 228/1151, Canton despatches about the plague, June–July 1894; and FO 228/1133, Leg. 155, 1894.
46. FO 228/1190, Canton, 1 July 1895, and 32, 1895; FO 228/1223, Canton 1, 1896; and FO 228/1321, Canton, 5 July 1899, and 33, 1899.
47. FO 228/1249, Canton 1, 1897.
48. FO 228/1357, Amoy, 8 Oct. 1900.
49. FO 228/1281, Amoy, 25 Jan. 1898; and FO 228/1357, Amoy, 14 July 1900.
50. FO 228/823, Amoy 5, 1886.
51. FO 228/427, Amoy 7, 1867; and IUP, Vol. 15, p. 83.
52. Giles, *Koolangsoo*.
53. R. Swinhoe, 'Catalogue of the Mammals of China...', *Proceedings of the Scientific Meetings of the Zoological Society of London for the Year 1870*, p. 626; and FO 228/1113, Amoy 5, 1893.
54. FO 228/565, Amoy 60, 1876; FO 228/696, Amoy 11, 1882; and FO 228/1222, Amoy 7, 1896, and FO 228/1248, Amoy 13, 1897.
55. FO 228/721, Amoy reply to Leg. 11, 1883.
56. FO 228/521, Amoy 6, 1873; and FO 228/764, Swatow 29, 1884.
57. FO 228/671, Amoy 14, 1881.

58. FO 228/671, Amoy 19, 1881.

59. L. Marchant (ed.), *The Siege of the Peking Legations: A Diary: Lancelot Giles* (University of Western Australia Press, 1970), pp. xxiv–xxv.

60. FO 228/623, Amoy 25, 1879; FO 228/645, Amoy 38, 1880; and FO 228/671, Leg. 1 to Amoy, 1881.

61. FO 228/645, Amoy 30, 32, 36, 45, 51, and 57, and Leg. 6 and 8 to Amoy, 1880; FO 228/643, F.O., 11 Nov. 1880; FO 228/671, Amoy 2 and 9, 1881; and FO 17/857, Leg. 14, 1881.

62. FO 228/510, F.O. 54, 1872; FO 228/621, F.O. 67, 1879; FO 228/855, Swatow 6, 1887; and FO 228/1446, F.O. treaty 3, 1903, Leg. minute.

63. FO 17/626, Leg. 6, 1872; FO 228/600, Leg. circular to consuls, 12 Sept. 1877; FO 228/1446, Leg. treaty 21, 1903; and FO 228/1567, Leg. circular to consuls 10, 1904.

64. FO 228/587, Canton 25B, 1877; FO 228/752, Foochow 2, 1884; and FO 228/789, Canton 4, 1885.

65. FO 228/875, Amoy 13, 1889; and FO 228/521, Amoy 15, 1873.

66. FO 228/405, Amoy 3 and Leg. 5 to Amoy, 1866.

67. FO 228/469, Amoy 13 and Leg. 7 to Amoy, 1869; and FO 17/783, Leg. 196, 1878.

68. FO 228/565, Amoy 21, 1876.

69. FO 228/427, Amoy 5, 1867; FO 228/489, Amoy 9, 1870; FO 228/606, Amoy, 26 Feb. 1878; FO 228/848, Amoy, 4 July 1887; and FO 228/852, Kiukiang, 31 Dec. 1887.

70. FO 228/1357, Amoy, 14 July 1900.

71. IUP, Vol. 15, p. 83.

72. FO 17/813, Leg. cons. 47, 1879; FO 17/1084, Leg. cons. 18, 1886; FO 228/1225, Foochow 11, 1896; Wilkinson, *Early Days*; and FO 228/1645, Leg. 216, 1907 (Hosie on Foochow).

73. FO 228/1225, Foochow 11, 1896; FO 228/725, Foochow 41, 1883; PRO 30/33/8/9, Brady to Satow, 6 Feb. 1904; and FO 228/1644, Leg. cons. 50, 1904.

74. FO 228/1065, Foochow 14, 15, 19, and 21, 1891; FO 228/1056, Leg. tel. to Foochow, 27 Sept. 1891; and FO 228/1061, Foochow accts. 15, 1891.

75. FO 228/1357, Foochow 18, 1900, and 1 Mar. 1900; and FO 228/1335, MacDonald to Werner, 22 May 1900.

76. FO 228/642, F.O. 74, 1880.

77. FO 17/782, Leg. 168, 1878.

78. PRO 30/33/8/1, Mansfield to Satow, 21 Sept. 1905; and FO 228/472, Leg. to Foochow, 16 Dec. 1869, and FO 17/557, F.O. cons. 18, 1870.

79. FO 228/513, Sinclair's quarrels with subordinates, 1872.

80. FO 228/610, Foochow, 2 Aug. 1878; FO 17/897, Leg. 119, 1882; FO 228/676, Foochow 31, 1881; and FO 17/904, Foochow 11 to F.O., 1882, and F.O. minutes thereon.

81. FO 17/815, Sinclair to F.O., 18 Apr. 1879; FO 391/19, Wade to Hammond, 1 Feb. 1870; FO 17/761, Wade to F.O., 1 Oct. 1877; and FO 17/813, Leg. cons. 47, 1879, and F.O. minutes thereon.

82. FO 17/897, Grosvenor to Cockerell, 13 Sept. 1882, and Currie's minute on Leg. 119, 1882; FO 17/923, Wade separate 2, 1883; and FO 17/958, Foochow 16 to F.O., 1884.

83. FO 228/521, Foochow 5, 1873; FO 228/831, Foochow, 3 Aug. 1886; and FO 228/889, Foochow 8, 1890.

84. FO 228/1324, Foochow, 3 Oct. 1899.

85. FO 228/1084, Foochow 5–7, 19, and 21–4, 1892.

86. FO 228/1225, Foochow, 4 Jan. 1896; and FO 228/1254, Foochow, 31 Mar. 1897.

87. FO 228/1194; and FO 228/1172, O'Conor to Sanderson, 23 Sept. 1895.
88. FO 228/1254, Foochow 13, 1897; FO 228/1285, Foochow 12, 1898; and FO 228/1357, Foochow 32 and 33, 1900.
89. For example, FO 228/346, Ningpo 12, 22, and 25, 1863; and FO 228/365, Ningpo 3 and 20, 1864.
90. FO 17/698, Leg. 89, 1875, and F.O. minutes thereon.
91. IUP, Vol. 11, p. 134, and Vol. 20, p. 138.
92. For example, FO 228/865, Ningpo 4, 1888; and FO 228/1087, Ningpo 3, 1892.
93. FO 228/890, Ningpo to Leg., 1890.
94. For example, FO 228/613, Ningpo, 25 Feb. 1878; FO 228/802, Ningpo 41, 1885; FO 228/1160, Ningpo 19, 1894; and FO 228/1267, Playfair to MacDonald, 25 Sept. 1898.
95. FO 228/1227, Ningpo, 1 Jan. 1896.
96. FO 228/701, Ningpo 6, 1882.
97. Morse, *International Relations*, Vol. III, p. 123; and IUP, Vol. 19, p. 479.
98. IUP, Vol. 14, p. 400; and FO 228/592, Shanghai 3, 1877.
99. FO 17/835, Leg. 70, 1880.
100. FO 228/474, Shanghai 105, 1869; and FO 17/529, Leg. 101, 1869.
101. FO 17/587, Leg. 178, 1871.
102. FO 228/571, Shanghai 20, 1876.
103. FO 17/424, Leg. 45, 1865; FO 17/451, Leg. 18, 1866, with F.O. minutes thereon, and FO 228/404, F.O. 113, 1866; FO 391/19, Wade to Hammond, 1 Feb. 1870; FO 17/529, Leg., 6 Dec. 1869, and F.O. minutes thereon; FO 228/487, F.O. 21, 1870; FO 228/684, Shanghai 54, 1881; FO 228/705, Shanghai 27 and 55, 1882; and FO 17/965, Wade to Granville, 12 Jan. 1884, and F.O. minute thereon.
104. FO 391/2, Alcock to Hammond, 25 Sept. 1870.
105. FO 17/767, Pauncefote's memorandum, Sept. 1877, and Tenterden's minute, Oct. 1877.
106. FO 97/555; FO 17/1685, Davidson's minute, 26 June 1905; FO 17/1903, Howard to Walsham, 31 Dec. 1889 (chief judge's views); FO 17/1205, Hannen to Sanderson, 2 Nov. 1893; IUP, Vol. 20, pp 229-31; and FO 17/1518.
107. FO 391/1, Alcock to Hammond, 14 Aug. 1865.
108. FO 228/380, F.O. 168, 1865.
109. FO 391/2, Alcock to Hammond, n.d.
110. *London and China Express*, supplement, 27 Nov. 1918, B. Brenan's reminiscences.
111. FO 17/499, Leg. 189, 1868; Elliston, *Shantung Road Cemetery*; and FO 17/558B, Winchester to F.O., 6 June 1870.
112. FO 228/411, Shanghai 6, 1866; and FO 228/401, Leg., 1 Dec. 1866.
113. FO 17/451, Leg. 26, 1866; and FO 17/988, F.O. circular to consuls, 30 Apr. 1885.
114. FO 228/425-6, F.O. 39, 70, and 130, 1867; FO 228/433, Shanghai 76 and 87, 1867; FO 228/446-7, F.O. 68 and 218, 1868; FO 228/461, chief judge 10 to Leg., 1868; FO 228/444, Leg. 185, 1868; FO 17/689, Treasury to F.O., 10 Feb. 1874; *North-China Herald*, 24 July 1869; FO 228/504, Shanghai 55, 1871; FO 17/1331, solicitors to F.O., 24 Aug. and 7 Sept. 1897; and FO 17/469C, Wade to Alston, 14 Dec. 1863.
115. IUP, Vol. 11, p. 718.
116. FO 228/514, Shanghai 59 and Leg. 30 to Shanghai, 1872.
117. FO 228/585, Amoy, 13 Dec. 1877.
118. IUP, Vol. 29, pp. 9-90; and FO 391/2, Alcock to Hammond, 3 Aug. 1869.
119. FO 17/673, Leg. 104, 1874, and F.O. minutes thereon; and FO 17/698, Leg. 120 and 137, 1875, and F.O. minutes thereon.

120. FO 17/767, Medhurst to F.O., 24 Jan. 1877; Tregonning, *Under Chartered Company Rule*, pp. 130–1; and *Journal of the Royal Asiatic Society of Great Britain and Ireland*, Vol. 18 (London, 1886), p. xxiii.
121. FO 17/1394, F.O. minute on Jamieson's resignation letter, 14 Feb. 1899; N.A. Pelcovits, *Old China Hands and the Foreign Office* (American Institute of Pacific Relations, 1948), pp. 254 and 268; and FO 228/1516, Leg. 396, 1904.
122. Fairbank *et al.*, *I.G. in Peking*, Vol. 2, p. 1345; and *London and China Express and Telegraph*, 3 Mar. 1927, obituary.
123. FO 17/1386, Leg. tel., 10 Mar. 1899, and despatch cons. 55, 1899; and FO 228/1309, Shanghai accts. 21, 1899.
124. FO 17/1424–5 and 1427; FO 671/257, Fraser to Warren, 18 June 1900; and FO 17/1426, F.O. tel. 39 to Shanghai.
125. PRO 30/33/7/1, Sanderson to Satow, 11 Aug. 1900.
126. FO 228/1740, F.O. 101, 1910; and FO 369/285, Leg., 2 Apr. 1910, F.O. minutes.
127. FO 369/285, Leg. cons. 112, 1910, Campbell's minute.
128. FO 17/1424–5, Bertie's minute, 5 Sept. 1900; PRO 30/33/8/22, Brenan to Satow, 11 Jan., 30 Mar., and 29 June 1901; and FO 17/1490, Leg. cons. 29, 1901.
129. FO 228/1468, Leg. 113, 1903; and *The Times*, obituaries, 2 and 3 Mar. 1927.

Notes to Chapter 9

1. FO 228/439, Swatow 14, 1867; FO 17/523, Leg. 89, 1869; Mayers *et al.*, *Treaty Ports*, pp. 230 and 232; and FO 17/548, Leg. 94, 1870.
2. FO 228/1291, Swatow, 12 July 1898; and FO 228/1193, Swatow, 24 July 1895.
3. FO 228/293, Swatow 13, 15, and 16, 1860, and FO 228/315, Swatow 6, 10, 16, and 23, 1861; and FO 228/354, Swatow 31, 1863.
4. FO 228/396, Swatow 16 and Leg. 10 to Swatow, 1865.
5. FO 228/373, Swatow 35 (sic), 1864.
6. FO 228/293, Swatow 13, 1860; and FO 228/354, Swatow 11, 1863.
7. FO 228/315, Swatow 53, 1861; FO 228/396, Swatow 1 to Alcock, 1865; FO 228/419, Swatow 7, 1866; and FO 228/479, Swatow 30, 1869.
8. FO 391/8, Robertson to Hammond, 29 Oct. 1865 and 9 Jan. 1868; FO 228/428, Canton 40, 1867; and FO 17/508, Wade to Hammond, 29 Feb. 1868.
9. FO 228/439, Swatow 5 and 6 to Alcock, 1867; FO 17/501, Leg. 300, 1868; FO 228/458, Swatow 14, 1868; FO 228/466, F.O. 34, 1869; FO 17/592, Leg. cons. 95, 1871; and FO 17/1093, Howard to Walsham, 31 Dec. 1889, and FO 228/1807, Swatow, 19 May 1911.
10. FO 228/293, Swatow 7 and 9, and Leg. 5 to Swatow, 1860; FO 228/315, Swatow 25 and Leg. 12 to Swatow, 1861; FO 228/439, Swatow (Cooper) 5 and 14, 1867; and FO 228/425, F.O. 60, 1867.
11. FO 17/501, Leg. 303, 1868; and FO 17/509, Cooper's father to F.O., 27 Apr. 1868.
12. FO 228/458, Swatow 11 and 13 to Alcock, 1868; and FO 17/518, Leg. 22 and 23 to Stanley, 1869, and F.O. minutes on both.
13. FO 228/470, Canton 7, 10, and 13, 1869; FO 228/472, Swatow 3, 5, 6, 8, 10, and 12, 1869; FO 17/520, Leg. 12, 1869; FO 228/480, Leg. 21 to Swatow, 1869; and FO 391/8, Robertson to Hammond, 6 Feb. 1869.
14. FO 228/466, F.O. 54, 1869.

15. FO 17/523, Leg. 89, 1869, and F.O. minutes thereon; FO 17/528, Leg. cons. 78, 1869, and F.O. minute thereon, and FO 17/549, Leg. 94, 1870.
16. IUP, Vol. 10, p. 413; FO 17/656, Leg. 234, 1873; FO 228/855, Swatow, 21 Apr. 1887; and King, *In the Chinese Customs Service*, p. 39.
17. FO 228/566, Canton 12, 1876; FO 228/574, Leg. to Swatow 2, 1876; FO 228/1068, Swatow 8, 1891; FO 228/1248, Swatow 11, 1897; and FO 228/1291, Swatow, 12 July 1898.
18. King, *In the Chinese Customs Service*, Chapters II and III; and IUP, Vol. 11, p. 145.
19. Mayers *et al.*, *Treaty Ports*, p. 235; and IUP, Vol. 8, p. 527, and Vol. 18, p. 503.
20. FO 228/880, Swatow 7, 1889.
21. FO 228/557, Swatow 17 and Leg. 6A to Swatow, 1875; FO 228/552, Canton 34 and Leg. 7 to Canton, 1875; FO 228/891, Swatow, 29 Aug. 1890; and FO 228/711, Swatow 2, 1883.
22. FO 228/513, Swatow 13, 1872; FO 228/534, Swatow, 6 May 1874; FO 228/595, Swatow, 10 Mar. 1877; FO 228/660, Swatow 4, 1880; and FO 228/806, Swatow 21, 1885.
23. FO 228/711, Swatow 1, 15, 18, and 28, 1883; FO 228/671, Amoy 17, 1881; and FO 17/666, B.C.G. Scott to F.O., 12 Sept. 1873.
24. FO 228/1248, Swatow tels., 28 Oct. and 5 Nov., and despatch 20, and Leg. to Swatow tel., 7 Nov., and despatch 3, all of 1897; FO 228/1291, Swatow 13 and 15, 1898; and FO 228/1330, Swatow 2, 1899.
25. FO 228/1363, Swatow, 2 Jan. 1900; FO 228/1291, Swatow, 12 July 1898; FO 228/867, Swatow 4, 1888; FO 228/855, Swatow, 21 Apr. 1887; FO 228/1193, Swatow, 24 July 1895; and FO 228/1330, Swatow 10, 1899.
26. FO 17/628, Leg. 56, 1872; FO 17/635, Leg. cons. 39, 1872; FO 228/512, Canton 4, 1872; FO 17/652, Leg. 4, 1873; FO 17/719, Leg. 11, 1876; and FO 228/718, F.O. 122, 1883.
27. FO 228/566, Canton, 1 Apr. 1876; FO 17/1307, Leg. cons. 34, 1883; FO 228/799, Hoihow 10, 1885; FO 17/1093, Howard to Walsham, 31 Dec. 1889; FO 228/1213, Hoihow accts. 4 and 15, 1896; FO 228/1362, Hoihow, 6 May 1900; FO 228/1345, Hoihow accts. 12, 1900; and FO 228/1405, Hoihow, 30 Apr. and 10 Aug. 1901.
28. FO 17/903, Leg. 59, 1882; FO 228/1145, Marshall to Bennett, 17 Oct. 1894; FO 228/1212, Chinkiang tel., 27 July 1896; FO 228/1289 and 1405, copies of entries in Hoihow birth register, 1897 and 1900; and FO 228/1181, Pakhoi, 4 Nov. 1895, and FO 228/1213, Hoihow accts. 11, 1896.
29. FO 17/1024, Leg. cons. 82, 1886; FO 17/1084, Leg. cons. 46, 1886; IUP, Vol. 15, pp. 444 and 631; FO 228/709, Hoihow 25, 1883; and FO 228/1183, Hoihow 9, 1895.
30. FO 228/680, Hoihow 6 and 10 and Leg. 3 to Hoihow, 1881; and FO 228/1120, Hoihow, 25 Apr. 1893.
31. FO 228/512, Canton 24, 1872; FO 391/12, Robertson to Hammond, 11 May 1876; FO 17/754, Leg. 77, 1877; FO 228/756, Pakhoi 3, 1884; and IUP, Vol. 15, pp. 45–7 and 685–6, and Vol. 21, pp. 36–7.
32. IUP, Vol. 15, p. 83.
33. IUP, Vol. 12, pp. 347–50; FO 228/683, Pakhoi 22 and 23, 1882; FO 228/704, Pakhoi 27 and 33, 1882; FO 17/816, Pakhoi 4 to F.O., 1879, and FO 17/810, Leg. 51, 1879; FO 228/853, Pakhoi 9, 1887; IUP, Vol. 17, p. 676; FO 228/1122, Pakhoi 2, 1893; FO 228/1329, Pakhoi 2, 1899; and FO 228/1364, Savage to Satow, 14 Dec. 1900.
34. FO 17/761, Leg. cons. 60, 1877; FO 228/587, Canton, 27 Aug. 1877; FO

228/599, Harvey to Leg., 25 Aug. 1877; FO 17/852; J. Foster, *Men-at-the-Bar* (London, 1885), p. 207; and *London and China Express*, 25 Apr. 1913, obituary.
35. FO 17/810, Leg. 76 and 81, 1879.
36. FO 228/683, Pakhoi 11 and 28, 1881; FO 228/803, Pakhoi, 12 Jan. 1885; FO 228/1183, Pakhoi, 6 July 1895; FO 228/728, Pakhoi 10, 1883; and FO 228/803, Pakhoi 8, 1885.
37. FO 228/704, Pakhoi 24, 1882; FO 228/803, Pakhoi 8 and 21, 1885, and Pakhoi, 14 Apr. and 9 Oct. 1885; FO 228/835, Pakhoi 2, 1886, and 8 Apr. 1886; FO 228/853, Pakhoi 4, 1887; and *London and China Express*, birth announcements, 1878, 1880, and 1883.
38. FO 228/865, Pakhoi 1, 1888; FO 228/1258, Leg. to Pakhoi, 2 Apr., and Pakhoi, 30 Apr., 1897; FO 228/1289; FO 228/1274, Pakhoi accts. 2, 1898; and FO 228/1364, Pakhoi, 15 Oct. 1900.
39. FO 228/592, Shanghai 19, 1877; IUP, Vol. 13, p. 368; FO 228/709, Wenchow 5, 1883; and FO 228/598, Wenchow 20, 1877, IUP, Vol. 12, p. 731, and FO 228/1167, Wenchow 7, 1894.
40. For example, 13 in 1884 and 19 in 1891 (IUP, Vol. 15, p. 83, and FO 228/1069, Wenchow 8, 1891).
41. FO 228/554, Ningpo 13, 1875; FO 228/709, Wenchow 10, 1883; and FO 228/1167, Wenchow, 27 Oct. 1894, and FO 228/1144, Foochow accts. 12, 1894.
42. FO 228/598, Wenchow 1 and 8, 1877; FO 228/592, Shanghai 19, 1877; FO 17/1093, Howard to Walsham, 31 Dec. 1889; FO 17/1045, Leg. cons. 153, 1904; FO 228/1094, Wenchow 6, 1892; and FO 228/709, Wenchow 6, 1883.
43. FO 17/1047, Leg. cons. 85, 1887; FO 228/881, Wenchow 2, 1889; FO 228/1062, Wenchow accts. 8a, 1891; FO 369/12, Ningpo to F.O., 14 Nov. 1906; and FO 228/1648, Ningpo accts. 14, 1907.
44. IUP, Vol. 13, p. 369, and FO 228/598, Wenchow 8, 1877; FO 228/770, Wenchow 7, 1884; and FO 228/598, Wenchow 20, 1877.
45. FO 228/770, Wenchow 16, 19, and 25, and Leg. 2 and 3 to Wenchow, 1884.
46. FO 228/1052, Hosie to Tratman, 3 Jan. 1890; FO 228/892, Wenchow 1 and 5, 1890; and FO 228/1197.
47. FO 17/1431, O'Brien-Butler to F.O., 20 July 1900; FO 228/1696, Wenchow 3, 1908; FO 17/1421, Leg. cons. 86, 1900; and FO 17/1643, F.O. cons. 14, 1904.
48. FO 17/1084, O'Conor to Currie, 16 June 1886; FO 228/868, Wenchow 6, 1888; *London and China Express*, marriage announcement, 1876, and FO 681/1, wife's death, Nov. 1876; and FO 17/1090, Stronach to F.O., 14 Jan. 1889, and F.O. minutes thereon.
49. Berkshire Record Office D/E Dd F4/13, Crawford's letter of 1 Feb. 1872; FO 228/851, Hong Kong to Leg., 30 Dec. 1887; FO 228/1039, Leg. accts. 3 to Kiukiang and related correspondence, 1888, FO 228/1045, Kiukiang tels., 10 and 19 Jan. 1889, and FO 228/883, F.O. 22, 1890; FO 228/1093, Leg. accts. tel. to Newchwang, 29 Feb. 1892, and FO 228/1087, Leg. tel. 1 to Newchwang and Newchwang 1, 1892; and FO 228/1103, Leg. tel. to Tamsui, 17 Oct. 1893.
50. FO 17/1291, tailors to F.O., 11 Nov. 1896; FO 228/1258, Leg. 2 to Wenchow and Wenchow 4, 1897; FO 228/1291, Wenchow 2 and Leg. 1 to Wenchow, 1898; and FO 228/1267, Playfair to MacDonald, 25 Sept. 1898.
51. FO 228/1275, Wenchow 6 and Leg. 2 to Wenchow, 1898; FO 17/1408, Treasury to F.O., 7 Mar. 1899, and F.O. minutes thereon; FO 17/1385, Treasury to F.O., 18 Mar. 1899; FO 228/1309, Wenchow accts. 4, 1899; and *Foreign Office Lists*.
52. FO 228/1286, Leg. tel. to Newchwang, 13 Nov. 1898; FO 228/1328, Allen to MacDonald, 23 Feb. 1899; FO 17/1386–7, Leg. cons. 21 and 91, 1899; FO 17/1768, Bax-Ironside to Bertie, 15 May 1899; FO 228/1309, Wenchow accts. 9,

1899; FO 228/1304, Wenchow Customs surgeon to F.O., 13 Sept. 1899; and *Foreign Office Lists.*

53. FO 228/1249, Canton 12, 1897; IUP, Vol. 21, p. 216; and FO 228/1329, Samshui, 9 Oct. 1899.

54. FO 228/1274, Samshui accts. 6, 1898; FO 228/1308, Kiukiang accts. 3, 5, and 6, 1899; and FO 228/1327, Brady to Fulford, 11 Nov. 1899.

55. Lambeth Palace Shanghai marriage registers; PRO 30/33/9/6, Fox to Satow, 29 June 1903; FO 228/1329, Samshui, 9 Oct. 1899; and FO 228/1358, Samshui, 6 Feb. 1900.

56. FO 369/8, Little to F.O., 30 Dec. 1905; FO 228/1411, Samshui, 8 Jan. and 9 July 1901; FO 228/1429, Satow to Little and to Office of Works, Shanghai, 16 July 1902.

57. FO 228/1329, Samshui, 20 Jan. 1899; FO 228/1358, Samshui, 5 Oct. 1900; and FO 17/1489, F.O. cons. 80, 1901.

58. FO 228/1240, Canton accts. 13 and 14, 1897; FO 228/1253, Wuchow 1, 1897, and 28 Sept. and 21 Oct. 1897; FO 228/1242, Wuchow accts. 5, 1897; IUP, Vol. 21, p. 348; and FO 228/1696, Wuchow, 5 July 1908.

59. FO 228/1241, Leg. tel. accts. 4 to Newchwang and Newchwang accts. 7, 1897; and FO 228/849, Canton 58, 1887.

60. FO 228/1242, Wuchow accts. 10, 1897; FO 228/1275, Wuchow accts. 7 and 11, 1898; FO 228/1309, Wuchow tel., 7 Feb. 1899; FO 228/1345, Newchwang tel., 29 Jan. 1900, and accts. 2A, 1900; *DNB 1922–1930*, p. 433 (Hosie's early life); and FO 228/1506, Wuchow 24, 1903.

61. FO 228/1309, Wuchow accts. 8 and 9, 1899.

62. FO 228/1270–1, F.O. 116 and 180, 1898; FO 228/1297, Hausser, 4 May 1898, and Leg. tel. to Hausser, 10 June 1898, and despatch 2, 1898; FO 228/1275, Mrs Hausser to MacDonald and MacDonald's minute thereon; FO 228/1300, F.O. 28, 1899; and FO 228/1295, Leg. 86, 1899.

63. FO 228/1412, copy of entry in Wuchow birth register, 1900; FO 17/1490, Leg. cons. 63, 1901, and Satow to Barrington, 15 Aug. 1901; FO 228/1535, Amoy accts. 14, 1904; and FO 228/1789, Jordan to Hausser, 24 Apr. 1911.

64. FO 17/1076, Treasury to F.O., 26 July 1888; FO 17/1087, Leg. cons. 21, 1889; FO 228/1240, Canton 23, 1897; and FO 17/1366, F.O. to Treasury, 10 Nov. 1898.

65. FO 228/1223–4, Canton 28, 1896, and Werner to MacDonald, 30 Sept. 1896; and FO 228/1249, Canton 21, 1897, and FO 228/1236, Leg. 6 to Canton, 1897.

Notes to Chapter 10

1. FO 391/19, Wade to Hammond, 22 June 1867; FO 228/358, Leg. 2, 1864; FO 228/435, Chinkiang 5 and Harvey to Alcock, 2 Mar. 1867; FO 17/449, Alcock to Hammond, 31 May 1866; FO 391/2, Alcock to Hammond, 2 Apr. 1869; and FO 17/475, Leg. 85, 1867.

2. FO 17/1557, petition, 28 Oct. 1902; FO 369/287, petition, 20 Sept., and letter to F.O., 20 Oct. 1910.

3. FO 17/452, Leg. 52, 1866.

4. FO 17/475, Leg. 81, 1867, and Hammond's minute thereon; FO 228/559, Wade to Ryder, 17 June 1875; and FO 228/541, Shanghai 96 and Leg. 72 to Shanghai, 1874.

5. IUP, Vol. 12, p. 271; and FO 228/792, Chinkiang, 9 Feb. 1885.

6. Mayers *et al.*, *Treaty Ports*, p. 423; and FO 228/370, Leg. 2 to Chinkiang, 1864.

7. FO 228/886, Chinkiang 7, 1890; FO 228/1080, F.O. 173, 1892; and FO 228/1082, Chinkiang 7, 1892.

8. FO 228/627, Chinkiang 1, 2, 5, and 21 and Leg. 4 to Chinkiang, 1879; FO 228/829, Oxenham to Walsham, 4 Nov. 1886; and FO 228/649, Chinkiang 11, 1880.

9. FO 228/698, Chinkiang 6, 1882; and FO 228/1214, Tientsin accts., 27 May 1896.

10. FO 228/829, Chinkiang 29, 1886, and Oxenham to Walsham, 4 Nov. 1886; FO 228/850, Chinkiang, 29 July 1887; FO 228/862, Chinkiang, 2 May and 11 Aug. 1888; FO 228/1153, Chinkiang, 17 July 1894; and FO 228/1359, Willis to Cockburn, 10 May 1900.

11. FO 228/872, F.O. 56, 1889.

12. FO 228/876, Chinkiang 1–3, 1889; FO 17/1140, Mansfield to Sanderson, 15 Oct. 1892; and *London and China Express*, death announcement, 1892.

13. FO 228/1252, Chinkiang, 6 July and 7 Oct. 1897; FO 228/1359, Willis to Cockburn, 10 May 1900; FO 228/886, Chinkiang, 15 Jan. 1890; and FO 228/1061, Allen to Brady, 30 July 1891. For pig-shooting see Rasmussen, *China Trader*, Chapters VIII and IX.

14. IUP, Vol. 14, p. 63; FO 228/371, Kiukiang, 11 Oct. 1864; and FO 228/314, Kiukiang 8, 9, 13, and 16, 1861.

15. FO 228/314, Kiukiang 35 and 36, 1861; FO 228/330, Kiukiang 3, 4, and 12, 1862, and Leg. to Kiukiang, 2 July 1862; FO 17/379, Hughes to F.O., Oct. 1862, and FO 228/352, Kiukiang 1, 4, and 22, 1863.

16. FO 228/1180, Brady to O'Conor from Ichang, 8 Feb. 1895.

17. FO 17/698, Leg. 120, 1875.

18. FO 17/785, Wade's memorandum, 15 July 1878; and FO 17/1084, O'Conor to Currie, 22 Dec. 1885. For specimens of Baber's verse see Giles, *Glossary*, pp. 169–70, and H. Yule (ed.), *The Book of Ser Marco Polo* (London, 1929), third edition), Vol. I, p. xxvi.

19. *T'oung Pao*, first series, Vol. I, obituary.

20. FO 17/630, Leg. 105, 1872, and Hammond's minute thereon; FO 17/632, Leg. 193, 1872; and FO 228/521, Tamsui 2, 1873.

21. FO 228/371, Kiukiang 9, 1864; IUP, Vol. 9, pp. 17–18, and Vol. 15, p. 609; FO 17/557, F.O. (Granville), 16 Dec. 1870, and FO 17/593, F.O. cons. 16, 1871; FO 228/852, Kiukiang, 31 Dec. 1887; and FO 228/1119, Kiukiang 6, 1893.

22. FO 228/679, Kiukiang 8, 1881; and IUP, Vol. 15, p. 83.

23. For example, FO 228/833, Kiukiang 19, 1886; and FO 228/1157, Kiukiang 2, 1894.

24. For example, FO 228/553, Kiukiang 4, 1875; and FO 228/1066, Kiukiang 9 and 11, 1891.

25. FO 228/1290, Wuhu 11, 1898.

26. Werner, *Autumn Leaves*, p. 484; and FO 228/1049, Leg. tel. to Kiukiang, 14 Nov. 1890.

27. For example, FO 228/1836, Nanking 54, 1912; FO 228/3347, Leg. tel. 300, 1921; and FO 228/3279, Nanking, 9 Apr. 1923.

28. FO 228/1195, Kiukiang 2, 8, 10, 13, and 14, 1895; FO 228/1227, Kiukiang 5, Beauclerk's minute thereon, and Leg. 2 to Kiukiang, 1896; and *London and China Express and Telegraph*, 25 Dec. 1924, obituary.

29. FO 228/1327, Kiukiang 8 and Leg. 2 to Kiukiang, 1899.

30. FO 228/313, Hankow 1 and 44, 1861; FO 228/331, Hankow 4, 20, and 32

and Leg. 10 and 17 to Hankow, 1862; FO 228/878, Hankow 8, 1889; FO 228/351, Hankow, 10 Mar. 1863, and Hankow 38 and 39 and Leg. 13 to Hankow, 1863; and FO 17/394, Leg. 138, 1863.

31. FO 228/358, Leg. 80, 1864; FO 228/370, Leg. to Hankow, 14 Dec. 1864; FO 228/392, Hankow 10 to Wade and Leg. 25 to Hankow, 1865; FO 17/508, F.O. to Webster, 9 Apr. 1868; FO 228/446, F.O. 116, 1868; and FO 17/570.

32. FO 17/820, Webster to F.O., 17 July 1879.

33. FO 228/392, Hankow 16 and Leg. 11 to Hankow, 1865.

34. FO 228/878, Hankow, 2 Sept. 1889; FO 228/392, Hankow 2, 4, and 7 to Alcock, 1865; and FO 228/401, F.O. 64, 1866.

35. FO 228/416, Hankow 9–11 and Leg. 4 to Hankow, 1866; and FO 228/436, Hankow 6, 1867.

36. 1861 census, Kirkcudbrightshire, Buittle parish.

37. PRO 30/33/15/1, entry for 11 Aug. 1862.

38. FO 228/355, Tientsin 13, 22, 23, and 26 and Leg. 9, 14, and 17 to Tientsin, 1863; FO 17/392, Leg. 39, 1863; and FO 17/410, Wade to Hammond, 29 Oct. 1864.

39. FO 228/358, Leg. 24, 1864; England and Wales marriage registers, 1865; FO 391/2, Alcock to Hammond, 18 Apr. 1868 and 1 and 3 Jan. 1869, also Adkins to Alcock; FO 228/436, Hankow 37, 40, and 46 and Leg. 12 to Hankow, 1867; and FO 17/497, Leg. 78, 1868, and Stanley's minute thereon.

40. FO 228/553, Hankow 53, 1875; FO 228/629, Hankow, 8 Dec. 1879; FO 228/700, Hankow 16, 1882; FO 228/864, Hankow 15, 1888; and FO 228/1226, Hankow 17, 1896.

41. IUP, Vol. 10, p. 153; FO 228/553, Hankow 15, 1875; and FO 228/677, Hankow 10, 1881.

42. FO 17/1093, Howard to Walsham, 31 Dec. 1889; FO 228/1041, Hankow accts. 8 and 13, 1888, and 27 Apr. 1888; FO 228/1085, Hankow, 5 Dec. 1892; and FO 228/1308, Hankow accts. 19, 1899.

43. FO 228/1257, Hankow 5, 1897.

44. Mayers et al., Treaty Ports, pp. 441–2; FO 228/1226, Hankow 26, 1896; FO 228/331, Hankow 13, 36, and 55, 1862; FO 228/878, Hankow, 1 June and 2 Sept. 1889; FO 228/553, Hankow 15, 1875; FO 228/1065, Hankow 2, 1891; and FO 228/1189, Hankow 2, 1895.

45. FO 228/700, Hankow 3 and 12, 1882.

46. FO 228/1281, Amoy, 1 July 1898.

47. FO 228/372, Newchwang 20 and Leg. 9 to Newchwang, 1864; FO 228/379, F.O. 8, 1865; FO 17/586, Leg. 163, 1871; FO 17/630, Leg. 101, 1872; FO 17/679, Wade to Tenterden, 27 Jan. 1874; FO 228/648, Leg. 9 to Chefoo, 1880, and FO 17/835, Leg. 48, 1880; and FO 233/69, Thistleton Dyer to Leg., 3 Sept. 1884, and FO 17/966, Jervoise's minute, 4 Sept., and letter to War Office, 5 Sept., 1884.

48. FO 228/889, Hankow 12, 1890; FO 228/1065, Hankow 14, 19, 40, and 41, 1891; and FO 17/1117, Gardner to Jervoise, 20 Nov. 1891, and F.O. minutes thereon.

49. FO 228/1077, Gardner to Walsham, 9 July 1892; FO 228/1085, Hankow tels., 17 Aug. and 20 Aug., despatches 20, 26, and 27, letter, 4 Oct., and O'Conor's minute thereon, and Leg. tel. to Hankow, 19 Aug., all of 1892; FO 228/1075, Leg. tel., 24 Dec. 1892; FO 17/1140, F.O. tel. to Hankow, 19 Aug. 1892; FO 17/1148, Hankow to F.O., 20 Aug. 1892, and F.O. minutes thereon; FO 228/1078–80, F.O. tel. 40 and despatches 140, 144, and 234, 1892; and FO 17/1161, Leg. cons. 5, 1893.

50. FO 228/1061, Hankow accts. 6, 1891; FO 17/1140, Gardner to Sanderson, 7 Jan. 1892; FO 17/1205, Leg. cons. 1, 1894; FO 228/1133, Leg. 200, 1894; and FO

228/1085, Hankow, 4 Oct. 1892, O'Conor's minute.
51. FO 17/982, Leg. 303, 1885; and FO 17/1164, O'Conor to Jervoise, 27 Jan. 1893.
52. FO 228/569, Leg. to Kiukiang, 22 Nov. 1876; FO 17/753, Leg. 4, 1877; FO 228/569, Hankow 45, 1876; FO 228/583, F.O. 135, 1877; FO 228/591, Ichang 1, 5, 13, and 23, 1877; FO 17/756, Leg. 164, 1877; FO 17/789, King to F.O., 20 Aug. 1878; FO 17/820, King to F.O., 2 Jan. 1879; and FO 228/652, Ichang 5, 1880.
53. FO 17/785, Leg. cons. 27, 47, and 58, 1878; and FO 17/843, F.O. to Crawford, 26 Jan., Treasury to F.O., 16 Feb. and 28 May, and Crawford's father to F.O., 9 Apr., all of 1880.
54. Berkshire Record Office D/E Dd F4/33, Crawford's letter, 3 July 1878.
55. IUP, Vol. 12, p. 655; and FO 228/652, Ichang 5, 1880.
56. FO 228/678, Ichang 2, 1881, and Ichang, 6 Feb. and 7 Aug. 1881; FO 228/973, Ichang accts. 10, 1881, and accts. 6 and 8, 1882; FO 17/860, Leg cons. 53, 1881; and IUP, Vol. 13, p. 447, and Vol. 14, pp. 52–3.
57. FO 17/993, Gardner to Hertslet, 14 Feb. 1885; FO 17/1307, Ichang accts. 5 and Leg. cons. 34, 1883; FO 228/1021, Newchwang accts. 7, 1885; FO 17/1057, Treasury to F.O., 28 Jan. 1887; FO 17/1106, Treasury to F.O., 11 Apr. 1890; FO 228/1119, Ichang, 24 Mar. 1893; and FO 228/1227, Ichang 7, 1896.
58. FO 228/1021, Newchwang accts. 7, 1885; FO 228/1000, Ichang accts. 6, 1883; FO 228/726, Ichang 2, 1883; FO 228/754, Ichang 1, 1884; FO 17/955, Leg. cons. 22, 1884; and FO 228/797, Hankow 9, 1885.
59. King, *In the Chinese Customs Service*, pp. 36–8.
60. FO 17/556, Leg. cons. 95, 1870; FO 17/813, Leg. cons. 47, 1879; FO 17/955, Leg. cons. 6, 1884; FO 228/995, Leg. accts. 6, 1883, and accts. 10, 1884, to Taiwan; FO 228/807, Taiwan 20, 1885; FO 228/798, Leg. 5 to Ichang, 1885; FO 228/1022, Ichang accts. 3, 1885; FO 228/864, Ichang 15, 1888; FO 228/869, A. Little to Leg., 7 Apr. 1888; FO 228/872, F.O. 4, 1889; FO 17/1084, O'Conor to Currie, 16 June 1886; FO 17/1087, Leg. cons. 45, 1889; FO 17/1101, Leg. cons. 17, 1890; FO 228/495, Tamsui 4, 1870, and *London and China Express*, marriage announcement, 1895, and death announcement, 1916; and *Foreign Office Lists*.
61. FO 17/1116, Leg. cons. 65, 1891; IUP, Vol. 18, pp. 414–15; FO 228/1066, Ichang 13, 18, 22, 24, 35, and 39, 1891; FO 17/1145, Connemara to Sanderson, 2 Feb. 1892; FO 228/1086, Ichang 4 and 10, 1892; and FO 228/1119, Ichang, 20 July 1893.
62. FO 228/1157, Ichang 18 and 19, 1894; FO 228/1066, Ichang 32, 1891; FO 228/1180, Ichang, 8 Feb. 1895; FO 228/1195, Ichang 7, 8, and 12, 1895; IUP, Vol. 20, p. 494; FO 228/1289, Ichang 1, 1898; and FO 17/1490, Satow to Barrington, 15 Aug. 1901.
63. FO 228/1290, Wuhu 2, 1898; FO 228/1258, Wuhu 9, 1897; FO 228/892, Wuhu 13, 1890; and FO 228/839, Wuhu, 21 July 1886, and 10, 1886, and Leg. 6 to Wuhu, 1886.
64. FO 228/709, Leg. minute on Wuhu 1, 1882.
65. FO 228/1069, Ford to Walsham, 13 May 1891, and Wuhu 7 and 13, 1891; England and Wales marriage registers, 1890; and Lambeth Palace register of Shanghai baptisms, 1891.
66. FO 228/1090, Wuhu 20, 1892; FO 228/1127, Wuhu 8, 1893; and FO 228/1192, Wuhu 1 and 9, 1895.
67. FO 17/1245, Leg. cons. 66, 1895; FO 228/1241, Shanghai accts. 18, 1897, and Leg. to Shanghai, 4 May 1897; FO 228/1255, Shanghai 6 and 40, 1897; and FO 17/1512, F.O. to Treasury, 7 Dec. 1901.
68. FO 228/1258, Shasi 3, 1897; IUP, Vol. 20, pp. 169–99; FO 228/1274, Shasi tel., 13 Apr. 1898, and accts. 11, 1898, and Leg. accts. 6 to Shasi, 1898; FO

228/1291, Shasi 5, 6, and 9, 1898; FO 228/1308, Leg. accts. 1 to Ichang, 1899; Lambeth Palace Shanghai marriage registers, 1899; and FO 17/1512, F.O. to Treasury, 7 Dec. 1901.

69. Morse, *International Relations*, Vol. III, pp. 124 and 159; FO 228/1296, Leg. 325, 1899; FO 228/1308, Hankow, 11 Dec. 1899; FO 17/1421, Leg. cons. 8 and 10, 1900, and tel., 5 Feb. 1900; and FO 17/1512, F.O. to Treasury, 7 Dec. 1901.

70. FO 228/1295, Leg. 147, 1899; and FO 17/1645, Leg. cons. 144, 1904.

71. FO 228/1406, Nanking 18, 1901; FO 228/1790, Sundius to Jordan, 28 June 1911; PRO 30/33/8/22, Warren to Satow, 12 Jan. 1901; and FO 17/1490, Satow to Cockerell, 9 Apr. 1901.

Notes to Chapter 11

1. FO 228/441, Tientsin 3, 1867; FO 17/474, Leg. 13, 1867; Mayers *et al.*, *Treaty Ports*, pp. 473–4; and FO 17/813, Leg. 47, 1879.

2. FO 228/280, Tientsin 1 and 2, 1860. Home leaves were from Oct. 1862 to Mar. 1865 and from Apr. 1870 to summer 1872.

3. FO 17/761, Leg. cons. 58, 1877; FO 17/760, F.O. cons. 67, 1877; *London and China Express*, death announcement, 1877; FO 17/786, Mongan to F.O., 3 July 1878; and FO 17/814, Mongan to F.O., 11 Mar. and 9 June 1879, with Cockerell's minute on the latter, and F.O. to Mongan, 10 June 1879.

4. FO 228/441, Tientsin 14, 1867; FO 17/642, Treasury to F.O., 2 Jan. 1872; Mayers *et al.*, *Treaty Ports*, p. 465; FO 17/704, Leg. cons., 11 Nov. 1875; FO 17/729, Leg. cons. 25, 1876; and FO 17/767, F.O. to Treasury, 31 Dec. 1877.

5. IUP, Vol. 29, pp. 237–491; FO 17/635, Tientsin 48, 1872; FO 391/11, Robertson to Hammond, 25 May 1873; FO 228/496, Tientsin 64, 1870; FO 17/583, Leg. 100, 1871; FO 17/592, Leg. cons. 73, 1871; and FO 17/737, Swinhoe to F.O., 1876.

6. *London and China Express*, marriage announcement, 1864; FO 17/592, Leg. cons. 102, 1871, and F.O. minutes thereon; FO 391/2, Alcock to Hammond, 26 May 1868; FO 17/556, Leg. cons. 98 and 100, 1870; FO 391/20, Wade to Hammond, 11 Apr. 1872; and FO 17/635, Leg. cons. 73, 1872, and FO 17/634, F.O. cons. 33 and 72, 1872.

7. FO 228/1238, Leg. 68, 1897; FO 228/1253, Tientsin 8, 1897; and FO 228/1228, Tientsin 13, 1896.

8. FO 228/1214, Tientsin accts. 6, 1896.

9. FO 17/813, Leg. cons. 47, 1879; Morse, *International Relations*, Vol. II, p. 255; FO 228/1214, Tientsin, 27 May 1896; and FO 17/923, Leg. 76, 1883. For examples of Brenan's contacts with Li see FO 228/1100, Leg. 44, 57, and 62, 1893.

10. FO 17/1023, Leg. cons. 55, 1886.

11. For example, FO 228/636, Tientsin 27, 1879; FO 228/663, Tientsin 46, 1880; and FO 228/687, Tientsin 19, 1881.

12. FO 17/633, Leg. 213, 1872.

13. FO 228/516, Tientsin 38 and 42, 1872; IUP, Vol. 15, p. 571; and FO 228/1089, Tientsin 6, 1892.

14. Jordan, *Chinese I have Known*; FO 228/1238, Leg. 23, 1897; FO 228/1166, Tientsin 81, 1894; and FO 228/1201, Tientsin 48, 1895.

15. Morse, *International Relations*, Vol. III, pp. 206 and 244; FO 17/1428, Tientsin 21, 1900; and FO 228/1347, Tientsin accts. 20, 1900.

16. *London and China Express and Telegraph*, 2 June 1927, obituary; FO

228/1347, Tientsin accts. 34, 1900; and FO 369/362, Campbell to F.O., 3 Mar. 1911.

17. FO 228/1064, Chefoo, 25 Sept. 1890; FO 17/1093, Howard to Walsham, 31 Dec. 1889, and FO 17/1685, F.O. minutes on Manson to F.O., 29 May 1905; IUP, Vol. 18, p. 490, and Vol. 19, p. 58; FO 228/1152, Chefoo, 4 July 1894; and FO 228/1191, Chefoo, 2 Oct. 1895.

18. FO 228/316, Chefoo 1, 1861; FO 228/350, Leg. 7 and 8 to Chefoo, 1863; FO 391/1, Alcock to Hammond, 29 Mar. 1864; FO 17/410, Wade to Hammond, 12 Sept. 1864; FO 228/376, Chefoo 5 and Leg. 4, 10, and 11 to Chefoo, 1864; and FO 17/430, Leg. 250, 1865.

19. FO 228/316, Chefoo 6, 1861; FO 228/335, Leg. 4 and 6 to Chefoo, 1862; FO 228/493, Chefoo 24 and 27, 1870; FO 228/558, Chefoo 3, 1877; and FO 228/1251, Chefoo, 5 Oct. 1897, FO 228/1295, Leg. 134, 1899, and FO 228/1359, Chefoo 3, 1900.

20. FO 228/376, Leg. to Chefoo 10, 1864; FO 228/434, Chefoo 39 and Leg. 10 to Chefoo, 1867; and FO 228/454, Chefoo 6 and 10 and Leg. 6 to Chefoo, 1868.

21. FO 228/538, Chefoo 11, 1874; FO 17/592, Leg. cons. 73, 1871; FO 17/730, Leg. cons. 62 and 67, 1876; and FO 682/506, Cooper's letters to Mayers, Aug.–Oct. 1874.

22. FO 17/813, Leg. cons. 47, 1879; FO 17/564–5, Tenterden's memorandum, 13 June 1870; and FO 17/955, Leg. cons. 55, 1884.

23. FO 228/538; and Hornby, *Autobiography*, pp. 240–5.

24. FO 17/730, Leg. cons. 74, 1876; FO 17/737, Swinhoe to F.O., 1876; FO 681/17, Chefoo death register, 1876; and England and Wales death registers, 1878.

25. FO 17/923, Leg. 62 and 74, 1883; FO 17/930, Leg. cons. 36, 1883; FO 17/955, Leg. cons. 7, 1884; and FO 228/746, Leg. 1 to Chefoo, 1884.

26. FO 228/828, Chefoo 24, 1886, and Leg. minute thereon.

27. FO 228/876, Chefoo 4, 5, and 7–12, 1889; and FO 228/1191, Chefoo, 3 Jan. and 3 Apr. 1895.

28. FO 228/1348; FO 233/126, Campbell to MacDonald, 25 Mar. 1900; and FO 228/1332, Leg. 83, 1900.

29. FO 228/314, Newchwang 1, 1861; FO 228/332, Newchwang 30, 1862; Mayers *et al.*, *Treaty Ports*, pp. 540–1; and IUP, Vol. 11, p. 124.

30. FO 228/314, Newchwang 5, 1861; FO 228/525, Newchwang 12, 1873; IUP, Vol. 13, p. 486; FO 228/703, Newchwang 1, 1882; FO 228/865, Newchwang 6, 1888; and FO 228/3701, Newchwang 9, 1927.

31. IUP, Vol. 11, p. 123.

32. Mayers *et al.*, *Treaty Ports*, p. 540; FO 17/592, Leg. cons. 127, 1871; FO 228/314, Newchwang 11, 1861; FO 17/500, Leg. 244, 1868; FO 17/592, Leg. cons. 127, 1871; FO 228/353, Newchwang 12 and 36, 1863; Hornby, *Autobiography*, p. 250; and FO 17/453, Hornby to Stanley, 1 Sept. 1866.

33. FO 228/314, Newchwang 1, 2, and 10, 1861; FO 228/332, Newchwang 12 and 19, 1862; and FO 17/427, Leg. 165, 1865.

34. FO 228/457, Newchwang 23 and 24, 1868.

35. FO 228/424, Leg., 24 Apr. 1867; FO 228/426, F.O., 9 July 1867; FO 228/442, Wade to Alcock, 15 July, and Beatty to Alcock, 24 July, 1867; FO 17/497, Leg. 115, 1868; FO 228/457, Newchwang 5, 1868; and FO 656/9.

36. IUP, Vol. 8, p. 564.

37. FO 228/457, Newchwang 21, 23, and 24, 1868; and FO 228/418, Newchwang 27, 1866.

38. For example, FO 228/314, Newchwang 14, 1861; and FO 228/418, Newchwang 6, 1866.

39. FO 17/450, Leg. 105, 1866; FO 228/314, Newchwang 10, 1861, and FO

228/801, Newchwang, 20 Jan. 1885; FO 228/332, Newchwang 23 and 24, 1862; and FO 228/394–5, Newchwang 5, 6, and 13, 1865.

40. For example, FO 228/332, Newchwang 23, 1862; FO 228/505, Newchwang 3 and 7, 1871; and FO 228/525, Newchwang, 20 Oct. 1873, and 13 and 20, 1873.

41. FO 228/395, Newchwang 19, 1865; FO 228/418, Newchwang 1, 1866; and FO 228/353, Newchwang 33 and Leg. 18 to Newchwang, 1863.

42. FO 228/372, Newchwang 21, 1864; FO 228/353, Newchwang 33, 1863; FO 228/372, Meadows to Bruce, 14 May 1864, Newchwang 21 and 30, and Leg. 5 and 10 to Newchwang, 1864; and FO 17/459, Hammond's minute on F.O. copy of Newchwang 6, 1866.

43. FO 17/501, Leg. 302 and 310, 1868; and FO 391/2, Alcock to Hammond, 8 Dec. 1868.

44. FO 228/525, Newchwang 13, 1873; and FO 228/617, Newchwang 1, 1878.

45. FO 17/588–9, Leg. 222 and 241, 1871; FO 17/592, F.O. cons. 64 and 77, 1871; FO 17/635, Leg. cons. 18, 1872; FO 228/801, Newchwang, 20 Jan. 1885, and FO 17/993, Gardner to Hertslet, 14 Feb. 1885; and Hosie, *Manchuria*, pp. 1 and 152.

46. See, for example, 1892 Newchwang correspondence in FO 228/1087.

47. FO 228/1196, Newchwang 12 and 78, 1895.

48. FO 228/1159, Newchwang 17, 20, 25, 42, and 59, 1894; and FO 228/1196, Newchwang tel., 5 Mar. 1895, and despatch 70, 1895.

49. FO 228/1251.

50. FO 228/1328, Newchwang 46, 1899; and FO 228/1358, Newchwang 18 and 20, 1900.

51. FO 228/1358.

52. FO 17/926, Leg. 54, 1883; FO 17/955, Leg. Corea [Korea] cons. 9, 1884; FO 228/781, Leg. 310 and 392, 1885; FO 228/1423, Leg. tel. 149, 1902; FO 17/1557, F.O. to Treasury, 7 July 1902; and FO 97/555, F.O. to Treasury, 6 Jan. 1891.

53. FO 228/1021, Baber to O'Conor, 17 Sept. 1885; and FO 17/1084, O'Conor to Currie, 22 Dec. 1885.

54. Jordan, *Chinese I have Known*; FO 17/903, Leg. cons. 11, 1882, FO 17/938, Baber to F.O., 19 June and 17 Dec. 1883, and FO 17/989, Leg. cons. 49, 1885; FO 228/1042, Seoul accts. 4, 1888; and *T'oung Pao*, first series, Vol. I, obituary.

55. FO 228/830, Parker to Walsham, 22 and 25 Nov. 1886; FO 17/1046, Leg. cons. 29, 1887; FO 17/1025, India Office to F.O., 12 Dec. 1888; and *Foreign Office Lists*.

56. FO 228/1029, Leg. tel. to Foochow, 6 Nov. 1886, and Foochow accts. 17, 1886; and PRO 30/33/7/11, Leg. memorandum.

57. FO 228/830; FO 228/850, Seoul 2, 1887; and FO 228/854, Shanghai tel., 27 Jan. 1887.

58. FO 17/1101, Leg. cons. 17 and 52, 1890; and FO 97/555, Leg. tel. 11, 1891.

59. FO 228/1056, Parker to Brady, 19 Nov. 1891, and Leg. minute thereon; FO 228/1076, Leg. tels. to Hoihow 1892; and FO 228/1120, Parker to O'Conor, 8 Dec. 1893.

60. FO 17/1250, Parker to F.O., 10 Jan., 1 June, and 8 and 18 July 1895, and F.O. minutes thereon; FO 228/876, Parker to Walsham, 15 Nov. 1889, FO 228/889, Foochow 3, 12, and 17, 1890, and PRO 30/33/7/11, Parker's printed letter of 8 Mar. 1901; and *T'oung Pao*, Vol. XXIV, obituary.

61. FO 228/1274, Seoul accts. 13–15, 1898.

62. FO 678/1886.

63. FO 228/538, Jordan to F.O., 12 Feb., and F.O. to Jordan, 16 Feb., 1874; FO 17/737, CSC to F.O., 5 and 14 Feb. 1876; FO 17/785, Leg. cons. 18, 1878; FO 17/835, Leg. cons. 17, 1880; FO 228/971, Canton, 26 July 1880, and accts. 11,

1880; and FO 17/903, Leg. cons. 64, 1882.
64. FO 17/835, Leg. cons. 23, 1880; FO 228/1000, Hoihow accts. 5, 1883; FO 17/955, Leg. cons. 15 and 57, 1884; FO 17/1024, Leg. cons. 82, 1886; *DNB 1922–1930*, p. 462 (date of marriage); and FO 17/1084, F.O. cons. 69, 1885.
65. FO 228/359, F.O. 13, 1864; FO 17/557, F.O. (Clarendon) cons. 15, 1870; FO 17/989, Leg. cons. 65 and 72, 1885; FO 17/988, F.O. cons. 68, 1885; and FO 17/1023, Leg. cons. 20 and 58, 1886.
66. FO 17/1084, Leg. cons. 56, 1887; FO 17/1087, Leg. cons. 33, 1889; and *Foreign Office Lists*.
67. FO 228/1214, Seoul accts. 7, 1896; FO 17/1282, Leg. cons. 51, 1896; FO 228/1265, Leg. tels. 41 and 47, 1898; FO 228/1272, F.O. tel. 37, 1898; FO 228/1262, Leg. 32, 1898; and *Foreign Office Lists*.
68. *Foreign Office Lists*; and PRO 30/33/7/5, Grey tel. to Satow, 3 Mar., and Satow tel. to Grey, 4 Mar. 1906.

Notes to Chapter 12

1. FO 17/675, Leg. 181, 1874; *The Journey of Augustus Raymond Margary*, p. 330; FO 391/12, Robertson to Hammond, 1 July and 23 Sept. 1875; and Morse, *International Relations*, Vol. II, Chapter XIV.
2. FO 17/617–18, tables of results in examinations in July 1864, Apr. 1865, and July 1866, F.O. minute on Suffield's letter of Apr. 1866, and Margary to F.O., Aug. 1866, and F.O. minutes thereon; and FO 228/425, F.O. 26, 1867. For relationship to A.H. Layard see *The Journey of Augustus Raymond Margary*, p. xiv.
3. FO 17/628, Leg. 75, 1872; and *Foreign Office Lists*.
4. *The Journey of Augustus Raymond Margary*; Morse, *International Relations*, Vol. II, pp. 287 and 294; and FO 228/1172, Leg. 348, 1895.
5. FO 17/737, C. Layard to F.O., 26 Jan. 1876; FO 17/767, Mrs Margary to F.O., 18 Jan. and 16 May, and F.O. to Mrs Margary, 6 July 1877; FO 228/658, Shanghai 48, 1880; and E. Milliken (comp.), *Brighton College Register, 1847–1922. With brief biographical notes* (Brighton, 1922).
6. FO 17/587, Leg. 187, 1871; Morse, *International Relations*, Vol. II, p. 302; FO 228/886, Chungking 5, 1890, and FO 228/1064, Chungking 6, 1891; and FO 17/835, Leg. cons. 56, 1880.
7. IUP, Vol. 20, p. 496.
8. FO 228/973, Chungking accts. 5, 1881; FO 228/726, Ichang 1, 1883; FO 17/1101, Leg. cons. 42, 1890; FO 228/1345, Ichang tel., 28 Dec. 1900, and FO 17/1490, Leg. cons. 28 and 55, 1901; and FO 369/1091, Leg. cons. 182, 1918.
9. FO 228/1240, Chungking accts. 8, 1897; IUP, Vol. 20, p. 494; and author's personal knowledge.
10. FO 228/674, Parker to Grosvenor, 15 July 1881; FO 228/1050, Chungking accts. 10, 1890; and FO 228/1273, Chungking accts. 9, 1898.
11. FO 228/1253, Chungking, 1 Feb. 1897; FO 228/1284, Chungking, 30 Apr. 1898; FO 228/1323, Chungking, 14 Feb. 1899; PRO 30/33/8/5, Campbell to Satow, 11 Feb. 1905; and FO 228/1864, Chungking accts. 14, 1913.
12. FO 17/903, Leg. cons. 10, 1882; and FO 228/1307, Chungking accts. 7, 1899.
13. FO 17/1031, Hosie to F.O., 31 Mar. 1886; FO 228/1035, Chungking accts. 9, 1887; FO 17/1145, Treasury to F.O., 27 July 1892; and FO 17/1160, F.O. cons. 25, 1893.
14. FO 228/674, Parker to Wade, 12 Nov. 1881; and FO 17/1084, Wade to F.O., 21 Jan. 1884.

15. FO 228/674–5, Chungking, 5 July 1881 *et seq.*; Parker, *John Chinaman*, pp. 100 *et seq.*; and FO 17/903, Leg. cons. 8, 1882.

16. FO 17/1018, Leg. 233, 240, and 244, 1886; FO 228/829; and FO 17/1046, Leg. cons. 21, 1887.

17. FO 228/1193; FO 228/1225; and FO 228/1253, Chungking, 1 May 1897.

18. FO 17/1396, Tratman to F.O., 23 Apr. and 20 Aug. 1899; FO 17/1490, Satow to Cockerell, 9 Apr. 1901; FO 17/1644, Satow to Hardinge, 12 Feb. 1904; FO 369/10, Tratman to F.O., 26 May 1906; and England and Wales probate records, 1945.

19. IUP, Vol. 21, p. 127; FO 228/1193, Chungking 12, 1895; FO 228/1403, Chungking 12, 1901; and FO 17/1317, Leg. cons. 4, 1897.

20. *Eton College Register, Part III, 1862–1868* (privately printed, Eton, 1906); FO 228/1193, Swatow, 15 Jan. 1895; FO 17/1301, Leg. cons. 35, 1895; FO 228/1185, Leg. to Singapore, 28 June 1895; FO 228/1182, Singapore to Leg., 9 Aug. 1895; FO 228/1213, Shanghai accts. 10 and Leg. accts. 9 to Shanghai, 1896; and FO 228/1273, Chungking accts. 9, 1898.

21. FO 228/1284; FO 228/1323; FO 228/1295, Leg. 23, 1899; FO 228/1386, MacDonald to Villiers, 24 Aug. 1899; and FO 228/1304, Litton from Kweiyang, 9 Apr. 1899.

22. FO 228/1307, Leg. tel. to Litton, 9 June 1899; FO 17/1386, Leg. cons. 66, 1899; FO 228/1323, Litton from Kweiyang, 3 May 1899; and FO 228/1301, F.O. 144, 1899.

23. FO 228/1592, Chungking 5 and Leg. 2 to Chungking, 1905; FO 228/1573, F.O. 241, 1905; FO 369/8, Satow to Cockerell, 13 Nov. 1905, and F.O. minutes thereon; PRO 30/33/9/10, Satow to Wilton, n.d., and Wilton to Satow, 21 Apr. 1906.

24. FO 17/1421, F.O. minute on Leg. 79, 1900; FO 17/1430, F.O. minute preceding F.O. tel. to Chungking, 27 Nov. 1900, and Sanderson's minute on Chungking to F.O., 19 Aug. 1900; FO 228/1359, Chungking, 15 Dec. 1900; and FO 17/1490, Satow to Cockerell, 9 and 26 Apr. 1901.

25. FO 228/1275, Wuhu accts. 2, 1898; FO 17/1498, Fraser to F.O., 30 July and 4 Nov. 1901, and F.O. minutes thereon, and F.O. to Fraser, 15 Nov. 1901; and information kindly supplied by bursar, Trinity Hall College.

26. FO 17/1106, Baber's father to F.O., 11 Dec. 1890; Parker, *China Past and Present*, pp. 182–3; Hosie, *Western China*, p. xx; and Baber, 'Travels and Researches', pp. 1, 53, and 105.

27. FO 228/608, Baber to Fraser, 3 May 1878.

28. FO 228/781, Leg. 469, 1885; and FO 228/851, Chungking, 7 Feb. 1887.

29. FO 17/949, Leg. 54, 1884; and FO 17/1169, Kew to F.O., 4 Sept. 1893.

30. FO 17/1425, Leg. 66, 1895; FO 17/1317, Leg. 46 and 62, 1897; FO 228/1239, Leg. 156, 1897; FO 17/1366, F.O. to India Office, 1 Dec. 1898; FO 228/1347, Tengyueh accts. 2 and 5, 1899; FO 228/1383, Tengyueh accts. 6, 1901; FO 228/1411, Tengyueh, 20 Dec. 1901; FO 228/1434, F.O. 198, 1902; and FO 228/1756, Tengyueh 6, 1910.

31. FO 228/1327, Jamieson to Bax-Ironside, 4 Aug. 1899, and Tengyueh 4 and 8, 1899.

32. FO 228/1327, Tengyueh 6, 7, and 9, 1899; and J.F. Fraser, *Round the World on a Wheel...* (London, 1899).

33. Morse, *International Relations*, Vol. II, p. 411; FO 228/1171, Leg. 228, 1895; IUP, Vol. 21, pp. 387–94; FO 228/1283, Ssumao 1 and 6, 1898; and FO 228/1274, Ssumao accts. 4, 1898.

34. FO 228/1330, Ssumao tel., 2 July 1899; FO 228/1327, Tengyueh 2, 1899; FO 228/1283, Ssumao 6, 1898; and FO 228/1263, Leg. 167, 1898.

35. FO 228/1307, Litton from Chungking tel., 10 June 1899; FO 228/1330, Litton from Canton, 31 July 1899, and Ssumao 2, 1899; FO 228/1309, Ssumao accts. 4, 1899; and FO 17/1431, Bertie's minute of 15 Dec. 1900 on trade report.

36. FO 228/1354, India to Leg., 7 Apr. 1900; FO 228/1363, Litton, 15 Feb. 1900; FO 228/1309, Ssumao accts. 6, 1899; and FO 228/1411, Tengyueh 1, 1901.

Notes to Chapter 13

1. FO 17/555, Leg. cons. 58, 1870; and FO 17/1093, Howard to Walsham, 31 Dec. 1889.

2. FO 228/313, Taiwan 1, 4, 5, and 10 and Leg. 5 to Taiwan, 1861, and Swinhoe from Amoy, 21 Nov. 1861; FO 228/330, Tamsui 11, 1862, and Swinhoe from Amoy, 20 May 1862; FO 17/379, Swinhoe to F.O., 20 Nov. and 12 Dec. 1862, with Hammond's minute on the former; and FO 228/319, F.O. 120, 1862. For descriptions of Tamsui see FO 228/881, Tamsui, 9 Mar. 1889, and FO 228/892, Tamsui 8, 1890.

3. FO 228/330, Tamsui 31A, 1862; FO 17/390, Leg. 33, 1863, and Hammond's minute thereon; FO 228/339, F.O. 157, 1863; FO 228/341, Kuper to Leg., 19 May 1863; and FO 228/360, F.O. 104, 1864.

4. FO 228/351, Tamsui 11, 14, and 16, 1863.

5. FO 228/351, Leg. 1, 5, 7, and 16 to Tamsui, 1863, and Tamsui, 3 Mar. 1863; and FO 228/360, F.O. 131, 1864.

6. FO 228/374, Braune from Foochow, 9 Mar. 1864, and Tamsui 11, 1864; and FO 17/408, Leg. 69, 1864.

7. IUP, Vol. 6, p. 219; and FO 228/374, Tamsui, 1 Feb. 1864, and Tamsui 11, 16, 29, and 32 and Leg. 6 to Tamsui, 1864.

8. Mayers et al., Treaty Ports, p. 298; FO 17/1023, Leg. cons. 3, 1886; FO 228/379, F.O. 29, 1865; FO 17/429, Leg. 199, 1865; FO 228/596, Taiwan 20 and 22, 1877; FO 228/420, Taiwan 8, 1866; and FO 17/452, Leg. 51, 1866.

9. FO 228/374, Taiwan 32 and 40, 1864; FO 228/397, Taiwan 31, 40, 44, 45, and 48 and Leg. 25 to Taiwan, 1865; FO 17/429, Leg. 204, 1865; FO 228/420, Taiwan 2, 1866; FO 17/450, Leg. 115, 1866; and FO 17/476, Leg. 97, 1867.

10. FO 228/397, Leg. 9 and 30 to Taiwan and Taiwan 25, 1865, Leg. to Taiwan, 3 July 1865, and Taiwan, 16 Aug. 1865; FO 228/420, Leg. 4 to Taiwan, 1866; and FO 17/476, Leg. 117, 1867.

11. FO 228/405, Amoy (Swinhoe) 1, 1866; and FO 228/420, Taiwan 12, 1866.

12. FO 17/476, Leg. 113, 1867; FO 228/440, Taiwan 19, 1867; and FO 228/451, Carroll, 22 Jan. 1868.

13. FO 228/397, Taiwan 45, 1865; FO 17/478, Alcock to Hammond, 18 Nov. 1867; and FO 17/497, Leg. 125, 1868.

14. FO 228/459; IUP, Vol. 29, pp. 93–149; FO 228/463, Swinhoe, 28 Nov. 1868, and 9, 1869; FO 391/2, Alcock to Hammond, 3 Jan., 26 Feb., 18 June, and 31 July, 1869; FO 17/522, Leg. 68, 1869; and FO 17/632, Leg. 193, 1872.

15. FO 228/481, Taiwan 5, 15, and 23, 1869; FO 391/2, Alcock to Hammond, 5 July 1869; FO 228/469, Amoy 15, 1869; and North-China Herald, 12 Aug. and 23 Sept. 1869.

16. FO 678/1832; FO 917/69; and FO 391/2, Adkins to Alcock.

17. FO 17/555, Leg. 42, 1870.

18. FO 228/459, Swinhoe, 26 Dec. 1867; FO 391/1, Hammond to Alcock, 6 May 1869; FO 228/466, F.O. 78, 1869; FO 228/463, Swinhoe, 20 July 1869; FO 17/524,

Leg. 102, 1869; and FO 228/468, F.O. 199 and 207, 1869.

19. FO 228/463, Swinhoe, 19 July 1869, and FO 17/557, F.O. cons. 49 (Clarendon) and cons. 24 (Granville), 1870; FO 17/635, Leg. cons., 1 May 1872; FO 17/658–9, Leg. cons. 47 and 78, 1873; and England and Wales death registers, 1877 (Mr I.C. Orr, HM Diplomatic Service, kindly drew attention to the cause of death there stated).

20. FO 391/2, Alcock to Hammond, 5 July 1869; FO 228/495, Taiwan 1, 6, and 12 and Leg. 3 to Taiwan, 1870; IUP, Vol. 2, p. 437; FO 17/548, Leg. 94, 1870; FO 17/592, Leg. cons. 95 and 104, 1871; FO 17/635, Leg. cons., 1 May 1872; and FO 17/641, Cooper's medical certificates of 2 May and 15 Oct. 1872.

21. FO 228/495, Taiwan 15 and 21, 1870; W. Pickering, *Pioneering in Formosa* (London, 1898), pp. 236–7; and FO 17/583, Leg. 34, 1871.

22. FO 228/570, Taiwan 10, 1876; FO 228/616, Taiwan, 28 Aug. 1878; IUP, Vol. 13, p. 662, and Vol. 14, p. 114.; Fo 17/930, Leg. cons. 48, 1885; and FO 228/1199, Tainan 12, 1895.

23. FO 228/807, Taiwan 1, 11–13, and 26 and Leg. 3 to Taiwan, 1885; and FO 228/780, Leg. 215, 1885.

24. FO 228/807, Taiwan 20, 31, 33, 39, and 42, 1885; FO 228/781, Leg. 473, 1885; and FO 228/852, Foochow, 5 Feb. 1887.

25. FO 17/555, Leg. cons. 55, 1870, and FO 17/658, Leg. cons. 45, 1873; FO 17/813, Leg. cons. 61, 1879, and FO 17/860, Leg. cons. 21, 1881; FO 17/930, Leg. cons. 11, 1883, and FO 17/955, Leg. cons. 6, 1884; FO 17/1024, Leg. cons. 73, 1886; and FO 228/807, Taiwan 6, 1885.

26. Hummel, *Eminent Chinese*, Vol. I, pp. 527–8; FO 228/867, Taiwan 5, 1888; and FO 228/1089, Tainan, 17 Nov. 1892.

27. FO 228/1125, Leg. 7 to Tainan, 1893; and FO 17/1161, Leg. cons. 45 and 57, 1893.

28. H. McAleavy, *Black Flags in Vietnam* (London, 1968), pp. 100–4; Morse, *International Relations*, Vol. III, p. 52; FO 228/1199; and FO 228/1172, Leg. 416, 1895.

29. FO 228/1173, Hurst to Beauclerk, 19 Nov. 1895; FO 228/1181, Tainan accts. 21, 1895; FO 17/1281, F.O. to O'Conor, 8 Jan. 1896, and O'Conor's reply; and FO 228/1208, Beauclerk to Bourne, 30 Jan. 1896.

30. FO 228/1164, Tainan 7, 1894; FO 228/1178, F.O. 163, 1895; and IUP, Vol. 11, p. 174.

31. FO 228/397, Leg. 4 to Taiwan, 1865; FO 228/380, F.O. 104, 1865; FO 17/557, F.O. (Granville), 16 Dec. 1870; FO 228/521, Taiwan 8, 1873; FO 228/420, Taiwan 16, 1866; FO 228/554, Tamsui 21 and 23 and Leg. 3 to Tamsui, 1875; and FO 17/760, F.O. 67, 1877.

32. IUP, Vol. 11, p. 162; FO 17/476, Leg. 117, 1867; FO 228/455, Tamsui 12, 1868; FO 228/481, Tamsui 14, 21, and 23, 1869; *The Journey of Augustus Raymond Margary*, p. 17; FO 17/642, Treasury to F.O., 2 Jan. 1872; FO 228/505, Tamsui 12, 1871; FO 228/554, Tamsui 12, 1875; FO 228/892, Tamsui 8, 1890; and FO 228/999, Tamsui accts. 5, 1883.

33. FO 228/405, Tamsui 18, 1866; FO 17/476, Leg. 117, 1867; IUP, Vol. 2, pp. 230 and 474; and FO 17/555–6, Leg. cons. 58 and 95, 1870.

34. IUP, Vol. 11, p. 162; FO 228/845, F.O. 37, 1887; FO 228/892, Tamsui 8, 1890; and FO 228/837, Tamsui 11, 1886.

35. For example, FO 228/495.

36. FO 228/440, Tamsui 21, 1867; FO 228/554, Tamsui 4, 1875; FO 228/570, Tamsui 7, 1876; and FO 228/635, Tamsui, 15 May 1879.

37. FO 17/496, Leg. 20, 1868; FO 17/729, Leg. cons. 25, 1876; FO 228/713, Tamsui 8, 1882; FO 228/881, Tamsui, 27 Mar. 1889; FO 17/1093, Howard to

Walsham, 31 Dec. 1889; FO 228/892, Tamsui 8, 1890; and FO 17/1116, Leg. cons. 63, 1891.

38. FO 228/481, Tamsui 13 and 20 and Leg. 7 to Tamsui, 1869, and Taiwan 33, 1869.

39. FO 17/477, Leg. 140 and 161, 1867; FO 17/501, Leg. 299, 1868; FO 228/808, Tamsui 7, 1885; FO 228/837, Tamsui 11, 1886; and England and Wales probate records, 1907.

40. FO 228/765; FO 228/781, Leg. 449, 1885; FO 228/808, Tamsui 13, 1885, and 6 May 1885, and Leg. 13 to Tamsui, 1885; and FO 228/788, Amoy, 12 Mar. 1885 (erroneously dated 1884).

41. FO 228/855, Tamsui 8, 1887; FO 228/867, Tamsui, 7 July and 23 Oct. 1888; FO 228/881, Tamsui, 9 Mar. 1889; FO 17/1093, north Formosa residents to F.O., 31 July 1889; and Hummel, *Eminent Chinese*, Vol. I, p. 528.

42. Morse, *International Relations*, Vol. III, pp. 51–2; and FO 228/1200.

Notes to Chapter 14

1. FO 17/679, Wade to Tenterden, 10 July 1874.

2. FO 17/679, Leg. cons 10, 1874; FO 17/703, F.O. cons. 4, 1875; FO 17/704, Leg. cons. 44, 1875; and FO 17/711, CSC to F.O., 3 July 1875.

3. FO 17/1057, CSC to F.O., 27 May 1887; and FO 17/1230, F.O. to universities, 23 May 1894.

4. For example, Watters, H.A. Giles, and W.S.F. Mayers. For Watters' sinology see *T'oung Pao*, second series, Vol. II, obituary.

5. For example, McL. Brown and W.C. Hillier. See Committee on Oriental Studies, Satow's evidence, QQ. 1908–10.

6. Fourth Report of Royal Commission on Civil Establishments, Q. 29, 430.

7. FO 17/784, F.O. cons. 41, 1878; and FO 228/1346, Shanghai accts. 39, 1900, and PRO 30/33/8/22, Brenan to Satow, 21 Nov. 1900.

8. FO 17/642, F.O. to CSC, 14 Feb., and CSC to F.O., 11 Mar., 1872; CSC Seventeenth Report, PP 1872, XIX, p. 200; CSC Eighteenth Report, PP 1874, XVI, p. 208; and CSC Eighth Report, PP 1863, XX, p. 224.

9. For example, Townsend and one of his contemporaries. See *In Memoriam. Walter Ewen Townsend*, p. 25.

10. King's College calendars; and FO 369/66, Leg. cons. 26, 1907.

11. See, for example, FO 17/1106, Piper to F.O., 21 Feb. 1890.

12. FO 17/999, F.O. to universities, 11 Nov. 1885, and F.O. note about CSC press advertisements.

13. See Appendix II.

14. FO 17/1103, F.O. minute of ? Aug. ? Sept. 1890.

15. FO 17/1229.

16. 1871 census, Hertfordshire, Cheshunt, 4 Waltham Cross Road.

17. FO 881/7205, correspondence and minutes (1896–9) regarding student interpreters' entrance examination.

18. FO 17/1903, Howard to Walsham, 31 Dec. 1889; and FO 17/1161, Leg. cons. 2, 1893.

19. FO 17/785, Leg. cons. 37, 1878; FO 17/1047, Leg. cons. 65, 1887; FO 17/564–5, Tenterden's memorandum, 13 June 1870; and FO 17/556, Leg. cons. 28, 1870, F.O. minute.

20. FO 17/478, Leg. 175, 1867, and Alcock to Hammond, 18 Nov. 1867.

21. FO 17/767, F.O. to Treasury, 8 Nov., and Treasury to F.O., 1 Dec., 1877; and FO 17/903, Leg. cons. 64, 1882, and FO 17/966, Blake to Fitzmaurice, 15 Oct. 1884, enclosing statement of juniors' grievances.

22. Second Report of Select Committee on Diplomatic and Consular Services, Q. 1774; FO 17/513, Treasury to F.O., 14 Sept. 1868, Hammond's minute; FO 17/897, Leg. cons. 68, 1882, and F.O. minutes thereon; and FO 17/965, Treasury to F.O., 4 Feb. 1884.

23. FO 228/1109, Shanghai accts. 8, 1893.

24. FO 228/1830, Kiukiang accts. 15, 1912.

25. FO 17/559, Ningpo to F.O., 9 Mar. 1870; and FO 228/1345, Ningpo accts. 4, 1900.

26. See, for example, FO 228/1035, Ningpo, 10 Nov. 1886; FO 228/1152, Chefoo 27, 1894, and FO 228/1212, Chefoo accts. 3, 1896; FO 228/1192, Chinkiang, 20 May 1895; and FO 228/1227, Foochow 11, 1896.

27. See, for example, FO 228/1192, Chinkiang, 13 Apr. 1895; and FO 228/1240, Foochow accts. 9, 1897.

28. FO 350/5, Jordan to J.R. Harding, 5 May 1908; and FO 228/1029, Ningpo accts. 6, 1886, and FO 228/1035, Ningpo, 10 Nov. 1887.

29. FO 228/539, Kiukiang 8, 1874.

30. FO 17/843, Miss Middleton to F.O., 11 July 1880; and FO 369/812, Miss Swinhoe to F.O., 20 Aug. 1915.

31. FO 228/367, Shanghai 31, 1864.

32. Jones, British Diplomatic Service, p. 150.

33. FO 17/897, Leg. 68, 1882.

34. FO 17/1084, Leg. cons. 80, 1885, and Currie's reply to Walsham's tel. 10, 1887; FO 17/1093, Howard to Walsham, 31 Dec. 1889; and FO 17/1490, Leg. cons. 63, 1901.

35. For example, FO 17/923, Leg. separate 2, 1883; FO 17/730, Leg. cons. 82, 1876; and FO 17/1084, O'Conor to Currie, 22 Dec. 1885 and 16 June 1886.

36. For example, FO 17/1498, F.O. to M.F.A. Fraser, 15 Nov. 1901.

37. FO 228/1021, Spence to O'Conor, 20 Dec. 1885; FO 228/1018, O'Conor to Spence, 18 Jan. 1886; FO 17/1023, Leg. cons. 10, 1886; FO 17/1032, F.O. to Treasury, 30 Jan. and 13 Feb., and Treasury to F.O., 10 Feb. and 6 Mar., 1886; FO 17/1090, Spence to F.O., 4 Dec. 1889; and London and China Express, death announcement, 1890.

38. FO 228/1221, Bourne to Jordan, 23 July 1896.

39. FO 17/619, Sir T. Abdy to F.O., Apr. 1868; FO 228/446, F.O. 69, 1868; FO 17/538, Alcock to Hammond, 18 July 1868; London and China Express, 12 Aug. 1910, obituary; and Who Was Who.

40. FO 228/355, Tientsin 52 and Leg. 40 to Tientsin, 1863; FO 228/375, Leg. 13 to Tientsin, 1864; FO 228/379, F.O. 70, 1865; and Who Was Who. For a criticism of the F.O. see his China (London, 1912, fourth edition), p. 411.

41. FO 17/448, Leg. 39, 1866. For his subsequent varied career see entries in Couling, Encyclopaedia Sinica, King and Clarke, China Coast Newspapers, and Colonial Office List for 1889 (London, 1889), also T'oung Pao, second series, Vol. II, obituary.

42. FO 228/315, Swatow 45 and Leg. 20 to Swatow, 1861; FO 228/325, Foochow 12B and Leg. 11 to Foochow, 1862; and FO 369/923, George to F.O., 2 Nov. 1917, and F.O. minutes and reply.

43. FO 881/7205, O'Conor to Sanderson, 12 Feb. 1897; and FO 17/1084, O'Conor to Currie, 22 Dec. 1885.

44. FO 17/680, Leg. cons. 128, 1874; and FO 17/701, Leg. 185, 1875.

45. The significance of this was appreciated at too late a stage of research for the

proportion to be quantified.

46. PRO 30/33/15/1, entry September 1862; FO 17/390, Leg. 6, 1863; FO 17/393, Bruce to ?Hammond, 2 Aug. 1863; FO 17/448, Leg. 39, 1866, and F.O. minutes thereon; FO 17/711, Currie's minute, 17 Mar. 1875; FO 17/792, G.A. Smith to F.O., 6 Feb. 1878, and F.O. minutes thereon; and *Foreign Office Lists*, for example, 1901, p. 272.

47. FO 17/1230, Tours to F.O., 11 and 13 Sept. 1892; and FO 17/1229, Wilton to F.O., 2 Aug. 1890, and F.O. minutes thereon.

48. FO 17/1072, Baber to F.O., 21 Dec. 1888; and FO 369/2017, Leg. 563, 1928.

49. *London and China Express*, supplement, 27 Nov. 1918, Jamieson's 'To Peking in the Sixties'.

50. FO 17/452, Leg. 59, 1866; *Where Chineses Drive*, p. 29; FO 228/1049, Leg. to Office of Works, Shanghai, 15 Sept. 1890; *In Memoriam. Walter Ewen Townsend*, p. 20; and FO 228/1263, Leg. 245, 1898.

51. FO 369/561, Leg. cons. 28, 1913.

52. For example, FO 17/449, Leg. 87, 1866; FO 17/587, Alcock to Granville, 17 July 1871; FO 17/729, Leg. cons. 40, 1876, F.O. minutes; FO 17/1490, F.O. minutes, June 1900; FO 17/1512, Office of Works to F.O., 8 July 1901; and FO 369/561, Leg. cons. 28, 1913, F.O. minute.

53. FO 369/1091, Treasury to F.O., 25 July 1919; FO 369/561, Leg. cons. 28, 1913; and FO 17/910, Office of Works to F.O., 11 Aug. 1882, Pauncefote's minute.

54. FO 17/1366, Warren to F.O., 19 July 1898, and F.O. reply.

55. FO 369/285, Leg. cons. 112, 1910, Tyrrell's minute.

56. FO 17/1490, Satow to Barrington, 15 Aug. 1901; FO 17/1498, Perkins to F.O., 15 Jan. 1901, Barrington's minute thereon and subsequent action: PRO 30/33/7/1, Cockerell to Satow, 12 Apr. 1901; FO 369/204, Board of Education to F.O., 18 June 1909, F.O. minute; PRO 30/33/7/3, Cartwright to Satow, 30 June 1904; and Jones, *British Diplomatic Service*, p. 157.

57. FO 228/446, F.O. 106, 1868; FO 17/499, Leg. 220, 1868, and F.O. minute thereon.

58. FO 17/679, Leg. cons. 34, 1874, F.O. minute; FO 17/1076, Treasury to F.O., 4 Dec. 1888; FO 17/1087, F.O. cons. 24, 1889; and FO 17/1309.

59. FO 17/787, Pedder to F.O., 2 Aug. 1878.

60. FO 17/737, F.O. to Taylor's brother; FO 228/1180, Amoy, 15 July 1895; and FO 228/1287, Chinkiang 9, 1898.

61. IUP, Vol. 2, p. 409; and FO 228/1180, Chefoo accts. 6, 1895.

62. For example, FO 228/1213, Ichang accts. 10, 1896, and FO 228/1208, Leg. accts. 10 to Ichang, 1896; and FO 228/1274, Shasi tel., 13 Apr. 1898.

63. FO 17/860, Leg. cons. 25, 1881.

64. For some account of the Chinese secretary's work see the author's 'Documents in Chinese from the Chinese Secretary's Office...', *Modern Asian Studies*, 17, 2 (1983), pp. 239–55.

65. FO 17/679, Leg., 27 Jan. 1874, Tenterden's minute.

66. FO 228/780, Leg. 159, 1885; and Fourth Report of Royal Commission on Civil Establishments, Q. 29,297.

67. FO 17/407, St. John to Alston, 5 Jan. 1864; FO 228/448, Canton 36, 1868; FO 17/592, Leg. cons. 84, 1871, and Wade to Hammond, 20 Oct. 1871; FO 17/628, Leg., 6 Apr. 1872, and Hammond's minute thereon; FO 17/679, Leg., 27 Jan. 1874; FO 17/680, Leg. cons. 128, 1874, and FO 17/761, Leg. cons. 32, 1877; FO 17/697, Leg. 1, 1875, and F.O. minutes thereon; FO 17/729, Leg., 4 May 1876, and F.O. minutes thereon; FO 17/727, Leg. 209, 1876, F.O. minutes; and FO 17/813, Leg. cons. 48, 1879, and Tenterden's minute thereon.

68. FO 17/779–80, Leg. 26 and 60, 1878 (see also FO 17/636, Leg. cons. 102,

1872); FO 17/793, Prime Minister's Office to F.O., 26 Aug. 1878; FO 17/831, Leg. 73, 1880; FO 682/136A, Wade to Li Hung-chang, 3 Nov. 1879, and Li's reply of 9 moon 26 day; and FO 682/325/1, Ting Jih-ch'ang to Wade, 1880.

69. FO 17/1093, Howard to Walsham, 31 Dec. 1889, Currie's minute; FO 228/1263, Leg. 178, 1898; PRO 30/33/7/2, Barrington tel. to Satow, 22 Jan., and Satow tel. to Barrington, 24 Jan., 1902; FO 228/1434, F.O. 168, 1902; and FO 371/5335, Leg. 474, 1920.

70. FO 17/1076, Currie's minute, 15 Mar. 1889; and FO 17/1093, F.O. to Treasury, 1 Apr. 1889, and Howard to Walsham, 31 Dec. 1889, Currie's minute.

71. FO 17/451, Leg. 16, 1866, and F.O. minutes thereon; FO 17/679, Leg. cons. 32, 1874, FO 17/678, F.O. cons. 41, 1874, FO 17/730, Leg. cons., 20 Nov. 1876, FO 17/760, F.O. cons. 4, 1877, and FO 17/761, Leg. 32, 1877; FO 17/930, Leg. cons. 26, 1883; FO 17/923, Leg. 95, 1883; and FO 17/949, Leg. 67, 1884.

72. FO 17/910, CSC to F.O., 9 Nov. 1882; and *Foreign Office List, 1883*, p. 272.

73. FO 17/1087, Leg. cons. 39, 1889; FO 17/1103, E.F. Bennett to F.O., 1890, and Currie's minute thereon; and FO 228/1790, Leg. accts. 3 to Canton, 1911.

74. FO 369/202, Leg. cons. 5, 1909; and FO 369/1775, Leg. 409, 1922.

75. FO 228/1312, Shanghai 84, 1899; and FO 17/1421, Leg. cons. 30 and F.O. cons. 58, 1900.

76. FO 228/534, Canton, 6 Apr. 1874; FO 17/756, Leg. 154, 1877, and F.O. minutes thereon; FO 228/781, Leg. 377 and 478, 1885; FO 228/878, Hankow 2, 1889; FO 228/1440, Canton accts. 19, 1902; and FO 17/1606, Leg. cons. 68, 1903.

77. FO 369/8, Leg. cons. 157, 1905; FO 228/1616, Kiukiang tel., 7 Mar. 1906; and FO 228/1733, Tengyueh, 5 Nov. 1909.

78. FO 228/1181, Shanghai accts. 31, 1895; FO 17/1282, Leg. cons. 53, 1896; FO 369/8, Robertson to Cartwright, 28 Nov. 1905; and FO 369/11, Leg. cons. 59, 1906, and F.O. minute thereon.

79. Sir P. Manson-Bahr, *Patrick Manson* (London, 1962), p. 153.

80. PRO 30/33/7/2, Cartwright to Satow, 2 Nov. 1903.

81. FO 17/1169, F.O. to Treasury, 28 Oct., and Treasury to F.O., 2 Dec., 1893, and Sanderson's minute on the latter. For maiden name of Giles' first wife see FO 228/553, Hankow 1, 1875. For F.O. attitude to transfers away from the Far East see, for example, FO 17/597, Holt to F.O., 16 Dec. 1871, Hammond's minute.

82. For example, L.G.C. Graham was transferred from the China service. See FO 17/1651, Graham to F.O., 4 Nov. 1904, Sanderson's minute thereon, F.O. to Graham, 15 Nov. 1904, and *Foreign Office List, 1919*.

83. FO 369/454, F.O. reply to Treasury letter of 31 July 1912.

84. For example, PRO 30/33/8/2, B.C.G. Scott to Satow, 29 June 1901; and FO 228/1648, Hopkins to Kirke, 11 Oct. 1907.

85. FO 17/1102, Hughes to F.O., 8 Sept. 1890, Currie's minute thereon.

86. For example, FO 17/1257, F.O. to Treasury, 26 Feb. 1895 (Watters), and Beale to F.O., 16 Aug. 1895 (Parker).

87. FO 17/592, Leg. cons. 48, 1871; FO 17/635, Leg. cons. 27 and 35, 1872; FO 391/20, Wade to Hammond, 11 Apr. 1872; FO 17/666, Treasury to F.O., 25 Aug. 1873 (Neale); FO 17/1421, Leg. cons. 50 and 69, 1900; FO 17/1434, Peachey to F.O., 20 Mar. 1900; and FO 17/1452, F.O. minutes, July 1900 (Peachey).

88. FO 17/786, Mongan to F.O., 3 July 1878; FO 228/999, Tientsin accts. 10, 1884 (Davenport); FO 228/1214, Tientsin accts., 27 May 1896 (Bristow); PRO 30/33/8/2, Scott to Satow, 27 May 1901; and FO 228/1377, F.O. 230, 1901 (Carles).

89. FO 17/564-5, memorandum by Abbott (later Lord Tenterden), 2 Jan. 1870.

90. FO 391/1, Alcock to Hammond, 24 Jan. 1866; FO 17/538, Alcock to Hammond, 18 July 1868; FO 391/2, Alcock to Hammond, 1 Jan. 1869 (Payne); FO

17/659, Leg. cons. 80 and 93, 1873; FO 17/679, Leg. cons. 19, 1874; and FO 17/688, F.O. to Murray, 7 Oct., and Murray's brother to F.O., 5 Nov., 1874 (Murray).

91. FO 17/538, Alcock to Hammond, 18 July 1868; FO 228/447, F.O. 252, 1868; FO 17/642, Payne to F.O., 10 Apr. 1872, and F.O. reply (Payne); and FO 17/634, F.O. cons. 72, 1872 (Howlett).

92. FO 17/1683, F.O. to Bennett, 18 Feb. and 8 Mar., Bennett to F.O., 26 Feb., and F.O. minute thereon, 1905; and FO 17/1685, F.O. to Treasury, 11 May, and related minutes, and Treasury to F.O., 15 June, 1905.

93. FO 228/425, F.O. 94, 1867, and FO 17/694, Treasury to F.O., 24 Sept., and F.O. reply, 1873; FO 17/360, F.O. 175, 1864, and FO 17/528, Leg. cons. 45, 1869, F.O. minutes; and FO 17/538, solicitors to F.O., 13 Feb. 1869.

94. FO 391/2, Alcock to Hammond, 18 Apr. 1868; FO 17/556-7, Leg. cons. 89 (to Clarendon), cons. 28 (to Granville) with F.O. minute thereon, and F.O. (Granville), 16 Dec. 1870; FO 391/19, Wade to Hammond, 17 Mar. and 18 July 1871; and FO 17/592-3, Leg. cons. 85 and F.O. cons. 45, 1871.

95. FO 17/635-6, Leg. cons. 4, 43, and 128, 1872; FO 228/515, Leg. 7 and 9 to Hankow and Hankow 31 and 32, 1872, and Hankow, 4 Nov. 1872; FO 228/517, Hornby to Wade, 1 Aug. 1872; FO 17/633, Leg. 223, 1872; FO 17/643, Hammond to Mrs Caine, 22 Aug. 1872; FO 17/652, Leg. 10, 1873; *North-China Herald*, 26 July and 2 and 9 Aug. 1873, reports of court proceedings; FO 17/694, Hornby cons. 13 to F.O., 1873; FO 228/524, Shanghai 51 and 56, 1873; Hornby, *Autobiography*, p. 310; and FO 17/666, Treasury to F.O., 14 Aug. 1873.

96. FO 228/524, Shanghai 98, 1873; FO 17/694, Balfour to F.O., 29 Dec. 1873, Tenterden's minute, 25 Feb. 1874, and F.O. 4 to Shanghai, 1874; FO 17/679, Leg. cons. 21, 1874; FO 228/540, Shanghai 5 and 13, 1874; England and Wales probate records, 1920; Hornby, *Autobiography*, p. 310; and *The Times*, marriage announcement, 19 Sept. 1900.

97. FO 228/1226, Hankow, 27 Apr. 1896, and 30, 1896; FO 228/1212, Leg. tel. to Hankow, 12 May 1896, and Hankow accts. 8, 1896; FO 17/1282, Leg. cons. 24, 1896; FO 228/1213, Leg. accts. 38 to Shanghai, 1896; FO 228/1241, Shanghai accts. 23, 1897; and FO 17/1366, F.O. to Treasury, 21 Jan. 1898.

98. FO 17/592, Leg. cons. 107, 1871; FO 17/679, Leg. cons. 20 and 40, 1874, and Tenterden's minute on the latter; FO 17/689, Mitford to Tenterden, 30 July 1874; FO 17/678, F.O. cons. 60, 1874; FO 228/576, Fraser to Wade, 31 Dec. 1875, and Wade to Fraser, 25 Mar. 1876 (Fraser); FO 391/19, Wade to Hammond, 26 Jan. 1867; FO 228/441, Tientsin 43 and Leg. 19 to Tientsin, 1867; FO 17/592, Leg. cons. 30, 1871; FO 17/635, Leg. cons., 1 May 1872; and FO 17/658, Leg. cons. 13, 1873 (Goddard).

99. FO 17/562, Carroll to F.O., 20 Sept. 1870, F.O. minutes; FO 17/730, Leg. cons. 82, 1876, and F.O. minutes thereon; and FO 17/761, Leg. cons. 4 and 19, 1876.

Notes to Chapter 15

1. FO 228/1341, Salisbury to MacDonald, tel., 21 Sept. 1900.
2. FO 228/2510, Leg. tel. 3 to Shanghai, 1906.
3. Lo Hui-min, *Correspondence of G.E. Morrison*, Vol. I, p. 166.
4. FO 228/1663, Pakhoi 18, 1907; FO 228/1734, Tientsin, 18 Oct. 1909; and FO 228/1757, Canton, 22 July 1910.

5. FO 228/1452, Amoy 5, 1902; and FO 228/1724, Amoy 14, 1909.
6. FO 228/4302, Amoy, 25 Apr. 1930.
7. FO 228/2137, Chefoo 6, 1909.
8. FO 228/1797, Amoy, 18 July 1911.
9. FO 228/1625, Chinkiang, 9 Aug. 1906.
10. FO 228/1734, Tientsin, 14 Jan. 1909.
11. For example, FO 228/1762, Nanking 44, 1910.
12. FO 228/1696, Wuchow, 5 July 1908; and FO 228/1692, Amoy 10 and Chinkiang 50, 1908.
13. FO 228/1486, Tientsin accts. 27, 1903; FO 228/1594, Tientsin, 14 Jan. 1905; FO 228/1664, Hankow, 8 July 1907; and FO 228/1697, Hankow 2, 1908.
14. FO 17/1645, Leg., 2 Nov. 1904, and F.O. minute thereon; FO 228/1535, Canton accts. 23 and 30, 1904; FO 228/1548, Canton 118, 1904; FO 228/1576, Canton accts. 3, 1905; FO 228/1614, Canton accts. 6, 1906; and FO 228/1569, Leg. 2, 1905.
15. FO 228/1948, Leg. 18 to Mukden, 1915.
16. FO 228/1550, Chungking, 30 Oct. 1904.
17. FO 228/1406, Nanking 19, 1901.
18. FO 228/1659, Chinkiang 21, 1907; FO 228/1728, Chinkiang 34 and 46, 1909; and FO 228/1759, Chinkiang 7 and 12, 1910.
19. FO 228/1564, Wuchow 2, 7, and 8, 1904; and FO 228/1594, Wuchow 1, 1905.
20. FO 228/1645, Leg. 216, 1907; and FO 228/1594, Wuchow 12, 1905.
21. FO 228/2873, Ichang 65 and 66, 1921, and Leg. minute on the latter.
22. FO 371/11693, Wellesley's minute on Leg. 369, 1926; and FO 228/4121, Teichman's minute on Tsinan 28, 1930.
23. FO 228/1569, Leg. 222, 1905.
24. FO 228/1660, Chungking, 30 June 1907; and FO 228/1731, Ningpo, 24 Dec. 1909.
25. FO 228/1693, Chengtu, 20 July 1908; and FO 228/1759, Ichang, 1 Jan. 1910, and Jordan's minute thereon.
26. FO 228/1458, Hankow tels. 54, 59, 60, and 109, and despatch 54, 1902, Leg. tel. 51 to Hankow, 1902, and Hankow, 23 Aug. 1902; and FO 228/1423, Leg. 339, 1902.
27. FO 228/3430, Changsha 3 and Hankow 31, 1926, and Leg. minutes on the latter.
28. FO 228/3254, Mukden 37, 1923.
29. FO 228/1389, Ningpo 35, 1901.
30. FO 228/1692, Chinkiang 50, 1908.
31. FO 228/1714, Canton accts., 9 Mar. 1909; and FO 228/1826, memorandum by Tours, 11 Sept. 1914.
32. FO 228/1648, Shanghai 97, 1907.
33. FO 228/2510, Pitzipios to Warren, 18 Dec. 1905.
34. See, for example, FO 228/1648, Wuchow accts. 3, 1907; FO 228/1716, Shanghai accts. 35, 1909; and FO 228/1934, Chungking accts. 9, 1915.
35. FO 369/565, Bristow to F.O., 29 Nov. 1913.
36. FO 228/1464, Tientsin 43, 1902.
37. FO 228/1594, Tientsin, 14 Jan. 1905; FO 228/1734, Tientsin, 14 Jan. 1909; and FO 228/1756, Tientsin accts. 5, 1910.
38. FO 228/1693, Ichang 5, 1908.
39. FO 228/1958, Leg. cons. 93, 1916; and FO 369/866, Leg. cons. 84 and 136, 1916.
40. PRO 30/33/9/1, Willis to Satow, 9 Sept. 1903; FO 228/1614, O'Brien-Butler

to Kirke, 28 Nov. 1906; FO 228/1645, Leg. 216, 1907; FO 228/1569, Leg. 222, 1905; and FO 228/1555, Kiukiang 13, 1904.
41. FO 17/1490, Leg. cons. 33, 1901, Satow to Cockerell, 9 Apr. 1901, and F.O. minute on the latter.
42. FO 17/843, CSC to F.O., Mar. 1880; and *Journal of the North China Branch of the Royal Asiatic Society*, Vol. LIII (Shanghai, 1922), obituary.
43. See, for example, FO 228/1664, Hankow, 8 Apr. 1907, and FO 228/1761, Hankow 66, 1910, and 21 July 1910.
44. FO 228/1458, Hankow, 23 Aug. 1902; FO 228/1647, Hankow accts. 21, 1907; FO 369/9, Satow to Cartwright, 11 Jan. 1906; and FO 350/5, Jordan to Campbell, 9 July 1908.
45. PRO 30/33/7/9, Hillier to Satow, 9 Jan. 1901; and FO 228/790, Canton 66, 1885.
46. FO 228/1501, Nanking, 6 Jan. 1903.
47. Lo Hui-min, *Correspondence of G.E. Morrison*, Vol. I, p. 155; PRO 30/33/8/10, Fraser to Satow, 31 Dec. 1901; FO 228/1457, Hankow 1 and 2, 1902; FO 228/1502, Hankow tels., 14 and 20 Apr. 1903; FO 228/1440, Hankow accts. 27, and Leg. accts. 20 to Hankow, 1902; FO 228/1595, Hankow, 11 July, 16 Oct., and 26 Dec. 1905; FO 228/1632, Hankow, 9 Jan. 1906; and FO 228/1664, Hankow, 16 Apr. 1907.
48. FO 228/1381, Canton accts. 7, 1901; FO 17/1504, Colonial Office to F.O., 18 May 1901, and F.O. minutes thereon; PRO 30/33/8/2, Scott to Satow, 27 May 1901; PRO 30/33/7/1, Satow tels. to Lansdowne, 31 May and 7 June 1901; and FO 17/1490, Satow to Barrington, 15 Aug. 1901.
49. For example, FO 228/1384, Canton 8 and 9, 1901.
50. FO 17/1490, Satow to Cockerell, 9 Apr., and Leg. tel., 31 May, 1901; PRO 30/33/8/23, Mansfield to Satow, 7 May 1902; FO 17/1490, Satow to Barrington, 15 Aug. 1901; PRO 30/33/7/2, Satow tel. to Barrington, 18 Jan. 1902; FO 17/1644, Satow to Hardinge, 12 Feb. 1904; PRO 30/33/8/2, Scott to Satow, 24 May 1902; FO 228/1440, Canton accts. 9, 1902, and tel., 20 May 1902; and FO 17/1543, Mansfield to F.O., 7 Aug. 1902.
51. PRO 30/33/8/2, Scott to Satow, 22 Sept. 1903; FO 17/1606, Leg. cons. 117, 1903; FO 17/1677, Satow to Cartwright, 9 May 1905; FO 228/1548, for approximate date of Scott's return to Canton in 1904; and FO 228/1576, Canton accts. 18, 1905.
52. FO 17/1677, Satow to Cartwright, 9 May 1905, F.O. minute; and FO 228/2623, Canton, 12 Sept. 1907.
53. FO 228/1454, Canton, 24 Oct. 1902; and FO 228/1498, Canton 22 and 31, 1903.
54. Wilkinson recorded the blood-sipping in private papers. See also FO 228/1594, Leg. tel. 1 to Wuchow and Wuchow tel., 6 May, 1905, and Lo Hui-min, *Correspondence of G.E. Morrison*, Vol. I, p. 407.
55. FO 228/1499, Chengtu 2 and 7, 1903; FO 228/1807, Tengyueh, 31 Mar. 1911; FO 228/1660, Chengtu, 1 June 1907; FO 350/4, Jordan to Campbell, 13 June 1907; FO 228/2712, Leg. 194, 1916; and FO 228/1661, Canton, 19 Jan. 1907, and 44, 1907.
56. FO 881/8972, Colonial Office to F.O., 6 June 1903, F.O. minute thereon, and Satow to Hardinge, 15 June 1903; FO 228/2156–8; FO 228/3291, Shanghai, 6 Feb. 1922, and FO 405/272, Leg. 250, 1933; FO 228/1694, Canton, 22 Aug. 1908; and FO 228/1724, Canton, 23 July 1909.
57. FO 228/1569, Leg. 154, 1905; and FO 228/1677, F.O. 79, 1908.
58. FO 228/2151; and FO 369/201, Leg. tel., 2 Jan. 1909.
59. FO 228/1740, F.O. 127, 1910.

60. FO 228/1797, Canton tel. and private letter, both 9 June 1911; FO 228/1785, Lugard to Jordan, 10 July 1911; and FO 800/245, Max Müller to Alston, 2 Nov. 1910.

61. FO 228/2440–1, F.O. 1 and 47, 1911; FO 228/3484, Jamieson to Alston, 28 Sept. 1922; and FO 228/2712, May to Jordan, 25 Aug. 1916.

62. FO 228/1411, Tengyueh 1, 1901; FO 228/1441, Leg. tel. to Ningpo, 8 Mar., Ningpo tel., 9 Mar., and Ningpo, 4 Dec., all of 1902; PRO 30/33/8/21, Wilkinson to Satow, 10, 11, and 14 Mar. 1902; FO 228/1504, copy of death register entry, 12 Mar. 1902; FO 228/1425, Leg. cons. 21, 1902, and tel., 17 Mar. 1902; PRO 30/33/7/9, Townley to Satow, 12 Feb. 1903; FO 228/1508, Wilkinson to Satow from Maymyo, 1 Oct. 1903; FO 228/1506, Tengyueh 3, 1903; and FO 228/1727, Chengtu 38, 1909.

63. For Mackinnon see FO 17/1490, Satow to Barrington, 15 Aug. 1901; PRO 30/33/8/9, Brady to Satow, 6 Feb. 1904; FO 228/1486, Litton to Ottewill, 10 Nov. 1903; FO 17/1606, Leg. cons. 118 and 130, 1903; FO 228/1537, Litton to Ottewill, 9 Jan. 1904; FO 228/1535, Canton accts. 4, 1904, Satow's minute, and accts. 19, 1904; FO 17/1644, Satow to Hardinge, 12 Feb. 1904; PRO 30/33/8/2, Campbell to Satow, 9 Jan., – Feb., 10 Apr., and 15 May 1904; FO 17/1676–7, Satow to Cockerell, 23 Mar. 1905, and F.O. cons. 81, 1905; PRO 30/33/7/4,. Cockerell to Satow, 13 July and 17 Aug. 1905; PRO 30/33/9/10, Mackinnon to Satow, 15 July 1905; PRO 30/33/8/1, Mansfield to Satow, 4 Oct. 1905; FO 369/9, Satow to Cartwright, 11 Jan. 1906; FO 369/11, Leg. cons. 51 and 127, Carnegie to Barrington, 25 July and 19 Sept., F.O. minutes, 28 Sept. and 3 Nov., and Leg. tel., 3 Oct., all of 1906; and FO 369/66, Carnegie to Barrington, 19 Feb., Mackinnon's father to Barrington, 12 Mar., Leg. cons. 11, and Amoy 1 to F.O., all of 1907.

64. FO 17/1644, Leg. cons. 75, 1904; FO 228/1434, F.O. 198, 1902; FO 228/1598, Tengyueh 1, 1905; FO 228/1562, Tengyueh 9, 1904; FO 228/1525, F.O. 226, 1904; FO 228/1557, Litton to Ottewill, Apr. 1904; and FO 228/1579, Tengyueh accts. 10, 1905.

65. FO 228/1461, Tengyueh 1, Leg. minute thereon, and amendments to draft of Leg. 4 to Tengyueh, all of 1902; FO 228/1562, Tengyueh 9, 1904; and FO 228/1508, Yunnanfu 18, 1903.

66. FO 17/1677, Leg. cons. 55, 1905; FO 369/8, Leg. cons. 148, Satow to Cockerell, 13 Nov., and Litton to F.O., 15 Dec., and F.O. minute thereon, all of 1905; and Foreign Office List, 1906.

67. FO 228/1579, Tengyueh accts. 15, 1905; FO 17/1612, F.O. 249, 1906; FO 369/8, Leg. 73 and cons. 47, 1906, and solicitors to F.O., 17 Feb. 1906; PRO 30/33/9/3, Ottewill to Satow, 26 Apr. 1906; and FO 917/1206.

68. FO 228/1461, Tengyueh 1, 1902, and FO 228/1598, Tengyueh 18, 1905; FO 800/245, Rose to Jordan, 22 Dec. 1909; and FO 228/1733, Rose to Jordan, 5 Nov. 1909.

69. FO 228/1807, Rose's paper, 26 Apr. 1911; FO 228/1733, Tengyueh 4, 1909, and 6 Aug. 1909; FO 228/1455, Chungking 19, 1902; FO 228/1733, Tengyueh, 21 Apr. and 27 May 1909; FO 228/1764, Tengyueh 36, 1910; and FO 228/1795, Tengyueh accts. 9, 1911, and FO 228/1756, Tengyueh 6 and 16, 1910, and Rose to Eastes, 30 July 1910.

70. FO 228/1733, Tengyueh, 8 and 22 Oct. 1909; FO 228/1764, Tengyueh, 11 July, 17 Oct., with Leg. minute thereon, and 25 Oct., and tel., 15 Oct., all of 1910; FO 350/7, Jordan to Campbell, 4 Aug. 1911; and FO 228/1947, Ningpo, 5 Oct. 1915.

71. FO 228/873, F.O. 103, 1889; FO 228/1523, F.O. 67, 1904; C. Skrine and P. Nightingale, Macartney at Kashgar (London, 1973), p. 151; and FO 369/1340, Leg. cons. 183, 1919.

72. FO 17/1644, Leg. cons. 47 and 70, 1904; FO 228/1555, Kongmoon 1, 1904, and 21 July and 31 Dec. 1904; FO 228/1536, Kongmoon tel., 7 June 1904, and accts. 20, 1904; FO 228/1592, Kongmoon, 31 Mar. 1905; FO 228/1832, Shanghai accts. 42, 1912; FO 228/1528, Tebbitt to Ottewill, 21 May 1904; PRO 30/33/7/10, Carnegie to Satow, 19 Apr. 1905; and FO 228/1569, Leg. 222, 1905.

73. FO 17/1677, Leg. cons. 11, 1905; FO 228/1591, Changsha 1, 2, and 10, 1905, and 5 July 1905; PRO 30/33/8/3, Flaherty to Satow, 23 Apr. 1905; FO 369/136, Leg. cons. 119, 1908; Hewlett, *Forty Years in China*, p. 50; and FO 228/1616, Leg. tels., 15 and 17 Sept. to Hankow and Hankow tel., 18 Sept. 1906.

74. FO 228/1628; FO 228/1662, Changsha 11, 1907; and FO 228/1714, Tsinan accts. 13, 1909.

75. FO 17/1160, F.O. cons. 21, 1893; FO 17/1205, Leg. cons. 39, 1894; FO 17/1490, Satow to Barrington, 15 Aug. 1901; PRO 30/33/8/9, Brady to Satow, 6 Feb. 1904; FO 369/10, Leg. cons. 30, 1906; FO 228/1680, Hankow, 9 Jan. 1908; FO 369/132, Leg. cons. 34, 1908, and Shanghai cons. 4 to F.O., 1908; FO 228/1793, Shanghai accts. 44, 1911; and *Foreign Office Lists*.

76. PRO 30/33/9/10, Hewlett to Satow, 25 Feb. 1904; Lambeth Palace marriage registers; and FO 228/1689, Fox to Kirke, 4 May 1908.

77. FO 228/3344, Teichman's minute on Chengtu 42, 1919; and FO 228/3584, Teichman's minute on Hewlett to Lampson, 19 Nov. 1927.

78. FO 228/1695, Changsha, 24 Oct. 1908; FO 228/1758, Changsha, 25 Jan. 1910; Hewlett, *Forty Years in China*, p. 52; FO 228/1714, Hewlett to Kirke, 21 Feb. 1909; FO 228/1726, Changsha, 1 Oct. 1909; FO 228/1758, Changsha, 25 Jan. 1910; FO 228/2184–5, Hankow tels. 22, 23, 26, 29, and 39, Hankow, 17 Apr., Leg. tel. to Hankow, 21 Apr., Hewlett from Hankow, 28 Apr., and Leg. 128 and 142, all of 1910; FO 800/245, Max Müller to Campbell, 4 July 1910; and FO 228/1753, Hankow accts. 17, 1910, and 15 July 1910.

79. FO 228/1592, Satow to Clennell, 1 Dec. 1905; FO 228/1628, Tsinan 3, 1906, Tsinan, 23 Apr. 1906, and Satow's minute on the latter; and FO 228/1662, Tsinan, 19 Nov. 1907.

80. FO 17/1644, Satow to Hardinge, 12 Feb. 1904; FO 17/1643, F.O. cons. 14, 1904; FO 369/67, Treasury to F.O., 14 Sept. 1907, and Leg. cons. 100, 1907; FO 228/1693, Antung 8 and 21, 1908; FO 369/203, Leg. cons. 16 and 17, 1909; FO 369/269, Dufferin's minute, 10 Aug., and F.O. to Russell, 16 Aug., 1909; FO 369/282, Russell to F.O., 19 Feb. 1910, and action thereon; *Foreign Office List*, 1921; and *Who Was Who*, 1941–1950.

81. FO 228/1716, Mukden, 3 Aug. 1909; FO 369/206, Leg. cons. 109 and 143, 1909; FO 369/811, Leg. cons. 28, 1915; and FO 369/811, Leg. cons. 28, 1915.

82. FO 228/1633, Mukden 2, 1906; FO 228/1789, Jordan to Mortimore, 15 Nov. 1911; FO 228/1681, Mukden accts. 5, 1908, and 28 Nov. 1908; and FO 228/1754, Mukden accts. 19, 1909.

83. FO 369/206, Leg. cons. 109 and 143,1909; FO 228/2383, Fox to Jordan, 14 July 1911; FO 369/363, Leg. cons. 27, 1911; FO 228/1803, Harbin 4, 1911; and FO 228/1873, Harbin, 11 Jan. 1913.

84. FO 228/1263, Leg. 154, 1898, and FO 228/1284, Chungking, 30 July 1898; FO 228/1478, F.O. 36, 1903; FO 17/1606, Leg. cons. 36, 1903; FO 228/1550, Leg. 9 to Chengtu, 1904, and Chengtu, 17 Dec. 1904; FO 228/1562, Tengyueh 9, 1904; and FO 228/1629, Chengtu 71A, 1906.

85. Hosie, *Western China*, pp. 85–6; PRO 30/33/8/5, Hosie to Satow, 5 Mar. and 25 May 1904, and Goffe to Satow, 5 June 1905; PRO 30/33/9/10, Hosie to Satow, 3 Mar. 1905; and FO 228/1591, Leg. tel. 8 to Chengtu, 1905.

86. PRO 30/33/8/5 and /9/10, Hosie to Satow, 18 July and 30 Oct. 1904 and 7 May 1905; PRO 30/33/8/2 and /5, Campbell to Satow, 13 Sept. and 30 Nov. 1904

and 11 and 18 Feb. 1905; PRO 30/33/9/10, Fox to Satow, 11 Mar. 1905; *The Times*, marriage announcement, 25 July 1905; FO 228/1660, Chengtu, 28 Feb. 1907; and FO 369/130, Leg. cons. 132, 1907.

87. FO 228/1660, Chengtu, 28 Feb. and 31 Mar. 1907; FO 228/1693, Chengtu, 28 Jan. 1908; FO 228/1904, Chengtu 47, 1914; FO 228/1800, Chungking, 14 Feb. 1911; and FO 228/1660, Chengtu, 4 Oct. 1907.

88. FO 369/201, Leg. cons. 26, 1909; and FO 228/1790, Chengtu, 5 June 1911.

89. FO 17/1644, Satow to Hardinge, 12 Feb. 1904; FO 350/4–5, Jordan to Campbell, 17 Oct. 1906 and 30 Apr. 1908; FO 228/1799, Chengtu tel. 5, tel., 15 Apr., despatches 7 and 40 with Leg. minutes on both despatches, and Leg. tel. 11 to Chengtu, all of 1911; and FO 228/1942, Chengtu 36, 1915.

Notes to Chapter 16

1. Clubb, *20th Century China*, pp. 55 and 58.
2. FO 800/119, Satow to Lansdowne, 8 Feb. 1901.
3. FO 228/3002, Macleay to Eastes, 27 Nov. 1923; and FO 228/3183, Amoy 26, 1923, Teichman's minute.
4. FO 228/3002, Wellesley to Macleay, 5 Apr. 1923; FO 228/2998, Canton 43, 1922; FO 228/2374, Mukden, 30 Jan. 1909, and FO 228/2384, Mukden, 28 Nov. 1911; FO 228/1838, Chengtu, 14 Dec. 1912; and FO 228/1840, Ningpo 23, 1912.
5. FO 228/2986, Mukden 70, 1919.
6. FO 228/1807, Tengyueh 27, 1911; FO 228/1835, Chinkiang 15, 1912, and 11 July 1912; FO 228/1843, Ichang 9, 1912; and FO 228/1593, Wuchow 16, 1915.
7. FO 228/3322, Hangchow 5, 1918; and FO 228/3284, Kiukiang, 21 July 1919.
8. FO 228/3288, Chefoo, 5 Feb. 1921.
9. FO 228/1804, Ningpo tel. 4, 1911; FO 228/1809, Wuhu tel., 14 Nov. 1911; FO 228/1801, Hangchow 16, 1911; FO 228/1803, Ichang 16, 1911; FO 228/1798, Changsha 45, 1911, and FO 228/1837, Changsha 9, 1912; FO 228/1797, Amoy 27 and 28, 1911; and FO 228/1800, Foochow 35, 1911.
10. FO 228/1798, Chefoo 13, 1911; and FO 228/1835, Chefoo, 11 Mar. 1912, and 10 and 15, 1912.
11. FO 228/1807, Swatow 35, 1911; and FO 228/1840, Swatow 6, 10 with Jordan's minute thereon, and 36, 1912, and 30 July 1912.
12. FO 228/2233, Pakhoi, 20 June 1907; and FO 228/1663, Pakhoi, 24 June 1907.
13. FO 228/1804, Major to Jordan 10 and 11, 1911.
14. FO 228/1800, Chungking 46 and 48, 1911, and FO 228/1785, Teichman to Chancery, 27 Dec. 1911; FO 228/1799, Chengtu 92, 93, and 94, 1911, and 23 Dec. 1911; FO 228/1827, Chengtu accts. 1 and 10, 1912; FO 228/1838, Leg. 1 to Chengtu, 1912; FO 350/8, Jordan to Tyrrell, 13 Mar. 1912; and FO 228/1870, Chungking 30, 1913, and 17 Nov. 1913.
15. FO 228/3273, Chungking, 27 June and 1 Oct. 1923.
16. *The Times*, 12 May 1939; and FO 228/1952, Yunnanfu, 2 Aug. 1915.
17. FO 228/2617, Nanking 24, 1910; FO 228/1801, Hankow tel. 52, despatch 92, with Jordan's minute thereon, despatch 101, and Hankow, 10, 20, and 29 Nov., all of 1911; and FO 228/1841, Hankow 17, 1912.
18. FO 228/1804, Nanking 36–41, and 44, 1911; FO 228/1836, Nanking 25, 1912; and FO 228/1831, Nanking accts. 9, 1912.

19. FO 228/1806 and FO 228/1844; and FO 350/8, Jordan to Tyrrell, 13 Mar., and Jordan to Langley, 4 Aug., both of 1912.
20. FO 228/1797, Canton tel. 57, 1911; and FO 228/1836, Canton 1 and 7 and tel. 6, 1912, and 15 Apr. 1912.
21. FO 228/1836, Canton 26 and tels. 26 and 39, with Jordan's minute on the latter tel., Leg. tel. 18 and despatch 28 to Canton, and Canton, 10 Sept., all of 1912.
22. Clubb, *20th Century China*, p. 49; FO 228/1874, Nanking, 28 Oct. 1913, and 88, 1913; FO 228/1852, Leg. 380, 1913; FO 228/1909, Nanking 1, 1914; and FO 228/1982, Nanking 146, 1916.
23. FO 228/1852, Leg. 407, 1913; and Rasmussen, *China Trader*, p. 118.
24. FO 228/1875, Leg. tel. 20 to Shanghai, 1913; and FO 228/3344, Chengtu 42, 1919, Jordan's minute. For Jordan's personal liking for China see FO 350/5–6, Jordan to Campbell, 12 Dec. 1907 and 18 Sept. 1908, and Jordan to Alston, 7 Jan. 1910.
25. For an example of treaty port internationalism see FO 228/1909, Newchwang 61, 1914.
26. FO 228/1946, Kiukiang, 9 Oct. 1915; FO 228/1947, Pakhoi, 24 Apr. 1915; FO 228/1909, Newchwang 44, 1914, FO 228/3283, Ichang, 6 Apr. 1918, and FO 228/2736, Swatow 11, 1916; FO 228/1942, Chefoo 3 and Leg. 2 to Chefoo, 1915; FO 228/1941, Canton, 30 June 1915, and Jordan's minute thereon; FO 228/1950, Jordan to Fraser, 16 Dec. 1915; FO 228/1907, Hankow 101, 1914; and Teichman, *Affairs of China*, p. 75.
27. FO 228/3502, Mukden, 2 Feb. 1922.
28. FO 369/386, Porter to F.O., 3 Sept., F.O. minutes thereon, and F.O. to Porter, 12 Sept. 1914; FO 369/389, F.O. tel. 233, 1914; FO 369/808, Jordan to Alston, 30 Mar. 1915; FO 228/1950, Jordan to Rose, 17 Aug. 1915; FO 369/920, Leg. cons. 86, 1917; FO 228/2001, Leg. tel. to Hoihow, 6 June 1917; FO 369/984, Leg. tels. 969 and 987, and F.O. minutes on the latter; and FO 228/2000, Leg. to Amoy, 24 Sept. 1917.
29. FO 228/2987, Tsinan 19, 1920.
30. FO 228/1913, Tsinan 24 and 29, 1914, and Leg. to Tsinan, 28 Nov. 1914.
31. FO 228/2753, Yunnanfu tel. 54, 1915, letter, 30 Dec. 1915, and tel. 5, 1916, and Leg. tel. 31 to Yunnanfu, 1915: FO 228/1981, Leg. tel. 1 to Mukden, 1916; and FO 228/1985, Yunnanfu, 2 Aug. 1916, Jordan's minute.
32. FO 228/2736, Canton 63, 1916.
33. FO 228/3011, F.O. 51, 1925, and Leg. minutes thereon.
34. FO 228/2712, Canton 115 and 119, 1916; and FO 228/2993, Ichang 46, 1921.
35. FO 371/12398, FO 371/12400–1, FO 371/12416, and FO 371/12474, Tengyueh 35 and 37, 1926, and 1, 1927, with F.O. minutes on all three, India Office to F.O., 19 Jan. 1927, and Leg. tels. 46 and 290, 1927; and FO 228/3275, Tengyueh 36, 1926.
36. FO 228/3488, Wuchow tel., 21 Feb., tel. 3 and despatches 5, 6, and 10, Leg. tel. 6 to Canton and despatch 23 to Canton, Canton tels. 3 and 4, and Jamieson tel. from Wuchow, 2 Mar., all of 1919; and FO 369/1396, Leg. 119, 1920.
37. FO 228/2784, Harbin tel. 42 and despatch 51, 1921; and FO 228/3254, Leg. to Tengyueh, 26 July, Sly to Teichman, 30 July, Tengyueh 21 and 24, and Yunnanfu 22, all of 1923.
38. FO 228/3272, Swatow, 8 Oct. 1921.
39. FO 228/2996, Orpen-Palmer to Alston, 3 May 1922, and Leg. 185, 1922; FO 369/1942, Turner to Kelsey, 7 Oct. 1927; and FO 369/2188, Treasury to F.O., 30 Dec. 1931.
40. FO 228/2980, Changsha 10, 1918, and 1 Apr. 1918.

41. FO 228/3172–3, Kiukiang 23, 1920, and 23 Oct. 1920, and Kiukiang 6, 1922; and FO 228/3528, Hankow 15, 27, and 30 and Leg. 76, 1923.

42. FO 228/1971, Chengtu accts. 7, 1916.

43. Teichman, *Eastern Tibet*, Parts III–V; FO 228/2582–4, F.O. tel. 193, Leg. tel. 17 to Chengtu, Leg. tel. to King, 4 Sept., and Chengtu 69, all of 1913; and FO 228/2584, Tachienlu 19, 1914.

44. *China as it Really Is*; and FO 228/2583–7, Tachienlu 10, 1913, and 19 and 23, 1914, Leg. tel. 130, 1914, and F.O. tels. 119, 128, and 334, 1914, with Jordan's minute on the last.

45. FO 228/2960, Tachienlu 29, 1921; King, *China in Turmoil*, p. 38; FO 228/2587, Chengtu tels. 14 and 15 and Leg. tels. 5 and 6 to Chengtu, 1915; FO 371/2318, Leg. 92, 1915, and F.O. minutes thereon; FO 228/2588, Leg. tel. 225, 1915; and FO 228/2749, F.O. 12, 1916.

46. FO 228/2588, F.O. tel. 211 and Leg. tel. 289, 1915; and FO 228/1971, Chengtu accts. 7, 1916.

47. FO 17/1644, Leg. cons. 37, 1904; FO 228/1755, Shanghai accts. 20, 1910, and FO 369/365, Coales to F.O., 3 June 1911; and FO 228/2749, Tachienlu 1, 3, and 5, 1917, Chengtu tel., 28 Apr. 1917, Leg. tel. 18 to Chengtu, 1917, and F.O. tel. 316, 1917.

48. See Teichman, *North-West China*.

49. FO 369/1099, Leg. cons. 92, 1919.

50. FO 228/2749, Tachienlu 18, 1917; FO 228/2956–7; and FO 371/5330, Leg. 663, 1920.

51. FO 369/1592, Leg. 110 and 494, 1921; FO 228/2960–2, Tachienlu, 21 June 1920, and Teichman's minute thereon, Tachienlu 24, 1920, and 48, 1921, and King to Barton, 26 Mar. 1921; FO 369/1774, Leg. tel. 135, 1922; and FO 228/2963, Leg. 482, 1923.

52. Rin-chen Lha-mo, *We Tibetans* (London, 1926), p. vii; FO 369/1885, Pratt's minute, 1 Dec. 1925, and succeeding F.O. minutes; FO 369/2076, Ellen Wilkinson to Noel Baker, 5 Sept. 1929, and reply; FO 369/2129, L'Estange Malone to Dalton, 8 July 1930, and reply; and England and Wales probate records, 1950.

53. FO 228/3257, Chengtu 48, 1924.

54. FO 228/1942, Chengtu, 16 Aug. 1915.

55. FO 228/1752, Chengtu accts. 17, 1910, and FO 228/1837, Chungking 8, 1912; FO 228/1942, Chengtu 28 and 69 and Leg. minute on the latter, Chengtu, 28 May and 16 Aug., and Leg. to Chengtu, 1 July and 4 Oct., all of 1915; and FO 228/1979.

56. FO 369/866, Fox to F.O., 6 June 1916; FO 228/1973, Ichang, 1 Mar. 1916, and accts. 8, 1916; FO 369/1095, Leg. cons. 95, 1919, and Hewlett to F.O. from leave, 23 July 1919; FO 369/1100, Leg. cons. 170, 1919; and FO 369/2074, Leg. 89, 1929.

57. FO 228/2001, Chengtu accts. 1, 1917; FO 228/2744; FO 228/2981; FO 228/2986–90, including Teichman's minute on Chengtu 57, 1920.

58. FO 369/1592, Leg. 110, 1921.

Notes to Chapter 17

1. FO 17/1490, Satow to Barrington, 15 Aug. 1901; F.O. confidential print 7973, July 1903, evidence to Walrond committee on consular service; FO 369/66, Leg. cons. 26, 1907, and minutes by Cartwright and Langley thereon; FO 369/184,

F.O. minutes, 16 Dec. 1905 and 19 Feb. 1906 quoting Satow's views, also Barrington's minute, May 1908; and FO 369/432, F.O. to CSC, 31 May 1911. For persons making recommendations see, for example, FO 369/10, list of nominations for Oct. 1906 entrance examination.

2. FO 369/1319, report of Steel-Maitland committee on consular service, 1919, Appendix I.

3. Grafftey-Smith, *Bright Levant*, p. 5. For China entrants' backgrounds see Appendix II.

4. T. Beck, *Heroes of the Horrors* (New York, 1975), p. 108.

5. FO 369/528 (20780), F.O. minutes, 1912.

6. FO 369/528, Leg. cons. 137, 1911.

7. FO 369/66, Leg. cons. 26, 1907, and CSC to F.O. 3 Oct. 1907; FO 369/269, CSC to F.O., 6 Nov. 1909; and FO 228/1888, F.O. cons. 78, 1914, Jordan's minute.

8. FO 369/342, CSC to F.O., 7 Oct. 1910, and F.O. minute thereon; FO 369/432, F.O. to CSC, 23 Mar., and CSC reply, 26 Mar., 1911; FO 369/435, CSC to F.O., 27 Sept. 1911, F.O. to Treasury, 23 Nov. 1911, and Treasury reply; FO 369/528, CSC to F.O., 1 and 18 Oct. and 8 Dec. 1912, Leg. cons. 107, 1912, with F.O. minutes on the last three, and F.O. to CSC, 31 Oct. 1912; FO 369/686, Leg. cons. 50, 1914; FO 228/1826, Barton to Jordan, 27 Nov. 1914; FO 369/808, Leg. cons. 175, 1914; FO 369/641, CSC to F.O., 22 Oct. 1913, and F.O. minutes thereon; and FO 369/811, Leg. cons. 40, 1915.

9. FO 369/432, Leg. 26, 1911, and F.O. to CSC, 31 May 1911; and FO 369/528 (20780), F.O. minutes, 1912.

10. FO 369/1097, DOT to F.O., 26 July 1919; and FO 369/1345, CSC to F.O., 23 Dec. 1919; and FO 369/1348, reply to Parliamentary Question, 18 Nov. 1919.

11. See FO 369/2246, Ingram to Crowe, 21 July 1932.

12. FO 369/2199, CSC to F.O., 29 Dec. 1930 and 26 Sept. 1931.

13. FO 369/1349 (K 3333), Sherwood's minute, 3 Jan. 1920.

14. FO 369/1799, F.O. to CSC, 1 and 23 May, and CSC to F.O., 15 May, 1922; FO 369/2141, CSC to F.O., 23 Apr. and 9 and 15 May 1930; FO 369/2199, CSC to F.O., 15 May 1931; FO 369/2257, CSC to F.O., 5 Apr. 1932, Crowe's minute; and FO 369/2400, CSC to F.O., 3 Apr. 1935, F.O. minute.

15. FO 369/1940, Montgomery to Lampson, 25 Apr. 1927; FO 369/2129, Montgomery to Lampson, 16 Oct. 1930; and FO 369/2141, CSC to F.O., 30 Oct. and 24 Nov. 1930, and Crowe's minute on the latter.

16. See, for example, FO 369/2257, CSC to F.O., 13 Oct. 1932; FO 369/2316, report of F.O. committee on Levant service, Jan. 1933; FO 369/1885, Leg. tel. 503, 1926, Crowe's minute;. FO 369/2357, Crowe to Mounsey, 14 Aug. 1934; and FO 371/18101, Crowe to Orde, 7 Sept. 1934, Scott's minute.

17. FO 369/1940, Leg. tel. 1724, 1927, Crowe's minute.

18. FO 369/1776 (K 18952), F.O. minutes on discontent in the Far Eastern services, 1922; FO 369/641, Treasury to F.O., 3 Jan. 1913, F.O. minute; FO 369/1886, Macleay to Butler, quoted in Crowe's minute on Leg. tel. 503, 1926; and FO 369/2020, Leg. 1264, 1928.

19. FO 369/2316, report of F.O. committee on Levant service, Jan. 1933; FO 369/1867, Leg. 144, 1925; FO 369/1088, Leg. cons. 183, 1918; FO 369/1437 (K 1541), undated DOT memorandum about pay, 1920; and FO 369/921, China Association to F.O., 15 Feb. 1917.

20. FO 369/1885, Leg. tel. 503, 1926, Crowe's minutes; and FO 369/2347, Cadogan to Scott, 9 June 1934.

21. FO 369/1940, Montgomery to Lampson, 25 Apr. 1927.

22. FO 369/2129, Montgomery to Lampson, 16 Oct. 1930.

23. FO 369/1940, Leg. 246, 1927, and Leg. tel. 1724, 1927, Crowe's minute.

24. FO 369/1092, Leg. cons. 88, 1918, and cons. 89, 1919.
25. FO 228/1648, Hopkins to Kirke, 11 Oct. 1907; FO 228/1790, Sundius to Jordan, 28 June 1911; FO 369/454, Leg. cons. 58, Treasury to F.O., 31 July, and F.O. reply, and Treasury to F.O., 24 Aug., all of 1912, and Sundius to Alston, 23 Jan. 1913; and FO 369/559–60, further F.O. correspondence with Treasury about Sundius, and Leg. tel., 13 Mar., all of 1913.
26. FO 369/536, report of committee on consular service, 18 Nov. 1912; FO 369/1319, report of departmental committee on consular service, 19 Mar. 1919; FO 369/1940, Montgomery to Lampson, 25 Apr. 1927; FO 369/2020, Leg. 1264, 1928; FO 369/2073, Treasury to F.O., 14 Mar. 1929; FO 369/2243, Montgomery to Lampson, 18 Feb. 1932; and Platt, *Cinderella Service*, p. 225.
27. FO 369/282, Leg. cons. 7, 1910, and F.O. minutes thereon; FO 369/285, Max Müller to F.O., 2 Apr. 1910; and FO 369/982, Leg. tel. 270, 1918, and F.O. minute thereon.
28. FO 369/1090, Wilkinson to F.O., 10 Mar. 1919, privately printed correspondence relating to his retirement, and Gye's minutes of 3 and 12 Aug. 1919; and FO 369/1393, Butler's minute concerning Parliamentary Question, 2 Dec. 1919.
29. Cassels, W.S. Mayers, Mead, Miéville, H. Porter, Rose, Walker, and Wilton.
30. Gammon and Russell.
31. FO 17/1282, Leg. cons. 34, 1896; PRO 30/33/9/5, Hopkins to Satow, 2 Apr. 1901; FO 17/1490, Leg. cons., 15 Aug. 1901; FO 17/1685, Treasury to F.O., 23 June 1905; PRO 30/33/7/4, Cockerell to Satow, 13 July 1905; *London and China Express*, 24 Jan. 1913, obituary; and *The Times*, 23 Jan. 1913.
32. FO 228/1976, Tientsin accts. 6, 1916; and FO 369/865, Leg. cons. 18, and F.O. action thereon, Keown to F.O., 18 Apr., and F.O. minute thereon, and Leg. cons. 80, all of 1916.
33. FO 800/245, Max Müller to Alston, 2 Nov. 1910.
34. See other letters from Max Müller in FO 800/244–5. For another British diplomatist's adverse opinion of Max Müller see M. Gilbert. *Sir Horace Rumbold* (London, 1973), p. 22.
35. FO 369/1940, Leg. 246, 1927.
36. FO 369/2357, Leg. 533, 1934.
37. FO 369/536, report of committee on consular service, 18 Nov. 1912.
38. FO 17/1490, Leg. cons., 15 Aug. 1901; PRO 30/33/8/13, Clennell to Satow, 25 Jan. 1904; FO 17/1644, Satow to Hardinge, 12 Feb. 1904; PRO 30/33/7/10, Carnegie to Satow, 26 Apr. 1905; PRO 30/33/8/24, Warren to Satow, 17 Apr. 1904 and 8 May and 20 June 1905; FO 228/1630, Leg. to Foochow, 31 Oct. 1906; FO 369/205, Leg. cons. 84, 1909; FO 228/1804, Leg. to Ningpo, 4 Mar. 1911; FO 228/1793, Leg. accts. 1 and 7 to Ningpo, 1911; FO 350/1, Langley to Jordan, 29 Dec. 1911; FO 369/365, Leg. cons. 108, 1911, and F.O. minutes thereon; FO 369/452, Leg., 12 Dec. 1911, tel., 1 Feb. 1912, with F.O. minutes on both, Leg. cons. 28 and 71, 1912, and Sharkey to F.O., 8 July 1912, with F.O. minutes thereon; FO 228/1831, Leg. accts. 2 to Ningpo, 1912; FO 228/1832, Shanghai accts. 18,. 1912; FO 369/562, F.O. to Treasury, 23 Apr., and Treasury to F.O., 20 May, 1913, with F.O. minute on the latter; *London and China Express and Telegraph*, wife's death announcement, 1924; and England and Wales probate records, 1928.
39. FO 369/1096, Leg. cons. 37 and 55 and F.O. tel. 231, 1919; FO 369/1389, Sharkey to F.O., 22 Jan., F.O. to Byrne, 4 Feb., and F.O. to Treasury, 26 Apr., 1920; and medical directories.
40. FO 369/683, Leg., 15 Jan. 1914; and FO 228/1829, Werner to Jordan about Harding, 26 Mar., 2 Apr., and 30 May 1912.
41. FO 228/1861, Leg. correspondence about Werner with inspector-general of Customs and with Foochow residents; and FO 369/683, Werner to F.O., 5 Mar. and

31 July, and F.O. to Treasury, 7 Apr., 1914.
    42. FO 228/1632, Hankow, 21 Apr. 1906; FO 369/133, Leg. cons. 18, 93, and 96, with F.O. minutes on the last, F.O. confidential circular to China consular officers, 15 Aug., and Fletcher to F.O., 30 July and 7 Sept., with F.O. reply to the latter, all of 1908; FO 369/983, Leg. cons. 133 and 158, 1918; FO 228/2983, J.W. Jamieson to Jordan, 17 July 1918; FO 369/1396, Leg. 313, 1920; and *Foreign Office Lists.*
    43. FO 369/365, Leg. cons. 108, 1911; and FO 369/452, Jordan to Langley, 12 Dec. 1911.
    44. FO 228/1665, Mukden, 12 June 1907.
    45. FO 369/1319, report of departmental committee on consular service, 19 Mar. 1919, Annex V.
    46. See various references to wives by Phillips as inspector-general of consulates, for example, FO 369/2018, report on Shanghai, 23 Mar. 1928, FO 369/2020, report on Harbin, 15 July 1928, and FO 369/2021, report on Hankow, 4 Nov. 1928.
    47. PRO 30/33/9/10, Hosie to Satow, 7 May 1905; and Ogden, *Jessie Vera Ogden.*
    48. FO 369/286, Fraser to Jordan, 6 Aug., Jordan to Alston, 4 Sept., and Treasury to F.O., 13 Sept., 1910; and FO 228/1794, Shanghai accts. 42, 1911, and 27 Sept. 1911.
    49. FO 369/1774, Leg. 188 and 308, 1922, and Whitehall action on the latter, China Association to F.O., 31 May 1922, and Lady Fraser to F.O., 29 Sept. 1922.
    50. FO 369/922, Dufferin's minute on Fox's memorandum of 22 Feb. 1917.
    51. Platt, *Cinderella Service,* pp. 91-2; FO 369/1339, F.O. circular to consuls, 1 Nov. 1919; and *Foreign Office Lists.*
    52. FO 369/1772, Leg. tel. 47, 1922, F.O. minute; and FO 228/1957, Leg. 328, 1916.
    53. FO 369/1938, Leg. 364, 1927, Lampson to Gye, 12 Oct. 1927, and Whitehall minutes on both.
    54. FO 369/1938, Burdett to Crowe, 26 Jan. 1927, Crowe's minute; and FO 369/2392, Teichman to Scott, 24 Jan. 1935, and Scott's reply. For increasing Whitehall control over postings see FO 369/2461, Dunlop's memorandum, 15 Dec. 1937.
    55. FO 369/8, Little to F.O., 30 Dec. 1905, Leg. 44, 1906, and F.O. minutes on both.
    56. FO 228/1893, Jordan's undated minute immediately preceding Leg. cons. 48, 1914; FO 369/536, report of committee on consular service, 18 Nov. 1912 (mentioning Jordan's objection); and FO 228/1832, Shanghai accts. 63, 1912, Jordan's minute.
    57. PRO 30/33/7/10, Carnegie to Satow, 17 Oct. 1906.
    58. FO 17/1490, Leg. cons. 67, 1901, and Satow to Cockerell, 26 Apr. 1901.
    59. E. Satow, *A Diplomat in Japan* (London, 1921), p. 141; and Hewlett, *Forty Years in China,* p. 35.
    60. FO 17/1592, Leg. 25, 1901; FO 17/1490, Satow to Cockerell, 9 Apr., and Satow to Barrington, 15 Aug., 1901; and FO 17/1644, Satow to Hardinge, 12 Feb. 1904.
    61. FO 350/5-6, Jordan to Campbell, 28 Nov. 1907 and 29 July 1909; and FO 228/1662, Tsinan, 17 Sept. 1909.
    62. FO 369/2246, Crowe to Lampson, 5 Dec. 1932, led to the issue of a Lampson circular to consuls against insobriety, listed in FO 671/560 as unnumbered accts. circular of 30 Jan. 1933. No copy of the circular, famous in the service, has been traced.
    63. For an impression of Lampson's style towards consular subordinates see

Grafftey-Smith, *Bright Levant*, p. 238.

64. For example, FO 228/3159, Leg. 171, 1927.

65. FO 369/1938, Lampson to Gye, 12 Oct. 1927, FO 369/2017, Leg. tel. 128, 1928, and Whitehall minutes on both.

66. FO 228/1606, Leg. 204, 1906; FO 800/244, Jordan to Campbell, 8 Sept. 1909; FO 369/363, Leg. cons. 44, 1911; and FO 369/1775, Leg. 409, 1922.

67. FO 800/244, Max Müller to Alston, 13 July 1909, and F.O. minutes thereon; FO 228/1744, Leg. treaty 14, 1910, and F.O. treaty tel. 5, 1910; FO 369/287, Leg. cons. 131, 1910; FO 369/363, C.W. Campbell to F.O., 3 Mar., and F.O. reply, 11 Mar., 1911; and FO 350/1 and 7, F. Campbell to Jordan, 4 Mar., and Jordan's reply, 6 Apr., 1911.

68. FO 228/1750, Newchwang, 3 Sept. 1910, and Wilkinson to Max Müller, 3 Sept. 1910.

69. FO 800/299, Mckillop to Clark Kerr, 12 Apr. 1938, Clark Kerr to Cadogan, tel. 717, 1938, and Cadogan to Clark Kerr, tel., 11 May 1938.

70. FO 369/2261, examples of diplomatists' social discrimination against Levant consular officers quoted by Crowe to F.O. committee on Levant service; and Grafftey-Smith, *Bright Levant*, p. 13.

71. FO 17/592, Wade to Hammond, 20 Oct. 1871.

72. FO 228/1606, Leg. 204, 1906; and FO 369/1586, F.O. to Treasury, 27 July 1921.

73. No surviving copy has been found of this document, which is quoted from memory.

74. FO 369/363, Leg. cons. 44, 1911.

75. FO 369/2357, Leg. 533, 1934 (Brenan's views).

76. FO 369/1095, Leg. cons. 17, 1919. For Jordan's mastery of spoken Chinese see his *Chinese I Have Known*.

77. FO 17/1421, Leg. cons. 85, 1900, and F.O. minutes thereon; and FO 17/1490, Leg. cons. 63, 1901. For the final closure of Wenchow see FO 369/1772, Leg. 272, 1922.

78. FO 17/1490, Satow to Barrington, 15 Aug. 1901.

79. FO 228/1569, Leg. 222, 1905.

80. FO 369/12, Little to F.O., 14 Nov. 1906.

81. PRO 30/33/8/2, Campbell to Satow, 22 Feb. 1904; FO 17/1490, Satow to Barrington, 15 Aug. 1901; FO 228/1903, Amoy 8, 1914, Leg. minutes, and FO 369/1092, Leg. tel. 95, 1919; and FO 17/1354, Little to F.O., 28 Nov. 1898, F.O. minute, and FO 369/8, Little to F.O., 30 Dec. 1905, F.O. minutes.

82. FO 369/66, Little to Leg., 10 Oct. 1907.

83. FO 228/1789, Max Müller to Jordan, Apr. 1911; FO 369/1938, report on Nanking, 31 Dec. 1926, Crowe's minute; FO 369/2076, Gye? to Crowe, 13 June 1929; and FO 369/2305, Kelsey's undated minute (1933).

84. FO 228/1792, Harding to Jordan, 28 Sept. 1911; and FO 369/864, Willis to F.O., 22 Nov. 1916, and F.O. to Treasury arising therefrom.

85. FO 369/811, Leg. cons. 28, 1915, and FO 369/1100, Leg. cons. 142, 1919.

86. For example, FO 369/811, Leg. cons. 28, 1915, and FO 369/1100, Leg. cons. 142, 1919.

87. FO 369/2020, Leg. 1264, 1928; and FO 369/2246, Leg. 1466, 1932.

88. FO 228/1977, Wuhu, 3 Sept. 1916; FO 369/1595, Leg. 477, 1921; FO 369/1885, Office of Works to F.O., 7 Jan. 1926; and FO 228/2992, Ningpo, 22 Aug. 1921, Barton's minute.

89. FO 369/2020, Leg. 1264, 1928; and FO 369/2304, Leg. 1499, 1932.

90. FO 369/1939, Leg. cons. 6, 1927.

91. FO 17/1614, Treasury to F.O., 26 Nov. 1903; FO 369/2141, Kelsey's memorandum, 30 Oct. 1930, and minutes thereon; and FO 369/2126, Leg., 20 Feb. 1930.

92. FO 369/2261, Allchin's note, 8 July 1932, for F.O. committee on Levant service.

93. FO 369/1940, Leg. tels. 747 and 1599, and F.O. tel. 541, all of 1927; *Foreign Office Lists*; and FO 228/3085, Lampson's minute on F.O. paper F5764/10/10.

Notes to Chapter 18

1. FO 228/3276, Canton 31, 1923.
2. See Clubb, *20th Century China*, for example, pp. 66, 73, 104, and 106.
3. FO 228/2991, Yunnanfu 34, 1921.
4. FO 228/3276, Canton 28, 1921, and 30 Sept. 1924.
5. FO 228/2753, Canton 19, 1916; and FO 228/2982, Leg. 266, 1918; FO 228/1978, Canton 98, 1916, Canton, 15 June and 15 Sept. 1916, and Leg. to Canton, 29 Sept. 1916.
6. FO 228/2983, Canton 55 and 61, 1918; and FO 369/1097, Jordan tel. to Hardinge, 22 May 1919, and related papers.
7. FO 369/1390, Alston tel. to Wellesley, 1 Nov. 1920, Leg. tel. 479, 1920, Whitehall minutes thereon, and resulting exchanges between Leg. and Whitehall.
8. FO 228/2990, Canton 40, 1921.
9. FO 228/2291, Canton 52, 1921, Canton, 6 July 1921, and Alston's minute on the latter; and FO 228/3527, Canton 7 and 8, 1922, and FO 228/3484, Jamieson to Alston, 28 Sept. 1922.
10. FO 228/3484, Alston to Tyrrell, 10 Apr., Alston to Jamieson, 15 Sept., and Jamieson to Alston, 28 Sept., all of 1922; and FO 369/1774, Alston tel. to Crowe, 22 Mar. 1922.
11. FO 228/3000, Canton 6 and Leg. tel. 26, 1923; and FO 228/2873, Canton 109 and Leg. 126 to Canton, 1923.
12. FO 228/2874, Canton 39, 1924; FO 228/3503, Canton 190, 1924; FO 228/3008, Canton 9, 1925; FO 228/3011, Canton 29, 1925; and FO 228/3010, Leg. to Mukden, 20 Feb. 1925.
13. Clubb, *20th Century China*, p. 129.
14. FO 228/3011, Chengtu 17, 1925.
15. FO 228/3177, Shanghai 88, 1926.
16. FO 228/3291, Shanghai 122, 1925.
17. See, for example, FO 228/3142, Chefoo 14, 1925; FO 228/3147, Newchwang 17, 1925; FO 228/3277, Tsinan 27, 1925; FO 228/3285, Tientsin 148, 1925; and FO 228/3290, Mukden 48, 1925.
18. FO 228/3147, Yunnanfu 27 and 28, 1925; and FO 228/3151, Tengyueh 17, 1925.
19. FO 228/3006, Shanghai 122 and 127, 1924; and FO 228/3009, Leg. tel. 13, 1925.
20. FO 228/3141, Shanghai tel. 70, 1925; and FO 228/3019, Shanghai tel. 84, 1926.
21. FO 228/3177, Shanghai 88, 1926; FO 228/3291, Shanghai 157, 1925; and FO 228/3144, Leg. minute, 7 July 1925.
22. FO 228/3010, Chinkiang 3, 1925; FO 228/3142, Chinkiang 22, 1925; and FO

228/3150, F.O. 760, 1925.

23. FO 228/3142, Kiukiang 11 and 13 and Leg. 10 to Kiukiang, 1925; and FO 228/3284, Kiukiang 31, 1925.

24. FO 228/3141, Hankow tel. 19 and Leg. 8 to Hankow, 1925; and FO 228/3150, F.O. 774, 1925.

25. FO 228/3141, Nanking tels. 26 and 27, 1925; FO 228/3147, Nanking 57 and tel. 34, 1925; and FO 228/3151, Nanking 113, 1925, and Macleay's minute thereon.

26. FO 228/3144–6, Chungking tel., 6 July 1925, and despatch 24, 1925; FO 228/3012, Chengtu 23, 1925; FO 228/3273, Chungking 38, 1925; and FO 228/3014, Archer to Teichman, 28 Nov. 1925.

27. FO 228/3012, Chengtu 23, 1925; FO 228/3143–4, Chengtu tels. 10 and 11 and despatch 19, 1925; FO 228/3529, Chengtu 27, 1925; FO 228/3154, Chengtu tel. 2, 1926; and FO 228/3390, Chengtu 20, 1926.

28. FO 228/3142, Ningpo tels. 1 and 2, 1925; and FO 228/3280, Ningpo 25, 1925.

29. FO 228/3144, Canton 46, 47, and 50, 1925; FO 228/3012, Canton 74, 1925; FO 228/3018, Institute of International Affairs meeting, 28 June 1926, Jamieson's remarks; and FO 228/3020, Brenan to O'Malley, 2 Dec. 1926.

30. FO 228/3151, Canton 121, 1925; and FO 228/3153, Ashton-Gwatkin's memorandum, 3 Feb. 1926.

31. FO 228/3012, Leg. 278 and 679, 1925; FO 800/258, Stampfordham to Chamberlain, 21 Aug. 1925; and FO 228/3146–7, Canton 65 and 73, 1925, and minutes thereon by Palairet and Garstin.

32. FO 228/3152, F.O. tel. 3, 1926, and O'Malley to Strang, 10 Feb. 1926; and FO 228/3940, Hewlett to Lampson, 24 Mar. 1929.

33. FO 228/3018, Institute of International Affairs meeting, 28 June 1926, Jamieson's remarks and Macleay's minute thereon; and FO 800/259, Crowe to Wellesley, 21 Aug., and minutes by Wellesley and Chamberlain, 23 and 24 Aug., 1926.

34. FO 228/3144, Hoihow 9, 1925; FO 228/3152–3, Hoihow 3, 5, and 8, 1925; FO 228/3158, Canton tel. 14, 1927; and FO 228/3163, navy signal to Admiralty, 16 Apr. 1927.

35. FO 228/3142, Amoy, 9 June 1925; FO 228/3146, Amoy 14–16, 19, and 21, 1925, Amoy, 30 July 1925, and Hewlett to Turner, 4 Nov. 1925; and Hewlett, *Forty Years in China*, p. 158.

36. FO 228/3142, Foochow 20, 1925; and FO 228/3144, Foochow 22, 1925.

37. FO 228/3272, Swatow, 17 Apr. 1924; FO 228/3528, Swatow 10, 1924, and Swatow, 7 July 1924; FO 228/3430, Swatow, 30 Sept. 1924; and FO 228/3272, Swatow, 26 Mar. 1925.

38. FO 228/3011, Swatow 10, 1925.

39. FO 228/3012–3, Swatow 32, 43, 55, 57, 63 with Leg. minute thereon, and 79, 1925; FO 228/3146–7, Swatow 30, 31, and 34, 1925, and Swatow, 20 July 1925, with Garstin's minute thereon; FO 228/3529, Swatow 64, 1925, Garstin's minute; and FO 228/3151, Swatow, 9 Nov. 1925.

40. FO 228/3152, Leg. tel. 8 to Swatow and Swatow tel. 33, 1925, with Macleay's minute thereon; FO 228/3154, Swatow tels. 13–15, 1926; FO 228/3272, Swatow 77, 1926; FO 228/3154–6, Swatow 48 and 95, 1926; FO 228/3158–9, Foochow tels. 2 and 3 and despatch 3, 1927, and Swatow 5, 1927; FO 228/3161, Swatow 7, 1927; FO 228/3163, Canton tel. 39, 1927, and Swatow tel. 13, 1927, FO 228/3609, Swatow 22, 1927, and FO 228/3640, Swatow 9, 1927; and FO 228/3580–1, Swatow tel. 25 and despatches 46 and 49, 1927.

41. FO 369/2017, Leg. tels. 4 and 19, 1928, and minutes and action on both; and

FO 369/2076, Leg. tel. 568 and Yunnanfu 20, 1929.

42. FO 228/3159, Leg. 63, 1927.

43. FO 228/3018, Chungking tel. 2, 1926; FO 371/11693; Toynbee, *International Affairs*, 1926, pp. 312–13; FO 369/1937, Leg. 834, 1926, and 60, 1927; and FO 228/3586, Brenan to Clementi, 11 Sept. 1926 (text enclosed in F.O. 1045, 1927).

44. FO 228/3182, Amoy 59, 1922, and 25–7, 1923, with Leg. minutes on the 1923 despatches: FO 228/3002, Amoy 35 and 44, 1923, Leg. minutes on both, and Macleay to Eastes at Ichang, 27 Nov. 1923; and FO 228/3502, Ichang 7, 1924.

45. FO 228/3273, Chungking 38, 1925, Chungking political report, Mar. quarter, 1926, and Chungking 14 and 34, 1926; and FO 369/1937, Leg. 834, 1926.

46. FO 228/3017, Hankow tel. 65, 1926, Teichman's minute thereon, and O'Malley to navy, 21 July 1926; FO 228/3018–19, Hankow tels. 128 and 131, 1926, with Leg. minute on the former, and Hankow despatch 120, 1926; FO 228/3021, Teichman to Lampson from Hankow, 7 Mar. 1927; FO 228/3282, Hankow, 31 Dec. 1926; and FO 228/3157–8, Leg. tel. 173 to Hankow, 1926, Leg. 52, 1927, and Hankow tels. 3 and 5, 1927.

47. FO 228/3157–8, Leg. tel. 19, 1927, Cameron signal to Lampson, 7 Jan. 1927, and Hankow 1, 1927.

48. FO 800/259, Stampfordham to Chamberlain, 14 Jan. 1927; and FO 228/3158–9, F.O. tel. 6 and Leg. 6 to Hankow, 1927.

49. FO 228/3188, F.O. tel. 198, 1927, Lampson's minute.

50. FO 371/12433, Lampson to Wellesley, tels., 16 and 17 Feb., and Chamberlain's minute, 17 Feb., 1927; FO 800/261, Chamberlain to Lampson, 3 Aug. 1927; FO 369/1937, Crowe to Goffe, 9 Sept. 1927; and FO 369/1940, Leg. tel. 1724, 1927, Crowe's minute.

51. FO 228/3019, Kiukiang 23 and 28, 1926.

52. FO 228/3157, Kiukiang tels. 2 and 3 and despatch 1, 1927, and Leg. tel. 2 to Kiukiang, 1927.

53. FO 228/3189, Chinkiang 11, 1922; FO 228/3183, Leg. 21 to Amoy, 1922, and F.O. 541, 1923; FO 228/3281, Amoy, 7 Oct. 1922; and FO 228/3649, F.O. memorandum, 7 June 1927.

54. FO 228/3160–1, Ichang 3 and 4 and tel. 11, 1927.

55. FO 228/3159, Chungking 1, 1927, and Leg. minutes thereon; FO 369/1942, Leg. 895, 1927; FO 228/3163, Ichang, 23 Apr. 1927, and Leg. minute thereon; FO 228/3161, Leg. tel. 260 to Teichman at Hankow, 28 Mar. 1927; and FO 369/2019, report on Tientsin, 15 July 1928.

56. FO 228/3390, Chengtu 22, 1926; FO 228/3155, Chengtu 25, 1926; FO 228/3159, Chengtu 1, 1927; and FO 228/3157, Leg. tel. 2 to Chengtu, 1927.

57. FO 228/3390, Chengtu 22, 1926, Teichman's minute.

58. FO 228/3159, navy signal, 10 Feb. 1927; FO 369/1938, Leg. 205, 1927; and FO 369/2306, Leg. 435, 1933.

59. FO 228/3020, Yunnanfu 2, 1927.

60. FO 228/3190–1, Leg. tel. 441, 1927, and Chinkiang tels., 27 Mar. and 2 and 7 Apr. 1927; FO 228/3998, Chinkiang 1, 1929, Teichman's minute: FO 228/3635, Chinkiang 7, 8, and 10, 1927; and FO 228/3827, Tengyueh 7, 1927.

61. FO 228/3159, Leg. 171, 1927.

62. FO 228/3161–2, Leg. tel. 506, 1927, Nanking tel., 28 Mar. 1927, and Shanghai tel. 125, 1927; FO 228/3165, Nanking, 9 Apr. 1927; and FO 369/2075, Leg. 252, 1929.

63. FO 228/3162–3, Nanking tels., 27 Mar. and 7 Apr., Leg. tel. 674, and F.O. tel. 293, all of 1927; FO 228/3635, Hewlett from Nanking 35, 1927; and FO 228/3826, Shanghai 184, 1928.

64. FO 369/1940, Crowe to Gye, 18 Feb. 1928, and Leg. tel. 1724, 1927, Crowe's

minute; FO 369/2017, Treasury to F.O., 20 Mar., with F.O. minute thereon, Gye's minute, 14 June, and Treasury to F.O., 14 July, all of 1928; and FO 371/13177–8, Montgomery to Lampson, 18 Jan. 1928, and solicitors to F.O., 4 Oct. 1928, with F.O. minutes thereon.

65. FO 369/2075, Leg. 252, 1929, and Whitehall action thereon.

66. FO 228/3161–2, Leg. tel. 260 to Hankow (for Teichman), 1927; FO 228/3431, Leg. tels. to consulates, 25 Mar. 1927; and FO 228/3164, admiral's signal, 21 Apr. 1927.

67. FO 228/3158, Foochow tels. 2 and 3, 1927; FO 228/3278, Foochow 17, 1927; FO 228/3161, Foochow 13, 1927; and FO 228/3615, Foochow, 6 May 1927.

68. FO 228/3577, Shanghai 22, 1927; and Toynbee, *International Affairs*, 1926, p. 377.

69. FO 800/259, Chamberlain to Lampson, 16 Mar., and Lampson to Chamberlain, 3 May, 1927; FO 228/3577, Shanghai 22, 1927; FO 228/3586, Shanghai tel. 231, 1927, and FO 228/3640, Shanghai 32 and 70, 1927; and FO 800/262, Lampson to Chamberlain, 8 Apr. 1928.

70. FO 228/3158, F.O. tel. 49 and Canton tels. 12 and 13, 1927; FO 228/3153, O'Malley to Brenan, 23 Mar. 1926, and Canton 38, 1926; FO 69/249, Barrington to Lansdowne, 22 June 1903, and FO 69/268, Cockerell's minute, 11 May, and F.O. to Brenan, 23 June, 1905; PRO 30/33/7/4, Cockerell to Satow, 10 May 1905; FO 228/1578B, Leg. accts. tel. 39 to Shanghai, 1905, and Shanghai tel., 28 Oct. 1905; and *Foreign Office Lists*.

71. FO 228/3085, Canton tel. 1, 1927; FO 228/3154–6, Canton tels. 51, 73, 76, and 91 and despatch 149, 1926; and FO 228/3586, Brenan to Clementi, 29 Aug. and 11 Sept. 1926 (texts enclosed in F.O. 1045, 1927), and Canton 162, 1927.

72. FO 369/1885, Leg. 730, 1926, F.O. minute; FO 228/3162, Canton 31, 1927, Leg. to Canton, 23 Apr., and Canton, 14 May, 1927; FO 228/3703, O'Malley to Brenan, 15 Aug., and Lampson to Brenan, 20 Nov., 1927; and FO 228/4110, Lampson to Wellesley, 8 Oct. 1929.

73. FO 228/3154, Brenan to Teichman, 15 June 1926, and Canton 69, 1926; FO 228/3020, Canton, 2 Dec. 1926; and FO 228/3635, Canton 100, 1927.

74. FO 228/3276, Canton 49, 1927; FO 228/3194, Canton tel. 34, 1927; FO 228/3635, Canton 100, 1927; FO 228/3163, Canton tel. 39, 1927; FO 228/3586, Canton 162 and tels. 96, 100, and 101, and F.O. tel. 613, all of 1927; FO 228/3826, Canton 208, 1927; FO 228/3586, Canton tels. 113–19, 1927; and FO 228/3728, Canton 204, 1927, and Canton 8, 1928.

75. FO 228/3826, Canton 40, 1928; and FO 228/3734, Canton, 14 Dec. 1928.

76. FO 228/3585, Ningpo 48, 1927; and FO 228/3825–7, Swatow 18, Shanghai 57, Chungking 7, and Hankow 32, all of 1928.

77. FO 228/3157, Changsha 55, 1926.

78. FO 228/4004, Foochow 41, 1929; FO 228/3933, Chungking 41, 1929; and FO 676/121, Hankow 25 and 27, 1932.

79. FO 228/3706, Swatow 3, 1928.

80. FO 228/4127, Changsha 43, 1930.

81. See, for example, FO 369/2021, report on Changsha, 4 Nov. 1928.

82. FO 228/3141, F.O. 280, 1925, Teichman's minute.

83. FO 228/3183, Amoy, 17 July 1925, Garstin's minute.

84. FO 228/3019, Goffe to O'Malley, 15 Oct. 1926.

85. FO 228/3019, Wilkinson to O'Malley, 17 Nov. 1926.

86. FO 228/3278, Foochow 49, 1925, and 28, 1926.

87. FO 676/189, Yunnanfu 60 and 93, 1934, and Yunnanfu, 7 Aug. 1934.

88. Toynbee, *International Relations*, 1926, pp. 488 and 494.

89. See, for example, FO 405/269, F.O. tel. 294, 1931.

Notes to Epilogue

1. Platt, *Cinderella Service*, pp. 227–30.
2. FO 800/263, Lampson to Selby, 15 Nov. 1928.
3. FO 228/3933, Kiukiang 30, 1929, and Lampson's minute thereon.
4. FO 228/3999, Aveling tel. to Leg. from Nanking, 1 Nov. 1929.
5. FO 228/4302, Lampson tour series 135, 1930.
6. P. Atwell, *British Mandarins and Chinese Reformers* ... (Hong Kong, 1985), p. 162; and FO 369/2246, F.O. 621 and Leg. 1466, 1932.
7. Pratt, *War and Politics*, p. 204; and FO 405/270, Leg. 1914, 1931.
8. See, for example, FO 228/3143, Fox's memorandum, 20 June 1925.
9. FO 369/2350, Tuson to Kelsey, 3 July 1934.
10. FO 228/3913, Mukden 5, 1928 (confidential print F 2438/7/10), and Harbin 66, 1928.

INDEX OF PERSONAL AND
PLACE NAMES

REFERENCES in the text to British consular officers and their families, to other British civil officials and ministers of the Crown, and to Chinese office-holders are indexed, as are two references to King George V. The figures in brackets after consular officers' names refer to the numbers against which their names appear in Appendix II.

The place names indexed are those of consular posts, together with Hong Kong and Macao.

Other personal and place names are not indexed.

CHINA CONSULAR SERVICE POSTS IN MAINLAND CHINA, FORMOSA, AND KOREA

The international and internal boundaries shown are
those of 1910. The consular post at Kashgar was a
Government of India post.

OUTER M

•Kashgar

CHINESE TURKISTAN
(SINKIANG)

C H I

KOKONOR

TIBET

INNER TIBET

Tachien

S

N
↑

Tengyueh

YUN

Ssumao